The Encyclopedia of the Sword

The Encyclopedia of the Sword

NICK EVANGELISTA

Foreword by William M. Gaugler

GREENWOOD PRESS
Westport, Connecticut • London

Library of Congress Cataloging-in-Publication Data

Evangelista, Nick.
　　The encyclopedia of the sword / Nick Evangelista ; foreword by William M. Gaugler.
　　　　p.　cm.
　　Includes bibliographical references and index.
　　ISBN 0–313–27896–2 (alk. paper)
　　　1. Fencing—Encyclopedias.　2. Swordplay—Encyclopedias.
　　3. Swords—Encyclopedias.　　I. Title.
　　GV1143.2.E93　　　1995
　　796.8'6'03—dc20　　　　94–7426

British Library Cataloguing in Publication Data is available.

Library of Congress Catalog Card Number: 94–7426
ISBN: 0–313–27896–2

First published in 1995

Greenwood Press, 88 Post Road West, Westport, CT 06881
An imprint of Greenwood Publishing Group, Inc.

Printed in the United States of America

The paper used in this book complies with the
Permanent Paper Standard issued by the National
Information Standards Organization (Z39.48–1984).

10　9　8　7　6　5　4　3　2

Every reasonable effort has been made to trace the owners of copyright materials in this
book, but in some instances this has proven impossible. The author and publisher will
be glad to receive information leading to more complete acknowledgments in subsequent
printings of the book and in the meantime extend their apologies for any omissions.

This book is dedicated to the memory of my
fencing master, Ralph Faulkner

The history of the Sword is the history of humanity.

—*Richard F. Burton (1884)*

Contents

Foreword

The Encyclopedia of the Sword, Nick Evangelista's masterful and comprehensive publication, contains entries that deal with every aspect of the sword, from its construction to its use, as well as a vast amount of biographical data from the sixteenth century to the present.

In some ways the *Encyclopedia* is like a family album or scrapbook in which the personal fencing history of each of us can be traced. Every item, like the cup of tea and *petites madeleines* in Marcel Proust's *A la recherche du temps perdu*, is capable of evoking a vivid image. Indeed, certain poignant entries carry me back to my childhood. For example, "mensur" awakens memories of my parents' tales of student duels at Tübingen; "fencing school" elicits recollections of summer evenings spent sitting on the front lawn of Bela de Tuscan's *salle d'armes* in Detroit, and watching with fascination, through open windows, fencers in immaculate white uniforms executing rapid counter-parry-riposte exercises; and "swashbuckler movie" evokes the excitement and romance motion pictures such as *Captain Blood* (1935), *The Prisoner of Zenda* (1937) and *The Man in the Iron Mask* (1939) offered during the bleak and dispiriting years of the Great Depression.

The entry "books, fencing" also stimulates memories. During World War II, as I was growing up, I read every fencing book in the public library, including classics like Luigi Barbasetti's *The Art of the Foil* (1932), Julio Castelló's *The Theory and Practice of Fencing* (1933), and Joseph Vince's *Fencing* (1937). And when in 1943 Aldo Nadi's *On Fencing* appeared on the recent acquisitions shelf, I picked up the three-hundred-page volume and devoured it in a few hours.

Having read this book, I realized that I could no longer satisfy my appetite for swordplay in a vicarious manner; I now wanted to hold the weapon in hand, sense the vibrations of the steel, and learn everything there was to know about fencing technique—and not from any teacher, but from Aldo Nadi himself. Some years later I moved to Los Angeles and became Maestro Nadi's pupil.

The decades that followed took me from America to Europe, from Aldo Nadi's academy at Los Angeles to fencing schools in Geneva, Cannes, Monaco, Florence, Frankfurt, and Rome. From Aldo Nadi and Amilcare Angelini I learned the method of the Livornese-Pisan school; Edmond Durrieu introduced me to the traditional French system of instruction; and from Ettore Spezza, Giorgio Pessina, and Umberto Di Paola I learned the pedagogical method of the Roman-Neapolitan school, that is to say, the system of the Italian Military Master's School. Here the *Encyclopedia* provides the framework for a genealogical chart: Carlo Pessina, Director of the Italian Military Master's School, was a disciple of Giuseppe Radaelli, and the father and teacher of Giorgio Pessina. Eugenio Pini, whose father was the fencing master of the Naval Academy at Livorno, taught Beppe Nadi, who, in turn, was the teacher of his sons, Nedo and Aldo Nadi, and of Oreste Puliti and Gustavo Marzi. And Alfredo Angelini, whose father was also a fencing master, taught his son, Amilcare Angelini. The traditions of the Pessina, Nadi, and Angelini families continued well into the 1960s: Giorgio Pessina instructed Giulio Gaudini and Renzo Nostini, Aldo Nadi taught John Huffman and Janice York Romary, and Amilcare Angelini trained Erwin Casmir and Max Geuter.

How does one generation pass a tradition on to the next? Again, the *Encyclopedia* provides us with pertinent entries: "professional fencing teacher" and "Louis Rondelle." These bring to mind Rondelle's recommendation in his treatise, *Foil and Sabre: A Grammar of Fencing* (1892), that we establish in the United States "a normal school, where every man would be obliged to stand a rigid examination before he was permitted to teach." Such formal instruction is required for a teaching license in Europe. In France and Italy the candidate receives training in all aspects of fencing pedagogy, and, at the completion of his studies, must demonstrate his competence before a national commission of fencing masters. In Italy the examinations are held every year at the Accademia Nazionale di Scherma in Naples. When I took these in the 1970s they were administered in the Castel Nuovo, a magnificent thirteenth-century royal residence and fortress overlooking the Bay of Naples. The commission included Domenico Conte, Giorgio Pessina, and Ugo Pignotti. In retrospect, the splendor of the setting and the seriousness and rigor of the examinations made the event unforgettable.

As the reader will discover, the *Encyclopedia* is also a source for definitions of fencing terms, old and new. Among the old is the word "*intagliata.*" Not since the nineteenth century has anyone taught fencers this evasive action. Cesare Enrichetti, in *Trattato elementare teorico-pratico di scherma* (1871), describes the *intagliata* as the reverse of the *inquartata*; instead of swinging the rear foot to the outside of the line of direction, the leading foot is swung to the inside, and the thrust, rather than being delivered to the adversary's inside high line, is directed to his outside low line or flank. Now while few modern competitive fencers would be inclined to use the *intagliata*, it is, nevertheless, an action that can still be employed effectively on the stage.

Among the new expressions is "right-of-way." This concept, however, has its origins in dueling practice, and can be traced at least as far back as the sixteenth century. Camillo Agrippa, for instance, in *Trattato di scientia d'arme* (1553), notes that while some teachers advise drawing the sword arm back in order to deliver the thrust with greater force, he does not agree, for by keeping the arm well extended, he says, the weapon travels along a straight line, moves more rapidly, and therefore has the advantage. By pulling the arm back and then thrusting forward, he concludes, time is lost, and this offers the opponent the opportunity to counterattack.

By the beginning of the seventeenth century the importance of the straight arm, and the principle that arm motion must precede foot movement, can be found in every major Italian treatise on swordplay. Salvator Fabris, in *Sienza* [*sic*] *e pratica d'arme* (1606), writes, "There are some who, wishing to attack with the point, launch the arm with violence to give it greater force, [but] such a manner is not good . . . [for] one may be wounded in the time of this withdrawal of the arm." Nicoletto Giganti, in *Scola overo teatro* (1606), states that in executing the thrust one must first extend the arm; and Ridolfo Capo Ferro, in *Gran simulacro dell'arte e dell'uso della scherma* (1610), adds that in thrusting, the right arm should be extended in a straight line.

Subsequent Italian fencing literature follows the same line of reasoning despite the fact that dueling practice is no longer an essential factor in the development of contemporary fencing theory. For example, Giorgio Pessina and Ugo Pignotti, in their teacher-training manual, *Il fioretto* (1970), describe the execution of the lunge as follows: "Gradually—with absolute precedence of the point of the foil, and without jerkiness or withdrawal—one completes extension of the weapon arm, which is followed by forward inclination of the bust; thereafter, without the least interruption, one carries the right foot forward, shaving the surface of the ground."

The *Encyclopedia* also contains a plethora of facts concerning actors and films in which swordplay is prominent. For instance, although I knew that Basil Rathbone was a trained swordsman, I was not aware that he took fencing lessons regularly from Fred Cavens, yet the results of this practice should have been evident to me in films such as the *Mark of Zorro* (1940) and *Frenchman's Creek* (1944). Moreover, the fact that actors Henry Daniell and George Sanders lacked fencing skills came as no surprise, but that both men apparently disliked fencing was astonishing, given their frequent appearances in swashbuckler films.

Maestro Nadi observes in his autobiography, *The Living Sword* (1995), that in 1943, after his treatise *On Fencing* was reviewed in *Time* magazine, Paramount Pictures engaged him as fencing master for *Frenchman's Creek*. Regarding his work with the actors, Nadi comments: "I proceeded to teach Arturo de Cordova, the Mexican leading man of the picture, whose co-ordination, thank God, was good. But the man whom he had to fight, the late Ralph Forbes, was so lazy that it was practically impossible to make him do any work." Following *Frenchman's Creek*, Maestro Nadi arranged swordplay for a number of films, including *The Mississippi Gambler* (1953), a picture that is not memorable, but that has a fencing sequence that is. Nadi recreated, with considerable accuracy, a nineteenth-century French foil encounter, and contributed lines to the script which, to an astute observer, revealed the author's identity. These occur when Tyrone Power scores more than once with the same action, prompting his adversary to remark: "That same low-line hit again." And then Power's next opponent, who watched the bout, adds: "My compliments. . . . You have courage to let the point come so close before parrying." Both the low-line attack and delayed parry were typical of Nadi's fencing. Also listed in the cast of *The Mississippi Gambler* is Guy Williams, who five years later was awarded the title role in the Disney production of *Zorro*. The fencing sequences for this television series were also devised by Maestro Nadi.

In conclusion, *The Encyclopedia of the Sword* is the most important reference source of its kind currently available. In having brought this large undertaking to a successful end, our erudite and indefatigable colleague and friend, Nick Evangelista, has made a genuine contribution to the literature of fencing.

William M. Gaugler
Maestro d'Armi and Director
Military Fencing Masters Program
San José State University

Preface

The research for what follows began, I think, when I was born. I have always been interested in the sword and fencing and have absorbed information concerning the subject like a sponge.

As a child, I drew my own primitive comic books filled with blood-soaked swordplay. As a teenager, I voraciously began reading literature that abounded in fencing, starting with the fantastic creations of Edgar Rice Burroughs and Robert E. Howard: John Carter of Mars and Conan the Barbarian. Eventually, I graduated to the historical: *The Three Musketeers* by Alexandre Dumas, *The Prisoner of Zenda* by Anthony Hope, and *Captain Blood* by Rafael Sabatini, to name a few.

Finally, unable to content myself with fiction, I decided to learn to fence. At the age of twenty, I took up the sword, becoming a student of fencer veteran Ralph Faulkner. A former Olympic competitor (1928 and 1932) and a film fencing master, he had worked with the likes of Errol Flynn, Douglas Fairbanks, Jr., and Ronald Colman. He was seventy-nine the day I walked into his Hollywood school, Falcon Studios, for the first time.

Fencing was not easy. I wanted to be D'Artagnan. I was not, I found, D'Artagnan. My first lesson was so traumatic, it took me two weeks to get up the courage to go back for more. I did go back, though, and from that point on I never gave up fencing again.

I competed in fencing tournaments, a practical testing ground for what I learned. Once, after taking first place in a tournament and feeling rather large-headed, Mr. Faulkner said to me, "You fenced well. Now, let's talk about all

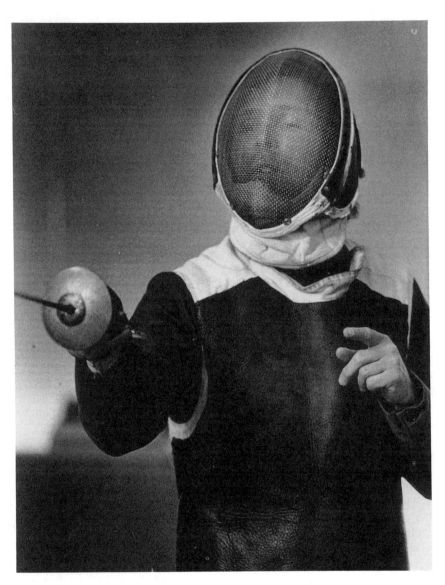

Fencing master. Photograph by Bob McEowen

the things you did wrong.'' I have never forgotten that little bit of truth about keeping one's performance in perspective.

In time, I went to Europe to study in fencing schools in Paris, Rome, Vienna, and Munich. I wanted to find out what fencing really was, in the places where it all started. I was drawn to traditional values. European fencing was, simply put, tough. There was no room to let things slide or to be halfhearted in my approach. Everywhere I went, I had to prove myself. Sometimes, I did well; sometimes, not so well. Although fencing was physically and psychologically draining, I learned.

Back in the United States, I applied what I had picked up, formulating thoughts and theories, dissecting fencing with scientific fervor. I began to see how the pieces of fencing fit together.

After years of constant study and practice, I became a fencing teacher. Beginning as Ralph Faulkner's assistant, in time, I opened my own school. Still, I studied and learned, this time, from my students. Each new fencer brought new problems that had to be overcome. Each new problem solved brought further focus to my art.

Today, I live on a farm in the Missouri Ozark Mountains—far away from the hectic muddle of southern California. The teaching and learning, of course, continue—even in the seemingly isolated confines of my rural setting. Fencing is not something one gives up easily. I am sure I never will.

I brought this mind-set and background, then, to the task of producing this volume. It was created to fill a particular need: to bring all aspects of sword knowledge under one roof. Numerous books have been written about the sword and fencing, almost all of them limited to one or two aspects of the weapon— historical, sporting, theatrical, or technical. Yet the sum of sword information is much, much more than any of these. All at once, the sword is a social and psychological symbol, a literary device, a romantic decoration, a sport tool, a movie prop, and, of course, a deadly weapon.

When I began writing *The Encyclopedia of the Sword,* I hoped to put together a reference source that would make sword facts, fencing theory, and related terms accessible to anyone in an easy-to-use form. Someone looking up the name of a particular sword, a fencing master, or a film with swordplay in it could open the book and easily locate needed information I had gleaned from dozens of unrelated sources.

To help readers, I have used asterisks to cross-reference material. An asterisk (*) following a word indicates that it may be found under its own alphabetized heading.

Two asterisks (**) following a word indicate that it may be explained in greater detail under a heading other than its own and will be located in the index.

I apologize if I have left out someone's favorite fencing master or fencer from my writings. I have tried to be true to my sources and include as many notables as possible but *The Encyclopedia of the Sword* is not infinite, nor am I omnis-

Faulkner School of Fencing around 1975. Author is in the front row, second from right. Photograph by Anita Evangelista

cient; it would be impossible for me to list every fencer who ever lived. I, of course, salute all the members of this noble art, science, and sport that the lack of time, space, and information kept out of this volume.

I would also like to mention that while I usually use the male point of view when writing about fencers (e.g.: "When a fencer picks up his foil, he . . ."), I am well aware that women play an equally important role in the sport. However, to adopt the "he/she, him/her" pronoun approach would have bogged down the text with useless verbiage and, perhaps, ended up creating a volume twice as big as this one already is. Political correctness was not my point in producing this book; to convey information was my goal. Suffice it to say that when I speak of modern fencing, I acknowledge fully that women are part of the equation.

Defining fencing terms had its challenges. In fencing there is no lack of definitions for terms. Unfortunately, they do not always jibe with one another. Fencing, from its inception centuries ago, has been a constantly growing, living thing, giving birth to new concepts, one moment brawling and unruly, the next systematic and refined, grabbing methods and holding them tenaciously, then vigorously tearing loose and discarding dead weight, continually naming and renaming itself. Thousands of fencing minds have shaped theories, molded concepts, and tested skills, each of them a little different, and—horror of horrors—all of them, in the minds of the originators, entirely "correct."

Even today, we run into murky waters when defining actions, actions that may have once been fully formed black-and-white realities. The straight arm rule in foil fencing is a prime example. Once, it was an unquestioned requirement of form that to establish one's position as a valid attacker, one had to fully straighten one's sword arm before lunging. There are many individuals now arguing that the rule really permits a "straightening" arm rather than a "straight" one. In some circles, the straight arm is totally ignored when a fencer begins his offensive drive, and priority in an attack is established not by the arm at all but merely by one's forward motion. This final concept allows, comically, that if a fencer has cardiac arrest on the fencing strip, as long as he falls forward, he is the attacker.

Ultimately, in developing definitions for *The Encyclopedia of the Sword*, I tried to combine written consensus with my own fencing experience of twenty-five years. And I stand behind what I have written.

Finally, I have tried to make *The Encyclopedia of the Sword* as complete and diverse as humanly possible. A reference book, I believe, is only as good as the information it does not leave out.

I hope, for those using this book, that I have achieved what I set out to do.

Acknowledgments

I would like to thank Colleen Walker Mar, former media relations director for the U.S. Fencing Association (USFA), for supplying me with vital sport fencing information, which I would otherwise have been unable to locate.

Thanks, too, to Jeff Tishman, former USFA historian and present editor of *The Swordmaster,* the official publication of the U.S. Fencing Coaches Association, for providing the odd date I needed to make this volume more complete.

Continued thanks to Polly Craus August, friend and former Olympic fencer, for her continued support of my personal efforts.

Certainly, thanks to Toney Aid for his concern.

Also, thanks to Terry and Allen Hampton for photocopy assistance.

Thanks to Dr. William Gaugler, director of the Military Fencing Masters program at San Jose State University, for our enjoyable discussions of fencing masters and fencing technique.

Finally, thanks to my wife, Anita, for simply putting up with both me and fencing over the years.

Introduction

There is a primal fascination with the sword. Its presence is almost magical, otherworldly. It is a weapon that exists in virtually all historic times. Moreover, barring slight variations in design, it is omnipresent around the world. One of man's oldest, most valued tools, for the Viking, the sword was his named companion, for the samurai, his very soul.

Today, the sword is part of our modern mythology. *The Three Musketeers, Robin Hood,* and *Zorro,* swordsmen all, have helped shape our ideas of fair play, bravery, and loyalty. The sword, then, is a vehicle that encodes our innermost aspirations for ourselves and humanity.

There are, however, vast contradictions to be found in the image of the sword. A multifaceted creation, it is a cruel weapon dealing out brutality and death and, at the same time, a thing of swashbuckling romance and a bringer of life and liberty. A sword can be an artistic creation or simply a utilitarian device for efficient killing. The sword has been a decider of history and a vital part of literature and drama; it has both ruled us and entertained us. It is a symbol— of justice, honor, independence, and manhood. Nevertheless, it cannot escape its link to the violent, despotic suppression of humankind.

By itself, the sword is nothing, an inanimate piece of sharpened metal. The men who used it brought it to life, devising intricate methods of manipulating it and employing it for noble and selfish purposes.

In modern times, the sword has proven an avenue of healthy diversion, an athletic outlet for aggressive energies otherwise frowned upon by society. In the sport of fencing, we are allowed to touch a past when men met in a physical and mental contest, one-on-one, honestly, without pretense, to settle differences and even scores.

Movies have added another dimension to the aura that tightly envelops the sword. Dashing celluloid swordsmen—Errol Flynn, Douglas Fairbanks, and Ronald Colman—stimulate our romantic leanings with their brave deeds rewarded and send us into flights of heroic fancy with their artful, albeit exaggerated, blade waving.

The sword, then, as removed as it is from what we call modern, normal, everyday life, is as much a part of our collective psyche as, perhaps, the automobile. It represents for us a simpler time, when men were not so bogged down in societal encumbrances—the rules and waiting lines, the speed limits and calorie counts—that we all must endure. It reminds us that we are part of nature's plan, the life-and-death process.

To keep the image in perspective, it is good to remember that in days gone by, one man, sword in hand, could influence kingdoms, that once upon a time, the fates of entire civilizations were settled by the sword.

The Encyclopedia of the Sword

A

ABDUCTION. A movement of the sword arm in which it deviates from the mid, or central, line of the body.
REFERENCE
Morton, E. D. *Martini A–Z of Fencing.* London: Queen Anne Press, 1992.

ABSENCE OF BLADE. Absence of blade occurs when fencers' blades are not in contact with each other. This term also refers to an instance when a fencer is on guard* but not covering a line* with his weapon.

By removing one's blade to a position where it cannot be dealt with directly, a fencer hopes to limit the number of offensive possibilities open to his opponent. This strategy has been found to be most effective when used against the neophyte fencer, who does not usually possess the experience necessary to cope with nonconventional fencing tactics.

Also known as *invito aperto.*
REFERENCES
Lownds, Camille. *Foil Around and Stay Fit.* San Diego: Harcourt Brace Jovanovich, 1977.
Palffy-Alpar, Julius. *Sword and Masque.* Philadelphia: F. A. Davis, 1967.

ABSTAIN. When fencing touches were decided by the observations of a bout director and four judges (rather than by the sensitivity of an electric scoring machine), any one of these officials was obliged, when he was unsure if a touch occurred, to abstain from the decision.
REFERENCE
Cass, Eleanor Baldwin. *The Book of Fencing.* Boston: Lothrop, Lee, and Shephard, 1930.

ACADEMIE D'ARMES DE LANGUEDUC. A renowned fencing school at Toulouse, France. Probably established by the Spanish when they exerted some influence there during the early 1500s. A highly respected and influential family of fencing masters, the Labats,* taught here from the end of the sixteenth century until the middle of the eighteenth.

The school was commonly known as the "Academie de Toulous."
REFERENCES
Castle, Egerton. *Schools and Masters of Fence.* London: George Bell, 1885.
McEvedy, Colin. *The Penguin Atlas of Modern History.* England: Penguin Books, 1972.
Wise, Arthur. *The Art and History of Personal Combat.* Greenwich, CT: Arma Press, 1971.

ACCELERATION. When attacking, "acceleration" refers to increasing the speed of one's action as one decreases the distance between one's self and one's opponent.
REFERENCE
Morton, E. D. *Martini A–Z of Fencing.* London: Queen Anne Press, 1992.

ACCIDENTS, MOVIE-RELATED FENCING. Movie sword fights are, of course, not the spontaneous events they appear to be but are rather well-rehearsed moments of expertly conceived movement. In an interview in 1974, actor Douglas Fairbanks, Jr.,* who starred in such classic swashbuckler films as *The Prisoner of Zenda* (1937)** and *The Corsican Brothers* (1941),** described the manner in which Hollywood sword duels are set up: "They would be designed and thought out in advance with as much care and attention as, let us say, Fred Astaire would work out a dance routine." That so much consideration is paid to these theatrical undertakings is understandable; the danger inherent in two people going at one another with swords, even dulled or blunted ones, is a historical reality. As Ralph Faulkner,* one of the film industry's great fencing coaches, once explained about the sword fights he worked on, "We were very careful. It didn't behoove you to forget an action, because someone might get his ears lopped off if you did." Just the same, accidents happen.

Errol Flynn* stated in his autobiography *My Wicked, Wicked Ways* (1959)** that actors are the most dangerous people to face with a sword because they don't really know what they're doing; they just want to look good. Flynn was true to his hypothesis, once nearly cutting off the thumb of fellow actor Christopher Lee while filming a sword fight for *The Warriors* (1955).**

The celebrated thespian Laurence Olivier,* proudly enumerating his many stage and film fencing-related injuries in an introduction for a volume on theatrical combat, *Techniques of the Stage Fight* (1967),** talked of countless cuts, bruises, rips, ruptures, strains, and sprains. He also mentioned being nearly electrocuted when he accidentally stuck his sword blade into some movie studio sound stage electrical equipment.

Commenting on the fencing scenes he considered most dangerous to stage, Ralph Faulkner was emphatic: "Those big melees aboard pirate ships were the worst! There were so many fellows in those battles who knew nothing about fencing or swords. They'd wave their blades around like there was no one within a mile of them, and all the time everyone would be so packed together you couldn't step a foot in any direction. There was always some guy who would haul off and stick his sword point in someone's ear. Or his eye! We got to where we'd give the worst brutes rubber-bladed swords.''

Actor Louis Hayward,* who starred in many successful swashbuckler films in the 1930s, 1940s, and 1950s, spoke about his most memorable fencing injury, which he suffered while filming *Anthony Adverse* (1936)**: ''I was fencing with Claude Rains, a delightful, charming man, but a rather awful swordsman. During one take, he got his sword point up under the wig I was wearing, and gave me quite a gash on the scalp. No one even knew I'd been wounded until we were done, and blood suddenly came trickling down my face.''

Fight arranger Fred Cavens* was conspicuous for producing safe movie sword fights. By insisting that the actors in his charge always be well-trained for their undertakings, he minimized the chances of disaster striking. Yet even his work was marred occasionally by the unforeseen mishap. During the filming of the climactic sword duel in *The Adventures of Robin Hood* (1938),** stuntman Fred Graham, doubling for Basil Rathbone,* took a tremendous plunge down a staircase and broke his ankle. In another Cavens fight, this time in *Against All Flags* (1952),** Errol Flynn narrowly escaped injury when a sword blade was thrust through his doublet by Anthony Quinn.**

In his book *The Moon's a Balloon* (1972), David Niven recounted a harrowing moment he experienced in a battle scene for *Bonnie Prince Charlie* (1947).** Running with a drawn sword, he (as the ''bonnie prince'') tripped and accidentally stuck his blade through the leg of an extra. Niven went on to add that it was then that he discovered the man had a wooden leg.

Another performer, John Loder, was not so lucky. In the midst of rehearsing a fencing routine with two stuntmen for *The Wife of Monte Cristo* (1946),** he was seriously wounded when one of his two opponents knocked the other's sword blade into Loder's thigh. The actor ended up with a deep cut and a trip to the hospital.

It should be noted that even fencing masters are not exempt from film fencing injuries. Participating in a duel for *Sword of the Avenger* (1948), Ralph Faulkner stepped on a piece of wire someone had carelessly left on the ground. Slipping, he pitched forward, face first, onto his adversary's sword. The point just missed his eye, leaving him with a scar he carried for the rest of his life.

William Hobbs,* the fencing supervisor for *The Three Musketeers* (1974)** and *Pirates* (1985),** has a formula for avoiding sword fight accidents. In his book *Techniques of the Stage Fight,* he advanced the following precepts: train an actor slowly, building up his confidence along the way; always work in adequate light; never allow combatants to work too close together; check weapon grips before any fight, making sure they are not slippery; check the floor for objects one might trip or slip on; wear gloves; always warm up; and never attempt to use any weapon in a duel other than the ones with which you have specifically trained.

REFERENCES

Behlmer, Rudy. *The Adventures of Robin Hood.* Wisconsin: University of Wisconsin Press, 1979.

Evangelista, Nick. "Won By the Sword." *Silver Circle News* (Spring 1979).

Flynn, Errol. *My Wicked, Wicked Ways.* New York: G. P. Putnam's Sons, 1959.

Hobbs, William. *Techniques of the Stage Fight.* London: Studio Vista, 1967.

Niven, David. *The Moon's a Balloon.* New York: G. P. Putnam's Sons, 1972.

Richards, Jeffrey. *Swordsmen of the Screen.* Boston: Routledge and Kegan Paul, 1977.

ACCIDENTS, THEATRICAL STAGE FENCING. Fencing on the theatrical stage, while theoretically safer than dueling or sport fencing, has still managed to inflict a number of serious injuries on actors over the years.

In Shakespeare's time, there was always the possibility of unwanted intrusions by unruly audience members during stage fights. Such encounters, of course, could lead to disaster for both actors and spectators.

It has been noted that old-time stage fights were often fierce and sometimes not overly rehearsed. During the climactic fencing scene between Henry Irving and Squire Bancroft in the nineteenth-century play *The Dead Heart,* only the final thrust was rehearsed. The rest of the fight, night after night, was totally improvised. Considering the energy both men put into their parts—plus the fact that Henry Irving was nearsighted—it is a wonder neither actor was ever seriously injured.

When accidents in plays did occur, however, they ranged from sword hands or heads being bashed, to fingers being cut off, to the occasional death. There was also the unforeseen problem of swords flying into the audience.

The nineteenth-century writer Bram Stoker (the creator of Dracula) once observed in a newspaper review of a London stage production of *Romeo and Juliet* that the swordplay was so spirited that on most evenings at least one member of the cast needed medical attention.

Famed actor Laurence Olivier,* in writing about his own fencing injuries on stage, spoke of broken bones, countless sword cuts, a sword-thrust wound in the chest, and torn muscles. He also mentioned nearly cutting the thumb off a fellow actor in a 1935 play.

REFERENCES

Hobbs, William. *Techniques of the Stage Fight.* London: Studio Vista, 1967.

Morton, E. D. *Martini A–Z of Fencing.* London: Queen Anne Press, 1992.

ACKNOWLEDGMENT OF TOUCHES. In the early days of fencing, acknowledging touches was considered one of the honor points of fencing, even in informal practice situations. So, it is understandable that when fencing was set up on an official, organized level, acknowledging touches was written into the rules. However, by 1932, this concept was abolished.

Today, among serious fencers, acknowledging touches is still looked upon as a given in practice settings.
REFERENCE
Morton, E. D. *Martini A–Z of Fencing.* London: Queen Anne Press, 1992.

ACTORS—MOVIE FENCERS. While numerous actors have tried their hand at swordplay in films over the years, only a handful have excelled at it. Natural athletes or dedicated students of fencing, they made it all look exciting and effortless.

Sadly, the vast majority of actors who have fenced in films have fallen somewhere between, adequate at best and totally embarrassing at worst.

Actors who have fenced in films include:

Performer	Fencing Example
Silent Films	
Douglas Fairbanks, Sr.	*The Mark of Zorro* (1920)
Ramon Novarro	*Scaramouche* (1923)
Rudolph Valentino	*Monsieur Beaucaire* (1924)
John Barrymore	*Don Juan* (1926)
John Gilbert	*Bardelys the Magnificent* (1926)
Sound Films	
Robert Donat	*The Count of Monte Cristo* (1934)
Basil Rathbone	*Captain Blood* (1935)
Henry Wilcoxon	*The Crusaders* (1935)
Walter Abel	*The Three Musketeers* (1935)
Paul Lukas	*The Three Musketeers* (1935)
Leslie Howard	*Romeo and Juliet* (1936)
Frederic March	*Adventures of Cellini* (1936)
Alan Hale	*The Prince and the Pauper* (1936)
Ronald Colman	*The Prisoner of Zenda* (1937)
Errol Flynn	*The Adventures of Robin Hood* (1938)
Louis Hayward	*The Man in the Iron Mask* (1939)
Don Ameche	*The Three Musketeers* (1939)
Tyrone Power	*The Mark of Zorro* (1940)
Douglas Fairbanks, Jr.	*The Corsican Brothers* (1941)
George Sanders	*The Black Swan* (1942)
Jon Hall	*Arabian Nights* (1942)
Arturo de Cordova	*Frenchman's Creek* (1944)
Paul Henried	*The Spanish Main* (1945)
Randolph Scott	*Captain Kidd* (1945)

Charles Laughton	*Captain Kidd* (1945)
Bob Hope	*Monsieur Beaucaire* (1946)
Patric Knowles	*Monsieur Beaucaire* (1946)
Henry Daniell	*The Bandit of Sherwood Forest* (1946)
Cornel Wilde	*Forever Amber* (1947)
Orson Welles	*Black Magic* (1947)
Gilbert Roland	*Pirates of Monterey* (1947)
Larry Parks	*The Swordsman* (1947)
Laurence Olivier	*Hamlet* (1948)
Raymond Burr	*The Adventures of Don Juan* (1948)
Gene Kelly	*The Three Musketeers* (1948)
Robert Coote	*The Three Musketeers* (1948)
Gig Young	*The Three Musketeers* (1948)
Van Heflin	*The Three Musketeers* (1948)
Burt Lancaster	*The Flame and the Arrow* (1950)
Jose Ferrer	*Cyrano de Bergerac* (1950)
John Carroll	*The Avengers* (1950)
Ricardo Montalban	*Mark of the Renegade* (1951)
Gregory Peck	*Captain Horatio Hornblower* (1951)
Richard Greene	*Lorna Doone* (1951)
Jean Peters	*Anne of the Indies* (1951)
Robert Douglas	*At Sword's Point* (1952)
Alan Hale, Jr.	*At Sword's Point* (1952)
Maureen O'Hara	*At Sword's Point* (1952)
Robert Taylor	*Ivanhoe* (1952)
Jeff Chandler	*Yankee Buccaneer* (1952)
Sterling Hayden	*The Golden Hawk* (1952)
James Mason	*The Prisoner of Zenda* (1952)
Anthony Quinn	*Against All Flags* (1952)
Stewart Granger	*Scaramouche* (1952)
Ricard Todd	*The Story of Robin Hood* (1952)
Lou Costello	*Jack and the Beanstalk* (1952)
Victor Mature	*The Veils of Bagdad* (1953)
Richard Burton	*The Robe* (1953)
John Derek	*Mask of the Avenger* (1953)
Jeffrey Hunter	*Princess of the Nile* (1954)
Robert Wagner	*Prince Valiant* (1954)

Alan Ladd	*The Black Knight* (1954)
Robert Stack	*The Iron Glove* (1954)
Rock Hudson	*The Golden Blade* (1954)
Laurence Harvey	*King Richard and the Crusaders* (1954)
Tony Curtis	*The Purple Mask* (1955)
Peter Finch	*The Warriors* (1955)
David Niven	*The King's Thief* (1955)
Vincent Price	*Casanova's Big Night* (1956)
John Wayne	*The Conqueror* (1956)
Grace Kelly	*The Swan* (1956)
Danny Kaye	*The Court Jester* (1956)
Louis Jordan	*Dangerous Exile* (1958)
Kirk Douglas	*Spartacus* (1960)
Steve Reeves	*Morgan the Pirate* (1960)
Charlton Heston	*El Cid* (1961)
Rory Calhoun	*Marco Polo* (1962)
Jean-Pierre Cassel	*Cyrano and D'Artagnan* (1962)
Rod Taylor	*Seven Seas to Calais* (1962)
Albert Finney	*Tom Jones* (1963)
Ross Martin	*The Great Race* (1965)
Mel Ferrer	*El Greco* (1966)
Doug McClure	*King's Pirate* (1967)
Donald Sutherland	*Start the Revolution Without Me* (1970)
Frank Langella	*The Mark of Zorro* (1974)
Michael York	*The Three Musketeers* (1974)
Frank Finlay	*The Three Musketeers* (1974)
Christopher Lee	*The Four Musketeers* (1975)
Ryan O'Neal	*Barry Lyndon* (1975)
Malcolm McDowell	*Royal Flash* (1975)
Alan Bates	*Royal Flash* (1975)
Stanley Baker	*Zorro* (1975)
Gene Wilder	*Sherlock Holmes' Smarter Brother* (1975)
Robert Shaw	*Swashbuckler* (1976)
James Earl Jones	*Swashbuckler* (1976)
Sean Connery	*Robin and Marian* (1976)
Oliver Reed	*The Prince and the Pauper* (1977)
Marty Feldman	*The Last Remake of Beau Geste* (1977)

Peter Ustinov	*The Last Remake of Beau Geste* (1977)
Harvey Keitel	*The Duellists* (1977)
Keith Carradine	*The Duellists* (1977)
Beau Bridges	*The Fifth Musketeer* (1977)
Lloyd Bridges	*The Fifth Musketeer* (1977)
Richard Chamberlain	*Man in the Iron Mask* (1977)
George Hamilton	*Zorro, the Gay Blade* (1981)
Arnold Schwarzenegger	*Conan the Barbarian* (1982)
Peter O'Toole	*My Favorite Year* (1982)
Mark Hamill	*Return of the Jedi* (1983)
Peter Boyle	*Yellowbeard* (1983)
George Segal	*The Zany Adventures of Robin Hood* (1984)
David Carradine	*Warrior and the Sorceress* (1984)
Michael Douglas	*Jewel of the Nile* (1985)
Robert De Niro	*The Mission* (1986)
Mandy Patinkin	*The Princess Bride* (1987)
Cary Elwes	*The Princess Bride* (1987)
Christopher Guest	*The Princess Bride* (1987)
Val Kilmer	*Willow* (1988)
Michael Caine	*Without a Clue* (1988)
Mel Gibson	*Hamlet* (1990)
Kevin Costner	*Robin Hood* (1991)
Robin Williams	*Hook* (1991)
Dustin Hoffman	*Hook* (1991)
Raul Julia	*The Addams Family* (1992)
Eric Roberts	*By the Sword* (1993)
F. Murray Abraham	*By the Sword* (1993)

REFERENCES

Halliwell, Leslie. *Halliwell's Filmgoer's and Video Viewer's Companion.* New York: Charles Scribner's Sons, 1988.

Maltin, Leonard. *Leonard Maltin's Movie and Video Guide 1993.* New York: Penguin Books, 1993.

Richards, Jeffrey. *Swordsmen of the Screen.* Boston: Routledge and Kegan Paul, 1977.

ACTORS—STAGE FENCERS. The first theatrical fencers were, of course, stage actors. In the early days of the theater, especially in Shakespeare's time, to become a successful actor necessitated not only developing one's histrionic skills but devoting a good amount of time to the study of fencing. Since dueling was an accepted part of everyday life from the Middle Ages until the end of the eighteenth century, it was inevitable that swords should command a significant position in many, if not most, plays.

Even after the custom of fighting with blades had died away in real life, fencing remained a beloved part of the theatrical scene, so much so that, as British fencing master William Hobbs wrote in his book *Techniques of the Stage Fight* (1967): "Many a bad play was devised as an excuse for a terrific combat."

By the nineteenth century, according to writer David Caroll in his book *The Matinee Idols* (1972),

a primary qualification for matinee stardom was swordfighting ability. A melodrama was incomplete without a climactic duel between hero and villain. . . . Most actors took their stage fights seriously and considered them a kind of art. A few performers neglected authenticity completely and clanked swords disinterestedly, waiting for an appropriate amount of time until one of them suddenly fell dead for no apparent reason other than ennui. . . . But most were conscientious about their battles.

For much of the present century, actors have had little stage fencing to engage in outside the realm of Shakespearean dramas and comedies.

Actors who fenced on stage include:

Eighteenth century:

John Bannister, Thomas Caufield, David Garrick, John Henderson, Charles Macklin, and William Smith.

Nineteenth century:

Squire Bancroft, Edwin Booth, Coquelin, Ben Greet, Martin Harvey, Henry Irving, Edmund Kean, Henry Kimble, Richard Mansfield, Henry Marston, Forbes Robertson, Frederick Robinson, Fred Terry, and Herman Vezin.

Early twentieth century:

Gerald Du Maurier, Halliwell Hobbs, Matheson Lang, Eric Mayne, Lewis Waller.

Mid-twentieth century:

John Barrymore, Jose Ferrer, John Gielgud, Laurence Olivier, Ralph Richardson, and Orson Welles.

Modern times:

Richard Burton, Richard Chamberlain, Charlton Heston, Frank Langella, Peter O'Toole, Christopher Plummer, Jon Voight, and David Warner.

REFERENCES
Benet, William Rose. *The Reader's Encyclopedia.* New York: Thomas Y. Crowell, 1965.
Halliwell, Leslie. *Halliwell's Filmgoer's and Video Viewer's Companion.* New York: Charles Scribner's Sons, 1988.
Hobbs, William. *Techniques of the Stage Fight.* London: Studio Vista, 1967.
Richards, Jeffrey. *Swordsmen of the Screen.* Boston: Routledge and Kegan Paul, 1977.

ACTORS—TELEVISION FENCERS. When a character on a television series happens to be either rich, worldly, or dashing, there is a good chance that, at some time during the run of the show, the actor portraying that character will have a chance to fence—fencing being something in the collective consciousness that rich, worldly, and dashing people do as a matter of course.

If said actor, sometime during his career, ever fenced in a swashbuckler film, then swordplay, already identified with that individual, is even more likely to occur.

Occasionally, in the case of actors whose performance emphasis is on comedy, fencing becomes a humorous gimmick.

Actors who have been called on to fence on television include:

1950s

    Lucille Ball (as Lucy Ricardo): "I Love Lucy," 1951–1955.

    Elinor Donahoe (as Betty Anderson): "Father Knows Best," 1954–1960.

    Louis Jordan** (star): "The Man Who Beat Lupo," *Ford Theatre,* 1957.

    Errol Flynn* (star): *"Errol Flynn Theatre,"* 1957.

    Guy Williams** (as Zorro): *"Zorro,"* 1958–1959.

    James Mason** (star): "A Sword for Marius," *Alcoa GoodYear Theatre,* 1959.

1960s

    Patrick MacNee (as John Steed): "The Avengers," 1960–1968.

    Gene Barry (as Amos Burke): "Burke's Law," 1963–1965.

    Roger Moore (as Simon Templar): "The Saint," 1963–1968.

    Robert Culp (as Kelly Robinson): "I Spy," 1965–1968.

    Diana Rigg (as Mrs. Peel): "The Avengers," 1965–1967.

    Guy Williams** (as John Robinson): "Lost in Space," 1965–1968.

    Don Adams (as Maxwell Smart): "Get Smart," 1965–1970.

    William Shatner** (as James Kirk): "Star Trek," 1966–1969.

    Leonard Nimoy** (as Mr. Spock): "Star Trek," 1966–1969.

    Patrick McGoohan (as Number Six): "The Prisoner," 1967.

1970s

    Fernando Lamas (guest star): "Dan August," 1970.

    David Carradine (as Kane): "Kung-Fu," 1972–1974.

    Henry Winkler (as the Fonz): "Happy Days," 1973–1983.

    Ricardo Montalban** (as Roarke): "Fantasy Island," 1977–1985.

    Robert Wagner** (as Jonathan Hart): "Hart to Hart," 1979–1983.

    Benny Hill (star): "The Benny Hill Show," 1970s.

1980s

    John Hillerman (as Higgins): "Magnum P.I.," 1980–1989.

    Pierce Brosnan (as Remington Steele): "Remington Steele," 1982–1984.

    John Saxon (guest star): "Fantasy Island," 1983.

    Charo (guest star): "Fantasy Island," 1983.

    Lee Van Cleef** (as the ninja master): "The Master," 1984.

1990s

Rodney Dangerfield (as the guardian angel): "Rodney," 1990.

Duncan Regehr** (as Zorro): "The New Zorro," 1990s.

REFERENCE

Halliwell, Leslie. *Halliwell's Filmgoer's and Video Viewer's Companion.* New York: Charles Scribner's Sons, 1988.

ACTOR'S PARRY. The parry* of seconde, when performed with a wide sweep of the blade, lends itself particularly well to the melodrama of the theatrical sword fight, hence its name.

REFERENCE

Morton, E. D. *Martini A–Z of Fencing.* London: Queen Anne Press, 1992.

ADVANCE. To move toward one's fencing opponent.

After mastering the on-guard* position, "advancing" is the first movement a novice fencer learns. The advance (in the case of a right-handed fencer) begins with a forward step with the right foot—heel first—and ends by bringing the left foot up.

On the surface, one of the simplest components of fencing, the ability to advance smoothly is the basis of a fencer's offensive control. A smooth advance helps to maintain balance and to set up proper attacking distance. It also regulates one's ability to attack quickly.

In mastering the advance, the feet must never be slid. Also, they should always be the same distance apart at the end of the action as they were when the action began.

REFERENCE

Palffy-Alpar, Julius. *Sword and Masque.* Philadelphia: F. A. Davis, 1967.

AFRICAN SWORDS. Swords of Africa come in a wide variety of shapes and sizes—from the straight, North African Crusader-style swords, Dankali swords, and Congo swords to the sabrelike *khopsh,** Wasa, and Gaboon swords to the sickle swords of Abyssinia.

REFERENCE

Burton, Richard F. *The Book of the Sword.* London: Chatto and Windus, 1884.

AGENTE. An Italian fencing term for "on the attack."

REFERENCE

Morton, E. D. *Martini A–Z of Fencing.* London: Queen Anne Press, 1992.

AGRIPPA, CAMILLO. (c. 1550). Milanese architect, mathematician, engineer, and fencer.

Camillo Agrippa was a true man of his period. In his book, *Schools and Masters of Fence,* fencing historian Egerton Castle notes: "Like many of his contemporaries, and especially his friend Michelangelo, who did not find his stupendous works sufficient to quench his super-abundant energy, Agrippa devoted much of his time to practice in the schools of fence."

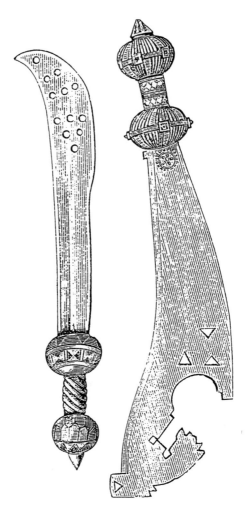

African swords

A highly educated man, Agrippa attacked fencing with a scientific curiosity. Not being a formal teacher, he was not constrained by ideas already ingrained in the fencing world. Finding numerous errors and needless complications in the styles of swordsmanship then being espoused, he used his knowledge as an engineer to develop a natural method of combat based on human movement.

Besides creating a simplifed style of fighting, Agrippa was one of the first writers on the subject of fencing to advocate the use of the sword's point against an opponent. His book, *Trattato di Scientia d'Arme,*** was published in 1553.

DI.M. CAMILLO AGRIPPA
TRATTATO DI SCIENZA
D'ARME.
ET VN DIALOGO IN DETTA
MATERIA.

In Venetia Appreßo. Roberto
Meglietti anno 1604.

Italian scholar and fencer Camillo Agrippa

REFERENCES

Castle, Egerton. *Schools and Masters of Fence.* London: George Bell, 1885.

Wise, Arthur. *The Art and History of Personal Combat.* Greenwich, CT: Arma Press, 1971.

ALAUX, MICHAEL. French fencing master (1923–1974).

Receiving his fencing master's degree in 1947, Michael Alaux became an outstanding figure in the French fencing world. In 1962, the French government awarded him the Palme Academique for services rendered to the sport of fencing. Alaux was the fencing master of the great French fencer Christian d'Oriola.

In 1956, Alaux came to the United States to become fencing master at the New York Fencers Club. He was U.S. Olympic team coach in 1964, 1968, and 1972.

Michael Alaux contributed a chapter entitled "The Épée" to the *Sports Illustrated Book of Fencing* (1961), and authored *Modern Fencing* (1975).

REFERENCE

Gradkowski, Richard. "Michael J. Alaux." *American Fencing* (March/April 1975).

ALBERICH. In Germanic legends, Alberich was the king of craftsmen dwarves who lived underground. Among other things, these individuals produced magic swords for the gods and heroes. Their work included the swords *Tyrfing, Balmung,* and *Gram.*

REFERENCE

Leach, Maria, ed. *Funk and Wagnalls Standard Dictionary of Folklore, Mythology, and Legend.* San Francisco: Harper and Row, 1972.

AL DISTACCO. An attack or riposte performed by detaching one's blade from the blade of one's opponent.

REFERENCE

Morton, E. D. *Martini A–Z of Fencing.* London: Queen Anne Press, 1992.

ALFIERI, FRANCESCO. (c. 1600). Italian fencing master and head of the fencing academy at Padua, Italy.

Alfieri's style of fencing, while artistically rendered in copiously illustrated volumes and, of course, presented as original, actually brought nothing new to the practice of swordplay. His teachings were simply a reworking of already accepted ideas and differed little from the principles devised by Ridolfo Capo Ferro,* who preceded Alfieri by forty years.

Alfieri wrote two volumes on fencing, *La Scherma di F. Alfieri* (1640) and *La Spadone di F. Alfieri* (1653). He also produced a book on the effective display of banners.

REFERENCES

Castle, Egerton. *Schools and Masters of Fence.* London: George Bell, 1885.

Wise, Arthur, *The Art and History of Personal Combat.* Greenwich, CT: Arma Press, 1971.

ALL-JAPAN KENDO FEDERATION. The All-Japan Kendo Federation,

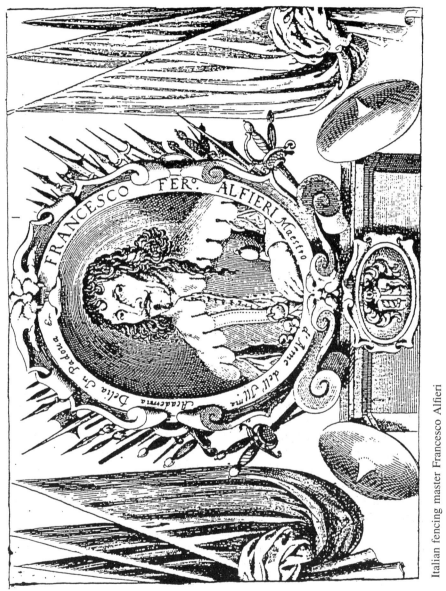

Italian fencing master Francesco Alfieri

founded in 1928, was organized to promote kendo,* or Japanese fencing, in that country on a nationwide basis. They gave membership to all professional and amateur dojo* (schools) and to any individual kendoist who was able to pass a set of examinations at a dojo.

The organization assumed the responsibility of holding examinations through which kendoists are classified and of officially granting said ranks. They also oversee the teaching that takes place in kendo schools, making sure that standards of excellence are regularly met by both instructors and students. These ideals, maintained with care and diligence, are looked on as the cornerstone of the sport, giving it its individual character and spirit.

The first president of the All-Japan Kendo Federation was Masataro Fukuda, who held the office for twenty years.

REFERENCE

Sasamori, Junzo, and Gordon Warner. *This Is Kendo.* Vermont: Charles E. Tuttle, 1984.

A L'OUTRANCE. In medieval times, *a l'outrance* referred to knightly combat with swords, lances, or other weapons, in which anything was allowed. Meaning "to the utterances," or, in modern terms, "to the death," tournaments *a l'outrance* were responsible for the demise of countless knights. The remarkable thing is that this was considered sport.

Thought to be a vital testing ground for war, these contests were such a part of life in the Middle Ages that even outraged protests from the church (underscored by threats of excommunication for those involved in the carnage) were unable to stem their popularity. One contest in the year 1180 had over 3,000 armed and mounted participants. The biggest events, always replete with an air of sweeping pageantry, easily attracted thousands of spectators.

Once the action was well under way, the scenes of carnage were always pretty much the same: mounted knights galloping mercilessly over knights on foot; men, crazed with blood-lust, swinging swords wildly at anything that moved; the bloody bodies of the wounded and dead littering the ground. The fighting would end only when a signal to quit was given or when one combatant, often near suffocation in armor so badly dented it could be removed only with the aid of a blacksmith, was unable to remain standing.

The most famous participant in these dangerous matches was a twelfth-century knight named William Marshal.* In fifteen years of active competition, he fought successfully over 500 times.

The tournament *a l'outrance* eventually gave way to contests in which more emphasis was placed on pomp rather than bloodletting. The show became the important thing. Controlled and stylized, these exchanges rarely exacted anything worse than a few bruises. Old-timers looked on this new form of play with contempt.

REFERENCES

Douglas, Jackie, ed. *Quest for the Past.* New York: Reader's Digest Association, 1984.
Slope, Nicholas. *The Book of Medieval War Games.* New York: Harper and Row, 1984.

AMA GOI KEN. A Japanese sword with the image of the Amakurikara, or rain dragon, used as a decoration on the blade. The weapon was a ceremonial temple sword,* with a straight, double-edged blade.
REFERENCE
Stone, George Cameron. *A Glossary of the Construction, Decoration, and Use of Arms and Armor.* New York: Jack Brussel, 1961.

AMAKUNI. (c. A.D. 600). The earliest known swordsmith in Japan.
REFERENCE
Stone, George Cameron. *A Glossary of the Construction, Decoration, and Use of Arms and Armor.* New York: Jack Brussel, 1961.

AMA NO MURAKUMO TSURUGI. In Japanese samurai lore, Ama No Murakumo Tsurugi was a legendary sword drawn from the tail of the eight-headed dragon by folk hero Susano-O no Mikoto and was kept in the temple of Ise until given to Prince Yamoto Dake.

Tradition has it that while trapped in a burning field by his enemies during a fierce battle, Yamoto used his sword to cut his way clear through the grass. After this, the weapon was known as Kusunagi no Tsurugi, the grass-mowing sword.

In 1935, the 2,000-year-old sword was moved to the Atsuta Shrine at Nagoya, Japan. The occasion, held in great regard by the entire country, was marked by a national holiday and a celebration in which over 500,000 took part.

Also known as "the Divine Sword of Japan" and "Rusanagino Tsurugi."
REFERENCES
Menke, Frank G. *The Encyclopedia of Sports.* A. S. Barnes, 1955.
Stone, George Cameron. *A Glossary of the Construction, Decoration, and Use of Arms and Armor.* New York: Jack Brussel, 1961.
Turnbill, Stephen. *The Book of the Samurai.* New York: Gallery Books, 1982.

AMATEUR FENCER. According to the U.S. Fencing Association (USFA)*, a fencer is deemed an amateur if he practices fencing solely for his own pleasure, relaxation, and/or health, without ever receiving any financial profit from his efforts.

A fencer may, however, under special circumstances receive specific financial assistance or financial compensation, as defined by the bylaws of the USFA, without endangering his amateur status: during periods of training for competitions and during competitions themselves, or in case of need because of training for, and participation in, the Olympic Games.* To qualify for these highly controlled exemptions, a fencer must first obtain official permission from the USFA.

An amateur fencer may also receive money for writing, editing, or publishing articles or books on all aspects of fencing without endangering his amateurism. The guiding assumption here is that the fencer is capitalizing on his ability as a writer or artist, rather than on his fencing skills.

By the same token, an actor may fence in a movie or play and receive money for his work without being considered a professional fencer.

A fencer will not have standing as an amateur if he is a professional athlete or coach in another sport.

REFERENCES

U.S. Fencing Association. *Operations Manual.* Colorado Springs, CO: U.S. Fencing Association, 1985 and 1991.

AMATEUR FENCERS LEAGUE OF AMERICA. On April 22, 1891, the Amateur Fencers League of America (AFLA) was founded in New York City, becoming the official guiding force behind amateur fencing in the United States. Before that, this function was administered by the Amateur Athletic Union. The first president of AFLA was Dr. Graeme M. Hammond, from 1891 to 1925.

The mandate for the AFLA, according to its bylaws, was to disseminate information about fencing, to establish a nationwide program of fencing competitions, to promote the development of fencing clubs and schools throughout the country, and to oversee the United States' international fencing effort.

In 1949, in order to establish better communication among U.S. fencers, the AFLA began *American Fencing,* a magazine designed to highlight the latest fencing news and trends. *American Fencing* was founded by longtime fencing Olympian Jose R. de Capriles and William L. Osborn.

In 1981, in an effort to update its image, the AFLA formally changed its name to the U.S. Fencing Association.* Its headquarters is presently in Colorado Springs, Colorado.

REFERENCES

Amateur Fencers League of America, ed. *Fencing Rules and Manual.* New York: Amateur Fencers League of America, 1970.

Johnson, Emily B. "From the President." *American Fencing* (September/October 1981).

AMATEUR FENCING TEACHER. At one time an amateur fencing teacher was just that—an amateur involved in an activity simply for the love of it, without receiving any financial remuneration for his efforts. In time this concept was changed to include reimbursement for "out-of-pocket expenses for travel and subsistence in connection with group coaching."

Today, an amateur fencing teacher may receive, within limits set and sanctioned by the U.S. Fencing Association,* money for his services.

A fencing coach is not considered an amateur, however, if he is a professional athlete or coach in another sport.

REFERENCES

Amateur Fencers League of America. *Fencing Rules and Manual.* New York: Amateur Fencers League of America, 1970.

U.S. Fencing Association. *Operations Manual.* Colorado Springs, CO: U.S. Fencing Association, 1985 and 1991.

AMIDA TAGANE. The name for the decoration of radiating lines from the center of a Japanesen tsuba (sword guard).

REFERENCE
Stone, George Cameron. *A Glossary of the Construction, Decoration, and Use of Arms and Armor.* New York: Jack Brussel, 1961.

ANALYSIS. The mental process, orally recounted, employed to describe an exchange between two fencers. The purpose of this analytical approach is to determine who has touched whom.
REFERENCE
Handelman, Rob. "Fencing Glossary." *American Fencing* (February/March 1978).

ANATOMICAL GRIP. Any type of modern pronged grip that has been designed to fit the contours of the hand.

Also known as pistol grip* and orthopedic grip.*
REFERENCE
Palffy-Alpar, Julius. *Sword and Masque.* Philadelphia: F. A. Davis, 1967.

ANDERSON, BOB. (c. twentieth century). British film fencing master.

Bob Anderson's work, characterized by a sound, basic, straightforward approach to fencing, includes swordplay in such films as *Moonraker* (1958), with George Baker; *Barry Lyndon* (1975), with Ryan O'Neal; *The Highlander* (1985), with Sean Connery and Christopher Lambert; *The Princess Bride* (1987), with Cary Elwes and Mandy Patinkin; and *By the Sword* (1993), with Eric Roberts and F. Murray Abraham. The last two are, by far, Anderson's best work to date.

Based on the best-selling 1973 novel by William Goldman, *The Princess Bride* was a parody of the swashbuckling genre. While comic in nature, the swordplay was nevertheless handled with respect. Because of this, it has some of the best-staged fencing moments in the last thirty years.

By the Sword, set in present times, deals with the world of modern fencing. Much of the action takes place, in fact, in a fencing school. The swordplay, of which, understandably, there is an abundance, is highly effective.

Early in his fencing career, Maestro Anderson was an amateur competitive champion, winning a number of Britain's most prestigious tournaments. He was also a member of the British Olympic fencing team in 1948 and 1952. Before becoming involved in film work, he also spent some time as his country's national coach.

Anderson has said of his film fencing: "My style of sword fencing draws heavily on my experience as a sabre fencer. . . . I usually put together a basic routine as it comes into my head, paying particular attention to getting the rhythm right. Other than the safety factor, the most important element in the final choreographed fight is the change of blade rhythm. If a fight goes along with the same tempo, it gets rather boring." The fencing master particularly enjoys movie swordplay reminiscent of Errol Flynn and Douglas Fairbanks.

Bob Anderson has written one book on fencing, *Better Fencing—Foil* (1973).

Italian fencing master Domenico Angelo around 1760

REFERENCES
Cragg, Tom. "Darth Vader and the Three Musketeers." *American Fencing* (Fall 1993).
Ivie, Mark Evan. "Club Fencer Goes Hollywood." *American Fencing* (Summer 1993).
Morton, E. D. *Martini A–Z of Fencing*. London: Queen Anne Press, 1992.

ANGELO, DOMENICO. (1716–1802). Italian-born fencing master.

Perhaps more than any other man, Domenico Angelo was responsible for fencing's becoming what it is in modern times. While the sword had primarily been used as a killing tool until the mid-1700s, Angelo, through his influence on the fencing world as a renowned teacher—his students included the rich, the noble, and the famous of Europe—turned its application toward sport, with an emphasis on developing health, poise, and grace. Through him we gain the image of the fencing master as a man of breeding, a combination teacher, sportsman, historian, artist, scientist, and philosopher.

Born in Leghorn, Italy, in 1716, Angelo first studied fencing in Pisa; as expected, his initial training was in the Italian method of swordplay. Later, moving to Paris, he studied the French style with Teillagory, acknowledged as one of the greatest swordsmen in all of Europe.

Eventually establishing his own reputation as both a talented amateur swordsman and horseman, Angelo moved to England in the mid-1700s and settled in London. Before long, due, in great part, to his gentlemanly accomplishments, he found himself in the center of London's high society.

In 1763, at the urging of his many friends, Angelo began teaching fencing professionally. This move was brought about, in great part, by an encounter with the foremost swordsman in Ireland, a Dr. Keys. Keys, a jealous rival of Angelo's, challenged the Italian to a public demonstration of skill, which, in those days, amounted to a bloodless duel.

The exhibition took place at a London tavern before an assemblage of noblemen, gentlemen, and ladies. Never having met Keys before, Angelo used his scientific approach to fencing to quickly determine his opponent's strengths and weaknesses. Finding that the Irishman's fencing style consisted of little more than brute force, Angelo determined to let him attack repeatedly and use up all his energy. He, on the other hand, concerned himself with maintaining a calm, graceful defensive approach. Once Keys had hopelessly tired himself out (without ever landing a single touch), Angelo proceeded to pick the doctor apart, and, as later described by the master's son in his *Reminiscences of Henry Angelo, with Memoirs of His Late Father and Friends,* published in 1828, he planted "twelve palpable hits on the breast of his enraged antagonist."

As news of this highly dramatic meeting spread, Angelo's popularity soared. From this point on, his fortune was made. He received so many requests for lessons from prospective students, he could hardly refuse to open his own school.

Angelo's fencing instruction was, as described by historian Arthur Wise in his study *The Art and History of Personal Combat,* "sound and methodical." It was a combination of techniques useful for both practice and serious fighting (duels of honor were still, of course, an accepted part of daily life). Yet in his teaching we can see the groundwork being laid for modern fencing.

In his book *The School of Fencing,*** first published in 1763, there is an emphatic insistence never before seen in fencing manuals that fencing should be practiced assiduously as a sport to improve one's physique. (In the original edition, paid for by his students and patrons, Angelo himself posed as one of the fencers for all forty-seven illustrations; many of his friends stood for his opponent.)

Domenico Angelo lived to the age of eighty-six and taught right up to a few days before his death. His school continued to flourish in England, dominating the European fencing perspective for the next 100 years.

REFERENCES
Angelo, Domenico. *The School of Fencing.* London: H. Angelo, 1787 edition.
Aylward, J. D. *The House of Angelo.* London: The Batchworth Press, 1953.
Castle, Egerton. *Schools and Masters of Fence.* London: George Bell, 1885.

ANGELO, HENRY (HARRY). (c. 1750). English fencing master and son of Domenico Angelo,* the founder of modern fencing.

Studying fencing in Paris under Motet, then known all over the Continent, according to historian Egerton Castle,* as the greatest living fencer, Henry Angelo became an accomplished fencer and teacher in his own right.

By 1787, Henry was running his father's school. Specializing in cavalry swordsmanship, his clientele included the Light Horse Volunteers of London and Westminster.

He was responsible for two books on fencing. The first was produced under his direction: *Hungarian and Highland Broadsword* (1798), a collection of twenty-four illustrations (by Thomas Rowlandson) depicting various attacks and defensive fencing positions, mostly for encounters on horseback. The second volume, *A Treatise on the Utility and Advantages of Fencing,* was published in 1817.

Published in 1828, Henry Angelo's *Reminiscences of Henry Angelo, with Memoirs of His Late Father and Friends* concentrated on personal anecdotes concerning famous people rather than on fencing topics.

REFERENCES
Angelo, Henry. *Hungarian and Highland Broadsword.* London: C. Roworth, 1798.
Castle, Egerton. *Schools and Masters of Fence.* London: George Bell, 1885.

ANGELO, HENRY C. (c. 1800). Son of Henry (Harry) Angelo.* The last fencing master in the dynasty founded by Domenico Angelo.*

An expert in the use of naval hand weapons, Henry C. developed effective systems for the employment of the cutlass and the boarding pike.

His book *Angelo's Bayonet Exercise* (1857) was a primer for the British military for many years.

Henry C. Angelo retired from fencing in 1866, relinquishing control of his famous school to his longtime partner, William McTurk.

REFERENCES
Aylward, J. D. *The House of Angelo.* London: The Batchworth Press, 1953.
Castle, Egerton. *Schools and Masters of Fence.* London: George Bell, 1885.

ANGELO FAMILY, THE. A dynasty of fencing masters established by the great Domenico Angelo,* the son of a wealthy Italian merchant.

The Angelo School of Arms, begun officially in London in 1763 (although its founder was giving lessons as early as the mid-1750s), dominated Europe's fencing scene for well over 100 years. The Angelos stressed scientific swordsmanship, turning fencing into a true game of strategy.

Domenico Angelo taught smallsword play to the cream of England's society, including King George III. Domenico's son Henry,* or Harry as he was known, was a Hungarian and Highland broadsword master. Henry's son, Henry C.,* the last of the line of Angelo fencing masters, interested himself in the use of naval weapons. He retired from fencing in 1866, turning over his practice to his partner William McTurk, thereby ending, for good, the family's long hold on the art of the sword.

The Angelo school had numerous locations in London during its existence. Its initial site was on Carlisle Street, followed by its most famous incarnation at the Opera House in the Haymarket (where bouts between many of Europe's greatest fencers were held). This was followed by the Old Bond Street establishment (the cavalry sabre was especially practiced here), and finally James Street (the final home of the Angelo operation).

Over the years the Angelo family's friends included such illustrious personages as the actor David Garrick, the artists Thomas Gainsborough and Sir Joshua Reynolds, the playwright Richard Sheridan, the composer Johann Christian Bach (son of Johann Sebastian Bach), the infamous adventurer Chevalier d'Eon, political reformers John Wilkes and Horne Tooke, and many members of England's noblest houses.

The youngest son of Henry Angelo, William Henry ("Old William"), also taught fencing, first at Oxford and later at the Angelos' James Street local. Due to a hand injury, he was impelled to strap his weapon to his wrist when he worked.

Another member of the family, Domenico's brother John Xavier, known too as "Angelo Tremamondo," taught fencing in Scotland. Known to his students as "Mr. Ainslie," he continued there successfully until his death in 1804.

REFERENCES

Aylward, J. D. *The House of Angelo.* London: The Batchworth Press, 1953.
Castle, Egerton. *Schools and Masters of Fence.* London: George Bell, 1885.
Morton, E. D. *Martini A–Z of Fencing.* London: Queen Anne Press, 1992.

ANNEAU. In the 1500s, as sword-handling techniques, spurred by a rapid growth in the popularity of fencing, grew increasingly more complicated, the old-style crossbar* sword guard, basic and simple in its design, no longer afforded the protection to the hand it once had. The *anneau,* a metal ring on one or both sides of the sword guard, was added to the weapon to improve hand safety.

The *anneau* eventually became part of a more complex arrangement of rings on the sword called the "counterguard."

REFERENCES
Castle, Egerton. *Schools and Masters of Fence*. London: George Bell, 1885.
Grancsay, Stephen V. *Arms and Armor*. New York: Odyssey Press, 1964.
Stone, George Cameron. *A Glossary of the Construction, Decoration, and Use of Arms and Armor*. New York: Jack Brussel, 1961.

ANNULMENT. To take an otherwise valid* touch away from a fencer because he has violated a rule in gaining that touch.

REFERENCE
Stevenson, John. *Fencing*. London: Briggs, 1935.

ANSPACH, PAUL. (c. 1900). Belgian fencing champion.

Between 1908 and 1920, Paul Anspach won four Olympic medals for épée: two gold, one silver, and one bronze.

In 1914, Anspach assisted in arranging the rules of fencing for international use.

REFERENCE
Wallechinsky, David. *The Complete Book of the Olympics*. New York: Penguin Books, 1984.

AOR. One of the five Greek Homeric names for the sword. The *aor* was a weapon possessing a broad, stout, strong blade.

In the *Iliad,* Homer's tale of the Trojan Wars, Ulysses drew his *aor* in battle and dug a furrow one cubit (from seventeen to twenty-two inches) wide.

The *aor,* according to historian Richard Burton, was also a sword carried by the gods Neptune and Apollo. In the former case, it was described as a "dreadful tapering sword" and "thunderbolt-like."

REFERENCES
Burton, Richard F. *The Book of the Sword*. London: Chatto and Windus, 1884.
Stone, George Cameron. *A Glossary of the Construction, Decoration, and Use of Armors and Armor*. New York: Jack Brussel, 1961.

APPEL. A stamp of the front foot. Using this motion helps to continue the force of an unsuccessful initial attack when a fencer wishes to immediately continue his offensive drive without first returning to the on-guard position.

Some old-time swordsmen, such as sixteenth-century fencing master Salvator Fabris,* suggested that the appel could be used to upset an opponent. "Some, when making feints, move more with their feet than their swords, stamping as much as they can, trying to frighten the enemy . . . before striking him." He warns, however, "This may sometimes be effectual in the schools especially, where the floor being made of boards is consequently highly resonant, but out in the open, in the fields, where the ground is not sonorous, no such effect can be produced."

Labat,* famed master of the 1600s, according to historian Egerton Castle, stressed that feints of attacks could be accentuated with a slight movement of the foot.

Also known as an *impetinata.*

REFERENCES
Castle, Egerton. *Schools and Masters of Fence*. London: George Bell, 1885.
Palffy-Alpar, Julius. *Sword and Masque*. Philadelphia: F. A. Davis, 1967.

APPUNTATA. A type of time thrust.*

In the case of the *appuntata,* the time thrust is made as a *remise* * (an immediate continuation of one's attack in the same line after being parried) against an indirect riposte (a counterattack, following a successful parry, that leaves the line in which the parry was made).

When the *appuntata* is executed with the proper timing, the initial attacker, by placing his extended blade in the path of his opponent's indirect riposte, both blocks the completion of the final action of the indirect riposte and scores a touch at the same time.

REFERENCE
Palffy-Alpar, Julius. *Sword and Masque*. Philadelphia: F. A. Davis, 1967.

A-PROPOS. To immediately take advantage of a favorable situation created by one's opponent.

REFERENCE
Handelman, Rob. "Fencing Glossary." *American Fencing* (February/March 1978).

ARCHES. On an Italian foil,* two metal bars that curve from opposite edges of the guard to join that weapon's crossbar.

Also known as the *archetti.*

REFERENCE
Morton, E. D. *Martini A–Z of Fencing*. London: Queen Anne Press, 1992.

ARMED AND UNARMED. From the Middle Ages to the 1600s, "armed" was a term that referred to the wearing of armor rather than the act of carrying arms. A man without armor was said to be "unarmed," even when outfitted with numerous weapons.

REFERENCE
Stone, George Cameron. *A Glossary of the Construction, Decoration, and Use of Arms and Armor*. New York: Jack Brussel, 1961.

ARMING GIRDLE. The arming girdle was a sword belt worn with armor.

REFERENCE
Stone, George Cameron. *A Glossary of the Construction, Decoration, and Use of Arms and Armor*. New York: Jack Brussel, 1961.

ARMING SWORD. The arming sword was a short, thrusting sword used primarily as an auxiliary weapon. In the early Middle Ages, it was hung in readiness from the saddle when on horseback or slid through rings on the belt when on foot.

REFERENCES
Stone, George Cameron. *A Glossary of the Construction, Decoration, and Use of Arms and Armor*. New York: Jack Brussel, 1961.
Wilkinson, Frederick. *Swords and Daggers*. New York: Hawthorn Books, 1967.

ARMITAGE, NORMAN. (1907–1972). U.S. fencing champion.

Norman Armitage was a member of the U.S. Olympic fencing team from 1928 to 1956. He was U.S. national champion sixteen times and runner-up nine times.

REFERENCE

Goldstein, Ralph, ed. "Norman C. Armitage." *American Fencing* (May/June 1972).

ARMOR. Simply put, armor is a covering worn for protection against weapons. Whether in the primitive form of dried animal hides or sophisticated metal plates, it allowed the warrior, soldier, or knight, by filling most defensive needs, to focus primarily on an offensive approach to personal combat.

The relationship between armor and fencing is an ambivalent one. While armor obviously afforded certain advantages in a sword fight, at the same time, by acting as a defensive crutch, it retarded the development of blade-handling skills. During the Middle Ages, the heyday of armor usage, swords were little more than glorified "can openers," hacking and whacking devices, whose sole purpose was to find a way through armor.

It was only when armor finally fell into disuse in the 1500s–being literally blown out of service by the introduction of armor-piercing firearms into warfare—that complex offensive and defensive systems of swordplay began to appear.

But armor did not go down without a fight. To withstand musket fire, it was made heavier and heavier. Unfortunately, according to French soldier and writer François de la Noue (1531–1591), armor became so ponderous, it was impossible to wear for any length of time. Before long, troops were refusing to wear their armor on marches. At last, it was too much to bear even in battle.

By the beginning of the seventeenth century, the wearing of armor was reduced to a mostly ceremonial level.

Today, armor has come full circle with the development of protective gear—the mask, thick jacket and pants, and glove—for the modern sport fencer.

REFERENCES

Castle, Egerton. *Schools and Masters of Fence.* London: George Bell, 1885.

Norman, Vesey. *Arms and Armor.* London: Octopus Books, 1964.

Stone, George Cameron. *A Glossary of the Construction, Decoration, and Use of Arms and Armor.* New York: Jack Brussel, 1961.

Vebell, Edward. *Sports Illustrated Book of Fencing.* Philadelphia: J. B. Lippincott, 1962.

ARMOR—JAPANESE. The Japanese character is strongly expressed in their armor (*katchu*)—the armor of the samurai. A concern for beauty, a Japanese obsession, can be seen in equipment designed as much for the eye as for the battlefield. The highly developed sense of tradition of the Japanese is apparent in that once the essential form of their armor was established in the tenth century—style changes dictated by period tastes aside—it basically remained the same for over 700 years. Moreover, the lightness and flexibility of the armor were highly suited to the Japanese physique.

Like its Western counterparts, the main focus of the Japanese armor was of a defensively offensive nature; that is, by taking on all defensive needs, it allowed the wearer to pursue an entirely offensive mode of fighting.

With regard to types of armor (of which there were many over the centuries), the *yoroi,* a heavy, ornate, boxlike armor, was the earliest. Lighter armor, called *haramaki* (a variant of armor called *do-maru,* which was previously worn only by foot soldiers)—whose main innovation was in its open back construction—was devised. Yet even this style had its drawbacks. Because the small metal plates making up the armor were connected by countless cords of colored silk lacing—a system called *kebiki-odoshi*—the armor easily absorbed and held great amounts of moisture, not only increasing its weight dramatically but also providing a suitable home for lice and ants. The *tachi-do* style was an attempt to make the armor more comfortable by redistributing its weight, but it, too, became difficult to wear for long periods. *Tosei-gusoku,* a term meaning "modern armor," was the final outcome. Here, the individual armor plates were replaced by solid strips of metal; also, fewer cords—a lacing method called *sugake-odoshi*—were used. *Okegawa,* one of the last armor styles designed, employed large, solid plates. It was created to withstand encounters with firearms.

The lacing used in the construction of Japanese armor gave it its characteristic flexibility. The lacing was also highly decorative and colorful.

A samurai's armor was made up of at least twenty-three items. However, it was often referred to as *roku gu,* or "six pieces": helmet, mask, body armor, thigh armor, gauntlets, and leg guards.

Armor pieces included:

Kabuto: helmet.

Menpo: steel face mask.

Yodare-kake: neck guard.

Hai-date: thigh protectors.

Sune-ate: leg guards.

Do: breastplate.

Kote: arm guards.

Sode: large shoulder protectors.

The Japanese were also heavy users of chain mail, making more varieties than all the rest of the world put together.

REFERENCES

Sasamori, Junzo, and Gordon Warner. *This Is Kendo.* Vermont: Charles E. Tuttle, 1984.

Stone, George Cameron. *A Glossary of the Construction, Decoration, and Use of Arms and Armor.* New York: Jack Brussel, 1961.

Storry, Richard. *Way of the Samurai.* New York: Galley Press, 1978.

Turnbull, S. R. *Samurai Armies.* London: Osprey, 1979.

ARMOR—WESTERN. The story of Western armor might be described as a story of self-preservation molded in metal. Before circumstances finally relegated it into oblivion, armor's development and alteration, more than anything else, was an ongoing attempt to keep one step ahead, defensively speaking, of new and increasingly lethal weapons of war.

Metal armor has been around for about 40,000 years. Its earliest form was small copper or bronze scales sewn or riveted to a backing of cloth.

In ancient Greece, however, the emphasis in fighting was placed on agility and strength for one's protection rather than body armor. Protective gear included strong, crested helmets, heavy, round shields, short breastplates (or cuirasses), and little else.

The Romans also scorned elaborate armor. The armor that was employed could not be allowed to get in the way of extended marches and active troop maneuvering in battle. The common soldier wore a coat of banded leather and metal and an iron head piece. Officers' outfits included bronze breastplates and iron bands that covered the shoulder.

After the fall of the Roman Empire in A.D. 410, armor returned to a more primitive style: simple leather coats, wooden shields, and iron caps.

By 1066, the time of the Norman invasion of England, armor had evolved into complete suits of mail. The varieties of mail were many—from tiny plates, to rings, to metal studs. All were attached to leather or cloth undercoats. Head coverings continued as simple metal caps.

The next step in the evolution of armor (a period lasting from 1180 to 1250) was chain mail. More complex in its construction than earlier forms of mail, this armor consisted of the interlinking of tiny metal rings (as many as 100,000 might be used for a single shirt). The head might now be entirely covered by a flat-topped steel helmet.

Around 1250, the reinforcement of chain mail began in the form of metal plates (in the beginning, provided mainly for the knees, normally a highly vulnerable spot for a man on horseback). Around this time, to improve vision, movable visors were added to the helmet.

Toward the close of the thirteenth century, banded mail, overlapping metal rings on strips of leather, had almost completely replaced chain mail. It is believed that this type of armor was devised to withstand the deadly piercing effect of arrows propelled by the newly introduced longbow.

Slowly but surely, metal plate began to supersede mail. Steel breastplates became common. Shoulder and leg coverings, separate from mail, were brought into use. To increase comfort, the *gambeson,* a body covering stuffed with wool, was worn beneath the armor.

By the time of the Battle of Crécy, in 1346, there were armor suits made up entirely of plates.

From this point on, according to Stephen Grancsay in his book *Arms and Armor* (1964), "the construction of a workable metal skin for man was a challenge that fired the imaginations of craftsmen and engineers."

The designing of armor reached new heights in the fifteenth and sixteenth centuries, becoming a skill that combined art with metallurgy. The products of this period have been described as being "vibrant" and "full of life."

The emphasis turned to suits of complete body armor formed perfectly to follow the contours of the human body. The custom tailoring of these outfits was looked on as essential. Knights, of course, were willing to pay high prices for such equipment.

The next important development in body armor, introduced in response to the appearance of firearms in combat, also became the last such development. Existing armor proved to be no match for the firepower of a musket and so became useless. Plate that would withstand bullets was then produced to remedy the situation. But it was, by necessity, extremely thick and heavy. Heavy, of course, equaled uncomfortable. Soldiers refused to wear such ponderous attire. In some cases, they purposefully "lost" it on the way to battle.

By the mid-1600s, body armor was, for the most part, a thing of the past.

REFERENCES

Ashdown, Charles. *European Arms and Armor.* New York: Brussel and Brussel, 1967.

Grancsay, Stephen V. *Arms and Armor.* New York: Odyssey Press, 1964.

Norman, Vesey. *Arms and Armor.* London: Octopus Books, 1972.

ARMORER. An armorer is defined as one who makes or repairs armor.

The craftsmen of the Middle Ages and the Renaissance were often highly secretive about the exact methods they used in their creative processes, relegating what they did to the realm of great mysteries. The armorer was a case in point. The minute details of his work were jealously guarded from all but the most trusted eyes. This is quite understandable since, in an age of constant warfare, quality armor that looked good and could be counted on to save lives commanded considerable respect and large sums of cash. Family fortunes were made by keeping certain techniques out of the hands of competitors. An armorer, upon whom kings and nobles depended, might even achieve knighthood. Towns became famous for their skilled armor makers.

A side effect of the armorer's reluctance to part with his knowledge, especially by setting it down on paper, which could be stolen, is that we are left without contemporary treatises describing the specifics of old-time armor making.

REFERENCES

Grancsay, Stephen V. *Arms and Armor.* New York: Odyssey Press, 1964.

Norman, Vesey. *Arms and Armor.* London: Octopus Books, 1964.

Thomas, Bruno, Ortwin Gamber, and Hans Schedelmann. *Arms and Armor of the Western World.* New York: McGraw-Hill, 1964.

ARMORER—SPORT. In modern terms, an armorer is a technician present at most fencing tournaments whose responsibility is to check weapons for eligibility in that day's competition and also to repair faulty weapons.

The armorer inspects the weapons of competing fencers for safety or structural violations and tests whether said weapons are in adequate working order going into the tournament. To clarify this further, it should be noted that electric foils, sabres, and épées—that is, weapons wired for use on an electric scoring machine—are mandatory for all contests sanctioned by the U.S. Fencing Association and the Federation Internationale d'Escrime (world).

With this factor of electronics in the competitive fencing picture, the need for the armorer to repair weapons becomes clearly of critical importance. Electrical fencing weapons—like any other electrical devices—sometimes stop functioning properly (the continued violent nature of their employment being the chief cause), and when this happens they must be fixed promptly. Too many malfunctioning weapons could bog down a tournament, easily bringing it to a complete standstill.

The armorer must also have the ability to deal with the rest of electrical fencing's battery of accessories: body cords, cable reels, floor cables, and scoring boxes (although these items create problems much less frequently than weapons).

Through his efforts, the armorer ensures that fencers can concentrate on their fencing rather than problems generated by technological breakdown. It is safe to say that it would be impossible to carry on an efficient, safe fencing tournament without the presence of a competent armorer.

REFERENCES

U.S. Fencing Association. *Operations Manual.* Colorado Springs: U.S. Fencing Association, 1985.

Volkman, Rudy. *Electrical Fencing Equipment.* Arvee Press, 1974.

ARMOR MAKERS. While most armorers of the Middle Ages worked on an anonymous basis, those of the Renaissance, spurred by newly organized professional guilds, proudly expressed their individuality to the world. The best were Italians and Germans, followed by the French, Spanish, Dutch, and English.

These men not only were able businessmen and accomplished manufacturers of quality equipment (becoming so proficient at their craft that they could, if called upon, outfit an entire army in a few days) but also created pieces of armor that are considered works of art.

Noted Italian armorers include Petrajolo Negroni (c. 1380), Tomasso dei Negroni (c. 1445), Ercole de Fideli (c. 1465), Giovanni Marco Missaglia (c. 1500), Damiano dei Negroni (c. 1500), Filippo Barini (c. 1532), Francesco Negroli (c. 1539), Bartolommeo Campi (c. 1540), Giocomo Filippo (c. 1541), Pompeo della Chiesa (c. 1570), and Luccio Piccinino (c. 1578).

Noted German armorers include: Hans Grunewalt (c. 1440), Lorenz Helmschmeid (c. 1480), Kaspar Rieder (c. 1485), Christian Treytz (c. 1490), Konrad Seusenhofer (c. 1500), Wilhelm von Worms (c. 1501), Wolfgang Grosschedel (c. 1515), Koloman Helmschmied (c. 1520), Desiderius Helmschmied (c. 1536), Kunz Lochner (c. 1548), Conrad Richter (c. 1550), Anton Peffenhauser (c. 1570), Jacob Halder (c. 1576), and Armand Bongarde (c. 1678).

Noted armorers in other countries include: William Pickering (c. 1610) and Richard Hoden (c. 1686) of England, Pierre Reddon (c. 1572) of France, and Jacob Topf (c. 1619) of Austria.

REFERENCES

Grancsay, Stephen V. *Arms and Armor.* New York: Odyssey Press, 1964.

Norman, Vesey. *Arms and Armor.* London: Octopus Books, 1964.

Thomas, Bruno, Ortwin Gamber, and Hans Schedelmann. *Arms and Armor of the Western World.* New York: McGraw-Hill, 1964.

ARMORY. Armories can be classified into two types: places where arms are kept and places where arms are made.

Between the years 1200 and 1400, the church initiated the first stockpiles of arms and armor in the form of collected funeral arms. This effort was to preserve these artifacts for religious reasons and to keep continuous family records that could serve, if necessary, as legal evidence. To collect arms and armor for purely historical and artistic motives became a by-product of the new enlightened thinking engendered by the Renaissance.

For most of the Middle Ages, armories of the manufacturing kind carried on their business in Europe with little note. But, from 1400 until 1700, centers sprang up where the art of producing arms and armor was raised to its highest levels of craftsmanship.

The armories of Milan, Italy—particularly those run by the Missaglia and Negroli families—were doubtlessly the most distinguished in all of Europe, turning out not only technically and functionally superior equipment for armies but also artistic triumphs for kings and dukes.

German armories were Milan's closest rival. The best one, established by the Helmschmied (meaning "helmet maker") family, was in Augsburg. Other successful factories were situated in Nuremberg, Innsbruck, Landshut, and Dresden.

Armories of lesser importance could be found in Greenwich, England; Paris; Brussels; The Hague, Holland; Brescia, Italy; and Arboga, Sweden.

These armories did not spring up in their particular locations by chance. Armories were highly dependent on certain external conditions for their existence: available iron, abundant supplies of charcoal, running water, and financial and political support for workshops from noble sources.

REFERENCES

Grancsay, Stephen V. *Arms and Armor.* New York: Odyssey Press, 1964.

Thomas, Bruno, Ortwin Gamber, and Hans Schedelman. *Arms and Armor of the Western World.* New York: McGraw-Hill, 1964.

ARREBATAR. In the seventeenth-century Spanish style of swordplay, *arrebatar* meant to cut with the entire arm from the shoulder.

REFERENCE

Castle, Egerton. *Schools and Masters of Fence.* London: George Bell, 1885.

ART, THE SWORD IN. The sword appears as a motif in art from the earliest of historic times. It has been employed in sculpture, painting, and illustration in

A medieval armory

terms both literal and symbolic, with themes both religious and secular, and in settings both historic and fantastic.

Ancient Egyptian art depicts scenes where both kings and soldiers brandish swords. The Greeks and Romans joined the sword with their statuary of gods and heroes. They further incorporated it in friezes and on vases illustrating combat scenes, such as on the fourth-century B.C. relief decorating a sarcophagus called the *Tomb of Alexander,* which presents the Greek victory at Granicus in 334 B.C.

During the Middle Ages, the utilization of the sword in art was a regular occurrence. In illuminated manuscripts like the *Bible of San Isidor de Lleo*

The Bayeaux Tapestry

(1162), the *Maciejowski Bible* (1250), *The History of Jerusalem* (1250) by William of Tyre, the *Psautier of St. Louis* (1270), and *Tristen et Yseut* (c. 1400) by Maitre Luces, sword-wielding knights are shown locked in mortal combat continually. Perhaps the most notable artistic production of medieval times was the *Bayeux Tapestry* (1077). This vivid work portraying the Norman invasion of England in A.D. 1066 provides numerous images of soldiers engaged in savage swordplay.

This artistic outlook continued into the Renaissance. Here we find portraits of the rich and noble, where the sword has been relegated to the position of a mere piece of wearing apparel.

Michelangelo,* repeatedly brought the sword into his work. He even produced a series of drawings for a text on fencing by the scholar Camillo Agrippa,* *Trattato di Scientia d'Arme* (1553).

Paintings of this period in which the sword appears in one context or another include *The Rout of San Romano* (1450) by Paolo Uccello, *The Capture of Constantinople by the Latins* (c. 1550) by Jacopo Tintoretto, *The Fall of the Rebel Angels* (1562) by Pieter Brueghel, *The Battle of Cador* (1577) by Titian, *William van Heythuysen* (1600) by Frans Hals, *The Portrait of Tommaso of Savoy* (1634) by Anthony Van Dyck, *The Surrender of Breda* (1635) by Diego Velázquez, *The Defense of Cadiz* (1650) by Francisco Zurbarán, and *The Conspiracy of Claudius Civilis* (1661) by Rembrandt.

In his biblically oriented drawing entitled *Expulsion from Paradise,* sixteenth-century artist Albrecht Dürer depicts Adam and Eve being driven from the Garden of Eden by an angel armed with a sword.

Eighteenth- and nineteenth-century romantic artists produced paintings and illustrations that, if not glorifying the sword outright, at least placed it in colorfully dramatic territory. During this period, we find William Hogarth's painting of the aftermath of a smallsword fight, *The Killing of the Earl* (1743); Thomas Rowlandson's etching of fencing master Domenico Angelo's* fencing school, *Angelo's Haymarket Room* (1787); Jean-Léon Gérôme's emotional *The Duel After the Masquerade Ball* (1853); Ferdinand Delacroix's exciting *Lion Hunt* (1855); and Jean-Louis Meissonier's jaunty *A Cavalier at the Time of Louis XIII* (1850).

Notable for its lack of romantic sentiment is Francisco Goya's *The Duelists* (c. 1800), a work portraying the sword fight as an ugly act engaged in by brutes.

Late–nineteenth-century French artist Maurice Leloir* produced over 200 sword-related drawings for an edition of Alexandre Dumas's *The Three Musketeers* that, to this day, have never been equaled for their cavalier dash. Another successful French illustrator, Gustave Doré, employed sword-toting angels in many of his rather ethereal drawings.

Modern artists Howard Pyle* and N. C. Wyeth* produced numerous paintings (used as book illustrations) that heavily exploited the sword. These efforts cast the weapon in an adventurous light. Subject matter included pirates, knights,

Vikings, and the ever popular Robin Hood.* More recently, Frank Frazetta,* an artist of much power and energy, has created paintings and drawings of fantastic worlds filled with barbarian swordsmen.

The East, both Middle and Far, has its share of sword-adorned art. While often of a symbolic nature—as in the case of the fourteenth-century Tibetian statue of a Buddha waving a double-edged sword representing the separation of the temporal of life from the eternal—it also devotes itself to mythic themes—such as the nineteenth-century Indian painting entitled *Vishnu as Varaha, the Cosmic Boar, Slays a Demon General,* in which two opposing armies, swords drawn, meet in a pitched battle while the god Vishnu flies overhead dispatching justice. Old Japanese paintings and drawings dwell on the sword in the guise of samurai themes. This art is, more often than not, epic in scope, incorporating events involving Japan's greatest warriors. The medieval paintings *The Battle of Shizugatake* and *The Burning of Sanjo Palace* are examples of this. The prints of nineteenth-century artist Kuniyoshi, in particular, have done much to shape the heroic sentiments with which the samurai is presently regarded.

It should not be forgotten that the sword itself has a place as an art object. Many swords over the centuries were not created as weapons but as decorative accoutrements for nobility. Designed by talented craftsmen such as the sixteenth-century masters Giovanni Cechino, Antonio Piccinino, and Johann Michel, these arms commonly exhibit dazzling hilts of inlayed gold, silver, and jewels fitted with intricately etched blades. Today such pieces as the sword of Emperor Frederic II of Hohenstaufen (1197), the golden rapier of Maximilian II (1552), the sword of Henry, Prince of Wales (1607), and the sword of Duke Maximilian I of Bavaria (1613) are museum pieces of considerable value.

REFERENCES

Burnham, Sophy. *A Book of Angels.* New York: Ballantine Books, 1990.

Burton, Richard F. *The Book of the Sword.* London: Chatto and Windus, 1884.

Campbell, Joseph, with Bill Moyers. *The Power of Myth.* New York: Doubleday, 1988.

Koch, H. W. *Medieval Warfare.* New York: Crescent Books, 1978.

Norman, Vesley. *Arms and Armor.* London: Octopus Books, 1972.

Pitz, Henry C. *Howard Pyle.* New York: Bramhall House, 1965.

Turnbull, Stephen R. *Samurai.* New York: Gallery Books, 1982.

ARTISTS AND IGNORANTS. Terms that seventeenth-century Scottish fencing master Sir William Hope* applied to fencers with true knowledge of their art (artists) and those who fenced a physical game without thought (ignorants). He had much contempt for the latter.

Hope suggested that when an artist fenced with an ignorant, sharps—fencing weapons with an inch of point beyond the button—should be employed to teach the poor swordsman his false ways.

REFERENCE

Castle, Egerton. *Schools and Masters of Fence.* London: George Bell, 1885.

ASHI. The *ashi* were two small collars, or lugs, on the scabbard of a *tachi*,*
the earliest form of single-edged sword in Japan. From these points the weapon
was hung by cords that connected to a sword belt.

In Japanese, the word *ashi* means "leg" or "foot."

The space between the lugs was called *ashima.*

REFERENCES

Sasamori, Junzo, and Gordon Warner. *This Is Kendo.* Vermont: Charles E. Tuttle, 1984.

Stone, George Cameron. *A Glossary of the Construction, Decoration, and Use of Arms
and Armor.* New York: Jack Brussel, 1961.

ASIDEVATA. The legendary sword (*khadga*) created by the Hindu god
Brahma, the lord of all creation, according to the sage Vaishampayana, a master
in the art of war. Asidevata was "fifty thumbs long and four thumbs broad."
Brahma gave it to Shiva, the destroyer, who used it in battle against demons
known as Asuras. After that, it was passed on, in turn, to Vishnu, god of pres-
ervation, and finally, Indra, king of the gods.

When Indra was finished with Asidevata, he entrusted it to the guardians of
the World-quarters, and they gave it to Manu, son of the Sun, for use against
evil. Since then, the sword has remained in his family.

REFERENCES

Brown, Joe David. *India.* New York: Time-Life Books, 1967.

Burton, Richard. *The Book of the Sword.* London: Chatto and Windus, 1884.

Parrinder, Geoffrey, ed. *World Religions.* New York: Facts on File, 1971.

Stone, George Cameron. *A Glossary of the Construction, Decoration, and Use of Arms
and Armor.* New York: Jack Brussel, 1961.

ASIL. One of a pair of swords usually worn by the Mahratta people of central
India. The *asil* was characterized as strong but not very sharp, as opposed to
the other weapon, the *sirohi* (*seyre*), which was very sharp but extremely brittle.

Also known as an *asseel.*

REFERENCE

Stone, George Cameron. *A Glossary of the Construction, Decoration, and Use of Arms
and Armor.* New York: Jack Brussel, 1961.

ASSAD ULLAH. (c. 1580). Sword maker.

Assad Ullah was the most famous of the Persian swordsmiths, living in the
town of Isfahan during the reign of the great military leader Shah Abbas (1587–
1622). His blades were celebrated for their beautiful appearance and fine balance.

The signature Assad Ullah placed on his blades was counterfeited widely by
less competent craftsmen wishing to increase the value of their own work; so,
today, a weapon bearing the name of Assad Ullah is not necessarily from that
master's workshop.

REFERENCES
Stone, George Cameron. *A Glossary of the Construction, Decoration, and Use of Arms and Armor.* New York: Jack Brussel, 1961.
Wilkinson, Frederick. *Swords and Daggers.* New York: Hawthorn Books, 1967.

ASSAULT. A friendly, informal encounter between two fencers, as opposed to a lesson or a bout, where touches to determine a result are kept.

From the earliest times, every fencing school of standing had rules, enforced by custom, that governed the assault. Fencers were expected to display the utmost control, avoiding time hits, riposting only when one's adversary had recovered, and so on. These demands were employed, more than anything else, to avoid facial wounds. Fencing masks,* while available, in one form or another, since the 1700s, were thought of as unnecessary for expert fencers, who were expected to "place" their hits on their opponent's chest. This was, as observed by historian Egerton Castle,* a far cry from the old-time fencing of the sixteenth century, from which "men never left but covered with bruises, perchance minus an eye or a few teeth!"

Until fairly recently, counting touches outside competition was unheard of. According to fencing champion Leo Nunes,* in an article in *American Fencing* magazine, to do so when he began fencing in the early part of the twentieth century "was considered unsportsmanlike and discourteous; good manners . . . demanded that both fencers should leave the strip with the illusion of being equal."

Today, fencers in a practice setting usually have the option of keeping or not keeping score.

Ultimately, aside from old-time "good manners," the major value of the assault is, by not keeping score, to place the emphasis of the fencing encounter on the development of technique rather than acquiring touches. By removing the pressure of winning and losing, a fencer has a better chance to focus on what he is doing and how he is doing it.

An assault is also sometimes called "free play" or "loose play."

REFERENCES
Castle, Egerton. *Schools and Masters of Fence.* London: 1885.
Nunes, Leo G. "Loose Play and Practice Bouts." *American Fencing* (January/February 1974).
Palffy-Alpar, Julius. *Sword and Masque.* Philadelphia: F. A. Davis, 1967.
U.S. Fencing Association, ed. *Operations Manual.* Colorado Springs, CO: U.S. Fencing Association, 1985.

ASSAULT DE GALA. A fencing exhibition at a festivity or social event.

REFERENCE
Morton, E. D. *Martini A–Z of Fencing.* London: Queen Anne Press, 1992.

ASSYRIAN SWORDS. Assyrian swords came in both cutting and thrusting varieties. Blade length averaged sixteen inches; hilt length, five inches. Hilts were often richly decorated.

REFERENCE
Burton, Richard F. *The Book of the Sword.* London: Chatto and Windus, 1884.

ASWAR. A name for the scimitar-like sword originating in the north central section of India (Rajputana), according to Colonel James Tod, in his book *Annales and Antiquities of Rajaat'han* (1905).

REFERENCE
Stone, George Cameron. *A Glossary of the Construction, Decoration, and Use of Arms and Armor.* New York: Jack Brussel, 1961.

ATTACK. An offensive fencing action in which the primary concern is to hit one's opponent.

There are two basic types of fencing attacks: simple* and composed.* In the simple attack, made up of timing and speed, one attempts to hit one's opponent before he can respond defensively. The composed attack is made up of a feint to lure an opponent into making a defensive response (parry), followed by an evasion, with one's blade, of that response.

Forward motion is the foundation of every attack. While the nature of footwork has changed over the centuries, the basic ability to move in and touch one's adversary remains vital.

During the seventeenth century, swordsmen fought in a circular fashion. An attack was customarily delivered by making a pass, that is, closing with one's opponent by passing one foot in front of the other.

Since the 1700s, sword encounters have been waged in a straight line. Here, the lunge, an action in which the back leg is used to push a fencer toward his target, supplanted the pass as the main method of presenting an attack.

In instances when the distance separating two fencers rules out lunging, the *fleche,* or jumping attack, can be employed to cover the area quickly.

The modern sport of fencing, in an effort to promote proper weapon usage, has developed rules that determine which fencer in any given encounter has initiated an attack and if that attack is valid or not.

With regard to fencing strategy, all attacks should be based on how one's opponent defends himself. There are four questions to be answered in formulating any attack: (1) What is my opponent doing?, (2) How is he doing it?, (3) What can I do to take advantage of him?, and (4) Can I actually accomplish what I've decided to do? By continually paying attention to these points, a fencer is more likely to find success with his attacks than if he simply does what he feels like doing.

REFERENCES
Castle, Egerton. *Schools and Masters of Fence.* London: George Bell, 1885.
Palffy-Alpar, Julius. *Sword and Masque.* Philadelphia: F. A. Davis, 1967.
U.S. Fencing Association, ed. *Operations Manual.* Colorado Springs, CO: U.S. Fencing Association, 1985.
Wise, Arthur. *The Art and History of Personal Combat.* Greenwich, CT: Arma Press, 1971.

ATTACK INTO PREPARATION. Attacking into preparation means to launch a counterattack* as an opponent is in the process of setting up his own offensive action. When performed correctly, it catches the other fencer completely off guard, because his focus is on attacking, and he is unprepared to act defensively.

An attack into preparation might consist of an evasion of a strong beat followed by a lunge, or it might be a simple straight hit* launched as an opponent performs a halfhearted, bent-arm feint.* The sudden, unexpected nature of the move—that is, the maner in which it is timed—is its most telling feature.

An attack into preparation is also referred to as an "action in time."
REFERENCE
Palffy-Alpar, Julius. *Sword and Masque.* Philadelphia: F. A. Davis, 1967.

ATTACK WITH AUTHORITY. Attacking with strong—and continual—pressure against an opponent's blade, a pressure that deflects the controlled blade out of line.

Also called an "attack with opposition."
REFERENCE
Morton, E. D. *Martini A–Z of Fencing.* London: Queen Anne Press, 1992.

AUF STOSS UND HIEB. A German fencing term meaning cut-and-thrust play, which was popular in German university dueling societies from the sixteenth century until the nineteenth century.
REFERENCE
Castle, Egerton. *Schools and Masters of Fence.* London: George Bell, 1885.

AURIOL, YVES. (1937–   ). French-born fencing master.

One of the top-ranked fencing coaches in the United States, Yves Auriol has coached U.S. teams for the Olympics (1980, 1984, 1988, and 1992), the Pan American Games (1987 and 1991), the World Championships (1986, 1990, and 1991), and the World University Games (1977 and 1979).

He has taught such fencing champions as Michael Marx, Robert Marx, and Molly Sullivan.

Auriol is presently head fencing coach of Notre Dame University.
REFERENCE
Walker, Colleen. *1992 United States Fencing Association Media Guide.* Colorado: ColorTek Printing, 1992.

AVANCES. The forward portions of one's target area beyond the torso of the body: in épée, the sword arm and front leg; in sabre, the sword arm.
REFERENCE
Morton, E. D. *Martini A–Z of Fencing.* London: Queen Anne Press, 1992.

AVANTAGE. A slight curve in the blade of a modern fencing weapon that allows for its proper bend when a touch is made.
REFERENCE
Morton, E. D. *Martini A–Z of Fencing.* London: Queen Anne Press, 1992.

AVENGER'S SWORD. A magic sword of Scandinavian legend. It was said to have a will of its own, killing on its own when it wished to. It sometimes even turned on its owner.
REFERENCE
Leach, Maria, ed. *Funk and Wagnalls Standard Dictionary of Folklore, Mythology, and Legend.* San Francisco: Harper and Row, 1972.

AWASE-DO. In Japan, a small whetstone on which sword blades were ground.
REFERENCE
Stone, George Cameron. *A Glossary of the Construction, Decoration, and Use of Arms and Armor.* New York: Jack Brussel, 1961.

AXELROD, ALBERT. (1921–   ). American fencing champion.

One of the foremost fencers in the United States, Albert Axelrod began his competitive career in high school in the 1930s.

A New York-based fencer, he was a member of five Olympic teams (1952, 1956, 1960, 1964, and 1968) and four Pan-American teams (1955, 1959, 1963, and 1967). He was U.S. national foil champion four times (1955, 1958, 1960, and 1970), placing second eight times. In addition, he placed fifth in the 1958 World Championships and was second four times in a row in the Pan-American Games.

Perhaps Axelrod's greatest feat was taking third place in the individual foil event of the 1960 Olympics** in Rome. This was the first Olympic fencing medal for a U.S. fencer since the U.S. sabre team finished third at the 1948 London Olympics and the first individual fencing medal since Joseph Levis* took second in individual foil at the 1932 Los Angeles Olympic Games. Axelrod was thirty-nine years old at the time of his Olympic achievement.
REFERENCES
Goldstein, Ralph, ed. "Axelrod Receives Hall of Fame Award." *American Fencing* (January/February 1974).
Grombach, John V. *The 1972 Olympic Guide.* New York: Paperback Library, 1972.

AYDA KATTI. The national sword of Coorg, an ancient principality in southern India (now in the province of Malabar).

The *ayda katti* has a very broad, heavy blade. It is curved and single-edged and wider at the tip than at the hilt. Its sharpness is on the concave side. The weapon has no hand guard.

Scabbardless, the sword was simply passed through a flattened metal ring attached to a belt and carried on the back.
REFERENCE
Stone, George Cameron. *A Glossary of the Construction, Decoration, and Use of Arms and Armor.* New York: Jack Brussel, 1961.

$\mathcal{B}$

BABANGA. A leaf-shaped sword with a squared-off end, made at Batta on the Gaboon River in the north of Sumatra and used by the Mpangwe people there.
REFERENCES
Burton, Richard F. *The Book of the Sword*. London: Chatto and Windus, 1884.

BABYLONIAN SWORD. The Babylonian sword is simply described as being short and straight.
REFERENCE
Burton, Richard F. *The Book of the Sword*. London: Chatto and Windus, 1884.

BACKSWORD. The backsword has been characterized as both a version of a broadsword* and a kind of sabre.* This lack of a singular definition becomes clear when, on examination, one finds weapons called ''backswords'' resembling both styles of swords. Some backswords have curved, pointed, sabrelike blades; some have straight, blunted blades set in basket hilts,* causing them to resemble the Scottish basket-hilted broadsword.* The key feature of all backswords is that they have single-edged blades.

By the 1700s, the term ''backsword'' referred specifically to a weapon with a straight, slender, blunted, single-edged blade (average length: thirty-two inches), used in military exercises and staged prizefights.*
REFERENCES
Castle, Egerton. *Schools and Masters of Fence*. London: George Bell, 1885.
Palffy-Alpar, Julius. *Sword and Masque*. Philadelphia: F. A. Davis, 1967.
Reid, William. *Weapons Through the Ages*. London: Peerage Books, 1984.

BACKSWORDING. According to fencing historian Egerton Castle,* backsword play was an art "requiring not so much science and agility as coolness and muscular vigor."

Backswording was, in fact, a very stylized type of fencing. The on-guard position was held in the line of either high seconde* or low tierce*; parries were performed only in pronation*; and fighting was always carried out in close quarters.

The action consisted of cuts and parries made in rapid succession, until, worn down by the aggressively vigorous play, one of the combatants was hit. Feints, because of the swift exchanges, were little used, and when they were, they were kept extremely simple.

Backsword fighting on stage, which consisted of two men hacking bits off each other until one of them was no longer able to continue, became a much-loved public entertainment in early eighteenth-century England. In time, this sport gave way in popularity to boxing.

Practice for backsword fighting was carried out with basket-hilted* wooden swords called "singlesticks,"* which became a popular sport in itself in England.

REFERENCES

Castle, Egerton. *Schools and Masters of Fence.* London: George Bell, 1885.

Stone, George Cameron. *A Glossary of the Construction, Decoration, and Use of Arms and Armor.* New York: Jack Brussel, 1961.

Wise, Arthur. *The Art and History of Personal Combat.* Greenwich, CT: Arma Press, 1971.

BACKWARD LUNGE. An old-time fencing trick employed when the maneuvering distance between two fencers had been reduced to a length where blade manipulation was impossible. By extending the rear leg backward and lowering the free arm, a fencer assumed the lunge position, which then created enough room for launching an offensive action.

Also known as an *echappement.*

REFERENCE

Morton, E. D. *Martini A–Z of Fencing.* London: Queen Anne Press, 1992.

BADELAIRE. A sixteenth-century sabre, with a short, falchion*-shaped blade (curved and broad, with its widest area near the point) and a straight grip protected by curved crossbars* (quillons).

REFERENCE

Stone, George Cameron. *A Glossary of the Construction, Decoration, and Use of Arms and Armor.* New York: Jack Brussel, 1961.

BAD FENCING. Bad fencers are not a modern phenomenon. They have, in fact, always been a part of the fencing scene.

During the fifteenth and sixteenth centuries, without any fixed technique to draw upon, bad fencing was, more than anything else, a matter of opinion. Every fencing master who opened his own school, as one might expect, avowed that all styles but his own were faulty. Today, with the perspective of hundreds of years behind us, we can see that most early combat methods, without exception, were rife with poor concepts. Some of the more fanciful actions actually bordered on suicidal.

As the thrusting rapier came into vogue in the late sixteenth century, it ran up against the long-entrenched cutting sword with a crash that resounded through the fencing world. Immediately, which was the better weapon became the prime argument of the day. Each faction believed fervently that the other was incredibly bad and often came to blows and thrusts over which was right. English fencing master George Silver, one of the last proponents of the cutting sword, called rapier play "schoole trickes and jugling gambalds." He reasoned that so many had been killed in rapier fights only because of the weapon's "length and unwieldiness thereof." Moreover, believing as he did, he spent much time defaming masters—mostly foreigners—who taught the use of the rapier. Rapier men, on the other hand, simply viewed the cutting sword as inept and crude. While most recriminations during these years were doubtlessly prompted by jealousy, rapier play eventually proved, through direct application, to be the more effective method of eliminating enemies.

The Spanish method of swordplay, devised during the sixteenth century along the lines of geometric patterns and overblown, esoteric philosophy by the masters Jeronimo de Carranza and Don Luis Pacheco Narvaez and later elaborated by the French master Girard Thibaust, was looked on by everyone outside Spain as utter nonsense. As was noted by Egerton Castle in his book *The Schools and Masters of Fence* (1885), "How the Italian and French masters must have laughed."

As fencing grew more scientifically standardized, picking out the truly bad fencer became easier. In the late seventeenth century, the great English fencing master Sir William Hope labeled fencers without true knowledge of swordplay "ignorants." These, he observed, were fencers who believed they were good but, in truth, had little knowledge of actual technique, relying mainly on force for their victories. Hope recommended such fencers be introduced to "sharps," practice weapons with a tiny bit of point exposed, to teach them the true level of their ineptness.

Encounters between able fencers and bad fencers are part of fencing lore. One such meeting took place between the famed eighteenth-century Italian fencer Domenico Angelo* and Dr. Keys, presumed to be the greatest swordsman in Ireland. In a public bout at the Thatched House Tavern in London, the two men met before an assemblage of society's most notable personages. A scientific fencer, Angelo perceived at once that his opponent was a "tirailleur, jeu de soldat—Anglicized, a poker" and, by merely keeping his distance, allowed his powerful, but thoughtless, opponent to tire himself out with useless flailing, after which Angelo easily defeated him.

In the last century, fencers who constantly indulged in the practice of attacking into their opponent's attack without deflecting the other's blade or performing some sort of evasive movement were looked upon as uncontrolled, uncouth, and disruptive and were often disqualified from competitions.

Modern fencing rules—especially those for foil—are based on the common sense one would employ using weapons with sharp points. Poor fencers of today never really master these concepts and continue to fence on a totally reactive level. They attack with bent arms, pay no attention to rules of priority, display poor form, lack any sense of timing or distance, and possess absolutely no point control. Moreover, they never learn to think in the language of fencing, the most important aspect of the game. They rely, rather, as did poor swordsmen in days of old, on strength, speed, and aggression. Unfortunately, in the context of today's competitive climate, such an approach often does quite well in terms of winning bouts—up to a point—actually learning to fence taking much longer than the direct implementation of force against an opponent. Hence, until a fencer learns to fence (in the classical sense), he may find himself at the mercy of the bulldozing competitor. Many, then, feeling a need to win, opt for the quick fix, meeting force with force and, of course, never discover the inner game of fencing. This can be looked upon as human nature, perhaps, but it does not excuse bad fencing. In the end, fencing is systematic; it is scientific; it is thoughtful. Fencing is control. Everything else is governed by chance and, hence, is bad fencing.

REFERENCES

Castle, Egerton. *Schools and Masters of Fence.* London: George Bell, 1885.
Morton, E. D. *Martini A–Z of Fencing.* London: Queen Anne Press, 1992.
Palffy-Alpar, Julius. *Sword and Masque.* Philadelphia: F. A. Davis, 1967.
Stevenson, John. *Fencing.* London: Briggs, 1935.

BADIK. A sword originating in Java. It had a short blade possessing a curved edge and a straight back. The hilt was shaped like the grip of a pistol.

REFERENCE

Stone, George Cameron. *A Glossary of the Construction, Decoration, and Use of Arms and Armor.* New York: Jack Brussel, 1961.

BALANCE—PHYSICAL. Establishing a strong sense of physical balance is crucial to every fencer's development. Balance is determined primarily by where the fencer places his center of gravity. Generally, proper balance is achieved by distributing one's weight equally on both legs, bending one's knees slightly to lower the center of gravity, and, at the same time, maintaining an upright torso. When these points are observed, the center of gravity is located where it does the most good: midway between the feet, and in the abdominal area of the body.

On the other hand, randomly concentrating one's weight on either one leg or the other almost always leads to problems. For instance, in the lunge position, a shifting of one's balance too far forward—caused by reaching for a touch— puts a strain on the bent front leg, drastically diminishing a fencer's ability to come back on guard quickly and safely.

The feet also play an important role in maintaining balance. The front foot should always point straight ahead; the rear foot should always be positioned at a right angle to the front foot. Heels are lined up. The feet, on an average, are separated by a distance of a foot to a foot and a half. This gives the fencer a solid base upon which to rest his weight.

Finally, there is the rear arm. Almost always a neglected part of a fencer's anatomy, it acts as a counterbalance when one is either on guard or in a lunge.

There may be times when the center of gravity must be shifted slightly to facilitate certain fencing maneuvers; but, when this is the case, a solidly developed sense of balance allows a fencer to work outside his normal attitude without experiencing a loss of control.

REFERENCES

Palffy-Alpar, Julius. *Sword and Masque.* Philadelphia: F. A. Davis, 1967.

Szabo, Laszlo. *Fencing and the Master.* Budapest: Franklin Publishing House, 1977.

Vebell, Edward. *Sports Illustrated Book of Fencing.* Philadelphia: J. B. Lippincott, 1962.

BALANCE—SPIRITUAL. The goal of every samurai* was to achieve a spiritual balance that could be carried into combat. This ideal was influenced greatly by the philosophy of Zen.* Entering a fight without fearing death, being able to meet an opponent without anger, giving up ego, and possessing a feeling of oneness with nature—these were the elements of balance.

Attaining balance, a samurai was said to have "shin," or spirit. Then, it was believed, sword technique would flow through one's body and limbs as if independent of the mind.

REFERENCES

Musashi, Miyamoto. *A Book of Five Rings.* New York: Overlook Press, 1974.

Nitobe, Inazo. *Bushido: The Warrior's Code.* Burbank, CA: Ohara, 1979.

Suzuki, Daisetz. *Zen and Japanese Culture.* Princeton, NJ: Princeton University Press, 1973.

BALDRIC. A belt, of either cloth or leather, worn across the shoulder as a support for a sword.

Also spelled "baldrick" and "baudrick."

REFERENCE

Stone, George Cameron. *A Glossary of the Construction, Decoration, and Use of Arms and Armor.* New York: Jack Brussel, 1961.

BALESTRA. The *balestra* is an action made up of a short, forward jump followed by a lunge. The lunge should be initiated immediately on the completion of the jump.

This action is also called a "jump-lunge."

REFERENCE

Palffy-Alpar, Julius. *Sword and Masque.* Philadelphia: F. A. Davis, 1967.

BANDEROLLE. In sabre fencing, a chest cut.

REFERENCE

Handelman, Rob. "Fencing Glossary." *American Fencing* (February/March 1978).

BANDOL. A Javanese sword with a hooked point.

Also referred to as a *bandul.*

REFERENCE

Stone, George Cameron. *A Glossary of the Construction, Decoration, and Use of Arms and Armor.* New York: Jack Brussel, 1961.

BARBASETTI, LUIGI. (c. 1875). Italian fencing master.

A pupil of the great master Giuseppe Radaelli,* Luigi Barbasetti went on to become, perhaps, more distinguished than his teacher. He was one of those few masters whose unique perspective and foresight were instrumental in ushering fencing into a modern mode compatible with twentieth-century thought.

Barbasetti began his teaching in his homeland. However, in 1894, he moved to Vienna, Austria, to take charge of the Austro-Hungarian Central Fencing School. His sabre technique, a pure Italian style favoring the delivery of cuts with forearm movements from the elbow, was so well received, it quickly replaced the teaching of the Hungarian master Joseph Keresztessy.

Barbasetti's foil style was of the Italian-French school, that is, the classical French approach to fencing molded to the Italian temperament.

Maestro Barbasetti also taught in Germany and France. His books include *The Art of the Foil* (1932) and *The Art of the Sabre and the Épée* (1936).

REFERENCE

Morton, E. D. *Martini A–Z of Fencing.* London: Queen Anne Press, 1992.

BARKUR. A flat club-sword used by the Aborigines of Queensland, Australia. It was five feet long and six inches wide. The grip was large enough for only one hand. The weapon was manufactured from a small tree trunk.

The *barkur* was held in one hand and hung down over the back. Swung forward and downward with a quick jerk, it was reported capable of splitting a man's skull.

Known also as a *worran.*

REFERENCE

Stone, George Cameron. *A Glossary of the Construction, Decoration, and Use of Arms and Armor.* New York: Jack Brussel, 1961.

BARRAGE. In the finals of a fencing tournament, when two fencers have the same number of wins and hits, the winner is determined by a single bout called a barrage (tie) bout.

In the case of two teams being tied in the finals, a single barrage bout is held between one representative from each team.

REFERENCE

U.S. Fencing Association. *Operations Manual.* Colorado Springs, CO: U.S. Fencing Association, 1985.

BARRYMORE, JOHN. (1882–1942). American film actor.

As a stage actor, John Barrymore was especially noted for his stage performance as Hamlet; as a film actor, for his roles as the great lover Don Juan and the evil hypnotist Svengali.

Good looks and great personal charm made Barrymore a natural for swashbuckling, costume adventures in which swordplay played a significant role. That he was also one of the greatest actors America has ever produced only made his characterizations more appealing.

On stage as Hamlet (1923), Barrymore had more than ample opportunity to hone his fencing talents (101 performances on Broadway and three months at the prestigious Haymarket Theatre in London). Apparently, from the sweeping critical praise of his work, he was not found wanting on any level.

Barrymore's fencing ability was first captured for posterity in the silent film *Don Juan* (1926). The story, rather than a retelling of the Don Juan legend, was pure Hollywood. This new Don Juan (Barrymore) is interjected into the Italian court of Cesare Borgia. Intrigue follows romantic entanglement follows intrigue, culminating with Don Juan's falling in love for the first time in his life. Eventually, to save the woman of his dreams from a vicious mauling by her degenerate husband, Don Juan crosses swords and daggers with the unpleasant spouse and kills him. (Masterfully staged by Fred Cavens,* this complex duel ranks as one of the screen's most thrilling sword combats.) Don Juan is now thrown into prison for murder. However, he soon escapes and flees with his ladylove. The film ends with another sword fight, this time on horseback. Don Juan ends up saving the day once more by single-handedly routing a troop of Cesare Borgia's henchmen, who have been sent to apprehend the pair.

Although he was drinking heavily at that time in his life, Barrymore's fencing was both energetic and artful.

Other films in which John Barrymore fenced include *When a Man Loves* (1927), *General Crack* (1929), and *Romeo and Juliet* (1936).

REFERENCES

Fowler, Gene. *Good Night, Sweet Prince.* New York: Viking Press, 1944.
Richards, Jeffrey. *Swordsmen of the Screen.* Boston: Routledge and Kegan Paul, 1977.

BASELARD. A short sword carried by civilians in the fourteenth and fifteenth centuries. The blade was straight and tapering (average blade length: 22.5 inches). The hilt was shaped like a capital "I." The quillons* were straight.

Because of its intermediate length, the baselard is sometimes listed as a dagger.

REFERENCES

Stone, George Cameron. *A Glossary of the Construction, Decoration, and Use of Arms and Armor.* New York: Jack Brussel, 1961.
Wilkinson, Frederick. *Swords and Daggers.* New York: Hawthorn Books, 1968.

BASKET HILT. A heavy sword guard in which the hand was completely enclosed by a system of wide, connecting bars (counterguards*). Designed to be an effective protection against the cut, rather than the thrust, it proved to be the best kind of guard for military, especially cavalry, weapons. Because of its sturdiness, the basket hilt could be used equally well as a "knuckleduster" (brass knuckles) when fighting took place at close quarters.

While usually associated with the Scottish broadsword,* the basket hilt actually originated in Italy. This variety, or *schiavona**-type, had a much more elaborate basket than did its Scottish relative.

REFERENCES

Castle, Egerton. *Schools and Masters of Fence.* London: George Bell, 1885.

Wilkinson, Frederick. *Swords and Daggers.* New York: Hawthorn Books, 1967.

BASKET-HILTED BROADSWORD. A broadsword with a hilt of interwoven metal strips. While blades were most likely single-edged, double-edge forms do exist. Such weapons were always used for cutting rather than thrusting.

Up to three grooves might be cut into the length of the wide blade to both lighten and strengthen it.

The two most noteworthy varieties of the basket-hilted broadsword are the Italian *schiavona** and the Scottish Highland broadsword.* Of the two, the former is the older sword.

REFERENCES

Castle, Egerton. *Schools and Masters of Fence.* London: George Bell, 1885.

Stone, George Cameron. *A Glossary of the Construction, Decoration, and Use of Arms and Armor.* New York: Jack Brussel, 1961.

BASTARD SWORD. Also known as a "hand-and-a-half" sword, the bastard sword was a long, straight-bladed weapon dating from 1490, with a plain cross guard, long grip, and rounded pommel. Blades averaged forty inches in length, but some were as long as fifty inches.

The bastard sword was usually used with one hand, but the grip had just enough room on it to hold it with two or three fingers of the free hand, if added cutting force was desired.

This style of arms came into vogue in England in the mid-1300s but found popularity in Germany much earlier.

The term *bastard* undoubtedly comes from the fact that the sword, because of its design, has no legitimate claim to being classified as either a single-handed or two-handed weapon.

REFERENCES

Ashdown, Charles. *European Arms and Armor.* New York: Brussel and Brussel, 1967.

Stone, George Cameron. *A Glossary of the Construction, Decoration, and Use of Arms and Armor.* New York: Jack Brussel, 1961.

BATED AND UNBATED. A slang reference to swords that were either made harmless for practice (bated) or left sharp (unbated).

REFERENCE

Burton, Richard F. *The Book of the Sword.* London: Chatto and Windus, 1884.

BATTAVILE. An archaic and little-used term used to describe a feint* made to distract an opponent with the intent of grabbing his sword.

REFERENCE
Morton, E. D. *Martini A–Z of Fencing.* London: Queen Anne Press, 1992.

BATTERY AND BEATING. In his book *Complete Fencing Master* (1692), the celebrated swordsman Sir William Hope* refers to "battery" as "striking with the edge and foible of your sword [the weak portion of the blade, closest to the point] against the edge and foible of your adversary." "Beating," he says, "is done with the forte of your sword [the strong portion of the blade, closest to the guard] on the foible of your adversary."

The beat, he suggests, is more useful for taking control of an adversary's weapon than is the battery.

REFERENCES
Castle, Egerton. *Schools and Masters of Fencing.* London: George Bell, 1885.
Stone, George Cameron. *A Glossary of the Construction, Decoration, and Use of Arms and Armor.* New York: Jack Brussel, 1961.

BATTRE DE MAIN. Parrying* with the free hand, which is not allowed in modern fencing.

REFERENCE
Morton, E. D. *Martini A–Z of Fencing.* London: Queen Anne Press, 1992.

BAVETTE. The *bavette* or "bib," is a padded fabric (cloth or plastic) extension on a fencing mask that protects the neck. The *bavette* may either be fastened to the mask with snaps or be sewn to it. According to the rules of international competition, the bavette, for safety purposes, must be of the "sewn in" variety.

In foil fencing, the *bavette* is part of the "off target" area. In sabre and épée fencing, however, it is subject to valid touches.

The *bavette* must be colored white in keeping with the traditional color of fencing uniforms (when touches are judged by the eye alone, blade contact on a white surface is easier to discern than blade contact on a colored surface).

REFERENCES
U.S. Fencing Association. *Operations Manual.* Colorado Springs, CO: U.S. Fencing Association, 1985.
Vebell, Edward. *Sports Illustrated Book of Fencing.* Philadelphia: J. B. Lippincott, 1962.

BEAT. The beat is a basic component of fencing technique that goes back to fencing's origins. It is an offensive action that knocks an opponent's blade aside as a preparation to attack. It is always and only used offensively. (To knock an opponent's blade away defensively is a "parry.") It is employed most often to simply overpower, but it also has a number of secondary applications.

The beat can be used to remove a blade that is held on guard with its point "in line" (i.e., a weapon that is held out with a straight arm, the point menacing an opponent's target area). This must be accomplished so that when one attacks, one does not inadvertently throw oneself onto a waiting weapon, a primary concern in fencing (especially when swords had sharp tips).

The heavy beat can be used to knock away an opponent's blade, opening up a particular line (area) into which one wishes to attack.

Beating an opponent's blade with quick, light taps serves to distract or annoy. Establishing a break in an opponent's concentration leaves him more vulnerable to attack.

A firm beat can be used to threaten, forcing a response: either a parry, which can then be deceived (evaded); a successful parry followed by a riposte (counterattack), which can then itself be parried and riposted against; or a stop thrust, which can be enveloped with a bind.

In days when duelling was still in vogue, the beat could be used to disarm. This was accomplished by either knocking the weapon out of the hand of an adversary or swatting the sword aside so that it might be grabbed at the hilt.

The beat is also known by the names *battement, battuta,* and *passement.*

REFERENCES

Angelo, Domenico. *The School of Fencing.* London: H. Angelo, 1787.

Palffy-Alpar, Julius. *Sword and Masque.* Philadelphia: F. A. Davis, 1967.

U.S. Fencing Association. *Operations Manual.* Colorado Springs, CO: U.S. Fencing Association, 1985.

Vebell, Edward. *Sports Illustrated Book of Fencing.* Philadelphia: J.B. Lippincott, 1962.

BEAT PARRY. A parry* that lightly beats an opponent's attacking blade aside. It is made by a snapping action from the fingers. The advantage of such a parry is that it does not move out of line, so it is difficult to evade. Moreover, it leads smoothly and quickly to an immediate riposte.

Also called a *picco* parry, a *tec* parry, a *tac* parry, a "detached parry," *parade au tac,* parry *de tac, parata di pico,* "a sling parry," a "tap parry," a "Bertrand parry," and a "rebounding parry."

REFERENCES

Morton, E. D. *Martini A–Z of Fencing.* London: Queen Anne Press, 1992.

Palffy-Alpar, Julius. *Sword and Masque.* Philadelphia: F. A. Davis, 1967.

BEAUMONT, CHARLES DE. (c. twentieth century). British fencing champion and fencing master.

Charles de Beaumont was one of England's greatest modern fencers. He was Britain's national épée champion from 1936 to 1938 and once more in 1953. He was also a renowned sabre man.

He was captain of the British fencing team in 1936, 1948, and 1952.

Serving as president of the British Empire Fencing Association, Beaumont worked tirelessly at establishing a strong fencing program in his homeland.

Charles de Beaumont wrote a number of books on fencing, including *Modern British Fencing* (1949), *Fencing* (1951), *Fencing Technique in Pictures* (1955), *Modern British Fencing, 1948–1956* (1958), *Fencing, Ancient Art, Modern Sport* (1960), and *Modern British Fencing, 1957–1964* (1966).

REFERENCES

Beaumont, Charles de. *Fencing Technique in Pictures.* London: Hulton Press, 1955.

Morton, E. D. *Martini A–Z of Fencing.* London: Queen Anne Press, 1992.

BEHEADING SWORD. One of the favorite weapons for dispatching condemned criminals in previous centuries was the beheading sword. The blade was long, with a rounded or squared-off "point." The balance was set forward in the blade, making it unwieldy for combat but extremely effective in creating the sweeping force needed to produce a decapitating cut. The guard was of simple cruciform design. The grip, as one might expect, was long enough to be used with both hands.

Asian beheading swords usually had curved blades.

One of the most famous victims of the beheading sword was Anne Boleyn (the second wife of Henry VIII), who was executed at the Tower of London in 1536.

The United States, which has always tended toward more prosaic methods of dispatching criminals, has one recorded sword beheading, which took place in Massachusetts in 1644.

In Asia, the practice of beheading criminals was carried on as late as the 1940s.

The beheading sword is also known as a "heading" sword, an "executioner's" sword, a "headsman's" sword, the "Sword of Justice," and the *schasfrichter's* sword.

REFERENCE

Burton, Richard. *The Book of the Sword.* London: Chatto and Windus, 1884.

BELADAH. A type of sabre* used in Borneo. The weapon possessed both a general hand guard* and a finger guard.*

Also known as a *belabang.*

REFERENCE

Stone, George Cameron. *A Glossary of the Construction, Decoration, and Use of Arms and Armor.* New York: Jack Brussel, 1961.

BELGIAN GRIP. The Belgian grip, a modern invention, was the first of the type known as "orthopedic,"* "anatomical,"* or "pistol."* Used only on foils and épées, it was originally designed as an aid for weak or damaged hands. However, it quickly found its way into mainstream use—first in France—when it was postulated that it helped alleviate some of the odd balance found in "electrical" weapons. In fact, its popularity soared because of the extra strength it was able to inject into a fencer's game.

Once the only grip of its type, today the Belgian grip has numerous imitators.

REFERENCES

Clery, Raoul. "A Props d'Un Accident." *Escrime* (February/March 1983).

Palffy-Alpar, Julius. *Sword and Masque.* Philadelphia: F. A. Davis, 1967.

BELL GUARD. A term for the circular, convex metal hand protection on a modern foil and épée.

Also called a "cup," a "shell," a *coquille,* a *coccia,* or simply a "guard."

REFERENCES
Palffy-Apar, Julius. *Sword and Masque*. Philadelphia: F. A. Davis, 1967.
Stone, George Cameron. *A Glossary of the Construction, Decoration, and Use of Arms
    and Armor*. New York: Jack Brussel, 1961.

BENT ARM ATTACK. The age-old technical defect of unsuccessful fencers
and doomed duelists.

In sport fencing, by lunging with a bent sword arm rather than one perfectly
straight, an attacker launches himself forward without first establishing priority
for his action, thereby inviting a decisive stop thrust from his opponent.

The shortcomings of a bent arm attack are twofold: (1) it shortens the length
of an attacker's reach during a lunge; and (2) it increases the amount of time
needed to deliver a blade point to its target. A stop thrust, therefore—if it has
itself been executed with a straight arm and, further, with proper timing—will
both establish right-of-way for the defender and, by instituting an arm and
weapon extension that exceeds in length the oncoming incorrect offensive maneuver, invariably lands well in advance of it, stopping the poorly trained transgressor in his bewildered tracks.

In a real sword fight, attacking with a bent sword arm would, of course, lead
to a quick, painful death on the sharp point of an adversary's blade.

REFERENCES
Morton, E. D. *Martini A–Z of Fencing*. London: Queen Anne Press, 1992.
Stevenson, John. *Fencing*. London: Briggs, 1935.

BERSAGLIO. In Italian, an opening in an opponent's defense that may be
taken advantage of.

REFERENCE
Morton, E. D. *Martini A–Z of Fencing*. London: Queen Anne Press, 1992.

BERTRAND, BAPTISTE. (?–1898). French fencing master.

Considered the legitimate successor to the great master Angelo,* Baptiste
Bertrand was the founder of a fencing dynasty that continued well into the
twentieth century.

Setting up his school in London in 1857, he created an academic atmosphere
that made his establishment the most popular *salle* in all of England. He did
much to popularize fencing for women. He was also a noted fight arranger for
the stage.

Disconcertingly, some of the accomplishments of Baptiste Bertrand have
been, at times, transposed to his son Felix,* also a noted master of fencing. This
was probably because by employing the single name "Bertrand," as father and
son sometimes did, and perhaps because Felix assisted his father, their work
was mistakenly intermingled by those writing about them. Fight arranger William Hobbs in his 1967 book on stage combat credits Baptiste's stage fencing
activities to Felix. Eleanor Cass, in her volume *The Book of Fencing* (1930),
further muddled the matter by confusing the exploits of another French fencing

Baptiste Bertrand

master named Bertrand, François-Joseph Bertrand,* with those of Baptiste (they were not even related) and by turning Baptiste into "Felix Senior" and Felix into "Felix Junior." She even identified a photograph of Baptiste as "Felix."

Baptiste Bertrand wrote a number of works on fencing, including an untitled book usually referred to as *Memorial of Fencers* (1893).

REFERENCES

Cass, Eleanor Baldwin. *The Book of Fencing*. Boston: Lothrop, Lee, and Shepherd, 1930.

Hobbs, William. *Techniques of the Stage Fight*. London: Studio Vista, 1967.

Morton, E. D. *Martini A–Z of Fencing*. London: Queen Anne Press, 1992.

BERTRAND, FELIX. (?–1930). British fencing master.

The son of the great Baptiste Bertrand,* Felix was a world-famous master in his own right. Taking over Salle Bertrand in 1898, upon the death of his illustrious father, he equaled the efforts of the elder Bertrand in every way.

REFERENCE

Morton, E. D. *Martini A–Z of Fencing*. London: Queen Anne Press, 1992.

BERTRAND, FRANCOIS-JOSEPH. (c. nineteenth century). French fencing master.

Known as the "Napoleon of foil," François-Joseph Bertrand was one of the most renowned masters of his time. Undefeated in professional competitions, he was said to be highly original in his teaching techniques.

Bertrand popularized the *tac* or beat parry, which instantly detaches from an opponent's blade and flows, without hesitation, into a riposte (sometimes called a "Bertrand" riposte). Moreover, in a break with tradition, he favored the stop hit and time hit, which had long been held in disfavor. He also stressed the development of a fencer's footwork.

REFERENCE

Morton, E. D. *Martini A–Z of Fencing*. London: Queen Anne Press, 1992.

BERTRAND, LEON ("PUNCH"). (?–1980). British fencing master.

Representing the last generation of the great Bertrand fencing master clan, Professor Leon assumed the position of head instructor of Salle Bertrand upon the death of his father, Felix, in 1930. As able as his ancestors in his office, he did especially well in the creation of champion female fencers.

A fencer through and through, he even spent his vacations from his salle fencing in other countries, especially Italy.

During World War II, Bertrand put aside his fencing chores to join the RAF. After the war, he returned to fencing; however, Salle Bertrand was never able to reclaim its earlier glory, and by the early 1950s, the once-proud school ceased to exist. Nevertheless, Professor Bertrand continued to teach fencing until his death in 1980.

Leon Bertrand's books on fencing include *Cut and Thrust* (1927) and *The Fencer's Companion* (1935).

REFERENCE

Morton, E. D. *Martini A–Z of Fencing*. London: Queen Anne Press, 1992.

BESNARD, CHARLES. (c. 1600). French fencing master.

With the teachings of Charles Besnard, we see a final ascendancy of the French style of fencing over the Italian style.

In Besnard's book, *Le Maistre d'Arme Liberal* (1653), we observe the beginnings of a transition from old-fashioned, heavy rapier play to the new, energetic smallsword fighting. With smaller, lighter weapons in mind, Besnard stressed point work above all else, cutting now being considered totally obsolete. He established the lunge as the primary method of delivering an attack. He defined the lines of attack and defense in a way that would not seem altogether strange to a modern fencer. He also condemned the then-prevalent practice of the single-action counterattack, called *stesso tempo,** replacing it with a definite separation between the parry and the riposte. Furthermore, he stated that defense was to be accomplished with the blade alone, the free hand no longer being deemed practical or safe for stopping an attack. Body evasions, while not completely forbidden in combat, were nevertheless discouraged.

Finally, Besnard introduced the formal salute* into the beginning of a sword fight.

REFERENCES

Castle, Egerton. *Schools and Masters of Fence.* London: George Bell, 1885.

Wise, Arthur. *The Art and History of Personal Combat.* Greenwich, CT: Arma Press, 1971.

BHAWANI. The sword belonging to Sivaji, prince of Maratha-land, a state in western India.

Sivaji, born in 1627, was the founder of the Mahratta power in India. Leading his people against the dominant Moslem rule in 1659, Sivaji eventually controlled all of the western portion of his country.

Bhawani was described as "a Genoa blade, four feet in length and of fine temper." There was a spike attached to the hilt, which could be used for thrusting at an opponent. The grip was said to be unusually small.

A prized relic of the Mahrattas, the blade was often called upon before battles for assistance.

Originally, the sword was said to reside at Sattara, but, in time, other weapons reputed to be the true Bhawani surfaced in other parts of India.

REFERENCES

Burton, Richard. *The Book of the Sword.* London: Chatto and Windus, 1884.

Stone, George Cameron. *A Glossary of the Construction, Decoration, and Use of Arms and Armor.* New York: Jack Brussel, 1961.

BILBO. A small rapier with a shell guard.* It was named after the Spanish town of Bilboa. The average blade length was just over thirty-four inches.

While the rapier ceased to be the weapon of fashion by the end of the 1600s, the Spanish continued to make the *bilbo* until the nineteenth century.

REFERENCES

Stone, George Cameron. *A Glossary of the Construction, Decoration, and Use of Arms and Armor.* New York: Jack Brussel, 1961.

Wilkinson, Frederick. *Swords and Daggers.* New York: Hawthorn Books, 1968.

BIND. When a fencer holds an on-guard* position with a straight arm and his point "in line" (i.e., menacing the target area of the person he is fencing with), his opponent is required to remove this threatening obstacle before carrying out his own offensive action. A fencer, by the rules of fencing, is discouraged from freely lunging onto an already presented point. If the weapons being used had sharp points, the reason for this would become readily, if not painfully, apparent.

One of the most effective ways to remove an "in line" blade is with a bind. The bind, in effect, takes hold of an opposing weapon in one line, envelops it, and moves it into a line where it is no longer a threat.

The dynamics behind the bind is leverage. Basically, when a weaker portion of one blade is engaged by a stronger part of another blade, a lever action may be initiated against the less-powerful weapon. By maintaining continued blade contact and maneuvering the binding blade in a half-circle motion as one extends one's arm, the captured weapon is automatically turned aside. Once this is accomplished, a lunge should immediately follow to complete the attack.

The effectiveness of the bind is mirrored in how long it has been part of sword-fighting techniques. Noted fencing master Sir William Hope* recommended its usage in his book *Scots Fencing Master* in 1687. Angelo's *School of Fencing,* * written in 1763, discussed its application.

The only major change in the bind is that it is no longer used for the purpose of disarming an opponent. In modern fencing, play comes to a halt when a fencer drops his weapon.

Other terms describing binding actions include *flaconnade, fianconata, envelopement,* "transfer," *trasporto di ferro,* "undercounter," "gathering up," *liement, riporto.* "transport," "transverse," "wrapping it up," and "circular transfer."

REFERENCES

Angelo, Domenico. *The School of Fencing.* London: H. Angelo, 1787 edition.

Bower, Muriel, and Torao Mori. *Fencing.* Dubuque, IA: Wm. C. Brown, 1966.

Castle, Egerton. *Schools and Masters of Fence.* London: George Bell, 1885.

Palffy-Alpar, Julius. *Sword and Masque.* Philadelphia: F. A. Davis, 1967.

BLACKBEARD. (?–1718). Infamous pirate captain. Real name: Edward Teach.

Born in Bristol, England, Edward Teach, alias Blackbeard, became one of the most-feared pirates of the early eighteenth century.

So nicknamed because of the long, black whiskers he wore, Blackbeard operated off the North Carolina coast, attacking any ship—merchantman or pirate—that came within his reach. He said he was the devil and more often than not lived up to his claim. To heighten his fierce image, he would stick lighted matches in his beard.

In 1718, the governor of Virginia, fed up with Blackbeard's pillaging, sent out two ships to hunt down and capture the pirate. When confronted with the attacking military vessels, commanded by Lieutenant Robert Maynard, Blackbeard, in his usual fashion, decided to fight rather than run. The pirate captain opened fire with his cannons. In spite of this, Maynard managed to board Blackbeard's ship.

In the hand-to-hand sword battle that followed, Blackbeard was wounded twenty-five times before he was finally shot to death by Lieutenant Maynard himself. Afterward, his head was cut off and returned to Virginia, where it was put on public display.

Blackbeard, as a dramatic character, has turned up in numerous movies, including *Blackbeard the Pirate* (1952),* *Anne of the Indies* (1951),* and *Blackbeard's Ghost* (1968).

REFERENCES

Franklin, Walter. *Famous American Ships.* New York: American Heritage, 1954.
Richards, Jeffrey. *Swordsmen of the Screen.* Boston: Routledge and Kegan Paul, 1977.

BLACK PRINCE, THE. (1330–1376). Edward, Prince of Wales, eldest son of King Edward III of England.

One of England's greatest military leaders, Edward, the Black Prince, participated in the battles of Crécy (1346) and Poitiers (1356), two of the most overwhelming military defeats for the French by English hands during the Middle Ages.

In the first instance, Edward fought under the leadership of his father, the king. The English army numbered perhaps 20,000, the French 40,000. The French, who attacked without order, were cut down by English longbow archers. The young prince fought at the head of one of the main battle groups. He was knighted for his efforts.

In the latter confrontation, Edward himself commanded an army of 8,000 against a French force of 16,000. Once again, the English, employing superior strategy, routed the French, this time taking the king of France (Jean II) captive for good measure.

Traditionally, the Black Prince has been looked on as a protector of English holdings and upholder of English rights in France. At worst, he might be described as a freebooter, who plundered the French countryside without mercy (among other things, he was responsible for taking numerous knights and nobles hostage, letting them go only after great ransoms were paid). At best, he might be described as an avid "fund-raiser" for the English Crown.

The epithet "Black Prince," once thought to denote the wearing of black armor by Edward, actually referred to his demeanor in combat.

In 1369, Edward was stricken with dysentery, which was further complicated by dropsy. He never recovered from the general debility that followed.

He died in 1376 at the age of forty-five.

The adventures of the Black Prince were depicted in film in *The Warriors*

(1955),* which starred Errol Flynn.* In this tale, Edward was presented as a swashbuckling, romantic swordsman.

REFERENCES

Churchill, Winston S. *The Island Race.* London: Corgi Books, 1972.

Thomas, Tony, Ridy Behlmer, and Clifford McCarty. *The Films of Errol Flynn.* New York: Citadel Press, 1969.

Tuchman, Barbara. *A Distant Mirror.* New York: Alfred A. Knopf, 1984.

BLACKWELL, HENRY. (c. 1700). British fencing master.

Henry Blackwell believed that fencing was "the only proper qualification for constituting a Man a Gentleman." His teaching, it has been said, while not particularly original, at least contained much sound advice.

Blackwell wrote two books on fencing: *The English Fencing Master* (1705) and *The Gentleman's Tutor for the Small-Sword* (1730).

REFERENCES

Castle, Egerton. *Schools and Masters of Fence.* London: George Bell, 1985.

Morton, E. D. *Martini A–Z of Fencing.* London: Queen Anne Press, 1992.

BLADE. The blade is the extended part of the sword, above the guard, used for cutting or thrusting on the offensive side and parrying on the defensive side.

A blade may be either straight or curved and have an edge (*le fil, il filo,* or *die Scharfe*) for cutting or a point (*la pointe, la punta, die Spitze,* or *der Ort*) for thrusting; sometimes it possesses both.

The earliest sword blades were made of copper (4000 B.C.). After that came bronze (3000 B.C.), iron (800 B.C.), and finally, steel (A.D. 1300).

Blade length and weight vary with the type of sword manufactured and the period in history when it was produced. For instance, blades of the Middle Ages were, by and large, long and heavy, because their main function was to penetrate armor. The rough-and-tumble style of fencing employed during the early Renaissance dictated that blades, while generally lighter than previous forms, still needed to retain a certain stout quality in their overall structure. A need for a more refined and efficient style of combat during the 1700s caused blade length and weight to decline drastically.

The characteristics of blades produced today are influenced by the element of sport in swordplay. Possessing a lightness and flexibility never imagined during earlier ages, modern blades reflect the superfast exchanges that take place on the modern fencing strip.

The advent of electrical scoring machines in fencing has also had an effect on the nature of blade construction. Blades destined for electrical use must be specially wired to fit into this technological advancement in swordplay. A thin wire, inset into the metal, runs the length of the blade, attaching to a special "button" at the tip that depresses with the pressure of a touch and at the hand guard to a socket (fastened to the guard) into which an extending electrical "body" cord is plugged.

The blade may also be called *la lame, la lama,* and *die klinge.*

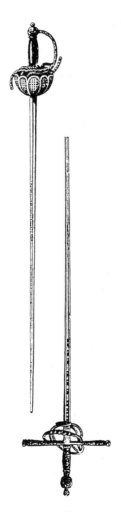

Blades of seventeenth-century rapiers

REFERENCES
Burton, Richard F. *The Book of the Sword.* London: Chatto and Windus, 1884.
Volkman, Rudy. *Electrical Fencing Equipment.* Arvee Press, 1975.
Wilkinson, Frederick. *Swords and Daggers.* New York: Hawthorn Books, 1967.

BLADE, PARTS OF.

Edge: the side of the blade. In the case of swords designed for cutting, the blade is sharp on one or both edges.

Point: the sharp tip of a blade used for thrusting.

Foible: the weak, flexible (thinnest) part of a blade.

Forte: the strong, rigid (thickest) part of a blade.

Shoulder: the spot where the blade proper meets the tang. The shoulder of the blade fits against the guard.

Tang: the part of a blade that fits down into the grip of the sword.

Button: the flattened tip on a sport weapon; also the surface of the tip to be depressed on an electric blade.

Ricasso: the portion of a rapier blade between the guard and the crossbars or quillons.

Fuller: a groove or grooves cut into the face of a blade to make it lighter. Wrongly called a "blood-gutter."

False edge: in the case of a blade with only one cutting edge, this is the nonsharp side of a cutting weapon.

Right edge: in the case of a sword with only one cutting edge, this is the sharp side of a cutting weapon.

Point d'arret: a blade tip with little sharp points or a flat cone with an edge, to catch the material of an opponent's fencing outfit.

REFERENCES
Burton, Richard F. *The Book of the Sword.* London: Chatto and Windus, 1884.
Castle, Egerton. *Schools and Masters of Fence.* London: George Bell, 1885.
Palffy-Alpar, Jules. *Sword and Masque.* Philadelphia: F. A. Davis, 1967.
Wilkinson, Frederick. *Swords and Daggers.* New York: Hawthorn Books, 1967.

BLADE IN LINE. When the point of one fencer's weapon is directed with an extended arm at any spot on an opponent's target area, the blade is said to be in line.

A fencer may merely stand on guard* with his blade in line so as to threaten and confound his adversary. Having one's blade in line is also a necessity to achieve validity—"right of way"*—as an attacker.

REFERENCES
Palffy-Alpar, Julius. *Sword and Masque.* Philadelphia: F. A. Davis, 1967.
U.S. Fencing Association. *Operations Manual.* Colorado Springs, CO: U.S. Fencing Association, 1985.

BLADE LENGTH—HISTORICAL.

Ancient

Egyptian sword blade: 17 to 36 inches

Etruscan sword blade: 14 to 25 inches

Greek sword blade: 14 to 25 inches

Trojan sword blade: unknown

Roman sword blade: 19 to 27 inches

Jewish sword blade: 18 inches

Early Medieval

Frankish sword blade: 30 inches

Saxon sword blade: 30 inches

Danish sword blade: 30 inches

Medieval

Sword blade: 40 inches

Two-handed sword blade: 60 to 70 inches

Sixteenth Century

Rapier blade: 50 to 65 inches

Sword blade: 36 inches

Seventeenth Century

Rapier blade: 36 to 40 inches

Small sword blade: 31 to 40 inches

Military sword blade: 30 to 40 inches

Eighteenth Century

Smallsword blade: 32 inches

Military sword blade: 38 inches

Nineteenth Century

Smallsword blade: 30 inches

Military sword blade: 30 inches

Twentieth Century

Military sword blade: 30 inches

REFERENCES

Ashdown, Charles. *European Arms and Armor.* New York: Brussel and Brussel, 1967.

Burton, Richard F. *The Book of the Sword.* London: Chatto and Windus, 1884.

Palffy-Alpar, Julius. *Sword and Masque.* Philadelphia: F. A. Davis, 1967.

Wilkinson, Frederick. *Swords and Daggers.* New York: Hawthorn Books, 1967.

BLADE LENGTH—JAPANESE.

Ken (double-edged sword): 16 inches

Tachi (early single-edged sword): 17 to 26 inches

No-Dachi (extra long sword): 48 inches

Katana (long sword): 30 inches

Wakizashi (short sword): 16 to 20 inches

Ninja-Ken (ninja sword): 24 inches

REFERENCES

Stone, George Cameron. *A Glossary of the Construction, Decoration, and Use of Arms and Armor.* New York: Jack Brussel, 1961.

Wilkinson, Frederick. *Swords and Daggers.* New York: Hawthorn Books, 1967.

Wujcik, Erick. *Weapons and Assassins.* Detroit: Palladin Books, 1983.

BLADE LENGTH—MODERN.
BLADE LENGTH—MODERN. The maximum length of modern sport blades is regulated by the rules of the Internationale Federation d'Escrime.

While blades may not, for any reason, exceed the maximum length allowed, they may be shorter.

Foil blade maximum length: 35-7/16 inches (90 cm)

Épée blade maximum length: 35-7/16 inches (90 cm)

Sabre blade maximum length: 34-41/64 inches (88 cm)

The shortest blade manufactured—for small children—is 29-3/4 inches long.
REFERENCE
U.S. Fencing Association. *Operations Manual*. Colorado Springs, CO: U.S. Fencing Association, 1985.

BLADE MAKING—EASTERN. Arabic bladesmiths relied on steel with a high carbon content. The best, known as Damascus blades, have been legendary for their sharpness since the Crusades.

While the actual technique used for creating such blades had been lost for centuries, metallurgists in the 1970s rediscovered—during experiments designed to explore the properties of extra strong metals called superplastic metals—the way in which Damascus steel came about.

The process, they found, was generated by rolling out metal (much like kneading pastry dough) during a period of extremely high heating.

The legends that sprang up during the Middle Ages concerning the way Damascus steel was produced were as numerous as they were odd. One story reported that before the metal was forged, it was fed to chickens mixed in their grain. The bird droppings were then melted to retrieve the steel. Another tale stated that the sword blade, heated for its final working, was cooled by plunging it through the body of a muscular, active slave, so that the slave's strength would be infused into the metal. Still another account proclaimed that the desired effect was realized by quenching a hot blade in the urine of a goat that had been fed on a diet of ferns for three days.
REFERENCES
Trefil, James. "Supersteel of the Ancients." *Science Digest* (February 1983).
Wilkinson, Frederick. *Swords and Daggers*. New York: Hawthorn Books, 1967.

BLADE MAKING—JAPANESE. The art of Japanese blade making was unique: putting a hard shell of metal completely around a softer inner structure.

Impurities in the outer "skin" were removed by a systematized procedure in which the metal was repeatedly beaten and folded. This created an extremely hard piece of metal. A similar process was followed for the inner metal, only much less beating and folding were employed.

Wrapping the soft core with the outer metal, the blade was then carefully beaten into shape.

The manner in which the blade's cutting edge was hardened, though, was the most critical step in the whole operation. The entire blade was covered with a thick coating of clay, after which the layer on the edge was carefully scraped off to expose the metal below. After that, the whole thing was heated and plunged into water. This rapid cooling created an extremely hard edge on the uncovered surface, while the rest of the blade, protected by clay, retained a more flexible nature.

At this point, the blade was examined for flaws. If it passed inspection, it was given to a polisher. If it was found to be lacking in any way, it was destroyed.

There were a number of ways of testing a blade of quality. One was that it should be able to cut a common blade in half without having its edge nicked. Another, which is slightly more apocryphal, was that if the blade was held in running water, it should be able to cut the stem of a lotus as the flower floated by.

It is interesting to note the great reverence with which the Japanese blade maker approached his work. When producing a blade, he would wear a ceremonial costume and decorate his forge with religious symbols, the idea being to promote purity and strength in the finished product.

REFERENCES

Nitobe, Inazo. *Bushido: The Warrior's Code.* Burbank, CA: Ohara, 1983.
Stone, George Cameron. *A Glossary of the Construction, Decoration, and Use of Arms and Armor.* New York: Jack Brussel, 1961.
Wilkinson, Frederick. *Swords and Daggers.* New York: Hawthorn Books, 1967.

BLADE MAKING—WESTERN. Early techniques for producing sword blades in Europe left much to be desired. In turn, copper and bronze were used; but, because both are relatively soft metals, neither held an edge for very long. Finally, iron, much harder than either copper or bronze, was employed, but even here the quality of the final product varied greatly. The carbon content of the metal was the chief factor determining the hardness of a blade, but centuries went by before this was understood.

The outcome of inadequate manufacturing know-how was graphically illustrated in Roman accounts of clashes with Frankish warriors. The Franks, it was noted, had to stop fighting periodically and straighten their soft iron sword blades beneath their feet.

Eventually, a method whereby a hard cutting edge of steel was welded onto a softer piece of iron was devised. Called pattern welding, it was popular as a bladesmithing technique until the end of the ninth century.

Secret formulas for blade making were often rumored, but probably the most important factor in the creative procedure was the smith's own experience and skill.

During the tenth century, metal-smelting skills improved to the point where old blade-making systems became obsolete. First, furnaces were enlarged, which allowed the melted iron to absorb more carbon; second, the ability to work impurities out of the metal was refined.

By the twelfth century, blade making was a highly standardized and polished craft.
REFERENCE
Wilkinson, Frederick. *Swords and Daggers.* New York: Hawthorn Books, 1967.

BLADE PARTS—JAPANESE.

Point: *kisaki*

Blade curvature: *sori*

Back of blade: *muni*

Blade groove: *hi*

Tang: *nakago*

Edge sections: *boshi, monouchi, yakiba, jigane, shinogi, nioi, niye, ryonome, habakimoto,* and *temoto*

REFERENCE
Stone, George Cameron. *A Glossary of the Construction, Decoration, and Use of Arms and Armor.* New York: Jack Brussel, 1961.

BLIND. In fencing, to blind an opponent refers to performing an action that masks one's true intent.

Blind may also refer to a fencer who is incapable—for whatever reason—of looking at an opponent and figuring out what he is actually doing.
REFERENCE
Stevenson, John. *Fencing.* London: Briggs, 1935.

BLIND FENCING. Extraordinary as it may seem—fencing being such a sight-oriented activity—there is fencing for the blind. Carried out under supervision of sighted fencers, blind persons approach the game basically through their sense of touch, which can both help them set up their distance and tell them where their opponent's blade might be. Another approach adds the idea that blind fencers regularly use electric weapons, so that they might, through the buzzing of the scoring box, gain instant recognition of successful actions.

As sight can sometimes be deceiving (leading one into making incorrect assumptions that lead to unsuccessful responses), it has been recommended, more than once, that sighted fencers practice actions blindfolded so that they might develop blade sensitivity (*sentement du fer*) to a higher degree.

During the eighteenth century, a blind fencing master named Langford gave lessons regularly. Needing to be told only the length of his student's weapon, he worked, of course, entirely by touch.

On a fanciful level, during the 1960s, the Japanese film industry produced Zatuichi, the blind swordsman. Lacking sight, Zatuichi (played by Shinntaru Katsu) had developed all his other senses to such levels that he was able to perform remarkable feats of swordplay. He could actually hear the angle and speed at which his opponent's blade approached him. He was so adept, that he

The boar's thrust

was even able to successfully oppose and dispatch numerous foes at one time. Zatuichi films include *The Blind Swordsman's Vengeance* (1966), *Zatuichi* (1968), and *Zatuichi Meets Yojimbo* (1971).
REFERENCES
Mintz, Marilyn D. *The Martial Arts Film.* New York: A. S. Barnes, 1978.
Morton, E. D. *Martini A–Z of Fencing.* London: Queen Anne Press, 1992.
Waffa, Joseph. "The Blind Can Also Fence." *American Fencing* (November/December 1978).

BLUNTS. A term used during the seventeenth century to describe a pointless weapon used in practice. In principle, this was the forerunner of the fencing foil.*
REFERENCES
Castle, Egerton. *Schools and Masters of Fence.* London: George Bell, 1885.
Stone, George Cameron. *A Glossary of the Construction, Decoration, and Use of Arms and Armor.* New York: Jack Brussel, 1961.

BOAR'S THRUST. The special "killing" thrust of Scottish fencing master Donald McBain.*
　　The boar's thrust consisted of a swordsman's dropping beneath an opponent's attacking blade by going down to the ground with his free hand and bent left knee and, at the same time, thrusting upward with his own weapon point.

Described in McBain's fencing manual, *The Expert Sword-Man's Companion* (1728).
REFERENCE
Wise, Arthur. *The Art and History of Personal Combat.* Greenwich, CT: Arma Press, 1972.

BODY CORD. In modern sport fencing, where an electrical scoring machine is used, the body cord is an electrical cord run beneath a fencer's jacket and up the length of his arm. One end of this cord plugs into a socket on the underside of the fencer's weapon guard*; the other end is attached to an adjustable line extending from a reel box. Still another cable runs from the reel box to the scoring apparatus,** completing the fencer's hookup to his electrical "touch-sensing" circuit.
REFERENCE
Volkman, Rudy. *Electrical Fencing Equipment.* Arvee Press, 1975.

BODY EVASION. Previous to the adoption of the parry* as the primary means of defense in sword fighting, moving one's body out of reach of an opponent's thrusting weapon was an accepted method to avoid being hit. This included ducking, twisting, or simply stepping out of line. These "displacements" were also designed to allow a swordsman to strike his enemy at the same moment he escaped injury.

These moves had names like *sbasso, intagliata, inquartata, passata sotto,* and *volting.*

While swords retained a quality of heaviness—a feature that consequently slowed down movement—body evasions proved to be of practical use. However, with the advent of the smallsword—the lightness of which promoted quick exchanges—these actions were no longer considered trustworthy.

At this point the use of the sword blade itself to deflect an oncoming attack became the standard measure of defense.

Body evasions are still used in modern fencing, but not with any frequency. More than anything else, they are looked upon as tricks.
REFERENCES
Castle, Egerton. *Schools and Masters of Fence.* London: George Bell, 1884.
Palffy-Alpar, Julius. *Sword and Masque.* Philadelphia: F. A. Davis, 1967.

BOGU. Specifically, the armor of kendo,* or Japanese fencing. This includes the *men* (mask), the *kote* (arm guards), the *do* (the chest protector), and the *tare* (waist protector).
REFERENCE
Sasamori, Junzo, and Gordon Warner. *This Is Kendo.* Vermont: Charles E. Tuttle, 1984.

BOKKEN. The wooden practice sword of Japan; developed around A.D. 400.

Fashioned from red oak, white oak, or loquat, the *bokken* was put into use as an alternative to practicing with real, potentially lethal weapons, which previously had been a swordsman's only choice.

The *bokken* is usually 100.5 centimeters long, with the center of balance about two-thirds of the way from its tip.

The *bokken* proved to be a great boon to both teachers and students of the sword, allowing them—by removing the threat of imminent death or maiming from practice encounters—to focus more intent and energy into their actions, thereby perfecting skills that would otherwise be stifled for safety's sake.

Just the same, even the employment of the *bokken* did not remove all peril from training sessions. Serious damage could still be caused to a fencer if the weapon's stout oak blade connected squarely with his head or spinal column.

Famed sixteenth-century swordsman Miyamoto Musashi,* who fought more than sixty duels without a loss, often used the wooden sword as his weapon of choice, even against foes with standard metal weapons. Frequently, he killed his opponents outright; on other occasions, he merely beat them soundly.

In time, the *shinai*—a flexible, harmless sword made from bamboo—replaced the *bokken* in the teaching of Japanese swordsmanship.

Today, the *bokken* is used to practice basic movements and *kata* (practice routines of kendo*).

REFERENCES

Lewis, Peter. *The Way to Martial Arts.* New York: Exter Books, 1986.
Musashi, Miyamoto. *A Book of Five Rings.* Translated by Victor Harris. New York: Overlook Press, 1974.
Nakano, Yasoji. *Fundamental Kendo.* Japan: Japan Publications, 1973.
Sasamori, Junzo, and Gordon Warner. *This Is Kendo.* Vermont: Charles E. Tuttle, 1984.

BOKU-TO. A piece of wood carved in the shape of a sword that was carried by Japanese medical men. Of a purely ornamental nature, the *boku-to* was hollowed out and fitted with compartments for medicines.

REFERENCE

Stone, George Cameron. *A Glossary of the Construction, Decoration, and Use of Arms and Armor.* New York: Jack Brussel, 1961.

BOLO. A general term in the Philippine Islands for a sword or long-bladed knife.

REFERENCE

Stone, George Cameron. *A Glossary of the Construction, Decoration, and Use of Arms and Armor.* New York: Jack Brussel, 1961.

BONETTI, JERONIMO. (c. 1590). Italian fencing master.

Son of fencing master Rocco Bonetti, Jeronimo succeeded his father as the master of his London school of defense. Like his father, he was the object of much hatred by less-prosperous English masters.

Jeronimo was eventually killed in a sword duel with an Englishman named Cheese. The Bonetti school then passed into the hands of Jeronimo's partner, Vincentio Saviolo.

An unflattering account of Jeronimo Bonetti's death was detailed by George Silver* in his *Paradoxes of Defence* (1599).**

REFERENCE
Castle, Egerton. *Schools and Masters of Fence.* London: George Bell, 1885.

BONETTI, ROCCO. (c. 1570). Italian fencing master.

Rocco Bonetti was a popular rapier master in England during the latter part of the sixteenth century. He was, however, hated by English fencing masters, who were jealous of his success. A particularly savage appraisal of his skills was drawn by George Silver* in his *Paradoxes of Defence* (1599).**

In the book, Silver describes his version of a sword fight between Bonetti and an Englishman, Austen Bagger, "a verie tall Gentleman," who, although quite drunk, easily defeats the Italian.

Despite George Silver's opinion of Rocco Bonetti's abilities with a sword, the Italian was nevertheless regarded highly enough as a teacher by his students to need the assistance of his son Jeronimo to run his busy London-based school.

REFERENCE
Castle, Egerton. *Schools and Masters of Fence.* London: George Bell, 1885.

BONNAFOUS, JUSTIN. (c. nineteenth century). American fencing master.

One of America's first U.S.-born fencing masters. He taught for years at the Philadelphia Fencing Club.

REFERENCE
Cass, Eleanor Baldwin. *The Book of Fencing.* Boston: Lothrop, Lee, and Shephard, 1930.

BONNEY, ANNE. (c. 1700). An Englishwoman pirate who sailed the West Indies in the early eighteenth century.

Legend has it that Anne Bonney became a pirate not for the plunder but for the sheer love of adventure. It was said she had many love affairs, a few of which were ended by cutlass duels.

She was finally captured in 1720 and sentenced to death, but the sentence was never carried out. At this point, Anne Bonney disappeared and was never heard from again.

The Anne Bonney character is often a staple of the modern pirate movie. She is usually depicted as very aggressive, even ruthless, and quite able with a sword. But, as one might expect, she always falls for the hero, who invariably tames her.

"Anne Bonney" films include *The Spanish Main* (1945), *Anne of the Indies***
(1951), *Against All Flags*** (1952), *Captain Kidd and the Slave Girl* (1954), and *The King's Pirate*** (1967).

REFERENCE
Richards, Jeffrey. *Swordsmen of the Screen.* Boston: Routledge and Kegan Paul, 1977.

BOOK OF FIVE RINGS, A. *A Book of Five Rings* (Go Rin No Sho) is a book of combat tactics—for both warfare and individual encounters—written by Japan's greatest swordsman, Miyamoto Musashi.* Composed in 1645, the volume was Musashi's personal vision of how to attain enlightenment in the dangerous business of dispatching one's enemies in violent circumstances. The "five rings" of the title refers to the five approaches one might take to achieve this end.

In poetic fashion typical of the Japanese people, Musashi compared the path toward true understanding with the characteristics of the elements. "The Ground Book" dealt with understanding the ways of the world. "The Water Book" covered the spirit. "The Fire Book" was about fighting. "The Wind Book" took into account old traditions of strategy. The last book, "The Book of the Void," discussed the development of intuitive enlightenment through the act of embracing nothingness, which, according to Musashi, was the truth that encompassed all other truths.

In the 1980s, *A Book of Five Rings* became a primer for modern businessmen.
REFERENCES

Musashi, Miyamoto. *A Book of Five Rings.* Translated by Victor Harris. New York: Overlook Press, 1974.

Sasamori, Junzo, and Gordon Warner. *This Is Kendo.* Vermont: Charles E. Tuttle, 1984.

BOOKS, FENCING. The literature of fencing is as diverse as it is vast. It ranges from the highly fanciful, such as Girard Thibault's* *Academie de l'Epee* (1628) to the highly practical *The School of Fencing* by Domenico Angelo* (1763).

The first-known work on fencing, *Flos Duellatorum,* was published in Italy in 1410, although the first work of any any real importance, *Opera Nova* by Achille Marozzo,* did not appear until 1550.

Early fencing books were filled with verbose philosophies and poorly defined actions. Favorite attacks were often tricks. But as time went on and more thoughtful individuals found their way into fencing, books began appearing that reflected creative and scientific approaches to swordplay. The best of these include Angelo Viggiani's* *Lo Schermo* (1575), Vincentio Saviolo's* *His Practice* (1595), Salvator Fabris'* *De lo Schermo* (1606), Ridolfo Capo Ferro's* *Gran simulacro dell'arte e dell uso della Schermo* (1610), and Charles Besnard's* *Le Maistre d'Arme Liberal* (1653).

Later books, such as Sir William Hope's* *The Complete Fencing Master* (1692), M. Olivier's* *Fencing Familiarized* (1771), and Guillaume Danet's* *L'Art des Armes* (1767), continued to define and refine the fencing process.

Modern volumes on fencing tend to be individual interpretations of the age-old subject.

Fencing books include:

Talhoffer's Fechtbuck, Hans Talhoffer (1467).

Opera Nova, Achille Marozzo (1536).

Trattato di scientia d'arme, Camillo Agrippa (1553).

De la Philosophia de las Armas, Heronimo de Caranza (1569).

Ragione di addoprar sicuramente l'Arme, Giacomo di Grassi (1570).

Grundtliche Besschreibung der Freyen, Joachim Meyer (1570).

Traicte contenant les secrets du premier sur l'espee seule, Henry de Sainct-Didier (1573).

Nuovo et breve modo di Schermire, Alfonso Fallopia (1584).

His True Art of Defence, Giacomo di Grassi (1594).

His Practice, Vincentio Saviolo (1595).

Libro de las grandezas de la Espada, Don Luis Pacheco de Narvaez (1599).

Paradoxe of Defence, George Silver (1599).

Trattato in Materia di Scherma, Marco Docciolini (1601).

De lo Schermo, Salvator Fabris (1606).

Teatro, Nicoletto Giganti (1606).

Traite, ou instruction pour tirer des armes, Hieronime Cavalcabo (1609).

Gran simulacro dell'arte dell'uso della Scherma, Ridolfo Capo Ferro (1610).

New Kunstliches Fechtbuch, Jacob Sutor (1612).

The Schoole of the Noble and Worthy Science of Defence, Joseph Swetnam (1617).

Academie de l'Espee, Girard Thibault (1626).

L'Exercise des armes ou le maniement du fleuret, Jean Baptiste le Perche du Coudray (1635).

La Scherma, Francesco Alfieri (1640).

A Book of Five Rings, Miyamoto Musashi (1645).

Il vero maneggio della Spada, Alexander Senesse (1660).

Le Maistre d'armes, Andre de Liancour (1686).

Scots Fencing Master, Sir William Hope (1687).

L'Arte de l'Epee, Labat (1690).

The Sword-Man's Vade-Mecum, Sir William Hope (1691).

The Complete Fencing Master, Sir William Hope (1692).

The English Fencing Master, Henry Blackwell (1705).

A New, Short and Easy Method of Fencing, Sir William Hope (1705).

The English Master of Defense, Zachary Wylde (1711).

Leib-beschirmende und Feinden Trotz-bietende Fecht-Kunst, Johann Schmidt (1713).

Hope's New Method of Fencing, Sir William Hope (1714).

A Vindication of the True Art of Self-Defence, Sir William Hope (1724).

Observations on the Gladiator's Stage-Fighting, Sir William Hope (1725).

The Expert Sword-Man's Companion, Donald McBane (1728).

A Treatise on Fencing, J. Miller (1738).

The School of Fencing, Domenico Angelo (1763).

L'Art des Armes, Guillaume Danet (1766).

Fencing Familiarized, Olivier (1771).

Nouveau traite de l'art des armes, M. C. Navarre (1775).

The Art of Fencing, James Underwood (1787).

Questions sur l'art en fait d'armes, Labat (1796).

Hungarian and Highland Broad Sword, Henry Angelo (1798).

Cudgel-Playing Modernized and Improved, Captain Sinclair (1800).

Traite de L'Art des Armes, de la Boessiere (1818).

The Reminiscences of Henry Angelo, Henry Angelo (1830).

Notes on Duels, Lorenzo Sabine (1859).

Histoire de l'escrime, Emile Merignac (1883).

The Book of the Sword, Richard F. Burton (1884).

Schools and Master of Fence, Egerton Castle (1885).

Fencing, H. A. Dunn (1889).

The Broadsword as Taught by the Celebrated Italian Masters Signors Masiello and Ciullini, Francis Wright (1889).

Broadsword and Singlestick, C. Phillipps-Wolley (1890).

The Swordsman, Alfred Hutton (1891).

Old Swordplay, Alfred Hutton (1892).

Foil and Sabre, Louis Rondelle (1892).

Fencing, Edward Breck (1894).

A Complete Bibliography of Fencing and Dueling, Carl Thimm (1896).

Secrets of the Sword, Cesar de Bazancourt (1900).

The Art of Fencing, Louis and Regis Senac (1904).

Swordplay for Actors, Fred Blakeslee (1905).

How to Fence, Maurice Grandiere (1906).

The Sentiment of the Sword, Richard F. Burton (1911).

Cut and Thrust, Leon Bertrand (1927).

The Book of Fencing, Eleanor Cass (1930).

Theory of Fencing, Julio Castello (1931).

The Art of the Foil, Luigi Barbasetti (1932).

The Theory and Practice of Fencing, Julio Castello (1933).

Fencing, John Stevenson (1935).

The Science of the Sword, Vincent Knowles (1935).

German Swordplay, Edwin Emerson (1936).

Foil Fencing, Henry Uyttenhove (1936).

Fencing Tactics, Percy Nobbs (1936).

Fundamentals of Foil Fencing, Joseph Vince (1937).

On Fencing, Aldo Nadi (1943).

Academic Fencing, Alfred Finckh (1946).

Modern Fencing, Clovis Deladrier (1948).

Modern British Fencing, C.–L. de Beaumont (1950).

Fencing with the Foil, Roger Crosnier (1951).

Fencing, C.–L. de Beaumont (1951).

The House of Angelo, J. D. Aylward (1953).

Fencing with the Sabre, Roger Crosnier (1954).

Fencing Technique in Pictures, C.-L. de Beaumont (1955).

Sports Illustrated Book of Fencing, Edward Vebell (1962).

This Is Kendo, Junzo Sasamori and Gordon Warner (1964).

The Duel, Robert Baldick (1965).

Fencing, Muriel Bower and Torao Mori (1966).

Sword and Masque, Julius Palffy-Alpar (1967).

Swords and Daggers, Frederick Wilkinson (1967).

Techniques of the Stage Fight, William Hobbs (1967).

The Art and History of Personal Combat, Arthur Wise (1971).

Better Fencing, Bob Anderson (1973).

Fundamental Kendo, Yasoji Nakano and Nariaki Sato (1974).

Fencing and the Master, Laszlo Szabo (1977).

Foil Around and Stay Fit, Camille Lownds (1977).

Fencing Is for Me, Art Thomas (1982).

The Fencing Book, Nancy Curry (1984).

Fencing Everyone, William Gaugler (1987).

Martini A–Z of Fencing, E. D. Morton (1992).

REFERENCES

Castle, Egerton. *Schools and Masters of Fence.* London: George Bell, 1885.

Conroy, Tom. "Checklist of Fencing Books." *American Fencing* (November/December 1981).

Wise, Arthur. *The Art and History of Personal Combat.* Greenwich, CT: Arma Press, 1971.

BOOKS, SWORD-RELATED. There are numerous volumes dealing with the development, construction, and decoration of the sword. These include:

A Critical Inquiry into Ancient Armour, Samuel Meyrick (1824).

Ancient Armor and Weapons in Europe, John Hewitt (1855).

Arms and Armor, David Boutell (1867).

Arms and Armor, Paul Lacombe (1867).

The Sword of Japan, Thomas McClatchie (1873).

Illustrated History of Arms and Armor, Auguste Demmin (1877).

The Book of the Sword, Richard F. Burton (1884).

Schools and Masters of Fence, Egerton Castle (1885).

Decoration of Swords and Sword Furniture, Edward Gilbertson (1894).

Japanese Sword Blades, Edward Gilbertson (1897).

The Sword and Centuries, Alfred Hutton (1901).

Fire and Sword in the Cacasus, Luigi Villiari (1906).

Spanish Arms and Armor, Albert Calvert (1907).

The Sword and Same, H. L. Joly (1913).

Handbook of Arms and Armor, Dean Bashford (1915).

Catalogue of European Court and Hunting Swords, B. Dean (1929).

Sword, Lance, and Bayonet, Charles Ffoulkes (1938).

Nippon-To—The Japanese Sword, I. Hakusui (1948).

The Naval Officer's Sword, H. T. Bosanquet (1955).

Irish Swords, G. A. Hayes-McCoy (1959).

The Small Sword in England, J. D. Aylward (1960).

A Glossary of the Construction, Decoration, and Use of Arms and Armor, George Cameron Stone (1961).

The Sword in Anglo-Saxon England, H. R. Ellis-Davidson (1962).

Swords and Daggers, J. F. Hayward (1964).

Arms and Armor of the Western World, Bruno Thomas, Ortwin Gamber, and Hans Schedelmann (1964).

Sword in the Age of Chivalry, R. Ewart Oakeshott (1964).

Arms and Armor, Stephen Grancsay (1964).

Japanese Sword Smiths, W. M. Hawley (1966).

Swords and Daggers of Indonesia, Vaclav Solc (1966).

Swords and Daggers, Frederick Wilkinson (1967).

European Arms and Armor, Charles Ashdown (1967).

Highland Weapons, William Mackay (1970).

Arms and Armor, Vesley Norman (1972).

Weapons Through the Ages, William Reid (1976).

Weapons and Armor, Harold Hart (1978).

English Weapons and Warfare, 449–1660, A. V. B. Norman and Don Pottinger (1979).

Knights, Julek Heller (1982).

Weapons and Assassins, Erick Wujcik (1983).

Martini A–Z of Fencing, E. D. Morton (1992).

REFERENCES

Burton, Richard F. *The Book of the Sword.* London: Chatto and Windus, 1884.

Stone, George Cameron. *A Glossary of the Construction, Decoration, and Use of Arms and Armor.* New York: Jack Brussel, 1961.

Wilkinson, Frederick. *Swords and Daggers.* New York: Hawthorn Books, 1967.

BORDON-DANZA. A Basque religious sword dance performed by two lines of men facing one another. It has been suggested this ceremony is connected with the summer solstice.

REFERENCE

Leach, Maria, ed. *Funk and Wagnalls Standard Dictionary of Folklore, Mythology, and Legend.* San Francisco: Harper and Row, 1972.

BORSODY, LASZLO. (c. 1900). Hungarian fencing master.

Borsody, along with Italo Santelli,* did much to modernize sabre technique in Hungary. He strongly believed in the simplicity of movement. He also championed the light, maneuverable sabre used today and the conventions by which it is employed.

It is ironic that Borsody, a master swordsman, should have been killed in a pistol duel.

REFERENCES

Morton, E. D. *Martini A–Z of Fencing.* London: Queen Anne Press, 1992.

Palffy-Alpar, Julius. *Sword and Masque.* Philadelphia: F. A. Davis, 1967.

BOSHI-MONO. In Japan, the name for a blade that has been retempered. These blades are always of inferior quality.

REFERENCE

Stone, George Cameron. *A Glossary of the Construction, Decoration, and Use of Arms and Armor.* New York: Jack Brussel, 1961.

BOTTA. An old fencing term referring to an attacking action from its beginning to completion.

Also known as *bott* and *botte.* The French equivalent would be *coup.*

REFERENCES

Castle, Egerton. *Schools and Masters of Fence.* London: George Bell, 1885.

Stone, George Cameron. *A Glossary of the Construction, Decoration, and Use of Arms and Armor.* New York: Jack Brussel, 1961.

BOTTA LUNGA. A term employed in the fifteenth century to describe a lunge, which, while basic to modern fencing, was highly revolutionary for its time period.

Italian fencing master Nicoletto Giganti* was the first to clearly explain the principles behind the *botta lunga* in his book *Teatro* (1606). Even by today's standards, his meaning was quite clear: "Place thyself in a firm attitude, rather collected than otherwise, so as to be capable of further extension. Being thus on guard, extend thy arm and advance the body at the same time, and bend the right knee as much as possible, so that thy opponent may be hit before he can parry."

By the mid-1600s, the *botta lunga* was well entrenched as a standard part of swordplay.

REFERENCES

Castle, Egerton. *Schools and Masters of Fence.* London: George Bell, 1885.

Stone, George Cameron. *A Glossary of the Construction, Decoration, and Use of Arms and Armor.* New York: Jack Brussel, 1961.

BOTTA SEGRETA. In the early days of fencing's history, when agility and cunning played a greater role in combat than science and art, every swordsman of note claimed to have a *botta segreta*—or secret attack—that, if executed properly, would easily penetrate any defensive action encountered.

The search for secret offensive moves became an obsession among fencers, not unlike the alchemist's pursuit of the fabled gold-creating philosopher's stone. An attack that could not be stopped was, in a way, as good as gold. It meant certain fame and fortune for the possessor.

A treasured *botta segreta* might be passed on to a favored student as a gift (if that student agreed to take a oath never to use it against the teacher). Then again, some fencing masters would give up their special move to anyone if the price was right.

There was nothing mystical—or even scientific—about secret attacks. By and large, they were sets of tricks, pure and simple. Almost anything a swordsman could think of and execute could find its way into a *botta segreta*. Attacks might include tumbling, tripping, jumping, grabbing blades. Of course, when they did work, it was due mainly to their momentary uniqueness. Once the element of surprise was gone, there was little to be said for them. That these fabulous *bottes* have not survived their inventors is an indication of their true worth.

REFERENCES
Castle, Egerton. *Schools and Masters of Fence.* London: George Bell, 1885.
Stone, George Cameron. *A Glossary of the Construction, Decoration, and Use of Arms and Armor.* New York: Jack Brussel, 1961.

BOTTE DE NOAILLES. A stop hit* between the eyes. A specialty of a sixteenth-century member of the French Noailles family, from whom the counterattack derived its name.
REFERENCE
Morton, E. D. *Martini A–Z of Fencing.* London: Queen Anne Press, 1992.

BOTTE DE PAYSAN. This action, as described by French fencing master le Sieur De La Touche* in his book *Les vrays principes de l'espee seule* (1670), essentially turned the sword into a bayonet.

The *botte de paysan* was performed by gripping one's sword blade in the left hand (while still holding the grip of the weapon firmly in the right hand), beating aside the opponent's blade, closing with him on a pass, and stabbing him in the belly.
REFERENCE
Wise, Arthur. *The Art and History of Personal Combat.* Greenwich, CT: Arma Press, 1971.

BOTTE DE SAINT-EVREMONT. A supposedly unstoppable thrust created by the famous French duelist Saint-Evremont, the exact nature of which has been lost.
REFERENCE
Morton, E. D. *Martini A–Z of Fencing.* London: Queen Anne Press, 1992.

BOUT. Two fencers are said to be engaged in a bout when the score of their encounter is kept.

In sport fencing—foil,* sabre,* and épée*—a bout has been won when one fencer scores five valid touches* before his opponent does.

Foil and sabre bouts have always been decided by five touches. Not so, however, in the case of the épée. In the early days of épée competition, a bout lasted for only one touch. Because fencing with the épée was supposed to reflect the reality of an actual duel—where one solid hit on a wrist or kneecap would pretty much end an encounter—the single-touch event was looked on as the only true indicator of skill. Eventually, it was decided that, while this made an épée bout more true to life, it was not very sporting (basically, allowing absolutely no room for error). So, the bout touch requirement was increased to five, putting the épée on a par with foil and sabre.

The one-touch épée bout still survives in the Olympic modern pentathlon competition.

Until quite recently, women fenced four-touch bouts. But, with the concept of equal rights taking a firm grip on the world in the 1970s, this convention was flatly rejected as sexist. Women now fence the same number of touches in their bouts as men do.

REFERENCES

Palffy-Alpar, Julius. *Sword and Masque.* Philadelphia: F. A. Davis, 1967.

U.S. Fencing Association. *Operations Manual.* Colorado Springs, CO: U.S. Fencing Association, 1985.

Wilkinson, Jack, ed. *Rules of the Game.* New York: Paddington Press, 1974.

BRAHE, TYCHO. (1546–1601). Danish astronomer and astrologer.

One of the great astronomers of the Renaissance, Tycho Brahe, discoverer of stars and mapper of the sky, also fought a sword duel in which he lost part of his nose. To remedy this noticeable lack, he wore a copper nose cover of his own design.

REFERENCE

Cave, Janet, ed. *Mysteries of the Unknown: Cosmic Connections.* VA: Time-Life Books, 1990.

BRAND. A sword with a long, narrow, quadrangular blade hung from the saddle.

The brand was used entirely for thrusting.

Also known as a *bronde.*

REFERENCES

Burton, Richard F. *The Book of the Sword.* London: Chatto and Windus, 1884.

Stone, George Cameron. *A Glossary of the Construction, Decoration, and Use of Arms and Armor.* New York: Jack Brussel, 1961.

BRANDESTOC. An ax or war hammer with a long, swordlike blade hidden inside the handle. It was simply pulled out if needed.

REFERENCE

Stone, George Cameron. *A Glossary of the Construction, Decoration, and Use of Arms and Armor.* New York: Jack Brussel, 1961.

BRANSTOCK. In Norse mythology, Branstock was a gigantic oak into which the god Odin thrust the magic sword Gram. Only the hero Siegfried was able to remove it from the tree.
REFERENCE
Leach, Maria, ed. *Funk and Wagnalls Standard Dictionary of Folklore, Mythology, and Legend.* San Francisco: Harper and Row, 1972.

BRAQUEMAR. A broad, short, double-edged sword, used especially during the sixteenth century. However, the name has been applied to a number of different sword forms—large and small—as long as they had a broad blade.

The name was probably derived from the word *braquet,* which meant, basically, a broadsword.

Also known as a *braquemart* and *malchus,* after the personage of Malchus in the Bible, whose ear was cut off by St. Peter, supposedly with such a weapon.
REFERENCES
Castle, Egerton. *Schools and Masters of Fence.* London: George Bell, 1885.
Stone, George Cameron. *A Glossary of the Construction, Decoration, and Use of Arms and Armor.* New York: Jack Brussel, 1961.

BRAS ARME. The sword arm.
REFERENCE
Handleman, Rob. "Fencing Glossary." *American Fencing* (February/March 1978).

BREAKING THE ATTACK. A counterattack, such as a beat,* on an opponent's blade as he makes a feint.*
REFERENCE
Morton, E. D. *Martini A–Z of Fencing.* London: Queen Anne Press, 1992.

BREAK THE GAME. Parrying a feint.*
REFERENCE
Morton, E. D. *Martini A–Z of Fencing.* London: Queen Anne Press, 1992.

BREAST PROTECTORS. For women to compete safely and comfortably in fencing, rounded aluminum plates are worn within the jacket to protect the breast area.

The rules of fencing, as set down by the U.S. Fencing Association, make breast protectors a requirement for all organized competitions.
REFERENCE
U.S. Fencing Association. *Operations Manual.* Colorado Springs, CO: U.S. Fencing Association, 1985.

BRITISH FENCERS, NOTED.

Nineteenth Century

Harry Angelo,* Richard Burton,* George Chapman,* William Desborough, Cosmo Duff-Gordon, Charles Herries,* Alfred Hutton,* Al Miller-Hallet.

Evan James

Early Twentieth Century (1900–1949)

Edward Amphlett, John Blake, I. D. Campbell-Gray, T. A. Cook, Archie Corble, C. Leaf Daniell, Percival Davson, Charles de Beaumont,* P. G. Doyne, Arthur Everitt, Vice-Admiral Granville, Cecil Haig, G. V. Hett, Martin Holt, Evan James, C. A. Kershaw, John Lloyd, A. Ridley Martin, Sydney Martineau, Robert Montgomerie, Rene Paul, A. E. Pelling, A. G. Pilbrow, Charles Robinson, Edgar Seligman, F. G. Sherriff, F. H. Townsend, Roger Tredgold, O. G. Trinder, P. M. Turquet.

Modern Times (1950–)

David Acfield, Michael Alexandre, M. J. Amberg, Bob Anderson,* William Beatley, Nick Bell, Owen Bourne, Robert Bruniges, Harry Cook, Arnold Cooperman, Rodney Craig, Geoffrey Grimmet, Nick Halsted, Pierre Harper, William Harrison, Henry Hoskyns, Michael Howard, Peter Jacobs, Allan Jay, Ralph Johnson, Alex Leckie, John Llewellyn, Neal Mallett, Angus McKenzie, Richard Oldcorn, Barry Paul, Graham Paul, Raymond Paul, Steve Paul, John Pelling, J. Philbin, Ulrich Wendon.

REFERENCES

Cass, Eleanor Baldwin. *The Book of Fencing.* Boston: Lothrop, Lee, and Sheperd, 1930.
Morton, E. D. *Martini A–Z of Fencing.* London: Queen Anne Press, 1992.
Wallechinsky, David. *The Complete Book of the Olympics.* New York: Penguin Books, 1984.

BRITISH WOMEN FENCERS, NOTED. Wendy Ager, Ann Brannon, Peggy Butler, Hillary Cawthorne, Gladys Daniel, Gladys Davis, Muriel Freeman, Mary Glen-Haig, Wendy Grant, Susan Green, J. Heather Guinness, Clare Halsted, Toupie Lowther, Linda Martin, Gwen Nelligan, T. M. Offredy, Edith Roberts, Gillian Sheen, Susan Wrigglesworth.

REFERENCES

Morton, E. D. *Martini A–Z of Fencing.* London: Queen Anne Press, 1992.
Wallechinsky, David. *The Complete Book of the Olympics.* New York: Penguin Books, 1984.

BROADSWORD. A sword with a straight, wide, single-edged blade, often employing a basket-type hilt. An average blade length would be 36 inches.

The broadsword was the favorite military sword of the seventeenth, eighteenth, and nineteenth centuries (although it was also used in the sixteenth century). It was also the weapon commonly used by the lower classes.

One version of broadsword, the Highland broadsword,* was adopted as the national sword of Scotland. Another, the *schiavona,*,* was Italy's version of the weapon.

REFERENCES

Castle, Egerton. *Schools and Masters of Fence.* London: George Bell, 1885.
Wilkinson, Frederick. *Swords and Daggers.* New York: Hawthorn Books, 1967.

BROCHIERO. A small shield used in personal combat during the early sixteenth century. When employed, it was always held at arm's length.

Also called a *broquel.*

REFERENCES

Castle, Egerton. *Schools and Masters of Fence*. London: George Bell, 1885.

Stone, George Cameron. *A Glossary of the Construction, Decoration, and Use of Arms and Armor*. New York: Jack Brussel, 1961.

BROKEN GUARD. In sabre, when an attacking blade, deflected by the weapon guard, secondarily makes contact with a valid* target area, it is said to have "broken the guard," and no touch is scored. However, if the guard and target are touched at the same time, the attack is allowed.

REFERENCE

Morton, E. D. *Martini A–Z of Fencing*. London: Queen Anne Press, 1992.

BROKEN TIME. A temporary alteration in the normal tempo of a fencing action. When performed intentionally, such a timing change is used to confuse an opponent.

REFERENCE

Morton, E. D. *Martini A–Z of Fencing*. London: Queen Anne Press, 1992.

BRUSSELS ACADEMY. During the seventeenth century, Brussels was the site of a successful fencing academy that had been established during Spanish occupation of Belgium 100 years before.

To maintain its continued importance in the fencing world, the academy held periodic grand tournaments, awarding prizes of richly decorated arms, which were presented with much pomp in public ceremonies.

REFERENCE

Castle, Egerton. *Schools and Masters of Fence*. London: George Bell, 1885.

BUCK, TIMOTHY. (c. 1700). English fencing master and stage fighter.

Buck was said to be a "solid Master," and "even when grown decrepid [sic], his old Age could not hide his uncommon Judgement. He was a Pillar of his Art, and all his Followers, who excelled, built upon him."

REFERENCE

Castle, Egerton. *Schools and Masters of Fence*. London: George Bell, 1885.

BUCKLER. The buckler was a small, usually round shield used primarily in personal combat. Worn on the wrist, it was considered as much a part of fashion as it was a defensive tool and was sold in clothing shops. It was in common use from the thirteenth to the seventeenth centuries.

Many bucklers came equipped with a sharp spike set in the middle, which allowed them to be used offensively as well as defensively. In general, these protuberances were between four and five inches in length, but some were as long as twelve inches. These latter types were meant to be used to break an opponent's blade.

One style of buckler even came with a pistol built into its frame, the gun barrel protruding where the spike would normally have been situated.

The sword and buckler

Because the buckler was employed only in conjunction with a "cutting" sword, it fell into disuse when the newfangled rapier, with its thrusting blade, replaced the sword as the weapon of choice in Europe. (The buckler was not effective against the thrust.)

England, as it turned out, became the last bastion for the buckler, mainly because the English adamantly rejected the rapier, in favor of the sword, as their national weapon. A hatred of things "foreign" (the rapier was an Italian/Spanish invention) and a propensity for tradition doubtlessly sparked most of the resistance.

But even the English could not hold out forever against the obvious killing efficiency of the rapier. By the mid-1600s, the sword and buckler were a thing of the past.

Also called a *bokeler.*

REFERENCES

Burton, Richard F. *The Book of the Sword.* London: Chatto and Windus, 1884.

Castle, Egerton. *Schools and Masters of Fence.* London: George Bell, 1885.

Stone, George Cameron. *A Glossary of the Construction, Decoration, and Use of Arms and Armor.* New York: Jack Brussel, 1961.

BULLFIGHTING. A highly stylized public spectacle—especially in Spain and Mexico—in which a bullfighter, called a matador, engages and usually executes a fighting bull with a sword. The sword is a long, thin-bladed weapon, with a simple cross hilt and a knuckle guard. The point is slightly curved.

Bullfighting terms with regard to the sword include:

Bajonazo: a faulty but effective sword thrust

Delantero: placement of the sword too far forward on the bull's neck

Espada: sword

Estocada: sword thrust

Estoque: a sword used to kill bulls

Descabello: the coup de grâce; also, a short sword used by matadors to sever the spinal cord of a bull too weak to charge

La muerte: the downward curve of the last third of a sword blade

Media estocada: a sword thrust in which only half of the blade enters the bull

Mozo de espada: the sword handler who takes care of the matador's equipment

Recibiendo: a method of killing a bull in which the matador stands completely still and receives a charging bull on his sword

REFERENCE

Fulton, John. *Bullfighting.* New York: Dial Press, 1971.

BURROUGHS, EDGAR RICE. (1875–1950). American writer of adventure stories whose most famous novel is *Tarzan of the Apes* (1914).

While Edgar Rice Burroughs's greatest claim to fame is his jungle tales of Tarzan (a character that has become a worldwide institution), he also penned numerous volumes of exotic, swashbuckling fantasies set on other planets. Perhaps the best of these was the ''John Carter of Mars'' series. These dealt with an American soldier of fortune who inexplicably finds himself on Mars, a planet full of loathsome monsters, beautiful maidens in desperate need of rescue, and muscular, sword-wielding adversaries. Titles included *A Princess of Mars* (1917), *The Chessmen of Mars* (1922), *A Fighting Man of Mars* (1931), and *Swords of Mars* (1936).

Swordplay is a constant in Burroughs's writing, as typified in *The Mad King* (1926), a *Prisoner of Zenda*-esque novel:

Barney Custer had been a pupil of the redoubtable Colonel Monstery, who was, as Barney was wont to say, one of the thanwhomest of fencing masters.

Quickly Maenck fell back to give place to Stein, but not before the American's point had found him twice to leave him streaming with flesh wounds.

Other Burroughs adventure novels in which swordplay figures include *At the Earth's Core* (1922), *The Outlaw of Torn* (1927), and *Pirates of Venus* (1934).

REFERENCES

Burroughs, Edgar Rice. *The Mad King.* New York: Ace Books, 1970.

Lupoff, Richard. *Edgar Rice Burroughs: Master of Adventure.* New York: Ace Books, 1965.

BURTON, RICHARD. (1925–1984). Versatile Welsh actor of stage, film, and television. His greatest acclaim came from his *Hamlet** on Broadway (1961) and his role as King Arthur in the musical *Camelot* (1960).

With a rich, full voice and dynamic theatrical bearing, Burton was a natural for heroic historical movies, yet, surprisingly, he starred in only a few such films, like *The Robe* (1953), *Alexandre the Great* (1956), and *Cleopatra* (1962). His forte was Shakespeare on stage, and *Hamlet* was the role that made him famous.

Wrote critic Kenneth Tynan of Burton's stage work, ''He has lashed himself to his own main-mast, steering directly by his own star, the star of absolute self-trust which is within all the best actors and whose courses are unalterable, even by failure.''

He also starred on stage in Shakespeare's *King John, Twelfth Night, Coriolanus, The Tempest, Henry V,* and *Othello.*

REFERENCES

Bragg, Melvyn. *Richard Burton: A Life.* Boston: Little, Brown, 1988.

Halliwell, Leslie. *Halliwell's Filmgoer's and Video Viewer's Companion.* New York: Charles Scribner's Sons, 1988.

BURTON, SIR RICHARD F. (1821–1890). English explorer, author, and fencer.

In 1884, Sir Richard F. Burton wrote a remarkable history of the sword. The tome, *The Book of the Sword,* an outgrowth of his love of fencing and weaponry, covered everything from metallurgy to how to determine the center of percussion

The writer Sir Richard F. Burton

on a sword blade. It also discussed in great detail the swords of ancient Egypt, Africa, Assyria, Persia, Greece, and Rome.

Burton's own personal views on the subject of the sword were woven into the text. He thought there was nothing finer in the world than the sword and the pursuit of knowledge concerning its history and use. He called the sword ''a gift of magic.''

It is interesting that, for all its astonishing scholarship, the author not only had trouble finding a publisher for *The Book of the Sword,* but the publication itself was a financial failure. Burton had planned two additional volumes, *The Sword Fully Grown* and *Memoirs of the Sword,* but these never got beyond the planning stage.

Burton's fencing career began when he was a boy living with his family in Italy. His training encompassed aspects of both the French and Italian schools. He became, it was said, a passionate fencer. He was a fencing champion at Oxford, and later he was looked upon as one of the most expert swordsmen of his age. "Fencing," he once said, "was the great solace of my life."

Addressing the game itself, Burton observed:

Again, men of thought cannot ignore the intrinsic value of the sword for stimulating physical qualities. The best of calisthenics, this energetic educator teaches the man to carry himself like a soldier. A compendium of gymnastics, it increases strength and activity, dexterity and rapidity of movement. Professors calculate that one hour of hard fencing wastes forty ounces of perspiration and respiration. The foil is still the best training tool for the consensus of eye and hand; for the judgment of distance and opportunity; and, in fact, for the practice of combat. And thus swordsmanship engenders moral confidence and self-reliance while it stimulates a habit of resource; and it is not without suggesting, even in schools, that "curious, fantastic, very noble generosity proper to itself alone."

REFERENCES
Benet, William Rose. *The Reader's Encyclopedia.* New York: William Y. Crowell, 1965.
Brodie, Fawn M. *The Devil Drives.* New York: W. W. Norton, 1967.
Burton, Richard F. *The Book of the Sword.* London: Chatto and Windus, 1884.

BUSHI. The early name for a Japanese warrior.
REFERENCE
Sasamori, Junzo, and Gordon Warner. *This Is Kendo.* Vermont: Charles E. Tuttle, 1984.

BUSHIDO. The code of the samurai* in feudal Japan. Bushido means "way of the warrior." The sources of this life system were Zen Buddhism, Confucianism, and Shintoism. In many ways Bushido paralleled the code of chivalry followed by European knights; yet in other ways it was distinctly Japanese.

Bushido stressed courage, loyalty, honesty, and self-control. It also allowed for suicide as a way of reclaiming one's lost honor.

The sword, through this demanding code, became the "soul of the samurai." At the age of five, a samurai boy was given a wooden sword. From that point on, he was never without a weapon. The samurai's *katana* (long sword) was often an object of deep veneration. Even to step over a weapon lying on the floor was considered a great personal insult to the owner.

The spirit of Bushido became the guiding force of Japan for centuries and can still be seen in aspects of that country's culture today.

REFERENCES
Nitobe, Inazo. *Bushido: The Warrior's Code.* Burbank, CA: Ohara, 1983.
Suzuki, Daisetz. *Zen and Japanese Culture.* Princeton, NJ: Princeton University Press,
     1959.

BUTTERFLY GUARD. A type of hand guard employed on the eighteenth-century smallsword. Made up of two small shells, it resembled a butterfly.
REFERENCE
Morton, E. D. *Martini A–Z of Fencing.* London: Queen Anne Press, 1992.

BUTTON. The flattened tip of a fencing weapon, fashioned so as to make it harmless for practice. In its earliest form, the button was about the size of a golf ball. Today, the button of a standard sport blade is approximately 3/16 of an inch across.

The button on an electric weapon is a product of modern technology. A depressible tip wired to an electrical plug beneath the hand guard forms the basis of the weapon's scoring system. Regulated by a spring inside the housing of the unit, the button causes a touch to be registered on an electric scoring machine when it is pushed in by firm contact.
REFERENCES
Palffy-Alpar, Julius. *Sword and Masque.* Philadelphia: F. A. Davis, 1967.
Volkmann, Rudy. *Electrical Fencing Equipment.* Arvee Press, 1975.

C

CADENCE. The rhythm in which a fencing move is executed.

Unconsciously repeating a fencing action with the same cadence over and over can set up a dangerous pattern that can be taken advantage of by one's opponent.

However, done on purpose, repetition of a rhythm can be used to subconsciously—almost hypnotically—guide another fencer into a timing sense that, if changed quickly, throws him off guard.

A constant awareness of cadence—both one's own and that of one's opponent—is a vital element in the formulation of fencing strategy.

REFERENCE

Palffy-Alpar, Julius. *Sword and Masque.* Philadelphia: F. A. Davis, 1967.

CALNAN, GEORGE. (1900–1933). U.S. fencing champion.

George Calnan was the first American to become a medalist in an individual Olympic fencing event since the 1904 St. Louis Olympics, taking third place in épée at the 1928 Amsterdam games. He also won two medals at the 1932 Los Angeles Olympics: a third-place medal for team foil and another third-place medal for team épée.

On a national level, Calnan was the U.S. men's individual foil champion from 1925 to 1928 and then again from 1930 to 1931. He was also the U.S. men's individual épée champion in 1923.

Calnan, a navy officer, was killed in the crash of the dirigible *Akron* off the coast of New Jersey in 1933.

REFERENCE

Grombach, John V. *The 1972 Olympic Guide.* New York: Paperback Library, 1972.

CAMBIAMENTO. To change the line of engagement.

Also known as *camineering*.
REFERENCE
Morton, E. D. *Martini A–Z of Fencing.* London: Queen Anne Press, 1992.

CAMELOT. The traditional home of King Arthur and his knights of the Round Table. In some versions of the Arthurian legends, the court divided its time between two locations, depending on the time of year. Camelot was where the court spent Christmas, while during Pentecost it moved to Caerleon (or Carduel).

Arthur derived his authority to rule his court from the ownership of the sword Excalibur.*
REFERENCE
Benet, William Rose. *The Reader's Encyclopedia.* New York: Thomas Y. Crowell, 1965.

CAMMINANDO. Attacking on the advance. This consists of straightening the sword arm and stepping forward at the same moment, after which the lunge is immediately employed.

Also known as attacking *en marchant.*
REFERENCE
Morton, E. D. *Martini A–Z of Fencing.* London: Queen Anne Press, 1992.

CAMPILAN. A Malayan sword, originally the weapon of the Dyaks of Borneo. It has a long, straight, single-edged blade (average length: twenty-eight inches), wider at the point than at the hilt. The grip is carved from wood. The weapon is often decorated with tufts of goat hair.

The scabbard of the *campilan* was fashioned of two separate pieces of wood so that when a single lashing was cut, it would fall away from the sword, making it unnecessary to draw the blade.

Also called a *kampilan.*
REFERENCES
Solc, Vaclay. *Swords and Daggers of Indonesia.* London: Spring Books, 1966.
Stone, George Cameron. *A Glossary of the Construction, Decoration, and Use of Arms and Armor.* New York: Jack Brussel, 1961.

CANNELURE. As the form of blades changed from the heavy sword to the more slender and lengthy rapier, a method both to increase blade strength and to lessen blade weight was needed. It was found that by placing a groove—the *cannelure*—down the middle of the blade, this could be accomplished. The *cannelure* also removed any whippy quality from the blade.
REFERENCES
Burton, Richard F. *The Book of the Sword.* London: Chatto and Windus, 1884.
Castle, Egerton. *Schools and Masters of Fence.* London: George Bell, 1885.

CAPO FERRO, RIDOLFO. (c. 1600). Italian fencing master ("Master of the most excellent German Nation in the famous City of Sienna").

Of all the masters of his time, Capo Ferro was doubtlessly most responsible

Inventive Italian fencing master Ridolfo Capo Ferro

for fixing the principles of fencing in the seventeenth century. His book, *The Great Simulacrum of the Use of the Sword* (1610),** was both comprehensive and intelligent, and the ideas he set down were improved upon very little for the next hundred years.

Perhaps his most important contribution to fencing was establishing, once and for all, the lunge as the primary method for delivering an attack.

REFERENCES

Castle, Egerton. *Schools and Masters of Fence.* London: George Bell, 1885.

Wise, Arthur. *The Art and History of Personal Combat.* Greenwich, CT: Arma Press, 1971.

CAPRICE. On a sport sabre,* the arc of metal that connects the guard* to the grip. It is, in effect, the knuckle guard.

REFERENCE

Handelman, Rob. "Fencing Glossary." *American Fencing* (February/March 1978).

CARE OF OLD SWORDS. Rust is the greatest enemy of old swords, and it is recommended that it be removed as quickly as possible. It has been recommended that it be scratched off with a copper coin. Copper, being softer than steel, does not mark the blade surface.

The blade may be cleaned with a brush and detergent to remove dirt, but if this is done, the weapon should be dried thoroughly and immediately, or it will rust badly.

Polishing may be done most effectively with an oiled emery cloth, steel wool, or jeweler's emery.

Steel hilts may be cleaned in the same manner as blades.

The weapon should then be covered with a layer of oil to prevent further damage.

Excessive handling of swords, because of hand moisture and the wearing off of protective oil, causes new rust spots, so weapons should be cleaned and reoiled after such contacts. Also, weapons should never be stored in damp places.

REFERENCE

Wilkinson, Frederick. *Swords and Daggers.* New York: Hawthorn Books, 1967.

CARRANZA, JERONIMO DE. (c. 1550). Spanish fencing master. Sometimes called the "inventor of the science of arms."

Carranza is the author of a ponderous, but influential, volume on swordsmanship, *De la Philosofia de las Armas,* written in 1569. The book, which dominated Spanish fencing thought for centuries, expounded theories of fencing based on the principles of geometry and grand, mysterious metaphysical "truths." It was, as one might anticipate, a very difficult method of swordplay to master.

Probably the greatest value of Carranza's system was that it stressed developing a calm mental outlook in combat. That his teachings produced many fine swordsmen is doubtlessly due, in great part, to this single factor.

REFERENCES
Castle, Egerton. *Schools and Masters of Fence.* London: George Bell, 1885.
Wise, Arthur. *The Art and History of Personal Combat.* Greenwich, CT: Arma Press, 1971.

CARTER, JOHN. Swordsman hero created by writer Edgar Rice Burroughs* in 1912.

As an earth man who inexplicably found himself transported to Mars, John Carter became the archetypical fantasy-adventure protagonist. With duty and honor as his basic motivating principles, he bravely plunged headlong into one exciting adventure after another in a series of novels. Sword fights and princess-saving were his specialties.

The John Carter novels include *A Princess of Mars* (1917), *The Gods of Mars* (1918), *The Warlord of Mars* (1919), *Thuvia, Maid of Mars* (1920), *The Chessmen of Mars* (1922), *The Mastermind of Mars* (1928), *A Fighting Man of Mars* (1931), *Swords of Mars* (1936), *Synthetic Men of Mars* (1940), *Llana of Gathol* (1948), and *John Carter of Mars* (1964).

REFERENCE
Lupoff, Richard A. *Edgar Rice Burroughs: Master of Adventure.* New York: Ace Books, 1965.

CARTHAGINIAN SWORDS. The swords of Carthage were made of bronze, copper, tin, and brass. Blades were of the short, leaf-shaped variety. Carthage, of course, stopped employing swords when, during the Punic Wars, it was expunged from the earth by the armies of Rome in 146 B.C.

REFERENCE
Burton, Richard F. *The Book of the Sword.* London: Chatto and Windus, 1884.

CARTOONS, FENCING IN. Due to the strong animal orientation of cartoons, most of the fencing action over the years has been carried on by humanesque rodents, dogs, cats, bugs, and the like. The action is rarely anything but simplistic and is often represented by a mad flurry of arms and swords.

Fencing can be found in cartoons featuring Mickey Mouse, Bugs Bunny, and Tom and Jerry. Tom and Jerry's *The Two Mouseketeers,* a musketeer mouse versus a cardinal's guard cat, won an Academy Award in 1951.

Disney's feature-length cartoon *Robin Hood* (1973) substituted animal characters for the well-known humans of the Robin Hood legend (a fox for Robin Hood, a bear for Little John, a lion for Prince John, and so on). The featured swordplay was presented with the usual Disney concern for form and movement.

The popular, but silly, Teenage Mutant Ninja Turtles brought martial arts, including swordplay, to young audiences beginning in the late 1980s, with average animated action.

Pseudohuman examples of animated fencing can be found in Max Fleischer's Popeye cartoon *Aladdin and His Wonderful Lamp* (1938), with Popeye/Aladdin fencing with a table leg against an evil genie wielding a huge sword; Fleischer's *Gulliver's Travels* (1939); and Mr. Magoo's *Cyrano de Bergerac* (1964).

Hanna and Barbara, creators of the ever-popular *Flinstones* and *Yogi Bear* cartoons, produced an animated version of Alexandre Dumas's classic adventure novel *The Three Musketeers* (1967), with an emphasis on realism. While the animation itself was on the cheap side, the fencing, if nothing else, concerned itself with believable blade movement.

Two 1980s Saturday morning television series, the short-lived "Zorro" (1984) and the popular "He-Man" (1983–1985), featured regular helpings of swordplay. The "Zorro" program, while rather silly for the most part, managed to create some surprisingly stylish cartoon fencing that often looked as though it had been patterned after movie sword fights.

Ralph Bakshi's adult-oriented *Lord of the Rings* (1983) has given us perhaps the most violent depiction of cartoon swordplay to date. Striving for a sophisticated and graphic kind of animation, Bakshi incorporated much blood—heads being lopped off, rampant death and destruction, and so on—into his action sequences.

REFERENCES

Halliwell, Leslie. *Halliwell's Filmgoer's and Video Viewer's Companion.* New York: Charles Scribner's Sons, 1987.
Katz, Ephraim. *The Film Encyclopedia.* New York: Perigee, 1979.

CASE OF RAPIERS. Two swords used simultaneously in combat. They were employed in the same manner as the sword and dagger—one weapon being used offensively and one being used defensively. Usually the swords were twins and were carried in the same scabbard. To facilitate this, each weapon guard was flattened on one side.

The obvious advantage of using a second sword, instead of a dagger, was that it gave a swordsman a longer reach with his defensive blade. Just the same, the two-rapier fencing style never became very popular, no doubt because it took considerable dexterity and skill to wield them both effectively at the same time.

REFERENCES

Castle, Egerton. *Schools and Masters of Fence.* London: George Bell, 1885.
Palffy-Alpar, Julius. *Sword and Masque.* Philadelphia: F. A. Davis, 1967.

CASTELLO, JULIO. (1882–1973). Spanish fencing master.

Learning to fence at the Royal Academy in Madrid, Julio Castello was a highly successful professional fencer in the early years of this century. He taught fencing in Spain, Argentina, and Cuba.

Coming to the United States in 1914, Castello began coaching immediately at the New York Athletic Club. In the 1920s, he taught briefly at Yale and Columbia universities. He was also a coach to the U.S. Olympic fencing team in 1924.

In 1927, Castello accepted the post of fencing master at New York University, a position he continued in until the late 1940s. In that time, he produced numerous champions.

The year 1947 brought retirement from mainstream fencing, although he continued to teach on an unofficial basis until he was in his eighties.

A case of rapiers, from Marozzo's *Opera Nova*

Jack Espinosa tells of a famous story concerning Castello, the venerable old master. One evening, while observing a fencing class conducted by one of his longtime pupils, "Papa" Castello, as he was called, observed two fencers, obviously, by their manner, new to the game, approach the group. They declined an offer to join in the class because, as they proclaimed, they "already knew how to fence." They simply wanted to work out at the other end of the room. Permission was granted, and the two "swordsmen" commenced battering each other with sabres. A quiet, gentle man, Castello attempted to ignore the flailing combatants; however, his fencing sensibilities, honed by decades of dedicated practice, were finally strained beyond their limits. He winced with every ferocious clash. He clenched his teeth with every untutored, uncontrolled action. Finally, as the story goes, he could take no more of it and walked slowly across the room to where the offenders were carrying on their brutalities.

He stopped in front of the belligerents and announced himself: "Excuse me."

The two stopped.

"Yes, sir?"

"I have a question to ask," the maestro said.

"Yes?"

Castello, the world-famous fencing master, had a look of pained consternation on his face. As if fencing, he motioned with his hand.

He paused, as if searching for just the right words.

Finally, he spoke.

"What . . . game . . . is this?" he asked.

Julio Castello produced two books, *Theory of Fencing* (1931) and *The Theory and Practice of Fencing* (1933).

Castello's two sons—Hugo and James—became respected fencing masters in their own right.

REFERENCES

Espinosa, Jack. "That's What Game This Is." *American Fencing* (March/April 1981).

Tishman, Jeffrey. "Julio Martinez Castello, Maestro des Armes." *American Fencing* (March/April 1973).

CASTLE, EGERTON. (1858–1920). English novelist, historian, and fencer.

Egerton Castle wrote a popular series of romantic novels (in collaboration with his wife, Agnes) at the turn of the century, but he is best remembered for his history of swordplay, the acclaimed *Schools and Masters of Fence* (1885). Generated by the writer's own personal passion for fencing, it is, by far, one of the most readable books on the development of swordplay ever produced, covering the art from its earliest blood-soaked days right up into its incarnation as a noble and thoroughly healthful sport.

Said Castle of fencing in this book:

Fencing is an exercise which well repays anyone who has the perseverance to submit to the drudgery of its early stages. The "Artist"—to use Sir William Hope's quaint expression—finds work for his head as well as for his limbs in every kind of personal combat; but this is especially the case with fencing, where it is possible for the observant swordsman to use his perceptive faculties in the discrimination of his opponent's characteristics, and assuming that practice has sufficiently gymnasticized his body, to find intellectual enjoyment in devising different plays for different adversaries.

"In a good fencer the head works as much as the body," say the best masters; to become such a good fencer, however, very long practice is necessary.

Ars longa, vita brevis. The art of fence is undoubtedly a long one to master; nevertheless, it would be difficult to discover any swordsman of standing who regrets the time he has devoted to it; it is a wonder that comparatively so few men take up swordsmanship in earnest.

Castle was eventually given the honorary title of "Maestro di Scherma" by the Academy of Fencing of Paris.

REFERENCES

Benet, William Rose. *The Reader's Encyclopedia.* New York: Thomas Y. Crowell, 1965.

Castle, Egerton. *Schools and Master of Fence.* London: George Bell, 1885.

Morton, E. D. *Martini A–Z of Fencing.* London: Queen Anne Press, 1992.

CATTIAU, PHILIPPE. (c. 1900). French fencing champion.

Philippe Cattiau took second place in individual foil at the 1920 and 1924 Olympics. His 1920 Olympic foil team took second; his 1924 Olympic foil team

Egerton Castle, the author of *Schools and Masters of Fence*

took first; his 1928 Olympic foil team took second; his 1932 Olympic foil team took first; and his 1932 Olympic épée team also took first.

Cattiau was world épée champion in 1929 and 1930.

REFERENCES
Palffy-Alpar, Julius. *Sword and Masque.* Philadelphia: F. A. Davis, 1967.
Wallechinsky, David. *The Complete Book of the Olympics.* New York: Penguin Books, 1984.

CAVALCABO, HIERONIMO. (c. 1600). Italian fencing master and founder of a long line of French fencing masters.

Cavalcabo was one of the first fencing masters of the "new" school, attempting to bring a studied, rational approach to swordplay. While his method still contained many old-style concepts, his terminology contained more precise definitions for offensive and defensive positions than had previously been ascribed to fencing attitudes.

His book on fencing, published in 1609, earned him the post of fencing master to the court of Henry IV of France.

Cavalcabo's father, Zacharia, and his son, Cesar, were also fencing masters of note.

REFERENCE
Castle, Egerton. *Schools and Masters of Fence.* London: George Bell, 1885.

CAVATIONE. The Italian name for a disengage, or moving from one line to another line, passing beneath an opponent's blade. It means, literally, "drawing away."

Also known as *cavazione.*

REFERENCES
Castle, Egerton. *Schools and Masters of Fence.* London: George Bell, 1885.
Palffy-Alpar, Julius. *Sword and Masque.* Philadelphia: F. A. Davis, 1967.

CAVENS, FRED. (1887–1962). Belgian-born movie fencing master.

A professor of fencing by the age of twenty-one, Fred Cavens, by his grasp of the inner workings of swordplay, was a natural for a career in swashbuckler films. Able to interject a strong sense of style and intent into his visual creations, he was responsible, more than anyone else, for bringing into existence the majority of the silver screen's most exciting sword duels.

Moving to the United States in the early 1920s, Cavens gravitated immediately to Hollywood. His first picture was a broad spoof of swashbuckler films— Max Linder's *The Three Must-Get-Theres* (1922). A parody of Douglas Fairbanks's successful *The Three Musketeers* (1921), it was an immediate success.

Impressing even the redoubtable Fairbanks with his dramatic style and his technical grasp of fencing, Cavens quickly established himself as Hollywood's leading film fencing master. By 1924, Cavens was the fight arranger on all of Fairbanks's swashbuckler epics. His first was *Don Q, Son of Zorro* (1925). This

Film fencing master Fred Cavens appearing before the camera in *The Count of Monte Cristo*

was followed by *The Black Pirate* (1926) and *The Iron Mask* (1929). The improvement in Fairbanks's fencing skill in these films over his earlier efforts was the direct result of Cavens's ability to effectively channel the actor's frenetic energies in a focused manner.

Other silent movies that benefited from Cavens's touch were *Dorothy Vernon of Haddon Hall* (1924), *Don Juan* (1926), *When a Man Loves* (1927), and *General Crack* (1929).

When Hollywood switched to sound—a painful change for many of the film industry's old-time members—Cavens made the transition without a hitch.

In 1934, he helped breathe life back into the nearly defunct swashbuckler genre when he directed the fencing in *The Count of Monte Cristo.*** This vehicle established Cavens, once and for all, as the movie studios' first choice in theatrical fencing masters.

Following this success, Cavens devised fencing routines for *The Three Musketeers* (1935), *Captain Blood* (1935),** *The Prince and the Pauper* (1937), *The Adventures of Robin Hood* (1938),** *The Sea Hawk* (1940),** *The Corsican Brothers* (1941), *The Black Swan* (1942), *The Spanish Main* (1945), and *The Adventures of Don Juan* (1949),** among others.

Perhaps Cavens's most dramatic and artistic triumph came in 1940 with the making of *The Mark of Zorro.*** The swordplay in this film is, without a doubt, the yardstick by which all other movie duels must be measured. The climactic duel between Tyrone Power and Basil Rathbone is staged without a musical score to enhance the action. The fencing itself becomes a symphony of sound and movement, creating its own rhythm and mood. Starting out slowly, it then builds, faster and faster, to the final, inevitable thrust. As a fight to the death, it has power and elegance.

Discussing his approach to film swordplay, Cavens once explained: "For the screen, in order to be well photographed and also grasped by the audience, all swordplay should be so telegraphed with emphasis that the audience will see what is coming. All movements—instead of being as small as possible, as in competitive fencing—must be large, but nevertheless correct."

The Hollywood of the 1950s, with its focus on the more "significant" elements of life—the human psyche, Communism, and out-of-control teenagers—looked on the subject of swashbuckler films as too lightweight for further serious attention. This was thus a time of considerable inactivity for all film fencing masters, including Cavens. Still, Cavens managed to find avenues in which to exercise his considerable talent during this period. *Cyrano de Bergerac* (1950), *Anne of the Indies* (1951), *At Sword's Point* (1952), and *Casanova's Big Night* (1954) were a few of his 1950s projects.

Cavens's final contribution to his profession was the fencing in the successful 1958–1959 Disney television series, "Zorro."**

Over the years, Fred Cavens was expertly assisted by his son Albert, who was a skilled theatrical swordsman in his own right.

REFERENCE
Richards, Jeffrey. *Swordsmen of the Screen.* Boston: Routledge and Kegan Paul, 1977.

CAVER. An exaggerated angulation of the sword arm employed in an attack, riposte, or counterattack, the purpose of which is to move one's attacking blade around an opponent's defensive position.

Also called "cave," "*coup* cave," *angolazione,* and "angulation."

REFERENCE
Handelman, Rob. "Fencing Glossary." *American Fencing* (February/March 1978).

CELEBRITY FENCERS. Fencing, with its innate sense of the dramatic, its tradition and color, and its need for balance, clear thinking, and self-discipline, has always appealed to people of a creative, forceful, and individualistic nature. Therefore it should not be surprising that many celebrated personalities of history and modern times have been attracted to the art of the sword.

Celebrity fencers include:

Sir Richard Burton (1821–1890), English explorer/author

Lord Byron (1788–1824), English poet

John Dickson Carr (1906–1976), American mystery writer

Egerton Castle (1858–1920), English novelist

Benvenuto Cellini (1500–1571), Italian Renaissance artist

Christian IV (1577–1648), King of Denmark

Winston Churchill (1874–1965), British statesman

Baron Pierre de Coubertin (1863–1937), founder of modern Olympics

Chevalier Charles d'Eon (1728–1810), French spy/adventurer

Neil Diamond (1941–), American pop singer/song writer

Alexandre Dumas (1802–1870), French novelist

Edward VII (1841–1910), King of England

Jose Ferrer (1909–1992), American actor

Paul Gallico (1897–1976), American novelist

David Garrick (1717–1779), English actor

George III (1738–1820), King of England

George IV (1762–1830), King of England

Robert Goulet (1933–), American actor/singer

Robert Hays (1948–), American actor

Robert Heinlein (1907–1988), American science fiction writer

Henry III (1551–1589), King of France

Henry IV (1553–1610), King of France

Henry VIII (1491–1547), King of England

Edmund Kean (1787–1833), English actor

Louis XIII (1601–1643), King of France

Marcel Marceau (1923–   ), French mime

Guy de Maupassant (1850–1893), French author

Michelangelo (1475–1564), Italian Renaissance artist

Wolfgang Mozart (1756–1791), Austrian musical genius

George Patton (1885–1945), American army general

Basil Rathbone (1892–1967), British actor

Marshal Maurice Saxe (1696–1750), French general

REFERENCES

Lane, Hana. *World Almanac Book of Who.* New York: World Almanac, 1980.

Morton, E. D. *Martini A–Z of Fencing.* London: Queen Anne Press, 1992.

Palffy-Alpar, Julius. *Sword and Masque.* Philadelphia: F. A. Davis, 1967.

CELTIC SWORD, THE. Celtic (or Keltic) swords came in both straight- and curved-bladed varieties. Blades were made of either bronze or iron. Hilts were fashioned of bronze, ivory, wood, or bone. Both thrusting and cutting swords exist.

REFERENCE

Burton, Richard F. *The Book of the Sword.* London: Chatto and Windus, 1884.

CENTER OF GRAVITY. The position of balance on a sword.

Found on swords in the middle of the forte (strong portion of the blade), the center of gravity was once considered the proper spot for parrying.*

Modern sport foils and épées, with a blade lightness never achieved by their old-style counterparts, have a center of gravity no more than an inch and a half from the *coquille.** The sport sabre's center of gravity is found slightly farther up on the blade, about three inches from the hand guard.

REFERENCES

Burton, Richard F. *The Book of the Sword.* London: Chatto and Windus, 1884.

Palffy-Alpar, Julius. *Sword and Masque.* Philadelphia: F. A. Davis, 1967.

CENTER OF PERCUSSION. The spot on a cutting sword's blade that is the ideal point at which a blow should be struck. When the exact center of percussion is met, the whole force of the blow becomes most effective.

Italian Giacomo di Grassi* was the first fencing master to have thoughts on this subject. He detailed his theories in his book *Ragione di addoprar sicuramente l'arme* (1570).

REFERENCES

Burton, Richard F. *The Book of the Sword.* London: Chatto and Windus, 1884.

Castle, Egerton. *Schools and Masters of Fence.* London: George Bell, 1885.

CENTRAL GUARD. The on-guard position of the sword hand, which places it halfway between the lines of quarte* and sixte.* While derided by some, who claim that by not closing off one line or the other, a fencer weakens his game by leaving himself open to the possibility of being attacked in either line instead of just one, it does, in fact, create a balanced position from which to parry that does not readily lead to a loss of control. Thus, in fact, the central guard strengthens one's defensive ability.

REFERENCES

Morton, E. D. *Martini A–Z of Fencing*. London: Queen Anne Press, 1992.

Vebell, Edward. *Sports Illustrated Book of Fencing*. Philadelphia: J. B. Lippincott, 1962.

CERCLE. In the late seventeenth century, French fencing master Philibert de la Tousche* taught a parry he called *cercle,* which corresponds to the modern parry of septime* (the low, inside line, with the sword hand in supination, or palm up).

REFERENCE

Castle, Egerton. *Schools and Masters of Fence*. London: George Bell, 1885.

CERCLE LES ONGLES EN DESSOUS. Eighteenth-century French fencing master P.J.F. Girard's* name for a parry corresponding to a modern "seconde" parry* (a parry covering the low-outside line, with the sword hand in pronation, or palm down).

REFERENCE

Castle, Egerton. *Schools and Masters of Fence*. London: George Bell, 1885.

CERCLE LES ONGLES EN DESSUS. P.J.F. Girard's* name for a low-inside line parry, with the hand in supination. The same as a modern "septime" parry.*

REFERENCE

Castle, Egerton. *Schools and Masters of Fence*. London: George Bell, 1885.

CERCLE MYSTERIEUX. A geometric pattern upon which seventeenth-century French fencing master Girard Thibault* based his fanciful and ponderous philosophy-laden theories of swordplay.

The circle—the radius of which measured the length of a sword blade—was based on the highly artificial Spanish system of fencing created by Jeronimo de Carranza* and Don Luis Pacheco de Narvaez.* Bisected by intersecting lines, the cercle mysterieux was touted to provide foolproof offensive footwork patterns when attacking one's adversary.

In his book, *The Academy of the Sword,*￼ published in 1628, Thibault states, without hesitation, that by stepping properly across imaginary intersecting lines (labeled from "A" to "Z") within the circle, not only would one be fully protected, but one's adversary would automatically and irresistibly end up being stuck on the end of one's sword. He further promised that even with a small amount of practice, any man could become an expert swordsman using his methods.

In Spain, where it was the fashion to fight according to artificial rules, *The Academy of the Sword* managed to further entrench ideas about fencing that had little to do with reality, ideas that persisted well into the eighteenth century. Elsewhere, it was looked upon as simply ridiculous.

Also called the "mysterious circle."

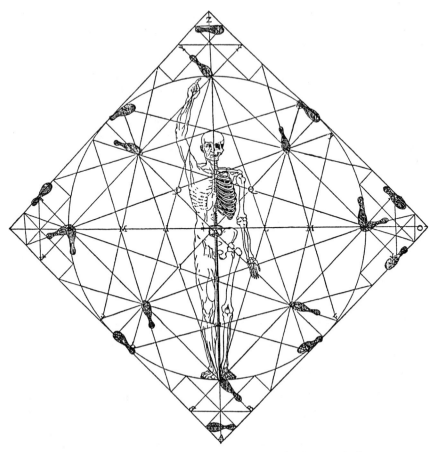

The geometric pattern upon which the Spanish school of fencing was built

REFERENCES

Castle, Egerton. *Schools and Masters of Fence*. London: George Bell, 1885.
Wise, Arthur. *The Art and History of Personal Combat*. Greenwich, CT: Arma Press, 1971.

CERCLE, PARADE DE. A guard described by eighteenth-century French fencing master Guillaume Danet* in which the sword hand was held as high as one's mouth, while the sword point was kept low. Here, by "a swift movement of the wrist," the blade was moved in a circle. Once it met an opponent's weapon, a riposte in the line of quarte was to immediately follow.

REFERENCE

Castle, Egerton. *Schools and Masters of Fence*. London: George Bell, 1885.

CETRULO, DEAN. (1919–). United States fencing champion.

Dean Cetrulo was the U.S. individual foil champion in both 1941 and 1947.

He was the U.S. individual sabre champion in 1948. He was also a member of the U.S. Olympic foil and sabre teams in 1948. In the team sabre event, his team took third place, winning a bronze medal for the United States.

Aside from sport fencing, Dean Cetrulo occasionally delved into theatrical swordplay. In 1946, he played the role of "Valvert," Cyrano de Bergerac's* blustering opponent in the "Duel in Rhyme,"** in Jose Ferrer's* award-winning Broadway stage production of *Cyrano de Bergerac*.

He later worked as a fencing double for Cornel Wilde in the films *The Bandit of Sherwood Forest* (1946),** and *At Sword's Point* (1952).**

Dean Cetrulo also acted as a technical consultant for a Hardy Boys mystery book, *The Clue of the Broken Blade* (1970),** by Franklin W. Dixon.
REFERENCES
Conwell, Charles. "Boyhood Hero." *American Fencing* (July/August/September 1992).
Mar, Colleen Walker. *1993 U.S. Fencing Association Media Guide.* Colorado Springs: ColorTek Printing, 1993.
Wallechinsky, David. *The Complete Book of the Olympics.* New York: Penguin Books, 1984.

CHALCOS. A name Homer gave to the Greek sword. It means copper or bronze.
REFERENCE
Burton, Richard F. *Book of the Sword.* London: Chatto and Windus, 1884.

CHAMBERLAIN, RICHARD. (1935–   ). American television, stage, and film actor.

First becoming popular on the long-running television series "Dr. Kildare," Richard Chamberlain eventually moved to England, where he turned to more demanding roles on the stage and in film. His highly acclaimed *Hamlet* established him as an actor of considerable regard.

After returning to the United States, Chamberlain starred in a widely acclaimed stage production of *Cyrano de Bergerac*** at the prestigious Ahamanson Theatre in Los Angeles. The swordplay, staged by fight arranger Anthony de Longis,* was noted for its liveliness.

In the 1970s, Richard Chamberlain starred in a number of costume films. These include *Julius Caesar* (1970), *The Three Musketeers* (1974),** *The Four Musketeers* (1975),** *The Count of Monte Cristo* (1976),** *The Man in the Iron Mask* (1977),** and *Shogun* (1980).**

Always a bit more effete than dashing, Chamberlain nevertheless managed always to handle himself well with a sword.
REFERENCES
Halliwell, Leslie. *Halliwell's Filmgoer's and Video Viewer's Companion.* New York: Charles Scribner's Sons, 1988.
Katz, Ephraim. *The Film Encyclopedia.* New York: Perigee, 1979.

CHANGE. The act of moving one's blade from one line* to another line. This may be repeated a number of times quickly to confuse or upset an opponent.

Making changes in a broken tempo also helps keep a fencer from becoming too static in his delivery.
REFERENCE
Palffy-Alpar, Julius. *Sword and Masque.* Philadelphia: F. A. Davis, 1967.

CHANGING PARRY. When a direct parry-risposte action is met by a parry that changes lines rather than remaining in the same line as the riposte, that parry is said to be a changing parry.
REFERENCE
Palffy-Alpar, Julius. *Sword and Masque.* Philadelphia: F. A. Davis, 1967.

CHAPMAN, GEORGE. (c. 1840). British fencing master.
George Chapman founded the London Fencing Club in 1848.
As a teacher, he broke with tradition to advocate that a beginner's initial instruction in fencing should be in defense rather than offense.
Chapman wrote one book on fencing, *Foil Practice* (1861).
REFERENCE
Morton, E. D. *Martini A–Z of Fencing.* London: Queen Anne Press, 1992.

CHASSE-COQUIN. A foil of a heavy, stiff nature. It was said that this type of weapon was favored primarily by poor fencers, the ignorant, the heavy-handed, and the poorly taught, who relied on power and an aggressive nature as their greatest fencing attributes.
Also known as a "poker."
REFERENCE
Morton, E. D. *Martini A–Z of Fencing.* London: Queen Anne Press, 1992.

CHASSELOUP-LAUBAT, MARQUIS DE. (c. 1880). French nobleman and fencer. Son of a noted general in the army of Napoleon.
In 1913, the first international civilian association for fencing, the Federation Internationale d'Escrime (FIE), was established. The following year, the Marquis de Chasseloup-Laubat, one of the group's founders, organized and set down the technical rules of fencing adopted by the FIE. He was assisted by fellow FIE member Paul Anspach.*
Because of the outbreak of World War I, the Marquis' work was not issued until 1919.
REFERENCE
U.S. Fencing Association, ed. *Operations Manual.* Colorado Springs, CO: U.S. Fencing Association, 1985.

CHECK. In the midst of a forward step, the action is broken by a sudden retreat or a lunge. Such an action is made to startle one's opponent and thereby interfere with his timing.
REFERENCE
Palffy-Alpar, Julius. *Sword and Masque.* Philadelphia: F. A. Davis, 1967.

CHEREB. A Hebrew sword. The chereb was mentioned 250 times in the Old Testament. Its root word, according to Sir Richard Burton* in his volume *The Book of the Sword* (1884),** means "to waste."

Originally, the chereb was made of copper and finally, of iron. It was not a very big weapon. The blade was short, straight, and stiff. Some were double-edged; some, single-edged.

The Hebrew sword, rather than being a constant piece of apparel, was worn only during times of trouble.

REFERENCES

Burton, Richard F. *The Book of the Sword.* London: Chatto and Windus, 1884.

Stone, George Cameron. *A Glossary of the Construction, Decoration, and Use of Arms and Armor.* New York: Jack Brussel, 1961.

CHERKESSKA. A sabre dance of the northern Caucasus Mountains. Full of athletic leaps and turns, it is performed only by men.

REFERENCE

Leach, Maria, ed. *Funk and Wagnalls Standard Dictionary of Folklore, Mythology, and Legend.* San Francisco: Harper and Row, 1972.

CHESS. Because of its heavy emphasis on mental input—on developing and building strategies and counterstrategies that may be used against one's opponent—fencing is often compared with the game of chess. Fencing has, in fact, long been considered a very intellectual sport. The "chess" analogy has almost become a cliché in the fencing world.

In 1987, Dr. Aladar Kogler,* head national coach for the United States, made a survey of fourteen top European fencing masters—masters who consistently developed strong contenders in world-class competition—to find out just how much emphasis, if any, was actually being placed on the mental, chesslike side of fencing. The coaches, responding entirely on the basis of their own personal experience, overwhelmingly stressed mind development as the most important factor in their training programs.

Based on his findings, Dr. Kogler was able to put together an extremely clear picture of how the mental and physical factors were blended to create successful fencers. They were as follows: 40.7 percent mental; 31 percent technical; and 28.3 percent physical.

REFERENCES

Evangelista, Nick. "Engarde." *Intro* (October 1984).

Kogler, Aladar A. "A Study of the Attributes of World Class Fencers." *American Fencing* (March/April/May 1987).

CHIKUTO. A Japanese fencing stick made from bamboo. Average length: thirty-six inches.

Same as *shinai,* the name commonly used today.

REFERENCE

Stone, George Cameron. *A Glossary of the Construction, Decoration, and Use of Arms and Armor.* New York: Jack Brussel, 1961.

CHILDREN AND THE SWORD. At first glance, children and swords might appear to be mutually exclusive topics, swordplay being an activity of high physical input and a certain amount of personal risk; but this is not, in fact, the case. Children have probably been involved in fencing as students, and even combatants, as long as fencing has been taught. This was true of children of the noble and wealthy in particular because they, more than anyone else, could afford the expensive luxury of study. This has definitely been the case since the Renaissance, when the sword became as much a personal attachment as it was a military tool.

Children certainly would not have been permitted by their parents to attend gatherings in early schools of fence—those dark, evil dens of iniquity housing the dregs of society; more likely fencing masters were hired to provide private lessons for young fencers. The rough and tumble methods of training were toned down extensively for children, but essentially they had to follow the same route to knowledge as their older counterparts.

We find examples of children armed with swords throughout history and art. Famed Renaissance artist Benvenuto Cellini (1500–1571) talked in his autobiography of numerous sword-oriented encounters. When he was fifteen, he witnessed a duel between his thirteen-year-old brother and a man of twenty. His brother severely wounded the other but was set upon with rocks by members of his enemy's family and knocked unconscious. Soon after this, Cellini had his own intimate experiences with sword fights. Of the first he chose to relate, he said, ''Then we each of us drew our swords with spirit; but the fray had hardly begun when a crowd of persons intervened.''

Shortly after this event, he sought out the expert skills of an old swordsman named Bevilacqua, who had fought over twenty duels and was thought to have once been the finest fencer in Italy. Later, Cellini described attacking a man from ambush with his sword: ''My blow descended on the shoulder of Luigi; but the satyrs who doted on him, had steeled his person round with coats of mail and such-like villainous defences; still the stroke fell with crushing force. Swerving aside, the sword hit Pantasilea [Luigi's female companion] full in the nose and mouth.'' He added, ''Then I turned upon the others boldly with my sword. . . . During this hurly-burly, some of the soldiers and captains wounded themselves with their own arms.'' The artist, it should be noted, was sixteen years old at the time of these adventures. Cellini's rather bloodthirsty activities with the sword continued well into his adulthood.

Of course, we have Shakespeare's* classic play *Romeo and Juliet* (1596)** with which to further our impressions of sword combat among the young. In old Verona, Italy, the boys run amuck in the streets, swords drawn, taunting and battling one another with the fervor of hardened duelists. In the course of events, Tybalt kills Mercutio; Romeo kills Tybalt; and Romeo dies by his own hand. Not a happy fencing tale by any means.

In the classical paintings and portraits of earlier times, we see the young pictured with swords as a matter of course. This is true of Michelangelo da

Caravaggio's *The Fortuneteller* (1610), Anthony Van Dyck's *William, Prince of Orange, and Princess Mary of England* (1641), and Nicholas de Largillier's *The Family of Louis XIV* (c. 1700).

During the eighteenth century, the study of the sword took on a new air of refinement and respectability and, more than ever before, young boys were directed into fencing by their parents to enhance their courtly manners and bearing. Domenico Angelo,* perhaps the most celebrated fencing master of his age, was engaged to teach, among others, the children of English kings.

While residing in Italy, Austrian musical genius Wolfgang Mozart* received fencing lessons as a child at the behest of his father, Leopold. Presumably this was done to help ground the boy in the real world, giving him a strong physical outlet to balance his musical activities. Nineteenth-century author Sir Richard Burton* fenced as a child, as did twentieth-century statesman Winston Churchill,** and the actors Basil Rathbone* and Jose Ferrer.*

Moreover, many world champion fencers had their start in the game at an early age. Fencing giants Nedo* and Aldo Nadi* both began taking lessons from their fencing master father Beppi almost as soon as they could walk. Giorgio Santelli,* the great U.S. Olympic coach, had the same sort of opportunity, commencing his training with his father Italo at the age of six. Two great Olympians, Edoardo* and Dario** Mangiarotti, both began fencing at the age of eight. German fencer Helene Mayer* took up fencing before the age of ten; she was the women's fencing champion of Germany at thirteen and at seventeen she won a gold medal at the 1928 Olympics. Famed Cuban fencer Ramon Fonst* was sixteen years old when he won his first Olympic gold medal in 1900.

In the realm of present-day fencing, the U.S. Fencing Association* has had a well-developed blueprint for young fencers since 1971 in the Junior Olympic Program. This undertaking provides both competitive outlets and training camps for youthful fencers. The world fencing body, the Federation Internationale d'Escrime,* has held world champion fencing tournaments for young competitors since 1950.

But what of actually teaching children to fence? There are some pronounced pitfalls to the undertaking that should always be addressed. Such an education should follow a process that is both slow and methodical, fully developing a strong base upon which to build fencing talent. It takes a good deal of time to develop the abstract thought process that turns a mere student into a true fencer, and to overlook or underestimate this fact can leave an individual forever stuck on a narrowly defined, superficial physical track for the remainder of their fencing career. Moreover, should a child rush into bouting and pick up bad fencing habits that are constantly reinforced through unrestrained competition, those habits will be nearly impossible to shed later in life.

This problem of inadequate and improper training in modern children's fencing has been observed by successful U.S. coach Michael D'Asaro.* "Our junior fencers," he states, "are very, very weak in basic fundamentals, i.e., the guard position, advance, retreat, lunge, holding the weapon, simple attack, parry, riposte, basic strategy and tactics, and point control.'' D'Asaro is hopeful, however, and has proposed an intensive training program based on international fencing standards to raise the essential skills of younger fencers.

From a purely practical standpoint, fencing among children, when closely observed, is really little more than a game of poking. Boys and girls of large stature frequently excel in the competitive setting not so much because of ability but because of their size and strength. Hence, winning should be kept in perspective, to deter the young athlete from developing conceit regarding his fencing gifts.

Even with its emphasis on hard work and dedication, fencing should be fun for the child fencer. An overbearing parent or coach looking out for his own reputation can change fencing into a highly unpleasant activity, distorting it, causing the goals of a truly fascinating art to be lost in a cloud of bad feelings.

When properly approached, fencing has been noted to develop a child's self-confidence, poise, sense of uniqueness, and, most certainly, independent thought.

REFERENCES

Cellini, Benvenuto. *The Life of Benvenuto Cellini.* New York: Brentano's, 1900.

D'Asaro, Michael. ''Do We Really Need a J. O. Program?'' *American Fencing* (May/ June 1986).

Levey, Michael. *17th and 18th Century Painting.* New York: Dell, 1967.

Mar, Colleen Walker. *1993 U.S. Fencing Association Media Guide.* Colorado Springs: ColorTek Printing, 1993.

Morton, E. D. *Martini A–Z of Fencing.* London: Queen Anne Press, 1992.

Shakespeare, William. *Romeo and Juliet.* New York: P. F. Collier, 1901.

Stevenson, John. *Fencing.* London: Briggs, 1935.

Wallechinsky, David. *The Complete Book of the Olympics.* New York: Penguin Books, 1984.

CHI-NAGASHI. Meaning ''blood channels.'' The name commonly given to the grooves in the blades of Japanese swords. In actuality, the grooves were made to lighten and strengthen the blades.

REFERENCE

Stone, George Cameron. *A Glossary of the Construction, Decoration, and Use of Arms and Armor.* New York: Jack Brussel, 1961.

CHINESE MARTIAL ARTS FILMS, SWORDPLAY IN. Besides various unarmed forms of combat, swordplay is often a featured part of Chinese martial arts films, especially films of a historical nature. The action is usually broad and choppy and very stylized. More than occasionally, an unarmed hero will battle (successfully) a sword-wielding villain.

Story lines in these movies usually revolved around the theme of simple revenge.

Chinese films that feature swordplay include *The One-Armed Swordsman* (1968), *The Crimson Charm* (1968), *The Rivals* (1968), *The Golden Swallow* (1969), *Lady Hermit* (1969), *Have Sword Will Travel* (1969), *The New One-Armed Swordsman* (1970), *Beach of the War Gods* (1970–1973), *Zatuichi and*

the One-Armed Swordsman (1970), *The Invincible Eight* (1970), *Trilogy of Swordsmanship* (1971), *Fists of Fury* (1971), *The Killer* (1971), *Five Fingers of Death* (1971), *When Taekwando Strikes* (1973).
REFERENCES
Glaessner, Verina. *Kung Fu, Cinema of Vengeance.* London: Lorrimer, 1974.
Mintz, Marilyn D. *The Martial Arts Film.* New York: A. S. Barnes, 1978.

CHISA KATANA. The *katana** was the standard long sword of the samurai.* The *chisa katana* was a sword about half as long as the *katana* (the blade was usually eighteen inches in length).

During the seventeenth century, the *chisa katana* was the only weapon allowed to be worn by nobles while in attendance at the shogun's court.
REFERENCES
Stone, George Cameron. *A Glossary of the Construction, Decoration, and Use of Arms and Armor.* New York: Jack Brussel, 1961.
Turnbull, Steven R. *The Book of the Samurai.* New York: Gallery Books, 1982.

CHISEL-EDGED. A blade in which one side is completely flat, while the other is tapered, at first gradually and then quite markedly, the closer one gets to the cutting edge.
REFERENCE
Stone, George Cameron. *A Glossary of the Construction, Decoration, and Use of Arms and Armor.* New York: Jack Brussel, 1961.

CHOKU-TO. A prehistoric Japanese sword. The blade was straight and single-edged.
REFERENCE
Stone, George Cameron. *A Glossary of the Construction, Decoration, and Use of Arms and Armor.* New York: Jack Brussel, 1961.

CHOOSING A MODERN FENCING WEAPON. Modern fencing weapons, even weapons of the same style, vary in their nature to one degree or another. When purchasing a foil, sabre, or épée where there are numerous items to pick from, often hefting one weapon after another is the only way to find a suitable choice.

Blades come in light, medium, and heavy forms; and only a fencer's inner voice ends up being the final factor in deciding which one to fence with. Fencers who compete in tournaments often pick heavier blades to approximate fencing with electric weapons, which are often more weighty than the average standard blade.

As for weapon grips, each style of handle has its own unique qualities. The Italian grip* promotes the use of the entire arm as a lever, where overpowering one's opponent becomes the goal. The French grip* fosters a more subtle style of fencing, where control comes from finger manipulation of the weapon. The pistol grip* gives a fencer a strong hand, which, like the Italian grip, ends up enhancing one's muscular strength.

REFERENCES

Palffy-Alpar, Julius. *Sword and Masque*. Philadelphia: F. A. Davis, 1967.

Vebell, Edward. *Sports Illustrated Book of Fencing*. Philadelphia: J. B. Lippincott, 1962.

CHOOSING A SWORD IN THE EIGHTEENTH CENTURY. According to eighteenth-century fencing master Domenico Angelo* (author of *The School of Fencing***):

A person should proportion his sword to his height and strength, and the longest sword ought not to exceed thirty-eight inches from pommel to point.

You should not fail observing, when you choose your blade, that there be no flaws in it; these flaws appear like black hollow spots, some long ways, others cross the blade; the first of these are frequently the cause of the blade's breaking.

The temper of the blade is to be tried by bending it against any thing, and it is a bad sign when the bending begins at the point; a good blade will generally form a half circle . . . , and spring back again; if it should remain in any degree bent, it is a sign the temper is too soft. . . . Those which are stubborn in the bending are badly tempered, often break, and very easily.

REFERENCE

Angelo, Domenico. *The School of Fencing*. London: H. Angelo, 1787 edition.

CHOOSING A SWORD IN THE SEVENTEENTH CENTURY. According to seventeenth-century Italian fencing master Ridolfo Capo Ferro,* a man's sword should be twice the length of the arm.

REFERENCE

Castle, Egerton. *Schools and Masters of Fence*. London: George Bell, 1885.

CHOOSING A SWORD IN THE SIXTEENTH CENTURY. Spanish fencing master Don Luis Pacheco de Narvaez* stated, rather vaguely, that a man's sword should be proportional to his height.

Englishman George Silver,* in his *Paradoxes of Defence* (1599),** also said of procuring the proper sword that the weapon should be neither too short nor too long. "Every man," he noted, "ought to have a weapon according to his own stature." He was, of course, speaking of the cutting sword rather than the thrusting rapier, which he hated.

REFERENCE

Castle, Egerton. *Schools and Masters of Fence*. London: George Bell, 1885.

CHOPPER. A rather crude term describing the more basic cutting swords— those with broad, heavy blades. These include the European cutlass* and falchion,* as well as numerous Arab, African, and Asian weapons, some of which were little more than meat cleavers.

REFERENCE

Stone, George Cameron. *A Glossary of the Construction, Decoration, and Use of Arms and Armor*. New York: Jack Brussel, 1961.

CHOPPING. The term used for making a cut* in backsword* play.

REFERENCE
Castle, Egerton. *Schools and Masters of Fence.* London: George Bell, 1885.

CHOREOGRAPHY OF FILM SWORDPLAY. Over the years, producing swordplay for films has changed but little.

To begin with, once a film project has been decided upon, and the actors chosen for the respective parts, a fencing master is brought in to train those who will be handling swords. The training may be relatively short (over a period of a week or two) or long (lasting up to a few months).

Then, the director and fencing master get together to plan the fencing scenes. The master, of course, supplies the specifics of the combat. The director, working with his assistants, takes the action and breaks it up into close-ups, special angles, long shots, or whatever might be called for.

At this point, the actors are brought in to begin work on their routines. The routines, normally speaking, are learned in phrases (i.e., small pieces of action containing several exchanges between adversaries). Doubles may also be brought in to engage in some of the rougher business.

When a fencing scene is finally shot, all the short phrases—with actors and stunt doubles intermingled in a manner that creates the most impressive effect—are edited together to create an exciting whole.

REFERENCE
Behlmer, Rudy. "Swordplay on the Screen." *Films in Review* (June/July 1965).

CHOREOGRAPHY OF STAGE SWORDPLAY. Stage fencing choreography, while taught and learned much like its counterpart for movie work, has one major difference in its execution: while a film sword fight is usually performed in bits and pieces and later edited into a whole scene, a stage sword fight must be accomplished all at once.

To facilitate this elongated type of theatrical combat, stage sword duels are often broken up into segments or routines, each segment taking place on a different part of the stage. This way, each bit of action is connected to a special spot and is, thus, offset from the rest of the fight, making it easier to recall. Without such breaks, a duel of two or three minutes would be difficult to accomplish.

To be as free of errors as possible, of course, is vital when an actor is on stage. Forgetting a parry or adding an improvised thrust could be a highly dangerous mistake.

British fencing master William Hobbs* produced a highly instructive and entertaining book, *Techniques of the Stage Fight* (1967),** which dealt in detail with sword combat on stage.

REFERENCES
Hobbs, William. *Techniques of the Stage Fight.* London: Studio Vista, 1967.

CHUJO FAMILY, THE. Founded by Nagahide Chujo during the fourteenth century, the Chujo family served the Kamakura shogunate as fencing masters for generations.

REFERENCE

Sasamori, Junzo, and Gordon Warner. *This Is Kendo.* Vermont: Charles E. Tuttle, 1984.

CHUNDRIK. A Javanese sabre* with an inward curved blade and a straight, carved hilt.

REFERENCE

Stone, George Cameron. *A Glossary of the Construction, Decoration, and Use of Arms and Armor.* New York: Jack Brussel, 1961.

CHURA. A short, heavy sword-knife in common use among the hill tribes of Afghanistan.

REFERENCE

Stone, George Cameron. *A Glossary of the Construction, Decoration, and Use of Arms and Armor.* New York: Jack Brussel, 1961.

CINCTORIUM. The sword used by Roman generals in the fourth century B.C. It was so called because of where it was worn on the body—*cinctorium* referring to the waist, just above the hips.

REFERENCE

Burton, Richard F. *The Book of the Sword.* London: Chatto and Windus, 1884.

CINQUEDA. A bladed weapon used from 1450 to 1550. The name was derived from the width of the blade, which was supposed to be "five fingers" across at the hilt.

Some blades were no more than eight inches long; others were long enough—over eighteen inches—to be considered small swords. All were straight and double-edged.

The *cinqueda* might be used in conjunction with a full-length sword in sword and dagger play.

Also, called an *anelace, anelac,* or *sangdede.*

REFERENCES

Stone, George Cameron. *A Glossary of the Construction, Decoration, and Use of Arms and Armor.* New York: Jack Brussel, 1961.

Wilkinson, Frederick. *Swords and Daggers.* New York: Hawthorn Books, 1967.

CIRCULAR FENCING STYLE. Previous to the introduction of the lunge into fencing in the early seventeenth century—the lunge, by the nature of the action, guided combat into a straight line—men fought with swords in a circular fashion, moving around one another much in the same manner of modern boxers.

When an opening was perceived by one fencer, he would begin his attack by advancing the rear foot forward—called "passing."* After a few such steps, he would then be within striking range, cutting at some exposed portion of his adversary.

The defender might attempt to sidestep the oncoming blade, parry with his shield or dagger if he had one, or simultaneously block the attack with his sword while thrusting vigorously in a counterattack.

REFERENCES
Castle, Egerton. *Schools and Masters of Fence.* London: George Bell, 1885.
Wise, Arthur. *The Art and History of Personal Combat.* Greenwich, CT: Arma Press, 1971.

CIRCULAR PASSAGE. A full circle made with the point of the blade. This places the blade in the exact same position it was in before the movement was begun.
REFERENCE
Palffy-Alpar, Julius. *Sword and Masque.* Philadelphia: F. A. Davis, 1967.

CLADIBAS. The long, heavy sword of the Celtic Gauls. The name comes from the Latin *gladius,* the popular Roman name for a sword. The iron blade of the *cladibas* was two-edged, rounded at the tip, and about three feet long. Usually of incredibly poor quality, these swords, it was reported, bent, broke, or became dull on enemy (Roman) helmets.

Also called *cladias* or *claidas.*
REFERENCE
Burton, Richard F. *The Book of the Sword.* London: Chatto and Windus, 1884.

CLAYBEG. A Scottish word meaning "small sword."

The term should be applied to the basket-hilted* broadsword* or "Highland broadsword"* (which is sometimes called, incorrectly, a *claymore,** or "great sword").
REFERENCE
Morton, E. D. *Martini A–Z of Fencing.* London: Queen Anne Press, 1992.

CLAYMORE. From the Scottish *claidheamah mor,* meaning "great sword."

Originally, the claymore was a two-handed sword used by the Scots through the 1400s and 1500s. It had a heavy, straight blade up to sixty inches long. The quillons (cross guards), slanting toward the blade, were straight. The grip, often bearing an interwoven Celtic pattern, was also straight. The weapon was noted for its fine balance.

Sword hilts for the claymore were manufactured on the island of Islay, off the west coast of Scotland.

By the 1700s, the two-handed sword had passed into disuse. The name "claymore," however, was now applied to the basket-hilted broadsword* that became Scotland's national weapon. This name transference probably occurred because many of the old-style claymore blades were simply cut down and converted to basket-hilted weapons.
REFERENCES
Mackay, William. *Highland Weapons.* Scotland: An Comunn Gaidhealach, 1970.
Wilkinson, Frederick. *Swords and Daggers.* New York: Hawthorn Books, 1967.

CLOAK. For a time, the cloak served as a useful supplement to the sword in dueling.

Cloak and rapier play

The cloak, wrapped twice around one's free arm, could be used to block attacks. It could also be tossed in the face of an opponent, momentarily blinding him. Or it could be thrown over someone's sword blade to render it useless.

The cloak as a fighting tool became obsolete when it proved ineffective against the light, quick-moving thrusting weapons that appeared at the end of the seventeenth century.

REFERENCES
Castle, Egerton. *Schools and Masters of Fence.* London: George Bell, 1991.
Palffy-Alpar, Julius. *Sword and Masque.* Philadelphia: F. A. Davis, 1967.

CLOSE DISTANCE. A fencer has achieved close distance when he can reach his opponent with his blade simply by extending his arm. In this case, no lunge is necessary.

Also known as "close quarters" or "infighting."

REFERENCE
Palffy-Alpar, Julius. *Sword and Masque.* Philadelphia: F. A. Davis, 1967.

CLOSED LINE. When a fencer has moved his weapon so far in one particular direction that he has eliminated that side of his target area from being intruded on, the line is said to be closed.

Some fencers will close one line on purpose to draw their opponent into an action that can go only the other way.

A line may also be closed involuntarily when a desperate fencer, reacting without control, makes an extremely wide parry. This type of defensive action is easily evaded because, as it shrinks down one line, it proportionally opens up the opposite line, giving an attacker easy access to his adversary's target area.

REFERENCES
Curry, Nancy. *Fencing.* Pacific Palisades, CA: Goodyear, 1969.
Palffy-Alpar, Julius. *Sword and Masque.* Philadelphia: F. A. Davis, 1967.

CLOTHING IN MODERN FENCING. A fencer is required to be adequately protected by his clothing at all times. The material must be in good condition and of a sufficiently strong nature to withstand the stress of fencing.

A fencer's clothing must not be designed or constructed in such a way that it will catch or obstruct an opponent's weapon.

Lastly, all clothing, including socks, must be white. In the early days of fencing competition, this was so to make it easier to judge touches (colored material often camouflaged all but the most obvious hits). Today, with electronic scoring machines taking all the guesswork out of touches, the main reason for white clothing is simply tradition.

The clothing of the fencing master, on the other hand, is traditionally of colored material—often black or dark blue—to immediately offset the teacher from his pupils.

REFERENCE
U.S. Fencing Association, ed. *Operations Manual.* Colorado Springs, CO: U.S. Fencing Association, 1985.

CLUDEN. Roman "shutting" sword. The blade slid down into the handle of the weapon.
REFERENCE
Burton, Richard F. *The Book of the Sword.* London: Chatto and Windus, 1884.

COB'S TRAVERSE. Taking a step backward instead of making a parry. This action was named after an Elizabethan ruffian named Cob, who, whenever he discovered that his opponent was more than a match for him, would merely run away.
REFERENCE
Morton, E. D. *Martini A–Z of Fencing.* London: Queen Anne Press, 1992.

COLICHEMARDE. A type of dueling sword that came into vogue during the late seventeenth century. An offshoot of the small sword, it was invented by Count Konigsmark—a marshal of France under Louis XIV—from whom its name is imperfectly derived.

The *colichemarde* is noted for its triangular blade, the shape of which is wide and heavy along the forte and slender and flat toward the tip. The change in thickness is very abrupt. The overall design was supposed to give the blade strength for parrying with the lower part of the weapon, while creating a light, highly maneuverable point. Proving to be extremely effective in combat because of this, the *colichemarde* was the favorite dueling sword through the reign of Louis XIV.

Interestingly, the development of this weapon actually altered the way in which personal combat was waged. Due to its easy handling, actions that were otherwise impossible to manage with ponderous old-style swords now became common to fencing, including attacking over the top of an opponent's weapon (*coupe*), multiple feints, and circular parries.

The *colichemarde* disappeared from use quite suddenly around 1720. It has been suggested this was because of its extreme costliness to produce. Another theory was that its slightly odd appearance clashed with current fashion.

Today, some museums incorrectly list any blade of triangular shape as a *colichemarde* blade.

Also known as a *conichemarde* or *konigsmark.*
REFERENCES
Burton, Richard F. *The Book of the Sword.* London: Chatto and Windus, 1884.
Castle, Egerton. *Schools and Masters of Fence.* London: George Bell, 1885.
Wilkinson, Frederick. *Swords and Daggers.* New York: Hawthorn Books, 1967.

COLLECTIONS, SWORD AND ARMOR. The earliest collections of swords and armor were made by the church during the Middle Ages in the form of acquired funeral arms. With the coming of the Renaissance, men began developing a critical sense of history and the passage of time, plus a desire to possess objects of artistic merit, and so began assembling weapons, first, of the great and, then, more common varieties. This was, of course, done by kings and noblemen, who had both the time and funds to undertake such ventures.

Perhaps the most famous collection of swords and armor of the Renaissance was the "Heroes' and Vassals' Armory" museum of Archduke Ferdinand II of Austria (1529–1595), which was situated at the castle of Ambras, in Innsbruck. Assembling a collection made up of family arms and armor, plus common, everyday arms, Ferdinand eventually added equipment of almost every outstanding military leader of his time. The museum was eventually absorbed into Austria's Imperial Museum in 1889.

Other collectors of weapons and armor included Francis I of France (1494–1547), Henry II of France (1519–1559), Philip II of Spain (1527–1598), Louis XIII of France (1601–1643), Elector Christian II of Saxony (1583–1611), Maximilian I of Bavaria (1573–1651), and Louis XIV of France (1638–1715).

Some of the greatest collections of the Renaissance were assembled in Vienna, Madrid, Munich, Dresden, Berlin, Paris, London, Stockholm, Copenhagen, Turin, and Florence.

In time, institutional museums continued the systematic collection of weapons and armor. This, of course, was augmented by the collecting proclivities of the wealthy.

Modern outstanding collections of swords and armor can be found at the Tower of London, the Wallace Collection, and the Victoria and Albert Museum in London; the Kunsthistorisches Museum in Vienna; the Musee Royal de L'Armee in Brussels; the Musee de L'Armee in Paris; the Museo Nazionale in Florence; the Museo Nazionale di Castel S. Angelo in Rome; the Real Armeria in Madrid; the George F. Harding Museum in Chicago; the Metropolitan Museum of Art in New York; and the Smithsonian Institution in Washington, D.C.

REFERENCES

Thomas, Bruno, Ortwin Gamber, and Hans Schedelmann. *Arms and Armor of the Western World.* New York: McGraw-Hill, 1964.
Wilkinson, Frederick. *Swords and Daggers.* New York: Hawthorn Books, 1967.

COLMAN, RONALD. (1891–1958). British film actor.

Ronald Colman was the epitome of the dashing English hero. With his dark good looks, sophistication, and mellow, flowing voice, he became an archetype upon which all other British leading men of the 1920s, 1930s, and 1940s were judged.

Colman is probably best remembered for his role in the 1937 *Prisoner of Zenda*** (also starring Madeleine Carroll and Douglas Fairbanks, Jr.*). As Rudolf Rassendyll, an English gentleman adventurer who is called upon to masquerade as his kidnapped look-alike cousin, the ruler of the tiny kingdom of Ruritania, he imposed his own unique personality on a part that seemed to have been created especially for him (even though it was first realized by author Anthony Hope in 1894).

Not a skilled fencer by any means, Colman, because of his dashing image, still found himself called on to pick up the sword from time to time. *The Prisoner of Zenda* was no exception. Yet, for all his obvious lack of athletic prowess,

Ronald Colman (left) in *The Prisoner of Zenda*

his demeanor under fire somehow overrode his shortcomings. His witty delivery of banter during sword-grinding clenches with villain Fairbanks, Jr., made the entire encounter a delight to watch. (In most of the highly physical sequences, the actor was doubled by veteran fencing master Ralph Faulkner.*)

Other films in which Ronald Colman fenced include *The Night of Love* (1927), *Two Lovers* (1928), and *If I Were King* (1938).

REFERENCES
Evangelista, Nick. "Won by the Sword." *Silver Circle News* (Spring 1979).
Quirk, Lawrence J. *The Films of Ronald Colman.* NJ: Citadel Press, 1977.

COLPO D'ARRESTO. Italian term for "stop thrust."
REFERENCE
Palffy-Alpar, Julius. *Sword and Masque.* Philadelphia: F. A. Davis, 1967.

COMBINED FEINTS. Feints made up of different simple* and/or composed* attacks used to evade a series of the same parries,* lateral* or counter,* or a combination of lateral and counterparries.
REFERENCE
Morton, E. D. *Martini A–Z of Fencing.* London: Queen Anne Press, 1992.

COMBINED WEAPONS. An oddity of weapons design during the sixteenth and seventeenth centuries, combined weapons were unique joinings of pistols built onto swords, daggers, axes, and spears.
REFERENCE
Stone, George Cameron. *A Glossary of the Construction, Decoration, and Use of Arms and Armor.* New York: Jack Brussel, 1961.

COMEDY FENCING IN THE MOVIES. Comedy fencing in the movies, over the years, has fallen into two basic categories: incredibly good and painfully silly. When approached with serious intent, the resultant display of swordsman-ship, besides being funny, has an underlying sense of artfulness. As a matter of fact, the humor is enhanced by the quality of the swordplay. The rest, lacking any understanding of fencing, ends up being hollow and, sadly, not very funny. There are many more examples of the latter approach to comedy fencing captured on film than the former.

Douglas Fairbanks, Sr.,* responsible for much of the swashbuckling on the silver screen during films' silent era, managed to work a broad humor into much of his swordplay. From *The Mark of Zorro* (1920),** to *The Iron Mask* (1929),** one finds a lighthearted sense of childlike regard for fencing. Villains get their behinds poked, and inventive, humorous sword stunts abound.

Perhaps the most successful example of comedy fencing during this early period, however, was created for silent star Max Linder's parody of Douglas Fairbanks's *The Three Musketeers* (1921)**—*The Three Must-Get-Theres* (1922).** The swordplay, supervised by fencing master Fred Cavens,* was de-signed to out-Fairbanks Fairbanks for outlandish flamboyance. Fairbanks himself like the action so much that he hired Cavens to oversee the fencing in the remainder of his adventure films.

In more modern times, the best example of comedy fencing in films, without a doubt, is Danny Kaye's brilliant send-up of a swashbuckler, *The Court Jester* (1956).** Every sword stunt ever devised for film was given a broad twist, from candle cutting to casually dueling while pouring and drinking wine. Kaye, playing a simpleton, got around his character's blatant mental and physical inadequacies by being turned into a dashing hero while under a witch's hypnotic spell. This premise allowed for an even greater range of gags as Kaye was constantly being changed from hero to klutz and back again any time someone snapped his fingers. The fencing was directed by fencing master Ralph Faulkner.

Bob Hope* was able to pull off a humorous duel in his 1946 *Monsieur Beaucaire,** mostly by the sheer force of his comic personality. Hope, as Beaucaire, the barber, masquerades as a dashing nobleman marked for murder. The comedian's fencing never rises above wild sword waving, but his wisecracks are always on target. Just to be on the safe side, the silly stuff was offset by some straight swordplay by his character's heroic ally.

Perhaps the most stylish comedy fencing routine of all time was created by fencing master Jean Heremans* for dancer Gene Kelly in the *The Three Musketeers* (1948).** More of a dance than a duel, this five-minute fight scene is full of humor ranging from highly subtle to almost slapstick. Guided by his highly developed sense of timing, Kelly was more than up to the task of translating Heremans's stunts into an all-out fight scene worthy of Douglas Fairbanks.

Start the Revolution Without Me (1970), starring Gene Wilder and Donald Sutherland, is another parody of the swashbuckler genre that managed to create some effective moments of comedy fencing. The story, set during prerevolutionary France, deals with two sets of mismatched twins (mixed up at birth)— one pair, cowardly peasants; the other, ruthless and incredibly neurotic aristocrats. When they are mistaken for each other, craziness begins.

Richard Lester's *The Three Musketeers* (1974),** which starred Michael York, Oliver Reed, Richard Chamberlain, and Frank Finlay, was an interesting and successful blend of both serious and humorous swordplay staged by British fight arranger William Hobbs.* A duel in an inn, where the musketeers steal food for supper while they pretend to fight, is a good example of the film's lighter approach.

Royal Flash (1975), based on a popular novel by George MacDonald Fraser, was a moderately successful attempt at swashbuckling humor. Starring Malcolm McDowell and Alan Bates, the film was a parody of the classic *The Prisoner of Zenda.* Harry Flashman, a bully and coward, is blackmailed into standing in for a prince whom he greatly resembles. The catch, unbeknownst to him, is that he is to be assassinated. Actually, the best part of the proceedings was the obligatory climactic sword duel between Flashman (McDowell) and his nemesis, Rudi Starnberg-Hentzau (Bates). It was well staged, although quite unheroically for Flashman, who has numerous mishaps during the fighting, such as his pants catching on fire.

The Princesss Bride (1987), one of Hollywood's more recent delvings into costume adventure films, brought some old-time class to a highly original comic fencing routine between actors Mandy Patinkin and Cary Elwes. As Inigo Montoya (Patinkin) and the man in black (Elwes) cross swords, they exchange banter about historical swordplay styles, fence matter-of-factly with either hand, and perform extravagant gymnastic feats, while generally maintaining the warmest personal regard for one another.

Adequate humorous fencing moments can be found in the Ritz Brothers' musical *The Three Musketeers* (1939), Gene Wilder's *Sherlock Holmes's Smarter Brother* (1975), and Cheech and Chong's *Corsican Brothers* (1983).

There is silly fencing galore in the Three Stooges' *Restless Knights* (1935), Abbott and Costello's *Jack and the Beanstalk* (1952), Bob Hope's copy of *Monsieur Beaucaire, Casanova's Big Night* (1956), Monty Python's *Monty Python and the Holy Grail* (1975), and *Dr. Detroit* (1982).

Some films where the humorous fencing fell completely flat were *Swashbuckler* (1976), Peter Sellers's *The Prisoner of Zenda* (1979), *Yellowbeard* (1983), Roman Polanski's awful *Pirates* (1985), and Mel Brooks's uneven *Spaceballs* (1987). These efforts were especially disappointing because of the talent and money that went into their creation.

REFERENCES

Halliwell, Leslie. *Halliwell's Filmgoer's and Video Viewer's Companion*. New York: Charles Scribner's Sons, 1988.
Richards, Jeffrey. *Swordsmen of the Screen*. Boston: Routledge and Kegan Paul, 1977.
Thomas, Tony. *Cads and Cavaliers*. New York: A. S. Barnes, 1973.

COMICS, FENCING IN. For years, comics were the prerogative of muscle-laden heroes sporting assorted superpowers and of large, anthropomorphic animals. Although Mickey Mouse or Donald Duck would occasionally be called on to cross swords with some villainous rat or dog, fencing normally had very little to do with the world of graphic storytelling.

The one area where swordplay did abound was in the *Classics Illustrated* comic books of the 1950s and 1960s. Based on the great stories of the world—from Homer's *Iliad* to Alexandre Dumas's *The Three Musketeers***—these "illustrated novels" brought the world of classical literature to life for a whole generation of children in desperate need of book reports. There was usually plenty of swordplay to be found in the adventure-oriented comics. Often it was depicted crudely. Once in a while, though, the art managed to achieve an amazing amount of class for comicbooks. As a source for fencing art in comics, it was the most constant and varied.

The one other major source of fencing in comics in the 1950s was the EC comic book line. From *Two-Fisted Tales* to *Piracy* to *Valor,* the swordplay in these alternatives to the standard comic fare was usually depicted with a grim, graphic quality that—along with the publishing house's *Tales from the Crypt, Crime Suspenstories,* and *The Vault of Horror*—earned EC the enmity of parents all over America, an enmity that eventually helped drive the company virtually out of business. Nevertheless, the artists who worked on these tales have become the greats of modern American illustrating: Reed Crandall, Wallace Wood, Angelo Torres, Al Williamson, Jack Davis, Roy Krenkel, and Frank Frazetta.*

(It is interesting to note that after all the fuss that was made over EC comics in the 1950s, they are now being fondly republished in their entirety—in book form—by Russ Cochran, a comic publisher and Tarzan aficionado situated in the small town of West Plains, Missouri.)

Two, more mainstream, and popular sources of illustrated swordplay could be found in Hal Foster's *Prince Valiant* and Alex Raymond's *Flash Gordon.* Here, the art was elegantly rendered and always with a strong emphasis on romanticism.

With the rise of "sword-and-sorcery" literature in the mid-1960s came a flood of alternative (sometimes called "underground") comics that often featured fantasy-adventure tales that abounded in gory sword combat. One of the most notable was *Witzend,* produced by artist Wallace Wood.

In the 1970s, this "realistic" form was legitimated and mainstreamed by a line of illustrated fantasy/horror magazines—*Creepy, Eerie,* and *Vampirella.* Enlisting the talents of former EC alumni Frank Frazetta, Reed Crandall, Angelo Torres, and Al Williamson, among others, and eventually adding a new generation of illustrators to their stable—like Gray Morrow, Ken Kelly, Estaban Maroto, and Sanjulian—these publications placed a heavy emphasis on innovative, quality graphics.

Eventually, the establishment publishing companies discovered the fantasy genre, and suddenly comics were inundated with swashbuckling action and swordplay. DC Comics came out with titles like *The Viking Prince, Weird Worlds, Sword of Sorcery,* and even *The Three Musketeers.* Marvel Comics had *Conan the Barbarian* and *King Kul.* Gold Key Comics published *John Carter of Mars.* King Comics issued an updated *Flash Gordon.* Keeping in step with industry decency standards, bloodshed was always minimal.

Today, dozens of comic titles employ swordplay, many from alternative comic publishing companies. Approaches to the subject matter range from the down-to-earth to the completely offbeat. Protagonists include barbarian warriors, ninja, samurai, tough, two-fisted modern adventurers, and even large, humanesque turtles.

REFERENCES

Feiffer, Jules. *The Great Comic Book Heroes.* New York: Dial Press, 1965.

King, Stephen. *Danse Macabre.* New York: Everest House, 1981.

O'Neil, Denny, ed. "Weird Worlds." *Weird Worlds.* New York: National Periodical Publications, 1972.

Stewart, Bhob, ed. *Piracy.* West Plains, MO: Russ Cochran, 1988.

COMMANDING THE SWORD. When dueling was still in vogue, commanding the sword was the act of closing with an opponent and seizing his sword with one's free hand. Special gloves, or gauntlets, were made for this purpose.

In modern fencing, this action is illegal.

REFERENCES

Castle, Egerton. *Schools and Masters of Fence.* London: George Bell, 1885.

Wise, Arthur. *The Art and History of Personal Combat.* Greenwich, CT: Arma Press, 1971.

COMPASSES. As explained by the Spanish fencing master Don Luis Pacheco de Narvaez* at the beginning of the seventeenth century, compasses were the steps taken when fencing in the circular fashion of the period.

The proper stepping distances were as follows:

The *pasada:* a step of twenty-four inches.

The *pasada simple:* a step of about thirty inches.

The *pasada doble:* a movement consisting of two *pasadas,* alternating the right foot with the left foot.

REFERENCES

Castle, Egerton. *Schools and Masters of Fence.* London: George Bell, 1885.

Stone, George Cameron. *A Glossary of the Construction, Decoration, and Use of Arms and Armor.* New York: Jack Brussel, 1961.

COMPOSED ATTACK. In fencing, for every defensive action made, there is an offensive action designed to break through it. That is the science of fencing. When simple attacks—attacks made up entirely of timing and speed—are no longer able to get past an opponent's defensive system, the composed attack may be used to create the needed openings.

A composed attack is made up of a feint of an attack, followed by a deception of a parry or parries. Because of its reliance on strategy for success, rather than basic physical attributes, it is considered an advanced fencing action.

The initial component of the composed attack, the feint, is an action of threat designed to create a desire on the part of an opponent to protect himself by parrying. The fencer making the feint then deceives (avoids) the defensive action by maneuvering his weapon out of the way of the parry. This creates an opening for the attacker, who may then lunge.

It is important to remember that if the feint looks like a feint instead of an attack in progress, it is not likely that the defending fencer will feel intimidated enough to make a parry. Because its only value is visual, the feint must be presented in such a way that it carries all the menace of an actual attack.

The second part of the composed attack, the deception, can best be described as an evasive action. To be effective, it should be guided by the fingers rather than the entire arm. This keeps the point movement small and precise. Executing a deception that is too large may allow the defender time to make a second parry.

The two basic composed attacks are the one-two and the *doublé*. The difference between the two is that the one-two evades a lateral parry (a parry that moves in a straight line), while the *doublé* evades a counterparry (a parry that moves in a circle).

Composed attacks can also be made by combining simple attacks—disengages, *coulés,* and *coupés*—with simple attacks, such as a *coulé*-disengaged or a disengage-*coupé*; or by combining simple attacks with composed attacks, such as a *coupé*-one-two or a *coulé-doublé*.

Knowing the type of parry an opponent will be making is the key to making successful composed attacks. A fencer finds this out by making enough exploratory feints to discover how his opponent defends himself.

The composed attack is also known as a "composite" attack and "compound" attack.

REFERENCES

Palffy-Alpar, Julius. *Sword and Masque.* Philadelphia: F. A. Davis, 1967.

Vebell, Edward. *Sports Illustrated Book of Fencing.* Philadelphia: J. B. Lippincott, 1962.

COMPOSITE PARRIES. A series of successive parries that keep numerous feints of an attack in check. They may be either a string of lateral or counterparries or a combination of both.

Also known as "compound parries."

REFERENCE

Palffy-Alpar, Julius. *Sword and Masque.* Philadelphia: F. A. Davis, 1967.

CONAN. A popular heroic pulp fiction barbarian swordsman created by writer Robert E. Howard.*

The Conan stories, first published in pulp magazines of the 1930s, enjoyed a newfound popularity beginning in the late 1960s, when adventure fantasy fiction suddenly took hold of the public's imagination.

An exceptional swordsman-cum-warrior, Conan usually found his way out of problems not through finesse but through smashing or slicing to tiny bits whatever stood in his way. His opponents ranged from brawny warriors to wizards to unspeakable monsters.

Conan became so popular that after all of his two dozen original adventures found their way into print, other writers—notably, L. Sprague de Camp, Bjorn Nyberg, and Lin Carter—began penning new Conan tales.

In recent years, Conan has found his way into comic books, art posters, and movies.

The Conan stories, it should be noted, have inspired countless imitators.

Books of collected Conan adventures include *Conan the Adventurer* (1966), Howard; *Conan the Conqueror* (1967), Howard; *Conan the Usurper* (1967), Howard and de Camp; *Conan the Warrior* (1967), Howard; *Conan* (1968), Howard, de Camp, and Carter; and *Conan of the Isles* (1968), de Camp and Carter, to name a few.

REFERENCES
Carter, Lin. "Buccaneers and Black Magicians." In *Conan the Buccaneer,* ed. L. Sprague de Camp and Lin Carter. New York: Lancer Books, 1971.
de Camp, L. Sprague. "Introduction." *Conan the Adventurer,* ed. Robert E. Howard. New York: Lancer Books, 1966.

CONTRA CAVATIONE. An action first described by Italian fencing master Salvator Fabris* in the early seventeenth century.

When one swordsman attacked by disengaging his weapon (i.e., moving from one line to the opposite line by passing beneath an opponent's blade), it was advocated that one could interrupt this maneuver by launching one's own disengagement, which would put the attacker back into his original line.

Historian Arthur Wise, in his book *The Art and History of Personal Combat,* states that this was the first suggestion of the counterparry in fencing, because the circular movement created by the *contra cavatione,* in effect, established an exclusive defensive situation rather than simply being part of a counterattack.

Adding a time thrust (an extension of one's blade into an opponent's attack) to the *contra cavatione* could be used to add an offensive element to the action if needed.

REFERENCES
Castle, Egerton. *Schools and Masters of Fence.* London: George Bell, 1885.
Wise, Arthur. *The Art and History of Personal Combat.* Greenwich, CT: Arma Press, 1971.

CONTRAPRINSE. A sixteenth-century term for a double disarm, or counter-seizure, that is, both combatants grabbing away the weapon of the other in an involuntary exchange. Usually, the weapon was grasped at the hilt, rather than on the blade.

Such an action takes place in Shakespeare's *Hamlet,*** where Prince Hamlet trades weapons with Laertes in the famous duel from that play.

The *contraprinse* is not allowed in modern fencing.

REFERENCES
Castle, Egerton. *Schools and Masters of Fence.* London: George Bell, 1885.
Shakespeare, William. *Hamlet.* Edited by Louis B. Wright and Virginia LaMar. New York: Washington Square Press, 1970.

CONTRE POSTURA. Guard positions advocated by the earliest masters of fencing referred only to stances from which attacks might be launched. Separating defensive measures from offensive ones was thought unwise.

As defined by seventeenth-century fencing master Salvator Fabris,* the *contre postura,* or *contre guardia,* was the first fencing attitude devised to hold within its application the modern concept of a guard held with defensive purposes in mind.

Fabris stated that in his opinion it was best to adopt a guard position that was similar to the one taken by one's opponent. Moreover, the sword should be positioned so that one fencer could not hit the other simply by thrusting forward.

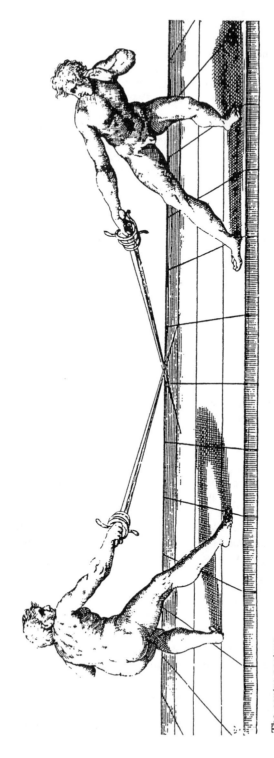

The contre postura

REFERENCES
Castle, Egerton. *Schools and Masters of Fence.* London: George Bell, 1885.
Wise, Arthur. *The Art and History of Personal Combat.* Greenwich, CT: Arma Press, 1971.

CONTRES. A French term from the seventeenth century referring to circular (counter) parries.
REFERENCE
Castle, Egerton. *Schools and Masters of Fence.* London: George Bell, 1885.

CONTRETEMPS. A term used by fencing master Sir William Hope* in the late 1600s to describe a thrust made into an attack in which hits were exchanged.
   Today, the term refers to a "time thrust" or "time hit."
REFERENCE
Castle, Egerton. *Schools and Masters of Fence.* London: George Bell, 1885.

CONTROL POINT. A term from the sixteenth century referring to displacing the point of an adversary's weapon.
REFERENCE
Morton, E. D. *Martini A–Z of Fencing.* London: Queen Anne Press, 1992.

CONTRO-TEMPO. *Contro-tempo* (counter time) describes a defensive-offensive action that is employed in opposition to a counterattack;* in essence, a counterattack against a counterattack. For example, when one fencer executes a counterattack in time against against his opponent, the latter may defeat this move by either parrying and riposting in counter time or performing a time thrust* in counter time.
   The term has also been used to simply describe a time thrust employed when there is a hesitation in time between the attacker's feint and the action following the feint.
   Also known as *contre temps*, "counter tempo," and *conta tempo.*
REFERENCES
Palffy-Alpar, Julius. *Sword and Masque.* Philadelphia: F. A. Davis, 1967.
U.S. Fencing Association, ed. *Fencing Rules and Manual.* Colorado Springs, CO: U.S. Fencing Association, 1984.

CONVENTIONAL EXERCISES. A formal type of fencing exercise in which certain limited attacks and parries may be practiced without any competitive angle getting in the way. Where the lesson situation deals with form and technique, conventionals add the element of intent, but without the complications of bouting.
   Usually, conventionals have one fencer attacking for a specified number of times, while the other fencer defends.
   A common conventional exercise has one fencer attempting disengages and

one-twos, while his opponent, who is required not to retreat, performs only lateral parries. Also, the defender is normally allowed to riposte.

The main purpose of conventional exercises is neither to score a hit nor to keep from being hit but to perfect the important elements of offensive and defensive actions that lead naturally to touches and effective parries. Timing, distance, the ability to make threatening feints and efficient deceptions, point control, controlled parries and ripostes, and, of course, a relaxed attitude under fire should always be the main focus of such practice.

Conventional exercises have been recognized as a vital part of fencing instruction since the seventeenth century. The French called them *tirer au mur;* the English, "parrieing and thrusting a plain thrust." A more colorless term was "thrusting at the wall."

Also called reciprocal exercises.

REFERENCES

Castle, Egerton. *Schools and Masters of Fence.* London: George Bell, 1885.

Palffy-Alpar, Julius. *Sword and Masque.* Philadelphia: F. A. Davis, 1967.

Szabo, Laszlo. *Fencing and the Master.* Hungary: Franklin Printing House, 1977.

CONVENTIONAL WEAPON. In the sport of fencing, conventional weapons are those weapons that have rules that guide the way they are employed. The foil* and the sabre* are conventional weapons.

The épée,* having few rules governing its use, is a nonconventional weapon.*

REFERENCE

U.S. Fencing Association, ed. *Operations Manual.* Colorado Springs, CO: U.S. Fencing Association, 1985.

CONVENTIONS. Conventions are the rules of fencing. They cover the use of weapons, weapon construction, personal behavior, and the method by which fencing bouts are conducted. Foil* and sabre* are covered by strict rules governing their use.

Many of the rules come from a time when men fought with sharp weapons and reflect a commonsense approach to fencing. When men fought with deadly weapons, they found out quickly what worked and what did not work—by who got killed. These observations became the basis for conventions.

For instance, one rule of foil fencing is that the attacker must have a straight arm to gain right-of-way (i.e., the right to hit one's opponent). This rule points out two facts. First, if you attack with a bent arm, you will not have as long a reach as you would have with a straight arm, so you are less likely to reach your target. Second, if you attack with a bent arm, and your opponent extends his arm straight, he will have a longer reach than you, allowing him to hit first. Hence, the straight arm is the most advantageous position for an attacking foil fencer. Common sense.

A rule common to both foil and sabre states that all correctly executed attacks must be either parried or completely avoided. If the weapons being used could kill, one would definitely try to defend one's self before trying to hit the attacker.

Anything less could be fatal. Again, common sense. By and large, without conventions, sharp points and cutting edges would be the only effective way to decide who got what touch.

The épée has a limited number of conventions guiding the way in which it is used, because it was designed to reflect what might happen in a real fight situation. Essentially, with épée, the idea is to simply hit your opponent before he hits you. One of the few rules governing épée fencing is that the free hand—the hand not holding the weapon—may not be employed either offensively or defensively. Another is that the épée may not be thrown at one's opponent. Such restrictions promote weapon control rather than relying on tricks. (These particular conventions also apply to the foil and sabre.)

Adhering to the strictures of conventions also helps develop control over one's actions.

REFERENCES

Palffy-Alpar, Julius. *Sword and Masque.* Philadelphia: F. A. Davis, 1967.
U.S. Fencing Association, ed. *Operations Manual.* Colorado Springs, CO: U.S. Fencing Association, 1985.

CONVERSATION OF THE FOIL. The swift, complex, back-and-forth exchanges encountered in foil fencing have aptly been described as a "conversation." The analogy comes out of the notion that the use of the foil must be a civilized affair. While one fencer attacks (talks), the other fencer must defend (listen). Moreover, as in any civilized social intercourse, this position changes from one participant to the other as necessity dictates. Thus, the metaphor becomes obvious.

This symbolical aspect of the sport has been so connected with conversation that fencing terms have even found their way into modern language as terms of communication. Verbal "thrusts," "parries," "ripostes," and "repartee" have long been considered part of eloquent dialogue.

REFERENCE

Beaumont, C-L. de. *Fencing in Pictures.* London: Hulton Press, 1955.

CONVERSION. The act of changing the sword hand from supination to pronation, or vice versa.

REFERENCE

Handleman, Rob. "Fencing Glossary." *American Fencing* (February/March 1978).

COPERTINO. A vertical, forward gliding pressure on an opponent's blade that ends in a straight, detaching thrust.

REFERENCE

Palffy-Alpar, Julius. *Sword and Mask.* Philadelphia: F. A. Davis, 1967.

COQUILLE. A cup-style hand guard. *Coquille* means "shell."

This type of guard was first used on the rapier and probably originated in Spain. Popular among swordsmen from the very start, it proved to be an ideal protection for the hand against thrusting weapons, much more so than old-fashioned crossbar guards—even ones with elaborate weaves of metal strips.

The shell guard actually began as a simple addition to the crossbar hilt. Two small, solid plates were set on either side of the blade. Eventually these were increased in size and joined to form one large single cup.

The *coquille,* surviving the test of time, is used on modern sport weapons. The guard size of the foil, sabre, and épée differs according to needs and application of each weapon.

The foil *coquille* is used simply as a general protection for the hand, which is otherwise not part of the target area (12 centimeters in diameter).

The sabre *coquille* includes a convex knuckle guard for defending the hand, primarily against cutting actions (15 centimeters).

The épée *coquille* is the main protection for the hand, the single most vulnerable spot on an épée fencer (13.5 centimeters).

While the blade on the foil and sabre constitutes the primary parrying portion of those weapons, the *coquille* of the épée is often used in executing parries. This defensive technique is employed to ensure that the épée's point is always being directed at one's opponent.

The *coquille* is also known as *la coccia, das stichblatt,* and cup guard.
REFERENCES
Palffy-Alpar, Julius. *Sword and Masque.* Philadelphia: F. A. Davis, 1967.
Wilkinson, Frederick. *Swords and Daggers.* New York: Hawthorn Books, 1967.

CORPORATION DES MAITRES EN FAIT D'ARMES. A group of fencing masters in France given special rights and privileges by the monarchy. From the time of Henri III to Louis XIV, these masters held an absolute monopoly over the teaching of swordplay in the kingdom.

A degree of *maitre en fait d'armes* was awarded only after six years of apprenticeship under some member of the corporation and a public trial of skill with three other members.

The Corporation des Maitres en fait d'Armes was eventually broken up by the French Revolution.
REFERENCE
Castle, Egerton. *Schools and Masters of Fence.* London: George Bell, 1885.

CORPORATION OF FENCING MASTERS IN SPAIN. The established fencing masters of Spain, as a group, set down requirements for admittance to their ranks that were both rigid and lengthy, requiring much study and training. Aspiring teachers were supposed to master, in theory and practice, all weapons. Then, in their "final exam," they were required to fight the whole board of their examiners, first one at a time, and then all together. Only the stoutest of individuals, by all accounts, managed to pass the necessary tests.
REFERENCE
Castle, Egerton. *Schools and Masters of Fence.* London: George Bell, 1885.

CORPORATION OF MAISTERS OF DEFENCE. In England, in an effort to encourage the practice of martial exercises and to reduce the amount of evil perpetrated by independent swordsmen, King Henry VIII incorporated a company of the most celebrated fencing masters of the day, giving them and only them the right to teach the art of swordplay in England.

To become an accredited fencing master, applicants first had to become students and take degrees. They then were publicly tested in the use of weapons. Anyone who did not follow this prescribed method to masterhood was visited by a group of professed masters who, eager to protect their monopoly, made certain, through threats or force, that the interloper was put out of business.

The places where official swordsmanship was taught were well known. Usually they were theaters, halls, or simply large enclosures with space sufficient for spectators. Ely Place in Holborn, the Bell Savage on Ludgate Hill, the Curtain in Hollyweel, the Gray Friars in Newgate, Hampton Court, the Bull in Bishopsgate Street, the Clink, Duke's Place, Salisbury Court, Bridewell, and the Artillery Gardens were among the most popular fencing locations.

REFERENCE

Castle, Egerton. *Schools and Masters of Fence.* London: George Bell, 1885.

CORPS A CORPS. Means "body to body." Essentially, *corps a corps* refers to body contact between two fencers.

Because of their sometimes brutal and potentially dangerous nature, both deliberate and accidental forms of body contact are discouraged by the rules of modern fencing. Initially, in a fencing bout, a single infraction is accompanied by a warning; thereafter, penalties are issued.

It is considered a sign of poor fencing not to be able to control one's maneuvering distance well enough to avoid continually precipitating the *corps a corps.*

REFERENCES

Palffy-Alpar, Julius. *Sword and Masque.* Philadelphia: F. A. Davis, 1967.

U.S. Fencing Association, ed. *Operations Manual.* Colorado Springs, CO: U.S. Fencing Association, 1985.

CORSICAN BROTHERS FILMS. The adventure tale of twin brothers separated at birth who share the same feelings has been popular with the public since it was written in 1845. As a subject for film, it was adapted for the screen almost as soon as film companies began turning out movies.

The first *The Corsican Brothers* was made in England in 1898, followed by a second British effort in 1902. The next versions came from the United States in 1908, 1915, 1919, 1941, and 1953. Ten years later, the French produced a remake. The last version, to date, was a British film made in 1984.

The subject of Corsican twins—of a mismatched variety—was used for comedy purposes in the 1970 spoof of costume-adventure films, *Start the Revolution*

*Without Me,*** and in Cheech and Chong's 1983 bathroom humor swashbuckler, *The Corsican Brothers.*

Douglas Fairbanks, Jr.'s *The Corsican Brothers* (1941) is by far the best of all versions.

REFERENCES

Druxman, Michael B. *Make It Again, Sam.* New York: A. S. Barnes, 1975.

Halliwell, Leslie. *Halliwell's Filmgoer's and Video Viewer's Companion.* New York: Charles Scribner's Sons, 1988.

Richards, Jeffrey. *Swordsmen of the Screen.* Boston: Routledge and Kegan Paul, 1977.

COUDRAY, JEAN BAPTISTE LE PERCHE DU. (c. 1630). French fencing master.

A pupil of Pater, the most famous fencing master in the days of Louis XIII, Coudray was the first of France's "modern" masters to put forth his ideas in book form.

His treatise, *L'Exercise des armes ou le maniement du fleuret,* was published in 1635.

REFERENCE

Castle, Egerton. *Schools and Masters of Fence.* London: George Bell, 1885.

COULÉ. The *coulé* is a simple attack, made up entirely of timing and speed, that runs lightly along an opponent's blade. *Coulé* means "running."

As a feint of an attack, the *coulé* is especially effective because of the blade contact, which is in itself overtly threatening, both physically and visually.

Mentioned in fencing texts as far back as the eighteenth century, the *coulé* was known as a *glizade.*

Also known as a "glide," *glise,* "glide thrust," graze, or "running glide."

REFERENCES

Castle, Egerton. *Schools and Masters of Fence.* London: George Bell, 1885.

Palffy-Alpar, Julius. *Sword and Masque.* Philadelphia: F. A. Davis, 1967.

COUNTERATTACK. Simply put, a counterattack is an attack launched against an attack.

In foil* and sabre* practice, the counterattack most often employed is the riposte,* an offensive extension of the blade made by a fencer after he has defended against an attack by first executing a successful parry.* A riposte may further be carried out following the parry of an opponent's riposte. According to the rules governing the use of the foil and sabre, under normal circumstances a counterattack should not be undertaken against a properly performed attack, or riposte, until a valid parry has been accomplished.

Yet, there are odd times in fencing when blade extensions into an adversary's oncoming attack may be instituted without a parry preceding them. These counterattacks are called stop thrusts* (or cuts*) and time thrusts* (or cuts*). For them to be effective, however, the fencer performing them must not be hit by his opponent.

It should be noted that the foil and sabre regulations dealing with counterattacks were instituted, in part, to discourage offensive actions that merely promote simultaneous (double) touches, an occurrence that would prove highly unsatisfactory if blades had sharp points or edges.

In épée* fencing, where the object is simply to hit before being hit, a parry is not necessary to carry out a successful counterattack.

In the early decades of swordplay's rough and tumble development, counter-offensive moves without parries were, for the most part, carried out automatically, such maneuverings at that time being the only acceptable form of defense against swords that could best be described as stiff and ponderous. When an attack came, one would attack into it, simultaneously attempting to either side-step or duck beneath the advancing blade, or to block it with one's own weapon and hit in one encompassing motion. When swords grew lighter and, hence, more manageable—thus speeding up swordplay movement—constantly engaging in these forms of counterattack became risky and were relegated to only occasional use.

The counterattack is also known as a "counteraction," "counteroffensive action," or *attaco responsivo.*

REFERENCES

Castle, Egerton. *Schools and Masters of Fence.* London: George Bell, 1885.

Morton, E. D. *Martini A–Z of Fencing.* London: Queen Anne Press, 1992.

Palffy-Alpar, Julius. *Sword and Masque.* Philadelphia: F. A. Davis, 1967.

COUNTER-CAVEATING. In England, during the late 1600s, counter-caveating was the term used to describe a circular parry. It was considered applicable to every line.

Sir William Hope,* the most famous English fencing master during the seventeenth century, spoke enthusiastically of the move, stating that, "it crosseth and confoundeth all feints; yea, not only feints, but in a manner all lessons which can be made with a small sword." He ended by saying that once a fencer had mastered it, he should never use another parry.

REFERENCE

Castle, Egerton. *Schools and Masters of Fence.* London: George Bell, 1885.

COUNTERGUARDS OF THE SWORD. The counterguard refers to a portion of the hand fortification—often a complex interweaving of bars and/or rings—of the sword. Basically, any extra guard section added beyond the ever-present cross-hilt,* cup guard,* and knuckle bow* (although, occasionally, the knuckle bow is regarded as part of the counterguard arrangement).

Various counterguard designs were produced because of the inability of the basic old-style crossbar sword design to adequately shield the weapon hand from attack.

Also known as *la contregarde, l'elsa, la contraguardia,* and *der Bugel.*

The counterparry as it was envisioned during the seventeenth century

REFERENCES
Burton, Richard F. *The Book of the Sword.* London: Chatto and Windus, 1884.
Castle, Egerton. *Schools and Masters of Fence.* London: George Bell, 1885.

COUNTERING. In old fencing terms, countering meant to meet an attack with a counterattack, rather than following the more modern practice of making a parry.
REFERENCE
Castle, Egerton. *Schools and Masters of Fence.* London: George Bell, 1885.

COUNTERPARRY. The counterparry is a defensive maneuver with the blade that covers the target area in a circular fashion, to be specific, a complete circle. It moves either clockwise or counterclockwise.

In its earliest incarnation, the Italian fencing master Salvator Fabris* called it *contra cavatione;* the English called it ''counter-caveating.''

In modern fencing, the counterparry is considered a more advanced action than the lateral parry, which moves in a linear fashion, because it takes a trained mind to initiate circular movement. For the most part, when reacting without the benefit of experience, a fencer will move his blade defensively in a back-and-forth lateral fashion.

The composed attack known as the *doublé* was designed to evade the counterparry. By moving in the same direction as the counterparry, it keeps one step ahead of the sweeping circular movement, basically outrunning it until an opening is created.

Until the light, easily managed smallsword came into use in the eighteenth century, counterparries were discouraged, for the most part, by the fencing establishment because weapons were simply too heavy to carry out the action quickly and effectively.

Because its circular movement passes briefly through all lines, the counterparry was once considered a kind of magical, universal parry. Used in such a fashion, however, it tended to throw the play into disorder.

Also called a "circular parry," a "*contre* parry," an "acquired parry," a *circolazione,* a "collecting parry," an "elliptical parry," a "round parry," a "thought parry," and a "twiddle."

REFERENCES
Castle, Egerton. *Schools and Masters of Fence.* London: George Bell, 1885.
Morton, E. D. *Martini A–Z of Fencing.* London: Queen Anne Press, 1992.
Palffy-Alpar, Julius. *Sword and Masque.* Philadelphia: F. A. Davis, 1967.

COUNTERRIPOSTE. After an attack has been successfully parried by a fencer, the defender's counterattack, or riposte, usually follows. When this initial riposte is successfully parried by the previous attacker, his counter-counterattack or, simply, counterriposte is the next proper response to be carried out.
REFERENCE
Palffy-Alpar, Julius. *Sword and Masque.* Philadelphia: F. A. Davis, 1967.

COUP. In fencing, the old French term for the action of an attack from its beginning to its conclusion. The Italians called the coup *botta.*
REFERENCE
Castle, Egerton. *Schools and Masters of Fence.* London: George Bell, 1885.

COUP D'ARRET. French term for the stop thrust.*
REFERENCE
Palffy-Alpar, Julius. *Sword and Masque.* Philadelphia: F. A. Davis, 1967.

COUP DE GRACE. The finishing stroke against an opponent with sword or dagger. Known also as a "mercy stroke."

A special dagger known as a *misericorde,* or "dagger of mercy," was often employed for the purpose of administering a death blow to someone who was mortally wounded.
REFERENCE
Castle, Egerton. *Schools and Masters of Fence.* London: George Bell, 1885.

COUP DE JARNAC. A fencing move first employed by Guy Chabot de Jarnac* in his famous duel with François de Vivonne La Chastaigneraye in 1547.

The action consisted of cutting an opponent on both thighs so that he could no longer stand and, hence, no longer fight.
REFERENCE
Baldick, Robert. *The Duel.* New York: Spring Books, 1970.

COUP DOUBLE. The French term for "double touch."
Also known as an "encounter" or "exchanged hits."
REFERENCE
Palffy-Alpar, Julius. *Sword and Masque.* Philadelphia: F. A. Davis, 1967.

COUP DROIT. This offensive action is a single, direct thrust that arrives without any hesitation. It is delivered in a straight line, by one complete movement.
Also called a "straight hit" and "straight thrust."
REFERENCE
Palffy-Alpar, Julius. *Sword and Masque.* Philadelphia: F. A. Davis, 1967.

COUPÉ. The *coupé* is a simple attack moving from one line to the opposite line passing over the top of an opponent's blade. *Coupé* means "cut over." In Italian, the term is *tagliata.*
The *coupé,* it should be noted, may be accomplished only in the high line.
As a feint, the *coupé* is highly effective. The movement of a blade point being raised and then dropped quickly possesses a strong degree of visual threat.
When the *coupé* (*coupée*) was first introduced in the late 1600s, apparently little value was attached to the action. The eighteenth-century fencing master Guillaume Danet* even discouraged its use, believing it "a dangerous mode of attack, often resulting in interchanged thrusts." He felt the action should be restricted to ripostes. However, in time, the *coupé* was to become a distinguishing feature of the French school of fencing.
Slight variations on the *coupé* proper included the *botte coupée* and the *quarte coupée sous les armes.*
Other names for the *coupé* include *cavazione angolata* and the "cut over the point."
REFERENCES
Castle, Egerton. *Schools and Masters of Fence.* London: George Bell, 1885.
Palffy-Alpar, Julius. *Sword and Masque.* Philadelphia: F. A. Davis, 1967.

COUP FOURRES. Defined by eighteenth-century French fencing master Guillaume Danet* as "interchanged thrusts," that is, repeated parry-riposte exchanges between combatants.
In modern fencing, this form of byplay is inevitable. In Danet's time, such actions were considered highly dangerous and were to be avoided if possible.
REFERENCE
Castle, Egerton. *Schools and Masters of Fence.* London: George Bell, 1885.

COUP JETE. A hit that is made by sliding the hand along the grip during the execution of an attack. This is done so that one's reach may be increased.

While, according to the rules of fencing, one may hold a weapon's grip at any point, to employ this action during the course of an attack is forbidden.

Also known as a "thrown hit."

REFERENCE

Morton, E. D. *Martini A–Z of Fencing*. London: Queen Anne Press, 1992.

COUP LANCE. A *coup lance* has occurred when a fencer, already in the process of attacking, lands a touch immediately after the director has, for whatever reason, called "Halt."

Nevertheless, the touch is allowed.

REFERENCE

Morton, E. D. *Martini A–Z of Fencing*. London: Queen Anne Press, 1992.

COUP SEC. A meeting of blades that is both crisp and firm.

REFERENCE

Morton, E. D. *Martini A–Z of Fencing*. London: Queen Anne Press, 1992.

COURT SWORD. An elaborately decorated smallsword worn by noblemen, as the name implies, at court. While the weapon was functional as a sword, its main purpose was to act as a fashion accessory.

The court sword was also known as the "Sword of Fashion."

REFERENCE

Palffy-Alpar, Julius. *Sword and Masque*. Philadelphia: F. A. Davis, 1967.

COUSTIL A CROC. A fifteenth-century, single-handed short sword with a straight, double-edged blade, which could be used as a dagger.

REFERENCE

Castle, Egerton. *Schools and Masters of Fence*. London: George Bell, 1885.

COUTEAU DE BRECHE. In its simplest form, a *couteau de breche* is a sword blade attached to one end of a staff used from the 1400s through the 1600s.

Also called a *couse*.

REFERENCE

Stone, George Cameron. *A Glossary of the Construction, Decoration, and Use of Arms and Armor*. New York: Jack Brussel, 1961.

COVER. In fencing terms, to cover means to close off a particular portion of one's target area with one's blade, leaving no room for an opponent to attack in that line.

REFERENCE

Palffy-Alpar, Julius. *Sword and Masque*. Philadelphia: F. A. Davis, 1967.

COVERING. Moving an opponent's weapon sufficiently away from one's valid target area by employing a slight pressure from one's blade.

REFERENCE

Morton, E. D. *Martini A–Z of Fencing*. London: Queen Anne Press, 1992.

COWARD'S PARRY. Retreating when attacked rather than using one's blade to stop an opponent.

Also called the "ninth parry" (in fencing, there are eight legitimate parries) and "parrying with one's feet."
REFERENCE
Morton, E. D. *Martini A–Z of Fencing.* London: Queen Anne Press, 1992.

CRAB. A derisive term used to describe a fencer who is unable to keep his heels lined up when advancing, retreating, and lunging. This effect—at the very least, unattractive—when left unchecked, eventually leads to a loss of balance.
REFERENCE
Morton, E. D. *Martini A–Z of Fencing.* London: Queen Anne Press, 1992.

CRAB CLAW HILT. A style of rapier hilt employing four down-curving cross-bars* in conjunction with a large *coquille.** When turned upside down, the entire construction resembles a crab.
REFERENCE
Wilkinson, Frederick. *Swords and Daggers.* New York: Hawthorn Books, 1967.

CRAQUEMARTE. A seventeenth-century cutlass* used by common sailors. It was quite heavy.
REFERENCE
Stone, George Cameron. *A Glossary of the Construction, Decoration, and Use of Arms and Armor.* New York: Jack Brussel, 1961.

CREAN, PATRICK. (c. twentieth century). British fencing master.

Patrick Crean was probably the first twentieth-century fencing master in England to be employed specifically to arrange sword fights for the stage.

His film work includes *The Master of Ballantrae* (1953), starring Errol Flynn, and *The Sword of Sherwood Forest* (1960), a Richard Greene swashbuckler. Crean's work is always efficient and skillful, but rather undistinguished.
REFERENCE
Richards, Jeffrey. *Swordsmen of the Screen.* Boston: Routledge and Kegan Paul, 1977.

CROISE. Pronounced "quaw-zay." It means "to cross."

The *croise* is a defensive binding action—much like the offensive liement or bind—using the elements of leverage and envelopment to both block and hit an opponent in one sweeping motion. In essence, it is a parry and riposte combined into a single action.

As an attacker lunges, the defender angles his own blade slightly in opposition to the incoming weapon the moment the two make contact. When the defender does this, his blade point passes across the attacking blade, "crossing" it.

Rather than knocking the approaching blade away, as a standard parry would do, this action simply resists it. By catching the attacking blade on the foible (weak part) with a stronger portion of the parrying blade, the defender is able to easily guide the attacker's point away from his target area. He has, in effect, turned his blade into a lever, which automatically makes it the stronger of the two.

The defender does not simply want to block the attack, however. To create the optimum effective defensive action, one that does not allow the attacker to continue with his onslaught, a counterattack must be brought into play.

This follow-through is easily accomplished. At the moment the attacker's blade is crossed, the defender should instantly envelop it with a binding action. The bind is produced by directing the point of the defending blade in a half-circle motion. Such a movement not only ensnares the attacker's weapon but also drops the defender's point into direct line with the attacker's target area. Here, if the *croise* has been done correctly, complete and overwhelming control of the exchange is achieved.

The defender then extends his weapon slightly to meet his opponent as the momentum of the lunge carries the attacker forward, thus completing the counterattack.

It should be noted that no lunge is necessary with the *croise* because the attacker has already lunged.

Also, the defender's hand should be maintained at chest level throughout the *croise.* Otherwise, he runs the risk of breaking contact with the attacker's blade, which instantly invalidates the defensive action.

The *croise,* of course, can be done in either the high or low line. The difference is that with the high-line *croise,* the defender's blade moves on top of the attacker's blade. In the case of the low-line *croise,* it ends up moving below the attacker's blade.

Finally, while the *croise* can theoretically be performed in any line, it is executed most effectively in the outside lines of sixte (high-outside) and octave (low-outside). These lines require a minimum of maneuvering to achieve the desired result. *Croises* carried out in the inside lines of quarte (high-inside) and septime (low-inside) require too much overall blade and arm movement to successfully deflect the attacker's point. Hence, such *croises* are less efficient and more susceptible to evasive maneuvering on the part of an attacker than their outside counterparts.

Also known as a "twist."

REFERENCES

Beaumont, C-L. de, ed. *Fencing Technique in Pictures.* London: Hulton Press, 1955.
Palffy-Alpar, Julius. *Sword and Masque.* Philadelphia: F. A. Davis, 1967.

CROSNIER, ROGER. (c. twentieth century). French fencing master.

Son of the famous fencing master Leon Crosnier, who taught fencing in Scotland in the early years of the twentieth century.

Professor Roger Crosnier coached France's Olympic team in 1948 and Britain's Olympic team in 1952. He was also the coach for Britain's national team from 1949 to 1954.

Crosnier wrote a number of books on fencing: *Fencing with the Foil* (1951), *Fencing with the Sabre* (1954), *Fencing with the Epee* (1958), and *Fencing with the Electric Foil* (1961).

REFERENCE

Morton, E. D. *Martini A–Z of Fencing.* London: Queen Anne Press, 1992.

CROSSE BLOWE. In his book, *His Practice* (1595), sixteenth-century fencing master Vincentio Saviolo* uses the term *crosse blowe* to describe the *mandritti,** or all cuts delivered by a swordsman from the right side.

REFERENCES

Castle, Egerton. *Schools and Masters of Fence.* London: George Bell, 1885.

Wise, Arthur. *The Art and History of Personal Combat.* Greenwich, CT: Arma Press, 1971.

CROSS HILT. The bars (quillons*) crossing the sword blade near the handle for the purpose of protecting the hand. At one time in the sword's development, these "branches" were the only form of buffer for the hand.

The habit of kissing one's drawn sword to invoke a blessing was doubtlessly inspired by the simple "cross" design of the weapon (created by the crossbar design) and the obvious religious connotations it invoked.

REFERENCES

Burton, Richard F. *The Book of the Sword.* London: Chatto and Windus, 1884.

Castle, Egerton. *Schools and Masters of Fence.* London: George Bell, 1885.

CROSSING. In George Silver's* *Paradoxes of Defence* (1599),** crossing means to parry.*

REFERENCE

Castle, Egerton. *Schools and Masters of Fence.* London: George Bell, 1885.

CROSS-STEP. To advance or retreat by stepping one foot in front of, or behind, the other.

REFERENCE

Morton, E. D. *Martini A–Z of Fencing.* London: Queen Anne Press, 1992.

CSISZAR, LAJOS. (1903–   ). Hungarian-born American fencing master.

Arriving from Hungary in 1947, Lajos Csiszar quickly established himself as one of the United States' most outstanding fencing coaches. He was a U.S. Olympic coach in 1956, coach of the U.S. team at the World Championships in 1970, a Pan-American Games U.S. team coach in 1971, and an adviser to the U.S. Olympic team in 1972. He was also fencing master at Penn State University for twenty-six years.

REFERENCE

Goldstein, Ralph, ed. "Lajos Csiszar Retires." *American Fencing* (September/October 1974).

CUDGEL. A sturdy stick about the length of a sword fitted with a wickerwork basket hilt. Used for practicing broadsword exercises.

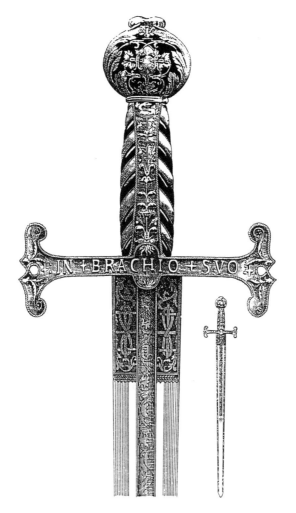

A sword with a cross hilt

No protection was employed in cudgeling. In his treatise on swordplay (1747), English fencing master Captain John Godfrey stated, ''I have purchased my knowledge . . . with many a broken Head and Bruise in every part of me.''

REFERENCES

Castle, Egerton. *Schools and Masters of Fence.* London: George Bell, 1885.

Stone, George Cameron. *A Glossary of the Construction, Decoration, and Use of Arms and Armor.* New York: Jack Brussel, 1961.

CUP HILT. A convex, usually round cup protecting the sword hand on a rapier. Considered a better protection against the thrust than open, bar-arrangement guards, both simple and complex, because of its solidity.

The term "complete cup" refers to a hilt design including crossbars and a knuckle guard combined with the cup.

The earliest cup hilts came from Spain.

The cup guard is the guard form used on the modern sport foil and épée. It may also be referred to a shell guard or *coquille** (which, in fact, means shell).
REFERENCES
Castle, Egerton. *Schools and Masters of Fence.* London: George Bell, 1885.
Palffy-Alpar, Julius. *Sword and Masque.* Philadelphia: F. A. Davis, 1967.

CURTANA. One of three swords brought before the sovereigns of England at their coronation. Known commonly as "the Sword of Mercy," it has a broad, straight, pointless blade.
REFERENCE
Stone, George Cameron. *A Glossary of the Construction, Decoration, and Use of Arms and Armor.* New York: Jack Brussel, 1961.

CURTIS, TONY. (1925–). American film actor.

With an always noticeable Brooklyn accent, Tony Curtis, aka Bernie Schwartz, at first glance seems like an odd choice for swashbuckler films. But an ever-present boyish enthusiasm and charm somehow managed to carry him through roles that would otherwise seem like blatant miscasting.

In his early career, Curtis starred in a handful of entertaining, light costume-adventure films. From playing an Arabian prince in *The Prince Who Was a Thief* (1951) to a medieval knight in *The Black Shield of Falworth* (1954), he attacked each role with an earnest enthusiasm, bounding and fencing across the screen as though born to the genre. His ability with a sword, guided by a natural athletic prowess, was always above average.

Eventually, he turned to more "serious" film roles.

Perhaps his best swashbuckling effort came in 1965, when he starred with Jack Lemmon and Natalie Wood in Blake Edwards's *The Great Race.* Here, he good-naturedly parodied his earlier adventurous movie image. As "the Great Leslie," a professional daredevil, he strode through episodes that took him from the old West to the frozen Arctic to a Hapsburgian-type European kingdom. His foil/sabre duel in a spoof of *The Prisoner of Zenda* is one of the best examples in recent years of film swordplay.

Other Tony Curtis films of the adventure variety include *Son of Ali Baba* (1952), *The Purple Mask* (1955), *The Vikings* (1958), *Spartacus* (1960), *Taras Bulba* (1962), *On My Way to the Crusades I Met a Girl Who . . .* (1969), and *The Count of Monte Cristo* (1975).**
REFERENCES
Lane, Hana, ed. *The World Almanac Book of Who.* New York: World Almanac, 1980.
Parish, James Robert, and Don E. Stanke. *The Swashbucklers.* NJ: Rainbow Books, 1976.

CUSPIS. The ancient Roman name for the point of the sword.
REFERENCE
Burton, Richard F. *Book of the Sword.* London: Chatto and Windus, 1884.

CUSTOMS, SWORD. Many customs exist around the sword. Kissing one's sword may act either as the sealing of a sacred oath, or as hommage toward one's superior. To break a man's sword blade is to degrade him. To give up one's sword is an act of submission. To present someone with a sword is to confer authority upon him.

In medieval times, the touching of a new knight's shoulder with the king's sword blade (dubbing) was a symbolic transference of the ruler's nobility to his subject, elevating him to his new position in society. A sword might be employed as a stand-in for an absent groom at his wedding. At an ancient Teutonic wedding, a sword was always given as a gift to the husband and the wife.

Ancient peoples frequently intertwined the sword with the birth of sons. The Britons of Roman times had a custom whereby the mother of a young male child would serve him his first meal upon the sword of his father: placing the food into the little one's mouth, she would pray to the gods that her son's death as an adult might occur amid arms. When a baby boy was born into a Viking household, the warrior father would symbolically impress upon him the nature of his future existence: laying a sword next to the infant he would announce loudly, "All that I leave you is this weapon. With it you must gain your livelihood and secure your future!"

The Japanese were serious creators of sword conventions. These customs always dealt with the issue of respect for the sword, the soul of the samurai.* A sword had to be situated in an honored spot within a home. To step over a sword laying on the ground was a grievous insult to its owner. A further custom held that to touch one's sword scabbard against another's in passing showed disrespect and disregard for that person and was a splendid way to pick a fight.

The Sikhs of India, a religious sect grounded in military traditions, had one supreme custom regarding the sword. They said when one drew one's blade, it could not be sheathed until it shed blood.

REFERENCES

Barber, Richard. *The Knight and Chivalry.* San Francisco: Harper and Row, 1982.
Burton, Richard F. *The Book of the Sword.* London: Chatto and Windus, 1884.
La Fay, Howard. *The Vikings.* Washington, D.C.: National Geographic Society, 1972.
Stone, George Cameron. *A Glossary of the Construction, Decoration, and Use of Arms and Armor.* New York: Jack Brussel, 1961.

CUT. The earliest form of attack in sword fighting. Using the sharpened side of a sword blade (edge) to administer a wound (as in actual combat) or touch (as in sport sabre fencing).

During the Middle Ages, swords were needed primarily to hack through heavy armor. The cut, then, was the only feasible method of delivering an attack. Thrusting weapon points would merely glance off metal plates.

Yet, even after armor was discarded, the cut continued as the favorite mode of attack, doubtlessly out of habit. Tradition being what it has always been in fencing, changes in technique often took decades to catch on.

Achille Marozzo,* sixteenth-century Italian fencing master and the author of

The cut

the first systematic book on fencing, classified cuts according to the direction from which they were delivered. Cuts coming from the right side were called *mandritti;* cuts from the left, *roversi.*

From the Italian *mano dritta* (meaning right hand), a *mandritto* action, executed with the right edge of a blade called *dritto filo,* could be *tondo,* a horizontally delivered circular cut; *fendente,* a vertically delivered downward cut; *motante,* a vertically delivered upward cut; or *sgualembrato,* an obliquely delivered downward cut.

Roversi cuts delivered with the right edge of the blade were given similar designations.

Cuts were also made with the opposite side of the blade, called the false edge, or *falso filo.* Cuts directed with this portion of the blade at the wrists were called *falso dritto,* and cuts directed at the knees were called *falso manco.*

During this period, little or no attention was paid to point work.

Marozzo's principles of swordplay dominated fencing thought and practice until the mid-sixteenth century, when the rapier, a thrust-oriented weapon, proved attacking with the point to be the most efficient form of personal combat.

The cut continued, however, in military swordplay, where close-distance fighting, on foot or horseback, created a necessity for the use of the sword edge.

Today, the sport of sabre fencing reflects the old-time use of the cut.

Also known as an *estafilade*.

REFERENCES

Castle, Egerton. *Schools and Masters of Fence.* London: George Bell, 1885.

Vebell, Edward. *Sports Illustrated Book of Fencing.* Philadelphia: J. B. Lippincott, 1962.

CUT-AND-THRUST WEAPONS. Swords designed for both cutting and thrusting (*fil et pointe*). These include some early rapiers,* sabres,* and numerous swords of ancient Assyria, India, and Japan.

REFERENCE

Burton, Richard F. *The Book of the Sword.* London: Chatto and Windus, 1884.

CUTLASS. A type of backsword, or single-edged weapon used entirely for cutting. The blade was about eighteen inches long. The name was derived from the French *coutelas,* meaning "large knife."

The name cutlass has been around since the 1400s and has been used to describe a wide variety of weapons of the same general style. In the eighteenth and nineteenth centuries, however, the term was confined to sabres employed on the high seas. These last weapons were usually plain, rugged, heavy-bladed, basket-hilted swords used, for the most part, by common seamen.

Also called a "cutlas," *cutilax,* "curtle axe," *coutelace, coutel* axe, *coutelas, coutel hache,* "cutlash," *coltello, coltellaccio,* and *cutlace.*

REFERENCES

Burton, Richard F. *The Book of the Sword.* London: Chatto and Windus, 1884.

Castle, Egerton. *Schools and Masters of Fence.* London: George Bell, 1885.

Wilkinson, Frederick. *Swords and Daggers.* New York: Hawthorn Books, 1967.

CUT-OVER. English for *coupé.*

REFERENCE

Morton, E. D. *Martini A–Z of Fencing.* London: Queen Anne Press, 1992.

CUTTING AND THRUSTING. The French term *tac et taille* refers to the ability to use a weapon for both cutting and thrusting.

REFERENCE

Burton, Richard F. *The Book of the Sword.* London: Chatto and Windus, 1884.

CUTTING EDGE. That portion of the sword blade—from the point to the hilt—reserved for cutting and slicing.

Also called *le fil, il filo,* and *die Scharfe.*

REFERENCE

Castle, Egerton. *Schools and Masters of Fence.* London: George Bell, 1885.

CUTTING SWORD. Any number of swords whose design and use feature the sharpened edge, or edges, of the blade.

Sir Richard Burton* states in his *Book of the Sword* (1884)** that the idea of the cutting sword was probably first suggested to man in nature, in certain grasses whose sharp blades have ability to cut to the bone and in various animal claws.

Cutting weapons include the sabre, broadsword, backsword, cutlass, hanger, scimitar, *dusack,* falchion, *spadone, espandon, spatha, zweyhander, flamberge, talwar, shashqa,* claymore, baselard, the *katana,* the *jin tachi,* and the *waki-zashi.*

REFERENCES
Burton, Richard F. *The Book of the Sword.* London: Chatto and Windus, 1884.
Castle, Egerton. *Schools and Masters of Fence.* London: George Bell, 1885.
Wilkinson, Frederick. *Swords and Daggers.* New York: Hawthorn Books, 1967.

CUTTING THE COUNTERPARRY. Normally, when a counterparry* is made, the blade tip defines a complete circle, ending up, in theory, exactly where it began. Sometimes, however, when executing a counterparry, the blade tip is improperly dropped at the end of the action, so that it cuts abruptly inward. Here, instead of parrying with the middle of the blade, creating a firm defensive action, contact is made with the foible (weak part). This, of course, undermines the parry. If the point drop is truly pronounced, contact with the oncoming weapon may be missed entirely.

REFERENCE
Morton, E. D. *Martini A–Z of Fencing.* London: Queen Anne Press, 1992.

CUTTING THE LINE. Defined as making a counterparry* in the opposite direction from which it normally may be expected to be made. For instance, when an attack is made into the line of quarte,* the counterparry one most often encounters is that of counter sixte.* When cutting the line, counter quarte is used. Likewise, counter quarte is usually the counterparry that deals with an attack into the line of sixte. But, to cut the line, counter sixte is used.

Cutting the line both blocks the attacking blade and binds it at the same time. The action works because of its unexpected nature.

A second definition explains cutting the line as performing a parry diagonally across the target area from the high line to the low line or from the low line to the high line.

Also known as ''crossing the line.''

REFERENCE
Morton, E. D. *Martini A–Z of Fencing.* London: Queen Anne Press, 1992.

CUT-UNDER. Corresponding to the high line's *coupé,** or cut-over, this attack is done in the low line, from septime to octave. As in its high-line counterpart, the sword arm must be drawn backward at the elbow to commence the action; however, in the case of the cut-under, the attacker's blade passes beneath the opponent's weapon point, rather than over its top.

REFERENCE
Morton, E. D. *Martini A–Z of Fencing.* London: Queen Anne Press, 1992.

CUT VERSUS THRUST. The original function of the sword was to cut. With a few minor exceptions in the history of personal combat, this was the case for hundreds of years. With the advent of the thrusting rapier in the late sixteenth century, however, a controversy arose in the fencing world over which approach to dueling with a sword was better—the cut or the thrust.

The matter was debated with a ferocity usually reserved for religious disagreements. Countless duels, in fact, were fought to establish which style of swordplay was superior.

Eventually, the thrust won out, simply because it proved to be the most efficient method of dispatching an opponent.

In the first place, the mechanics of cutting routinely exposed an attacker's arm and flank to his enemy's blade, while thrusting left one's body relatively covered. Second, the distance necessary to complete a thrust was much shorter than that needed to complete a cut (i.e., the shortest distance between two points is a straight line); hence, a thrust could be delivered more quickly and effortlessly than a cut. Last of all, since killing one's enemy was more often than not the reason for fighting, the thrust, when it hit, was often much more devastating than the cut.

The final stand of the old school of fencing thought came in England, where the cut of the sword was stubbornly defended against the thrust of the rapier.

George Silver,* noted sixteenth-century sword and buckler master, was typical of the English attitude in his unreasoning defense of the rapidly disappearing cut in swordplay. In his *Paradoxes of Defense* (1599),** he openly derided the modern rapier and its thrusting game.

Remarking on the thrusting method of fighting, Silver called it "Schooletrickes and jugling gambalds." He went on to say: "Bring me to a Fencer, I will bring him out of his fence trickes with good downe right blowes, I will make him forget his fence trickes I will warrant him."

Regardless of Silver's protestations and recriminations, by the midseventeenth century even the English had succumbed to the logical superiority of the thrust over the cut.

The sword point, having proven itself time and again under fire, was now supreme.

REFERENCES

Burton, Richard F. *The Book of the Sword.* London: Chatto and Windus, 1884.
Wise, Arthur. *The Art and History of Personal Combat.* Greenwich, CT: Arma Press, 1971.

CYRANO DE BERGERAC. (1620–1655). French swordsman, soldier, novelist, poet, and dramatist.

Cyrano de Bergerac, the historical personage upon whom Edmond Rostand* based his famous play, was an unpleasant, disorderly individual, in every sense a swashbuckler—in the old sense of the word—a loud and brutal bully.

Possessing a huge, unsightly nose, like his fictional counterpart, was doubt-

The cutting sword against the smallsword

Cyrano de Bergerac, from a nineteenth-century illustration

lessly at the bottom of his personality problem. Quarrelsome in the extreme, he would challenge anyone to fight who gave his nose a second glance. It has been written that he killed at least ten men in duels and that his nose became even more grotesque as a result of wounds he received in his various clashes.

But even legends have limits. To show how stories can be stretched out of proportion, the 1981 *American Heritage Dictionary* states quite emphatically that Cyrano de Bergerac "fought over 1,000 duels," which, as anyone with a knowledge of fighting knows, would have been impossible. First, the physical and mental stress of such a regimen would be unbearable. And second, no one could possibly survive that many potentially lethal encounters unscathed. By comparison, the great Japanese swordsman Miyamoto Musashi,* who also actively pursued dueling, fought sixty matches during his lifetime.

On a literary level, Cyrano's novel *Comical History of the States and Empires of the Moon* (1656), an account of an imaginary visit to the moon, has been called the first science-fiction story. His plays *The Pedant Tricked* (1654) and *The Death of Agrippina* (1653) are both recognized as works of considerable merit.

In 1653, he received a sharp blow to the head. Lingering in poor health for over fourteen months, he finally died in 1655, at the age of thirty-five.

REFERENCES

Benet, William Rose. *The Reader's Encyclopedia.* New York: Thomas Y. Crowell, 1961.

Fry, Horace B. "Preface." *Cyrano de Bergerac,* Edmond Rostand. New York: G. W. Dillingham, 1898.

𝒟

DACIAN SWORD. The sword of the Dacians—barbarians found in Eastern Europe (especially Hungary and Transylvania) during the early Roman Empire (27 B.C.–A.D. 100)—possessed a short blade that was somewhat sickle-shaped. Patterned after the ancient Egyptian *khopsh*,* the weapon may be likened to a sabre.*

REFERENCE

Burton, Richard F. *The Book of the Sword.* London: Chatto and Windus, 1884.

DAGGER. A short- to medium-length knife used especially for thrusting. The dagger could be employed both as an individual offensive weapon or in conjunction with a sword as a parrying device. The term "dagger" derives from the Celtic word *dag,* meaning "to stab."

During the Middle Ages, the dagger was initially carried in case one's sword became useless (i.e., it was dropped, broken, or there was insufficient space in which to wield it). It was also used in battle to administer a "mercy stroke" to a mortally wounded opponent.

The technique of utilizing the sword and dagger in swordplay was highly popular during the seventeenth century, but the practice quickly went out of fashion—except in Spain, where it continued well into the eighteenth century.

Types of daggers include the *dague a roulle, stiletto, main gauche, poignard* (also *poinard, pugnale,* and *punal*), *cinqueda,* dirk, *misericorde,* and *estradiot.*

REFERENCES

Castle, Egerton. *Schools and Masters of Fence.* London: George Bell, 1885.

Stone, George Cameron. *A Glossary of the Construction, Decoration, and Use of Arms and Armor.* New York: Jack Brussel, 1961.

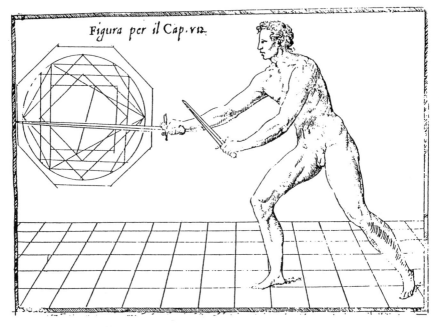

Figura per il Cap.vii.

The dagger being used in conjunction with the sword

DAGGER-SWORD. A leaf-shaped weapon used by the African Unyoro (in what is now Uganda). The short blade had a high rib down the middle. The guardless grip was wrapped with copper wire. The dagger-sword was used for both cutting and thrusting.

REFERENCE

Burton, Richard F. *The Book of the Sword*. London: Chatto and Windus, 1884.

DAIMIO NANAKO. A style of design used on mountings for Japanese swords in which the metal surface is cut diagonally with numerous V grooves at right angles, creating series of square pyramids.

REFERENCE

Stone, George Cameron. *A Glossary of the Construction, Decoration, and Use of Arms and Armor*. New York: Jack Brussel, 1961.

DAISHO. The pair of swords—one long, one short—worn by the samurai.* The longer (*dai*) weapon was the *katana*, the sword used for combat. The shorter (*sho*), or *wakizashi*, was employed as a supplemental sword for cutting off an enemy's head or for ceremonial suicide.

Upon entering the house of a host, a samurai would customarily leave his long sword at the door; the short sword he laid at his right when he sat on the floor.

When a visitor wished to demonstrate special respect for a host, both swords were left at the door.

REFERENCES

Brinkley, Captain F. *Samurai: The Invincible Warriors.* CA: Ohara, 1975.
Nitobe, Inazo. *Bushido: The Warrior's Code.* CA: Ohara, 1975.
Stone, George Cameron. *A Glossary of the Construction, Decoration, and Use of Arms and Armor.* New York: Jack Brussel, 1961.

DALWEL. A two-handed fighting sword of Burmese origin, whose two-foot-long blade was said to be of razor sharpness.

Also called a *dalwey.*

REFERENCE

Burton, Richard F. *The Book of the Sword.* London: Chatto and Windus, 1884.

DAL ZOTTO, FABIO. (1957–). Italian fencing champion.

Fabio Dal Zotto won the Olympic individual foil championship in 1976, at the age of nineteen. He also won a silver medal that same year in the team foil competition.

REFERENCE

Wallechinsky, David. *The Complete Book of the Olympics.* New York: Penguin Books, 1984.

DAMASCENING. Decorating the metal of swords, daggers, and armor by inlaying, or attaching, another metal. Often gold and silver were used for the purpose of damascening.

REFERENCE

Stone, George Cameron. *A Glossary of the Construction, Decoration, and Use of Arms and Armor.* New York: Jack Brussel, 1961.

DAMASCUS SWORD. A sword of extraordinary workmanship produced in Damascus, Syria, during the fifteenth century. The blades were fashioned from a steel that contained a high carbon content, making them both light and durable. The finished product contained a colored surface pattern that ranged from slightly mottled to a series of bars crossing the blade. The latter, prized above all other designs, was known as "Mohamet's Ladder."

Few examples of true Damascus swords exist. The problem when defining such a weapon is that Damascus was a marketplace for the Middle East, and swords were brought there from all over the region, especially Persia and India. All, when sold, ended up being called "Damascus." They may have been weapons of high quality, but that elusive Damascus nature was simply not present.

Today, any sword bearing a particular look and shape—particularly a long, slender, curved blade mounted on a pistol-style grip—may mistakenly be called "Damascus."

REFERENCES
Stone, George Cameron. *A Glossary of the Construction, Decoration, and Use of Arms and Armor.* New York: Jack Brussel, 1961.
Wilkinson, Frederick. *Swords and Daggers.* New York: Hawthorn Books, 1967.

DAMOCLES, THE SWORD OF. In the ancient Greek city of Syracuse, a courtier by the name of Damocles spoke in envious terms of the power, wealth, and happiness of his ruler, the tyrant Dionysius. Dionysius, to teach Damocles a lesson concerning the reality of kingship, invited him to a grand banquet at which he was seated beneath a large sword suspended by a horse hair. Afraid to move for fear of causing the hair to break, Damocles was unable to enjoy the banquet.

The lesson to be learned, of course, was that the life a king, for all its grandeur, was not to be envied, but rather that it was—with the threat of impending violence always hanging over one's head—an existence that could never be truly enjoyed.

REFERENCE
Leach, Maria, ed. *Funk and Wagnalls Standard Dictionary of Folklore, Mythology and Legend.* San Francisco: Harper and Row, 1972.

DAN. In Japanese fencing (kendo), the term *dan* refers to the rank or grade of the fencer.

The ranks are as follows:

judan: tenth grade (highest level)

kudan: ninth grade

hachidan: eighth grade

shichidan: seventh grade

rokudan: sixth grade

godan: fifth grade

yodan: fourth grade

sandan: third grade

nidan: second grade

shodan: first grade

A beginning kendoist must advance through a series of six classes, or *kyu,* before becoming eligible for the first *dan.* This may take up to five years.

Titles of *renshi* for levels four through six and *hanshi* for levels eight through ten may be awarded to a kendoist for contributing unique research to the field and taking a special examination.

REFERENCE
Sasamori, Junzo, and Gordon Warner. *This Is Kendo.* Vermont: Charles E. Tuttle, 1984.

Fencing according to the French master Danet

DANET, GUILLAUME. (c. 1750). French fencing master.

In his time, Danet was considered the final word in the French style of small-sword combat. As syndic, or official representative, of the royal fencing academy, he was a man of considerable influence. However, in attempting to affix many of his own terms and interpretations on recognized fencing actions of the day with his book *L'Art des Armes* (1767),** he managed to set a great portion of the French fencing establishment, a group rife with petty resentments and jealousies, against him.

Still, many of the things Danet taught have become standard fencing technique. He advocated a single "on guard" position as the starting point for all attacks and parries and disapproved of dodging instead of using the sword as the primary means of defense. He also encouraged the use of circular parries. Furthermore, his method of advancing and retreating is still in use today.

In spite of his many disagreements with his contemporaries, he was eventually appointed director of the Ecole Royale d'Armes.

It might be said of Danet, more than any other French master, that his teachings encouraged a moving away from old-style swordplay with sharp weapons to the more controlled approach of academic fencing. His ideas, then, form the foundation of modern fencing.

REFERENCES

Castle, Egerton. *Schools and Masters of Fence.* London: George Bell, 1885.
Wise, Arthur. *The Art and History of Personal Combat.* Greenwich, CT: Arma Press, 1971.

DANIELL, HENRY. (1894–1963). British film actor.

Henry Daniell was an anomaly in swashbuckler films: he had absolutely no fencing ability and even less desire to actually cross swords with anyone; yet, he found himself repeatedly faced with the prospect.

Daniell suffered from polio as a child and was quite awkward in his adult life because of it. According to film fencing master Ralph Faulkner:

It was an unfortunate bit of type-casting for Henry. He had this reputation as a swash-buckling bad guy from his appearance in Warner Brothers' *The Sea Hawk,*** in 1940. He was especially remembered for his fencing. The crazy thing of it was that he'd been heavily doubled by me in his fight scenes. He did almost nothing. That was an instance of Hollywood falling for its own hype.

Anyway, that led to Henry and me doing another picture together a few years later, *The Bandit of Sherwood Forest.*** In 1946, I think it was. Actually, he was about to turn down the picture flat; but when he learned that I was going to be handling the swordplay, he decided to hang in there. "I will play the part of the villain," he said slowly, in that droning British tone of his, "but fencing . . . fencing, Ralph—I loathe it!"

Henry Daniell also fenced in *The Exile* (1947).
REFERENCE
Evangelista, Nick. "Won by the Sword." *Silver Circle News* (Spring 1979).

DANPIRA. A Japanese sword.

Also called *dambira.*
REFERENCE
Stone, George Cameron. *A Glossary of the Construction, Decoration, and Use of Arms and Armor.* New York: Jack Brussel, 1961.

DAO. The national sword of the Naga people of Assam, a province in the northeast section of India.

The *dao* had a straight, stout blade (between nineteen and twenty-five inches long), squared off at the end and tapered downward so that it was narrowest at the hilt. The edge of the blade was chisel-edged. The weapon was without a guard or pommel. The grip was usually made of wood, especially bamboo root.

The *dao,* aside from being a weapon, was also used as a tool for building houses, clearing forest land, and fashioning household implements.
REFERENCE
Stone, George Cameron. *A Glossary of the Construction, Decoration, and Use of Arms and Armor.* New York: Jack Brussel, 1961.

D'ARTAGNAN. The protagonist of Alexandre Dumas's* classic novel *The Three Musketeers* (1844).**

Engaging in sword fights and serving the king and queen of France become the main pursuits of D'Artagnan upon his arrival in Paris in 1625. Straight from his country home in Gascony, he is eager to make a name for himself. His greatest desire is to become a musketeer.

The young man quickly joins forces with a small group of musketeers—

D'Artagnan

Athos, Aramis, and Porthos—three of the greatest swordsmen in France (after he inadvertently challenges each one to a duel).

Perhaps D'Artagnan's greatest moment in *The Three Musketeers* comes when, confronted and threatened by the guards of Cardinal Richelieu for dueling, he throws in his lot with Athos, Porthos, and Aramis against their hated rivals. As Dumas wrote: "It was one of those events which decide the life of a man." Outnumbered, five to four, the friends end up defeating their enemies soundly in a fierce flurry of swordplay. D'Artagnan proves himself a masterful swordsman by beating the cardinal's most dangerous henchman, Jussac.

Following a long string of adventures, our hero eventually accomplishes his goal and is appointed to the king's guards.

The further exploits of D'Artagnan are recounted in a series of novels by Alexandre Dumas known as the "D'Artagnan romances." They take the Gascon right up into old age to the moment, as a marshal of France, he is heroically killed in battle. These novels include *Twenty Years After* (1845) and *The Vicomte de Bragelonne* (1848–1850). The latter is often divided into four separate volumes—*The Vicomte de Bragelonne, Louise de la Vallier, Ten Years Later,* and *The Man in the Iron Mask.*

As an appealing entity of lasting literary merit, D'Artagnan has certainly withstood the test of time. Moreover, he has managed to leap beyond the bounds of his original story line, finding his way into numerous volumes penned by writers other than Dumas. A novel called *D'Artagnan,* by H. Bedford Jones, supposedly based on notes left by Dumas, was published in 1928. French authors Paul Feval and M. Lassez turned out a string of books in the 1920s called "The Years Between" novels; these detailed the adventures of D'Artagnan and Cyrano de Bergerac. D'Artagnan was also featured in an "adult" *Three Musketeers,* written by Tiffany Thayer, in 1943. A 1969 "young adult" book titled *Rapier for Revenge,* by Mildred Allen Butler, had Cyrano de Bergerac as a main character, with D'Artagnan in a supporting role. *The Four Musketeers,* a 1975 novel based on a screenplay for the film *The Four Musketeers* (1975), is perhaps the most recent fictional resurrection of the swashbuckling French swordsman.

As a theatrical character, D'Artagnan turned up as a very, very minor participant in Edmond Rostand's play *Cyrano de Bergerac* (1897). After Cyrano completes his famous "duel in rhyme," D'Artagnan walks up and congratulates him, after which he leaves, never to return in the proceedings.

He resumed his proper starring status, however, as a singing swordsman, no less, in a musical stage production of *The Three Musketeers* (1928), by composer Rudolf Friml.

The D'Artagnan character has been portrayed in film numerous times: 1908, 1911, 1913, 1916, 1921, 1935, 1939 (twice), 1948, 1952, 1953, 1961, 1962, 1964, 1974, 1975, 1977, and 1993.

Actors Douglas Fairbanks, Sr.* (1921 and 1929) and Gene Kelly* (1948) are perhaps the best-known "D'Artagnans."

REFERENCES

Benet, William Rose. *The Reader's Encyclopedia.* New York: Thomas Y. Crowell, 1965.
Dumas, Alexandre. *The Three Musketeers.* New York: Washington Square Press, 1961 (reprint).
Richards, Jeffrey. *Swordsmen of the Screen.* Boston: Routledge and Kegan Paul, 1977.

D'ARTAGNAN, CHARLES DE BAATZ. (1623–1673). French soldier and swordsman.

The historical personage upon whom Alexandre Dumas* based his main character in *The Three Musketeers* (1844).** Much of the real-life D'Artagnan's actual life is woven into the famous fictional work.

D'Artagnan's "life" was first portrayed in Gatien de Courtilz's (sometimes

Courtilz de Sandraz) apocryphal *Memoirs of M. d'Artagnan, Captain-Lieutenant in the First Company of the King's Musketeers* (1700 and 1704). This book contained many elements later employed by Dumas.
REFERENCE
Benet, William Rose. *The Reader's Encyclopedia.* New York: Thomas Y. Crowell, 1965.
Maurois, André. *Alexandre Dumas.* New York: Alfred A. Knopf, 1955.

DAS. A Burmese sword of the *dha* variety. Usually with a long, slightly curved blade, no hand guard, and a decorated grip.
REFERENCE
Stone, George Cameron. *Glossary of the Construction, Decoration, and Use of Arms and Armor.* New York: Jack Brussel, 1967.

D'ASARO, MICHAEL. (1939–   ). U.S. fencing master.
   Michael D'Asaro began fencing in high school. Becoming a champion in his senior year, he won a scholarship to New York University. Studying under the great Hungarian coach Csaba Elthes, he rose quickly in U.S. fencing ranks. In 1960, he was a member of the U.S. Olympic sabre team, which took fourth place that year. In 1962, D'Asaro was the U.S. national sabre champion.
   In time, D'Asaro became a fencing master and set up operations in San Jose, California, where he began developing his own line of champion fencers, including his own wife and son. D'Asaro also coached a number of Junior World Champion teams.
   In 1984, Michael D'Asaro was ranked No. 2 fencing coach in the United States by the United States Fencing Association.
REFERENCE
Dart, John. "No. 2 Fencing Coach Doesn't Make Five-Man Olympic Staff." *Los Angeles Times,* July 1984.
Van Waters, Roger. "An Interview with Mike D'Asaro." *American Fencing* (May/June 1977).

DEATHS, DUELING-RELATED. From the rough-and-tumble exertions of the cutting sword fight to the more studied thrusting mayhem of rapier play to the swift and energetic exchanges of smallsword fencing, the sword's primary purpose was to kill. Whether it was used to dispatch an opponent in personal combat or an enemy soldier in a pitched battle, spilling blood in an efficient manner was still the ultimate goal. Death, in a way, became a positive result— at least for the victor.
   Death could come instantly with a well-placed hit to a vital spot or days later from internal injuries caused by an intruding rapier point. Moreover, the outcome of a sword fight was not necessarily the cut-and-dried experience one might expect from watching the studied fencing in old swashbuckler movies. In confrontations of the blade, the winner sometimes died of wounds received, right along with the loser. Occasionally, death for both participants of a fight was

simultaneous. In his book *Paradoxes of Defence* (1559),** George Silver* tells us: "Two Captaines at Southhampton . . . fel at strife, drew their Rapiers, and presently, being desperate, hardie, or resolute, as they call it, with all force and over great speed, ran with their rapiers one at the other, and were both slain." Men fought with swords as a matter of custom, but not all of them were experts with the weapon they used.

The thrust, as history has shown us, proved to be more devastating than the cut. A man could often survive even maiming slices to the flesh and go on to win his duel; but a thrust of a few inches of steel into the throat or abdomen spelled certain death—if not from the wound itself, from infection. There was no effective medical treatment for a hole poked in a liver or a lung.

Sword fights were used to solve disputes. Knights of the Middle Ages fought duels of honor and of chivalry. They fought duels to determine the outcome of judicial disputes. Death became the predominant deciding factor of truth. A knight, for all his claims to righteousness, might be hacked to bits in single combat or die suffocating in armor that was too battered for air to reach him in tournament play with a hundred competitors. In medieval terms, God obviously smiled on a winner.

An example of a knightly encounter was the famous duel between the Lords Jarnac* and La Chastaigneraye* in 1547. The fight came about because of a supposed lie La Chastaigneraye had told King Francis I of France regarding what he believed to be a relationship of a sexual nature between Jarnac and Jarnac's mother-in-law. Jarnac took offense, said it was untrue, and issued a challenge. La Chastaigneraye was considered the greatest swordsman in France, yet, when honor was at stake, there was no alternative but to fight.

The duel was fought before the entire French court on July 10, 1547. La Chastaigneraye, of course, was considered the favorite. But Jarnac had a strategy. After a few energetic cuts had been made, and wounds were suffered on both sides, Jarnac made a pass at his enemy and sliced him on the left thigh. He quickly followed up by wounding La Chastaigneraye on the right thigh, at which point La Chastaigneraye fell to the ground. Presently, Jarnac called on his foe to acknowledge his lie, but the latter refused. La Chastaigneraye even attempted to rise up and strike Jarnac with his weapon but was unable to regain his feet. Eventually, Jarnac took La Chastaigneraye's sword and dagger away from him, and the king called a halt to the duel. Disgraced and humiliated by his loss, La Chastaigneraye rejected medical attention and quickly bled to death.

During the seventeenth and eighteenth centuries, private dueling became a mania all across Europe. France, a country known for its hot-tempered citizens, embraced the lethal fad, carrying it to new heights of butchery. Men fought over the slightest provocation—an imagined slight of one's mistress, jealousy of a reputation, or one individual's dislike of the color of another man's hat. From 1600 to 1780, according to historian Egerton Castle* in his book *Schools and Masters of Fence* (1885),** "40,000 valiant gentlemen [were] killed in single combats which arose generally on the most futile grounds."

The fatal outcome of a seventeenth-century duel

The Chevalier d'Andrieux, having killed seventy-one men in sword duels by the time he was thirty, was accosted by an opponent who announced, "Chevalier, you will be the tenth man I have killed." The chevalier replied, "And you will be my seventy-second." This, apparently, was as good a reason to fight as any. D'Andrieux then ran the man through, killing him on the spot.

Another notorious duelist, the Chevalier de Guise,* was best known for killing a father and son in successive encounters in 1613. The first duel, fought with the elderly Baron de Luz over a disputed historical fact, was concluded in a matter of seconds. The subsequent contest with the baron's son, fought with swords on horseback, was a desperate affair, but, once again, the savage and merciless de Guise was triumphant. He won by seizing his antagonist's sword arm and driving his own weapon through the young man's throat.

King Louis XIV, calling the incessant slaughter of his subjects a "monstrous frenzy,'' attempted to stamp out the practice of dueling by issuing over ten coercive edicts that threatened confiscation of property, torture, exile, and even death for anyone participating in these bloody pastimes. His legal interventions, however, did little to stem the flood tide of slain Frenchmen. Only time and a gradual waning interest in the sword as an expression of cultural identity managed to solve the problem.

England, never quite as fanatical as France over dueling, nevertheless had its share of personal combats. Old English swordsmen were never pleased with the influx of Italian fencing masters—with their newfangled rapiers—to their shores, and this loathing was repeatedly expressed in armed hostilities.

George Silver,* in his book *Paradoxes of Defence,*** describes a duel between a stalwart countryman named Cheese, ''a very tall man,'' and a certain Italian fencing master named Jeronimo Bonetti. Cheese, upset over Jeronimo's derisive attitude regarding English swordsmen, challenged the transgressor to fight. Bonetti, responding to the threat, drew his rapier and dagger and made himself ready in his best on-guard position. Despite his ''Italienated'' skill, however, according to Silver, ''Cheese with his Sword with two thrusts ran into the bodie and slue him.'' A quick and bloody end for a troublesome foreigner.

But, whatever the reason for crossing swords, the English often approached their strife with a civility that belied its murderous intent. A duel fought between Sir H. Bellasses and Tom Porter in 1667 attests to this strange juxtaposition of attitudes.

According to the famous diarist Samuel Pepys, a witness to the incident, these two friends, having had too much to drink at a dinner party, came to quarrel over some trivial matter, at which point Sir H. Bellasses gave Tom Porter a cuff on the ear. They would have fought immediately, but the other dinner guests prevented them.

Tom Porter left the scene and waited for Bellasses in the road. When the latter's coach approached, Porter stopped it and, as Pepys reported, ''bade Sir H. Bellasses come out. 'Why,' said Sir H. Bellasses, 'you will not hurt me coming out, will you?'—'No,' says Tom Porter. So out he went, and both drew. Tom Porter asked him whether he was ready. The other answered he was; and they fell to fight.''

Presently, they managed to wound one another, but Sir H. Bellasses took the worst of it. As it transpired, he was injured so badly he could not continue. Calling Porter to him, Pepys went on, Bellasses ''kissed him, and bade him shift for himself; 'for,' says he, 'Tom thou has hurt me; but I will make shift to stand on my legs till thou mayest withdraw, and the world not take notice of thee; for I would not have thee troubled for what thou hast done.' ''

Sir H. Bellasses died a few days later. As for Tom Porter, whose wound was also quite serious, Pepys merely remarked that he was ''ill.'' The writer finished his account with, ''It is pretty to see how the world talk of them, as a couple of fools, that killed one another out of love.''

The smallsword, the dueling weapon of the eighteenth century, became the ultimate killing weapon. With its lightness and needle-sharp point, it could be maneuvered in a way that allowed for maximum damage to an opponent. As was noted by Arthur Wise in his book, *The Art and History of Personal Combat* (1971), the smallsword, in its day, became the universal answer to the question, How do I kill my opponent?

By the end of the eighteenth century, duels with swords became almost non-existent. By 1780, men were no longer wearing weapons as part of their daily dress. Swordplay for the purpose of killing had transmuted into fencing as an athletic pursuit. Duels, for the most part, when they did come about, were handled with pistols.

France was probably the last country to give up the sword as a killing device, taking it clear into the first half of the twentieth century before it was finally swept aside forever by a world whose ancient attitudes were swiftly altered by the monumental intrusion of World War I.

REFERENCES

Baldick, Robert. *The Duel.* New York: Spring Books, 1970.

Castle, Egerton. *Schools and Masters of Fence.* London: George Bell, 1885.

Wise, Arthur. *The Art and History of Personal Combat.* Greenwich, CT: Arma Press, 1971.

DEATHS, FENCING-RELATED. For an activity so heavily entrenched in a history of violent bloodletting, modern fencing has proved to be a sport of relatively few fatalities. In a study appearing in the medical magazine *Lancet* in 1976, there were only four reported fencing fatalities between 1936 and 1976, and all, according to the article, "were due to a lack of proper equipment."

More recently, there was the death of Soviet fencer Vladimir Lapitsky, who was killed in the 1980 Moscow Olympics when his opponent's broken foil blade severed blood vessels in his chest. A British fencer was killed in 1983, when his opponent's épée blade snapped and stabbed him in the throat. In early 1983, a seventeen-year-old West German foil fencer was killed when his thirteen-year-old opponent's broken blade entered his heart.

But perhaps the best-publicized fencing fatality of the twentieth century was the death of Soviet world fencing champion Vladimir Smirnov* at the 1982 championship tournament in Rome, Italy. During a bout with a West German fencer, Smirnov's fencing mask was pierced by a broken foil blade that entered his eye and continued into his brain.

This spate of fencing deaths set off a controversy in the fencing world that led to a questioning of the quality of fencing uniforms, the structural makeup of fencing blades, the style of grips used on weapons, even the way modern fencing bouts are fought. As sometimes happens with heated disagreements, however, little actual change was effected.

Still, it is best to remember that, with hundreds of thousands of fencers participating in the sport worldwide every year, relatively few people are ever seriously injured, much less killed. As was noted by the late fencing master and

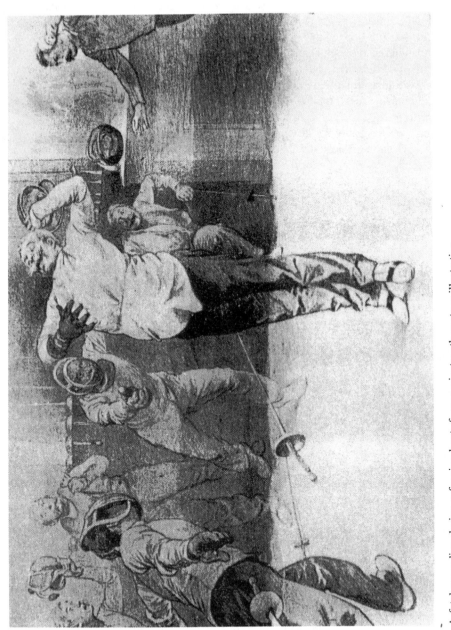

A fatal wounding during a fencing bout, from a nineteenth-century illustration

former Olympic competitor Ralph Faulkner,* "In spite of its apparent violent nature, fencing is, at its root, a sport of control. When approached with adequate precautions, and a proper knowledge of its workings, fencing is safe enough for even young children to participate in."

REFERENCES

Clery, Raoul. "A Propos D'un Accident." *American Fencing* (November/December 1983).

Conte, Mickey, ed. "How Safe Is Fencing?" *Southern California AFLA Newsletter* (March/April 1980).

Dart, John. "Danger: Fencing." *Los Angeles Times,* July 1984.

DECEPTION. Simply put, a deception is an evasion—made by the attacker—of an opponent's defensive action (parry). Normally, the deception follows a feint (threat) of an attack that has managed to draw one's adversary into making a parry. The deception, if successful, should then be followed by a lunge. The feint-deception combination, in essence, creates a hole in a defensive structure that can be exploited.

There are two types of deceptions: one that evades a lateral parry (a parry that travels in a straight line) and one that evades a counterparry (a parry that travels in a circle).

The deception that evades a lateral parry does so by dropping beneath it, causing the defender's blade to simply move out of the way. The deception that evades a counterparry does so by going in the same direction that the parry is traveling, in a sense, outrunning it. The type of deception used is always determined by the type of parry the defender decides to use.

A deception that is not followed immediately by a lunge—if it has been used to further misdirect an opponent—is considered a feint.

Deceptions may also be called "evasive thrusts" or "circulations."

REFERENCE

Palffy-Alpar, Julius. *Sword and Masque.* Philadelphia: F. A. Davis, 1967.

DECISIVE PLAY. This is defined as fighting with "sharps," that is, swords with points. The use of these, of course, produced results that were unmistakably apparent.

REFERENCE

Morton, E. D. *Martini A–Z of Fencing.* London: Queen Anne Press, 1992.

DEDANS. Pronounced "deh-dah." The inside line. Also taught as only the high inside line.

REFERENCE

Stevenson, John. *Fencing.* London: Briggs, 1935.

DEGAGÉ. A simple attack that travels from one line to another line by passing beneath an opponent's blade. In English the *degagé* is called a "disengage." Its name comes from the fact that when two blades are engaged (touching), this action disengages (separates) them.

The *degagé* is classified as an "indirect" simple attack because it changes lines.

The *degagé* was described by Italian fencing master Salvator Fabris* in his book *De lo Scherma, overo scienza d'arme* (1606). In 1653, French fencing master Charles Besnard* referred to the action as a *deliement.* Philibert de La Tousche,* in his *Les Vrays Principles de l'Espee Seule* (1670), was the first teacher to use the actual term *degagé.*

Also called a disengagement, a *degagément,* and a *cavazione,* old Italian masters called the *degagé* a *cavatione di tempo.*

REFERENCES

Castle, Egerton. *Schools and Masters of Fence.* London: George Bell, 1885.

Palffy-Alpar, Julius. *Sword and Masque.* Philadelphia: F. A. Davis, 1967.

DE GUISE, LOUIS, CHEVALIER. (c. 1600). French nobleman and fanatical duelist during the reign of Louis XIII.

Best known not for the number of men he dispatched but for killing a father and son in successive sword fights. Because of his high rank in the French court, de Guise was never punished for his dueling excesses.

REFERENCE

Baldick, Robert. *The Duel.* New York: Spring Books, 1965.

DEHORS. Pronounced "de-or." The outside line. Also taught as only the low outside line.

REFERENCE

Stevenson, John. *Fencing.* London: Briggs, 1935.

DE LA FALAISE, GEORGES. (c. 1900). French fencing champion.

Georges de la Falaise was the first world individual sabre champion, in 1906.

REFERENCE

Palffy-Alpar, Julius. *Sword and Masque.* Philadelphia: F. A. Davis, 1967.

DELFINO, GIUSEPPE. (1922–   ). Italian épée fencing champion.

Giuseppe Delfino took second place in the individual épée event at the 1956 Olympics. He took first place in individual épée at the 1960 Olympics. He was also a member of numerous championship Italian Olympic épée teams: 1952 (first), 1956 (first), 1960 (first), and 1964 (second).

REFERENCE

Wallechinsky, David. *The Complete Book of the Olympics.* New York: Penguin Books, 1984.

DE LONGIS, ANTHONY. (1950–   ). American combat choreographer for stage and film.

As a fight arranger, Anthony De Longis has managed to blend the skills of a fencer with the adroitness of Oriental martial arts. Inspired to get into film work because of his love of samurai movies, he quickly made a name for himself in action films and stage work.

His main influences in his developing technique were fencing master Ralph Faulkner* and martial artist Dan Inosanto, a former student of Bruce Lee.

De Longis has staged swordplay over the years for such classics as *Macbeth, Rashomon, Romeo and Juliet, Othello,* and *Hamlet.* His *Cyrano de Bergerac* (1973),** starring Richard Chamberlain, received especially good reviews. He has also worked closely with Universal Studios Tours to produce a "Conan the Barbarian Stage Spectacular" in which all sorts of swordplay are featured.

His film sword work includes *Sword and Sorcerer* (1983), *Warrior and the Sorceress* (1985), and *Masters of the Universe* (1987).

Always on the lookout for new combat skills to add to his repertoire, De Longis has even mastered the use of the bullwhip, which he was able to effectively channel into the film *Batman Returns* (1992).

In addition to his own theatrical activities, Tony De Longis was the stage combat instructor for the University of California–Los Angeles Theatre Arts Department for twenty years.

REFERENCES

Cavaleri, Ray. "Anthony De Longis." Resume. Los Angeles: Cavaleri and Associates, 1993.

De Longis, Anthony. "The Bullwhip—Catwoman's Weapon of Choice." *Inside Karate* (August 1992).

DEMARCHES. Described by sixteenth-century French fencing master Henry de Sainct Didier* in his book *Traicte Contenant les Secrets du Premier Livre sur l'Espee Seule* (1573)** as systems of stepping by which combatants should close distance or retreat. By modern standards, his actions were as unscientific and dangerous as they were complicated and lacking in reason.

REFERENCES

Castle, Egerton. *Schools and Masters of Fence.* London: George Bell, 1885.

Wise, Arthur. *The Art and History of Personal Combat.* Greenwich, CT: Arma Press, 1971.

DEMEANOR, FENCING. Early fencing masters, eager to add a sense of science to their art, were ever on the lookout for new angles upon which to formulate complex theories. One of these was the attempt to classify swordsmen according to their personalities, or humors, and thereby gauge specific actions to use against each type of individual.

For instance, sixteenth-century Spanish fencing masters Jeronimo de Carranza* and Don Luis Pacheco de Narvaez* talked at length of violent, natural, nervous, choleric, and phlegmatic swordsmen. They, of course, possessed the most elaborate remedies imaginable with which to counter each group—remedies couched in esoteric philosophy, secret knowledge, and geometrically oriented movement.

Over one hundred years later, the noted Scottish master William Hope* drew up his own list of character catagories. His roster included such labels as careless, slow, timorous, lax, calm, vigorous, hasty, judgmental, passionate, furious, and irregular. The ideal swordsman, concluded Hope, possessed a combination of three virtues: calmness, vigor, and judgment. Against these, he believed, nothing could stand.

While attempts to bring psychological awareness into personal combat were well intentioned, they were nevertheless too general and unspecific to be of any real use. Although men like Narvaez and Hope were skilled fencing masters, psychologists they were not.

In the end, as was noted by Egerton Castle* in his book *Schools and Masters of Fence* (1885), calmness under fire might have been the one valuable swordsman trait upon which to focus. Practiced coolness, observed Castle, "even with imperfect method, is of course of immense material use."

REFERENCE

Castle, Egerton. *Schools and Masters of Fence.* London: George Bell, 1885.

DEMI-CONTRE. A parry that moved in a half circle from the high line to the low line, or vice versa.

Today it is called a "semicircular" parry.

REFERENCES

Castle, Egerton. *Schools and Masters of Fence.* London: George Bell, 1884.

Palffy-Alpar, Julius. *Sword and Masque.* Philadelphia: F. A. Davis, 1967.

DEREK, JOHN. (1926–   ). American film actor, photographer, and husband of actress Bo Derek.

Early in his film career, Derek starred in numerous medium- and low-budget swashbuckler movies. His best costume-adventure film was his first, *The Rogues of Sherwood Forest* (1950), in which he played the son of Robin Hood.

Derek was convincing as a theatrical hero. Both good-looking and athletic, he was the picture of a dashing swordsman. His fencing—much of which was coached by film fencing master Ralph Faulkner*—always had an air of control about it. The greatest drawback to the actor's career was that he tested best, according to polls, mainly among adolescent girls.

John Derek also fenced in *Mask of the Avenger* (1951), *The Adventures of Hajji Baba* (1954), *Prince of Pirates* (1954), and *Omar Khayyam* (1957).

REFERENCES

Halliwell, Leslie. *Halliwell's Filmgoer's and Video Viewer's Companion.* New York: Charles Scribner's Sons, 1988.

Richards, Jeffrey. *Swordsmen of the Screen.* Boston: Routledge and Kegan Paul, 1977.

DERIVED ATTACK. An attack whose nature is set up in advance based on the previous responses of an opponent.

REFERENCE

Morton, E. D. *Martini A–Z of Fencing.* London: Queen Anne Press, 1992.

DEROBEMENT. An evasive slide off an opponent's parrying blade.

The derobement may be executed in conjunction with a *coulé* feint (a feint that runs—with contact—along an opponent's blade) that has caused a lateral parry. It can also be employed to escape an attacker's binding action.

The derobement never resists an opponent's blade pressure. When executed properly, the action involves a subtle, light slipping away.
REFERENCES
Handleman, Rob. "Fencing Glossary." *American Fencing* (February/March 1978).
Palffy-Alpar, Julius. *Sword and Masque.* Philadelphia: F. A. Davis, 1967.

DESSOUS. Pronounced "deh-soo." The low line. Also taught as only the low left line.
REFERENCE
Stevenson, John. *Fencing.* London: Briggs, 1935.

DESSUS. Pronounced "deh-see." The high line. Also taught as only the high right line.
REFERENCE
Stevenson, John. *Fencing.* London: Briggs, 1935.

DESTROYING PARRY. A parry* that negates the movement of an attack. That is, an opponent, engaged in the line of sixte, attacks into the line of quatre. A counterparry—counter sixte—is then made, taking the attacking blade back into the line of sixte, where it began.

Also called a "destructive parry."
REFERENCE
Morton, E. D. *Martini A–Z of Fencing.* London: Queen Anne Press, 1992.

DETACHED PARRY. A parry*—counter or lateral—that, once contact has been successfully established, rebounds instantaneously off an opponent's blade.
REFERENCE
Morton, E. D. *Martini A–Z of Fencing.* London: Queen Anne Press, 1992.

DETACHED RIPOSTE. A riposte* that instantaneously separates from one's opponent's parried blade and proceeds forward without further contact.
REFERENCE
Morton, E. D. *Martini A–Z of Fencing.* London: Queen Anne Press, 1992.

DEVELOPMENT. A type of thrust, described by mid–seventeenth-century fencing master Charles Besnard* in his book *Le Maistre d'Arme Liberal* (1653),** that strongly resembled a modern lunge. It was employed mostly by the French.

While not used with any real consistency among swordsmen of that time period, it was mainly brought into play when attacking into the line of quarte.* If the attack being used was of a complicated nature, the fencer often reverted to passing (stepping with one foot in front of the other to close distance).
REFERENCE
Castle, Egerton. *Schools and Masters of Fence.* London: George Bell, 1885.

DEVIAMENTO. In Italian, the deflection of an opponent's blade.
REFERENCE
Morton, E. D. *Martini A–Z of Fencing.* London: Queen Anne Press, 1992.

DEVIATION. The action of one blade pressing, always lightly, against another blade.
REFERENCE
Morton, E. D. *Martini A–Z of Fencing.* London: Queen Anne Press, 1992.

DHA. The national sword of Burma. The *dha* possessed a slightly curved, single-edged blade (between sixteen and twenty-four inches long). The guardless grip, fashioned of wood or ivory, was usually ornately decorated. While most examples of this weapon have sharp points, a few have been known to possess square ends.

The scabbard of the *dha* was fashioned of wood and worn over the shoulder.
REFERENCE
Stone, George Cameron. *A Glossary of the Construction, Decoration, and Use of Arms and Armor.* New York: Jack Brussel, 1961.

DHOUP. An Indian sword with a straight, blunt-ended, single-edged blade. The pommel is disk-shaped, with a spike on the end. The hilt is made up of a broad plate guard and a knuckle guard of considerable width.

The *dhoup* is also known by the name *khanda.*
REFERENCE
Stone, George Cameron. *A Glossary of the Construction, Decoration, and Use of Arms and Armor.* New York: Jack Brussel, 1961.

DIAMOND, PETER. (c. twentieth century). British fencing master.

During his lengthy career, Peter Diamond has staged fencing duels for the London Royal Opera House, the Old Vic, and Britain's National Theatre. For film, he staged the fencing in *Star Wars* (1977),** *The Empire Strikes Back* (1980),** and *Return of the Jedi* (1983).** He was also responsible for the 1989–1990 television series "The New Zorro,"** starring Duncan Regehr.
REFERENCE
Yenne, Bill. *The Legend of Zorro.* New York: Mallard Press, 1991.

DICKENS, CHARLES. (1812–1870). British novelist, best known for his classic books *Oliver Twist* (1837–1839), *A Christmas Carol* (1843), and *David Copperfield* (1849–1850).

A little-known fact about Charles Dickens is that he was an avid fencer. This grew out of his own theatrical career as an actor. He was a student of Salle Bertrand, the great fencing school of mid-Victorian England.

It is not unusual, then, that swordplay should have found its way into Dickens's writing. The novelist must have found it a simple task to create a scene based on his own personal experiences.

A scene from Charles Dickens's *Nicholas Nickleby*

In the novel *Nicholas Nickleby* (1883–1884), for instance, Dickens interjected a moment of theatrical swordplay encountered by the Nicholas character as he enters a theatrical establishment where he hopes to gain employment. The scene is, in fact, a humorous burlesque of stage combats:

Nicholas was prepared for something odd, but not for something quite so odd as the sight he encountered. At the upper end of the room were a couple of boys, one of them very tall and the other very short, both dressed as sailors—or at least as theatrical sailors, with belts, buckles, pigtails, and pistols complete—fighting what is called in playbills a terrific combat, with two of those short broadswords with basket hilts which are commonly used at our minor theatres. The short boy had gained a great advantage over the tall boy, who was reduced to mortal strait, and both were overlooked by a large heavy man, perched against a corner of a table, who emphatically abjured them to strike a little more fire out of the swords, and they couldn't fail to bring the house down, on the very first night.

The two combatants went to work afresh, and chopped away until the swords emitted a shower of sparks to the great satisfaction of Mr. Crummles, who appeared to consider this a very great point indeed. The engagement commenced with about two hundred chops administered by the short sailor and the tall sailor alternately, without producing any particular result, until the short sailor was chopped down on one knee; but this was nothing to him, for he worked himself about on one knee with the assistance of his left hand, and fought most desperately until the tall sailor chopped his sword out of his grasp. Now, the inference was, that the short sailor, reduced to his extremity, would give in at once and cry quarter, but, instead of that, he all of a sudden drew a large pistol from his belt and presented it in the face of the tall sailor, who was so overcome at this (not expecting it) that he let the short sailor pick up his sword and begin again. Then, the chopping recommenced, and a variety of fancy chops were administered on both sides; such as chops dealt with the left hand, and under the leg, and over the right shoulder, and over the left; and when the short sailor made a vigourous cut at the tall sailor's legs, the tall sailor jumped over the short sailor's sword, wherefore to balance the matter, and make it all fair, the tall sailor administered the same cut, and the short sailor jumped over his sword. After this, there was a good deal of dodging about, and hitching up of the inexpressibles in the absence of braces, and then the short sailor (who was the moral character evidently, for he always had the best of it) made a violent demonstration and closed with the tall sailor, who, after a few unavailing struggles, went down, and expired in great torture as the short sailor put his foot upon his breast, and bore a hole in him through and through.

REFERENCES
Benet, William Rose. *The Reader's Encyclopedia.* Thomas Y. Crowell, 1965.
Dickens, Charles. *Nicholas Nickleby.* New York: P. F. Collier, 1893.

DIG. An attack in which the sword hand is well out of line, while the blade point is angled inward toward the target.
REFERENCE
Morton, E. D. *Martini A–Z of Fencing.* London: Queen Anne Press, 1992.

DILLON-CAVANAGH, GEORGES. (c. 1900). French fencing champion.
Georges Dillon-Cavanagh, an Irish-Frenchman, was the first world individual foil champion, in 1906.
REFERENCE
Palffy-Alpar, Julius. *Sword and Masque.* Philadelphia: F. A. Davis, 1967.

DIMENSIONS OF HISTORICAL WEAPONS.

Prehistoric Period
Stone, bone, or wood swords—approximately 19 inches long.

Ancient Period

Greek sword—approximately 20 inches long; blade, 1-⅝ inches wide.

Roman sword—between 19 and 27 inches long; blade, 1-⅝ inches wide.

Medieval Period (up to first half of the sixteenth century)

Sword—about 40 inches long; blade, from 1-⅛ to 3-⅛ inches wide.

Two-handed sword—from 61 to 78 inches long; blade, between 1-⅝ and 2-⅜ inches wide.

Renaissance (beginning during the second half of sixteenth century)

Early rapier (cut and thrust)—approximately 50 to 55 inches long; blade, 1-⅛ inches wide.

Late Sixteenth Century

Rapier (thrust only)—approximately 65 inches long; blade, 1-⅛ inches wide.

Early Seventeenth Century

Rapier—between 39 and 50 inches long; blade, 1-⅛ inches wide.

Broadsword—approximately 41 inches long; blade, 1-¾ inches wide.

Mid-Seventeenth Century

Rapier—approximately 45 inches long; blade, 1-⅛ inches wide.

Military sword—between 39 and 43 inches long; blade, 1-½ inches wide.

Late Seventeenth Century

Rapier—approximately 45 inches long; blade, 1-⅛ inches wide.

Transition rapier—between 37 and 50 inches long; blade, between 1 and 1-⅛ inches wide.

Smallsword—between 31 and 40 inches long; blade, 1 inch wide.

Military sword—approximately 41 inches long.

Eighteenth Century

Smallsword—between 36 and 37 inches long; blade, 1 inch wide.

Military sword—between 30 and 39 inches long; blade, 1-½ inches wide.

Nineteenth Century

Smallsword—same as previous century.

Épée du combat—approximately 36 inches long; blade, 1 inch wide.

Dueling sabre—approximately 42 inches long; blade, ½ inch wide.

Military sword—between 33 and 39 inches long; blade, 1-½ inches wide.

Twentieth Century

Military sword—approximately 37 to 42 inches long; blade, 1 inch wide.

REFERENCES

Palffy-Alpar, Julius. *Sword and Masque.* Philadelphia: F. A. Davis, 1967.
Wilkinson, Frederick. *Swords and Daggers.* New York: Hawthorn Books, 1967.

DIMENSIONS OF WEAPONS—MODERN.

Foil—43 inches long.

Épée—43 inches long.

Sabre—41-⅜ inches long.

REFERENCE

U.S. Fencing Association, ed. *Operations Manual.* Colorado Springs, CO: U.S. Fencing Association, 1985.

DIRECT. Any offensive or defensive action in fencing that does not detour from one line into another line.

REFERENCE

Handelman, Rob. "Fencing Glossary." *American Fencing* (May/June 1978).

DIRECT. To control and judge the actions in a fencing bout.

REFERENCE

U.S. Fencing Association, ed. *Operations Manual.* Colorado Springs, CO: U.S. Fencing Association, 1985.

DIRECT ATTACK. An attack that is delivered, without hesitation, in a straight line* (i.e., the action must be executed in the same line in which the fencer is on guard).

Any change of line or break in timing within the attack automatically negates its "direct" status.

The direct attack is classified as a "simple"* attack.

Also called a "direct thrust," a "straight attack," and a *coup droit.*

REFERENCES

Handelman, Rob. "Fencing Glossary." *American Fencing* (February/March 1978).

Palffy-Alpar, Julius. *Sword and Masque.* Philadelphia: F. A. Davis, 1967.

DIRECT PARRY. A parry performed without changing from one high line* to the other high line or from one low line* to the other low line.

REFERENCE

Handelman, Rob. "Fencing Glossary." *American Fencing* (May/June 1978).

DIRECT PASSAGE. Direct movement of the sword blade from one line to another line. The direct passages are from quarte* to sixte* or from sixte to quarte; and from octave* to septime* or from septime to octave.

REFERENCE

Palffy-Alpar, Julius. *Sword and Masque.* Philadelphia: F. A. Davis, 1967.

DIRECTOR. The official overseer of a fencing bout.

The director controls the encounters between fencers, giving commands to those on the fencing strip to "begin" and to "halt" their actions; penalizes individuals for violations of rules; and acknowledges touches.

The director is aided by four judges, but the final decision of who has touched whom during any given fencing exchange is up to him.

During the early days of organized fencing competition, directing was done entirely by sight. Today, with the aid of electrical scoring machines, the director's job has been simplified greatly (the scoring box gives an immediate response when a touch—either "on target" or "off target"—has occurred; the director merely decides which fencer has established a "right-of-way," or valid right to hit). Directors work with scoring boxes at official fencing tournaments, that is, tournaments run by the U.S. Fencing Association (USFA).

Directors must follow the rules of fencing set down by the USFA and the Federation Internationale d'Escrime (FIE).

For many years, the expertise of a director depended entirely on his fencing experience. Today, the USFA holds clinics where proper directorial skills are taught, and directors are rated by their juridical abilities.

The director may also be called the president.

REFERENCE

U.S. Fencing Association, ed. *Operations Manual.* Colorado Springs, CO: U.S. Fencing Association, 1985.

DIRECT RIPOSTE. Following a successful parry,* a riposte* (counterattack) that is executed immediately in the same line in which the parry was made is said to be a direct riposte.

Also called a "straight" riposte.

REFERENCE

Palffy-Alpar, Julius. *Sword and Masque.* Philadelphia: F. A. Davis, 1967.

DIRK. Besides being the term for a dagger carried by Scottish Highlanders, a dirk was also a short sword carried by midshipmen of the English navy during the eighteenth and nineteenth centuries.

REFERENCE

Stone, George Cameron. *A Glossary of the Construction, Decoration, and Use of Arms and Armor.* New York: Jack Brussel, 1961.

DISARM. The act of relieving an opponent of his sword.

During the early days of swordplay, the art of grabbing an adversary's blade with one's free hand and wrenching it from his grasp was practiced as a matter of course. This was called a "seizure." Double seizures, where both swordsmen ended up trading weapons, were also taught. Examples of such devious actions are illustrated in Henry de Sainct Didier's* book, *Traicte Contenant les Secrets du Premier Livre sur l'Espee Seule* (1573).**

The disarm might also be accomplished with a strong beat or a spiral twist created by a binding action.

In its time, the disarm was considered a desirable ploy because, when delivered properly (i.e., with an element of surprise), it held less chance for personal

The disarm as pictured in Blackwell's *The Gentleman's Tutor*

injury than attempting to "outfence" an opponent. Too, with an enemy's weapon out of action, he could be forcibly encouraged to publicly admit to "wrongdoing," which, in many instances of dueling, was more desirable than simply silencing him. Certainly, if one did not wish to kill, disarming was a highly desirable alternative to sticking a foot of steel through someone.

Today, deliberate disarming actions are not tolerated in fencing. However, by the rules of the game, if one's opponent accidentally loses his weapon (in the course of receiving a beat or parry, for instance), a touch may be scored against the disarmed fencer if it lands before the dropped blade contacts the ground.

Also called *desarmo, sforzo,* or *desarmement.*

REFERENCES

Castle, Egerton. *Schools and Masters of Fence.* London: George Bell, 1885.

Palffy-Alpar, Julius. *Sword and Masque.* Philadelphia: F. A. Davis, 1967.

U.S. Fencing Association, ed. *Operations Manual.* Colorado Springs, CO: U.S. Fencing Association, 1985.

DISARMING ACT OF 1747. In 1745, the Jacobite army of Prince Charles Edward Stuart ("Bonnie Prince Charlie," the last pretender to the British throne) began an attempt to wrest control of England away from the ruling House of Hanover, then represented by George II, and restore it to the Stuart family (which had lost the Crown with the overthrowing of James II in 1689).

The following year brought the final showdown between the two opposing forces at the Battle of Culloden, in the Highlands of Scotland, on April 16, 1746.

Prince Charles's force had been recruited, to a great extent, from Scottish Highlands clans. Many of these Highlanders were little more than country boys who had joined the fight not so much out of political reasons but simply because their chiefs had told them to fight. The British regiments consisted of battle-seasoned veterans.

The rebel army, made up of around 5,000 men, met a British contingent, numbering over 9,000, head on. Armed mainly with swords and bucklers against cavalry and heavy cannon, the Scots fought bravely but in vain. Within an hour, they were routed, ending, once and for all, the Stuart family claim to the British monarchy.

For their part in the uprising, the Highlanders were dealt with severely. Besides imprisonment and death for many of them, heavy penalties were settled on the Scottish people as a whole. Among these was the Disarming Act of 1747, which declared that all Highlanders be deprived of their weapons—swords, dirks, bucklers, axes, and so on—and that any Highlander found guilty of possessing said weapons would face punishment of imprisonment or transportation, as a slave, to "His Majesty's plantations beyond the sea."

This law effectively stopped the use of swords in Scotland, thereby bringing an end to a practice that had been part of the Highlander's life for hundreds of years.

REFERENCES
Churchill, Winston S. *The Island Race*. London: Corgi Books, 1964.
Prebble, John. *Culloden*. England: Penguin Books, 1967.
Taylor, Iain Cameron. *Culloden*. Edinburgh: Highland Printers, 1965.

DISENGAGE. English for the simple attack *degagé*.
REFERENCE
Stevenson, John. *Fencing*. London: Briggs, 1935.

DISPLACEMENT OF TARGET. In foil and sabre play, when a fencer, to avoid being hit, removes his valid target area—through ducking or twisting—from the path of an attacking blade and subsequently presents an off-target area in its place (this includes placing an arm or hand in front of the chest, or ducking so that an on-coming blade hits one's mask), he has performed a displacement of target. This is not permitted by the rules of fencing.
REFERENCE
U.S. Fencing Association, ed. *Operations Manual*. Colorado Springs, CO: U.S. Fencing Association, 1985.

DISTANCE. The space for attacking or defending that separates two fencers.

Learning to establish proper distance is vital to successful fencing. The distance between two fencers constantly changes as they move up and down the fencing strip, and it is up to each individual to find the most advantageous spot for him to wage his offensive or defensive campaign.

A fencer who constantly finds himself too close when he attacks will have trouble fitting his blade into the space separating him from his opponent (this leads to the hasty and unpredictable jabbing of infighting). A fencer who lunges too far away from his target—no matter how good his form—will not hit with his weapon (leaning, with a subsequent loss of balance, often takes place).

Defensively, a fencer who does not learn to maintain an adequate defensive distance by retreating when an opponent closes with him will be constantly hard-pressed to parry in time to escape being hit, often receiving touches that could have been otherwise avoided with a simple backward step. Likewise, retreating too far out of distance as one parries an attack will prevent even an unstoppable counterattack from reaching its goal.

The synchronization of arm and hand actions with foot movement is vital to achieving proper fencing distance. Also, finding a comfortable lunging distance early in one's fencing career and working hard to maintain it from both stationary and mobile positions are other factors not to be overlooked.

It is interesting to note that even in the days of the old-time, rough-and-tumble sword masters—like Achille Marozzo* and George Silver*—proper distance was touted for its importance to fencing.

Distance has also been called "measure."

REFERENCES

Castle, Egerton. *Schools and Masters of Fence.* London: George Bell, 1885.
Palffy-Alpar, Julius. *Sword and Masque.* Philadelphia: F. A. Davis, 1967.
Szabo, Laszlo. *Fencing and the Master.* Hungary: Franklin Printing House, 1982.

DJOEMLOENG. A sword of Malaya.

REFERENCE

Stone, George Cameron. *A Glossary of the Construction, Decoration, and Use of Arms and Armor.* New York: Jack Brussel, 1961.

DO—ARMOR. A Japanese corselet (chest armor or, in modern terms, chest protector).

There are two styles of *do* armor: *do-maru,* which opens at the side, and *haramaki-do,* which opens at the back.

The *do* of today's kendoist* (Japanese fencer) is made of strips of stiff bamboo tied together tightly and covered with a heavy hide. It was first developed between 1765 and 1770 by Chuzo Nakanishi of Edo.

REFERENCES

Sasamori, Junzo, and Gordon Warner. *This Is Kendo.* Vermont: Charles E. Tuttle, 1984.
Stone, George Cameron. *A Glossary of the Construction, Decoration, and Use of Arms and Armor.* New York: Jack Brussel, 1961.

DO—ATTACK. In kendo,* a blow to the chest protector is called a *do* attack.

REFERENCE

Sasamori, Junzo, and Gordon Warner. *This Is Kendo.* Vermont: Charles E. Tuttle, 1984.

DO—PHILOSOPHY. In Japanese, the ultimate meaning of the word *do* is "way" or "path," as in "kendo"* (way of the sword) and "Bushido"* (way

of the warrior). Traditionally, it implies a road to self-understanding, perfection of technique, and spiritual growth.
REFERENCE
Lewis, Peter. *The Way to Martial Arts.* New York: Exter Books, 1986.

DOCCIOLINI, MARCO. (c. 1580). Italian fencing master.

While Docciolini introduced no particular innovations to fencing, through his writing we are allowed to see how important time thrusts were considered by swordsmen of the late sixteenth century. Such actions were, in fact, considered the best attacks.
REFERENCE
Castle, Egerton. *Schools and Masters of Fence.* London: George Bell, 1885.

DODHARA. A double-edged sword of India. The term, in fact, means ''double-edged.''
REFERENCE
Stone, George Cameron. *A Glossary of the Construction, Decoration, and Use of Arms and Armor.* New York: Jack Brussel, 1961.

DOGANE. A broad collar of metal fitted around the middle of a Japanese sword hilt.*
REFERENCE
Stone, George Cameron. *A Glossary of the Construction, Decoration, and Use of Arms and Armor.* New York: Jack Brussel, 1961.

DOGU. The entire collection of equipment of a kendoist.
REFERENCE
Sasamori, Junzo, and Gordon Warner. *This Is Kendo.* Vermont: Charles E. Tuttle, 1984.

DOHONG. A war sword of Dutch Borneo. The word itself implies bravery.
REFERENCE
Stone, George Cameron. *A Glossary of the Construction, Decoration, and Use of Arms and Armor.* New York: Jack Brussel, 1961.

DOIGHTE. Finger play.

The delicate finger manipulation of the fencing weapon, characteristic of the French school of fencing. It is created by a slight tightening and loosening of the fingers as the blade is being wielded.

The Italian style, controlled by the wrist rather than the hand, does not allow for such subtleties.
REFERENCES
Handelman, Rob. ''Fencing Glossary.'' *American Fencing* (May/June 1978).
Palffy-Alpar, Julius. *Sword and Masque.* Philadelphia: F. A. Davis, 1967.

DOJO. The Japanese fencing school or hall.

First established during the Muromachi period (1336–1568), when the art of swordplay began to flourish in Japan, these fencing establishments were instrumental in the formation of the samurai tradition. Early schools were Nen-ryu, Tenshin Shoden-shinto-ryu, Kage-ryu, and Chujo-ryu. Eventually, there were over 200 dojo in Japan.

One of the most honored and prosperous fencing schools in the entire country during the sixteenth and seventeenth centuries was the dojo of the Yagyu family. Serving the shogun and holding sway, technique-wise, for many years, the Yagyu masters have become folk heroes to their countrymen. Today, many famous old dojo in Japan have existed since medieval times.

Over the years, as weapons and equipment became standardized, a set method of fighting within the dojo was established. This was closely followed by a formal code of conduct between student and master. All of these innovations came to be called "kendo," or "way of the sword."

The modern dojo is treated with considerable respect by its members. In a way, because of the veneration held by the practitioners of kendo* for their art, the dojo might well be likened to a church. Whenever a kendoist enters or leaves his school, he bows to the building and to those present. A kendoist does not wear a hat in the dojo; nor does he smoke within its boundaries. Furthermore, each kendoist is responsible for some aspect of cleaning his dojo before and following each period of work (the floor, where practice takes place, receives special attention regarding its condition).

The construction of a dojo also has its own special guidelines. The floor must be made of highly polished hardwood strips, carefully joined together so there is no danger of exposed edges that might injure the kendoist, who performs his art barefooted. The floor must also be flexible enough to protect the fencer from impact damage to his feet and legs.

REFERENCES

Nakano, Yasoji, and Nariaki Sato. *Fundamental Kendo.* Japan: Japan Publications, 1974.

Sasamori, Junzo, and Gordon Warner. *This Is Kendo.* Vermont: Charles E. Tuttle, 1984.

DON JUAN. A legendary—but fictional—lover and swordsman.

Don Juan first appears in literary form in 1630, in Tirso de Molina's play *Burlador de Sevilla.* He is pictured as a tragic character—brave, arrogant, humorous—who is forced to kill (in a sword fight) the father of a girl he has dishonored. Eventually, Don Juan's enemies hound him to destruction.

The French dramatist Molière made use of Don Juan again in *Don Juan ou le Festin de Pierre* (1665). English playwright Thomas Shadwell revived him for an unimpressive *The Libertine* (1676). A milder Don Juan was sentimentalized and ultimately redeemed in Jose Zorrilla y Moral's *Don Juan Tenorio* (1844).

Other writers to employ the Don Juan theme were Alexandre Dumas,* Balzac, Flaubert, Pushkin, Lord Byron, and George Bernard Shaw.

The most famous working of the Don Juan story is, without a doubt, Mozart's monumental opera *Don Giovanni* (1787). Richard Strauss's tone poem *Don Juan* (1888) provides us with a musically idealistic and heroic interpretation of the legend.

In modern times, Don Juan has had numerous incarnations as a movie character. Here, he invariably loses most of his lecherous persona and assumes the role of the dashing swashbuckler and swordsman. The best known Don Juans have been John Barrymore (*Don Juan,* 1926**); Douglas Fairbanks, Sr. (*The Private Life of Don Juan,* 1934**); and Errol Flynn (*The Adventures of Don Juan,* 1949**).

REFERENCES
Benet, William Rose. *The Reader's Encyclopedia.* New York: Thomas Y. Crowell, 1965.
Richards, Jeffrey. *Swordsmen of the Screen.* Boston: Routledge and Kegan Paul, 1977.

D'ORIOLA, CHRISTIAN. (1929–   ). French fencing champion.
Christian d'Oriola became world foil champion in 1947 at the age of eighteen. In the years that followed, he won the event three more times: 1949, 1953, and 1954.

In his Olympic career, d'Oriola won individual foil championships at the 1952 and 1956 games. In team foil, he won medals in the 1948 (first), 1952 (first), and 1956 Olympics (second).

REFERENCES
Palffy-Alpar, Julius. *Sword and Masque.* Philadelphia: F. A. Davis, 1967.
Wallechinsky, David. *The Complete Book of the Olympics.* New York: Penguin Books, 1984.

DOUBLÉ. The *doublé* (pronounced ''du-blay'') is classified as a composed attack. It consists of a feint (threat) of disengage followed by a deception (evasion) of one counter (circular) parry.

A movement similar to the *doublé,* the *ricavatione* existed during the days of rapier play; but the *doublé* proper, needing a weapon of considerable lightness for its proper execution, did not come into common use until the highly maneuverable smallsword made its appearance on the fencing scene during the eighteenth century.

Also known as a ''circular disengage,'' a ''counterdisengage,'' and a *circolazione e finta.*

In a progression of counterparries deceived after a feint of disengage, the *doublé* is extended into the following:

Two counterparries deceived: a *triplé.*

Three counterparries deceived: a *quadruplé.*

Four counterparries: a *quintduplé*—and so on.

REFERENCES
Castle, Egerton. *Schools and Masters of Fence*. London: George Bell, 1885.
Morton, E. D. *Martini A–Z of Fencing*. London: Queen Anne Press, 1992.
Palffy-Alpar, Julius. *Sword and Masque*. Philadelphia: F. A. Davis, 1967.

DOUBLE BALTEUS. A Roman belt used for carrying sword and dagger.
REFERENCE
Burton, Richard F. *The Book of the Sword*. London: Chatto and Windus, 1884.

DOUBLÉ DE DOUBLÉ. Means *doublé** from the *doublé.*

This attack is made up of two *doublés,* each one going in the opposite direction. In its execution, the *doublé de doublé* is made up of a feint of disengage, an evasion of a counterparry, an evasion of a lateral parry, and an evasion of another counterparry.
REFERENCE
Stevenson, John. *Fencing*. London: Briggs, 1935.

DOUBLE-EDGED SWORDS. Traditional swords with two cutting edges. This type of weapon was the most dominant form of early sword, although single-edged weapons were by no means uncommon.

The basic advantage of a double-edged sword was that cuts could be administered from the inside line. or outside line without appreciably changing the position of the sword hand.

Double-edged swords came in single-handed and two-handed varieties.
REFERENCES
Burton, Richard F. *The Book of the Sword*. London: Chatto and Windus, 1884.
Castle, Egerton. *Schools and Masters of Fence*. London: George Bell, 1885.

DRAGON. The most popular design on Japanese swords and armor is that of the dragon. It represents powers of the air, or the spirit.
REFERENCE
Stone, George Cameron. *A Glossary of the Construction, Decoration, and Use of Arms and Armor*. New York: Jack Brussel, 1961.

DRESS, FENCING. Fencing's white uniform, while traditional, is a tradition only of modern times.

During the eighteenth century, men fenced in waistcoats (occasionally white), knee breeches, and stockings. Sometimes they even retained their hats. (While masks were in existence by the mid-1700s, they were rarely used, most fencers feeling that their skill was the only protection they needed.)

The dress of the early nineteenth century often included waist-length white jackets and masks (minus bibs); white, however, was still not mandatory.

White padded jackets were finally a requirement by the mid-1800s, but colored pants were still worn. Fencers often fenced in their street pants.

By the early twentieth century, the rules of fencing specified white jackets,

Women's nineteenth-century fencing garb

knickers, and socks, although gloves, masks, and shoes could still be of darker colors.

Today, conventions specify all-white for everything.

Women fencers once wore skirts—first black, then white—along with their jackets. Knickers eventually came into use along with skirts, although by the 1930s only knickers were officially acceptable for international competitions. Now, women no longer wear skirts while fencing, even informally.

REFERENCE

Morton, E. D. *Martini A–Z of Fencing.* London: Queen Anne Press, 1992.

DRESS SWORD. Any sword, usually one of a highly ornate nature, whose main function is to act as a decorative addition to a person's apparel.

In the days when swords were worn as a matter of course, dress swords were worn for ceremonial purposes or at court.

Today, the dress sword is normally limited to formal military dress.

REFERENCE

Wilkinson, Frederick. *Swords and Daggers.* New York: Hawthorn Books, 1967.

DRIMBA, IONEL. (1942–   ). Romanian fencing champion.

Ionel Drimba won the Olympic individual foil championship in 1968, with nineteen wins and two defeats.

In 1970, he defected to the United States.

REFERENCE

Wallechinsky, David. *The Complete Book of the Olympics.* New York: Penguin Books, 1984.

DUBBING. A medieval initiation ritual, dubbing was the ceremony of conferring knighthood on a young warrior. The new knight was always presented with a sword as a token of his achievement. Early accounts had this sometimes accompanied by a tap on the shoulder with a hand; this tap was later relegated to a sword. Often the phrase, "Be thou a knight," was spoken.

During the dubbing, the sword of the knight-to-be was blessed with a special prayer, such as this from the tenth century:

Harken, we beseech Thee, O Lord, to our prayers, and deign to bless with the right hand of Thy majesty this sword with which Thy servant desires to be girded, that it may be a defense of churches, widows, orphans, and all Thy servants against the scourge of pagans, that it may be the terror and dread of evildoers, and that it may be just both in attack and defense.

Another rite had the new knight being struck on the shoulder or neck with a sword three times to the prayer:

In the name of God, St. Michael, and St. George, I make thee a knight; be valiant, courteous, and loyal!

The dubbing ceremony ended with the knight's sword being girded on him by attendants.

Knighthood might be conferred by either a king or a high churchman.

REFERENCES

Barber, Richard. *The Knight and Chivalry*. San Francisco: Harper and Row, 1974.

Bulfinch, Thomas. *Bulfinch's Mythology*. New York: The Modern Library, 1934.

DUCRET, ROGER. (c. 1900). French fencing champion.

Roger Ducret took third in individual foil at the 1920 Olympics. His foil team took second place. At the 1924 Olympics, he took first in individual foil, second in individual épée, and second in individual sabre. Both his foil team and épée team took first. At the 1928 Olympic games, his foil team took second.

REFERENCE

Wallechinsky, David. *The Complete Book of the Olympics*. New York: Penguin Books, 1984.

DUEL. A highly regulated combat waged between two individuals to settle some point of honor. Until the nineteenth century, duels were fought chiefly with swords.

Duels were carried out, basically, on three different levels: (1) the judicial duel (also called trial by combat), which settled legal differences; (2) the duel of chivalry, which settled points of knightly conduct; and (3) the duel of honor, which settled occurrences in which someone's sense of personal integrity had been defamed.

Observed nineteenth-century French writer and critic Jules Janin of the duel: "A duel makes every one of us a strong and independent power, and constitutes out of each individual life the life of all; it grasps the sword of justice, which the laws have dropped, punishing what no code can chastise—contempt or insult."

Of course, to many, the duel was just a stylized form of murder.

REFERENCE

Baldick, Robert. *The Duel*. New York: Spring Books, 1970.

DUELING GAUNTLET. A metal or heavy leather glove (for the free hand only) created especially for parrying a thrust or grabbing an adversary's blade.

It was used mainly during the sixteenth and seventeenth centuries.

REFERENCE

Stone, George Cameron. *A Glossary of the Construction, Decoration, and Use of Arms and Armor*. New York: Jack Brussel, 1961.

DUELING SWORD. Originally, any sword used for the purpose of dueling, such as the *rapier*.

After the practice of wearing swords on a daily basis had come to a close, the dueling sword came to be a special weapon specifically designed for personal

A duel

combat. Its earliest form resembled that of a smallsword. By the end of the nineteenth century, however, it was much like a modern épée, possessing a stiff triangular blade, a large shell guard, and a simple grip.

When the dueling sword was employed, its razor-sharp tip was dipped in disinfectant.

Also called an *épée de combat* and an *épée de terrain*.

REFERENCES

Morton, E. D. *Martini A–Z of Fencing*. London: Queen Anne Press, 1992.

Stone, George Cameron. *A Glossary of the Construction, Decoration, and Use of Arms and Armor*. New York: Jack Brussel, 1961.

DUELISTS, NOTED. In the events of man, there have been countless individuals who have been compelled by either circumstances or inclination into armed sword combat with others. Some were obsessed with principles of honor; some were mere adventurers for whom life, even their own, meant little; still others were apparent sociopaths or psychotics of the worst kind, who went out of their way to instigate and fight duels. A few were doubtlessly motivated by a true sense of justice.

In most ages previous to modern times, these men were tolerated, even admired. Occasionally overstepping the bounds of behavior, even for societies noticeably blind to cruelty (as long as it was perpetrated on someone else), they were put to death for their bloodthirsty efforts by an outraged judicial system. More frequently, they became victims of their own excesses, dying in duels they themselves had provoked.

Noted duelists include:

Sixteenth century—La Chastaignerye, Guy Chabot de Jarnac, and the Comte de Quelus.

Seventeenth century—Chevalier d'Andrieux, Cyrano de Bergerac, George Villers 2nd Duke of Buckingham, Lord Herbert of Cherbury, Alexandre de Lameth, Julie de Maupin, Francois de Montmorency, Marquis de Tenteniac, and Legarde Vallon.

Eighteenth century—Comte d'Artois, Chevalier d'Eon, Jean-Louis, Donald McBane, Louis-Francois de Richelieu, Comte de Saint-Evremont, Poulain de Saint-Foix, Chevalier Saint-Georges, and Marquis Du Vighan.

Nineteenth century—General Dupont and Captain Fournier.

As duelists, General Dupont and Captain Fournier shared perhaps one of the strangest adversarial relationships in the history of personal combat. As a young officer in Napoleon's army, Dupont was ordered to deliver a disagreeable message to fellow officer Fournier, a rabid duelist. Fournier, taking out his subsequent rage on the messenger, challenged Dupont to fight. This sparked a succession of encounters, waged with sword and pistol, that spanned decades. The contest was eventually resolved when Dupont was able to overcome his opponent during a pistol duel, forcing him to promise never to bother him again.

One of the last duels on record occurred in 1958, between dance choreographer Serge Lifar and the Marquis de Cuevas over a disparaging remark the latter made concerning one of Lifar's ballets. Carried out with dueling swords, the affair was a brief one, ending with Lifar being wounded slightly on the arm.

REFERENCES
Baldick, Robert. *The Duel.* New York: Spring Books, 1970.
Morton, E. D. *Martini A–Z of Fencing.* London: Queen Anne Books, 1992.

DUI TEMPI. Means ''double time'' in Italian.

Dui tempi refers especially to the separation of the parry and the riposte, as opposed to combining a parry and hit into a single action.

Most old-time fencing masters were of the belief that the concept of *dui tempi*

Duelists

was a faulty one. Italian teacher Salvatore Fabris* remarks in his book *De lo Schermo* (1606):** "Although this method may succeed against certain men, nevertheless, it is impossible to consider it as good as that of parrying and striking at the same time. For the correct and only secure way of fighting is to meet your adversary's body at the same time as it presses forward, otherwise it will immediately retire safe and sound." He also says, "This method might succeed generally, but for the danger of being deceived." Finally, he maintains that any blow might be stopped by a movement that also covers the body.

The prejudice against *dui tempi* persisted until sword blades were shortened and lightened, thereby ensuring quicker defensive responses.

REFERENCE

Castle, Egerton. *Schools and Masters of Fence.* London: George Bell, 1885.

DUKN. A scymitar used by the people of Malay. A thick and heavy weapon, it was designed along the lines of a German cavalry sabre. The blade was double-edged at the point; hence, it could be used for both cutting and thrusting.

Known also as a *parang dedang.*

REFERENCE

Stone, George Cameron. *A Glossary of the Construction, Decoration, and Use of Arms and Armor.* New York: Jack Brussel, 1961.

DUKU. The sword of the seafaring people (Dyaks) of Borneo.

REFERENCE

Stone, George Cameron. *A Glossary of the Construction, Decoration, and Use of Arms and Armor.* New York: Jack Brussel, 1961.

DUMAS, ALEXANDRE. (1802–1870). French novelist and dramatist. The father of swashbuckling romances. Best known for his book *The Three Musketeers* (1844).**

Described by French historian Jules Michelet as "a force of nature," Alexandre Dumas has remained one of literature's greatest and most popular writers—worldwide—for nearly 150 years. An author of amazing prolificacy, he turned out nearly 300 volumes, while at the same time managing to live a life that rivaled any of his fictions for outright adventurousness.

Besides *The Three Musketeers,* Dumas's work includes *Twenty Years After* (1845), *The Man in the Iron Mask* (1848), *The Chevalier de Maison-Rouge* (1845), and *The Corsican Brothers* (1845).

An avid fencer, Dumas continually worked swordplay into his novels. Duels abound with joyous abandon.

In *The Chevalier D'Harmental* (1853), for instance, the author writes:

Roquefinette gave a cry which might have been taken for the roaring of a lion, and, bounding back a step, threw himself on guard, his sword in his hand. Then began between these two men a duel, terrible, hidden, silent, for both were intent on their work, and each understood what sort of an adversary he had to contend with. By a reaction very

Alexandre Dumas, author of *The Three Musketeers*

easy to be understood, it was now D'Harmental who was calm, and Roquefinette who was excited. Every instant he menaced D'Harmental with his long sword, but the frail rapier followed it as iron follows the loadstone, twisting and spinning round it like a viper. At the end of about five minutes the chevalier had not made a single lunge, but he had parried all those of his adversary. At last, on a more rapid thrust than the others, he came too late to the parry, and felt the point of his adversary's sword at his breast. At the same time a red spot spread from his shirt to his lace frill. D'Harmental saw it, and with a spring engaged so near to Roquefinette that the hilts almost touched. The captain instantly saw the disadvantage of his long sword in such a position. A thrust *sur les armes,* and he was lost; he made a spring backwards, his foot slipped on the newly waxed floor, and his sword-hand rose in spite of himself. Almost by instinct D'Harmental profited by it, lunged within, and pierced the captain's chest, where the blade disappeared to the hilt. D'Harmental recovered to parry in return, but the precaution was needless; the captain stood still an instant, opened his eyes wildly, the sword dropped from his grasp, and, pressing his two hands to the wound, he fell at length on the floor.

"Curse the rapier!" he murmured, and expired; the strip of steel had pierced his heart.

Dumas's work has been turned into numerous successful adventure films by Hollywood.

REFERENCES

Dumas, Alexandre. *The Chevalier D'Harmental.* New York: The Continental Press, 1900.

Hemmings, F. W. J. *Alexandre Dumas: The King of Romance.* New York: Charles Scribner's Sons, 1979.

Maurois, André. *Alexandre Dumas.* New York: Alfred A. Knopf, 1955.

DUNGEONS AND DRAGONS. Often known simply as "D & D," Dungeons and Dragons is the prototype fantasy role-playing game. Invented in 1974 by Gary Gygax, it owes its origins to the sword-and-sorcery fantasy fiction of Robert E. Howard and J.R.R. Tolkien. Because of its orientation, there is almost always an emphasis on sword-related activities.

There is actually no immediate goal in D & D, as one would find in, say, Monopoly. Instead, according to its creator, "The ultimate aim of the game is to gain sufficient esteem as a good player to retire your character—he becomes a kind of mythical, historical figure, someone for others to look up to and admire."

The proceedings of the game are overseen by a guiding personality known as the Dungeon Master. Encounters, of course, are not physical but are determined by rolling special dice. To complicate things, D & D has countless rules, which must be figured out by a complex mathematical system.

In his book, *The Straight Dope,* writer Cecil Adams describes D & D as "a game that combines the charm of a Pentagon briefing with the excitement of double-entry bookkeeping."

REFERENCE

Adams, Cecil. *The Straight Dope.* Chicago: Chicago Review Press, 1984.

DURATION OF FENCING BOUTS. The duration for bouts in foil, sabre, and épée is:

Four hits—five minutes

Five hits—six minutes

Eight hits—ten minutes

German dusack play

Ten hits—twelve minutes

The duration of "one-touch" épée bouts is one hit—five minutes.

REFERENCE
U.S. Fencing Association, ed. *Operations Manual*. Colorado Springs, CO: U.S. Fencing
Association, 1985.

DUSACK. Originating in Hungary, the *dusack* quickly became extremely popular among middle- and lower-class citizens of Germany. Used entirely for cutting, it was considered an excellent weapon, inexpensive and very simple to use.

The dusack was made from a single piece of iron, the upper portion of which was fashioned into a cutlasslike blade. The lower part was curved into a loop, which formed a combination grip and knuckle guard.

The *dusack* was used in Germany long after similar weapons in other countries had been discarded.

The two greatest masters of *dusack* play were Joachim Meyer* (*Grundtliche Beschreibung der freyen Ritterlichen und Adelichen kunst der Fechtens in allerley gebreuchlichen Wehren mit vil schonen und nutzlichten Figuren gezieret und furgestellet*, 1570**) and Jacob Sutor* (*Kunstliches Fechtbuch*, 1612**).

REFERENCES

Castle, Egerton. *Schools and Masters of Fence*. London: George Bell, 1885.

Stone, George Cameron. *A Glossary of the Construction, Decoration, and Use of Arms and Armor*. New York: Jack Brussel, 1961.

E

ECOLES DES ARMES. Written by Italian fencing master Domenico Angelo*
in 1763, this book (commonly known as *The School of Fencing*) is the all-time
classic volume on the subject of swordplay in particular and fencing in general.
A work of immense influence, it set the standards, in a highly scientific manner,
for smallsword combat during the mid- and late eighteenth century. Furthermore,
it was the first study to insist on the value of fencing for purely sport, health,
and cultural reasons. Even now, it contains much that is relevant for the modern
fencer.

Containing over forty excellent illustrations—all of which were posed for by
Domenico Angelo and his students—the book is also interesting as an artistic
endeavor.

A number of editions of *The School of Fencing* were produced during the
eighteenth century in French, English and French together, and English alone.
Edition dates include 1763, 1765, 1767, 1787, and 1799. It has since been
reprinted in facsimile form.

The School of Fencing manages to touch on all levels of thought more than
any other piece of writing on swordplay, and it is responsible for fencing evolv-
ing into what it is today.

REFERENCES

Angelo, Domenico. *The School of Fencing*. London: H. Angelo, 1787 edition.

Castle, Egerton. *Schools and Masters of Fence*. London: George Bell, 1885.

Wise, Arthur. *The Art and History of Personal Combat*. Greenwich, CT: Arma Press,
1971.

EDICTS AGAINST DUELING IN FRANCE. During the Middle Ages, the duel was looked upon by the establishment as a necessary part of human existence. Duels were used to settle important judicial disputes, to maintain one's honor, and to uphold the principles of chivalry.

In time, however, dueling outgrew its prescribed boundaries and spread with a manialike fervor across Europe. Dueling for the sake of dueling became as commonplace as any daily function of life. While no country remained untouched by this bloodthirsty fad, perhaps only France managed to raise the practice to its highest level of destruction.

Between 1600 and 1789, over 40,000 French aristocrats were killed in private sword fights. It was said that when friends met in the morning at the court of Louis XIII, their first question of the day was,

"Do you know who fought yesterday?"

The French became so adept at killing one another that the responsible elements of society began calling for official intervention to end the madness. But while many laws against fighting were drafted, few were actually put into effect.

Henry IV (king of France from 1589 to 1610) displayed a public distaste for dueling by producing a score of proclamations banning the practice. *The Edict of Blois,* issued in 1602, went so far as to condemn combatants to death. Yet dueling increased during Henry's reign, with over 4,000 noblemen being dispatched in "affairs of honor." This was undoubtedly due to the fact that the king privately looked on dueling with favor and could not bring himself to enforce his own laws. In nineteen years, he granted at least 7,000 pardons for dueling. Being lenient with duelists, of course, only tended to encourage them to greater heights of mayhem.

With Louis XIII* (king of France from 1610 to 1643), matters grew much worse. Dueling for no other reason than to enhance one's reputation was a common practice. On paper Louis, as to be expected, sternly prohibited dueling; but, like Henry before him, he was a frequent forgiver of dueling sins.

Only occasionally were prohibitions actually implemented. Perhaps the most infamous case was that of François de Montmorency, comte de Bouteville. A duelist without equal, he was in the habit of challenging anyone whose courage had been spoken of publicly. He was so blatant in his defiance of the king's edicts against private combats that, at last, it was a point of honor that Louis could do nothing but condemn him to death. De Bouteville, ever unrepentant, was summarily beheaded in 1627 in a public execution marked by considerable pageantry. A man of great vanity, he went to his death concerned only that his mustache would be mussed by the executioner's ax. It is safe to say, however, that even this display of royal displeasure did nothing to dampen the dueling spirit.

By the middle of the seventeenth century, dueling was so entrenched in French nature that no amount of legal condemnation could halt its progress.

Louis XIV (king of France from 1643 to 1715) published a total of ten edicts against dueling during his lifetime. His most famous, the Edit des Duels (1679), promised the death penalty for anyone taking part in a duel, even the seconds and thirds. It further stated that the participants would be deprived of all property and their letters of nobility. Furthermore, anyone killed in a duel would be denied a Christian burial. Just the issuing of a challenge was to be punished by exile.

Logically, this fearful edict should have ended dueling in France forever. But it did not. As the novelty of living peaceful lives wore off, the dueling habit quickly resurged. Before long, the king backed away from the issue, even going so far as to secretly express his admiration for duelists of particular accomplishment. That he actually promoted the growth of deadly swordplay by his official support of a national academy of fencing masters is well known.

Following the death of Louis XIV, all official bans on dueling were dropped.

REFERENCES

Baldick, Robert. *The Duel.* New York: Spring Books, 1970.

Castle, Egerton. *Schools and Masters of Fence.* London: George Bell, 1885.

Wise, Arthur. *The Art and History of Personal Combat.* Greenwich, CT: Arma Press, 1972.

EDICTS AGAINST FENCING SCHOOLS IN ENGLAND. Fencing schools have not always enjoyed the high regard in which they are held today as bastions of culture, healthful exercise, and sportsmanship. During their early days, they were quite often havens for the scum of society, dangerous men whose sole purpose for learning to fence was to use their murderous skills against the defenseless. Nowhere was this more true than in England. Perhaps it was because the English approached their swordplay with less scholarly discipline than, say, the Italians, Germans, and Spanish did. Anyway, English swordsmen were known bullies and ruffians. English fencing masters of the thirteenth and fourteenth centuries were usually placed in the same unsavory class with "rogues and vagabonds—and actors."

Because of this sad reputation, English fencing schools were often the subject of inhibiting edits, laws that either attempted to slow the spread of fencing or stamp it out altogether.

For example, in response to the wave of obnoxious "swordmen," as they were called, overrunning the city of London during the late thirteenth century, Edward I of England issued an edict in 1286 forbidding anyone to engage in fencing: "Whereas it is customary for profligates to learn the art of fencing, who are thereby emboldened to commit the most unheard-of villainies, no such school shall be kept in the city."

In 1311, fencing master Roger le Skirmisour, arrested for violating a fencing ban then in effect, was brought before the mayor of London. He was charged with "keeping a fencing school for divers men, and for enticing thither the sons of respectable persons so as to waste and spend the property of their fathers and mothers upon bad practices."

Henry VIII attempted to stop the spread of unsavory fencing establishments by awarding official patents to masters he deemed worthy to teach.

In the end, however, fencing schools prospered regardless of the laws passed to restrain them. Some did so out in the open; some went underground. Being the product of a brutal age, they were looked on, ultimately, in spite of the cries of a victimized and fearful citizenry, as a necessary evil.

REFERENCES

Castle, Egerton. *Schools and Masters of Fence.* London: George Bell, 1885.

Wise, Arthur. *The Art and History of Personal Combat.* Greenwich, CT: Arma Press, 1972.

EFFORT. An attack on an opponent's blade from the foible* to the forte.*

REFERENCE

Morton, E. D. *Martini A–Z of Fencing.* London: Queen Anne Press, 1992.

EFU NO TACHI. A *tachi** being the earliest type of single-edged sword in Japan, *efu no tachi* refers to a form of *tachi* reserved for the princes and nobles of the imperial retinue.

REFERENCE

Stone, George Cameron. *A Glossary of the Construction, Decoration, and Use of Arms and Armor.* New York: Jack Brussel, 1961.

EL CID. (1043–1099). Legendary medieval Spanish knight and swordsman.

Rodrigo Díaz de Vivar, known as El Cid (the lord) and El Campeador (the champion), fought against—and occasionally for—the Moors, who occupied his homeland for many years. His greatest feat was the conquest of Valencia.

Strangely, the deeds of this figure actually had little or no lasting impact on Spanish history. His appeal and continuing fame, no doubt, have more to do with the strength of his sword in battle and his ability to win fame and riches even when opposed by his superiors—the makings of a true folk hero.

El Cid has been the subject of numerous Spanish plays and epic poems.

REFERENCE

Benet, William Rose. *The Reader's Encyclopedia.* New York: Thomas Y. Crowell, 1965.

ELECTRICAL FENCING. The nature of electrical fencing, while in principle the same as nonelectrical fencing, has some distinct differences separating it from the latter.

The basic reason for developing electrical weapons was to simplify the method of judging touches. However, in making the directing process easier, fencing itself was presented with some new complications. Some were of a physical nature, and some were distinctly psychological.

Of all three sport weapons, the foil received the greatest change to its physical nature when it became electrified. To begin with, the weight/balance factor was altered dramatically from the "natural" feel of standard foils. This was due to the addition of a depressible button tip (plus protective tape) on the end of the blade and an electrical cord plug situated at the underside of the *coquille*. Too, a stiffer than average—and hence heavier—blade was needed to protect the fragile electric (copper) wire that was inset slightly into the length of the blade's surface. When one has become used to fencing with a standard foil, these factors can be quite disconcerting.

Also, the straightness of an electrical foil blade must be taken into account when bouting. An overly curved blade will cause the point to come in at a slight angle, preventing the button tip from depressing and registering a touch.

The electric épée, while receiving the same additions as its relative, was not thrown off quite as drastically as the foil. This was due to the already considerable bulk of the dueling weapon.

The electric sabre, possessing a different sort of touch-registering device than the other two weapons—a pair of sensors located on the underside of the hand guard rather than on the blade—has been changed the least by its electrification.

Another factor in the electrical picture is that, when competing, there is the constant possibility that one's weapon may malfunction. Fencing exchanges, while theoretically light and controlled, often become fast and furious; and even systems designed to stand up to a certain amount of continual abuse may break down. Button tips can jam; wire connections can break or develop shorts; sensors can stop sensing. Then, one is left with a piece of equipment that is useless until it is repaired. Sometimes, the scoring apparatus itself can stop operating. For these reasons, special electrical technicians (armorers), schooled in the workings of the implements of modern swordplay, have come to play an important role at fencing tournaments. Whenever possible, they are present at official events to handle the problems electrical fencing has generated.

Aside from physical difficulties, fencing with electrical weapons has also generated its share of mental hazards. There is a danger of what is sometimes called "fencing to the box." That is, whenever a maneuver is completed, a fencer may compulsively look over to see if his action has registered on the electrical scoring machine. The touch, accompanied by a loud buzzer and flashing lights, may be viewed subconsciously as a psychological perk, a reward, so to speak, for performing an attack or counterattack (the same sort of visual/audio hook is used overtly to signify "success" in video games; or think of Pavlov's famous trained dogs salivating hungrily at the sound of a bell). Unchecked, the bells and lights become a sought-after, psychologically pleasing public acknowledgment of accomplishment. The unwary fencer ends up spending more and more time looking for gratification than he does trying to relate to his opponent. Exchanges are halted in midstream as he turns to see if the machine has given its electrically generated approval. Meanwhile, his attention elsewhere, he is hit with a counterattack by his still-fencing opponent. Basically, the fencer has conditioned himself into a very bad habit.

A similar fencing pitfall arose in the early days of electrical foil fencing. With the electrical scoring box light to spur them on, fencers began to ignore right of way and simply tried to make their light go on first. Foil form and technique were abondoned, the weapon becoming a sort of second-class épée. It took four or five years before proper fencing principles were reimposed on the game, and the foil recovered its old sense of balance.

It has been said that the best way to fence electrically is to forget that you are fencing electrically. One's opponent and the commands of the director should be the only points of focus for a fencer during a bout.

REFERENCES

Evangelista, Anita. *Dictionary of Hypnotism.* Westport, CT: Greenwood Press, 1991.

Grombach, John V. *The 1972 Olympic Guide.* New York: Paperback Library, 1972.

Palffy-Alpar, Julius. *Sword and Masque.* Philadelphia: F. A. Davis, 1967.

Salter, Andrew. *Conditioned Reflex Therapy.* New York: Creative Age Press, 1949.

ELECTRICAL FENCING WEAPONS. The twentieth century ushered in a monumental change to fencing with the introduction of technology, in the form of electrical weapons, to the age-old art. These weapons are connected, via electrical cords, to a scoring machine that automatically registers touches both "on" and "off" target, thus removing all doubts as to when a valid touch has actually been scored.

The épée was the first weapon to go electric. It was introduced in 1931. This was followed by the foil in 1956.

For many years, the sabre remained the only nonelectrical weapon, mostly due to the technical difficulties in perfecting a mechanism that would register both cuts and thrusts. However, by the late 1980s, after much experimentation, a reliable electrical sabre system came into general use. It was introduced into a high-ranking event for the first time during an international tournament in 1986, but only for the finals. The first all-electric sabre contest of major proportions came three years later, at the 1989 World Fencing Championships in Denver.

REFERENCES

Axelrod, Albert, ed. "Special Notice for Sabre Fencers." *American Fencing* (December/ January/February 1989).

Palffy-Alpar, Julius. *Sword and Masque.* Philadelphia: F. A. Davis, 1967.

Stevens, Byron. "The New York International: Electric Sabre Arrives." *American Fencing* (July/August 1986).

ELECTRICAL SCORING MACHINE. The device used for sensing and announcing touches during modern fencing bouts. Touches are acknowledged via flashing lights and a loud buzzing sound.

Weapons are connected to the scoring machine by a series of electrical cords, lines, and cables.

Standard scoring machines originally contained a setting for operating in a foil fencing mode and one for operating in an épée fencing mode. Because the electrical sabre system is so different from the other two, with its inception it required its own distinct scoring box. Today, scoring machines can accommodate all three weapons.

The prototype of the scoring machine for the foil was invented in 1896 in England by Little. While similar in principle to modern scoring machines, it was unfortunately unable to differentiate between "on-target" and "off-target" touches.

The first official scoring machine was developed in France by Laurent and later improved upon by Pagan of Geneva, Switzerland. Designed for use with the épée, it was capable of measuring a difference of $\frac{1}{25}$ of a second between touches. While first used in an international tournament in 1931, it was not until 1933 that the Federation Internationale d'Escrime officially adopted it for use in major events. It saw its first Olympic action at the 1936 Berlin games. The capability of judging foil fencing was added to the scoring machine in the 1950s. Sabre, the final weapon to be electrified, was added in the 1980s.

The scoring machine may also be called the "box" or "recording apparatus."

REFERENCES

Byrnes, Joe. "Electric Sabre." *American Fencing* (June/July/August 1988).
Grombach, John V. *The 1972 Olympic Guide.* New York: Paperback Library, 1972.
Morton, E. D. *Martini A–Z of Fencing.* London: Queen Anne Press, 1992.

ELECTRICAL SHOCKS. One of the mishaps of modern electrical swordplay is the occasional shock to a fencer caused by a combination of his own heavy sweating and a short in his opponent's weapon system. With improved technology in weapons manufacture, however, this has become a fairly rare occurrence.

To protect against more serious injuries caused by a malfunction in the electrical system, a safety device called a ground circuit interruptor (GCI) has been brought into use. This mechanism impedes potentially harmful bursts of electrical energy into any electrical appliance.

There has been only one electrically induced fatality in all the years of electrical fencing. It occurred because of a faulty power plug on an épée scoring machine.

The idea that an electrical shock from a fencing weapon could cause death was employed fictionally in 1982 on the popular detective television series "Magnum P.I." In an episode entitled "Foiled Again," written by screenwriter and sometime fencer Tom Greene, an electrical scoring box used in a fencing tournament was secretly rewired to induce a fatal shock. The fencer inflicting the injury was Higgins (John Hillerman), one of the show's main characters. To make matters worse, the fatally injured fencer happened to be Higgins's hated, lifelong rival. Needless to say, Higgins was immediately suspected by the police of purposefully killing the other man. But, in the end, Magnum (Tom Selleck), the diligent private investigator, uncovered the true villain, thus saving the day in typical television-hero fashion.

REFERENCES
Byrnes, Joe. "Technical Talks." *American Fencing* (January/February 1984).
————. "Technical Talks." *American Fencing* (May/June 1984).
Greene, Tom. "Foiled Again." *Magnum P.I.* Universal Studios, 1982.

ELECTRIC ÉPÉE. The general setup of the electric épée system—from its button tip to the scoring box—is about the same as that of the electric foil.* Its differences are to be found in the manner in which it operates electrically. Because a touch anywhere on the body, from head to toe, produces a valid hit, there is no need for the circuitry to separate "on-target" and "off-target" responses, only to distinguish actual touches from point contact with the floor or an opponent's *coquille* (which produce no reaction from the scoring box).

Because there is no delineation of body target area in épée fencing (as would be the case in an actual sword fight), the épéeist has no need to wear a lame, as foil fencers are required to do. Nor is it necessary for the épée fencer to be grounded electrically. To guard against floor or *coquille* contact from being registered as valid touches, these two nonfencer areas are neutralized to contact. For the fencing strip, this is accomplished by surfacing its entire area with a thin copper or brass screen material.

The electric scoring machine has a setting that separates its épée functions from its foil functions.

REFERENCE
Volkman, Rudy. *Electrical Fencing Equipment.* Arvee Press, 1975.

ELECTRIC FENCING BLADE TIP. The point of the electric foil and épée blade is made up of a small cylinder capped with a round, flat tip which is set against the pressure of an inner spring. The tip is connected to a socket found beneath the hand guard by a coated copper wire indented into the length of the blade.

When it encounters a solid target, the tip depresses, causing an electric circuit to be completed (like turning on a light switch). This action immediately triggers a touch signaling system attached to the weapon via cables.

While electric tips are now required to be completely flat by the rules of fencing, early forms came in both flat and ridged varieties. The ridged tip, now illegal, was called such colorful names as "strawberry point," "beehive," "hedgehog point," and "mushroom head."

REFERENCES
Morton, E. D. *Martini A–Z of Fencing.* London: Queen Anne Press, 1992.
Volkman, Rudy. *Electrical Fencing Equipment.* Arvee Press, 1975.

ELECTRIC FOIL. Beginning at its point, the electric foil has a flat, depressible button tip attached to the metal blade. From the tip, a connecting copper wire is inset into the length of the blade and runs down to an electric plug that is situated on the underside of the hand guard. These spots make up the electric connections on the foil.

To hook up a foil to the electric scoring machine, a cord, called a "body cord," is inserted into the plug on the underside of the hand guard and fed up the fencer's fencing-arm jacket sleeve and through the jacket body to his back, where it is inserted into a plug from a line issuing from of a reel box situated at the end of the fencing strip (the body cord also has a special clip that attaches to the fencer's uniform, grounding him electrically). The reel line adjusts its length automatically, slidding in and out of the reel housing as the fencer advances and retreats. From the reel box, a long cable, called a "floor cable," is plugged into the scoring box, which is plugged into a wall outlet. This completes the electric connection.

When the button on the foil tip is depressed, a circuit is opened, which causes a touch to be registered on the scoring machine. However, for foil, "on-target" touches must be differentiated from "off-target" touches. For this to take place, the fencer must wear a specially designed vest, called a lame, over his fencing jacket. The exterior of this vest is inset with tiny, flexible copper threads, and its cut is that of the foil target area (the trunk of the body). When the foil makes solid contact with the copper-covered surface of the vest, a circuit is opened that triggers an on-target response on the scoring machine: a flashing colored light (either red or green, depending on which side of the fencing strip a fencer finds himself) and a loud buzz or ring. A touch off the vest opens another circuit, producing the "off-target" response on the scoring machine: a white light and a loud buzz or ring.

Sometimes called "the fourth weapon."

REFERENCE

Volkman, Rudy. *Electrical Fencing Equipment.* Arvee Press, 1975.

ELECTRIC SABRE. The electric functions of the sabre are totally unlike those of the foil or the épée. The blade itself has no touch-sensing capacity. All circuits are located on the underside of the hand guard. One sensor—the "capteur"—responds to the attacking fencer's accelerating forward movement; another one perceives blade contact on the special lame vest, glove, and mask the sabre fencer must now wear for bouting.

To keep cuts from registering on an opponent's weapon, the sabre is grounded.

Like the foil and épée, the electric sabre is connected—via cord, line, and cable—to the electric scoring machine. Unlike them, however, the sabre needs its own special scoring machine to perform its particular functions.

REFERENCES

Byrnes, Joe. "Technical Talks—Electrical Sabre." *American Fencing* (June/July/August 1988).

———. "Technical Talks—Electric Sabre Again." *American Fencing* (December/January/February 1989).

————. "Technical Talks—Electric Sabre Again." *American Fencing* (March/April/May 1989).

ELECTRUM MAGICUM. A superstitious belief that held sway during the Middle Ages that swordsmiths, under the influence of the stars, could create metal for swords and armor of supernatural strength, or *electrum magicum.*

This substance was supposedly composed of gold, silver, copper, and lead.

REFERENCE

Palffy-Alpar, Julius. *Sword and Masque.* Philadelphia: F. A. Davis, 1967.

ELEPHANT SWORD. The story of the elephant sword comes from early travelers to the East. Some accounts described it as a twelve-foot-long blade attached to an elephant's trunk. A more reasonable description has blades attached to the animal's tusks.

REFERENCE

Stone, George Cameron. *A Glossary of the Construction, Decoration, and Use of Arms and Armor.* New York: Jack Brussel, 1961.

ELTHES, CSABA. (1912–   ). Hungarian-born American fencing master.

Csaba Elthes began fencing at the age of thirteen at the insistence of his father, who, because Csaba was studying to become a lawyer and would eventually find himself in the upper levels of Hungarian society, might, perhaps, one day find himself in a duel.

In 1933, when he was twenty-one, Elthes studied fencing under the great Italo Santelli and Laszlo Borsodi. He quickly became a number one ranked fencer on his university team.

In 1951, Elthes became a fencing coach.

Leaving Europe in 1957, Elthes came to the United States and began teaching fencing immediately. By 1960, he was the U.S. Olympic team sabre coach.

In his years of teaching fencing, Csaba Elthes has coached countless individual champions and championship teams.

Said Elthes of his view of fencing: "In my teaching career I never considered who was talented and who was not because it was my principle always that in the fencing sport nobody is lost, nobody is hopeless. Everyone can be a good fencer if he has a good coach, has a love about fencing, and is diligent and tries hard and practices."

Csaba Elthes contributed a chapter entitled "The Sabre" to the *Sports Illustrated Book of Fencing* (1961).

REFERENCE

Axelrod, Albert. "Csaba Elthes, Coach of Champions." *American Fencing* (January/February 1987).

ELUDING THRUST OR CUT. An attack set into motion immediately on the heels of avoiding an opponent's attempt to bind* or beat* one's blade.

Blades engaged in the line of quarte

REFERENCE
Morton, E. D. *Martini A–Z of Fencing*. London: Queen Anne Press, 1992.

ENCLOSING. A term used by seventeenth-century English fencing master Sir William Hope* to describe closing ground with an opponent in an effort to seize his blade.
REFERENCE
Castle, Egerton. *Schools and Masters of Fence*. London: George Bell, 1885.

EN DEUX TEMPS. The term used by mid-seventeenth-century fencing masters to describe the principle of separating the parry* and riposte* into two separate actions.

Previous to this time, the "defensive" response of swordplay was an all-inclusive motion that attempted to block an opponent's attack and hit with a counterattack at the same time.
REFERENCE
Castle, Egerton. *Schools and Masters of Fence*. London: George Bell, 1885.

ENGAGEMENT. In modern terms, opponents' blades are said to be engaged when they are held in contact or placed in very close proximity to one another.

An older definition of engagement said that blades were engaged when the relative position of one weapon to the other was such that it blocked all possible attacks in the line it was guarding.

The old Italian masters called the engagement of blades *trovre di spada*.

REFERENCES
Castle, Egerton. *Schools and Masters of Fence.* London: George Bell, 1885.
Palffy-Alpar, Julius. *Sword and Masque.* Philadelphia: F. A. Davis, 1967.

EN GARDE. The term for a fencer's readiness either to attack or to defend. Also, "on guard."
REFERENCE
Palffy-Alpar, Julius. *Sword and Masque.* Philadelphia: F. A. Davis, 1967.

ENGLISH BROADSWORD. Similar to the Highland broadsword with its basket-hilted guard, the English broadsword was employed mainly as a military weapon. It enjoyed a particular popularity with Oliver Cromwell's army during the English Civil Wars (1642–1648).
REFERENCES
Morton, E. D. *Martini A–Z of Fencing.* London: Queen Anne Press, 1992.
Wilkinson, Frederick. *Swords and Daggers.* New York: Hawthorn Books, 1967.

ENGLISH SCHOOL OF FENCING. In its earliest form, the English school of fencing—solidified by Henry VIII in 1540, when he established the Corporation of Masters of the Science of Defence—was based on the use of the old-style cutting sword often used in conjunction with the buckler (shield). Such combat was looked upon by those who used it as the only true and honest form of sword fighting.

Not a style for weaklings, the English school promoted basically strong arms and strong blows to defeat one's enemy. This was exemplified by fencing master George Silver,* who thought there was nothing so good and noble as his English swordplay. He was especially of a mind that the cut was superior to the thrust.

The old English school eventually succumbed to foreign influences as the thrusting rapier, taught by Italians such as Vincentio Saviolo,* spread throughout the country. Here, English thought became Italian thought.

By the late seventeenth century, all foreign influences of swordplay had been absorbed and assimilated into the English temperament. As shown in the writings of fencing master Sir William Hope,* there were a simple honesty and a practicality displayed in English swordplay. It lacked frills. Even the making of feints was frowned upon. Beats and binds and disarms were common actions. One of the few innovations that could be found was the counter (circular) parry, which was looked upon with great enthusiasm as a kind of universal defensive action.

By the mid-eighteenth century, a new influence came into the English school of fencing. Guided by the genius of Italian master Domenico Angelo,* a "new" notion came into vogue, that fencing was no longer simply a killing skill but could be employed purely as an academic, athletic, artistic pursuit.

Eventually, even this school of thought, this refined notion of fencing, was tempered by the English mind, producing a modern, "manly," forceful game,

English swordsmen, from a sixteenth-century print

which could be categorized, perhaps, as typical of an empire-building, military people. While foreign masters—both French and Italian—continued to teach their thoughts, it appears that the British accepted only what suited them. Alfred Hutton,* one of the prime molders of British fencing during the late nineteenth century, was particularly adamant about what should and should not be included in the British game.

In 1931, the British Academy of Fencing Masters was created to solidify the British school into a body that could effectively teach and promote its ancient art in a completely sanctioned and organized manner. Its first president was Professor Leon Bertrand.*

REFERENCES

Castle, Egerton. *Schools and Masters of Fence.* London: George Bell, 1885.
Morton, E. D. *Martini A–Z of Fencing.* London: Queen Anne Press, 1992.

ENGLISH SWORD. While English swords varied in size over the years, their form remained relatively the same from the seventh until the sixteenth century: the straight, double-edged blade, the simple crossbar handguard, the plain grip, and the large pommel. The main differences included blade length, weight, point sharpness, and crossbar (quillon*) length.

Sword blades during Roman times were of the short, bronze variety, both straight and leaf-shaped. These were followed by iron swords and then steel.

In eighth-century Saxon England, the sword was doubled-edged and about 33 inches long. The blade was grooved to both lighten and strengthen it. As its tip was rounded, it was used exclusively as a cutting weapon. Later Saxon swords, influenced by those of invading Viking raiders, bore pointed, tapering blades, which made them equally serviceable for cutting or thrusting.

When the Normans invaded England in A.D. 1066, they introduced a longer sword than those of the Saxons. This weapon became the model for English swords thereafter.

In the sixteenth century, the English sword was supplanted by the Italian rapier.*

It should be noted that the English sword was often used in conjunction with a small, round shield called a buckler.*

REFERENCE

Castle, Egerton. *Schools and Masters of Fence.* London: George Bell, 1885.

Norman, A. V. B., and Don Pottinger. *English Weapons and Warfare 449–1660.* Englewood Cliffs, N.J.: Prentice-Hall, 1979.

EN MAIN. A French term meaning ''into the line of.''
REFERENCE
Morton, E. D. *Martini A–Z of Fencing.* London: Queen Anne Press, 1992.

ENVELOPMENT. A binding action where one fencer seizes his opponent's blade with his own weapon and leads it, without losing contact, in a circular motion that returns it to its original position.

Also a ''bind,''* an *enveloppment,* or *riporto.*
REFERENCE
Handelman, Rob. ''Fencing Glossary.'' *American Fencing* (May/June 1978).

EON, CHEVALIER CHARLES DE BEAUMONT D'. (1728–1810). French nobleman, diplomat, spy, swordsman, and transvestite.

The Chevalier Charles-Genevieve-Louis-Auguste-Andre-Timothee d'Eon was noted for two things: his ability with a sword and the fact that he often dressed publicly in women's clothing. It was rumored throughout his life that he was, in fact, a woman; but a postmortem carried out immediately after his death proved him to be definitely a man.

Like many noblemen of his time period, d'Eon was an avid duelist, so much so that Louis XVI, in an effort to curtail the chevalier's swordplay activities and thinking that wearing a dress would inhibit him in that pursuit, actually forbade him from wearing men's clothing anywhere within French borders. Once, when d'Eon disobeyed the order, he was thrown briefly into prison.

On a less bloodthirsty note, d'Eon also enjoyed a reputation as an amateur fencer. While living in England, he regularly fenced at Domenico Angelo's* famous school and occasionally gave lessons himself. He even posed for some of the illustrations in Angelo's acclaimed book, *The School of Fencing* (1763).

At the age of sixty, d'Eon engaged in a celebrated fencing match with the famous swordsman Chevalier de Saint-Georges,* who, was a third his age at the time. The encounter was arranged by the Prince of Wales and took place at Carlton House, a noted location for public fencing demonstrations. Despite being hampered by the dress he was wearing at the time, d'Eon scored seven strong touches against his young opponent.

The Chevalier d'Eon died in London at the age of eighty-three.

REFERENCES

Baldick, Robert. *The Duel.* New York: Spring Books, 1970.

Castle, Egerton. *Schools and Masters of Fence.* London: George Bell, 1885.

Gaillardet, Frederic. *Memoirs of the Chevalier d'Eon.* London: Corgi Books, 1972.

ÉPÉE. Evolved during the nineteenth century to teach fencers the necessities of actual combat, the épée is known as the "dueling sword" of modern sport fencing. It is referred to as a nonconventional weapon; that is, it has no special rules that restrict or direct the priority of touches ("right of way"); with épée, a touch is awarded to whichever fencer hits first.

The épée, like the foil, may score a touch only with the point of its blade. Too, its target area takes in an opponent's entire body, as would be the case in a real fight.

The overall length of a standard épée—from tip to pommel end—is 3 feet, 7 inches. Its weight is 27-1/8 ounces. The stiff blade is of triangular design; its length is 35-7/16 inches. The hand guard is 5-5/16 inches in diameter; its maximum depth is 2-11/16 inches. Considerably bigger than the foil guard, the épée *coquille's* large size reflects the special need to shield the épéeist's fencing hand from attacks.

The épée was the first sport weapon to be adapted to electrical use (1931).

The épée is sometimes called a "fencing iron" or a "fluking iron," the latter term referring to the épée being a weapon of chance rather than skill.

REFERENCES

Palffy-Alpar, Julius. *Sword and Masque.* Philadelphia: F. A. Davis, 1967.

U.S. Fencing Association, ed. *Operations Manual.* Colorado Springs, CO: U.S. Fencing Association, 1985.

ÉPÉE DE COMBAT. The weapon used in actual duels during the late nineteenth century and into the twentieth century. It was basically a modern épée* with a sharp point.

REFERENCE

Morton, E. D. *Martini A–Z of Fencing.* London: Queen Anne Press, 1992.

ÉPÉE DE PASSOT. A straight sword of medieval times.

REFERENCE

Morton, E. D. *Martini A–Z of Fencing.* London: Queen Anne Press, 1992.

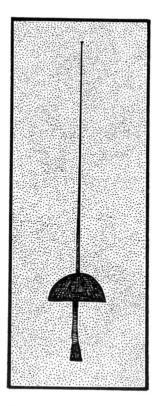

The épée

ÉPÉE DE SALLE. A practice dueling weapon, different from the real item only in that it had a protected tip.
REFERENCE
Morton, E. D. *Martini A–Z of Fencing*. London: Queen Anne Press, 1992.

ÉPÉE FENCING. Since the use of the épée should reflect the circumstances—both physical and psychological—of actual combat, the weapon has an application that uniquely fits these needs.

Because the entire body is subject to assault in épée combat, the weapon's on-guard position is designed to afford a fencer maximum protection. The sword hand is in a relaxed position of partial supination (palm up). The sword arm is kept relatively, although not completely, straight. Too much of a bend in the arm lessens a fencer's immediate reach and, at the same time, exposes the arm (at the bend) and the underside of the hand and wrist to attack. Conversely, a sword arm kept completely straight all the time will tire quickly. The épée's point should be kept level with—or slightly below—the hand but never higher, as this position, like a bent arm, exposes the hand and wrist to touches. Knees are bent; however, because the right leg—especially the knee and foot—are two of the closest body areas to an opponent's weapon, the bend should not be extreme. The point of one's weapon should continually menace the opposing fencer.

The fully extended lunge, as it is performed with the foil, is not used quite so frequently in épée fencing. This is because such a move runs the risk of leaving a fencer vulnerable to a multitude of counterattacks. An all-out lunge, say, to the body should be brought into play only when there is a sufficient opening in an opponent's guard. This can be achieved by preceding the attack with a feint, a strong beat, or a bind. Lacking the proper setup, one runs the risk of first being picked off by a counterattack that hones in on a closer target (i.e., the forearm).

Normally, half-lunges, accompanied by digs or jabs, can be extremely effective.

Of course, the underlying strength of épée fencing is the development of both offensive and defensive blade control. To be able to place one's point, at a moment's notice, anywhere on an opponent's body—even on a narrow wrist or a toe—is a skill to be sought after. To be able to defend without the protective element of "right of way" is vital.

Another important concept in the manipulation of the épée is "offensive defense" and "defensive offense." This means that a fencer should never slip into a mode of fencing that divides his offensive and defensive resources.

To become completely offensive in an action, without any regard to one's physical presentation, may expose a fencer's body to an effective counterattack. A proper attack, by and large, should incorporate a delivery that is efficient in terms of point movement and, at the same time, exposes as little of the attacker to his opponent's weapon as possible.

As for the defensive side, if a fencer allows himself to fall into a wholly protective frame of mind, he may find himself, rather than saved by his parries, altogether at his opponent's mercy. This can occur when a fencer, feeling extremely threatened, stops thinking and reacts. Often the defensive response is to pull one's arm back and raise one's weapon point to parry, as in foil fencing; and while this may momentarily halt an adversary's onslaught, it automatically sets some potentially ruinous and self-limiting factors into motion. First, the bent-arm "foil" parry exposes a vital target area—the hand and wrist—to a possible touch. Second, because there is no "right of way" to be considered in épée, the committed parrier may well be picked off by an insistent opponent whose attack continues unabated by conventions. Third, a weapon point moved out of line by performing a completely defensive parry no longer threatens an opponent, thus making it impossible to use one's blade offensively if the opportunity should arise. Fourth, the extra blade movement encountered in "foil" parrying may induce a loss of point control. The best defense, then, retains an element of offense. A maneuver that both blocks an opponent's attacking blade and, at the same time, retains a menacing point ends up being the most useful action. If a parry must, as a last resort, be separated from the counterattack, the sword arm should remain straight, and the épée blade should be angled in such a way that point movement is minimized.

Also, it should be noted that to avoid tying up the blade in detrimental defensive actions, the épée's enlarged *coquille* may sometimes be employed as a useful deflecting tool.

Ultimately, one's épée game should be kept relatively simple and uncomplicated. The intricacies of foil and the sweeping exchanges of sabre are not only unnecessary but dangerous. The épée is very much a game of the moment, where openings in an opponent's defense appear and disappear at the blink of an eye and where letting one's own guard down, even for an instant, may lead to disaster. To be a successful épéeist, then, means to be a balanced fencer in mind and body. It also helps to recall that the épée bout is the spiritual equivalent of a duel.

REFERENCES
Beaumont, C-L. de. *Fencing Technique in Pictures.* London: Hulton Press, 1955.
Palffy-Alpar, Julius. *Sword and Masque.* Philadelphia: F. A. Davis, 1967.
Vebell, Edward. *Sports Illustrated Book of Fencing.* Philadelphia: J. B. Lippinocott, 1962.

ÉPÉE RULES. The épée is a nonconventional weapon; that is, it has no rules regarding who should be doing what—attacking or defending—at any given time. Whoever manages to hit first is awarded the touch. For a touch to be valid, however, it must precede an opponent's adjoining offensive action by $1/25$ of a second. If two fencers strike simultaneously—a double touch—both are scored against (unlike in foil and saber competitions, where double touches are thrown out).

Some body contact—the *corps a corps*—is allowed in épée fencing (in foil and sabre it is penalized).

During épée's early days, a bout was settled by a single touch, as it might be in an actual duel. Today, following the lead of foil and sabre fencing, an épée bout lasts for five touches, which reflects more of the sport mentality of modern times. It should be noted, however, that in the Olympic pentathlon competition—where fencing is one of five sports competed in—the ''one-touch'' principle still applies.

The épée bout is fought on a strip six feet, seven inches wide and fifty-nine feet, one inch long.

The time allotted to a single épée bout is six minutes.

REFERENCE
U.S. Fencing Association, ed. *Operations Manual.* Colorado Springs, CO: U.S. Fencing Association, 1985.

ERROL FLYNN SOCIETY, INTERNATIONAL. Begun in 1977 in Great Britain, the International Errol Flynn Society is a group dedicated to the memory of actor Errol Flynn.

The society's founder, Eric Lilley, a driving instructor in Reading, England, tired of seeing the image of his boyhood hero run down in the media, got the idea of having a society that would uphold Flynn and the swashbuckling image he represented in his films.

The society sports honorary life memberships, held by former president Jimmy Carter, the Queen Mother of England, Olivia De Havilland, and Fidel Castro, to name a few. Today, the general membership, numbering over 1,500, is found worldwide.

Besides promoting the Errol Flynn image, Eric Lilley has used his organization to support charitable causes.

Lilley "fought a duel" in 1980 with a British actor, Oliver Tobias, who had announced in a magazine interview that he was a better swordsman than Errol Flynn. Tobias had called Flynn "a swordsman of indifferent merit," adding, "I wield the blade with greater skill." Lilley, taking umbrage at the remark, then sent out a press release announcing his displeasure with Tobias. Tobias followed this with a challenge. The two eventually met in an early morning skirmish that was covered by the British press. With sport sabres in hand, the society president and the actor "crossed swords" briefly and then shook hands. The event was used to raise money for a children's philanthropic organization.

REFERENCES

Lilley, Eric, ed. *The Errol Flynn Society Magazine: Sword II* (1979).
———. *The Errol Flynn Society Magazine: Sword III* (1983).

ESCRIMA. A form of stick fighting developed in the Philippines based on sword and dagger fighting techniques borrowed from invading Spanish armies in the sixteenth century and blended with the already existing form of personal combat known as Kali, a stick/empty hand/multiweaponed art.

While foreign conquerors attempted to stamp out *escrima,* rather than disappearing, it actually flourished, developing into numerous styles. As proof of its viability, it survived centuries of turmoil in the Philippines to become one of the most feared fighting arts in the world. It was employed successfully by Filipino fighting units against the Japanese during World War II. Today, it is still practiced among the Filipino community as both an exercise and a martial art.

REFERENCE

Inosanto, Dan, Gilbert, L. Johnson, and George Foon. *The Filipino Martial Arts.* Los Angeles: Know Now, 1980.

ESCRIME. The French word for "fencing."

ESCRIME LOISIR. Fencing for the pure enjoyment of it. Not to be confused with serious, competitive fencing.

REFERENCE

Morton, E. D. *Martini A–Z of Fencing.* London: Queen Anne Press, 1992.

ESPADA. The Spanish rapier of the eighteenth century. The blade of the weapon was five feet long.
REFERENCE
Pallfy-Alpar, Julius. *Sword and Masque.* Philadelphia: F. A. Davis, 1967.

ESPADACHIN. An old Spanish term for a swordsman.
REFERENCE
Castle, Egerton. *Schools and Masters of Fence.* London: George Bell, 1885.

ESPADIN. The name for the eighteenth-century Spanish smallsword.* It was in common use in Spain by the middle of the century.
REFERENCE
Palffy-Alpar, Julius. *Sword and Masque.* Philadelphia: F. A. Davis, 1967.

ESPADON. A fifteenth-century double-edged, two-handed sword used exclusively for cutting. In size, it was midway between a single-handed sword and a two-handed sword.

In his encyclopedic *Ancient Armour* (1824), Samuel Meyrick describes the weapon as a two-handed sword with a blade no more than two feet long.

Egerton Castle, in his *Schools and Masters of Fence* (1885), classifies the *espadon* as a long sword.

Also called a *spadone* and espadone.
REFERENCES
Castle, Egerton. *Schools and Masters of Fence.* London: George Bell, 1885.
Stone, George Cameron. *A Glossary of the Construction, Decoration, and Use of Arms and Armor.* New York: Jack Brussel, 1961.

ESPADRILLES. French fencing shoes.
REFERENCE
Morton, E. D. *Martini A–Z of Fencing.* London: Queen Anne Press, 1992.

ESQUIVE. The manner of avoiding touches by a rapid displacement of the body.
REFERENCE
Handelman, Rob. "Fencing Glossary." *American Fencing* (May/June 1978).

ESTOC. A sword with a long, narrow, quadrangular blade (30 inches long) used exclusively for thrusting. The first *estocs* were hung, without scabbards, from the saddle, but later models came equipped with scabbards. Rarely used as a primary weapon, the *estoc*'s original purpose was to take over when a horseman lost his lance.

The *estoc* was used from the thirteenth to the seventeenth centuries.

The term *estoc* was also applied to a sword specifically for cutting and thrusting. Much later, it was sometimes applied to the rapier.

REFERENCES

Castle, Egerton. *Schools and Masters of Fence.* London: George Bell, 1885.

Stone, George Cameron. *A Glossary of the Construction, Decoration, and Use of Arms and Armor.* New York: Jack Brussel, 1961.

Wilkinson, Frederick. *Swords and Daggers.* New York: Hawthorn Books, 1967.

ESTOC. A French term meaning a "thrust." Used by sixteenth-century French fencing master Henry de Sainct-Didier* as one of three forms of hitting an adversary.

Also called *estocada* by the Spanish.

REFERENCE

Castle, Egerton. *Schools and Masters of Fence.* London: George Bell, 1885.

ESTOCADE DE PASSE. The *estocade de passe,* according to Philibert de La Tousche,* was an offensive action performed by stepping with the left foot in front of the right and then bending the body over the thigh until the chin rested on the left knee. The left hand was placed on the ground for the sake of balance.

By its description, the *estocade de passe* was a highly exaggerated action of the sort much favored by La Tousche. Of course, it placed a fencer in a highly untenable position if it was stopped by an opponent.

REFERENCE

Castle, Egerton. *Schools and Masters of Fence.* London: George Bell, 1885.

ESTOCADE DE PIED FERME. An exaggerated, overreaching form of lunging described by seventeenth-century French fencing master Philibert de La Tousche.*

After the arm was extended, the fencer was to step forward with his right foot as far as he could manage. The right knee bending deeply, the body was then thrown forward until it rested on the thigh. The left leg was straightened. The left foot was turned on its side until the left ankle nearly touched the ground. The head was dropped as low as possible.

The term, meaning essentially "attack of firm footing," seems somewhat odd considering that the highly distorted nature of this action prevented any sort of quick recovery if it was parried by an opponent.

REFERENCE

Castle, Egerton. *Schools and Masters of Fence.* London: George Bell, 1885.

ETRUSCAN SWORD. The Etruscans, who occupied an area of Europe that would later become Rome, possessed swords with iron blades approximately twenty-five inches long. Rapier-like, these tapered to a sharp point. Sword sheaths were also made of iron.

The ceramics of the Etruscan people provide numerous illustrative examples of their swords, some of which were also of the sabre variety.

REFERENCE

Burton, Richard F. *The Book of the Sword.* London: Chatto and Windus, 1884.

EXCALIBUR. The legendary sword of King Arthur by which he derived his right to rule over Camelot* and the Knights of the Round Table. The way in which Arthur acquired the sword differs with the source of the story. In some versions, it was pulled from a stone, where it was magically embedded. In Sir Thomas Malory's *Le Morte d'Arthur* (1469), it was a gift from the mystical Lady of the Lake. When Arthur died, Excalibur was returned to its watery home by Sir Bedivere.

Excalibur has also been called "Escalibor," "Caliburn," and "Caledvwlch." A famous Irish blade called "Caladbolg," meaning "hard belly"—simply put, a sword "able to consume anything"—may also refer to this weapon.

REFERENCE

Benet, William Rose. *The Reader's Encyclopedia.* New York: Thomas Y. Crowell, 1965.

F

FABRIS, SALVATOR. (1544–16??). Sixteenth-century Italian fencing master.

Salvator Fabris brought together all that was best in sixteenth-century sword-play theory and practice into a single, highly workable system. His was a most practical approach that never forgot that what was being taught would be used in actual combat circumstances. To his credit, Fabris defined what he was talking about before he applied it to use, and he always proceeded from the general to the specific. It was perhaps his greatest strength that he was able to explain clearly actions that had, up to his time, been only partially understood.

Within the framework of his view of fencing, Fabris advocated a new approach to the idea of the on-guard position, that it could actually be used defensively, rather than simply a position from which to launch attacks. He explained how and when to use the disengagement* of blades, circular parries* and their deceptions,* and feints.*

Because of his popularity as a teacher, Fabris's insistence on the use of the thrust* over the cut* once and for all brought an end to the latter form of play in personal encounters.

Unfortunately, Fabris failed to remove himself from old-style swordplay on two very important points. Lacking an appreciation of the lunge, he sorely neglected its use, instead, holding fast to the principle of "passing"* (stepping) to close with an opponent. Also, he did not approve of *dui tempi,* the performing of the parry and riposte as two separate and distinct actions, maintaining steadfastly that *stesso tempo,* whereby a parry and a hit were accomplished in a single move, was the only way to approach defense. Thus, the master does not step fully into the modern school of swordplay.

Sixteenth-century fencing master Salvator Fabris

Fabris's book *De lo Schermo* (1606)** found such favor that five editions and at least five translations appeared during the seventeenth century.
REFERENCES
Castle, Egerton. *Schools and Masters of Fence.* London: George Bell, 1885.
Wise, Arthur. *The Art and History of Personal Combat.* Greenwich, CT: Arma Press, 1971.

FAIRBANKS, DOUGLAS, JR. (1909–   ). American film actor.
Never as athletic as his famous father, Douglas, Jr., was nevertheless a better actor. Charming and dashing, he appeared in a number of successful swash-buckler films during the 1930s and 1940s.
Beginning with his role of the dashing villain Rupert of Hentzau in the 1937

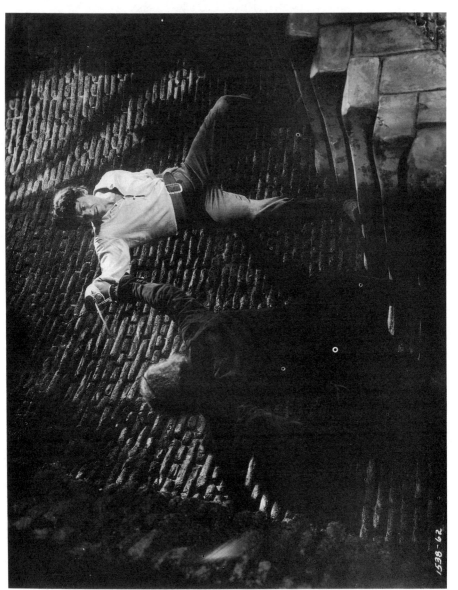

Douglas Fairbanks, Jr. (right), in *The Exile*

Prisoner of Zenda, Fairbanks went on to star in *The Corsican Brothers* (1941), *Sinbad the Sailor* (1946), *The Exile* (1947), and *The Fighting O'Flynn* (1949).

Fairbanks's most engaging and personally distinctive swashbuckling efforts were doubtlessly *Corsican Brothers* and *The Exile.*

The Corsican Brothers, also starring Akim Tamiroff, Ruth Warwick, and J. Carol Nash, was based on the novel by Alexandre Dumas.* Separated-at-birth Siamese twins, Lucien and Mario Franchi—the only surviving members of a family all but wiped out by a rival Corsican clan—battle injustice in their homeland. Complicating matters is the fact that the brothers share a mystical mental bond, continually experiencing each other's feelings. In the end, of course, good triumphs over evil, and justice is returned to Corscia.

Sword fights, staged by fencing master Fred Cavens,* abound. The final duel, fought one-on-one in a locked room, is both quickly paced and creatively artful.

The Exile, with Paule Croset and Henry Daniell,* was both written and produced by Douglas Fairbanks, Jr. A kind of swashbuckling fairy tale, the film tells the story of England's King Charles II following his flight from his homeland after being deposed by Oliver Cromwell and his "Roundhead" army. While living in Holland, Charles masquerades as a commoner to escape his enemies, falls in love with a farm girl, and occasionally engages in sword fights. Eventually, the king gives up his love to return to the English throne.

Fred Cavens created a short, exciting duel for Fairbanks set in a deserted mill. Charles is set upon by an assassin sent by Cromwell to kill him. The action quickly winds its way up a narrow stairway. When Charles's adversary's sword breaks, the king, ever the hero, throws away his weapon, and the two go at it man to man. The fight concludes with the villain's falling from the steps to his death far below.

Fairbanks, while not the best fencer in films, was still highly credible when he picked up a sword.

REFERENCES

Fairbanks, Douglas, Jr., and Richard Schickle. *The Fairbanks Album.* Boston: Little, Brown, 1975.

Richards, Jeffrey. *Swordsmen of the Screen.* Boston: Routledge and Kegan Paul, 1977.

FAIRBANKS, DOUGLAS, SR. (1883–1939). American film actor.

Douglas Fairbanks, Sr., was a Peter Pan, the perennial swashbuckler. His adventure movies were the best of their kind for their time. His acrobatic skills were thrilling to behold. His energies were boundless. He had a zest for life that unerringly came across in everything he did.

Fairbanks set the standard for swashbucklers when he starred in *The Mark of Zorro* (1920).** Lighthearted, dashing, brave, loyal, enthusiastic, idealistic, a swordsman through and through—this was the image he presented to the public. The public ate it up. From then on, while other actors tried their hand at swashbuckling, there was really only Douglas Fairbanks.

After *Zorro,* Fairbanks produced a string of top-rated films: *The Three Mus-*

Douglas Fairbanks, Sr., in *Don Q, Son of Zorro*

keteers (1921),** *Robin Hood* (1922),** *The Thief of Bagdad* (1924), *Don Q, Son of Zorro* (1925), *The Black Pirate* (1926), and *The Iron Mask* (1929). While there is something unique about each one of these films, Fairbanks's best work can be found in the final two.

The Black Pirate, also starring Billie Dove, Sam de Grasse, and Donald Crisp, was Fairbanks's salute to pirate adventures. The story deals with a nobleman out to avenge the death of his father, who was killed by pirates. Doug, of course, accomplishes what he sets out to do.

The swordplay, staged by fencing master Fred Cavens,* was lively and peppered with numerous grand stunts. Whether Fairbanks was crossing swords with a single opponent, as in his duel with the cruel pirate captain on the beach of a lonely island, or battling a dozen crazed, cutlass-waving pirates singlehandedly, as he does at the end of the film, Doug managed to carry out the task with grace and style.

The Iron Mask, with Marguerite de la Motte and Leon Barry, was Hollywood's last silent swashbuckler and, in truth, Fairbanks's swan song to the genre.

Fairbanks played the stalwart Gascon swordsman D'Artagnan in this filmed version of Alexandre Dumas's *The Man in the Iron Mask.* The story tells of twin sons born to King Louis XIII, one of whom must be hidden away to prevent the possibility of civil war. Louis, the older of the two, is the good son; Philippe, his brother, grows up in exile cruel and hateful. In time, a plot is hatched to put Philippe on the throne. Louis is kidnapped and imprisoned in the Bastille, where his face is covered by a grotesque iron mask. Eventually, he is saved by D'Artagnan and his musketeer friends, who, one by one, are killed in the service of their king.

Although now forty-five years old, Douglas Fairbanks was his usual athletic self, vaulting and climbing and swinging and fencing with a grace undiminished by age.

Doug's final costume film, *The Private Life of Don Juan* (1934), unfortunately, was a tired, colorless effort, lacking in all the virtues that had made his earlier movies successful. The tiny bit of fencing that did occur was without distinction.

While Douglas Fairbanks's image as an expert swordsman was often presented to the public by press agents, he was, for the most part, simply an actor who learned fencing routines for the roles he was playing. But he was a disciplined athlete and had excellent coordination, and these attributes made him look as good as any actor has ever looked with a sword.

A study of Fairbanks's films shows that his fencing skills improved dramatically from his first work in *The Mark of Zorro* to his final fencing scenes in *The Iron Mask.* It should also be noted that his image as a swordsman was enhanced greatly when he hired Fred Cavens to produce his movie fights. Cavens's expert ability was just what Fairbanks needed to whip his sometimes excessive energies into line.

Falchion play

REFERENCES
Behlmer, Rudy. "Swordplay on the Screen." *Films in Review* (June/July 1965).
Bodeen, DeWitt. "Douglas Fairbanks." *Focus on Film* (November/December 1970).
Richards, Jeffrey. *Swordsmen of the Screen.* Boston: Routledge and Kegan Paul, 1977.

FALCHION. A sword of the Middle Ages, coming into common use following
the Crusades. A kind of sabre, the falchion had a broad, slightly curved blade,
always widest near the point. It was used mainly by archers and men-at-arms.

The name "falchion" was derived from the Latin *falx,* through the Italian
falcione, which meant a scymitar, or the French *fauchon,* which meant a scythe.

Also known as a *fauchon.*

REFERENCES
Ashdown, Charles. *European Arms and Armor.* New York: Brussel and Brussel, 1967.
Castle, Egerton. *Schools and Masters of Fence.* London: George Bell, 1885.
Stone, George Cameron. *A Glossary of the Construction, Decoration, and Use of Arms
    and Armor.* New York: Jack Brussel, 1961.

FALSE ATTACK. The false attack is an attack—including a lunge—made not
to hit an opponent but to lure him into actually parrying and riposting. Here, if
evading his weapon has proved difficult, the riposte may be dealt with rather
than the parry.

False attacks may also be used simply to test the reactions of an opponent.

Any simple or composed attack may be used as a false attack.

Known, too, as a *fausse attaque* and an *attacco simulato.*

REFERENCE
Palffy-Alpar, Julius. *Sword and Masque.* Philadelphia: F. A. Davis, 1967.

FALSE EDGE. On a single-edged sword, a few inches of the back near the point was often sharpened to make the blade more effective for thrusting. This was called the "false edge" of the blade.
REFERENCE
Stone, George Cameron. *A Glossary of the Construction, Decoration, and Use of Arms and Armor.* New York: Jack Brussel, 1961.

FALSE GUARD. A short bar or widening of the blade in front of the true guard—found especially on two-handed swords.
REFERENCE
Palffy-Alpar, Julius. *Sword and Masque.* Philadelphia: F. A. Davis, 1967.

FALSE RIPOSTE. A riposte* made to be parried, so that the ensuing riposte issuing from one's opponent might be more easily met and disposed of. In theory, this opens the way for a final counterattack that, delivered with resolution, has an excellent chance of hitting.
REFERENCE
Morton, E. D. *Martini A–Z of Fencing.* London: Queen Anne Press, 1992.

FANTASY/ADVENTURE LITERATURE. The scope of fantasy/adventure writing spans the gamut from grim, blood-soaked barbarian 1930s pulp tales, in the manner of Robert E. Howard's *Conan** adventures, to more refined and noble fairy tale-like stories, such as William Morris's *The Well at the World's End* (1896), Lord Dunsany's *The Gods of Pegana* (1905), E.R.R. Eddison's *The Worm Ouroboros* (1926), and J.R.R. Tolkien's *Lord of the Rings* (1954–1956). Somewhere in between these extremes falls the Edgar Rice Burroughs* style of adventures, featuring heroic modern men thrown into swashbuckling, alien encounters, such as Burroughs's classic *A Princess of Mars* (1917).**

Many stories include elements of dark magic and wizards, evil, or strange science. Often there are evil, lusting, tough warrior women to be overcome or degenerate cavemenlike foes to outwit. Swordplay, of course, is almost always the avenue by which problems are solved.

Most of modern fantasy-adventure books have their roots somewhere in these types of stories. Examples include *The Tritonian Ring* (1953), by L. Sprague de Camp; *Strombringer* (1965), by Michael Moorcock; *The Wizard of Earthsea* (1968), by Ursula K. LeGuin; *Swords of Lankhmar* (1968), by Fritz Leiber; *The Wizard of Lemuria* (1965), by Lin Carter; *Brak the Barbarian* (1968), by John Jakes; and *Witch World* (1963), by André Norton.

In his book *Imaginary Worlds,* author Lin Carter remarks on the popularity of adventure/fantasy fiction, calling its readers "incurable romantics." Beyond that, he is not quite sure why people are drawn to it, remarking only on the dedication of such readers. Regarding its frequent descriptions as simply "escapist," he says that "virtually all reading—all music and poetry and art and drama and philosophy, for that matter—is a temporary escape from what is around us."

While there is no doubt as to the popularity of the genre, adventure/fantasy fiction does have its detractors. Stephen King, writing on the subject in *Danse Macabre,* a volume dealing with horror in literature and films, describes it essentially as stories "about the concept of power," the worst of which, he concludes, are about "people who have it and never lose it but simply wield it." He ends by labeling such "stuff" as "stories of power for the powerless."

Much of the adventure/fantasy genre also falls under the literary label of "swords and sorcery" fiction or "adult fantasy."

REFERENCES

Carter, Lin. *Tolkien: A Look Behind the Lord of the Rings.* New York: Ballantine Books, 1969.

———. *Imaginary Worlds.* New York: Ballantine Books, 1973.

King, Stephen. *Danse Macabre.* New York: Everest House, 1981.

Lupoff, Richard. *Edgar Rice Burroughs: Master of Adventure.* New York: Ace Books, 1965.

FAULKNER, RALPH. (1891–1987). American fencing master.

Ralph Faulkner began his adult life as a forest ranger and then switched to acting. Injuring his left knee in 1921 while making a film about lumberjacks, he was faced with being an invalid for the rest of his life. Looking for some sort of therapy for strengthening his damaged leg, Faulkner hit on fencing.

Fencing for fifty hours a week, Faulkner not only improved his knee but also ended up with a new direction for his life. Entering the world of organized fencing, he soon brought numerous championships under his belt. His crowning achievements to his competitive career were making the 1928 and 1932 U.S. Olympic fencing teams.

Faulkner eventually took his expertise with swords back to the theatrical world, becoming a professional film fencing master. His movie credits included such classics as *The Three Musketeers* (1935),** *Captain Blood* (1935),** *The Prisoner of Zenda* (1937),** *The Sea Hawk* (1940),** and *The Court Jester* (1956).**

Of film fencing, Faulkner explained: "Staging a film duel was no simple task. Planning often took weeks. And shooting, for various reasons, sometimes took months. We were very careful. It didn't behoove you to forget an action, because someone might get his ears lopped off if you did."

Faulkner's two best efforts were doubtlessly *The Prisoner of Zenda* and *The Court Jester.*

The Prisoner of Zenda, a story of political intrigue and adventure, starring Ronald Colman, Madelein Carroll, and Douglas Fairbanks, Jr., was Faulkner's first major job as a film fencing master. Overall, he found it to be a fairly straightforward affair, except for one incident:

Fencing master to the stars Ralph Faulkner

Toward the end of the picture, Ronnie Colman, as Rudolf Rassendyll, was to rush down some stairs and stop me from killing the king—also played by Colman. Ronnie was supposed to drive his sword into the wall right in front of my downward slashing sabre. I had an eight-inch-by-eight-inch piece of balsa wood placed in the wall, which was otherwise constructed of extremely hard wood. Balsa wood is so soft, you can drive a sword point into it with no trouble. But, since Ronnie had to do the stunt himself, I wanted to have the prop man put foam rubber into his sword guard for extra protection. And that, of course, took time. Well, a controversy developed about my holding up the shooting, so Ronnie said, "Anything Ralph wants me to do, I do."

The assistant director, however, didn't like actors, or fencing masters, telling him what to do. "I can do that stunt without any padding in the sword!" he said. So, I told him to go ahead. He took the weapon, rushed down the steps, missed the balsa wood, jammed the blade into the solid timber, and broke his thumb. Ronnie just looked at me, and raised an eyebrow.

The Court Jester, starring Danny Kaye, Glynis Johns, and Basil Rathbone, is considered by film critics to be one of Danny Kaye's best vehicles and one of the best-ever cinema spoofs of the swashbuckler genre. Kaye plays a simpleton who, through magical hypnosis, becomes a dashing swordsman hero, defeating evildoers and returning the rightful king to the throne of England. The main complication throughout is that Kaye's character is as easily brought out of his spell as he is put into it.

Faulkner's fencing scenes were both exciting and artistic. Moreover, he was able to interject a sense of humor into the action that is not often found in comedy swordplay.

Noted the fencing master:

Danny Kaye was a brilliant person, both mentally and physically. We had an almost impossible stunt where he had to fence while he poured wine into a cup and drank it— without once looking at his opponent, who was played by Basil Rathbone. Ever try patting your head and rubbing your stomach at the same time? It's something like that, only maybe twenty times more difficult. It was such a complicated maneuver, I had to double for Basil. It wasn't that he didn't have ability with a sword, but not being a professional swordsman, he just didn't have the precise timing that was needed to guide Danny through the routine. As for Danny, his extra-sharp mind and reflexes made up completely for his lack of fencing experience.

Other Faulkner efforts include *Anthony Adverse* (1936), *Zorro's Fighting Legion* (1939),** *The Thief of Bagdad* (1940), *The Fighting Guardsman* (1944), *The Foxes of Harrow* (1945), *The Bandit of Sherwood Forest* (1946),** *The Wife of Monte Cristo* (1946), *The Swordsman* (1947), *Sword of the Avenger* (1948), *Rogues of Sherwood Forest* (1950), *The Purple Mask* (1955), *Jason and the Argonauts* (1963), *The King's Pirate* (1967), and *Clash of the Titans* (1981).

Faulkner also taught sport fencing. Over the years, a number of his students went on to win national championships and compete on Olympic teams. Sewell Shurtz, Polly Craus, and Janice-Lee York were among his brightest pupils.

Ralph Faulkner continued to teach fencing until a few weeks before his death in 1987 at age ninety-five.

REFERENCES

Evangelista, Nick. "Won by the Sword." *Silver Circle News* (Spring 1979).

Hammer, Les. "Ralph Faulkner: The Last Swashbuckler." *American Fencing* (March/April/May 1987).

Richards, Jeffrey. *Swordsmen of the Screen.* Boston: Routledge and Kegan Paul, 1977.

FAUX TRANCHANT. The top one-third of a sport sabre blade opposite the cutting edge.

Also called the "false edge" and the *contre taille.*

REFERENCE

Handelman, Rob. "Fencing Glossary." *American Fencing* (July/August 1978).

FEATHER EDGE. An "on-guard"* position in which the left side of the body is turned away from one's opponent so that only the sword arm and right hip are visible. This is done to decrease the valid target area, but it is a position of extreme cramping and tension.

REFERENCE

Morton, E. D. *Martini A–Z of Fencing.* London: Queen Anne Press, 1992.

FEATHER PARADE. According to the teachings of Domenico Angelo,* the parry of sixte.* The name perhaps highlights a lightness in its execution.

REFERENCE

Morton, E. D. *Martini A–Z of Fencing.* London: Queen Anne Press, 1992.

FECHTEN. German term for fencing.

REFERENCE

Castle, Egerton. *Schools and Masters of Fence.* London: George Bell, 1885.

FECHTMEISTER. German term for fencing (*fecht*) master (*meister*).

REFERENCE

Castle, Egerton. *Schools and Masters of Fence.* London: George Bell, 1885.

FEDERATION INTERNATIONALE D'ESCRIME. Founded in 1913 by representatives from France, Italy, Great Britain, Germany, Holland, Bohemia, Hungary, Belgium, and Norway, the FIE, as it is generally known, immediately became the governing organization for the sport of fencing throughout Europe and then around the world.

In the execution of its duties, the FIE oversees all international fencing competitions and regulates the conduct of all national fencing bodies. One of its most valuable contributions to the game was to standardize rules, which, before its creation, varied somewhat from country to country.

REFERENCE
Belanger, Danielle, and Jean-Luc Duguary, ed. *Fencing.* Montreal: Organizing Commit-
    tee for the Games of the XXI Olympiad, 1976.

FEDERFECHTER. An association of fencing masters founded in Mecklen-
burg, Germany, around 1570. The Federfechter were proficient in the use of the
rapier* (*feder* being a slang word for rapier). Eventually, they moved their
headquarters to Prague.

The Federfechter were the arch rivals of the Marxbruder,* the original fencing
guild of Germany (the Marxbruder were masters of the two-handed sword*).
Whenever the rival groups met, a fight to prove superiority usually ensued.

REFERENCE
Castle, Egerton. *Schools and Masters of Fence.* London: George Bell, 1885.

FEET POSITION IN FENCING. Establishing proper foot placement in fencing is vital, for this factor helps a fencer maintain his balance. The feet create
a foundation upon which the fencer rests his weight. When the feet are not
aligned properly, losing one's balance becomes an inevitability.

Correct positioning of the feet begins with the on-guard* posture. To first
establish where the feet are to be set, bring them together at right angles, heels
touching. The right (front) foot points straight ahead, toward one's opponent;
the left (back) foot is held sideways to the right foot. Next, step forward with
the right foot so that a distance of at least a foot and a half separates the feet.
Having the feet too close together promotes a loss of balance; having the feet
too far apart makes moving quickly difficult. This distance should be kept constant while on guard.

In maintaining an advantageous foot arrangement, it may be helpful to think
of an invisible line extending forward from the heel of the back foot, and no
matter what one does—advancing, retreating, or lunging—the front foot stays
on this imaginary mark. While this situation may seem somewhat awkward at
first—a beginning fencer's feet tend to wander—sustaining it will prove beneficial.

The standard foot position might be altered when attempting various body
evasions or performing a *fleche.*

During the early stages of fencing's development, the way in which the feet
were arranged depended on the teachings of each individual fencing master.
Given the somewhat arbitrary "guard"* positions being advocated at the time
and the circular nature of approaching one's adversary, a swordsman's feet were
likely to be in a constant state of flux. Too, while few foot positions were much
more than adequate, some were, in fact, downright dangerous, if followed too
closely.

The Spanish were doubtlessly the greatest sticklers for where the feet should
go. They had their own specific positions for the feet that were based on geometry and esoteric philosophy.

As weapons grew lighter and more maneuverable—which promoted fencing in a straight line—the position for the feet became standardized in its modern form.

REFERENCES

Castle, Egerton. *Schools and Masters of Fence.* London: George Bell, 1885.

Palffy-Alpar, Julius. *Sword and Masque.* Philadelphia: F. A. Davis, 1967.

FEINT. The feint is, in effect, a lie. It is a false presentation of an attack—no lunge, therefore, is involved—designed to threaten an opponent into making a parry.

The feint may be used simply to determine how an opposing fencer defends himself (i.e., whether he uses lateral or counterparries). Its main application, however, is to draw a parry so that the defensive action may then be deceived (evaded).

Of course, to be effective, the feint must be made with the proper degree of force, so that one's adversary believes it to be an actual attack. Without this element of visual threat, a parry is unlikely to be made. Fencing master and former Olympian Ralph Faulkner* used to tell his students, "A feint should make your opponent faint."

Any form of attack—disengage, *coulé, doublé,* one-two, and so on—may be used as a feint.

The feint was considered a somewhat dangerous move by most old-time fencing teachers. It was felt that, by performing an action that was not really being used to hit, the attacker was left open to sudden counterattacks. Sixteenth-century master Rudolfo Capo Ferro* wrote, "[W]hen he feints, I thrust." His contemporary, Salvator Fabris,* thought the feint had its uses, but even he spent more time explaining how it should not be executed than how it should.

Feints gained a more widespread acceptance when the length and weight of swords had decreased enough to bring real speed into all maneuvering.

Also called the *finta, finto,* and *finda.* An older English term described feinting as "falsifying."

REFERENCES

Castle, Egerton. *Schools and Masters of Fence.* London: George Bell, 1885.

Palffy-Alpar, Julius. *Sword and Masque.* Philadelphia: F. A. Davis, 1967.

FEINTHORE. An old-time name for a bind* that takes an opponent's blade from the line of quarte* into the line of seconde.*

REFERENCE

Morton, E. D. *Martini A–Z of Fencing.* London: Queen Anne Press, 1992.

FENCE. The old-time name for the activity of swordplay.

The "art of fence" derived its name from the word "defence," the idea being that the sword was to be used not simply offensively—as it had been in the days of hacking and battering combat between armored knights—but also for the purpose of personal protection. In essense, the maneuvering of the sword was to create a figurative "wall" an adversary would be unable to penetrate with his own blade.

REFERENCE

Castle, Egerton. *Schools and Masters of Fence.* London: George Bell, 1885.

FENCER. Simply put, a fencer is one who fences.

In more ancient times, the term was applied to men who engaged in fighting with swords to injure or kill. Today, a fencer is more likely to engage in the sporting aspect of the activity.

REFERENCE

Castle, Egerton. *Schools and Masters of Fence.* London: George Bell, 1885.

FENCING. The art, science, and sport of fighting with swords or swordlike sport weapons.

The art of fencing is being able to regulate one's self so that every action performed is both controlled and well balanced, an efficient and visually pleasing blend of body and weapon.

The science of fencing is an understanding of the way all actions—both offensive and defensive—fit together. Everything in fencing's vast structure is based on human psychology, human movement, and physics. For every offensive action there is a defensive action to stop it; for every defensive action there is an offensive action to avoid it. The manner in which an opponent performs his offensive and defensive measures is then superimposed over this knowledge. Fully understanding these interactions allows a fencer to enter any fencing encounter, analyze its workings, and furnish himself with an accurate plan of operations, or strategy. In the end, following a scientific approach gives a fencer the opportunity to fully manipulate his adversaries and to use with consistency actions that have a universal application, rather than leaving everything to chance.

The sport of fencing is the ability to take what one knows about fencing and physically transform that information into physical fact, that is, achieve touches on a consistent, winning basis.

REFERENCES

Castle, Egerton. *Schools and Masters of Fence.* London: George Bell, 1885.

Palffy-Alpar, Julius. *Sword and Masque.* Philadelphia: F. A. Davis, 1967.

Vebell, Edward. *Sports Illustrated Book of Fencing.* Philadelphia: J. B. Lippincott, 1962.

FENCING, GENERAL HISTORY OF. The history of fencing has proceeded from the general to the specific, that is, from unrelated sets of tricks to scientific principles based on an understanding of the human condition.

The focus of early swordplay was on muscular strength and the ability to withstand a certain amount of physical punishment. As time went on, strategies involving the manipulation of one's weapon came into play.

Modern fencing. Photograph by Gretchen Knotts

Early sword fights often incorporated non-fencing maneuvers

For centuries, the cutting sword* held sway, and fighting techniques revolved around this fact. By the mid-sixteenth century, however, the thrusting weapon (rapier*) had come into vogue and began challenging the soundness of the cut. Eventually, the thrusting sword, because of its efficiency, won out over the cutting sword.

In the beginning a tool for protection and destruction, the sword, for many, was an indispensable part of everyday life. Fencing was, in effect, a killing art. But as customs changed, and the blade lost its once-unquestioned status in the world, its use detoured into an acquisition of culture and grace. By the end of the eighteenth century, the nature of fencing, for the most part, reflected a scholarly bent and a pursuit of personal growth.

From that point, fencing evolved into the sport it is today.

REFERENCES

Castle, Egerton. *Schools and Masters of Fence*. London: George Bell, 1885.
Palffy-Alpar, Julius. *Sword and Masque*. Philadelphia: F. A. Davis, 1967.
Wise, Arthur. *The Art and History of Personal Combat*. Greenwich, CT: Arma Press, 1971.

FENCING CLASSIFICATIONS. The modern fencer is classified by his achievement in organized competition, the highest rank being *A,* followed by *B, C, D, E,* and Unclassified. These levels are determined by the importance of the tournament and what place the fencer takes within the finals of that tournament. Higher-level tournaments, of course, produce a higher classification for those who win or finish close behind the winner. Lower-rated tournaments, as to be expected, engender lower ranks.

Tournaments are rated as follows: Group I-A (highest), Group I, Group II, and Group III (lowest). The rating for a tournament is determined by the level of its national importance, by the number of high-ranking fencers participating in the event, and, finally, by the overall number of fencers competing in the event.

REFERENCE

U.S. Fencing Association, ed. *Operations Manual.* Colorado Springs, CO: U.S. Fencing Association, 1985.

FENCING MASTER. A teacher of the art of fencing.

Early fencing masters were men who, lacking the funds for extensive protective armor, developed fighting techniques that depended rather on physical prowess and sword-wielding skills. Much of the fencing master's repertoire was based on trial and error and included such tactics as tripping, tumbling, kicking, punching, and even biting.

Most of these "scholars" were a rough lot drawn from the commoner elements of society; to a great degree, they were not individuals to be trusted. Fencing masters were routinely lumped in with every sort of unsavory type. Satan himself was said to be the first fencing master. In Thomas Dekker's *A Knight's Conjuring* (1607), the author wrote, "hee—'the devil'—was the first who kept a fence school, when Cayn was alive, and taught him that imbroccado by which he kild his brother; since which time he has made ten thousand free schollers as cunning as Cayn."

In time, though, men who considered the peculiarities and possibilities of the sword began to take over the fencing scene. Such masters were honored in their countries, and the best became the teachers to the noble houses of Europe. Kings even went so far as to protect them and their establishments from undue competition.

By the mid-eighteenth century the fencing master had evolved into a combination scholar/philosopher/artist/instructor and was looked upon as a purveyor of culture and breeding.

Today, the fencing master must be an athlete, teacher, and coach, a skillful interpreter and explainer of time-tested weapon-handling methods for sport and theatrical purposes, and even a dispenser of inspiration to his pupils.

REFERENCES

Castle, Egerton. *Schools and Masters of Fence.* London: George Bell, 1885.

Palffy-Alpar, Julius. *Sword and Masque.* Philadelphia: F. A. Davis, 1967.

Wise, Arthur. *The Art and History of Personal Combat.* Greenwich, CT: Arma Press, 1971.

FENCING MASTERS, NOTED.

Fifteenth Century: Diego de Valeria, Jayme Pons

Sixteenth Century: Camillo Agrippa, Rocco Bonetti, Jeronimo de Carranza, Don Luis Pacheco de Narvaez, Henry de Sainct-Didier, Giacomo di Grassi, Antonio di Manciolino,

Fencing master Martin Clery

Salvator Fabris, Ridofo Capo Ferro, Nicoletto Giganti, Hans Lebkommer, Achille Marozzo, Joachim Meyer, Hans Sachs, Vincentio Saviolo, George Silver, Jacob Sutor, Joseph Swetnam, Gerard Thibault

Seventeenth Century: Francesco Alfieri, Charles Besnard, Philibert De La Touche, Solomon de Faubert, Andre De Liancour, Sir William Hope, Wilhelm and Gottfried Kreussler, Labat, Jean Le Perche, Francesco Marcelli, Donald McBain, Morsicato Pallavicini, M. Teillagory

Eighteenth Century: Domenico and Harry Angelo, Henry Blackwell, Guillaume Danet, Henry de Faubert, Lorenz de Radaz, James Figg, P.J.F. Girard, John Godfrey, Heinrich Kreusler, La Boessiere, Sr., John McArthur, Motet, Don Juan Nicholas Perinat, Joseph Roland, J. Saint-Martin, Johann Schmidt, Captain Sinclair, M. Valdin, Anton Kahn, Zachery Wylde

Nineteenth Century: Henry Charles Angelo, William Henry Angelo, Albert Ayat, Luigi Barbassetti, Baptiste Bertrand, Felix Bertrand, François-Joseph Bertrand, Helene Bertrand, Justin Bonnafous, Bonnet, George Chapman, A. J. Corbesier, De Saint Martin, Franz Friedrich, Emile Gouspy, Alfred Hutton, H. H. Jacoby, Jean-Louis, Joseph Keresztessy, La Boessiere, Jr., Louis Lafaugere, the Loze family, Fernando Massiello, Emile Merignac, Morel, Beppe Nadi, Masaniello Parise, Pierre Prevost, Giuseppi Radaelli, George Roland, Louis Rondelle, Italo Santelli, Louis and Regis Senac, Louis Vauthier, Zanghery

Early Twentieth Century: Arlow, Borsody, Bouley, Louis Breton, Eurelio Camps, Catineau, Martin Clery, Antonio Conte, Coudurier, Dodier, Madame Froeschlen, A. Gautier, Felix Grave, Aurelio Greco, Grisier, Halasz, Jaquemard, Jeanty, Alphonse Kirchhoffer, Lovas, Luppi, Magrini, Giuseppe Mangiarotti, Alberto Marchionni, Lucien Merignac, Michoux, Jean-Baptiste Mimiague, Aldo Nadi, Nedo Nadi, Bela Nagy, Nerilac, A. Perigal, Eugene Pini, Camille Prevost, Rabou, Rakossy, the Roul Brothers, Don Adelardo Sanzi, Sassone, Edgar Seligman, Anthime Spinnewyn, Tagliapietra, Toricelli, Vizy

Mid-Twentieth Century: Bela Balogh, Zoltan Beke, Leon Bertrand, Eleanor Cass, Julio Castello, Roger Crosnier, Lajos Csiszar, Charles de Beaumont, Csaba Elthes, Ralph Faulkner, A. Garderer, Alfred Geller, L. Gerentser, Aladar Gerevich, Hans Halberstadt, B. Imregi, Karoly Lezak, Edward Lucia, A. Moldovanyi, Leon Paul, Rene Pinchart, Julia Jones Puglieser, Giorgio Santelli, Schlotzer, A. T. Simmonds, Laszlo Szabo, Gizella Tary, Tusnady, Imre Vass, Joseph Vince

Late Twentieth Century: Michael Alaux, Bob Anderson, Amilicare Angelini, Yves Aurial, Miklos Bartha, Michael Di Cicco, Mike D'Asaro, Umberto Di Paola, Livio Di Rossa, George Ganchev, William Gaugler, Wes Glon, Enzo Greco, Emmanuil Kaidanov, Ted Katzoff, Aladar Kogler, George Kolombatovich, Istvan Lukovich, Vladimir Nazlymov, Julius Palffy-Alpar, Niccolo Perno, Giorgio Pessina, Gerard Poujardieu, Ed Richards, Michel Sebastiani, Charles Selberg, Ettore Spezza.

When one considers the great numbers of men and women, both past and present, who have taught or are now teaching fencing, it is obvious that the listing here is no more than a convenient, rough sampling of individuals and should in no way be interpreted as an attempt to present a complete listing of noteworthy fencing masters.

REFERENCES

Castle, Egerton. *Schools and Masters of Fence.* London: George Bell, 1885.
Grombach, John. *The 1972 Olympic Guide.* New York: Paperback Library, 1972.
Morton, E. D. *Martini A–Z of Fencing.* London: Queen Anne Press, 1992.
Palffy-Alpar. Julius. *Sword and Masque.* Philadelphia: F. A. Davis, 1967.
Wise, Arthur. *The Art and History of Personal Combat,* Greenwich, CT: Arma Press.
    1971.

FENCING RULES. The technical rules of fencing—originally drawn up by Camille Provoste* in 1913—were set down as an official code the following year by the Marquis de Chasseloup-Laubat* and Paul Anspach.* They were adopted that same year by the International Congress of National Olympic Committees. But because of the outbreak of World War I, they were not issued until 1919. Over the years they have been revised numerous times.

The essence of the rules of fencing is that they cause a fencer to adhere to a commonsense approach to fencing—in lieu of sharply pointed weapons, which would teach faulty fencing without delay. Proper strategy is approved and rewarded; poor strategy is condemned and penalized.

The foil is the most structured weapon, rulewise, in fencing. The rules of foil fencing are not meant to limit a fencer's movement arbitrarily, however. They were established to force a fencer to develop self-control.

The sabre also has a specific code of operations designed to promote effective fencing.

The épée, because its usage, reflecting the come-what-may aspects of a real duel, is the least-structured weapon with regard to rules.

REFERENCES

Gaugler, William. "Right of Way and Fencing Time." *American Fencing* (July/August
    1986).
U.S. Fencing Association, ed. *Operations Manual.* Colorado Springs, CO: U.S. Fencing
    Association, 1985.

FENCING SCHOOL. The traditional learning place for the art of fencing.

In its early days, the fencing school was often a haven for the more unsavory elements of society, and fencing masters were classed with rogues and vagabonds. In many European countries edicts were passed to outlaw fencing schools, but, in spite of these laws, they continued unabated.

The Spanish are given credit for establishing the first "modern" fencing schools in the early fifteenth century. However, the Germans were the first to set up organized fencing academies on a widespread basis, protecting them jealously from all interlopers.

By the seventeenth century, fencing schools had cleaned up their image somewhat. In France, Spain, Germany, and England, for instance, the kings issued patents to favored fencing masters and protected their schools from outside competition.

The eighteenth century brought more changes to the fencing school. Codes

Domenico Angelo's eighteenth-century fencing school

of rules regulating fencing were enforced by custom. Schools became enclaves of culture and refinement, attracting both aristocrat and artist. The school of Domenico Angelo* in London was a shining example of this new attitude surrounding the fencing school.

Today, the fencing school may be anything from a college gymnasium to an empty store front. The students, by and large, represent a cross-section of modern society: doctors, truck drivers, secretaries, students, salesmen, actors, and so on. From its early beginnings in the darker regions of humanity, the fencing school has become a symbol of Old World values and uncommon athletic challenge for a mainstream world.

The fencing school may also be called a *salle de armes* or simply a *salle.*
REFERENCES
Castle, Egerton. *Schools and Masters of Fence.* London: George Bell, 1885.
Palffy-Alpar, Julius. *Sword and Masque.* Philadelphia: F. A. Davis, 1967.

FENCING STRIP. The fencing strip is the area of a tournament on which the actual fencing takes place. The surface of the strip may be made of earth, wood, linoleum, rubber, cork, plastic, or metallic mesh. The measurements of the strip vary for each fencing weapon.

Foil—length: 46 feet; width: between 5 feet, 11 inches and 6 feet, 7 inches.

Épée—length: 59 feet, one inch; width: between 5 feet, 11 inches and 6 feet, 7 inches.

Sabre—length: 59 feet, one inch; width: between 5 feet, 11 inches and 6 feet, 7 inches.

According to the rule book of the U.S. Fencing Association, although the strip length for épée and sabre is 59 feet, one inch, "[f]or practical reasons the actual length of the strip must be 46 feet."

The fencing strip may also be called the *piste* or "board."
REFERENCE
U.S. Fencing Association, ed. *Operations Manual.* Colorado Springs, CO: U.S. Fencing Association, 1985.

FENCING TOURNAMENT. According to the rules of the U.S. Fencing Association (USFA), the title "tournament" is the name give to all competitions.

Official tournaments, that is, those under the auspices of the USFA, are rated as to their importance.

In the United States, tournaments are held on a national, regional, and local basis.

International tournaments are subject to the control of the Federation Internationale d'Escrime, the world fencing organization.

An average fencing tournament, depending on the number of fencers involved, may be divided into preliminaries, semifinals, and finals. Larger tournaments may also include a quarter-finals.

REFERENCE
U.S. Fencing Association, ed. *Operations Manual.* Colarado Springs, CO: U.S. Fencing
    Association, 1985.

FENDENTE. In Italian fencing, a downward cut.
REFERENCE
Morton, E. D. *Martini A–Z of Fencing.* London: Queen Anne Press, 1992.

FER. In fencing, the French word *fer,* meaning iron, is synonymous for blade.
In fencing terms, *fer* has numerous applications:

Absence de fer (absence of the blade): the action of ending contact one has had with an
opponent's blade.

Attaque au fer (attack on the blade): actions executed on an opponent's blade, such as
a beat or a *froissement.*

Prise de fer (taking the blade): actions where one seizes an opponent's blade and controls
it, such as binds and *croises.*

A travers le fer (across the blade): an attack that is poorly parried so that it lands at the
moment of the parry.

REFERENCE
Handelman, Rob. ''Fencing Glossary.'' *American Fencing* (May/June 1978).

FERIRE A PIEDE FERMO. In Italian, to lunge* with the back foot remaining
firmly planted on the ground.
REFERENCE
Morton, E. D. *Martini A–Z of Fencing.* London: Queen Anne Press, 1992.

FERITE. In Italian, an offensive action.
REFERENCE
Morton, E. D. *Martini A–Z of Fencing.* London: Queen Anne Press, 1992.

FERMA. In Italian, a horizontal cut.
REFERENCE
Morton, E. D. *Martini A–Z of Fencing.* London: Queen Anne Press, 1992.

FERRARA, ANDREA. (c. 1550). Legendary sword blade maker.
    Little is actually known about Andrea Ferrara, and much controversy sur-
rounds him and his work. One source identifies him as Andrea dei Ferari, who
worked in Venetia during the latter half of the sixteenth century. Another story
has it that he traveled from Ferara, Italy, to Banff, Scotland, where he set up
his workshop.
    Whatever the case, Ferrara blades are noted, as one writer states, ''for their
great breadth, their suppleness and fine temper.''
    Unfortunately, countless counterfeit Ferrara blades exist, mostly dating from

the eighteenth century. Genuine blades are said to be two inches wide, with three grooves, and possess an inscribed gold orb and cross on both sides. But even here, there is no total agreement. Some blades bear double cross marks; some, a double diamond mark. On some blades, the maker's first name is spelled Andria, on others, Andrea. The spelling of his last name includes "Ferrara," "Ferara," and "Farara."

Ferrara blades, it should be noted, are found chiefly on swords of the Scottish Highlands.

REFERENCE

Mackay, William. *Highland Weapons.* Scotland: An Comunn Gaidhealach, 1970.

FERRER, JOSE. (1912–1992). Puerto Rican-born American stage and film actor best known for his film role of the large-nosed French swordsman/poet Cyrano in *Cyrano de Bergerac* (1950). Based on Edmond Rostand's* nineteenth-century play, *Cyrano* was a lavish, swashbuckling cinematic invention expertly fitted to the talents of Ferrer, who won an Academy Award for his efforts.

The character of Cyrano was not, however, new to Jose Ferrer. He had previously played the role on Broadway in 1946. For this stage production, which ran for a year, the actor studied fencing with famed Olympic coach Giorgio Santelli,* whom Ferrer viewed as the embodiment of Cyrano in both appearance and spirit.

The duel they created for the play, the action centerpiece of *Cyrano de Bergerac* known as the "Duel in Rhyme" (in which Cyrano engages in a sword fight and composes a poetic ballad at the same time), while obviously theatrical, was nevertheless free of moves false to fencing, what Ferrer described as "silly turns." The resulting combat consisted of cuts, thrusts, passes, and one spectacular disarm in which Cyrano binds his opponent's blade, flips it high into the air, and catches it (for the entire run of the show, to his credit, Ferrer never once dropped the airborne sword). Cyrano ends the duel with a one-two.*

For the movie version of *Cyrano de Bergerac,* Jose Ferrer worked with Hollywood's premiere fencing master Fred Cavens* and his son Albert.

This time around, thanks to the creative flexibility of film, the storyline was able to incorporate additional fencing that the play, limited by the fixed space of a theatre stage, could only hint at.

The compulsory "Duel in Rhyme," which took thirteen hours in front of the cameras to shoot, was both exciting and well-staged. A second sword fight—the "Fight with a Hundred Men" (only talked about in the play)—was a masterpiece of choreography, constructed in exchanges so simple and clean that one man fighting, and vanquishing, a large group of armed foes becomes not only believable but a thing of beauty to watch. Additional swordplay, as part of a sweeping battle scene, occurred in the latter part of the film. In all encounters, although sometimes doubled by Cavens, Ferrer handled himself superbly.

Ferrer reprised his role of Cyrano in *Cyrano and D'Artagnan* (1963), a French movie directed by famed film maker Abel Gance. Jean-Pierre Cassel played D'Artagnan.*

The actor took up the sword one last time, in 1977, in *The Fifth Musketeer,* playing the role of Athos in a reworking of Alexandre Dumas's *The Man in the Iron Mask.*

Interestingly, Jose Ferrer's involvement in fencing did not begin with the theatre. At age 10, coming across an old book on fencing by the famous master Regis Senac* and fired by its imagery, he soon began taking lessons. Later, at Princeton University, he fenced for the school, lettering in the sport. It was Ferrer's love of fencing that eventually led him to tackle the complex role of Cyrano de Bergerac.

REFERENCES

Conwell, Charles. "Boyhood Hero." *American Fencing* (July/August/September 1992).
Halliwell, Leslie. *Halliwell's Filmgoer's and Video Viewer's Companion.* New York: Charles Scribner's Sons, 1988.
Thomas, Tony. *Cads and Cavaliers.* New York: A.S. Barnes, 1973.

FICTIONAL SWORDSMEN. Fictional characters who fence run the gamut from those whose fencing is inherent in the individual to those from whom it simply springs as the situation demands (in the latter case, our belief system has been sufficiently suspended by the story line to accept swordplay as part of the situation).

Fictional swordsmen include:

Novels

D'Artagnan—*The Three Musketeers* (1844)

Ivanhoe—*Ivanhoe* (1819)

Rudolf Rasendyll—*The Prisoner of Zenda* (1894)

John Carter—*A Princess of Mars* (1912)

Peter Blood—*Captain Blood* (1922)

Conan—*Conan the Barbarian* (1930s)

Harry Flashman—*Royal Flash* (1970)

Sherlock Holmes—*The Seven Percent Solution* (1974)

Film

Zorro—*The Mark of Zorro* (1920/1940)

Luke Skywalker—*Star Wars* (1977)

Television

Maxwell Smart—*Get Smart* (1960s)

John Steed—*The Avengers* (1960–1968)

Simon Templar—*The Saint* (1963–1968)

Captain James Kirk—*Star Trek* (1966–1969)

Number 6—*The Prisoner* (1967)

The Fonz—*Happy Days* (1974–1983)

Comics

Prince Valiant—*Prince Valiant* (1937–)

Flash Gordon—*Flash Gordon* (1940s)

Plays

Romeo—*Romeo and Juliet* (1596)

Hamlet—*Hamlet* (1601)

Cyrano—*Cyrano de Bergerac* (1897)

Legends

Robin Hood—*The Merry Adventures of Robin Hood* (medieval)

King Arthur—*Le Morte d'Arthur* (medieval)

Sinbad—*The Arabian Nights* (Arabian)

Cartoons

Mickey Mouse—*Shanghaied* (1934); *Thru the Glass* (1936)

Popeye—*Aladdin and His Wonderful Lamp* (1938)

Peter Pan—*Peter Pan* (1953)

He-Man—*Masters of the Universe* (1980s)

Teenage Mutant Ninja Turtles—*Teenage Mutant Ninja Turtles* (1988); *The Incredible Shrinking Turtles* (1988).

REFERENCES
Benet, William Rose. *The Reader's Encyclopedia.* New York: Thomas Y. Crowell, 1965.
Halliwell, Leslie. *Halliwell's Filmgoer's and Video Viewer's Companion.* New York: Charles Scribner's Sons, 1988.
Lane, Hana, ed. *The World Almanac Book of Who.* New York: World Almanac, 1980.

FIELD OF PLAY. In fencing, the field of play refers to the area in which a fencing match is to take place. According to the official rules of fencing, it should have an even, level surface, giving neither an advantage nor disadvantage to any fencer.

The area designated for actual fencing in the field of play is called the *piste,*** strip,** or board.**

The field of play may also be called the "terrain."
REFERENCE
U.S. Fencing Association, ed. *Operations Manual.* Colorado Springs, CO: U.S. Fencing Association, 1985.

FIGG, JAMES. (1695–1734). Champion British prizefighter and master of swordsmanship.

Eighteenth-century prize fighter and fencing master James Figg

Called the ''Atlas of the Sword,'' James Figg (sometimes written as ''Fig'') was the most famous back swordsman of his time, demonstrating his skill time and again in public fencing bouts.

In Downes Miles's *Pugilistica* (1747), the author wrote of Figg: ''In him,

Strength, Resolution, and unparallell'd Judgement, conspired and blazed in all his actions. . . . He was just as much a greater Master than any other I ever saw, as he was a greater Judge of Time and Measure."

Another famous swordsman of the time and a student of Figg's, Captain John Godfrey,* wrote in 1747: "I chose to go mostly to Figg, and exercise with him; partly as I knew him to be the ablest Master, and partly, as he was of a rugged Temper, and would spare no Man, high or low, who took up a stick against him."

In all his years of public demonstrations of skill with the sword, Figg was beaten only once, and then he was said to have been ill.

James Figg is also generally acknowledged as England's first champion of bare-fist boxing.

REFERENCE
Castle, Egerton. *Schools and Masters of Fence.* London: George Bell, 1885.

FIGHTING GUILDS. In Europe during medieval times, organizations were set up among the middle classes to hand down fight skills from one generation to another. This practice was generally considered a practical safeguard against oppression.

REFERENCE
Castle, Egerton. *Schools and Masters of Fence.* London: George Bell, 1885.

FIGURE. Target situated on the left or right side of the fencing mask. This term is applied entirely to sabre fencing.

REFERENCE
Handelman, Rob. "Fencing Glossary." *American Fencing* (May/June 1978).

FIL. The cutting edge of the sword.

Also called the *filo* and *die Scharfe.*

REFERENCE
Burton, Richard F. *The Book of the Sword.* London: Chatto and Windus, 1884.

FILM FENCING MASTER. The man responsible for setting up and directing the swordplay to be filmed for a movie. The film fencing master also coaches the actors involved in the production and sometimes "doubles" for them (takes their place) in scenes where the action might be dangerous or is simply beyond an actor's abilities.

The film fencing master fills a very important position in a swashbuckler film's evolution, for it is upon his efforts that the fencing action—the element upon which the entire film hinges—either excels or falls flat. A number of expensively mounted swashbuckler films have been carried to a mediocre level by lackluster swordplay. On the other hand, a few otherwise average adventure epics have become classics because of well-staged, exciting sword duels.

In the days of silent movies, the first fencing teacher to be hired to direct the fencing in a film was a Belgian, Henry Uyttenhove.* Uyttenhove worked on films like *The Mark of Zorro* (1920),** *Robin Hood* (1922),** and *Scaramouche* (1923).**

He was soon followed by another Belgian fencing master, Fred Cavens,* who became the most successful director of fencing of the 1920s, 1930s, and 1940s. Caven's work included *The Black Pirate* (1926),** *The Adventures of Robin Hood* (1938),** *The Mark of Zorro* (1940),** *The Sea Hawk* (1940),** and *Cyrano de Bergerac* (1950).**

Ralph Faulkner* was one of the few Americans to become a successful film fencing master during Hollywood's "golden age." His films include *The Prisoner of Zenda* (1937),** *The Thief of Bagdad* (1940), *The Bandit of Sherwood Forest* (1946),** and the comedy classic *The Court Jester* (1956).**

The last of the top film fencing masters, also from Belgium, was Jean Heremans.* Heremans's film fencing direction included *The Three Musketeers* (1948),** *Scaramouche* (1952),** *The Prisoner of Zenda* (1952),** and *Prince Valiant* (1954).

Other supervisors of film fencing include Patrick Crean of *Master of Ballantrae* (1953); William Hobbs,* the fight arranger for *The Three Musketeers* (1974) and *The Four Musketeers* (1975); Bob Anderson,* the fencing master on *The Princess Bride* (1987) and *By the Sword* (1993); Victor Paul, the fencing coach for *Zorro, the Gay Blade* (1981) and *My Favorite Year* (1982); Anthony De Longis,* who guided the swordplay for *Warrior and the Sorceress* (1984) and *Masters of the Universe* (1987); and Ted Katzoff,** who put together the sword combat for Steven Spielberg's *Hook* (1992).**

Additional people involved in Film Fencing choreography include Aldo Nadi,* Albert Cavens,** Dave Sharpe, Peter Diamond,* Niccolo Perno, Robert O'Sullivan, and Dan Speaker.

REFERENCES
Behlmer, Rudy. "Swordplay on the Screen." *Films in Review* (June/July 1965).
Richards, Jeffrey. *Swordsmen of the Screen*. Boston: Routledge and Kegan Paul, 1977.

FINALE. The last portion of an offensive action, when an attack ends.
REFERENCE
Handelman, Rob. "Fencing Glossary." *American Fencing* (July/August 1978).

FINGER GUARD. The part of the sword hilt that protects the fingers against a cross cut.

The finger guard is usually formed by extending a curved bar, systems of bars, or plate from the quillons (crossbars) and/or the *coquille* (shell guard).

In combat situations, the stouter forms of the finger guards could be used as a sort of "brass knuckles" in close-quarters fighting.

Also known as the "bow," "counterguard," "knuckle bow," "knuckle guard," and the "ward iron."

The finger guard on a French sword

REFERENCES

Stone, George Cameron. *A Glossary of the Construction, Decoration, and Use of Arms and Armor.* New York: Jack Brussel, 1961.
Wise, Arthur. *The Art and History of Personal Combat.* Greenwich, CT: Arma Press, 1971.

FINGER LOOP. Some swordsmen had a practice of crossing their fingers over the sword's crossbar to strengthen their hold on the weapon. In some cases, a small, metal loop was added to the crossbar through which a finger could be inserted for this purpose.

The loop both kept the finger from slipping from its position and afforded it protection.

REFERENCE
Castle, Egerton. *Schools and Masters of Fence.* London: George Bell, 1885.

FINGERPLAY. The ability to guide the maneuvering of one's weapon with the fingers (instead of the arm or wrist). This produces small, decisive blade movements, rather than large, sweeping, muscular ones. The French grip is noted for inducing such manipulations.
REFERENCE
Morton, E. D. *Martini A–Z of Fencing.* London: Queen Anne Press, 1992.

FIRANGI. A cut-and-thrust, straight-bladed sword of the Mahratta people of India. The blades for these weapons were either imported from Europe by the Portuguese or made in a European style, hence the name *firangi,* meaning "foreigner."

Broadsword blades and rapier blades were both used. The hilts were fitted with broad hand guards and knuckle guards. Pommels were of the disk-type, with curved spikes on them.

Most *firangi* blades are of the seventeenth century, although some date from the sixteenth century.

Also known as a *firang* and a *phiranhi.*
REFERENCE
Stone, George Cameron. *A Glossary of the Construction, Decoration, and Use of Arms and Armor.* New York: Jack Brussel, 1961.

FIREARMS. The great irony of fencing, as we know it today, is that it came about as the direct result of the invention of firearms. Swordplay, in the days of knights, was a rather simple affair. Swords had only one purpose: offensive. They were large, bulky things designed to smash through an opponent's armor as quickly as possible. Science and skill had little to do with armed combat. Strength and effective armor were what usually ended up winning the day. The need for complex sword maneuvering was not a major concern.

But, when firearms were introduced into armed combat, all this changed. When bullets began piercing the armor knights wore, knights discarded that armor. Not only was it useless, but its weight made it difficult to get out of the way of the shooting. The shedding of metal suits, of course, improved mobility. However, it also left a major gap in the area of personal defense.

At this point, a new way of protecting one's self had to be devised. Sword-handling techniques became the method. In effect, the controlled movement of a blade became a fighting man's "armor."

In the beginning, the men who no longer wore armor turned to the most logical source of instruction: men who had never worn armor, that is, commoners. According to writer Egerton Castle,* "These 'sword-men,' whether jugglers in sport or gladiators in earnest, were, of course, in great request." Men unable to afford the luxury of outfitting themselves in armor plate, by necessity had to develop a certain facility with their swords for protection.

Early fencing styles were usually a crude hodgepodge of kicking, punching, tripping, and tumbling. Artfulness was still at a premium. To be truly effective, one had to depend heavily on sudden inspiration and raw courage. But, given hundreds of years of experimenting—sometimes in practice, sometimes in deadly earnest—fencing evolved into a refined set of offensive and defensive actions, which can be counted on to work again and again because they deal with well-studied aspects of human psychology and human movement.

REFERENCES
Castle, Egerton. *Schools and Masters of Fence.* London: George Bell, 1885.
Evangelista, Nick. "En Garde! Take a Stab at Fencing." *Intro Magazine* (October 1984).
Palffy-Alpar, Jules. *Sword and Masque.* Philadelphia: F. A. Davis, 1967.
Wise, Arthur. *The Art and History of Personal Combat.* Greenwich, CT: Arma Press, 1971.

FIREARMS—DEFENSE AGAINST WITH A SWORD. According to early teachings, the best tactic for a swordsman to use against a man with a musket was to approach him in a serpentine (zigzag) fashion, thereby making it difficult for the musketeer to aim his weapon.

REFERENCE
Wise, Arthur. *The Art and History of Personal Combat.* Greenwich, CT: Arma Press, 1971.

FIST SWORD. Actually not a sword at all but a stiletto-style dagger used in India. The blade was approximately nine inches long.

Also known as a *maushtika.*

REFERENCE
Burton, Richard F. *The Book of the Sword.* London: Chatto and Windus, 1884.

FITNESS, FENCING AND. Fencing, because of its continual, unrelenting by-play, is one of the most physically challenging sports in existence. However, it is a game in which strength is less of a factor than endurance and flexibility.

It has been estimated that an average fencing encounter burns approximately five calories per minute.

REFERENCE
Berland, Theodore. *The Fitness Fact Book.* New York: Signet Books, 1980.

FITTING MAKERS, JAPANESE SWORD. Fittings, that is metal decorations for weapon and scabbard, were considered an integral part of a Japanese sword's makeup. In most cases, these beautifully designed mountings also served a practical purpose, such as securing the sword blade within its wooden sheath, or strengthening the connection between a blade and its handle.

Typical of the Japanese obsession with artistic excellence in all things, entire schools were founded whose sole task was to create aesthetically pleasing fittings.

Noted sword fitting makers include:

Issander Joi, (1700–1761): One of the greatest designers of sword mountings of the eighteenth century. It was said his work displayed a keen sense of humor.

Haruaki (1786–1859): The most celebrated designer of fittings of the nineteenth century. He was awarded the title of *hogen,* the highest honor an artist could aspire to, by the Emperor.

Natsuo Kano (1828–1898): Designed sword fittings of extreme fineness. He also designed Japanese coins.

REFERENCE
Stone, George Cameron. *A Glossary of the Construction, Decoration, and Use of Arms and Armor.* New York: Jack Brussel, 1961.

FLAMBERGE. Originally, any large sword. In time, though, it came to mean a sword with a wavy or undulating edge, especially the *spadone* and *Zweyhander.*

By the latter part of the sixteenth century, the name *flamberge* was applied to a rapier with simple hilt arrangement consisting of only a shallow cut guard and quillons. The blade was usually more slender than that of the average rapier blade. According to the teaching of some fencing masters of the time period, this weapon could be easily transferred from the right hand to the left hand in combat. Because of its lightness, it was a favorite dueling sword of the seventeenth century. The *flamberge* is usually recognized as the first step in the transition of the rapier to the smallsword.

Also called a *flamberg.*
REFERENCES
Castle, Egerton. *Schools and Masters of Fence.* London: George Bell, 1885.
Stone, George Cameron. *A Glossary of the Construction, Decoration, and Use of Arms and Armor.* New York: Jack Brussel, 1961.

FLANC. Target area situated under the sword arm of a fencer.
REFERENCE
Handelman, Rob. ''Fencing Glossary.'' *American Fencing* (May/June 1978).

FLANCONNADE. A term used in eighteenth-century smallsword* fencing, referring to an attack directed toward an opponent's right flank.

Also called a *fianconata.*
REFERENCE
Morton, E. D. *Martini A–Z of Fencing.* London: Queen Anne Press, 1992.

FLECHE. *Fleche* means "arrow." It is a leaping or jumping attack made by throwing the torso forward as the left foot crosses in front of the right. Ideally, the action hits before the left foot touches the ground.

The main strength of the *fleche* is that it covers a considerable distance quickly, which, if done correctly, will catch an opponent completely off guard. Its main weakness is that, if unsuccessful, it leaves one in a position that is difficult to defend.

To maintain an element of surprise around the *fleche,* it should be used sparingly.

The *passe on avant* of the eighteenth century is considered the forerunner of the *fleche* as it is practiced in modern times.

Also known as the "running attack," a "flash," a "jump attack," and a *frecciata.*

REFERENCES

Palffy-Alpar, Julius. *Sword and Masque.* Philadelphia: F. A. Davis, 1967.

Vebell, Edward. *Sports Illustrated Book of Fencing.* Philadelphia: J. B. Lippincott, 1962.

FLEURET. The French term for the foil. It was derived from the foil's blunted tip, which resembled a flower bud.

REFERENCE

Castle, Egerton. *Schools and Masters of Fence.* London: George Bell, 1885.

FLICKING. Similar in appearance to fly casting in fishing, a fencer attempts to whip his blade at his opponent to gain a touch. Part of the lure of this action is that the blade point need not be "in line" for a touch to occur. The "flick" bends the flexible blade, popping its point downward into the target area. Moreover, the pressure produced by a flicking blade can cause an electric tip to depress even when it hits at a bit of an angle. Theoretically, the attacking blade may even bend enough to send its point around a parrying weapon to produce a hit.

A very imprecise action, flicking has been condemned by traditional fencers for its failure to produce consistent positive results. Unfortunately, as it is somewhat spectacular in appearance, flicking has attracted numerous less discriminating fencers to its ranks, producing a fad that has swept through the fencing world.

REFERENCE

Oliver, Bill. "To Flick or Not to Flick." *American Fencing* (Spring 1993).

FLYING CUT-OVER. An attack utilizing a beat from which a *coupé* is immediately executed.

REFERENCE

Morton, E. D. *Martini A–Z of Fencing.* London: Queen Anne Press, 1992.

FLYING FLANCONADE. A *coupé* followed by an attack to the flank.
Also called a *flanconade a la mouche.*
REFERENCE
Morton, E. D. *Martini A–Z of Fencing.* London: Queen Anne Press, 1992.

FLYING LUNGE. An attack in which the back foot leaves the ground during
the lunge and is placed down only as the front foot hits the floor. The purpose
of the flying lunge is to add a few more inches to the distance covered in one's
offensive action.
REFERENCE
Morton, E. D. *Martini A–Z of Fencing.* London: Queen Anne Press, 1992.

FLYING PARRY RIPOSTE. In sabre* fencing, a fencer may blend his parry*
riposte* maneuver together into a single, continuous sweeping motion, catching
the opponent's blade during the course of the action. This is known as a flying
parry riposte.
REFERENCE
Palffy-Alpar, Julius. *Sword and Masque.* Philadelphia: F. A. Davis, 1967.

FLYNN, ERROL. (1909–1959). Australian-born American film actor.
    While he acted in over fifty films of various types—from westerns to com-
edies to war movies—Errol Flynn is remembered first and foremost for his
swashbuckler films, the best of which include *Captain Blood* (1935), *The Adventures of Robin Hood* (1938), *The Sea Hawk* (1940), and *The Adventures of
Don Juan* (1949).
    From the mid-1930s until the late 1940s, Flynn reigned as the king of the
dashing swordsmen heroes of the screen. Not since the days of Douglas Fairbanks had there been an actor whose very bearing and personality so defined
the term "swashbuckler." Flynn was truly the ruler by which all other actors
of the genre were measured.
    Described as an indifferent swordsman, Flynn was nevertheless a natural ath-
lete and was easily able to give the impression of being able to handle a blade
with skill.
    In his autobiography, *My Wicked, Wicked Ways* (1959), the actor gave his
opinion of actors and fencing: "Actors are the most dangerous people to have
a duel with . . . because we don't know how to handle ourselves. . . . We come
out charging, whirling all around, forgetting prepared routines of swordplay."
    Of theatrical fencing's specific dangers, Flynn noted: "Anthony Quinn ran a
sword through my doublet and I nearly lost an eye." He also reported having
a sword tip accidentally stuck into his mouth on another occasion. Some years
later, he came close to slicing off actor Christopher Lee's thumb in a broadsword
fight.
    He finished by saying: "I don't know much about fencing, but I know how
to make it look good. You only have to stand still, and look forward, your head

Eroll Flynn (right) in *The Sea Hawk*

proud, and let the sword point straight out, you and the sword point both un-moving, and it is dramatic. Let the sword point dip two inches, and the gesture can look very clever and dangerous.''

Errol Flynn began his career as a movie swordsman with *Captain Blood* (1935), which was adapted from Rafael Sabatini's* famous 1922 novel. The film costarred Olivia de Havilland, and Basil Rathbone.

Captain Blood tells the story of a young Irish doctor who, after being unjustly convicted of treason against the Crown, is sent to the West Indies as a slave. Escaping his captivity, he then becomes a feared pirate. Eventually he wins the beautiful girl, defeats all the villains, and becomes the governor of Jamaica.

The main duel of the film, staged by Fred Cavens,* while certainly energetic, ends up being rather technically uninspiring. As Flynn and Basil Rathbone fence across a sandy island beach, neither exhibits much style or grace. Flynn looks particularly uneasy, even awkward, with his sword, at times hopping fitfully across rocks like a giant crab. Rathbone simply appears vaguely demented. Still, it was their first effort as screen swordsmen, and, to their credit, they both improved dramatically in their fencing by the time they did another swashbuck-ler film.

Flynn's greatest film triumph was doubtlessly *The Adventures of Robin Hood* (1940), which also starred Basil Rathbone, Olivia de Havilland, Claude Rains, Patric Knowles, Alan Hale, and Eugene Pallette. Writer Tony Thomas, in his book *The Great Adventure Films* (1976), characterized it as ''the most glorious of all adventure movies.''

Drawing heavily on the ancient Robin Hood legends, *The Adventures of Robin Hood* begins with Robin's being outlawed and ends with his aiding King Rich-ard the Lion-Hearted to defeat his treacherous brother, Prince John. In between, Robin Hood meets Little John, Friar Tuck, and Maid Marian, robs from the rich and gives to the poor, and wins an archery tournament.

Fencing master Fred Cavens staged the swordplay in *Robin Hood* with flair and imagination. While more than a little historically incorrect in its portrayal—the swords were modified to a lightness that allowed for fast-paced, vigorous exchanges that would have been unthinkable during the Middle Ages; also, offensive and defensive moves were included in the action that would not have been seen historically for another 900 years—the combat remains one of the best and most exciting examples of theatrical dueling ever filmed.

The Sea Hawk (1940) is another example of Flynn at his zenith as a swash-buckler. Also starring Brenda Marshall, Claude Rains, Alan Hale, and Henry Daniell, the film deals with the adventures of Captain Geoffrey Thorpe, a mem-ber of the Sea Hawks, who fight against the tyranny of Spain by attacking its treasure ships and New World colonies.

The film's climactic rapier duel between Flynn and Henry Daniell (again staged by Fred Cavens) was paced at a breakneck speed, with short pieces of action edited together to form a fight of epic proportions. The movement was uniformly clean and stylish. Flynn was doubled in the more hectic moments of the fight by stuntman Don Turner. Daniell, up to very little of the fencing, was doubled by fencing champion Ralph Faulkner.*

Flynn's final great swashbuckler film was *The Adventures of Don Juan* (1949), with Viveca Lindfors, Alan Hale, and Robert Douglas. Flynn starred as the legendary lover Don Juan, now world-weary and looking for a little peace and quiet. He, of course, never finds it. Women chase him, and men challenge him to duels. Eventually, he finds himself in the middle of a plot to overthrow the king and queen of Spain, which he quickly ends amid a flurry of rapier and dagger play. Still another Fred Cavens fight, this was the last time Flynn and the fencing master worked together.

Other Flynn swashbuckler vehicles include *The Prince and the Pauper* (1937), *Against All Flags* (1952), *Master of Ballantrae* (1953), *Crossed Swords* (1953), and *The Warriors* (1955).

REFERENCES

Flynn, Errol. *My Wicked, Wicked Ways.* London: Heinemann, 1960.

Richards, Jeffrey. *Swordsmen of the Screen.* Boston: Routledge and Kegan Paul, 1977.

Thomas, Tony, Rudy Behlmer, and Clifford McCarty. *The Films of Errol Flynn.* New York: Citadel Press, 1969.

FLYSSA. The sword of the Kabyle people of Morocco.

The *flyssa* has a long, single-edged blade (from twelve to thirty-nine inches long), straight along the back, with a long point. Its widest point is at its center of percussion, which is located one-third of its length from the tip.

The hilt of the weapon has no guard.

REFERENCE

Stone, George Cameron. *A Glossary of the Construction, Decoration, and Use of Arms and Armor.* New York: Jack Brussel, 1961.

FOIBLE. The weakest part of a sword blade (always the portion near the tip).

Also known as the "faible," the "feeble," the "weak part of the blade," and a *debole.*

REFERENCE

Burton, Richard F. *The Book of the Sword.* London: Chatto and Windus, 1884.

FOIL. The traditional practice weapon of modern fencing. The foil was conceived to teach a fencer the fundamentals of swordplay in a relatively danger-free way. In its original usage, however, the term "foil"—derived from the French *refouler,* or "to turn back"—referred to any weapon designed for the purpose of practice.

With specific regard to swords, the initial concept of the foil was simply to render a standard weapon harmless for practice by placing a covering of some kind over the cutting edge or tip of the blade. This might be done with a leather covering for the cutting edge or a special metal ball or even a piece of wood for the tip. This was described as "foiling" one's weapon (i.e., rendering it harmless).

Practice weapons, called rebated weapons, were in common use in fencing's early days. These were specially designed with blunted tips and dulled cutting edges. However, because they were no less heavy and stout than the actual swords they represented, they could create almost as much bodily injury as the real thing.

Finally, in an effort to establish a truly safe environment in the fencing school, light, flexible blades were designed to eliminate the accidental mayhem wrought by rebated or "foiled" weapons. By the late seventeenth century, these new-style blades—the prototypes of modern foil blades—were in common use. At first, they simply fitted onto standard hilts. By the mid-1700s, however, foils had their own distinct guards and grips, looking much like the weapons used today.

The modern foil blade is quadrangular. The maximum length of the weapon is 3 feet, 7 inches; the weight, 17-5/8 ounces. The maximum blade length is 2 feet, 11-7/16 inches. The tip, which is blunted, may be called either the *point d'arret* or simply the button.

There are numerous varieties of foil grips. The French and Italian grips are traditional. The former is a straight grip with a slight twist in it that fits neatly into the contours of the hand; the latter is a completely straight grip accompanied by crossbars around which a fencer wraps a finger or fingers.

In recent years, various forms of "pistol"-type grips have become popular. These, resembling a pistol (as the name implies), possess one or more prongs on the grip itself around which the fencer places his fingers.

The foil is, as has already been noted, the teaching weapon of fencing. It classifies as a "conventional weapon"; that is, it is a weapon whose usage is guided by rules. The rules, based on proper fencing practices, force a fencer to adhere to actions that benefit his fencing, thereby giving him control over himself and his situation.

The foil may hit only with its point and only on the trunk of an opponent's body.

Also known as a *fleuret,* "file," the *spada d'exerciso,* the "practice weapon," *fiorette*, and *fioretto*.

REFERENCES

Castle, Egerton. *Schools and Masters of Fence.* London: George Bell, 1885.
Morton, E. D. *Martini A–Z of Fencing.* London: Queen Anne Press, 1992.
Palffy-Alpar, Julius. *Sword and Masque.* Philadelphia: F. A. Davis, 1967.
U.S. Fencing Association, ed. *Operations Manual.* Colorado Springs, CO: U.S. Fencing Association, 1985.

FOILING. Foiling one's blade refers to the practice, during fencing's early days, of covering the cutting edge or tip in such a way as to render it harmless for practice encounters. This was done with metal balls or pieces of wood placed on the blade tip or with a leather sheath that covered the entire blade.

Still, it has been noted that such measures did not prevent injuries from happening on a regular basis.

Eventually, the foil*—a light, flexible practice weapon that takes its name from the act of rendering a weapon harmless—was created to remove virtually all chance of personal mishap from friendly sword crossings.
REFERENCE
Castle, Egerton. *Schools and Masters of Fence.* London: George Bell, 1885.

FOINING WEAPONS. Any thrusting weapon, such as a rapier.

Also called a *"foyning* weapon."
REFERENCE
Stone, George Cameron. *A Glossary of the Construction, Decoration, and Use of Arms and Armor.* New York: Jack Brussel, 1961.

FONST, RAMON. (1884–1959). Cuban fencing champion.

Ramon Fonst has been described as one of modern fencing's legends. Trained in France under the tutelage of the great French master Albert Ayat, Fonst rose quickly in the ranks of international competition.

At the age of sixteen, he won the Olympic championship in épée in 1900. He also took second place, behind his own teacher, in épée for amateurs and masters, a now-discontinued Olympic event.

In the 1904 Olympics, Fonst won both the individual foil and épée (he is, by the way, the only repeat winner in individual épée). In addition to these wins, he led the Cuban team to the first Olympic team championship in foil.
REFERENCES
Capriles, Miguel de. "Ramon Fonst and Nedo Nadi." *American Fencing* (September/ October 1976).
Grombach, John V. *The 1972 Olympic Guide.* New York: Paperback Library, 1972.
Wallechinsky, David. *The Complete Book of the Olympics.* New York: Penguin Books, 1984.

FORBIDDEN GAUNTLET. An armored glove that could be locked around the grip of a sword. It was considered foul play and unworthy of a knight to employ such a device in combat, as it gave an unfair advantage to the user.

A 1554 edict stated: "He that shall have a close gauntlet or anything else to fasten his sword to his hand shall have no prize."

Also called "locking gauntlet."
REFERENCE
Stone, George Cameron. *A Glossary of the Construction, Decoration, and Use of Arms and Armor.* New York: Jack Brussel, 1961.

FORCE. Attacks on an opponent's blade, especially beats* and binds.*
REFERENCE
Morton, E. D. *Martini A–Z of Fencing.* London: Queen Anne Press, 1992.

FORCONNADE. In French, a stabbing thrust in which the sword arm is immediately withdrawn. It is considered extremely poor fencing technique.
REFERENCE
Morton, E. D. *Martini A–Z of Fencing*. London: Queen Anne Press, 1992.

FORE-CUT. A cut made with the leading edge (fore-edge) of the sabre.*
REFERENCE
Morton, E. D. *Martini A–Z of Fencing*. London: Queen Anne Press, 1992.

FORMULE. In French, a specific plan for running a fencing competition.
REFERENCE
Handelman, Rob. "Fencing Glossary." *American Fencing* (May/June 1978).

FORTE. The strongest part of a sword blade (always the portion nearest the hilt).
   Also known as "the strong part of the blade."
REFERENCE
Burton, Richard F. *The Book of the Sword*. London: Chatto and Windus, 1884.

FORTE AU FOIBLE. In French, "strong to the weak." A basic defensive action of fencing, whereby the strong portion of one's blade opposes the weak portion of an opponent's blade.
REFERENCE
Handelman, Rob. "Fencing Glossary." *American Fencing* (May/June 1978).

FOUET. In French, the whipping action created by the flexible portion of a blade immediately after a parry.
   Also called "whip over."
REFERENCE
Handelman, Rob. "Fencing Glossary." *American Fencing* (May/June 1978).

FOUL BLOW. A touch that is executed before the director* of the bout* has given permission to begin fencing; also, a touch scored after the director has called for a halt in the action.
REFERENCE
Morton, E. D. *Martini A–Z of Fencing*. London: Queen Anne Press, 1992.

FRAZETTA, FRANK. (1928–   ). American illustrator.
   Perhaps the best-known modern illustrator for the sword-and-sorcery genre of literature.
   Frazeta began his professional art career at the age of sixteen as a comic book illustrator, a career that lasted for some twenty years.
   In the mid-1960s, Frazetta's art began appearing on the covers of paperback books, especially those devoted to fantastic subject matter. His work, often featuring muscular, barbarian swordsmen and scantily clad women, has been de-

scribed as ''powerful and sensuous'' and, over the years, has been much sought after by the publishing industry for magazine and book covers.

Frazetta's art, always immediately recognizable, has spawned numerous imitators.

Frank Frazetta's work has been collected in a number of volumes titled *The Fantastic Art of Frank Frazetta.*

REFERENCE

Ballantine, Betty, ed. *The Fantastic Art of Frank Frazetta.* New York: Charles Scribner's Sons, 1975.

FREE ARM AND HAND. The arm and hand not used to hold the sword.

In days gone by, the free arm and hand could be brought into play in combat. The free hand could wield a dagger, a cloak, a lantern, or any number of objects as defensive devices. When gloved with a mail or leather glove, the free hand itself might be used to parry with. On occasion, the free hand could also be employed to grab an opponent's sword away from him.

In modern fencing, the free arm and hand may not be used in blade exchanges with an opponent, according to the rules of the U.S. Fencing Association. The free arm is used exclusively for maintaining balance in the on-guard position and while lunging.

REFERENCES

Castle, Egerton. *Schools and Masters of Fence.* London: George Bell, 1885.

U.S. Fencing Association, ed. *Operations Manual.* Colorado Springs, CO: U.S. Fencing Association, 1985.

FREEZING. Distracting an opponent through the use of changes in speed and timing, rapid footwork, and weapon movement. When employed properly, these elements seem to almost hypnotize one's adversary, confusing him, setting up a false sense of security, or causing him to fixate on a particular element in the setup.

These actions, in effect, cause the ''victim'' to momentarily stop thinking, which slows down—''freezes''—his response time when an attack is finally launched against him.

REFERENCE

Morton, E. D. *Martini A–Z of Fencing.* London: Queen Anne Press, 1992.

FRENCH FENCERS, NOTED.

Foil

Rene Bougnol, Marcel Jacques Boulenger, Jehan Buhan, Henri Callot, Philippe Cattiau, Emile Coste, Jacques Coutrot, Debax, de Laborde, Pierre d'Hugues, Georges Dillon-Cavanagh, Christian d'Oriola, Roger Ducret, Andre Gardere, Edward Gardere, Lucien Gaudin, Eugene-Henri Gravelotte, Paskal Jolyot, Andre Labatut, Jacques Lataste, Jean-Claude Magnan, Henri Masson, Claude Netter, Christian Noel, Philippe Omnes, Daniel Revenu, Senat

The free hand used to grab an adversary's sword

The French foil

Épée

Gaston Alibert, Jean-Pierre Allemand, Philippe Boisse, Claude Bourgard, Georges Buchard, Gustave Buchard, S. Casanova, Phillippe Cattiau, Georges Dillion-Cavanagh, Emile Cornereau, Emile Cornic, George de la Falaise, Yves Dreyfus, Roger Ducret, Lucien Gaudin, Jacques la Degaillerie, Henri Lepage, Alexandre Lippman, Armand Massard, E. Moreau, Armand Mouyal, Eugene Oliver, Louis Perree, Rene Queyroux, Bernard Schmetz, Leon See, Leon Thiebaut, Edmond Wallace

Sabre

Claude Arabo, Regis Bonissent, G. J. Conraux, de Boissiere, Georges de la Falaise, B. de Lesseps, Roger Ducret, Serge Panizza, Marcel Parent, Leon Thiebaut

REFERENCE
Wallechinsky, David. *The Complete Book of the Olympics.* New York: Penguin Books, 1984.

FRENCH FOIL. As its name implies, the French foil originated in France. The French, wishing to separate their school altogether from the other predominant method of swordplay—the Italian school—developed a foil to fit their distinctive approach to combat.

In its original form, the French foil possessed a complicated hand guard (*pas d'anes*) made up of interwoven bars. The grip, short and square, was nevertheless held much like a modern French foil; that is, all fingers rested on the grip itself instead of having one or two wrapped around the hand guard. The blade was as long as that of the sword it stood for. In this form, the weapon was only slightly less cumbersome than its lethal counterpart.

By the end of the seventeenth century, the foil blade was drastically shortened to decrease its weight.

During the latter portion of the eighteenth century, the foil underwent more changes. Now patterned after the smallsword—the dueling weapon of this time period—the blade was shortened to its present length, and the complicated hand guard of previous days was replaced by a simple, light guard resembling the figure eight (called a *lunette,* meaning "spectacles"). The *lunette,* it should be noted, afforded little protection for the hand, so a padded glove became a necessary part of a fencer's equipment.

Overall, these changes in the French foil produced a maneuverable, flexible weapon, allowing for a style of fighting that was both quick and fluid.

Perhaps the most important development of the French foil, however, was the modern grip. The long handle is distinctive, possessing a slight curve, or twist, that allows it to fit perfectly into the contours of the sword hand.

The final change for the French foil came in the twentieth century when the *lunette* was abandoned for the more solid protection of the cup or shell guard.

REFERENCES

Burton, Richard F. *The Book of the Sword.* London: Chatto and Windus, 1884.

Castle, Egerton. *Schools and Masters of Fence.* London: George Bell, 1885.

Gaugler, William. "Labat and the Development of the French School." *American Fencing* (January/February 1987).

FRENCH GRIP. The French grip, for foil* and épée,* is a straight handle with a slight twist set into it. This construction allows the grip to fit neatly and comfortably into the folds of the sword hand, promoting finger manipulation of the weapon.

By the nature of its design, the French grip, is used best on an offensive basis when the sword hand is placed in complete supination* (palm up) and the thumb at three o'clock; defensively it is used most effectively with the sword hand in partial supination, the thumb positioned at one o'clock.

As the grip's name implies, it originated in France.

REFERENCES

Morton, E. D. *Martini A–Z of Fencing.* London: Queen Anne Press, 1992.

Palffy-Alpar. Julius. *Sword and Masque.* Philadelphia: F. A. Davis, 1967.

FRENCH SCHOOL OF FENCING. In the development of fencing, two approaches to the art became dominant: the Italian school and the French school. By the seventeenth century, the French school had become the more widely accepted of the two.

The Italian style, based on old-time rapier play, was a highly physical method

The French style of fencing, as taught by Labat

of fighting, and its interpretation, sadly, depended entirely on the master who taught it. But few Italian masters could agree on what was correct, and most felt that their teachings were the only valid ones.

The French, on the other hand, developed a more academic approach to fencing, which relied heavily on strategy for success. In practice, it was both smooth and flexible. Better still, the principles involved were universally adopted, making the French school of sword fighting an easier method to both teach and learn.

Following the French method of swordplay, a fencer was more likely to attempt to outthink his opponent rather than physically overpower him.

The principles incorporated into the old French school of fencing still survive today in the modern French approach. A strong emphasis on finger work with the foil allows for light attacks, subtle deceptions, and supple parries. It is a style that allows a less physically endowed fencer to compete on an equal basis against a more robust individual.

REFERENCES

Castle, Egerton. *Schools and Masters of Fence.* London: George Bell, 1885.

Pallfy-Alpar, Julius. *Sword and Masque.* Philadelphia: F. A. Davis, 1967.

FRENCH WOMEN FENCERS, NOTED. Brigitte Dumont-Gapais, Rene Garilbe, Brigitte Gaudin, Lylian Lecomte-Guyonneau, Pascale Trinquet.

REFERENCE

Wallechinsky, David. *The Complete Book of the Olympics.* New York: Penguin Books, 1984.

FROISSEMENT. In French, a fencing move of extremely intense pressure.

The *froissement* is accomplished by forcing an opponent's weapon aside—out of line—with a strong push from one's own blade. This is followed by an extension of the sword arm and a lunge.

Also known as a *sforzo*, an "expulsion," or simply "violent pressure."

REFERENCE
Palffy-Alpar, Julius. *Sword and Masque.* Philadelphia: F. A. Davis, 1967.

FUCHI. Meaning a "border" or "margin."

The *fuchi* is an ornamental ring around the hilt of a Japanese sword.

The two most celebrated families of makers of *fuchi* were the Nishi-gake and the Kasu-ga.
REFERENCE
Stone, George Cameron. *A Glossary of the Construction, Decoration, and Use of Arms and Armor.* New York: Jack Brussel, 1961.

FUCHS, JENO. (c. 1900). Hungarian sabre champion.

Jeno Fuchs took first place in individual sabre at the 1908 and 1912 Olympics. His team took first in team sabre at the 1908 and 1912 Olympics.
REFERENCE
Wallechinsky, David. *The Complete Book of the Olympics.* New York: Penguin Books, 1984.

FUDO. A Buddhist divinity often depicted on Japanese blades. Fudo is usually represented as seated on the brink of a precipice or on a rock surrounded by flames. In his right hand, he carries a sword; in his left, a rope intended for binding the wicked of the world.
REFERENCE
Stone, George Cameron. *A Glossary of the Construction, Decoration, and Use of Arms and Armor.* New York: Jack Brussel, 1961.

FUKURA. The curve of a Japanese blade near the point.

Fukura-kaku: sharply curved.

Fukura-sugu: nearly straight.

REFERENCE
Stone, George Cameron. *A Glossary of the Construction, Decoration, and Use of Arms and Armor.* New York: Jack Brussel, 1961.

FUORI TEMPO. In Italian, performing a fencing action in which one changes the timing of the movement.

Also called "out of time."
REFERENCE
Morton, E. D. *Martini A–Z of Fencing.* London: Queen Anne Press, 1992.

FUTARI. In kendo,* two opponents meeting in a match.
REFERENCE
Sasamori, Junzo, and Gordon Warner. *This Is Kendo.* Vermont: Charles E. Tuttle, 1984.

G

GAFFLET. A small cap fitted over the tips of smallswords* used in exhibition bouts during the eighteenth century. A tiny portion of the blade point fitted through the *gafflet,* allowing for demonstrable, if not dramatic, touches without seriously wounding an opponent.
REFERENCE
Morton, E. D. *Martini A–Z of Fencing.* London: Queen Anne Press, 1992.

GAGNE-PAIN. A term of the fourteenth and fifteenth centuries referring to a weapon—usually a sword—by which a soldier gained his bread.
    Also called a "gain-pain" or a "win-bread."
REFERENCE
Stone, George Cameron. *A Glossary of the Construction, Decoration, and Use of Arms and Armor.* New York: Jack Brussel, 1961.

GAINING ON THE LUNGE. Quickly increasing the distance one covers when attacking by bringing the rear foot forward so that it touches the heel of the front foot just before lunging. This moves the lunging spot forward suddenly, adding an element of surprise to the attack.
REFERENCE
Morton, E. D. *Martini A–Z of Fencing.* London: Queen Anne Press, 1992.

GAKI. One term for the art of swordplay in Japan.
    Also may be called "kendo" or *kenjutsu.*

REFERENCE
Stone, George Cameron. *A Glossary of the Construction, Decoration, and Use of Arms and Armor.* New York: Jack Brussel, 1961.

GALLIC SWORD. A short, cutting weapon of bronze used in early Rome. The blade was curved; the guard was a simple crosspiece. Called the Gallic sword because it was long popular among the Gallic people, it was also sometimes known as the "hero's arm."

The Gallic sword was one of the arms of the Roman auxiliary.
REFERENCE
Burton, Richard F. *The Book of the Sword.* London: Chatto and Windus, 1884.

GAMA ISHIME. A method of decorating portions of the metal of Japanese sword mountings so that it resembles the skin of a toad.
REFERENCE
Stone, George Cameron. *A Glossary of the Construction, Decoration, and Use of Arms and Armor.* New York: Jack Brussel, 1961.

GANADOS LOS GRADOS AL PERFIL. A circular, counterclockwise walk used by Spanish fencers during the seventeenth century to approach an opponent. The *ganados los grados al perfil* was continued until a suitable position for attacking was arrived at.

The action was described by Girard Thibault* in his book *L'Academie de l'Épée* (1628).**
REFERENCES
Castle, Egerton. *Schools and Masters of Fence.* London: George Bell, 1885.
Wise, Arthur. *The Art and History of Personal Combat.* Greenwich, CT: Arma Press, 1971.

GANCHEV, GEORGE. (c. twentieth century). Bulgarian fencing master.

Moving to England in the early 1970s, Maestro Ganchev opened a highly successful fencing school that ended up supplying the British fencing community with some of its brightest competitors.

Coach for the British saber team, Ganchev was also twice world professional sabre champion.

Eventually, the fencing master moved to the United States—Southern California—where he expertly plied his trade in a number of school locations.
REFERENCE
Morton, E. D. *Martini A–Z of Fencing.* London: Queen Anne Press, 1992.

GARCON DE SALLE. In old-time fencing terms, an apprentice fencing master.
REFERENCE
Morton, E. D. *Martini A–Z of Fencing.* London: Queen Anne Press, 1992.

GARDERE, EDWARD. (c. twentieth century). French fencing master.

One of the first fencing masters to adopt the use of the "orthopedic"* or "pistol" grip (a type of grip designed for fencers with damaged sword hands). He himself found such a weapon useful because he had lost several fingers from his hand in an accident. He eventually gave his name to one variety of orthopedic grip.

Gardere was also a former Olympian, having placed second in individual foil at the 1936 games in Berlin.

REFERENCES

Morton, E. D. *Martini A–Z of Fencing.* London: Queen Anne Press, 1992.

Wallechinsky, David. *The Complete Book of the Olympics.* New York: Penguin Books, 1984.

GAUDIN, LUCIEN. (1887–1934). French fencing champion.

Considered one of the greats of fencing, Lucien Gaudin was said to be the most graceful fencer of his day, "poetry in motion," as observed by the noted British master Felix Bertrand.*

Gaudin became the only other fencer besides Cuban Ramon Fonst* to win both the individual foil and épée events in a single Olympics (1928). He was forty-one years old at the time of these wins.

Other Gaudin Olympic efforts include:

Team foil (1920): Second place

Team foil (1924): First place

Team foil (1928): Second place

Team épée (1924): First place

In addition to these achievements, Gaudin was world épée champion in 1921.

In 1922, Lucien Gaudin participated in an unusual fencing exhibition that pitted his classical French technique against the Italian school as exemplified by the formidable Italian champion Aldo Nadi.* The Frenchman, in a hard-fought bout, won twenty touches to Nadi's eleven.

REFERENCES

Morton, E. D. *Martini A–Z of Fencing.* London: Queen Anne Press, 1992.

Wallechinsky, David. *The Complete Book of the Olympics.* New York: Penguin Books, 1984.

GAUDINI, GIULIO. (c. 1900). Italian fencing champion.

Between 1928 and 1936, six-foot, six-inch Giulio Gaudini won a number of Olympic medals for foil: three gold, four silver, and two bronze.

He was world foil champion in 1930 and 1934.

REFERENCES

Palffy-Alpar, Julius. *Sword and Masque.* Philadelphia: F. A. Davis, 1967.

Wallechinsky, David. *The Complete Book of the Olympics.* New York: Penguin Books, 1984.

French fencing champion Lucien Gaudin

GAUGLER, WILLIAM. (1931–   ). American fencing master.

William Gaugler established the first recognized fencing master training course—the Military Fencing Masters Program—in the United States in 1979, at San Jose State University, California.

The instruction, based on the classical system created by Italy's famed Scuola Magistrale di Scherma,* has three levels of certification: Military Instructor at Arms, Military Provost at Arms, and Military Master at Arms. According to Gaugler, "Written, oral, and practical examinations are required" for all levels, although for the last, and highest, rank, "candidates must complete a thesis." Study and testing cover all aspects of fencing theory and practice, as well as familiarity with international (F.I.E.) regulations and fencing safety.

In 1988, the Military Fencing Masters Program was awarded international accreditation by Niccolo Perno of the *Association Mondiale des Academies d'Armes Nationales* and the *Associazione Italiana Maestri di Scherma,* and Enzo Musumeci Greco of the *Accademia Nazionale di Scherma di Napoli.*

William Gaugler's own fencing training included study in Los Angeles with the great master Aldo Nadi*; in Italy with masters Ettore Spezza, Giorgio Pessina, and Umberto Di Paola; and in Germany with Amilcare Angelini.

Gaugler has written numerous articles over the years on fencing methodology and history. His work has appeared in the U.S. Fencing Association's *American Fencing,*** Italy's *Scherma,* France's *Escrime Internationale,* England's *The Sword,* and the professional journal *The Swordmaster.* In addition, he has written a book—*Fechten* (1983), which was subsequently translated into English *(Fencing Everyone,* 1987) and Italian *La scienza della scherma* (1992)—as well as one booklet—*Compilation of Fencing Terminology* (1994).

REFERENCES

Gaugler, William. "Evaluation of Fencing Masters Program Examinations." *American Fencing* (June/July/August 1988).

———. Curriculum Vitae. 1994.

GAUNTLET SWORD. A sword of the Mahrattas of India, the hilt of which is a gauntlet (armored glove).

REFERENCE

Stone, George Cameron. *A Glossary of the Construction, Decoration, and Use of Arms and Armor.* New York: Jack Brussel, 1961.

GAUTIER, A. (c. twentieth century). French fencing master.

A famous épée master, Professor Gautier moved to London in 1929, where he set up shop at the London Fencing Club. His students included the great fencer Charles de Beaumont.*

REFERENCE

Morton, E. D. *Martini A–Z of Fencing.* London: Queen Anne Press, 1992.

GAVIGLIANO. The crossbar on an Italian foil.

REFERENCE

Morton, E. D. *Martini A–Z of Fencing.* London: Queen Anne Press, 1992.

GAZEE. An old term for performing the one-two attack with a forward step.

REFERENCE

Morton, E. D. *Martini A–Z of Fencing.* London: Queen Anne Press, 1992.

GEMBI. A basket-type guard* on a Japanese sword.

REFERENCE

Stone, George Cameron. *A Glossary of the Construction, Decoration, and Use of Arms and Armor.* New York: Jack Brussel, 1961.

GEORGIADIS, JEAN. (c. 1896). Greek fencing champion.

Jean Georgiadis was the first individual sabre fencing champion of the Olympics, in 1896. He was also the first world sabre champion, in 1906.

REFERENCE

Wallechinsky, David. *The Complete Book of the Olympics.* New York: Penguin Books, 1984.

GEREVICH, ALADAR. (1910–   ). Hungarian fencing champion.

Aladar Gerevich competed in a total of six Olympics between 1932 and 1960. He was fifty years old in his final competition.

Gervich took third place in individual sabre at the 1936 Olympic games. In 1948, he took first in individual sabre. In 1952, he took second.

His team took first place in Olympic team sabre in 1932, 1936, 1948, 1952, 1956, and 1960.

Aladar Gerevich was world sabre champion in 1935, 1951, and 1955.

REFERENCES

Palffy-Alpar, Julius. *Sword and Masque.* Philadelphia: F. A. Davis, 1967.

Wallechinsky, David. *The Complete Book of the Olympics.* New York: Penguin Books, 1984.

GERMAN FENCERS, NOTED.

Men

Matthias Behr, Erwin Casmir, Gustav Casmir, Fritz August Gazzera, Tim Gerresheim, Mathias Gey, Jergen Hehn, Harold Hein, Walter Kostner, Alexander Pusch, Franz Rompza, Emil Schon, Dieter Wellmann

Women

Cornelia Hanisch, Hedwig Hass, Helene Mayer,* Helga Mees, Heidi Schmid, Erna Sondheim

REFERENCE

Wallechinsky, David. *The Complete Book of the Olympics.* New York: Penguin Books, 1984.

GERMAN SCHOOL OF FENCING. The German school of fencing for many years favored the two-handed sword, the *schwerdt.** This weapon was taught as a favored sword from 1480 until 1570 by the reigning fencing association of the time, the Marxbruder* (although the sword and buckler, the *dusack,* and the *braquemar* were also employed).

As practiced, the main elements in two-handed swordplay were muscular strength and supple wrists. The point of the weapon was rarely used; the cuts were, generally speaking, sweeping. The technique in the sword's manipulation, as noted by Egerton Castle* in his *Schools and Masters of Fence* (1885),* involved "a combined and opposite action of the two hands on the grip round an imaginary fulcrum. The sword being held with the left hand near or on the pommel, and the right near the quillon, in all cuts delivered from the right, the left hand was drawn backwards and the right pressed forward, and in all cuts delivered from the left, the action was the same, but the arms were crossed."

The German school included wrestling and tripping as part of its curriculum, and it gave attention to how the right knee might be driven into an opponent's groin when he was thrown to the ground.

Around 1570, the rapier was introduced by the society of the Federfechter* under the influence of the Italians. While there was much initial contention from the Marxbruder, the thrusting sword quickly became the weapon of choice.

By 1590, there was little difference between the Marxbruder and Federfechter.

The German school of fencing was noted for its strict observance of honor, discipline, and custom.

The eighteenth century saw the Germans develop a cut-and-thrust style of swordplay that was considered quite formidable. The free hand was often used to parry with, and the beat* was used with considerable frequency as a means of disarming an opponent.

During the nineteenth century, a highly stylized form of swordplay came into vogue among German university students. A weapon called a *schlaegar*—a basket-hilted sword* with a flat, pointless blade sharpened for a length of eight inches from the tip—was used in a stationary cut-and-parry game whose object was simply to slice one's opponent on the head or face. The main requirements for this form of dueling were endurance and plenty of courage.

Noted teachers in the German tradition include Joachim Meyer,* Johann Schmidt, and Friedrich Kahn.*

REFERENCES

Castle, Egerton. *Schools and Masters of Fence.* London: George Bell, 1885.

Wise, Arthur. *The Art and History of Personal Combat.* Greenwich, CT: Arma Press, 1971.

GERMAN SWORDS, ANCIENT. While early German swords were relatively short, later ones were up to three feet in length. Blades came both in leaf-shaped and straight varieties, and were invariably fashioned of bronze.

REFERENCE

Burton, Richard F. *The Book of the Sword.* London: Chatto and Windus, 1884.

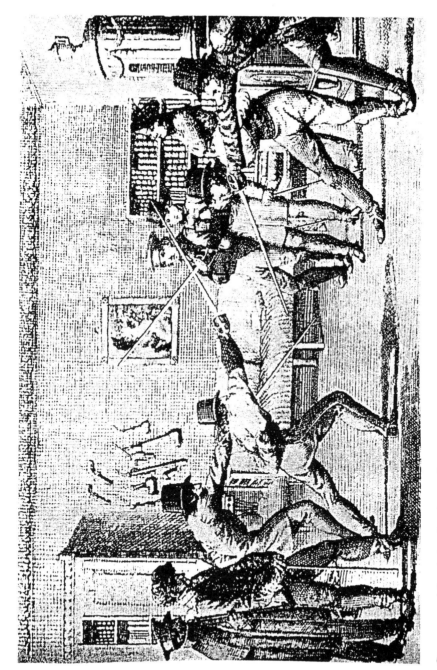

German swordplay during the nineteenth century

GIANDONATO. Sixteenth-century Italian sword maker. He is thought to have been the brother of Andrea Ferrara.*
REFERENCE
Stone, George Cameron. *A Glossary of the Construction, Decoration, and Use of Arms and Armor.* New York: Jack Brussel, 1961.

GIGANTI, NICOLETTO. (c. 1550). Italian fencing master.

Nicoletto Giganti was the first master of swordplay to clearly explain the lunge and to apply it to most attacks.

Strangely, Giganti later advocated a guard with the left foot forward and announced his intention to bring out a book that would show that all actions could be performed in this manner. This change in his perspective was not explained, nor was the book ever published.

Giganti's one book on fencing, *Scola overo Teatro,*** was published in 1606.
REFERENCES
Castle, Egerton. *Schools and Masters of Fence.* London: George Bell, 1885.
Wise, Arthur. *The Art and History of Personal Combat.* Greenwich, CT: Arma Press, 1971.

GIN-SAME. Silver plates covering the sides of a Japanese sword hilt. Usually embossed to resemble sharkskin.
REFERENCE
Stone, George Cameron. *A Glossary of the Construction, Decoration, and Use of Arms and Armor.* New York: Jack Brussel, 1961.

GIRARD, P.J.F. (c. 1700). A French naval officer and master of arms.

Girard was not an academic fencing master, yet the book he published in 1730 is one of the best of its time. The work contained over 116 illustrations representing the French school in opposition to the Italian, German, and Spanish styles.

He was the first to name the parry covering the low-inside line with the hand in pronation, Prime (One).* He was also an advocate of the counterparry,* which, up to his time, was frowned on by most masters as being too slow and, hence, too dangerous to use.
REFERENCES
Castle, Egerton. *Schools and Masters of Fence.* London: George Bell, 1885.
Wise, Arthur. *The Art and History of Personal Combat.* Greenwich, CT: Arma Press, 1971.

GIRDING ON THE SWORD. A biblical term used in reference to those adults who were able to serve as soldiers; also, the beginning of a campaign.
REFERENCE
Burton, Richard F. *The Book of the Sword.* London: Chatto and Windus, 1884.

French fencing master P.J.F. Girard

GIUOCO CORTO. Seventeenth-century Italian fencing master Alexander Senese's* term for fencing within measure* (proper distance), something he disapproved of as being dangerous.
REFERENCE
Castle, Egerton. *Schools and Masters of Fence.* London: George Bell, 1885.

GIUOCO LUNGO. As taught by the seventeenth-century Italian fencing master Alexander Senese,* *giuoco lungo* referred to fencing at long distance.*
REFERENCE
Castle, Egerton. *Schools and Masters of Fence.* London: George Bell, 1885.

GIUOCO PERFETTO. A rapid feint*-thrust* attack delivered without ever meeting an opponent's blade. This was, according to seventeenth-century fencing master Alexander Senese,* offensive perfection.
REFERENCE
Castle, Egerton. *Schools and Masters of Fence.* London: George Bell, 1885.

GIVING THE BLADE. Consciously presenting one's blade so as to be attacked, with the intention of employing some sort of counteraction to stop the assault.
REFERENCE
Morton, E. D. *Martini A–Z of Fencing.* London: Queen Anne Press, 1992.

GLADIATOR. From the Latin *gladius,* meaning "sword."

Gladiators were professional arena combatants usually, as the name implies, expert in the use of the sword, although they were often versed in the employment of other weapons as well.

The concept of gladiatorial combat was originated by the Etruscans, who allowed captives to fight for their lives.

In the pure Roman tradition, based on honor and skill, gladiators performed entirely on a voluntary basis. Spectacles would commence with combatants' demonstrating their abilities, en masse, with wooden swords, after which individual fights would be staged with real swords. At first, such fights were fought only until one opponent was disarmed.

However, as the Roman civilization disintegrated, the use of slaves, prisoners of war, and condemned criminals in gladiatorial spectaculars became the norm. By this time, most fights were fought to the death.
REFERENCE
Burton, Richard F. *The Book of the Sword.* London: Chatto and Windus, 1884.

GLADIUS. The sword most often identified with the Roman soldier. While it could be used for cutting, the *gladius* was chiefly a thrusting weapon. The length was twenty-two inches. The grip was six inches long. The blade was thick and heavy. Early forms were of bronze, but later swords were made of steel.

Roman gladiators

REFERENCE
Burton, Richard F. *The Book of the Sword.* London: Chatto and Windus, 1884.

GLAIVE. An old name for a sword, especially a broadsword.
   Also called a *glay.*
REFERENCE
Stevenson, John. *Fencing.* London: Briggs, 1935.

GLIDE. English for *coule.**
REFERENCE
Morton, E. D. *Martini A–Z of Fencing.* London: Queen Anne Press, 1992.

GLISSEMENT. In French, advancing with a slide of the front foot, as opposed
to a step.
   Also known as a "glide."
REFERENCE
Handelman, Rob. "Fencing Glossary." *American Fencing* (May/June 1978).

GLOVE. The earliest use for the glove in fencing was to wear it on the left
hand, so that one might parry with it. These gloves were made of mail or heavy
leather.
   Later, the glove was brought into use to protect the sword hand.

Today, the glove is a necessary part of the fencer's equipment. The rules of the U.S. Fencing Association specify that it must "in all circumstances, cover approximately half the forearm of the competitor's sword arm to prevent the opponent's blade entering the sleeve of the jacket."

Modern gloves are designed specifically for each fencing weapon.

REFERENCES

Castle, Egerton. *Schools and Masters of Fence*. London: George Bell, 1885.

U.S. Fencing Association, ed., *Operations Manual*. Colorado Springs, CO: U.S. Fencing Association, 1985.

GLOVE, FENCING. The glove worn on the sword hand for protection. It must, according to the rules of the U.S. Fencing Association, be white and cover approximately half the forearm to keep an opponent's blade from entering one's jacket sleeve.

Modern fencing gloves are usually made from leather. Varieties include gloves designed specifically for use with foil, sabre, or épée and gloves created to accommodate all three weapons.

The main difference between types of fencing gloves is the degree of padding and location of the padding.

The glove, of course, must be well fitted to a fencer's hand. A glove that is too loose will slip and bunch up, making it difficult to hold onto one's weapon; it may also rub and cause blisters. A glove that is too tight will constrict the muscles of the hand, slowing down blood circulation. This results in a fencing hand that, deprived of oxygen, tires out quickly.

REFERENCES

Palffy-Alpar, Julius. *Sword and Masque*. Philadelphia: F. A. Davis, 1967.

U.S. Fencing Association, ed., *Operations Manual*. Colorado Springs, CO: U.S. Fencing Association, 1985.

GOD, SWORD. Many ancient peoples worshipped some god that was associated with the sword. The Egyptians had Ramenma, Lord of the Sword. The Chaldean Bel possessed a flaming sword, as did Yehweh, the god of the Hebrews. The Babylonian god Merodach was a sword-god. It is written that the Assyrian god Assur-bani-pal destroyed the people of Arabia with a sword. The Scythians prayed to the fearful sword-god Nergal,** to whom they made human sacrifices. The Greeks had Ares**; the Romans, Mars.** Both gods, versions of the same entity, were linked to war and disease. The Scandinavians and Teutons venerated Odin or Wodin. At festivals, young Germans danced naked before their god of the sword amid brandished blades. The Hindus of India revered a sword created by the god Bramha called Asidevata,* which was said to have appeared in the sky above the Himalayas, shaking both the heavens and the earth.

REFERENCES

Burton, Richard F. *The Book of the Sword*. London: Chatto and Windus, 1884.

Velikovsky, Immanuel. *Worlds in Collision*. New York: MacMillan, 1950.

GODDARA. A Persian-Turkish sabre.*
REFERENCE
Stone, George Cameron. *A Glossary of the Construction, Decoration, and Use of Arms and Armor.* New York: Jack Brussel, 1961.

GOLIAH. A very heavy, slightly curved sword of central India used during the eighteenth century by men of rank.
REFERENCE
Stone, George Cameron. *A Glossary of the Construction, Decoration, and Use of Arms and Armor.* New York: Jack Brussel, 1961.

GOMOKU ZOGAN. A type of Japanese sword guard (*tsuba*) decoration, the whole surface of which is covered with bits of brass and copper wire brazed on iron. It is supposed to represent pine needles and branches floating on a mountain lake.
REFERENCE
Stone, George Cameron. *A Glossary of the Construction, Decoration, and Use of Arms and Armor.* New York: Jack Brussel, 1961.

GORDIAN KNOT. Gordias, the king of Phrygia, created a rope knot so intricately tied that it was foretold by an oracle that whoever should untie it would reign over all of Asia. Alexander the Great, according to the tale, upon encountering the Gordian knot, simply cut it in half with a single stroke of his sword.
REFERENCE
Benet, William Rose. *The Reader's Encyclopedia.* New York: Thomas Y. Crowell, 1965.

GOUSPY, EMILE. (c. nineteenth century). French fencing master.
Following a career as one of France's greatest swordsmen, Emile Gouspy came to the United States, where he taught at New York's Tennis and Racquet Club.
REFERENCE
Cass, Eleanor Baldwin. *The Book of Fencing.* Boston: Lothrop, Lee, and Shephard, 1930.

GRADOS. In the early Spanish school of fencing, this described the act of gaining an advantage over an opponent in combat through a series of steps around him.
REFERENCE
Castle, Egerton. *Schools and Masters of Fence.* London: George Bell, 1885.

GRAND SALUTE. The Grand Salute was a special salute done at old-time fencing exhibitions. Almost like a dance, it was performed without masks and consisted of a series of slightly exaggerated movements with sword in hand.

The sequence began with two fencers facing one another in a position of attention with arms held straight. They saluted each other, then to the right and to the left; after this, both fell into the on-guard position for five counts.

Guard positions as taught by Giacomo di Grassi

Presently, one fencer would lunge while the other parried in the line of prime,* and vice versa. Then it was back to the on-guard position for five more counts.

Next came various actions showing the basic methods of attack and defense. At the conclusion of this, with two stamps of the right foot, both returned to the position of attention.

Now, another salute to the right and left, followed by a return to on-guard, again for five counts.

The salute ended with a single stamp of the right foot, a final return to attention, and both fencers saluting each other one last time.

The Grand Salute was sometimes accompanied by music.

REFERENCE

Palffy-Alpar, Julius. *Sword and Masque.* Philadelphia: F. A. Davis, 1967.

GRANGER, STEWART. (1913–1993). British leading man and star of a number of swashbuckler films.

While he acted in over fifty films, Stewart Granger is best remembered for his work in two swashbuckler films: *Scaramouche* (1952) and *The Prisoner of Zenda* (1952).

Tall and dashing, Granger was always the cool, capable hero, somewhere between Errol Flynn and Ronald Colman in his image. His fencing was never flamboyant, but always competent.

Scaramouche ends up being Granger's trademark. Based on a novel by Rafael Sabatini, it tells the pre-French Revolution tale of Andre Moreau, who is out to avenge the death of his best friend, killed in a sword fight by the Marquis de Maynes (Mel Ferrer); but, to do so, he must learn to fence—and fence well. This, he, of course, does. Eventually, Andre crosses swords with his intended adversary in a crowded theater. The two duel from one end of the building to the other. In the end, Andre outfences the marquis, but, for some reason, is unable to run him through (he later learns that the nobleman and he are half-brothers).

The major duel in *Scaramouche,* guided by Belgian fencing master Jean Heremans, was the longest fencing sequence ever filmed, running a full six minutes and thirty seconds. According to MGM studio publicists, Granger and Ferrer had to memorize ''eighty-seven separate sword counts which incorporated twenty-eight stunts and situations.'' It was also noted that, due to wear on the blades, they used eighteen swords during the filming of the fight scene.

The Prisoner of Zenda, while more or less a carbon copy of the earlier classic film starring Ronald Colman, still stands as a solid piece of film work. The swordplay, again staged by Jean Heremans, was both dramatic and fast-paced.

Other films in which Stewart Granger fences include *Saraband* (1949), *Moonfleet* (1955), and *Swordsman of Siena* (1962).

REFERENCES

Parish, James Robert, and Don E. Stanke. *The Swashbucklers.* NJ: Rainbow Books, 1976.
Richards, Jeffrey. *Swordsmen of the Screen.* Boston: Routledge and Kegan Paul, 1977.
Thomas, Tony. *Cads and Cavaliers.* New York: A. S. Barnes, 1973.

GRASSI, GIACOMO DI. (c. 1550). Italian fencing master.

Grassi was the first to define the various parts of the sword blade with reference to their specific properties for offense or defense and to divide the fencer's body into lines, which he labeled inside (*di dentro*), outside (*di fuori*), high (*di sopra*), and low (*di sotto*).

He was also one of the pioneers in the theory of using one's sword for thrusting.

Grassi's system of swordplay, while not particularly innovative, was the one most commonly followed during the latter part of the sixteenth century.

Grassi wrote *His True Art of Defense,*** which was published in 1594, and later published in both English and German.

REFERENCES

Castle, Egerton. *Schools and Masters of Fence.* London: George Bell, 1885.
Wise, Arthur. *The Art and History of Personal Combat.* Greenwich, CT: Arma Press, 1971.

GRAVELOTTE, EUGENE-HENRI. (c. 1896). French fencing champion.

Eugene-Henri Gravelotte was the first individual foil fencing champion of the Olympics, in 1895.

REFERENCE

Wallechinsky, David. *The Complete Book of the Olympics.* New York: Penguin Books, 1984.

GREEK SWORDPLAY, ANCIENT. While their celebrated mythic heroes of old—the warriors of the Trojan War and before—often slugged it out with swords in contests of monumental proportions, the men of classical Greece never put much emphasis on learning the art of the sword. For them practicing with the sword fell somewhere after gymnastics, wrestling, foot races, and the like.

The Athenians, as described by the historian Demosthenes (384–322 B.C.), "were as rustics in the fencing school, who after a blow always guard the hit part and not before."

Even the great philosopher Plato (428–347 B.C.) denounced training with the sword as useless, remarking that neither masters nor their students ever became great military leaders. It is not surprising, then, that Greek literature of this period has few references to the weapon. It should be pointed out that Alexander the Great,** Hannibal, and Julius Caesar all spent time learning to fight with swords.

It is interesting that centuries later it was the Greeks—Jean Georgiadis* and Leon Pyros—who would win gold medals for fencing in the very first modern Olympic Game* in 1896.

REFERENCES

Burton, Richard F. *The Book of the Sword.* London: Chatto and Windus, 1884.

Wallechinsky, David. *The Complete Book of the Olympics.* New York: Penguin Books, 1984.

GREEK SWORDS. The ancient Greeks had a number of swords. The Greek infantry sword was a straight, two-edged weapon, somewhat broad in the blade and of equal width from hilt to point, which was beveled in its shape. The Greek cavalry preferred a sabre*-type sword.

The shapes of Greek swords take in all the variants: straight, curved, and leaf-shaped.

The Spartans had swords with blades no more than fifteen inches long. When derided for having such short swords, the Spartan reply was, "You only have to advance a pace."

Later Greek swords are more moderate, measuring up to twenty-five inches in length.

Swords were made of both bronze and iron.

REFERENCE

Burton, Richard F. *The Book of the Sword.* London: Chatto and Windus, 1884.

GRIP. The portion of the sword intended to be grasped by the hand.

Old-style grips were usually straight and varied in length according to the length of the sword.

There are many modern grips for fencing weapons: the French grip, with a slight twist and bend that fits the handle into the contours of the hand; the Italian grip, a completely straight design, with crossbars around which a fencer hooks one or two fingers; and numerous "pistol"-type grips, fitted with one or more prongs, or horns, which fit between the fingers, allowing for a more powerful hand hold (styles include Belgian, Visconti, American, German, Gardere, Spanish, and Rambeau grips).

The French grip, designed to be used in complete supination, cultivates finger control, which allows for a light, flexible style of fencing. The Italian grip, which is strapped to a fencer's wrist, allows for a vigorous, muscular approach to fencing in which the entire arm may be employed. Pistol grips, for the most part, promote power and a vicelike hold on one's weapon.

Today, the pistol grip, also known as an orthopedic or anatomical grip, is the most popular grip around the world.

The traditional covering for the sword grip is leather, but for modern sport weapons, the covering may also be made of plastic, rubber, twine, or metal.

The grip may also called a *fusee,* a "handle," a *poignee,* a *mancio,* and a "grasp."

REFERENCES

Burton, Richard F. *The Book of the Sword.* London: Chatto and Windus, 1884.

Morton, E. D. *Martini A–Z of Fencing.* London: Queen Anne Press, 1992.

Palffy-Alpar, Julius. *Sword and Masque.* Philadelphia: F. A. Davis, 1967.

Wilkinson, Frederick. *Swords and Daggers.* New York: Hawthorn Books, 1967.

GROMBACH, JOHN V. (1901–1982). U.S. fencer and U.S. army general.

John Grombach began fencing in the mid-1920s. He was a nationally ranked fencer until 1945. He was also the former secretary-general of the Federation Internationale d'Escrime, the organization governing fencing worldwide.

General Grombach authored *The 1977 Olympic Guide* (1972), a detailed sport-by-sport account of Olympic history. It, of course, included a chapter on fencing.

REFERENCES

Grombach, John V. *The 1972 Olympic Guide.* New York: Paperback Library, 1972.

Tishman, Jeffrey. "In Memoriam: John V. Grombach." *American Fencing* (November/ December 1982).

GRYPES. Old-time methods of grabbing an opponent's arm or sword and employing leverage, so that the weapon must be relinquished. They were extremely popular during the sixteenth and seventeenth centuries.

REFERENCE

Morton, E. D. *Martini A–Z of Fencing.* London: Queen Anne Press, 1992.

GUADAGNAREDI DI SPADA. An Italian fencing term for covering one's self when advancing by engaging an opponent's blade.
REFERENCE
Morton, E. D. *Martini A–Z of Fencing.* London: Queen Anne Press, 1992.

GUARD. Over the centuries, the sword guard has evolved from the simple to the elaborate and back to the simple again.

Early guards were plain crossbars* called quillons.* Side rings (*anneau*) were eventually added to shield the hand from cuts.

Then came a series of curved loops (*pas d'ane**) and bars (*countre-guards,** and knuckle guard*) to further protect the swordsman. While the quillons and knuckle guard remained intact, the large cup guard* (*coquille**), as an ideal defense against the thrust, soon took over for the *countre-guard* arrangement (which survived only in the military basket hilt*).

As swords became more streamlined, the cup guard became smaller and more shallow. In some cases, the guard was reduced to a simple bar shaped in the form of a figure eight (*lunette*).

Eventually, when the focus of fencing became almost exclusively that of sport, the cup guard alone was retained—except in the case of the sabre, which also kept the knuckle guard.
REFERENCES
Castle, Egerton. *Schools and Masters of Fence.* London: George Bell, 1885.
Grancsay, Stephen V. *Swords and Armor.* New York: Odyssey Press, 1964.
Palffy-Alpar, Julius. *Sword and Masque.* Philadelphia: F. A. Davis, 1967.

GUARD POSITIONS. The guard position (or guard) is defined as the most favorable position that a fencer can take to be equally ready offensively and defensively.

Early guards were for the most part fanciful inventions of various masters. They had little to do with defense and were considered simply a starting point for given attacks. They had names like *guardia di testa, coda lunga e larga,* and *becca cesa.*

Before long, the guard positions began to be identified numerically for simplification, such as *terza guardia* and *quarta guardia larga,* but the number position of a guard altered with each fencing master's teaching. Where the blade might be held, where the feet might be placed, and where the free hand was located all depended on one's teacher.

Ridolfo Capo Ferro,* one of the more progressive masters of the seventeenth century, said of the guard, "A guard is a posture with the arm and the sword extended in a straight line towards the middle of the attackable parts of an adversary, and with the body well established according to its own pace, so as to keep the adversary at a distance, and to strike him should he approach at his peril." Still, his ideas regarding guards were his own and were not necessarily shared by other masters.

Eventually, guards did become standardized as fencing itself solidified into a more uniform science.

Different weapons, of course, required different guards for their proper employment. The correct guard for the smallsword was different from the one used for the backsword. The backsword, for instance, had such curious-sounding guards as the "hanging guard," the "spadroon guard," and "St. George's guard."

In modern times, guard positions have become even more established. Each sport weapon has its own recognizable guard that is uniform throughout the fencing world.

For foil, the feet are placed at right angles, between a foot and a foot and a half apart. The forward foot points straight ahead. The knees are bent. The sword arm is bent slightly. The sword hand is at chest level in partial supination, the thumb at one o'clock. The point of the weapon is at the height of one's own eyes. The free arm is bent upward at the elbow, and held out from the body, at shoulder level, at a forty-five degree angle.

For épée, the body attitudes are almost the same as for foil, except that the arm is kept straighter, and the point of the weapon is held lower (it is, in fact, held in line with the opponent's target area).

For sabre, the guard position is the same as in foil, except that the hand is held in pronation.

REFERENCES

Castle, Egerton. *Schools and Masters of Fence.* London: George Bell, 1885.

Handelman, Rob. "Fencing Glossary." *American Fencing* (May/June 1978).

Vebell, Edward. *Sports Illustrated Book of Fencing.* Philadelphia: J. B. Lippincott, 1962.

GUDDARA. An Indian sabre with straight quillons* (crossbars), a pistol hilt, and a back-edged blade that widens toward the tip.

REFERENCE

Stone, George Cameron. *A Glossary of the Construction, Decoration, and Use of Arms and Armor.* New York: Jack Brussel, 1961.

GUPTI. An Indian sword cane quite common in northern and central India. They were often screwed into the scabbard,* which, according to Lord Egerton, a nineteenth-century weapons expert, made them nearly useless as weapons, as it took too long to draw them.

REFERENCE

Stone, George Cameron. *A Glossary of the Construction, Decoration, and Use of Arms and Armor.* New York: Jack Brussel, 1961.

GUPTI AGA. A divan sword, that is, a sword that was worn by an Indian prince when he was seated on a cushion giving audiences.

REFERENCE

Stone, George Cameron. *A Glossary of the Construction, Decoration, and Use of Arms and Armor.* New York: Jack Brussel, 1961.

𝓗

HABAKI. A metal ring surrounding a Japanese sword blade next to the guard*
that holds the sword blade steady in its scabbard. It may be of one or two pieces,
which are fashioned of both gold and silver.

The part of the sword blade covered by the *habaki* is referred to as the *habaki
moto.*

REFERENCE

Stone, George Cameron. *A Glossary of the Construction, Decoration, and Use of Arms
and Armor.* New York: Jack Brussel, 1961.

HADA. Meaning "skin." The watering marks on a Japanese sword blade.

Masama-hada: a straight grain.

Itama-hada: a curved grain.

Nachi-hada: a grain in the shape of a halved pear.

Matsu-hada: a ragged grain.

REFERENCE

Stone, George Cameron. *A Glossary of the Construction, Decoration, and Use of Arms
and Armor.* New York: Jack Brussel, 1961.

HAGAKURE. A book written in eighteenth-century Japan dealing with samurai
philosophy, thought, and action, as expressed and recalled by an elderly samurai,
Yamamoto Tsunetomo. It is based on the old man's conversations with a young
samurai, Tashiro Tsuramoto (who recorded the conversations).

The volume, beginning with the admonition that "the way of the samurai is found in death," has been described as a volume that is both anti-intellectual and antischolastic; and yet it is a book of great sincerity and, as such, accurately reflected the cult of the sword, the world of the samurai in old Japan.

The title means "hidden leaves."

REFERENCE

Tsunetomo, Yamamoto. *Hagakure.* Translated by William Scott Wilson. New York: Avon Books, 1979.

HAKAMA. The divided skirt worn by kendo* fencers.

REFERENCE

Sasamori, Junzo, and Gordon Warner. *This Is Kendo.* Vermont: Charles E. Tuttle, 1964.

HAKASE. A Japanese name for a sword.

REFERENCE

Stone, George Cameron. *A Glossary of the Construction, Decoration, and Use of Arms and Armor.* New York: Jack Brussel, 1961.

HAKIJIN. In Japanese, this refers to a naked sword blade.

REFERENCE

Stone, George Cameron. *A Glossary of the Construction, Decoration, and Use of Arms and Armor.* New York: Jack Brussel, 1961.

HAKO-MUNE. The square back of a Japanese sword blade.

REFERENCE

Stone, George Cameron. *A Glossary of the Construction, Decoration, and Use of Arms and Armor.* New York: Jack Brussel, 1961.

HAKUBYO. A method of decorating Japanese sword mountings that resembles brush strokes.

REFERENCE

Stone, George Cameron. *A Glossary of the Construction, Decoration, and Use of Arms and Armor.* New York: Jack Brussel, 1961.

HALAB. A sword used by the Sikhs of India. It has a grooved blade, finger guard, and disk pommel.

The *halab* is a variety of *talwar,* or Indian sabre.

Also called a *halat.*

REFERENCE

Stone, George Cameron. *A Glossary of the Construction, Decoration, and Use of Arms and Armor.* New York: Jack Brussel, 1961.

HALF-CIRCLE. A parry* described by seventeenth-century French fencing master Charles Besnard,* corresponding to the modern septime* parry (the low, inside line, with the hand in supination, or palm up).

REFERENCE
Castle, Egerton. *Schools and Masters of Fence*. London: George Bell, 1885.

HALF-DISENGAGE. Attacking from the high line* to the low line* or from the low line to the high line.
REFERENCE
Morton, E. D. *Martini A–Z of Fencing*. London: Queen Anne Press, 1992.

HALF-STANCE. A term describing an on-guard* position in which the chest is barely exposed.
REFERENCE
Morton, E. D. *Martini A–Z of Fencing*. London: Queen Anne Press, 1992.

HAMMASTI. An ancient Egyptian word meaning "the blade of the double sword." This may refer, according to British historian Richard Burton,* to a weapon with two distinct blades—one long and one short.
REFERENCE
Burton, Richard F. *The Book of the Sword*. London: Chatto and Windus, 1884.

HAND-AND-A-HALF SWORD. A long, straight-bladed sword of the fifteenth century, possessing a plain cross guard, a long grip, and a large, round pommel.

The hand-and-a-half sword was usually used with a single hand, but the grip was long enough to be grasped with two or three fingers of the free hand if one wished to give extra force to a blow.

Also called a "bastard sword," doubtlessly because, being more than a one-handed sword but somewhat less than a two-handed sword, it is not a legitimate member of either weapon family.
REFERENCES
Stone, George Cameron. *A Glossary of the Construction, Decoration, and Use of Arms and Armor*. New York: Jack Brussel, 1961.
Wilkinson, Frederick. *Swords and Daggers*. New York: Hawthorn Books, 1967.

HANGER. A light sabre used from the seventeenth through the eighteenth centuries. The single-edged blade (coming in both straight and curved varieties) was around twenty inches long. The hilt was made up of a short, down-curving quillon, a small shell guard, and a single knuckle bow.

The hilt is very often decorated with mythological or hunting scenes—hence, the sometime name of "hunting sword."

Also called a "whinger" or a "whinyard."
REFERENCES
Stone, George Cameron. *A Glossary of the Construction, Decoration, and Use of Arms and Armor*. New York: Jack Brussel, 1961.
Wilkinson, Frederick. *Swords and Daggers*. New York: Hawthorn Books, 1967.

HANGING GUARD. A sabre* guard in which the arm was extended, with the hand in pronation as high as the top of the head. The point of the sword was, conversely, held low.

The hanging guard was often called the "coward's guard" by fencing teachers because they considered it a very safe attitude to assume. It was also a difficult one from which to launch an offensive action.

The half-hanger was a guard halfway between the hanging guard and a medium guard, a position where the arm was extended straight out from the shoulder.

REFERENCE

Castle, Egerton. *Schools and Masters of Fence.* London: George Bell, 1885.

HARI ISHIME. A type of decoration used as a background on Japanese sword fittings. It is made up of small openings, as if the metal had been pricked with a needle.

REFERENCE

Stone, George Cameron. *A Glossary of the Construction, Decoration, and Use of Arms and Armor.* New York: Jack Brussel, 1961.

HARRYHAUSEN, RAY. (1920–). American film animator.

A creator of movie special effects, Ray Harryhausen has produced some of the most enthralling images in the history of film. Focusing on ancient myths, he has brought to "life" monster cyclops, sword-wielding skeletons, giant rampaging statues, dragons, dinosaurs, centaurs, and many other fantastic creatures.

Harryhausen is the master of "stop motion" animation camera work, that is, the art of taking a pliable miniature model, painstakingly moving various parts of its "body," and shooting one frame of movie film for each alteration. When the individual film frames are run continuously, the resulting effect is that the model actually appears to be alive.

Of special note are Harryhausen's animated skeleton sword fights in *The Seventh Voyage of Sinbad* (1958), and *Jason and the Argonauts* (1963), for their intricate interlacing of human and model action. The actors went through their fight routines alone, with the skeleton images—actually, animated miniatures—being added to the proceedings much later in Harryhausen's workshop.

In the case of *Jason and the Argonauts,* fencing master Ralph Faulkner* was engaged to train actor Todd Armstrong for his sword work as the hero Jason.

Other Harryhausen films include *The Golden Voyage of Sinbad* (1973), *Sinbad and the Eye of the Tiger* (1977), and *Clash of the Titans* (1981).

REFERENCE

Rovin, Jeff. *From the Land Beyond Beyond.* New York: Berkley Windover Books, 1977.

HA-TSUDA. The light color of a Japanese blade near the edge as opposed to the darker color of the rest of the blade.

REFERENCE
Stone, George Cameron. *A Glossary of the Construction, Decoration, and Use of Arms and Armor.* New York: Jack Brussel, 1961.

HATSUMI, MASAAKI. (1931–   ). Modern master of the Japanese discipline of *ninjutsu.**

Beginning in the 1950s, Dr. Hatsumi began his study of the ninja tradition, which includes the mastery of countless weapons—including the sword—and various forms of unarmed combat. He also learned the ninja* skills of diguise, horsemanship, stealth, and espionage.

Today, Dr. Hatsumi is the thirty-fourth Grandmaster of the Toqakure Rye style of *ninjutsu.* In 1981, he published *Ninjutsu,** a detailed account of ninja history and technique.

REFERENCE
Hatsumi, Masaaki. *Ninjutsu.* Burbank, CA: Unique, 1981.

HAUSA SWORD. A sword of the Sudanese in Africa. The hilt has straight, slightly flared quillons,* a disk pommel,* and a leather-covered grip. The blade is straight and double-edged.* Its overall length is nearly thirty-nine inches; the blade length, nearly thirty-four inches.

Many *hausas* are fitted with blades made in Europe.

REFERENCE
Wilkinson, Frederick. *Swords and Daggers.* New York: Hawthorn Books, 1967.

HAYWARD, LOUIS. (1909–1985). British (South African-born) film actor.

Louis Hayward, while never a swashbuckler of Errol Flynn's stature—his adventure films were usually of the grade B variety—still managed to hold his own with a sword or a lady in distress. During the last half of his acting career, he was pretty much typecast as a dashing swordsman.

Hayward was a competent film fencer.

The Man in the Iron Mask (1939) was perhaps Louis Hayward's best swash-buckler film effort. Based on Alexandre Dumas's* novel *The Man in the Iron Mask,* this movie version took some liberties with the original story. While the underlying tale continued to deal with twin sons (both played by Hayward) of Louis XIII of France, it had the added attraction of making one of the brothers good and the other one evil.

Exiled Philippe, raised by an aging D'Artagnan, grows up to become a dashing swordsman. His pampered brother, Louis, corrupted by his lifestyle, turns into a vicious, cowardly degenerate.

In the end, Louis is killed. Philippe then becomes king.

The swordplay, staged by Fred Cavens,* was rather lackluster, proving to be one of the fencing master's less effective efforts. Still, the film is worth seeing, if only for Louis Hayward's enthusiastic, versatile performance.

REFERENCE
Richards, Jeffrey. *Swordsmen of the Screen*. Boston: Routledge and Kegan Paul, 1977.

HEBREW SWORD. The basic sword of the Hebrews was originally of copper. This was followed by bronze and iron. It was not a large or heavy weapon. The blade was stiff, short, and straight.

The Hebrews also possessed longer-bladed swords used for both cutting and thrusting.
REFERENCE
Burton, Richard F. *The Book of the Sword*. London: Chatto and Windus, 1884.

HEIDELBERG. During the latter part of the nineteenth century, a particular form of sword fighting—called *schlaeger** fighting—arose in the universities of Germany, becoming a mania with the members of student fraternities. This was especially true of student groups at Heidelberg, where the practice reached its most virulent form. Indeed, Heidelberg is synonymous with such "dueling clubs."

The objective in *schlaeger* encounters was not to kill but simply to cut one's opponent on the head or face. As the dueling syndrome progressed, however, to be cut and so receive a facial scar—a true badge of honor among student duelists—was considered as much of a goal as winning one's duel. These "mutilations" were generically called "Heidelberg scars."
REFERENCES
Castle, Egerton. *Schools and Masters of Fence*. London: George Bell, 1885.
Wise, Arthur. *The Art and History of Personal Combat*. Greenwich, CT: Arma Press, 1971.

HEIJUTSU YOKUN. A book written by Japanese swordsman Adachi Masahiro (founder of the Shimbu-ryu school of swordsmanship) in 1790 on the proper training for a samurai.* The title means "essentials of swordsmanship."

Masahiro emphasized the importance of spiritual development over physical training and even mastery of technique as the true way to certain victory.

He stressed calmness. Fear of being killed or mental distractions of any kind were likely to affect the movement of the sword, thereby giving one's opponent a dangerous advantage. Masahiro stated flatly that in a fight a warrior should feel as if nothing crucial was happening. His behavior should be the behavior of everyday life. To act in this manner he called "the immovable mind."
REFERENCE
Suzuki, Daisetz. *Zen and Japanese Culture*. Princeton, NJ: Princeton University Press, 1973.

HEISS, GUSTAVE. (1904–1982). American fencer.

Gustave Heiss, a decorated combat veteran of World War II, won four U.S. national épée championships: 1933, 1934, 1936, and 1941. He also represented the United States in the 1932 and 1936 Olympics. He was a member of the 1932 Olympic épée team, which won a bronze medal.

REFERENCE

Huddleson, Mary, ed. "In Memoriam: Col. Gustave M. Heiss 1904–1982." *American Fencing* (September/October 1982).

HENTY, G. A. (1832–1902). English writer.

A writer of boys' adventure stories, G. A. Henty produced a number of books of a swashbuckling nature. His heroes were usually stalwart young men who were virtuous and brave to a fault.

His nineteenth-century works include *Won by the Sword, At Agincourt, Wulf the Saxon,* and *The Lion of the North.*

Swordplay is often encountered in Henty's tales, as in *Won by the Sword* (1899):

With a fierce oath the man pushed his way through those in front of him and drew his sword. He threw back his cloak to obtain full use of his sword arm.

With a roar of fury Beaufort rushed upon him. He was a good swordsman and personally brave, but his rage neutralized his skill, and after parrying two or three of his lunges Hector repeated the thrust with which he had that morning disabled de Vipont, and ran him through the shoulder.

REFERENCE

Henty, G. A. *Won by the Sword.* New York: Charles Scribner's Sons, 1899.

HERCULES, THE SWORD OF. Described as "the averter of destruction," the sword of Hercules, ancient Greece's legendary strong man, was said to be fashioned of alabaster, ivory, elektron (a mixed metal), and pure gold.

REFERENCE

Burton, Richard F. *The Book of the Sword.* London: Chatto and Windus, 1884.

HEREBRA. A Phoenician sickle-shaped sword.

REFERENCE

Burton, Richard F. *The Book of the Sword.* London: Chatto and Windus, 1884.

HEREMANS, JEAN. (c. twentieth century). Belgian fencing champion and film fencing master.

Jean Heremans was the fencing coach at the Los Angeles Athletic Club in 1948 when he was employed by MGM Studios to supervise the swordplay in their refilming of *The Three Musketeers,* starring Gene Kelly. Utilizing Kelly's athletic ability as a dancer, the fencing master produced some highly acceptable swordplay.

The Three Musketeers was followed by *The Prisoner of Zenda* (1952), *Scaramouche* (1952), *Prince Valiant* (1954), *Princess of the Nile* (1954), *The King's Thief* (1955), *The Swan* (1956), and *Swordsman of Siena* (1961).

While occasionally mechanical in his approach, more often than not, Heremans created fencing scenes that were both elaborate and exciting.

Heremans also holds the record for creating the longest sword fight on film. In *Scaramouche,* he put together a sword duel between Stewart Granger and Mel Ferrer lasting a full six minutes and thirty seconds.

REFERENCES
Behlmer, Rudy. "Swordplay on the Screen." *Films in Review* (June/July 1965).
Richards, Jeffrey. *Swordsmen of the Screen.* Boston: Routledge and Kegan Paul, 1977.

HERRIES, CHARLES. (c. 1794). British fencer.

Described as "the finest amateur of his day" by fencing master Harry Angelo of the famous Angelo family, Charles Herries never wore a fencing mask or jacket, because he thought they caused a fencer to become slack in his skills.

REFERENCE
Morton, E. D. *Martini A–Z of Fencing.* London: Queen Anne Press, 1992.

HEYAZASHI. In Japan, a very short sword worn in the house.

REFERENCE
Stone, George Cameron. *A Glossary of the Construction, Decoration, and Use of Arms and Armor.* New York: Jack Brussel, 1961.

HI. The grooves in a Japanese sword blade.

Also called *kesso.*

REFERENCE
Stone, George Cameron. *A Glossary of the Construction, Decoration, and Use of Arms and Armor.* New York: Jack Brussel, 1961.

HIEBCOMMENT. A set of rules governing a style of swordplay practiced by German university students toward the end of the eighteenth century. The system fostered a purely cutting technique, similar to English backswording. It eventually gave way to a more stylized mode of combat employing the *schlaeger.**

REFERENCE
Castle, Egerton. *Schools and Masters of Fence.* London: George Bell, 1885.

HIGHLAND BROADSWORD. A type of basket-hilted broadsword particular to Scotland. It may be distinguished from its Italian cousin, the *schiavona,* with its tendency toward complex, refined hand guard design, by a heavy, thick, simple style of metal weave.

Taking over as the weapon of preference from the old Scottish two-handed sword, the *claymore,* the Highland broadsword was often saddled mistakenly with the former's name. Popular from the seventeenth to the nineteenth century, it was carried as both a personal and military sword. The Highland broadsword was always employed as a cutting weapon: the flexible quality of its blade made point work unthinkable.

The very best Highland broadsword blades bore the name Andrea Ferara. Ferara blades, because of their extraordinary suppleness and temper, were much prized by Highland swordsmen. Because of this, countless counterfeits of lesser quality were constantly being produced to take advantage of the great demand.

Some blades spell the maker's name as "Andria" or "Andrea." On still others, "Ferara" is spelled "Ferera."

Strangely, for all the popularity of Ferara weapons, it is not known who Andrea Ferara actually was. It has been suggested he was Andrea dei Ferari, who made sword blades in Belluno, Italy, in the second half of the sixteenth century. Another theory identifies him as a swordsmith who moved to Scotland from Ferara, Italy.

Sword hilts for the Highland broadsword were manufactured on the island of Islay, off the west coast of Scotland.

In Scotland, the broadsword was often used in conjunction with a large, round shield called a target (or *targe*). The typical Scottish target was about twenty inches across and made of wood covered with stiff leather. Many had a spike as long as ten inches protruding from the center.

REFERENCES

Castle, Egerton. *Schools and Masters of Fence.* London: George Bell, 1885.

Mackay, William. *Highland Weapons.* Scotland: An Comunn Gaidhealach, 1970.

Stone, George Cameron. *A Glossary of the Construction, Decoration, and Use of Arms and Armory.* New York: Jack Brussel, 1961.

HIGH LINE. The area of a fencer's body comprising the upper torso (from the chest to the neck).

The high line includes the high-inside* lines of quarte* (4) and quinte* (5) and the high-outside* lines of sixte* (6) and tierce* (3). Quarte and sixte are "hand-in-supination"* positions; quinte and tierce are "hand-in-pronation"* positions.

In old fencing terms, the high line was referred to as *di sopra.*

The high line may also be called *dessus,** or *alta.*

REFERENCES

Castle, Egerton. *Schools and Masters of Fence.* London: George Bell, 1885.

Handelman, Rob. "Fencing Glossary." *American Fencing* (February/March 1976).

Palffy-Alpar, Julius. *Sword and Masque.* Philadelphia: F. A. Davis, 1967.

HIKIHADA. In early Japan, the *hikihada* was a scabbard cover used while traveling. Later, it was a leather sword case.

REFERENCE

Stone, George Cameron. *A Glossary of the Construction, Decoration, and Use of Arms and Armor.* New York: Jack Brussel, 1961.

HILT. The entire portion of the sword below the blade.

The hilt is made up of various sections: the guard* (or guards), the grip,* the

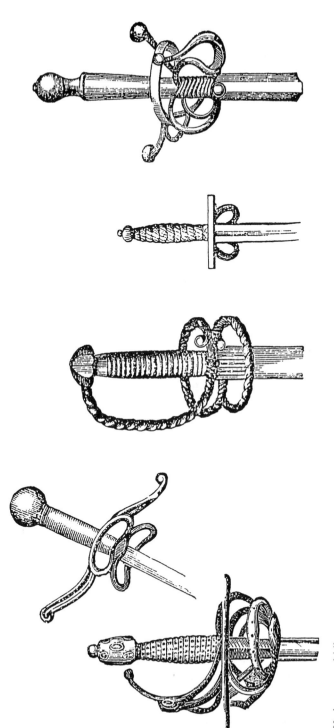

Various sword hilts

tang,* and the pommel.* It also comes in various forms: the simple "cross"-type hilt, the "cup" or "shell"-style hilt, and the "basket" hilt.

The hilt may also be called the "heft," *la manche, la manica, die Hilse,* and *das Heft.*

REFERENCES

Burton, Richard F. *The Book of the Sword.* London: Chatto and Windus, 1884.

Castle, Egerton. *Schools and Masters of Fence.* London: George Bell, 1885.

HIRA-TSUKURI. A Japanese sword blade that tapers uniformly from the back to the cutting edge.

REFERENCE

Stone, George Cameron. *A Glossary of the Construction, Decoration, and Use of Arms and Armor.* New York: Jack Brussel, 1961.

HI-SAKI-SHITA. A groove in a Japanese sword blade that does not go all the way to the point.

REFERENCE

Stone, George Cameron. *A Glossary of the Construction, Decoration, and Use of Arms and Armor.* New York: Jack Brussel, 1961.

HI-SAKI-UE. A groove in a Japanese sword blade that reaches the blade tip.

REFERENCE

Stone, George Cameron. *A Glossary of the Construction, Decoration, and Use of Arms and Armor.* New York: Jack Brussel, 1961.

HIT. The act of striking an opponent with one's sword.

In modern fencing, the method of making a valid hit is determined by the weapon being used. In foil fencing, a hit is scored with the point of the blade on the trunk of an opponent's body. With the épée, a hit may be scored anywhere on an opponent's body, but, once again, only with the blade point. The sabre hit is made on an opponent anywhere above the waist with either the blade's point or its cutting edge.

For hundreds of years, hits were scored in sport fencing by sight. Today, hits are recorded on an electric scoring machine.

The hit may also be called a "touch," a "point," a "score," *venie, veney,* or simply "touché."

REFERENCES

Palffy-Alpar, Julius. *Sword and Masque.* Philadelphia: F. A. Davis, 1967.

U.S. Fencing Association, ed. *Operations Manual.* Colorado Springs, CO: U.S. Fencing Association, 1985.

HITTITE SWORD. The Hittites, who ruled most of Asia Minor and Syria between 2000 and 1200 B.C., possessed a sword that was short and straight. Richard Burton described it as a "flesh chopper."

REFERENCE

Burton, Richard F. *The Book of the Sword.* London: Chatto and Windus, 1884.

HI UCHI BUKURO. A brocade bag hung from the scabbard of a sword in old Japan. It was often used to carry fire starting implements.
REFERENCE
Stone, George Cameron. *A Glossary of the Construction, Decoration, and Use of Arms and Armor.* New York: Jack Brussel, 1961.

HOBBS, WILLIAM. (c. twentieth century). British fencing master.

Learning to fence at the age of fourteen, William Hobbs became, first, a successful competitor in the sport of fencing and then a recognized master of stage fencing. He has staged sword fights for the Old Vic Company and the National Theatre Company of England.

Hobbs's approach to theatrical fencing suggests a realism that goes beyond the usual neatness of established theatrical combat, harking back to a time when art and brutality went hand in hand in swordplay.

In 1974, Hobbs directed the fencing in Richard Lester's *The Three Musketeers.*** The sword duels, following his historical approach, were both lively and highly physical, possessing an intent and sense of danger that fitted perfectly into the gritty atmosphere director Lester was attempting to interject into his work. The weapon combinations employed by Hobbs included sword alone, sword and dagger, sword and sword, sword and cloak, and sword and lantern.

Hobbs continued with this approach in the sequel to *The Three Musketeers, The Four Musketeers* (1975).**

Other Hobbs efforts include *Romeo and Juliet* (1968), *Macbeth* (1971), *Excalibur* (1981), *Monty Python's The Meaning of Life* (1983), and *Pirates* (1985).

In 1967, William Hobbs published a book, *Techniques of the Stage Fight,* which outlined his numerous theories on theatrical combat.
REFERENCES
Hobbs, William. *Techniques of the Stage Fight.* London: Studio Vista, 1967.
Richards, Jeffrey. *Swordsmen of the Screen.* Boston: Routledge and Kegan Paul, 1977.

HOKEN. A Japanese temple sword of the *ken** variety, that is, a sword possessing a straight, double-edged blade, occasionally widened near the tip. It was used only for ceremonial purposes.
REFERENCE
Stone, George Cameron. *A Glossary of the Construction, Decoration, and Use of Arms and Armor.* New York: Jack Brussel, 1961.

HOKKU. A Japanese poem of seventeen syllables. Such poems were often used to decorate sword mountings.
REFERENCE
Stone, George Cameron. *A Glossary of the Construction, Decoration, and Use of Arms and Armor.* New York: Jack Brussel, 1961.

HOLE IN THE HAND. An incorrect sword-hand position that creates a weakness in one's on-guard* position.
REFERENCE
Morton, E. D. *Martini A–Z of Fencing.* London: Queen Anne Press, 1992.

HOLE IN THE PARRY. A term describing a parry* that has been executed incorrectly.
REFERENCE
Morton, E. D. *Martini A–Z of Fencing.* London: Queen Anne Press, 1992.

HOLLYWOOD AND FENCING. From its earliest days, Hollywood has been fencing's most deceptive publicist. From anachronistic fighting techniques, to weapons of a specific time period mindlessly inserted in the wrong age, to ineptness presented as expertness, fencing has been twisted, chopped, and chewed up by many a film studio, to the point where few old-time swordsmen would recognize their art as the blade-waving mishmash often depicted on the movie screen.

A case in point of the Hollywood attitude was once related by film fencing master Ralph Faulkner*:

> In 1946, I was hired to work on *The Bandit of Sherwood Forest,*** which starred Cornel Wilde.* It was a "son of Robin Hood" movie, so it was, of course, set in the Middle Ages. Well, one day, early on in the production of the film, I was talking with Harry Cohn, the big boss at Columbia Pictures, about the type of swordplay we'd be using. After a bit, he took me down to his private screening room and showed me, of all things, the duel from *The Sea Hawk*** —one of my films. "I want the fight in my picture to be just like that," he told me. "Fine," I said. I could deliver that easily enough. "I especially like those swords," he continued. "I want swords just like those in my picture." This put me off a little. "But Harry," I explained, "those are rapiers. They weren't invented until five hundred years after our film takes place." Harry shook his head, and shrugged. "Oh, we can always get around that," he replied matter-of-factly.

REFERENCE
Evangelista, Nick. "Won by the Sword." *Silver Circle News* (Spring 1979).

HOLMES, SHERLOCK. The most famous character in detective fiction, Sherlock Holmes was created by Sir Arthur Conan Doyle in 1887.

A master of analytical detection, Holmes was also fashioned as a man of clear athletic capabilities. In Chapter 2 of the first Sherlock Holmes adventure story, *A Study in Scarlet* (1887), the detective's faithful assistant, Dr. Watson, identifies him as "an expert singlestick player, boxer, and swordsman."

Not until 1974, however, when author Nicholas Meyer penned *The Seven Per-Cent Solution,* a novel recounting a hitherto unknown episode in the "life" of Sherlock Holmes—an episode flavored with an interesting blend of historical and fictional personalities—was the master sleuth actually given a chance to display his fencing skills publicly.

Holmes crosses sabres with a certain Baron Von Leinsdorf, a Heidelberg-trained duelist, in an attempt to thwart a plot to plunge Europe into war (a number of years prior to World War I). Employing the knowledge that his opponent is weak on backhanded maneuvers, a fact observed during a prior tennis match, Holmes defeats Von Leinsdorf and saves the day.

REFERENCES

Benet, William Rose. *The Reader's Encyclopedia.* New York: Thomas Y. Crowell, 1965.

Doyle, Arthur Conan. *A Study in Scarlet.* New York: Berkley Publishing, 1963.

Meyer, Nicholas. *The Seven Per-Cent Solution.* New York: E. P. Dutton, 1974.

HOMERIC NAMES FOR SWORDS.

Chalos: a copper sword.

Xiphos: a generic name for a sword.

Phasganon: a two-edged, leaf-shaped sword.

Aor: a broad, stout, strong sword.

REFERENCE

Burton, Richard F. *The Book of the Sword.* London: Chatto and Windus, 1884.

HO-NOKI. The wood used to make scabbards* for Japanese swords. It was usually magnolia.

REFERENCE

Stone, George Cameron. *A Glossary of the Construction, Decoration, and Use of Arms and Armor.* New York: Jack Brussel, 1961.

HOPE, ANTHONY. (1863–1933). British novelist.

The author of numerous books, Anthony Hope is probably best known for his classic novel of swashbuckling adventure, romance, and political intrigue, *The Prisoner of Zenda* (1894).

The story deals with Englishman Rudolf Rassendyll, who, while on holiday in the tiny kingdom of Ruritania, is called upon to impersonate the king of that country—his twin cousin—who has been kidnapped.

Swordplay is encountered at the end of the story: "We were sword to sword. . . . Yes, we were man to man: and we began to fight, silently, sternly, and hard. Yet I remember little of it, save that the man was my match with the sword—nay, and more, for he knew more tricks than I. . . . He slipped; he fell. Like a dart I was upon him. I caught him by the throat and before he could recover himself I drove my blade through his neck."

While Hope's novel was not the first of its type, it was the most popular, starting a trend in fiction that lasted for more than ten years.

Rupert of Hentzau (1898) continued Rudolf Rassendyll's adventures.

REFERENCES

Benet, William Rose. *The Reader's Encyclopedia.* New York: Thomas Y. Crowell, 1965.

Hope, Anthony. *The Prisoner of Zenda.* New York: Heritage Press, 1966.

HOPE, BOB. (1903–   ). American (British-born) comedian.

Hollywood's perennial funnyman, Bob Hope was doubtlessly destined to surface in a swashbuckler spoof or two, and this he did with his characteristic wisecracking flair, as the comic coward who makes good.

In 1944, Hope starred in *Princess and the Pirate,* a hearty ribbing of pirate films. In 1946, he appeared in *Monsieur Beaucaire,* a comedy reworking of a popular novel by Booth Tarkington. Finally, in 1954, he made *Cassanova's Big Night,* a film where he got to "swashbuckle" and be a "great lover."

Never did Hope appear as anything but a klutz in these films. His fencing was always of the incompetent "sword-waving" variety. Yet, as in *Monsieur Beaucaire,* as a comedy device it was highly effective. In his book *Cads and Cavaliers,* author Tony Thomas notes of *Beaucaire:* "Duels are not easy to burlesque, but this one succeeded hilariously."

Occasionally, actors with more fencing ability were brought in to balance Hope's hopeless fencing antics.

REFERENCES

Halliwell, Leslie. *Halliwell's Filmgoer's and Video Viewer's Companion.* New York: Charles Scribner's Sons, 1988.

Thomas, Tony. *Cads and Cavaliers.* New York: A. S. Barnes, 1973.

HOPE, SIR WILLIAM. (1660–1724). English fencing master.

Although he never fought a duel in his life, William Hope produced the most important volumes on fencing in the English language in the latter half of the seventeenth century. He was, in fact, considered his nation's leading authority on fencing.

Moreover, while Hope covered at length the numerous ways of killing a man with a sword—in particular, the smallsword—his works hold within their pages the beginnings of the transition of fencing from a killing art to an art for its own sake.

William Hope's writings include *The Scots Fencing Master* (1687), *The Sword-Man's Vade-Mecum* (1691), *The Complete Fencing Master* (1692), *A New, Short and Easy Method of Fencing* (1707), *Hope's New Method of Fencing* (1714), *A Vindication of the True Art of Self-Defence* (1724), and *Observations on the Gladiator's Stage-Fighting* (1725).

REFERENCES

Castle, Egerton. *Schools and Masters of Fence.* London: George Bell, 1885.

Wise, Arthur. *The Art and History of Personal Combat.* Greenwich, CT: Arma Press, 1971.

HORIMONO. The decoration on Japanese sword blades.

REFERENCE

Stone, George Cameron. *A Glossary of the Construction, Decoration, and Use of Arms and Armor.* New York: Jack Brussel, 1961.

An illustration from Sir William Hope's *The Complete Fencing Master*

HORN, TEETH, AND BONE SWORDS. Animal by-products were long used by primitive peoples—such as Brazilian Indians, Polynesian islanders, and Eskimos—to enhance their wooden weapons, especially, wooden swords. The sharp points of horn and teeth and sharpened bone were set into wooden blade edges to create deadly cutting surfaces.

REFERENCE
Burton, Richard F. *The Book of the Sword.* London: Chatto and Windus, 1884.

HOWARD, ROBERT E. (1906–1936). Novelist and short story writer of fantasy adventures.

Howard specialized in writing stories about highly muscled barbarian swordsmen for pulp magazines during the 1930s. His tales are rich in fantastic imagery and dark sensuality and have inspired countless less worthy imitators.

He is probably best known for his Conan* the Cimmerian swordsman tales. These include the novel *Conan the Conqueror* (1935) and the short story collection *Conan the Adventurer* (1966).

The sword is ever-present in Howard's writing, as in his story "The Hand of Negral": "The soldiers fled, leaving Conan to fight the thing alone. And fight he did. Setting his feet squarely, he swung the great sword, pivoting on slim hips. . . . The sword flashed in a whistling arc of steel, cleaving the phantom in two."

Other Howard adventure books include *Solomon Kane* (1928), *King Kul* (1967), and *Wolfshead* (1968).

REFERENCE
Carter, Lin. *Imaginary Worlds.* New York: Ballantine Books, 1973.

HUFFMAN, JOHN. (1905–1979). American fencing champion.

John Huffman began his fencing career in 1922 at Yale University. In the years that followed, he studied under Giorgio Santelli and Aldo Nadi.

Huffman was a member of the 1928, 1932, and 1936 U.S. Olympic sabre teams. He was seven times U.S. national three-weapon champion; five times national saber champion; and three times national outdoor sabre champion.

In 1930, while studying at the University of Copenhagen, he also became the Danish national foil and sabre champion.

In the 1940s, Dr. Huffman helped pioneer the development of the world's first nuclear test reactor.

REFERENCE
Every, Dernell. "Dr. John R. Huffman, 1905–1979." *American Fencing* (March/April 1980).

HUKIM KHANI. A type of sword hilt* particular to Hyderabad, India. It had short quillons* with seals on the ends and drooping projections over the sword blade, a short grip, and a disk pommel.*

REFERENCE
Stone, George Cameron. *A Glossary of the Construction, Decoration, and Use of Arms and Armor.* New York: Jack Brussel, 1961.

HUNGARIAN BROADSWORD. Unlike the Highland and English broadswords, the Hungarian broadsword did not employ a basket-type hilt, but rather a simple curved knuckle guard. It was most often used as a cavalry weapon.

The art of Hungarian broadsword combat was a specialty of Henry Angelo,* who produced a book of illustrations picturing its implementation in battle, *Hungarian and Highland Broad Sword* (1798). Angelo was the son of famed Italian fencing master Domenico Angelo.*

The Hungarian broadsword is sometimes referred to as a sabre.
REFERENCES
Angelo, Henry. *Hungarian and Highland Broad Sword.* London: C. Roworth, 1798.
Castle, Egerton. *Schools and Masters of Fence.* London: George Bell, 1885.

HUNGARIAN FENCERS, NOTED.

Foil

Bela Bekessy, Laszlo Berti, Jozsef Gyuricza, Jeno Kamuti, Lajos Maszlay, Sandor Syabo, Istvan Szelei

Épée

Lajos Balthazar, Csaba Fenyvesi, Erno Kolczonay, Gyozo Kulcsar, Istvan Osztrics, Jozsef Sakovics

Sabre

Jeno Apathy, Bela Bekessy, Tibor Berczelly, Deyso Foldes, Jeno Fuchs, Janos Garay, Imre Gedovari, Aladar Gervich, Sandor Gombos, Zoltan Horvath, Endre Kabos, Rudolf Karpati, Pal Kovacs, Tamas Kovacs, Peter Maroth, Ervin Meszaros, Attila Petschaur, Tibor Pezsa, Gyorgy Piller, Sandor Posta, Laszlo Rajcsanyi, Zoltan Schenker, Jeno Szantay, Odon Terztyanszky, Peter Toth, Amon von Gregurich, Gyula von Ivanyi, Lajos Werkner, Bela Zulavszky

REFERENCE
Wallechinsky, David. *The Complete Book of the Olympics.* New York: Penguin Books, 1984.

HUNGARIAN SCHOOL OF FENCING. The Hungarian school of fencing is, essentially, a school devoted to the sabre. Developed in the mid-1800s by Maestro Joseph Keresztessy (called the ''father of Hungarian sabre fencing''), this style involved the wrist, which brought into play short swings of a circular fashion in both cuts and parries.

The Hungarian school was improved upon by Italian fencing master Italo Santelli,* who was invited by the Hungarian government in 1896 to coach its national team. Santelli remolded the Hungarian approach into a style of fencing that kept Hungary at the top of international fencing circles for decades.

Further technique improvements were added to the Hungarian style by the Hungarian master Borsody* and the Italian Luigi Barbasetti.*

Modern Hungarian masters of note include Bela Balogh, Zoltan Beke, Mikla Bela, B. Imregi, Istvan Lukovitch, A. Moldovanyi, Bela Nagy, and Laszlo Szabo.

REFERENCES
Palffy-Alpar, Julius. *Sword and Masque.* Philadelphia: F. A. Davis, 1967.
Wallechinsky, David. *The Complete Book of the Olympics.* New York: Penguin Books, 1984.

HUNGARIAN WOMEN FENCERS, NOTED. Ildiko Bobis, Erna Bogathy Bogen, Margit Dany, Margit Elek, Katalin Juhasz, Magdolna Kovacs-Nyari, Magda Maros, Ilona Schacherer-Elek, Ildiko Schwarczenberger, Gizella Tary, Ildiko Ujlaki-Rejto, Ilona Vargha.

REFERENCE
Wallechinsky, David. *The Complete Book of the Olympics.* New York: Penguin Books, 1984.

HUTTON, ALFRED. (1841–1910). British fencing master.

Alfred Hutton was one of a handful of men responsible, at the turn of the century, for breathing new life into the sport of fencing after it had fallen into the category of anachronistic, esoteric activities. He organized fencing exhibitions and lectures all over his country and, in time, formed his own *salle.*

A proponent of the French school of fencing, Maestro Hutton did much to modernize sabre technique as it was fenced at the time. He also attempted, unsuccessfully, to have the sword reinstated as a military combat weapon.

Hutton's theories can be found in his books, which include *Cold Steel* (1889), *The Swordsman* (1891), *Old Swordplay* (1892), and *The Sword and the Centuries* (1901).

REFERENCES
Morton, E. D. *Martini A–Z of Fencing.* London: Queen Anne Press, 1992.
Wise, Arthur. *The Art and History of Personal Combat.* Greenwich, CT: Arma Press, 1971.

HYPNOTISM. Hypnotism has been used to improve athletic performance for decades in sports such as baseball, tennis, boxing, track and field, and even skating. Well-known professional athletes like Nolan Ryan, Maury Wills, Don Sutton, Muhammad Ali, and Rod Carew have stated publicly that much of their success in sports has been due to the use of hypnosis.

It has been suggested in the past by some fencing experts that hypnosis could be used to improve concentration and promote relaxation on the fencing strip. However, in spite of its acknowledged successes, this has yet to find widespread acceptance.

On a fictional level, fencing and hypnosis have been blended into fantastic

British fencing master Alfred Hutton

combinations on occasion. In *Black Magic,*** a 1949 film starring Orson Welles* (based on Alexandre Dumas's novel *Joseph Balsamo*), an evil hypnotist, Cagliostro, uses his powers against the nobles of the court of Louis XVI. After nearly toppling the throne of France, Cagliostro is unmasked as a wicked traitor. Escaping, the villain is then trapped on the rooftops of Paris, where he fights a sword duel with a young army officer—''You cannot defeat my eyes!'' ''I'm looking at your sword point!''—who kills him.

The other major fencing/hypnotism movie—and probably the best—is Danny Kaye's *The Court Jester* (1954).* Hypnotism becomes the vehicle for turning Kaye's bumbling character into a dashing swordsman. Under the spell—''Tails of lizards, ears of swine, chicken gizzards soaked in brine, now your eyes and mine entwine, your will is broken, thou art mine!''—he is directed into all sorts of comic encounters. Unfortunately, he remembers nothing when the spell is broken. The ''hypnotically induced'' fencing, staged by fencing master Ralph Faulkner,* is by far the best comic swordplay on film.

REFERENCES

Drooz, Alan. ''Mind over Muscle.'' *Los Angeles Times,* August 9, 1984.
Evangelista, Anita. *Dictionary of Hypnotism.* Westport, CT: Greenwood Press, 1991.

I

IAIDO. The Japanese art of drawing the sword from its scabbard.*

In the days of the samurai,* *iaido* was called *iaijutsu* (sword-drawing art). The concept of the discipline was to be able to go on the offensive instantly, striking as one was unsheathing one's blade. For this reason, the skill was also called *battojutsu* (striking from the sheath).

Iaido, the descendant of the earlier form, is actually a development of the twentieth century. The emphasis now is on the character-building and spiritual aspects of the art. To mold form that is both aesthetically pleasing and combatively sound is the ultimate goal of the swordsman.

The full technique of *iaido* includes the drawing of the sword, the cut, and the return to the scabbard.

REFERENCES

Corcoran, John, and Emil Farkas. *Martial Arts.* New York: Gallery Books, 1983.

Lewis, Peter. *Martial Arts of the Orient.* New York: Gallery Books, 1985.

————. *The Way to Martial Arts.* New York: Exter Books, 1986.

ICHI-NO-ASHI. The upper band on the scabbard* of a *tachi,* the earliest form of single-edged Japanese sword. The *ichi-no-ashi* possesses a sling loop, so that it might be mounted on a sword belt.

Conversely, the lower band on the scabbard is called *ichi-no-sei.*

REFERENCE

Stone, George Cameron. *A Glossary of the Construction, Decoration, and Use of Arms and Armor.* New York: Jack Brussel, 1961.

IIZASA, CHOISAI. Legendary founder (pre-eighth century) of *kenjutsu,** Japan's art of sword fighting.

REFERENCE

Sasamori, Junzo, and Gordon Warner. *This Is Kendo.* Vermont: Charles E. Tuttle, 1984.

IMBRACCIATURA. A long shield sometimes used in conjunction with the sword during the sixteenth century.

REFERENCE

Castle, Egerton. *Schools and Masters of Fence.* London: George Bell, 1885.

IMBROCCATA. A thrust taught by sixteenth-century Italian fencing master Vincentio Saviolo.*

The *imbroccata* reached an opponent over his sword, hand, or dagger, traveling in a downward direction (even as far as the knee). It was delivered with the hand in pronation (palm down).

In modern fencing, *imbroccata* refers to a time thrust* that also blocks and guides an opponent's blade away in the line of seconde* (low-outside quarter). It is performed on the final measure* of an attack.

Also called *imbroccado.*

REFERENCES

Castle, Egerton. *Schools and Masters of Fence.* London: George Bell, 1885.

Palffy-Alpar, Julius. *Sword and Masque.* Philadelphia: F. A. Davis, 1967.

IMMOBILITE. To launch an attack from a completely static position.

REFERENCE

Handelman, Rob. "Fencing Glossary." *America Fencing* (May/June 1978).

IMPUGNATURA. The guard,* the handle,* and the pommel* of an Italian weapon.

REFERENCE

Morton, E. D. *Martini A–Z of Fencing.* London: Queen Anne Press, 1992.

INCARTATA. As taught by Vincentio Saviolo,* the *incartata* was a thrust* similar to the *imbroccata,** except that *a volte** (body evasion)—created by stepping to the right with the left foot and twisting the body sideways out of the way of an attack—was incorporated into the action.

In modern fencing, the *incartata* is a time thrust performed against an attack to the inside high line in its final movement, much as in the action of earlier times (including the body evasion). The oncoming attack may also be simultaneously blocked with the forte of one's weapon.

Also called *inquartata* and *inquarto.*

REFERENCES

Castle, Egerton. *Schools and Masters of Fence.* London: George Bell, 1885.

Palffy-Alpar, Julius. *Sword and Masque.* Philadelphia: F. A. Davis, 1967.

INDIRECT ATTACK. An indirect attack is any attack made in the opposite line* from which a fencer is initially engaged.*
REFERENCE
Palffy-Alpar, Julius. *Sword and Masque.* Philadelphia: F. A. Davis, 1967.

INDIRECT PARRY. Any parry* that travels into an opposite line* to stop an opponent's attack. This includes counterparries,* semicircular parries,* and changing parries.*
REFERENCE
Palffy-Alpar, Julius. *Sword and Masque.* Philadelphia: F. A. Davis, 1967.

INDIRECT RIPOSTE. Any riposte* that is not made immediately into the same line in which a parry* has been executed.
    This includes:

The riposte by disengage—a riposte passing beneath an opponent's blade into the opposite line.

The riposte by *coupé*—a riposte traveling over the top of an opponent's blade into the opposite line.

The riposte by one-two—a riposte made up of a feint of disengage followed by an evasion of one lateral parry.

The riposte by *doublé*—a riposte made up of a feint of disengage followed by the evasion of one counterparry.

    Indirect ripostes may also be made up of combinations of the aforementioned actions.
REFERENCE
Palffy-Alpar, Julius. *Sword and Masque.* Philadelphia: F. A. Davis, 1967.

INDONESIAN SWORDS. Indonesian swords—those of Sumatra, Nias, Java, Bali, Borneo, and the Celebes—cover the gamut of blade shapes: straight, curved, wavy, and leaf-shaped (blade length average is 24 inches). Some blades widen toward the tip and are used for cutting; others taper to a sharp point and are for thrusting. Grips are straight, made of wood or bone, and are often wrapped with cord or wire (grip length average is 5 inches). Pommels are usually carved shapes, especially animal and human heads.
    Swords include the *kris,* the *klevang, parang,* or *mandau,* the *sebua,* and the *gari telegu.*
REFERENCE
Solc, Vaclav. *Swords and Daggers of Indonesia.* London: Spring Books, 1966.

INFIGHTING. Fencing at a distance that is too close for normal maneuvering of the blade, usually within a foot or two of one's opponent. Infighting usually occurs when both fencers have attacked simultaneously on the advance and missed each other; or when one fencer, exhibiting a poor sense of distance, draws too close to his opponent.

Infighting usually consists of bent-arm jabbing and twisting and turning as each fencer attempts to successfully land a touch.

While some fencing masters teach infighting as a matter of course, others consider such techniques an excuse for poor distance.

Body contact, while engaged in infighting, is prohibited in foil and sabre fencing. In the case of épée, a minimum of contact is allowed as long as jostling does not occur.

Infighting may also be called "fighting at close quarters" or simply "closing."

REFERENCES

Lownds, Camille. *Foil Around and Stay Fit.* New York: Harcourt Brace Jovanovich, 1977.

Palffy-Alpar, Julius. *Sword and Masque.* Philadelphia: F. A. Davis, 1967.

INJURIES, FENCING. As one might expect considering its highly combative nature, fencing has its share of injuries. Any physical activity can be potentially risky. Yet, when stacked up against other sports, fencing shows itself to be a relatively safe pastime. A sports medicine study conducted in England in the early 1970s and published in the British medical journal *Lancet* (1976), reported that, per 10,000 hours examined, fencing had a mere 4.2 injuries. By comparison, soccer had 36.5 injuries.

More recently, a five-year inquiry carried out by the U.S. Fencing Association,* utilizing nearly 1,600 of its members, produced some illuminating facts about fencing hazards. Nearly 50 percent of those polled reported absolutely no injuries at all. Of the 842 who did disclose physical mishaps, 61 percent described them as having no real impact on their fencing, and 22 percent said they were not severe enough to keep them from fencing. Fifteen percent described their bodily traumas as "significant."

Factors contributing to injuries most often included poor fencing technique, inadequate warm-up, fatigue, dangerous fencing tactics, and faulty equipment.

Frequently reported injuries included muscle strains and sprains, tendonitis, cartilage and tendon tears, and minor lacerations. Fractures and punctures were relatively infrequent problems. The areas of a fencer's body most likely to suffer injuries were the ankles and knees.

REFERENCES

Carter, Cynthia, John Heil, and Eric Zemper. "What Hurts and Why." *American Fencing* (Spring 1993).

Conte, Mickey. "How Safe Is Fencing?" *Southern California AFLA Newsletter* (March/April 1980).

Moyer, Julie, and Jeff Konin. "An Overview of Fencing Injuries." *American Fencing* (April/May/June 1992).

IN LINE. A fencer's blade is said to be "in line" when his weapon's point is menacing some portion of his opponent's valid target* area.

Having one's point in line is part of what helps establish a fencer's legitimacy as an attacker. The other element is a straight arm.

REFERENCES

Curry, Nancy. *The Fencing Book.* New York: Leisure Press, 1984.

U.S. Fencing Association, ed. *Fencing Rules and Manual.* Colorado Springs, CO: U.S. Fencing Association, 1984.

INSIDE LINE. The portions of a fencer's target area on the palm side of his hand. These include the lines of prime* (one), quarte* (four), quinte* (five), and septime* (seven).

The inside line is made up of a high-inside line and a low-inside line. The lines of quarte and quinte make up the high-inside line; prime and septime make up the low-inside line.

In fencing's early days, the inside line was referred to as *di dentro.*

Also called *interna* and *dedans.*

REFERENCES

Castle, Egerton. *Schools and Masters of Fence.* London: George Bell, 1885.

Curry, Nancy. *The Fencing Book.* New York: Leisure Press, 1984.

Palffy-Alpar, Julius. *Sword and Masque.* Philadelphia: F. A. Davis, 1967.

INSTANCES. In the Spanish method of swordplay developed in the seventeenth century by Girard Thibault,* the manner in which a fencer approached his adversary was called an instance. These instances were determined by following specified intersecting geometric lines within a "mystical" circle.

REFERENCE

Castle, Egerton. *Schools and Masters of Fence.* London: George Bell, 1885.

INSUFFICIENT PARRY. A parry* that is too light to deflect an opponent's oncoming blade. Such an action often results in a touch for the attacker.

REFERENCE

Morton, E. D. *Martini A–Z of Fencing.* London: Queen Anne Press, 1992.

INTAGLIATA. A time thrust* practiced during the eighteenth century that was delivered by making a pass* to the left of an opponent when his attack came in the outside line.*

REFERENCE

Castle, Egerton. *Schools and Masters of Fence.* London: George Bell, 1885.

INTENT. The resolve that goes into executing an attack. Without true intent, any attack will likely fail.

Strategywise, intent may be reserved for any action following an initial attack, allowing a fencer to purposefully manipulate his adversary's counterattack.

Developing a strong feeling for intent and being able to project this visually help a fencer create feints of attacks that are both credible and threatening. A feint without a sense of intent behind it looks like what it is—a fake action—and will be unlikely to draw a parry from one's opponent.

Also, bringing a sense of intent into one's fencing lesson helps turn mere mechanical actions into actions that more resemble actual combat. This aids in shrinking the psychological gap between the structured lesson and the heated bout.

REFERENCE

Palffy-Alpar, Julius. *Sword and Masque.* Philadelphia: F. A. Davis, 1967.

INTENTION. The moment when a fencer actually intends to hit his opponent.

Some attacks are made to hit on the primary (first) action; some are meant to hit on a secondary action, the first action in the attack then being a kind of feint that the attacker wants to be parried. Saving one's intention for the secondary response helps a fencer get a timing jump on his opponent.

A third intention may follow a secondary intention, a fourth may follow a third, and so on down the line until one's desired result has been achieved.

The use of intention is an important part of the tactics of fencing.

REFERENCE

Palffy-Alpar, Julius. *Sword and Masque.* Philadelphia: F. A. Davis, 1967.

INTERCEPTION. A counteroffensive* action that blocks the passage of an opponent's blade into the line where it should have touched.

REFERENCE

Handelman, Rob. "Fencing Glossary." *American Fencing* (May/June 1978).

INTRECCIATA. A favorite attack of sixteenth-century Italian swordsmen. It consisted of a sliding action along an opponent's blade accompanied by prolonged heavy pressure (*froissement*),* followed by either a disengage* (*degagé*) or a bind* (*liement*).**

This action was first explained by Antonio Marcelli* in his book *Regole Della Scherma* (1686).**

REFERENCES

Castle, Egerton. *Schools and Masters of Fence.* London: George Bell, 1885.

Handelman, Rob. "Fencing Glossary." *American Fencing* (May/June 1978).

INVALID ATTACK. Any attack made when a fencer has not established the right to hit his opponent (right-of-way*).

An invalid attack is made when a fencer attacks with a bent arm, or his point is not menacing his opponent's target area; when a fencer attacks into his opponent's valid attack; when a fencer hesitates during an attack long enough for his opponent to claim the right-of-way; when an attacker continues attacking into a continuous parry*-risposte* action; and when a fencer violates any rules of proper fencing methodology or behavior during his execution of his attack (e.g., if a fencer parries with his free hand to gain a touch).

It should be noted that an invalid attack acquires validity over a valid one when a valid action misses hitting its target entirely, that is, in every one of the previous examples except the last one.

REFERENCE

U.S. Fencing Association, ed. *Operations Manual.* Colorado Springs, CO: U.S. Fencing Association, 1985.

INVALID PARRY. A parry that, for whatever reason, does not sufficiently deflect an incoming blade away from one's target area.

REFERENCE

U.S. Fencing Association, ed. *Operations Manual.* Colorado Springs, CO: U.S. Fencing Association, 1985.

INVALID TOUCH. Any touch made when a fencer executes an invalid attack.

Invalid touches also occur when a touch lands on the parts of a fencer's body that are considered off target* or when the side of the blade hits when only the point is allowed.

In electrical fencing, an invalid touch is also one that does not register on the scoring machine (even if otherwise correct regarding right-of-way,* and so on).

REFERENCE

U.S. Fencing Association, ed. *Operations Manual.* Colorado Springs, CO: U.S. Fencing Association, 1985.

INVITATION. In the French school of fencing, invitation refers to any on-guard* position held without contacting an opponent's blade.

The term may also be ascribed to any action made to tempt an opponent into attacking. Different types of invitations, of course, draw different responses. Opening a particular line, for instance, helps lead an attack into that area. An extended blade might draw either a beat or a bind. The use of an invitation, then, is a simple form of fencing strategy.

REFERENCES

Lownds, Camille. *Foil Around and Stay Fit.* New York: Harcourt Brace Jovanovich, 1977.

Palffy-Alpar, Julius. *Sword and Masque.* Philadelphia: F. A. Davis, 1967.

ITALIAN FENCERS, NOTED.

Foil

Giancarlo Bergamini, Edoardo Berti, Giorgio Bocchino, Andrea Borella, Stefano Cerioni, Federico Cesarno, Fabio Dal Zotto,* Manlio Di Rosa, Giulio Gaudini,* Gioacchino Guaragna, Edoardo Mangiarotti, Gustavo Marzi, Aldo Nadi,* Nedo Nadi,* Maro Numa, Ugo Pignotti, Oreste Puliti,* Georgio Santelli,* Antonio Spallino, Pietro Speciale

Épée

Carlo Agostini, Stefano Bellone, Giovanni Bredo, Luigi Cantone, Giancarlo Cornaggia-Medici, Giuseppe Delfino,* Dario Mangiarotti,** Edoardo Mangiarotti,* Virgilio Mantegazza, Carlo Pavesi, Saverio Ragno, Franco Riccardi, Gianluigi Saccaro

Sabre

Bino Bini, Wladimiro Calarese, Federico Cesarano, Gianfranco Dalla Barba, Gastone Dare, Arturo De Vecchi, Giulio Gaudini,* Michele Maffei, Gustavo Marzi, Fernando Meglio, Mario Montano, Aldo Nadi, Nedo Nadi, Luigi Narduzzi, Vincenzo Pinton, Oreste Puliti, Rolando Rigoli, Giovanni Scalzo

REFERENCE
Wallechinsky, David. *The Complete Book of the Olympics.* New York: Penguin Books, 1984.

ITALIAN FOIL. The Italian foil is based, in form, on the rapier,* the dueling sword of the seventeenth century. With its crossbar-oriented hilt, it allows for a firm grip, strong parries, and energetic attacks. Traditionally, the Italian foil's grip* is strapped to the wrist of its user with a leather thong, called a martingale,* to augment control. This causes the weapon's manipulation to emanate chiefly from the wrist and forearm (rather than from the fingers, as with the French* foil).

Over the years, the Italian foil has lost some of its popularity, first to the French foil, then to the various forms of pistol grip* foils. However, those who continue to employ it are fiercely dedicated to its unique nature.
REFERENCES
Morton, E. D. *Martini A–Z of Fencing.* London: Queen Anne Press, 1992.
Palffy-Alpar, Julius. *Sword and Masque.* Philadelphia: F. A. Davis, 1967.

ITALIAN GRIP. The Italian grip, for both foil and épée, is a streamlined version of the old-time rapier grip. It employs crossbars (*gavigliano*) beneath the handguard around which the fencer wraps one or two fingers, and a straight handle that is usually secured to the wrist with a strap.

By its construction, the Italian grip promotes a muscular style of fencing.
REFERENCES
Morton, E. D. *Martini A–Z of Fencing.* London: Queen Anne Press, 1992.
Palffy-Alpar. Julius. *Sword and Masque.* Philadelphia: F. A. Davis, 1967.

ITALIAN SCHOOL OF FENCING. In its earliest days, to refer to a single Italian school of swordplay would be a misnomer since each Italian master had his own highly individualized ideas about the way fencing should be conducted. Still, with the Italians we first see an attempt to organize fencing into a workable science.

Initially, fencing, as conducted by the Italians, was a rough, undisciplined game, which depended heavily on dash and violence. But, as time went on, workable systems began to emerge.

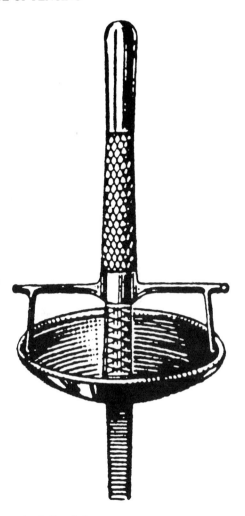

The Italian foil

Beginning, as everyone else did, with the edged sword, the Italians were among the first to adopt the thrusting rapier, quickly becoming the acknowledged masters of that weapon. Along the way, they invented the lunge, divided the body into lines, described the properties of the various portions of the sword and how best to employ them, and perfected the counterattack. If that was not enough, they were able to write about everything in such a way as to make it understandable.

While the Italian school had taken a secondary position to the French approach by the end of the seventeenth century, it is safe to say that fencing would not be what it is today without the input of masters like Achille Marozzo,

Italian swordplay according to Ridolfo Capo Ferro

Camillo Agrippa, Angelo Viggiani, Vincentio Saviolo, Nicoletto Giganti, and Ridolfo Capo Ferro.

The modern Italian school of fencing, based on old-time rapier play, clearly reflects the Italian temperament. It is a game that favors strength, speed, and agility. In foil, the arm and wrist come into constant play; powerful footwork is essential. The Italian sabre style, carried by the forearm, is one of short, but powerful, swings of the arm and dramatic counterparries,

Italian fencers are among the most accomplished international competitors.
REFERENCE
Palffy-Alpar, Julius. *Sword and Masque.* Philadelphia: F. A. Davis, 1967.

ITALIAN WOMEN FENCERS, NOTED. Irene Camber, Velleda Cessari, Maria Collino, Bruna Colombetti, Giovanna Massciotta, Antonella Ragno, Dorina Vaccaroni
REFERENCE
Wallechinsky, David. *The Complete Book of the Olympics.* New York Penguin Books, 1984.

ITO MAKI TACHI. A *tachi** (Japanese single-edged sword) with the upper portion of the scabbard* wound with braid or leather like the hilt* of its sword.
REFERENCE
Stone, George Cameron. *A Glossary of the Construction, Decoration, and Use of Arms and Armor.* New York: Jack Brussel, 1961.

J

JACKET, FENCING. The protective coat worn in fencing. The jacket, for competition purposes, must be white. It is usually made of cotton duck (canvas) or stretch nylon.

Fencing jackets are designed for each individual weapon. The foil jacket is cut so that it covers the target area for foil. It includes a *cuisard* (groin strap). By U.S. Fencing Association (USFA) rules, the material of the jacket must overlap the fencer's pants by at least ten centimeters when the fencer is in the on-guard position.

Sabre jackets are cut to the waist, covering that weapon's target area. Because of the inevitability of cuts to the sword arm, the jacket must include a double thickness of material for the sleeve down to the elbow. There may also be extra padding in the chest area. Like the foil jacket, the sabre jacket must overlap the pants by at least ten centimeters when the fencer is in the on-guard position.

The épée jacket, which is cut along the same lines as the foil jacket, must be of double thickness material in the sword arm.

Jackets incorporating the needs of foil, sabre, and épée are referred to as three-weapon jackets.

REFERENCE

U.S. Fencing Association, ed. *Operations Manual.* Colorado Springs, CO: U.S. Fencing Association, 1985.

JACOBY, H. H. (c. nineteenth century). French fencing master.

An honor student of the famous Joinville-le-Pont fencing school of France,

H. H. Jacoby came to America to teach in 1889. He became one of the pioneers of college fencing in America.

REFERENCE

Cass, Elanor Baldwin. *The Book of Fencing*. Boston: Lothrop, Lee, and Shephard, 1930.

JAPANESE BLADES. The Japanese sword blade derives its named from its length. The *jin tachi** (long sword) blade measures thirty-three inches and over; *katana** and *tachi** (standard-length, curved, single-edged swords) blades from twenty-four to thirty inches; *chisa katana** (medium-length sword) blades from eighteen to twenty-four inches; and *wakizashi** (short sword) blades from sixteen to twenty inches.

Unlike a Western blade—with its point,* forte,* foible,* shoulder,* and tang*—the Japanese blade is broken down into well over thirty parts, with each portion being assigned its own special name based on its characteristics.

Early Japanese sword blades come in both single- and double-edged varieties, but the blade of the generic samurai sword is almost always of the single-edged type.

The creating of a Japanese blade became an almost spiritual experience for its maker. Often much ceremony was involved in the final processes.

The method used by the most celebrated blade makers was to weld and double and weld four bars of iron five times, which produced 4,194,304 layers in the blade. The heating and cooling of the metal were approached with much care, for, when done properly, they produced a cutting edge that was extremely hard without being brittle and a body that was both soft and tough.

The blade of a Japanese sword was supposed to be able to cut off a man's head with a single stroke. It was not uncommon for the owner of a new sword to test it on the first peasant he met along the road. This murderous act was known as *tsujigiri.* Blades were also tested on the corpses of executed criminals, a test called *tamashigari.* Sometimes bodies were piled up, one on top of the other. It was said that a truly superior blade could slice through seven bodies with one cut. Murderers, individuals with skin diseases, and tattooed men were not used in the testing.

It was a common belief in Japan that the quality of a blade reflected the character of its owner. It was said that it was ''impossible for an evil-hearted man to retain possession of a famous sword.'' A man sought to live up to the attributes of a superior blade, and such a blade was often cherished by his family for centuries.

Once the blade was finished, it was usually decorated by a master craftsman.

Blades produced prior to 1600 are called *koto* (old); those made later are called *shinto* (new).

Famous Japanese blade makers include Munchechika (c. tenth century); Yoshimitsu (c. thirteenth century); and Kane-uji (c. fourteenth century).

REFERENCES

Brinkley, Captain F. *Samurai: The Invincible Warrior.* Burbank, CA: Ohara Books, 1975.

Stone, George Cameron. *A Glossary of the Construction, Decoration, and Use of Arms and Armor.* New York: Jack Brussel, 1961.

JAPANESE SWORDSMEN, FAMOUS. Over the centuries, Japan had a vast number of talented swordsmen whose prowess was heralded across the land. Many of these men, once they had developed their own approach to the use of the sword, opened schools whereby their techniques became established styles of personal combat. A strong underlying motivation of most of these swordsmen was a desire for perfection of style and spiritual enlightenment.

Thirteenth Century

Shigenobu Hayashizaki (c. 1280). Introduced the technique of rapidly drawing the sword from its scabbard, a skill that became vital to Japanese swordplay.

Fourteenth Century

Nagahide Chujo (c. 1380). Founder of his own school of swordplay, the Chujo-ryu school. He also acted as counselor to the shogun, who bestowed on him the title of "master swordsman."

Fifteenth Century

Bungoro Hikida (1437–?). Master swordsman and teacher.

Iko Aisu (1452–1538). Famed fencing master who, when he was no longer able to defeat his fencing opponents and pupils, retired to a secluded cave where he created a new style of swordplay.

Bokuden Tsukahara (1490–1572). Fought thirty-seven duels without a defeat. His skill was due to the great stress he placed on mastering numerous fencing styles and concentration. He also believed in developing patience.

Sixteenth Century

Muneyoshi Yagyu (1527–1606). Established the famous Yagyu school of fencing. Became fencing master to the shogun.

Munenori Yagyu (1571–1646). Son of Muneyoshi. Became a great swordsman and soldier. Served the shogun as his chief of police.

Tsunenaga Hasekura (1571–1622). A swordsman of exceptional ability, he was chosen by the shogun to travel to Spain and Italy to study those countries' customs.

Miyamoto Musashi* (1584–1645). Japan's greatest swordsman; won sixty duels. In 1645, he wrote the classic book on swordsmanship, *A Book of Five Rings.***

Seventeenth Century

Mataemon Araki (1591–1637). A skilled swordsman who avenged the killing of his retainer's younger brother.

Kagehisa Ittosai Ito (c. 1600). Established the "one sword" school of fencing called Kiriotoshi, whereby all fencing techniques were said to derive from one original technique.

Japanese swordsmen in action

Mitsuyoshi Yagyu (1607–1650). Known as Jubei, Mitsuyoshi is considered the real founder of the Yagyu school of swordplay, which, because of him, became the most successful style of its day. Also, served as a spy for the shogun.

Zesuiken Iba (c. 1690). Devised techniques for fighting with the long sword.

Eighteenth Century

Chuta Nakanishi (c. 1750). Desiring to instill safety into the learning of swordplay, Chuta invented protective gear that removed the more dangerous elements from practice sessions. He designed the *kote* (fencing glove), the *shinai* (bamboo sword), and the *do* (chest protector).

Nineteenth Century

Yamaoka Tesshu (1836–1888). Skilled swordsman, Zen master, and teacher. Trained his pupils in a method that was said to tap new sources of physical energy.

REFERENCES
Sasamori, Junzo, and Gordon Warner. *This Is Kendo.* Vermont: Charles E. Tuttle, 1964.
Suzuki, Daisetz. *Zen and the Japanese Culture.* Princeton, NJ: Princeton University
    Press, 1959.

JARNAC, GUY CHABOT, COMTE DE. (c. 1530). French nobleman and swordsman.

Known chiefly for his duel of chivalry with François la Chastaigneraye** (famed as the finest swordsman in France). Jarnac won the fight by unexpectedly cutting the ham of each of his opponent's legs so that he was unable to stand— a stroke known ever since as the coup de Jarnac.*
REFERENCE
Baldick, Robert. *The Duel.* New York: Spring Books, 1970.

JAUHAR. The grain, or watering, of Persian steel called Damascus.

It was produced by welding and twisting pieces of metal of varying degrees of hardness and composition.

Also called ''Jauhardar.''
REFERENCE
Stone, George Cameron. *A Glossary of the Construction, Decoration, and Use of Arms
    and Armor.* New York: Jack Brussel, 1961.

JEAN-LOUIS. (c. eighteenth century). French swordsman and fencing master.

A legendary swordsman, Jean-Louis fought numerous duels, in one of which he is reported to have employed a foil against an opponent armed with a dueling sword. Jean-Louis, as the story goes, after allowing his enemy to tire himself out, slashed him savagely across the face with his blade, which ended the combat at once. Another duel saw him kill or seriously wound eleven adversaries in a row.

During the early 1800s, Jean-Louis turned his skills to the teaching of fencing, opening a school that was popular into the 1830s.

REFERENCE
Morton, E. D. *Martini A–Z of Fencing.* London: Queen Anne Press, 1992.

JENA. A town in Germany known for its university fencing schools during the seventeenth and eighteenth centuries. The fencing was taught there for years by members of the Kreussler family.

The students of Jena were a particularly bloodthirsty lot and insisted on the privilege of being killed or at least seriously wounded long after the dueling custom elsewhere in Germany was to merely cut one's opponent on the head.
REFERENCE
Castle, Egerton. *Schools and Masters of Fence.* London: George Bell, 1885.

JEU DE FANTAISIE. Fencing of a highly romantic, stylized nature, much influenced by old-time techniques or flamboyant, theatrical swordplay. More play than serious fencing.
REFERENCE
Morton, E. D. *Martini A–Z of Fencing.* London: Queen Anne Press, 1992.

JEU DE SALLE. Friendly, relaxed practice fencing where a certain amount of experimental risk taking occurs due to the lack of importance of the encounter. Such bouts are underscored by their lack of aggressiveness or sense of serious intent.
REFERENCE
Morton, E. D. *Martini A–Z of Fencing.* London: Queen Anne Press, 1992.

JEU DE SOLDAT. The violent, clumsy performance of a poor fencer.
REFERENCE
Morton, E. D. *Martini A–Z of Fencing.* London: Queen Anne Press, 1992.

JEU DE TERRAIN. The swordplay of a real duel.
REFERENCE
Morton, E. D. *Martini A–Z of Fencing.* London: Queen Anne Press, 1992.

JIGANE. The portion of a Japanese blade that slopes toward the cutting edge.
REFERENCE
Stone, George Cameron. *A Glossary of the Construction, Decoration, and Use of Arms and Armor.* New York: Jack Brussel, 1961.

JIN-TACHI. A long, heavy, two-handed, single-edged Japanese sword. The *jin-tachi* was usually carried by an attendant to a noble.
REFERENCE
Stone, George Cameron. *A Glossary of the Construction, Decoration, and Use of Arms and Armor.* New York: Jack Brussel, 1961.

JINTO. A Japanese war sword.

REFERENCE
Stone, George Cameron. *A Glossary of the Construction, Decoration, and Use of Arms and Armor.* New York: Jack Brussel, 1961.

JI-TSUYA. The luster on the portion of a Japanese sword blade outside the portion closest to its edge.
REFERENCE
Stone, George Cameron. *A Glossary of the Construction, Decoration, and Use of Arms and Armor.* New York: Jack Brussel, 1961.

JIT-TE. A Japanese baton used for parrying. Most often, simply a rod with a hilt. Occasionally, it was shaped like a sword.
   Also called a *jittei* or a "fencer's baton."
REFERENCE
Stone, George Cameron. *A Glossary of the Construction, Decoration, and Use of Arms and Armor.* New York: Jack Brussel, 1961.

JOINING. An old fencing term for a disarming action.
REFERENCE
Morton, E. D. *Martini A-Z of Fencing.* London: Queen Anne Press, 1992.

JOINVILLE-LE-PONT. The famous nineteenth-century French army school center for fencing instruction and gymnastics. Founded in 1852, Joinville-le-Pont turned out most of France's great fencing masters.
   The school continues, to this day, to train teachers of fencing.
REFERENCE
Cass, Eleanor Baldwin. *The Book of Fencing.* Boston: Lothrop, Lee, and Shepherd, 1930.

JOKO-RYU. The ancient style of swordplay in Japan.
REFERENCE
Sasamori, Junzo, and Gordon Warner. *This Is Kendo.* Vermont: Charles E. Tuttle, 1964.

JOUR. An opening into which an attack may be launched.
REFERENCE
Morton, E. D. *Martini A–Z of Fencing.* London: Queen Anne Press, 1992.

JUDGE. An assistant to the director* of a fencing bout. Usually, there are four judges to a fencing strip—two on either side of the *piste.* It is the job of a judge to watch the fencer opposite him and verify touches landed against that individual.
REFERENCE
U.S. Fencing Association, ed. *Operations Manual.* Colorado Springs, CO: U.S. Fencing Association, 1985.

JUDGEMENT DE LA TOUCHE. A bout director's decision as to the priority,* validity,* penalty,* or annulment* of a touch.
REFERENCE
Handelman, Rob. "Fencing Glossary." *American Fencing* (May/June 1978).

JUJIE, LUAN. (1958–   ). Chinese fencing champion.
   Luan Jujie became the first Chinese to win an Olympic fencing medal, taking first in women's individual foil at the 1984 Olympics in Los Angeles. She had been fencing for ten years at the time of her victory.
REFERENCE
Huddleson, Mary, ed. "Notes from the Olympics." *American Fencing* (September/October 1984).

JUMGHEERDHA. A sword with a long, narrow, straight blade set onto a basket hilt. It was used by the Polygars of India.
REFERENCE
Stone, George Cameron. *A Glossary of the Construction, Decoration, and Use of Arms and Armor.* New York: Jack Brussel, 1961.

JURY. The director* of a bout and his four judges* (ground judges) constitute a jury. When using an electric scoring box to determine touches, the jury may be made up of a director and two judges.
REFERENCE
U.S. Fencing Association, ed. *Operations Manual.* Colorado Springs, CO: U.S. Fencing Association, 1985.

K

KABJA. In India, a sword hilt.*
Also called a *qabja.*
REFERENCE
Stone, George Cameron. *A Glossary of the Construction, Decoration, and Use of Arms and Armor.* New York: Jack Brussel, 1961.

KABUTO GANE. The pommel* of a Japanese state sword of the *tachi** variety.
Also called *tsuka gashira.*
REFERENCE
Stone, George Cameron. *A Glossary of the Construction, Decoration, and Use of Arms and Armor.* New York: Jack Brussel, 1961.

KABUZUCHI. The pommel* of a Japanese sword.
REFERENCE
Stone, George Cameron. *A Glossary of the Construction, Decoration, and Use of Arms and Armor.* New York: Jack Brussel, 1961.

KAIRAGAI. In Japan, a toy wooden sword.*
REFERENCE
Stone, George Cameron. *A Glossary of the Construction, Decoration, and Use of Arms and Armor.* New York: Jack Brussel, 1961.

KALAIPAYATTU. A centuries-old form of swordplay practiced by the men of Kerala, India. It was originally developed by the Nairs, a warrior caste similar to Japan's samurai.*

REFERENCE
Miller, Peter. "Kerala, Jewel of India's Malabar Coast." *National Geographic* (May 1988).

KAMAE. The basic postures, or guard positions,* in kendo* (Japanese fencing).

Chudan no kamae: holding the *shinai* (bamboo sword) at the center of the body.

Jodan no kamae: holding the *shinai* over the head.

Gedan no kamae: holding the *shinai* low.

Hasso no kamae: holding the *shinai* vertically at the right side of the head.

Wakigamae: holding the *shinai* at the right side of the body with the point of the weapon (*kissaki*) pointing back.

REFERENCE
Sasamori, Junzo, and Gordon Warner. *This Is Kendo.* Vermont: Charles E. Tuttle, 1984.

KAMAKIRI. In Japanese, a mantis.
A common decoration on Japanese swords. An emblem of bravery.
REFERENCE
Stone, George Cameron. *A Glossary of the Construction, Decoration, and Use of Arms and Armor.* New York: Jack Brussel, 1961.

KAMASHIMO ZASHI. In old Japan, a sword given to a boy the first time he put on ceremonial dress. It was short, with a plain, black scabbard. It was also worn by men with the court dress called *kama-shimo.*
It was the one sword that did not have to be left at the entrance of a house.
REFERENCE
Stone, George Cameron. *A Glossary of the Construction, Decoration, and Use of Arms and Armor.* New York: Jack Brussel, 1961.

KAMURI OTOSHI. A Japanese sword blade with a blunt back edge.
REFERENCE
Stone, George Cameron. *A Glossary of the Construction, Decoration, and Use of Arms and Armor.* New York: Jack Brussel, 1961.

KANTSCHAR. A seventeenth-century Russian sword. It possessed a very narrow blade with short quillons* that curved toward the tip of the weapon.
REFERENCE
Stone, George Cameron. *A Glossary of the Construction, Decoration, and Use of Arms and Armor.* New York: Jack Brussel, 1961.

KAPEE DHA. A sword of the Assam people of India. It had a short, broad blade.

REFERENCE
Stone, George Cameron. *A Glossary of the Construction, Decoration, and Use of Arms and Armor*. New York: Jack Brussel, 1961.

KARPATI, RUDOLF. (1920–   ). Hungarian sabre champion.

Rudolf Karpati won the individual sabre event at the 1956 and 1960 Olympics.

His team took first place in Olympic team sabre in 1948, 1952, 1956, and 1960.

Karpati was world sabre champion in 1954 and 1959.

REFERENCES
Palffy-Alpar, Julius. *Sword and Masque*. Philadelphia: F. A. Davis, 1967.
Wallechinsky, David. *The Complete Book of the Olympics*. New York: Penguin Books, 1984.

KASANE. The thickness of a Japanese sword blade at its back.

REFERENCE
Stone, George Cameron. *A Glossary of the Construction, Decoration, and Use of Arms and Armor*. New York: Jack Brussel, 1961.

KASKARA. The sword carried by the Baghirmi people of the Sahara. It had a straight blade with a plain cross guard.* Such weapons date back to the tenth century.

REFERENCE
Stone, George Cameron. *A Glossary of the Construction, Decoration, and Use of Arms and Armor*. New York: Jack Brussel, 1961.

KASTANE. The most common sword of Ceylon. The blades were often of European origin. Most were short, heavy, single-edged, and curved. The hilt of the *kastane* possessed two to four quillons* that curved toward the blade. The pommel* was usually carved in the likeness of a monster. Many bear the emblem of the Dutch East India Company, placing their date of origin in the eighteenth century.

REFERENCE
Stone, George Cameron. *A Glossary of the Construction, Decoration, and Use of Arms and Armor*. New York: Jack Brussel, 1961.

KATANA. The traditional Japanese samurai* sword.

The slightly curved blade of the *katana* is between twenty-four and thirty inches long. The hilt is from eight to ten inches long and usually covered in sharkskin wound with cord. The *tsuba* (hand guard) is a flat metal plate, usually decorated. The sword's lacquered scabbard* is most often made of magnolia wood.

The *katana* was so designed that it could be used with one or both hands.

Parrying was done with the flat of the blade to protect the weapon's cutting edge.

A *wakizashi** (short sword) was the traditional companion weapon of the *katana.*

The *katana* was considered the soul of the samurai.

REFERENCES

Nitobe, Inazo. *Bushiodo: The Warrior's Code.* Burbank, CA: Ohara, 1975.

Stone, George Cameron. *A Glossary of the Construction, Decoration, and Use of Arms and Armor.* New York: Jack Brussel, 1961.

KATANA KAKE. A sword stand or rack for a Japanese sword.

REFERENCE

Stone, George Cameron. *A Glossary of the Construction, Decoration, and Use of Arms and Armor.* New York: Jack Brussel, 1961.

KATANA ZUTSU. A sword case for a Japanese sword.

REFERENCE

Stone, George Cameron. *A Glossary of the Construction, Decoration, and Use of Arms and Armor.* New York: Jack Brussel, 1961.

KEEPING CAPTIVE. The act of keeping an opponent continually in the same line* of engagement.*

REFERENCE

Morton, E. D. *Martini A–Z of Fencing.* London: Queen Anne Press, 1992.

KEIKO. Kendo* practice.

REFERENCE

Sasamori, Junzo, and Gordon Warner. *This Is Kendo.* Vermont: Charles E. Tuttle, 1984.

KELLY, GENE. (1912–   ). American dancer and film actor.

While Kelly usually appeared in musicals, in 1948 he turned his unique abilities to the swashbuckler genre. Starring in *The Three Musketeers*** as D'Artagnan,* Kelly had a field day leaping and fencing across the screen. His athletically graceful dance skills and superb timing helped produce a characterization of Dumas's heroic Gascon that made his version of *Musketeers* one of the best.

Kelly's swordfight with the cardinal's guards "behind the Luxembourg," lasting five minutes, is the highlight of the film.

Despite his natural abilities as a swashbuckler, Kelly made no other such films.

REFERENCES

Halliwell, Leslie. *Halliwell's Filmgoer's and Video Viewer's Companion.* New York: Charles Scribner's Sons, 1988.

Thomas, Tony. *Cads and Cavaliers.* New York: A. S. Barnes, 1973.

Gene Kelly as D'Artagnan in *The Three Musketeers*

KEMPO. The rules of Japanese fencing.
REFERENCE
Stone, George Cameron. *A Glossary of the Construction, Decoration, and Use of Arms and Armor.* New York: Jack Brussel, 1961.

KEN. A Japanese term for a sword.
Ken also refers to the earliest form of Japanese sword in historic times (after A.D. 700). This weapon had a straight, double-edged blade, occasionally widened at the point, and a simple crossbar guard. It exists today only as a ceremonial object in temples.
The *ken* is also called *hojiu* or *tsurugi.*
REFERENCE
Stone, George Cameron. *A Glossary of the Construction, Decoration, and Use of Arms and Armor.* New York: Jack Brussel, 1961.

KENBU. The Japanese art of sword dancing. Dancers pantomime legendary heroes or famous battles.
Kenbu was formally introduced during the nineteenth century. While initially an entertainment, the art form was soon engaged in by samurai,* who found it improved their balance, timing, coordination, and breathing.
Kenbu is still practiced today in Japan.
REFERENCE
Corcoran, John, and Emil Farkas. *Martial Arts.* New York: Gallery Books, 1983.

KENDO. Kendo means "the Way of the Sword." Essentially, it is the classical art of Japanese swordplay. The concept goes back hundreds of years to the ancient samurai* warriors. As a sport, it is still practiced today.
Kendo is a highly systematized method of swordplay in which technique and individual spirit are held more important than simply striking an opponent. The practice of kendo develops self-discipline, character, and a sense of respect, as well as the physical aspects of timing, coordination, and balance. Underlying all of this is a search for spiritual awareness in the perfection of one's art.
Dedication is vital in kendo. Because the cultivation of technique is strictly observed, a student may practice footwork alone for a year before ever donning the uniform and armor of kendo and working out with other students. The attainment of the highest levels of the art can take a lifetime of work.
The weapon of kendo, the *shinai,** was developed in the eighteenth century. It is a bamboo sword wielded with two hands, unlike Western fencing weapons, which are held with one.
Differing from his Western counterparts, the kendoist calls out the target he is aiming for when making a touch. In part, this is done to ensure the accuracy of his intent; also, it helps the kendoist focus his energy in an efficient manner.

Kendo—a nineteenth-century depiction

Moreover, touches are determined by other criteria than just striking an opponent. One's form and directed energy are key factors in determining a valid hit. A proper touch theoretically would cut through an enemy's armor in battle.

Kendo, while predominantly a Japanese martial art, is practiced all over the world.

REFERENCES

Evangelista, Anita. "Kendo, Japanese Sword Fighting, Has Dual Nature as Art, Sport." *Los Angeles Times,* April 12, 1984.

Sasamori, Junzo, and Gordon Warner. *This Is Kendo.* Vermont: Charles E. Tuttle, 1984.

KENDO EQUIPMENT. Like Western fencing, kendo, or Japanese fencing, has its own distinctive equipment (*dogu*).

Keiogi: heavy cotton jacket

Hakama: cotton skirt-trousers

Tare: waist and hip protectors made of a heavy cotton material

Do: chest protector made of bamboo strips tied together

Hachimaki: a towel-like cloth for the head

Men: helmet with face mask

Kote: arm and hand guards

Shinai: bamboo sword

No shoes are worn in kendo.

REFERENCE

Sasamori, Junzo, and Gordon Warner. *This Is Kendo.* Vermont: Charles E. Tuttle, 1964.

KENDO IN THE UNITED STATES. Kendo was first brought to the United States in the 1920s and has been growing in popularity ever since. While traditionally an art performed by the Japanese community, it has attracted a number of non-Asian people to its ranks in recent years. As to be expected, though, Japanese names dominate the ranks of American kendo's most able and accomplished practitioners.

Noted kendoists in the United States include: Shunji Asari, Gene Eto, Midio Hattanda, Akio Hara, Maki Miyahara, Hidetsugo Miura, Ichiro Murakami, Pat Murasako, George Nakano, Steve Nakauchi, Osamu Okaniwa, Masaharu Shimoda, Yoshimichi Takeda, Kik Uyeji, Masashi Yamaguchi, and Takeshi Yamaguchi.

REFERENCE

Anderson, Anita. "Kendo, Japanese Sword Fighting, Has Dual Nature as Art, Sport." *The Los Angeles Times,* June 12, 1984.

KENDOISTS, NOTED. Since the founding of Japan's first kendo federation in 1909, many great exponents of the art have emerged. These include: Masataka

Inoue, Eiichi Kijima, Tokutara Kimura, Yutaka Kubota, Moriji Mochida, Torao Mori, Kinnosuke Ogawa, Goro Saimura, Junzo Sasamori, Kyutaro Takahashi, Shigeyoshi Takano, Gordon Warner, and Toshio Watanabe.
REFERENCE
Sasamori, Junzo, and Gordon Warner. *This Is Kendo.* Vermont: Charles E. Tuttle, 1984.

KENDOKA. Those who practice kendo.*
REFERENCE
Lewis, Peter. *Martial Arts of the Orient.* New York: Gallery Books, 1985.

KENDO RULES. In its original form, there were no rules or regulations in kendo* beyond those already established for fighting with actual swords.

Eventually, however, the new form of combat required regulations covering both etiquette and fighting.

Touches may be scored with either cuts* or thrusts.* But only eight specific areas of the body may be attacked. A point, however, is not awarded unless a blow has been delivered with full spirit and correct form.

The winner of a bout is the first kendoist to score two points, or the contestant with the higher score when the time limit of three or five minutes runs out.

A competitor may not step outside the match area, trip his opponent, strike or thrust at unprotected body parts of his opponent, grasp his opponent's *shinai,** or act in a disrespectful manner.
REFERENCES
Midgley, Ruth, ed. *Rules of the Game.* New York: Paddington Press, 1974.
Sasamori, Junzo, and Gordon Warner. *This Is Kendo.* Vermont: Charles E. Tuttle, 1984.

KENDO TARGET AREAS. Eight points may be attacked in kendo*: seven are with cuts,* and one is with a thrust.*

Hidari-men: a point on the left side of the *men* (mask) just above the left ear.

Men: a point directly at the peak of the face mask.

Migi-men: a point on the right side of the *men* just above the right ear.

Kote: a point just above the wrist joint on the right arm.

Hidari-kote: a point on the left wrist (allowed only when the left hand is at shoulder level or higher).

Migi-do: a point on the right side of the chest protector.

Hidari-do: a point on the left side of the chest protector.

Tsuki: the throat protector (the only spot where a thrust is allowed).

Any other spots are considered off target in kendo.
REFERENCE
Sasamori, Junzo, and Gordon Warner. *This Is Kendo.* Vermont: Charles E. Tuttle, 1984.

KENDO TERMS, GENERAL.

Aite: opponent

Aiuchi: tie match

Ateru: to strike, or score a point

Chikara: strength

Daisensei: teacher of the highest rank in kendo

Fumu: to step

Furu: to swing

Gokaku-geiko: practice between two opponents of equal ability

Hajime: begin match

Hanshi: an outstanding fencer of high rank

Hansoku: violation of a kendo rule

Harau: to parry by brushing away an opponent's weapon

Hikitate-geiko: practice in which a senior fener guides a junior

Iai: sword exercises employing a series of cuts and thrusts

Jiyu-renshu: free bouting

Kachinuki: a match in which a kendoist meets all opponents in succession until he is defeated, after which the winner goes on in the same fashion

Kakari-geiko: attack practice

Kangeiko: winter practice

Kankyaku: spectators at a kendo match

Katsu: to win

Keirei: formal bow

Maai: the distance between two contestants

Makeru: to be defeated

Mamoru: to defend

Metsuke: the point of observation

Renshu: training period

Sasu: to thrust a sword forward

Sensai: teacher

Shiai: contest

Shiaijo: contest area

Shimpan: referee

Shoshinsha: a beginner in kendo

Tai-atari: body contact

Taikai: a tournament

Ukedachi: counterattack

Ukeru: to block a blow

Utsu: to strike a blow

Waza: technique

Yame: halt

REFERENCE

Sasamori, Junzo, and Gordon Warner. *This Is Kendo.* Vermont: Charles E. Tuttle, 1984.

KENJO TSUBA. A type of sword guard* given as a gift to a superior in Japan.
REFERENCE

Stone, George Cameron. *A Glossary of the Construction, Decoration, and Use of Arms and Armor.* New York: Jack Brussel, 1961.

KENJUTSU. The art of Japanese swordsmanship mainly practiced during Japan's medieval period.

Kenjutsu consisted of training with the *katana,** or long sword. Techniques involved the development of cuts* and thrusts* and parrying.*

Targets were clearly defined in *kenjutsu,* and fighting followed strict rules. The sword was to be employed against only four points: the top of the head, the wrist, the side, and the leg below the knee. A dedicated swordsman took no pride in defeating his opponent in a dishonorable fashion. Those who did violate fencing codes suffered the possibility of being publicly rebuked by their masters.

There were numerous styles of swordplay within the confines of *kenjutsu.* Competition between schools was fierce, since a poor showing of one's methods could ruin a fencing master. A winning technique, on the other hand, usually meant fame and patronage from a wealthy lord.

Often, when an individual swordsman mastered one school of *kenjutsu,* he proceeded to travel around the country to encounter and learn other approaches to fencing. This was exemplified by Japan's great swordsman Miyamoto Musashi.

REFERENCES

Corcoran, John, and Emil Farkas. *Martial Arts.* New York: Gallery Books, 1983.

Sasamori, Junzo, and Gordon Warner. *This Is Kendo.* Vermont: Charles E. Tuttle, 1984.

KENUKI GATA TACHI. A form of *tachi** (old-style long sword) with the hilt* and blade made as a single piece. It was carried as a sign of mourning when visiting a temple.
REFERENCE

Stone, George Cameron. *A Glossary of the Construction, Decoration, and Use of Arms and Armor.* New York: Jack Brussel, 1961.

KENYE. A bag used to wrap a Japanese sword when it was to be stored in a case.

REFERENCE
Stone, George Cameron. *A Glossary of the Construction, Decoration, and Use of Arms and Armor.* New York: Jack Brussel, 1961.

KESSO. The grooves in a Japanese blade.
REFERENCE
Stone, George Cameron. *A Glossary of the Construction, Decoration, and Use of Arms and Armor.* New York: Jack Brussel, 1961.

KHADJA. A legendary sword of Hindu mythology. Introduced by Brahma and given by him to Shiva, it is sometimes described as a two-handed weapon six feet long.

Also called *As* or *Asi.*
REFERENCE
Burton, Richard F. *The Book of the Sword.* London: Chatto and Windus, 1884.

KHANDA. The oldest and most typical of Indian swords.

The *khanda,* a cut*-and-thrust* weapon, had a broad, straight blade, usually widening near the point (which was generally blunt). Occasionally doubled-edged, the single-edged variety was more the norm. The hilt* had a broad plate guard and a wide finger guard.* The pommel* was round and large. There was sometimes a spike on the pommel that could be gripped to make two-handed cuts.
REFERENCE
Stone, George Cameron. *A Glossary of the Construction, Decoration, and Use of Arms and Armor.* New York: Jack Brussel, 1961.

KHANDOO. A kind of Arab sword.
REFERENCE
Stone, George Cameron. *A Glossary of the Construction, Decoration, and Use of Arms and Armor.* New York: Jack Brussel, 1961.

KHARGA S'HAPNA. The Rajput (Indian) worship of the sword. The nine-day ceremony was very elaborate. The sword worshiped was a *khanda,* thought to be an enchanted weapon made by the god Vishvakarman (known as "the All-Maker").
REFERENCES
Parrinder, Geoffrey, ed. *World Religions.* New York: Facts on File, 1983.
Stone, George Cameron. *A Glossary of the Construction, Decoration, and Use of Arms and Armor.* New York: Jack Brussel, 1961.

KHARG BANAI. Meaning "the binding of the sword."

A Rajput (Indian) ceremony performed when a boy was old enough to bear arms.

Also called *yulwar bundai.*

REFERENCE
Tod, James. *Annales and Antiquities of Rajaat'han.* London: 1905.

KHOPSH. An ancient Egyptian sword. Its brass blade was sickle-shaped and double-edged. Some had small hand guards*; some had none.

The *khopsh* was used by both officers and their troops. A golden *khopsh* was carried by the pharoah.

Also called a *khrobi, kopis, knopsh,* or *kops.*

REFERENCE
Burton, Richard F. *The Book of the Sword.* London: Chatto and Windus, 1884.

KHYBER KNIFE. A smallsword, with a blade between fourteen and thirty inches long, used by the Indian tribes (especially the Afridis) living in or near the Khyber Pass between India and Afghanistan.

The blade is straight, heavy, and single-edged. The hilt* is without a guard.

Also called an "Afghan knife," a *charras,* a *charay,* a *churra,* and a *salawar yatagan.*

REFERENCE
Stone, George Cameron. *A Glossary of the Construction, Decoration, and Use of Arms and Armor.* New York: Jack Brussel, 1961.

KILIJ. The sabre* of Turkey.

The blade is broad and curved, although the curve ends eight or ten inches from the point. Because the weapon's curve is not continuous, it can be used for thrusting* as well as cutting.*

The hilt* is pistol-shaped. The guard* is a straight crossbar.

Also called a *kilig* or *qillij.*

REFERENCE
Stone, George Cameron. *A Glossary of the Construction, Decoration, and Use of Arms and Armor.* New York: Jack Brussel, 1961.

KIMI-BAN-ZEI. A saying often found carved on Japanese sword blades. It means, "Will cut for a thousand years."

REFERENCE
Stone, George Cameron. *A Glossary of the Construction, Decoration, and Use of Arms and Armor.* New York: Jack Brussel, 1961.

KINDACHI. A name for a Japanese wooden fencing sword.

REFERENCE
Stone, George Cameron. *A Glossary of the Construction, Decoration, and Use of Arms and Armor.* New York: Jack Brussel, 1961.

KIPPA. The sharp edge of a Japanese sword.

REFERENCE
Stone, George Cameron. *A Glossary of the Construction, Decoration, and Use of Arms and Armor.* New York: Jack Brussel, 1961.

KIROMONO. Grooves or hollows in a Japanese sword blade filled with crimson lacquer. These grooves are either carved images or writing.
REFERENCE
Stone, George Cameron. *A Glossary of the Construction, Decoration, and Use of Arms and Armor.* New York: Jack Brussel, 1961.

KISSING THE BUTTON. Sixteenth-century Spanish fencers would often show their disdain for practice opponents they considered inferior by making them "kiss the button," that is, hitting them in the mouth with their weapon. This was, of course, before the days of both fencing etiquette and fencing masks.
REFERENCE
Morton, E. D. *Martini A–Z of Fencing.* London: Queen Anne Press, 1992.

KLEDYV. The ancient Welsh sword.
The *kledyv* was a short thrusting sword, with a blade made of iron.
REFERENCE
Burton, Richard F. *The Book of the Sword.* London: Chatto and Windus, 1884.

KLEWANG. A Maylay sabre. It has a straight, single-edged blade widening at the point. Hilts vary in appearance.
Also called a *lamang.*
REFERENCE
Stone, George Cameron. *A Glossary of the Construction, Decoration, and Use of Arms and Armor.* New York: Jack Brussel, 1961.

KLOPFFECHTER. German swordsmen who, as late as the start of the seventeenth century, made their living by competing in prizefights at fairs that were held around the country.
REFERENCE
Castle, Egerton. *Schools and Masters of Fence.* London: George Bell, 1885.

KNICKERS. The traditional "knee breeches" of fencing.
Knickers, for competition purposes, must be white and must close below the knee. They are usually made of either heavy cotton duck or nylon.
REFERENCE
U.S. Fencing Association, ed. *Operations Manual.* Colorado Springs, CO: U.S. Fencing Association, 1985.

KNIGHT. The mounted, armored warrior of medieval Europe.
Knights lived by a complicated code of ethics (chivalry) that shaped their entire lives. Unfortunately, these rules mainly governed their interaction with their lords, other knights, kinsmen, and upper-class Christians. Most other folks—peasants, non-Christians, and the like—were fair game for knightly aggressions. When knights wanted to acquire more wealth, they went on raids to

Klopffechter exhibiting their fencing skills at a country fair

Combat between knights in the Middle Ages

other countries. Various Crusades to the Holy Land—where pillaging and plundering were not only acceptable but encouraged practices—are a case in point.

Knights were experts in the use of most weapons, including the sword. Their skills were often put on display in tournaments, where a large portion of their destructive energies could be channeled and dissipated in either mock combat or actual duels to the death.

Knightly combat skills were mostly of an offensive nature, as their defense was taken care of chiefly by the thick armor they wore from head to toe.

Famous historical knights include Rodrigo Diaz de Vivar, El Cid (1043–1099),* Edward, the Black Prince (1330–1376),* Bertrand du Guesclin (1320–1380), and William Marshall (1146–1219).*

REFERENCE

Barber, Richard. *The Knight and Chivalry.* San Francisco: Harper and Row, 1974.

KNIGHTS OF THE ROUND TABLE. The legendary followers of King Arthur at Camelot.*

The Knights of the Round Table were, by and large, expert soldiers and swordsmen, and much has been written about their exploits over the centuries.

The Knights of the Round Table—a nineteenth-century illustration

The most famous of King Arthur's minions were Sir Lancelot, Sir Galahad, Sir Tristram, Sir Gawain, and Sir Perceval.

The greatest quest of the Knights of the Round Table was the search for the Holy Grail.

Perhaps the most popular books concerning the Round Table knights are *Morte d'Arthur* (1469) by Sir Thomas Malory and *The Once and Future King* (1958) by T. H. White.

Movie versions of the Round Table legends are numerous. They include *Knights of the Round Table* (1954), *The Sword of Lancelot* (1961), *Camelot* (1967), and *Excalibur* (1980).

REFERENCES

Benet, William Rose. *Reader's Encyclopedia.* New York: Thomas Y. Crowell, 1965.

Bulfinch, Thomas. *Bulfinch's Mythology.* New York: Modern Library, 1934.

Halliwell, Leslie. *Halliwell's Filmgoer's and Video Viewer's Companion.* New York: Charles Scribner's Sons, 1988.

KNUCKLE BOW. A thin, curved bar extending from the hand guard* designed to protect the fingers from cuts. It could also be a series of connected bars or simply a wide metal strip.

In close combat, the knuckle bow could be used offensively in the same manner as brass knuckles.

Today, in modern fencing, the knuckle guard is found only on the sabre.

Also called "finger guard," "knuckle guard," "bow," or "counterguard."

REFERENCE

Burton, Richard F. *The Book of the Sword.* London: Chatto and Windus, 1884.

KOBUSHIGATA TSUBA. An oval hand guard* shaped somewhat like a closed fist. It was introduced to Japan in the sixteenth century.

REFERENCE

Stone, George Cameron. *A Glossary of the Construction, Decoration, and Use of Arms and Armor.* New York: Jack Brussel, 1961.

KODOGU. All the fittings (decorations) of a Japanese sword. The *tsuba** (guard), however, is not considered part of these items.

REFERENCE

Stone, George Cameron. *A Glossary of the Construction, Decoration, and Use of Arms and Armor.* New York: Jack Brussel, 1961.

KOGAI. A short skewer sometimes carried in the scabbard* of a sword. It was reportedly used to pierce the ankle vein of suffering and dying comrades after a battle. Another story said that it was sometimes left in the body of a dead enemy as an identifying mark of who killed him.

REFERENCE

Stone, George Cameron. *A Glossary of the Construction, Decoration, and Use of Arms and Armor.* New York: Jack Brussel, 1961.

KOGLER, ALADAR. (1933–   ). Hungarian-born fencing master.

One of the most respected coaches in the United States, Aladar Kogler has had a lengthy and productive career in fencing. Before coming to the United States, he coached the Czechoslovakian Olympic team in three Olympic games: 1972, 1978, and 1980. He produced eight World Fencing Championship finalists, a Junior World champion, and a World University Games champion, to name a few of his successes.

Since he moved to the United States, Dr. Kogler has been a coach for the U.S. Olympic fencing team (1988 and 1992), the U.S. Pan American Games fencing team (1987 and 1991), the U.S. World Championships fencing team (1985, 1987, 1990, and 1991), and the U.S. World University Games fencing team (1985 and 1989).

Kogler's students have included Olympian fencers Caitlin Bilodeaux, Robert Cottingham, and Steve Trevor.

Presently, Aladar Kogler is the head fencing coach for Columbia University. He also teaches at the New York Athletic Club and the New York Fencers Club.
REFERENCE
Walker, Colleen. 1992 *United States Fencing Association Media Guide.* CO: ColorTek
       Printing, 1992.

KOI-GUCHI. The open end of a Japanese sword scabbard.* The Japanese believe it looks like the mouth of a carp (*koi*).

The decorative ring or cap covering the mouth of the *koi-gushi* was called a *koi-guchi kanagu, kuchi-kane,* or *kuchi-gane.*
REFERENCE
Stone, George Cameron. *A Glossary of the Construction, Decoration, and Use of Arms
       and Armor.* New York: Jack Brussel, 1961.

KOI-GUCHI WO KIRU. In Japanese, to prepare to draw one's sword. It means, basically, to loosen the weapon in its scabbard.*
REFERENCE
Stone, George Cameron. *A Glossary of the Construction, Decoration, and Use of Arms
       and Armor.* New York: Jack Brussel, 1961.

KO-KATANA. A small knife carried in the scabbard* of a Japanese sword.

Also called a *kogatana, kozuka,* or *kodzuka.*
REFERENCE
Stone, George Cameron. *A Glossary of the Construction, Decoration, and Use of Arms
       and Armor.* New York: Jack Brussel, 1961.

KONGAVAL. A swordlike weapon classed as a "chopper." It had a curved blade set onto a long wooden handle.
REFERENCE
Stone, George Cameron. *A Glossary of the Construction, Decoration, and Use of Arms
       and Armor.* New York: Jack Brussel, 1961.

KONIGSMARK, COUNT. (c. 1650). Swedish nobleman and soldier.

Inventor of the *colichemarde,** a dueling sword that became highly popular from around 1680 until well into the eighteenth century.

The blade of Konigsmark's creation was highly unusual, having a wide, stiff, sometimes triangular forte and a narrow, flat, flexible foible. The overall effect, however, was that the weapon was extremely light, which meant it could be wielded with much ease.

REFERENCES

Castle, Egerton. *Schools and Masters of Fence.* London: George Bell, 1885.

Stone, George Cameron. *A Glossary of the Construction, Decoration, and Use of Arms and Armor.* New York: Jack Brussel, 1961.

KORA. The sword of Nepal. It has a heavy, single-edged, incurved blade that widens considerably at the point. The point usually ends in two concave curves. There is always an eye—a Buddhist symbol—inlaid on both sides of the blade.

Also called a *cora* or *khora.*

REFERENCE

Stone, George Cameron. *A Glossary of the Construction, Decoration, and Use of Arms and Armor.* New York: Jack Brussel, 1961.

KORNGOLD, ERIC WOLFGANG. (1897–1957). Czechoslovakian composer of film music.

Korngold was a child-prodigy composer and conductor in Vienna. Arriving in Hollywood in 1934, he went to work immediately for Warner Brothers Studio. His flowing, emotional melodies were highly suited to the films being produced by that company.

Korngold's style of music, often grand and heroic, was especially suited to the swashbuckler genre, and the great success of some of the now-classic adventure films of the 1930s and 1940s was doubtlessly due, in part, to his efforts.

The music Korngold wrote to highlight sword fights can almost not be separated from the action, as it fits so cleanly into every cut and thrust and parry made by the actors.

Korngold's swashbuckler film scores include *Anthony Adverse* (1936), *The Prince and the Pauper* (1937), *The Adventures of Robin Hood* (1938),* and *The Sea Hawk* (1940).*

Korngold won Academy Awards for his music in *Anthony Adverse* and *The Adventures of Robin Hood.*

REFERENCE

Katz, Ephraim. *The Film Encyclopedia.* New York: Perigee Books, 1979.

KOSHIATE. A carrier for a Japanese sword.

The *koshiate* was a wooden or leather device for holding the sword firmly in the belt. There were several kinds: the *rio-koshiate,* which held both the long

and short swords; the *kata-koshiate,* which held only a single weapon; the *tsutsu-koshiate,* a tube-shaped holder; and the *ita-koshiate,* a flat-board holder.
REFERENCE
Stone, George Cameron. *A Glossary of the Construction, Decoration, and Use of Arms and Armor.* New York: Jack Brussel, 1961.

KOTO. The Japanese term for swords and their makers before the seventeenth century.
REFERENCE
Stone, George Cameron. *A Glossary of the Construction, Decoration, and Use of Arms and Armor.* New York: Jack Brussel, 1961.

KOVACS, PAL. (1912–?). Hungarian sabre champion.

Pal Kovacs was forty years old when he won his first Olympic individual sabre championship in 1952. He had already taken third place in individual sabre at the previous Olympics in 1948.

His team won the Olympic team sabre events in 1936, 1948, 1952, 1956, and 1960.

Kovacs was world sabre champion in 1937 and 1953.
REFERENCES
Palffy-Alpar, Julius. *Sword and Masque.* Philadelphia: E. A. Davis, 1967.
Wallechinsky, David. *The Complete Book of the Olympics.* New York: Penguin Books, 1984.

KREUSSLER. A renowned family of fencing masters in German universities for over 200 years, beginning in the 1600s.

Wilhelm Kreussler, the founder of the dynasty and one of the first Marxbruder, had twelve children, most of whom became fencing masters of note. Moreover, many of their children became fencing masters, and their children also.

Heinrich, one of Wilhelm's descendants, is credited with having been instrumental in the establishment of the cut-and-thrust German school of fencing.
REFERENCE
Castle, Egerton. *Schools and Masters of Fence.* London: George Bell, 1885.

KUBIKURI. A Japanese short sword, or knife, used to cut off the head of a dead enemy. It had an incurved, chisel-edged blade.

The name *kubikuri* means ''head cutter.''
REFERENCE
Stone, George Cameron. *A Glossary of the Construction, Decoration, and Use of Arms and Armor.* New York: Jack Brussel, 1961.

KUGE-NO-TACHI. A Japanese long sword reserved for princes and nobles of the imperial retinue.

REFERENCE
Stone, George Cameron. *A Glossary of the Construction, Decoration, and Use of Arms and Armor*. New York: Jack Brussel, 1961.

KURIKATA. A projecting knob on a Japanese sword scabbard* that kept it from slipping through the wearer's sash.

REFERENCE
Stone, George Cameron. *A Glossary of the Construction, Decoration, and Use of Arms and Armor*. New York: Jack Brussel, 1961.

KUROSAWA, AKIRA. (1910–   ). Japanese film director.

While Kurosawa has produced a wide range of work, he is probably best known for his samurai films.

One of Kurosawa's early and most acclaimed efforts was *Rashamon* (1950), which told the story of a moment of violence from four separate points of view: the bandit killer (Toshiro Mifune*), the killed samurai (Masayuki Mori), the samurai's wife (Machiko Kyo), and a peasant woodcutter who viewed the entire episode (Takashi Shimura). The swordplay leading to the death varies in quality with each telling of the event.

Seven Samurai (1954), starring Takashi Shimura, Toshiro Mifune, Yoskio Inaba, Seiji Miyaguchi, Minoru Chiaki, Daisuke Kato, and Ko Kimura, is one of Kurosawa's most popular films. Seven wandering samurai are hired to protect a village of farmers from bandits. Eventually, inspired by their protectors—some of whom die in the ensuing conflict—the villagers, too, fight off their enemy. The swordplay is savage and frequent.

In 1961, Kurosawa directed *Yojimbo* (meaning bodyguard). A wandering samurai (Toshiro Mifune), coming to a small town corrupted by two contesting factions, skillfully pits the gangs against each other to rid the village of their foul influence. While there is considerable swordplay along the way, at the end of the film, the hero must defeat an opponent armed with a gun.

Other Kurosawa samurai films include *The Hidden Fortress* (1958) and *Sanjuro* (1962).

REFERENCES
Halliwell, Leslie. *Halliwell's Filmgoer's and Video Viewer's Companion*. New York: Charles Scribner's Sons, 1988.
Mintz, Marilyn D. *The Martial Arts Film*. New York: A. S. Barnes, 1978.

KUSARI TACHI. A Japanese long sword hung from a belt by chains.

REFERENCE
Stone, George Cameron. *A Glossary of the Construction, Decoration, and Use of Arms and Armor*. New York: Jack Brussel, 1961.

L

LABAT, LE SIEUR. (c. 1680). French fencing master.

Le Sieur Labat, one of a celebrated family of fencing masters teaching at Toulouse** from the end of the sixteenth century until the middle of the eighteenth, was instrumental in establishing an official French national school of swordplay in the seventeenth century. This school, which quickly took the lead in European fencing, distinguished itself from the already existing Italian school by modifying its practice weapon into one that stressed finger manipulation rather than muscular arm actions, by developing offensive actions that depended on a lack of blade contact rather than constant blade contact, and by placing a strong importance on the defensive side of fencing.

He also helped usher in, through his teaching methods, the smallsword as the accepted weapon of personal combat.

Labat produced two works on fencing: *L'art de l'Épée* (1690) and *L'art en fait d'armes* (1696). Experts have noted that these books, by and large, rank among the best studies of practical swordplay.

The name Labat is sometimes found spelled "L'Abbat."

REFERENCES

Castle, Egerton. *Schools and Masters of Fence.* London: George Bell, 1885.

Gaugler, William. "Labat and the Development of the French School." *American Fencing* (January/February 1987).

Wise, Arthur. *The Art and History of Personal Combat.* Greenwich, CT: Arma Press, 1971.

LA BELLE. When two fencers reach a 4-4 tie in their bout, the final touch—*la belle*—then decides the match.

Also known as the "assault point."

REFERENCE
Morton, E. D. *Martini A-Z of Fencing*. London: Queen Anne Press, 1992.

LA BOESSIERE. (c. 1740). French fencing master.

An influential member of the French academy of arms, La Boessiere's greatest gift to fencing was the invention of the fencing mask, which he cocreated with the famous fencer and duelist the Chevalier St. Georges.

La Boessiere's son, also a fencing master of repute, wrote a study of fencing, *Traite de l'Art des Armes* (1818). His career as a fencing teacher lasted well into the nineteenth century.

REFERENCE
Castle, Egerton. *Schools and Masters of Fence*. London: George Bell, 1885.

LADING BELONAJOENG LAMAH. A sabre* of Borneo. It had a short, heavy blade that widened toward the point, a pistol-shaped hilt, and no hand guard.

REFERENCE
Stone, George Cameron. *A Glossary of the Construction, Decoration, and Use of Arms and Armor*. New York: Jack Brussel, 1961.

LAFAUGERE, LOUIS. (c. 1800). French fencing master.

A strong fencer and popular teacher, Lafaugere is said to have remarked that the foil must be held like a small bird—not so tightly that it is crushed, not so loosely that it escapes.

Lafaugere wrote one book on fencing, *Traite de l'art de faire des Armes* (1825).

REFERENCE
Morton, E. D. *Martini A-Z of Fencing*. London: Queen Anne Press, 1992.

LAID ON. A term used to describe a sabre touch that has been rendered without force.

REFERENCE
Morton, E. D. *Martini A-Z of Fencing*. London: Queen Anne Press, 1992.

LALL-I-WALL. A narrow, curved sword with a very broad back used in the Indian state of Mysore.

REFERENCE
Stone, George Cameron. *A Glossary of the Construction, Decoration, and Use of Arms and Armor*. New York: Jack Brussel, 1961.

LANCASTER, BURT. (1913–1994). American leading man.

Because of an early background as a circus acrobat, Burt Lancaster was a natural as a swashbuckler in the movies. Warner Brothers Studios saw him as the perfect replacement for an aging Errol Flynn.* His earliest costume adventure was *The Flame and the Arrow* (1950), in which he played a William Tell-type hero. This was followed by *The Crimson Pirate* (1952), a freewheeling

Louis Lafaugere winning his celebrated bout with the Comte de Bondy

The landsknecht

spoof of pirate epics. The action emphasis in both pictures, however, was ac-
robatics rather than fencing.

Desiring to avoid typecasting, Lancaster quickly gave up swashbucklers entirely for historically more modern films.

REFERENCE
Katz, Ephraim. *The Film Encyclopedia*. New York: Parigee Books, 1979.

LANDSKNECHT. A broadsword named after the German mercenaries who
carried it during the fifteenth and sixteenth centuries. Its double-edged broad
blade was two feet long. The hilt consisted of two rings formed by the crossbar
being curved into a figure eight.

Also called a *lansquenette*.

REFERENCE
Castle, Egerton. *Schools and Masters of Fence.* London: George Bell, 1885.

LANGUETTE. The protruding flexible strip (fabric-covered wire) on top of the fencing mask that keeps the mask from slipping off.

Also called the "tongue."
REFERENCE
Morton, E. D. *Martini A–Z of Fencing.* London: Queen Anne Press, 1992.

LANTERN. During the days of dueling, the lantern was sometimes used in conjunction with the sword. It was employed in night fighting to blind one's opponent. Because of its solid nature, it could also be used to parry with if necessary.

The common approach to using the lantern was to hold it behind one's back and shine it suddenly, from this protected position, into an adversary's eyes.

A recommended defense against this form of attack was to quickly circle around the lantern user to avoid the blinding beam of light. Moreover, if carrying a cloak, one might throw it over the lantern. A thrust to the throat or face was then prescribed, for anyone "cowardly" enough to use a lantern might be wearing some sort of armor protection under his clothing.
REFERENCE
Angelo, Domenico. *The School of Fencing.* London: H. Angelo, 1787 edition.

LATCHEN BLADE. The common name for a thrusting sword blade whose shape, looking straight down the tip toward the hilt, resembles a diamond. This form, which dates from the earliest of times, produced a strong, stiff, and lasting weapon that was also extremely heavy.

Also known as the Saxon blade.
REFERENCE
Burton, Richard E. *The Book of the Sword.* London: Chatto and Windus, 1884.

LATERAL PARRY. A parry that covers the target area in a straight line.

The linear motion of the lateral parry is part of the human reaction pattern and, hence, is the basic parry of fencing, the obvious parry of a beginning fencer. Only when a fencer begins to control his game—that is, think in actual fencing terms—is he able to break away from the lateral parry and interject the more complex counterparry into his defense. Once this occurs, lateral and counterparries may be combined and exchanged at will, which creates a truly formidable defensive position.

Also called a "simple parry," an "instinctive parry," a "reaction parry," a "basic parry," and the "beginner's parry."
REFERENCE
Morton, E. D. *Martini A–Z of Fencing.* London: Queen Anne Press, 1992.

The lantern and sword against the cloak and sword

LA TOUSCHE, PHILIBERT DE. (c. 1650). French fencing master.

La Tousche devised an oddly exaggerated form of fencing, whereby attacks were delivered with lunges so drawn out and extreme that only an acrobatic contortionist could perform them. In one case, the head was supposed to be thrown so far forward that it would come to rest on one's knee.

He also established methods of using the rapier with both hands, a style that became popular in France during the latter part of the seventeenth century.

On a more practical note, La Tousche was responsible for coining the term *degagement* (disengage) to describe an attack moving from one line to another by passing beneath an opponent's blade. But, on the whole, he did very little to advance fencing theory.

La Tousche produced one book, *Les Vrays principes de l'espee seule* (1670).**

REFERENCE

Castle, Egerton. *Schools and Masters of Fence.* London: George Bell, 1885.

LEADING ACTION. Any offensive response that is accompanied by a step forward.

REFERENCE

Morton, E. D. *Martini A–Z of Fencing.* London: Queen Anne Press, 1992.

LEE, BRUCE. (1940–1973). Chinese martial arts movie star.

Star of a number of successful martial arts films—including *Fists of Fury* (1971), *The Chinese Connection* (1972), and *Enter the Dragon* (1973)—Bruce Lee was also the creator of his own martial arts style, *Jeet kune do.*

In forming the concepts for *Jeet kune do,* Lee borrowed heavily from fencing technique, simply substituting his arm for a foil. Lee made use of such moves as the stop hit, the riposte, the counterattack, and the parry.

Lee made use of the writings of Julio Castello* (*Theory of Fencing,* 1931), C.-L. de Beaumont* (*Fencing,* 1951), and Roger Crosnier* (*Fencing with the Sabre,* 1954).

REFERENCES

Mintz, Marilyn D. *The Martial Arts Film.* New York: A. S. Barnes, 1978.

Snyder, Joseph J. ''Bruce Lee's Adaptation of European Fencing Techniques.'' *American Fencing* (March/April 1983).

LEGAMENTO. In Italian, an engagement of the blades.

REFERENCE

Morton, E. D. *Martini A–Z of Fencing.* London: Queen Anne Press, 1992.

LELOIR, MAURICE. (c. 1890). French illustrator.

In the late nineteenth century, artist Maurice Leloir produced the definitive illustrations for Alexandre Dumas's *The Three Musketeers.** In a labor of love that lasted for two years, he drew 250 pictures (which were then engraved on

wood) for an 1895 edition of the book that have been imitated and even shame-
lessly copied since they first appeared. His depictions are works of interpretive
brilliance, at once complementing and enhancing the text in a way that no other
Musketeer illustrations have ever managed to do.

Actor Douglas Fairbanks, Sr.,* designed his film *The Three Musketeers*
(1921) around Leloir's classic illustrations.

REFERENCES

Dumas, Alexandre. *The Three Musketeers.* New York: D. Appleton, 1925.

Richards, Jeffrey. *Swordsmen of the Screen.* Boston: Routledge and Kegan Paul, 1977.

LE PERCHE, JEAN BAPTISTE. (c. 1630). French fencing master.

Le Perche has been called "the father of the modern French school of fencing" because he was the first master to insist on the importance of the riposte.
Unfortunately, the rest of his approach to swordplay was not much different
from that of other leading teachers of his day.

Still, his book, *L'Exercise des Armes ou le Maniement du Fleuret* (1635),**
contained principles of a far more useful nature than some volumes penned by
more favored fencing masters.

REFERENCE

Castle, Egerton. *Schools and Masters of Fence.* London: George Bell, 1885.

LESSON, FENCING. The various areas of fencing expertise covered by a
lesson include form, distance, offensive blade manipulation (simple and complex), defensive blade manipulation (simple and complex), footwork, strategy,
timing, and conventions. In the course of training, the subjects of philosophy,
psychology, history, physics, and theatrics may also be included.

While a modern fencing lesson can be, at its worst, a physical or mental
drain, lessons during fencing's formative years could be positively dangerous,
leaving either student or teacher cut and bruised, maimed for life, and even
dead.

A tragic example of such hazards occurred in 1607, when a Scottish nobleman, Lord Sanquhar, lost an eye during a fencing lesson with his teacher, John
Turner. In revenge for this accident, Sanquhar ordered men in his pay to kill
the fencing master, which they did. The offending peer was subsequently executed for the murder.

REFERENCES

Morton, E. D. *Martini A–Z of Fencing.* London: Queen Anne Press, 1992.

Palffy-Alpar, Julius. *Sword and Masque.* Philadelphia: F. A. Davis, 1967.

LEVIS, JOSEPH. (1905–). U.S. fencing champion.

The achievements of Joseph Levis have always ranked high in the annals of
American fencing. He placed eleventh in the individual foil at the 1928 Amsterdam Olympics, becoming the first U.S. fencer since the 1904 St. Louis games
to make an individual event fencing finals. Moreover, Levis continues to be the

A fencing lesson

only U.S. fencer since 1904 to finish above third in an Olympic competition, capturing second in the individual foil event at the Los Angeles Olympics in 1932. That same year, he also acquired a third-place medal in team foil. This makes him one of the few Americans to ever win more than one Olympic fencing medal.

In putting Levis's achievements into perspective, it is important to remember that his individual skills were being tested during Olympic games fully attended by the European fencing community. The only other time the United States had ever won fencing medals above third place in an individual—as opposed to team—event was at the previously mentioned 1904 games, which took place in St. Louis. At this time, however, few European nations even bothered to show up, partially out of a feeling that St. Louis was too far off the beaten track and partially out of disgust for the poor way the games were being handled by their organizers (even the founder of the Olympics, Baron de Coubertin, stayed away). In this setting, then, the United States had its all-time best showing in Olympic fencing, winning almost a dozen medals. So, while these victories are recognized as valid by the Olympic Committee, the St. Louis games were, in truth, little more than an American contest. This fact, of course, only accentuates the feats of Levis, who fought his way up against some of the best European swordsmen of his time.

Joseph Levis was the U.S. national foil champion in 1929, 1932, 1933, 1935, 1937, and 1954.

REFERENCES

Grombach, John V. *The 1972 Olympic Guide.* New York: Paperback Library, 1972.

Menke, Frank. *The Encyclopedia of Sports.* New York: A. S. Barnes, 1955.

Wallechinsky, David. *The Complete Book of the Olympics.* New York: Penguin Books, 1984.

LIANCOUR, ANDRE DE. (c. 1680). French fencing master.

Andre de Liancour was one of the most respected fencing masters of his time. While producing little that was actually new to fencing, he did manage to eliminate much of what was wrong with the French school. His style, then, was highly sound, if not original.

Liancour was one of the first to teach the *coupé,* an attack that passes over the top of an opponent's blade.

Also, he was quite explicit about using the proper foil. The master's foil, he noted, should be lighter than the student's, so that his arm might not tire while teaching for long periods. Moreover, the student's foil used during a lesson should be heavier than the one used in bouting, and it should have no hand guard, this to encourage proper parrying; it must also be shorter so that the student might be extra wary of time thrusts.

Liancour published one book—*Le Maistre d'armes* (1686)**—at the beginning of his career as a fencing master.

REFERENCE

Castle, Egerton. *Schools and Masters of Fence.* London: George Bell, 1885.

French fencing master Andre de Liancour

LIBERI, FIORE DEI. (c. 1400). Italian fencing master.

The author of the earliest known book on fencing, *Flos Duellatorum* (1410).
REFERENCE
Morton, E. D. *Martini A–Z of Fencing*. London: Queen Anne Press, 1992.

LINEA PERFETTA E LINEA RETTA. This action, as taught by seventeenth-century Italian fencing master Alexander Senese,* placed a swordsman on guard with his sword point always directly menacing his adversary.

REFERENCE
Castle, Egerton. *Schools and Masters of Fence.* London: George Bell, 1885.

LINEAR FENCING. Linear fencing, that is, fencing in a straight line, is a concept associated with modern fencing.

In earlier times, men fought in a circular fashion. This was due chiefly to the ponderous nature of old-style swords. To fight in a way that would not over-extend and overbalance a swordsman with his weighty weapon—and, hence, leave him off guard and open to devastating counterattacks—meant that most of his attack maneuvering was accomplished with his body rather than his blade. A circular advance toward one's adversary proved to be the best and most natural way to accomplish this.

Seventeenth-century Italian fencing master Ridolfo Capo Ferro, as the thrusting rapier took over for the cutting sword, first recognized the value of the linear approach to fencing. Yet, with excessive weight continuing to be a factor in blade construction, his ideas could never be fully realized and remained imperfect.

The development of the light and highly maneuverable smallsword changed this. Suddenly, a sword could be employed quickly and effectively in and of itself. Encumbered no more by heavy weapons, swordsmen now found it possible to attack an opponent with facility by simply lunging straight at him. This, of course, proved to be much more efficient and accurate than the circular style of swordplay. Also, a safe recovery—in case of an unsuccessful attack—by returning swiftly to an on-guard position and parrying an opponent's counterattack was now a relatively simple task.

These new developments, then, encouraged a fresh view of combat that transformed fencing into the linear game it is today.

REFERENCES
Castle, Egerton. *Schools and Masters of Fence.* London: George Bell, 1885.
Wise, Arthur. *The Art and History of Personal Combat.* Greenwich, CT: Arma Press, 1971.

LINEAS INFINITA. According to the early Spanish school of fencing, this term referred to two parallel lines on which two opposing swordsmen stood and along which they could move indefinitely without coming in reach of each other.

REFERENCE
Castle, Egerton. *Schools and Masters of Fence.* London: George Bell, 1885.

LINE OF ATTACK. The line or portion of an opposing fencer's target area into which an attack is delivered.

Also a theoretical line, sometimes called the axis, running parallel to the length of a fencing strip along which two competing fencers either advance upon each other or retreat.

REFERENCES
Morton, E. D. *Martini A–Z of Fencing.* London: Queen Anne Press, 1992.
Stevenson, John. *Fencing.* London: Briggs, 1935.

LINE OF DIRECTION. An imaginary straight line on the fencing strip upon which a fencer places both heels as he comes on guard.* When the heels have been lined up properly (the feet forming a right angle in relationship to each other), not only will proper balance be maintained while fencing, but a fencer is more likely to produce an effective lunge, with his momentum aimed directly into his opponent, rather than creating an oblique approach with his attack that invariably waters down forward impetus.

REFERENCE
Morton, E. D. *Martini A–Z of Fencing.* London: Queen Anne Press, 1992.

LINES. In the early days of swordplay, each fencing master had his own unique way of describing areas of the body to be attacked or defended. Much depended on the height at which one's sword was being held, how the blade was to be manipulated, and how the feet were placed. These attitudes were, generally speaking, highly eccentric and had little to do with logic or efficiency. Often their usefulness and appropriateness existed only in the minds of their creators.

In time, with the establishment of an accepted on-guard attitude in fencing—the body, the sword hand, the sword blade, and the feet being positioned in a way that was consistent from moment to moment—the fencer's anatomy could be reasonably sectioned off, academically speaking, in relationship to this uniformity. Such a move was taken to further enhance an ever-growing stock of universal fencing concepts.

Today, of course, this sectioning of the body is so entrenched in fencing thought that it is an unquestioned given of the sport.

To begin with, the torso of the body is divided into four equal quarters, or, in fencing terms, lines. Each line has two sword hand positions—one in supination (palm up) and one in pronation (palm down)—that may be used offensively or defensively in manipulating one's weapon. Which hand position is used determines the name of the line.

Because there are four supinated hand positions and four pronated hand positions, the total number of lines equals eight. These eight lines have names, which are numbers. The numbers, though, are traditionally identified in old French to maintain their uniquely Old World flavor. These are prime (1), seconde (2), tierce (3), quarte (4), quinte (5), sixte (6), septime (7), and octave (8). Prime, seconde, tierce, and quinte are pronation lines; quarte, sixte, septime, and octave are supination lines.

To further define sectioning, the lines are divided into high (*dessus*) and low (*dessous*), inside (*dedans*) and outside (*dehors*). The high line is defined as those quarters above the sword hand in the on-guard position; the low line, as those be-

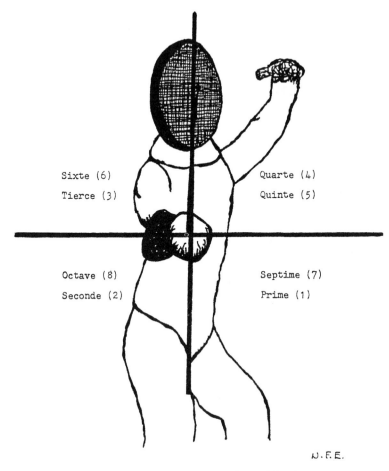

Sixte (6)   Quarte (4)

Tierce (3)   Quinte (5)

Octave (8)   Septime (7)

Seconde (2)   Prime (1)

N.F.E.

The eight body divisions, or lines, of fencing

low the sword hand. The inside line is made up of those quarters on the left side of the body; the outside line, those on the right side. This, then, gives us a high-inside line (quarte and quinte), a high-outside line (tierce and sixte), a low-inside line (prime and septime), and a low-outside line (seconde and octave).

The terms dessus, dedans, dessous, and dehors are sometimes used specifically to define the high right line, the high left line, the low left line, and the low right line, respectively.

By either raising or dropping the sword hand, one can also establish a high-low line (hand higher than normal) or a low-high line (hand lower than normal). These, however, are not consistently maintained because of their unbalanced nature.

REFERENCES

Castle, Egerton. *Schools and Master of Fence.* London: George Bell, 1885.

Palffy-Alpar, Julius. *Sword and Masque.* Philadelphia: F. A. Davis, 1967.

Vebell, Edward. *Sports Illustrated Book of Fencing.* Philadelphia: J. B. Lippincott, 1962.

LITERATURE, SWORD IN. The history of both classical and popular literature is replete with examples of the sword being used as an integral plot device for change, conflict, and resolution.

Examples in literature in which the sword plays an important role include:

The Bible

The Iliad (800 B.C.), Homer

La Morte d'Arthur (1469), Sir Thomas Malory

Romeo and Juliet (1596), William Shakespeare

Hamlet (1601), William Shakespeare

Don Quixote (1605), Miguel de Cervantes

A Faire Quarrell (1617), Thomas Middleton/William Rowley

Tom Jones (1749), Henry Fielding

Waverley (1814), Sir Walter Scott

Ivanhoe (1822), Sir Walter Scott

Taras Bulba (1835), Nikolai Gogol

The Three Musketeers (1844), Alexandre Dumas

Twenty Years After (1845), Alexandre Dumas

Barry Lyndon (1846), William Makepeace Thackeray

Chevalier d'Harmental (1853), Alexandre Dumas

Captain Fracasse (1861), Theophile Gautier

Lorna Doone (1869), R. D. Blackmore

The Prince and the Pauper (1881), Mark Twain

Bel-Ami (1885), Guy de Maupassant

Kidnapped (1886), Robert Louis Stevenson

The Black Arrow (1888), Robert Louis Stevenson

With Fire and Sword (1890), Henryk Sienkiewicz

Men of Iron (1892), Howard Pyle

The Prisoner of Zenda (1894), Anthony Hope

A Gentleman from Gascony (1895), Bicknell Dudley

Rupert of Hentzau (1898), Anthony Hope

Won by the Sword (1899), G. A. Henty

Monsieur Beaucaire (1900), Booth Tarkington

The Trail of the Sword (1900), Gilbert Parker

David versus Goliath, in the Bible

The Courtship of Morrice Buckler (1903), A.E.W. Mason

The White Company (1912), Arthur Conan Doyle

Under the Red Robe (1915), Stanley J. Weyman

A Princess of Mars (1917), Edgar Rice Burroughs

Captain Blood (1922), Rafael Sabatini

The Mad King (1926), Edgar Rice Burroughs

The Secret of the Bastille (1929), Paul Feval/ M. Lassez

Prince of Peril (1930), O. A. Kline

The Black Swan (1931), Rafael Sabatini

Salute to Cyrano (1931), Paul Feval

Conan the Conqueror (1935), Robert E. Howard

Musashi (1937–1939), Eiji Yoshikawa

Master-at-Arms (1940), Rafael Sabatini

Frenchman's Creek (1941), Daphne du Maurier

Chesapeake Cavalier (1949), Don Tracy

The Adventurer (1950), Mika Waltari

Stormbringer (1965), Michael Moorcock

The Hobbit (1965), J.R.R. Tolkien

The Worm Ouroboros (1965), E. R. Eddison

The Smith of Wootton Major (1967), J.R.R. Tolkien

Royal Flash (1970), George MacDonald Fraser

The Clue of the Broken Blade (1970), Franklin W. Dixon

The Broken Sword (1971), Poul Anderson

The Princess Bride (1973), William Goldman

The Seven Per-Cent Solution (1974), Nicholas Meyer

Shogun (1975), James Clavell

Conan of Aquilonia (1977), L. Sprague de Camp and Lin Carter

Mystery of the Samurai Sword (1979), Franklin W. Dixon

Two to Conquer (1980), Marion Zimmer Bradley

Seven Altars of Dusarra (1980), Lawrence Evans

Locksley (1983), Nicholas Chase

Gods of Riverworld (1983), Philip Jose Farmer

Sword of Winter (1983), Marta Rundall

Sensei (1983), David Charney

The Miko (1984), Eric Van Lustbader

Wishsong of Shannara (1985), Terry Brooks

Quest for Saint Camber (1986), Katherine Kurtz

King of Ys (1987), Paul and Karen Anderson

A Royal Quest (1987), Mary Lide

Knight and Knave of Swords (1988), Fritz Leiber

Lords of Vaumartin (1988), Cecelia Holland

Fortress of the Pearl (1989), Michael Moorcock

Knight of Shadows (1989), Roger Zelazny

Man of Mundania (1989), Piers Anthony

Race of Scorpions (1990), Dorothy Dunnet

The Seeress of Kell (1991), David Eddings

The Reckoning (1991), Sharon Kay Penman

The Magic of Recluse (1993), L. E. Modesitt, Jr.

Wayfinder's Story (1993), Fred Saberhagen

Golden Trillium (1993), Andre Norton

The Bastard Prince (1994), Katherine Kurtz

The prose in the preceding literature may be light, such as in Dumas's *The Three Musketeers:*

[B]ut D'Artagnan seized the moment at which, in this movement, the sword of Bernajoux deviated from the line: he freed his weapon, made a lunge, and touched his adversary on the shoulder.

It may be grim, as in George MacDonald Fraser's *Royal Flash:*

And with that he came in, foot and hand, and had me fighting for my life as I fell back across the hall. His blade was everywhere, now darting at my face, now at my chest, now slashing at my flank, now at my head—how I parried those thrusts and sweeps is beyond me, for he was faster than any man I'd ever met.

It may be flowery, as in Rafael Sabatini's *Captain Blood:*

"You do not take her while I live!" he cried. "Then I'll take her when you're dead," said Captain Blood, and his own blade flashed in the sunlight. . . . It was soon over. The brute strength upon which Levasseur so confidently counted, could avail nothing against the Irishman's practiced skill. When, with both lungs transfixed, he lay prone on the white sand, coughing out his rascally life . . .

It may be lurid, as in Don Tracy's *Chesapeake Cavalier:*

Bristoll's mouth twisted and he threw himself at Dale. Morley's sword slashed once, twice across Bristoll's face and the blood welled out of two cuts that striped the other man's cheeks.

It may even be comic, as in William Goldman's *The Princess Bride:*

"You seem a decent fellow," Inigo said. "I hate to kill you." "You seem a decent fellow," answered the man in black. "I hate to die." They touched swords.

In any case, the sword is there to win, to conquer, to avenge.

REFERENCES

Benet, William Rose. *The Reader's Encyclopedia.* New York: Thomas Y. Crowell, 1965.

Carter, Lin. *Imaginary Worlds.* New York: Ballantine Books, 1973.

Dumas, Alexandre. *The Three Musketeers.* New York: D. Appleton, 1925.

Fraser, George MacDonald. *Royal Flash.* New York: Alfred A. Knopf, 1970.

Goldman, William. *The Princess Bride.* New York: Ballantine Books, 1970.

Magill, Frank, ed. *Masterplots.* NJ: Salem Press, 1993.

Sabatini, Rafael. *Captain Blood.* New York: Bantam Books, 1976.

Tracy, Don. *Chesapeake Cavalier.* New York: Pocket Books, 1950.

LLAVE Y GOBIERNO DE LA DESTREZA. A technical term, according to sixteenth-century Spanish fencing master Don Luis Pacheco de Narvaez,* describing the instinct that prompts two combative opponents to circle each other when not actually striking.

These movements were perceived as a necessary part of swordplay as long as a standard method of engaging blades had yet to be recognized.

REFERENCE

Castle, Egerton. *Schools and Masters of Fence.* London: George Bell, 1885.

LOCKET. A ringed band on a sword scabbard. From this device the weapon is hung.

REFERENCE

Stone, George Cameron. *A Glossary of the Construction, Decoration, and Use of Arms and Armor.* New York: Jack Brussel, 1961.

LOGER. Placing the point of one's blade near an adversary's target area* in preparation for an attack.

REFERENCE

Handleman, Rob. "Fencing Glossary." *American Fencing* (May/June 1978).

LONG SWORD. The long sword was of the two-handed variety. It was invariably a cutting weapon and was always, because of its length and weight, used on foot. Blades of these weapons often reached five feet and more in length.

The long sword family includes the claymore, the *spadone,* the *espadon,* the *zweyhander,* and the *flamberge.*

Also called a "great sword."

REFERENCE

Castle, Egerton. *Schools and Masters of Fence.* London: George Bell, 1885.

LOUIS XIII. (1601–1643). The king of France from 1610 to 1643.

While passing numerous public edicts against dueling, Louis XIII did very little on a personal level to discourage the practice. In fact, pardons for duelists—swordsmen and otherwise—were a frequent feature of his reign.

REFERENCE

Baldick, Robert. *The Duel.* New York: Spring Books, 1970.

LOW LINE. The lower half of a fencer's torso.

The low line comprises inside and outside sections. The low-inside portion of a fencer's target area is made up of the lines of prime (1), where the sword hand is held in pronation, and septime (7), where the sword hand is held in supination. The low-outside portion is made up of the lines of seconde (2), where the sword hand is held in pronation, and octave (8), where the sword hand is held in supination.

Of the four positions, septime and octave are used most often in foil and épée fencing. In sabre fencing, prime and seconde are used most often.

Also called *dessous* or *bassa.*

REFERENCES

Palffy-Alpar, Julius. *Sword and Masque.* Philadelphia: F. A. Davis, 1967.

Vebell, Edward. *Sports Illustrated Book of Fencing.* Philadelphia: J. B. Lippincott, 1962.

LUCAS, GEORGE. (1945–). American filmmaker.

George Lucas created the highly successful *Star Wars* trilogy: *Star Wars* (1977), *The Empire Strikes Back* (1980), and *Return of the Jedi* (1983). These films espoused a kind of science-fiction-like samurai/Zen philosophy that caught the imagination of movie audiences around the world.

The films, starring Mark Hamill, Harrison Ford, Carrie Fisher, and Alec Guinness, recount the adventures of Luke Skywalker as he becomes a Jedi knight. Taught by mystical Obi-Wan Kanobi and the ancient Yoda, Skywalker progresses from a young, headstrong initiate to the ways of the Force (the binding energy of the universe) into an experienced warrior.

The swordplay, of which there is much, is performed with laserlike ''light sabres,'' which draw their energy from the aforementioned Force. The combat, staged by British fencing masters Peter Diamond* and Bob Anderson,* is simple but clean and based on kendo, the two-handed fencing of Japan.

It has been noted that the *Star Wars* films were influenced to a great degree by the samurai films of Akira Kurosawa* and by the writings of mythologist/philosopher Joseph Campbell,** especially his *Hero with a Thousand Faces* (1949).

REFERENCES

Cousineau, Phil. *The Hero's Journey: Joseph Campbell on His Life and Work.* New York: Harper and Row, 1990.

Halliwell, Leslie. *Halliwell's Filmgoer's and Video Viewer's Companion.* New York: Charles Scribner's Sons, 1988.

LUCIA, EDWARD. (1914–1984). Italian American fencing master.

Starting his fencing career in high school, Edward Lucia quickly moved on to become a student of famed maestro Giorgio Santelli. Eventually, Santelli chose him to be his assistant, after which he became a master in his own right.

In his years as a highly respected fencing teacher, Edward Lucia produced a number of champions, including four-time U.S. national women's foil champion

Harriet King** and Olympic bronze medalist Albert Axelrod.* His women's teams won two national championships.

Lucia served on the U.S. Olympic Fencing Committee, was twice awarded the U.S. Fencing Association Professional Certificate of Merit, and was elected to the Helms Hall of Fame.

Lucia collaborated with Giorgio Santelli* to produce one book, *Engravings in Steel* (1980).**

REFERENCES

Santelli, Giorgio, and Edward Lucia. "Engravings in Steel." *American Fencing* (May/ June 1980).

Sobel, Steve. "In Memoriam: Edward Lucia 1914–1984." *American Fencing* (January/ February 1985).

LUCKY SWORD. In early medieval times, when a swordsman was deemed "lucky" in battle, that luck was thought to rub off on his sword. This concept of transference also was believed to be true of courage and ability. These weapons, sung of as "ancient heirlooms" by the poets of old, were much prized by those who gained them.

REFERENCE

Norman, A. V. B., and Don Pottinger. *English Weapons and Warfare 449–1660.* Englewood Cliffs, N.J.: Prentice-Hall, 1979.

LUDI. Combat schools (*ludus gladiatorius*) of ancient Rome, where gladiators* learned and practiced the use of swords and other weapons.

With regard to swordplay, students began their instruction with wooden swords, practicing first on posts and later with various partners. Their final destination, of course, was the Roman public combat arenas, where their acquired skills would receive their ultimate test.

REFERENCE

Burton, Richard F. *The Book of the Sword.* London: Chatto and Windus, 1884.

LUNETTE. A hand guard* employed on the French foil* during the late nineteenth century. Consisting of two oval rings on either side of the grip, the *lunette* somewhat resembled a pair of spectacles, which gave the guard its name.

The *lunette* fell into disuse early into the twentieth century, and was replaced by the more functional saucer-shaped *coquille.**

Also called a "figure eight" guard.

REFERENCE

Morton, E. D. *Martini A–Z of Fencing.* London: Queen Anne Press, 1992.

LUNGE. The primary form of launching an attack in modern fencing.

While first introduced during the sixteenth century by the Italian master Nicoletto Giganti,* the lunge was not perfected until the eighteenth century. The main stumbling block in the original development of the lunge was the weight

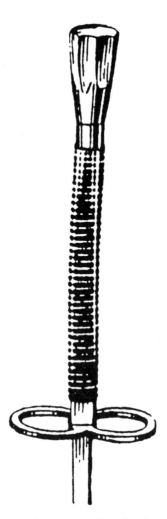

The lunette on a French grip

of the swords being used: they were simply too heavy for the kind of arm and leg extension the lunge required. It was not until the lightweight smallsword came into common use that the lunge became feasible.

The objective of the lunge is to increase one's reach dramatically while attacking. This is accomplished by stepping forward with the front leg at the same moment the sword arm is extended toward one's opponent.

Numerous factors work together to create an effective lunge:

1. The sword arm extends completely straight. This ensures that the attacker will have the full potential of his reach and that an opponent, by extending his arm, will not have a longer reach than the attacker does.

The lunge as it was envisioned at the beginning of the seventeenth century

2. The rear leg snaps straight at the knee, pushing the fencer forward. It is from this pistonlike action that the lunge receives its acceleration.

3. The front foot is picked up in a forward step. Unfortunately, this maneuver can be somewhat misleading, because none of the lunge's momentum should be generated by the step. A lunge, using the front leg to establish forward motion, creates a pulling response that not only has no real speed behind it but promotes an inward turn of the front foot that invariably leads to a loss of balance.

4. The free arm drops down from its upwardly bent on-guard position, straightening as it falls. This aids in the forward impetus of the lunge.

5. Once the free arm has dropped just below shoulder level, it now acts as an effective counterbalance.

6. As the free hand lowers, its palm should be turned into supination, another mechanism to promote balance.

7. The front foot continues forward until the proper distance for the lunge has been reached.

8. Landing on the heel, the foot drops flat, the toe pointing straight ahead.

9. The front knee pushes forward until it is directly over the front ankle. Once it reaches this point, the push stops. To go farther with the knee shifts the weight of the body too far forward, making it difficult to maintain balance and to return easily to the on-guard position.

10. The lunge has been completed.

Also known as *affondo, elonge,* and *botta lunga.*

REFERENCES
Castle, Egerton. *Schools and Masters of Fence.* London: George Bell, 1885.
Palffy-Alpar, Julius. *Sword and Masque.* Philadelphia: F. A. Davis, 1967.
Vebell, Edward. *Sports Illustrated Book of Fencing.* Philadelphia: J. B. Lippincott, 1962.

LUNGE ON THE ADVANCE. Straightening one's arm and stepping forward before employing the lunge.

The lunge on the advance is performed to close attacking distance on an opponent. It may be used (1) when a fencer begins his attack from outside his normal lunging distance or (2) to follow an opponent who retreats as he is being attacked.

REFERENCE
Stevenson, John. *Fencing.* London: Briggs, 1935.

LURE OF FENCING. There is a magical something about fencing, some otherworldly quality that sets it apart from other pursuits. Whether it is the romance of the sword, reaching back to the days of knights and musketeers; the individual challenge of one-on-one personal combat; or simply a way of achieving, through the blending of mind and body, a healthful exercise, fencing—esoteric and practical in the same breath—is one of man's universal preoccupations.

Perhaps the old-time fencers—unhindered by the modern distractions of elec-

tric weapons, politicized sport victories, and athletic equipment endorsements—
said it best.

The great eighteenth-century master Domenico Angelo* said of fencing:

Nothing can give elegance and freedom in greater degree than fencing. To acquire any
degree of proficiency in any art or science, a competent knowledge of theory must be
judiciously applied to practice. Fencing enables those who practice it to perform other
exercises with greater facility.

In fine, it has, among many others, two inseparable qualities: the agreeable and the
useful; the former, as it affords gentlemen a manly and dignified amusement; the latter,
as it forms the body and furnishes one with a facility of defense, whether it be for honor
or for life, when the one or the other is brought into question by any disagreeable
accident, or attack by those turbulent and dangerous persons whose correction is of
service to society in general.

Louis Senac,* one of America's earliest fencing masters, noted:

The practice of fencing is an excellent school of individual combat. It develops strength,
resistance, suppleness, power, quickness, precision, judgement, coolness, will, decision—
in short—all the natural or acquired qualities which distinguish the true fencer, whatever
the weapon. The foil cultivates these qualities to the highest degree. The physical benefits
of fencing are so numerous, in fact, that he that would enumerate them in detail must
needs possess a vast measure of endurance. Every muscle is brought into play, individ-
ually and in combination, and the system is invigorated surprisingly. As a stimulant, a
fencing bout is far more effective than the best tonic a physician could prescribe. So if
you are a victim of any sort of depressing affliction, try the fencing cure.

In everyday life the fencer has a distinct advantage over his disinterested, more prosaic
neighbor. He feels sure of himself at all times and under all conditions. His training has
rendered it impossible for him to strike an awkward pose. He will unconsciously make
movements that will attract favorable attention through their ease. The constant use of
his arms and hands has made him stronger than the ordinary man, and the consciousness
of this fact gives him confidence he would otherwise lack. In the business world he will
be able to stand unusual strain. The fresh blood and newly formed tissues will support
him through many crises when competitors are exhausted or even seriously ill through
their efforts.

Lord Desborough, one of England's noted nineteenth-century swordsmen, explained his view of fencing:

I always think the best description I have heard of it was given by professor Verbrugge.
. . . He had the supreme gift of making the lesson which he gave more interesting than
an assault, in fact, he turned it into a symphony. With him, fencing was a conversation
with the sword, and to make the conversation interesting each of the controversialists
had to be well-educated in the art of argument.

No conversation could take place unless your opponent understood the language. If
he merely parried carte and sixte, it was just like talking to a man who could only say
"yes" and "no," whereas if he understood the language of the sword he could reply to
your attack and counter-ripostes with every sort of argument and variation, which adds
intensely to the interest of an argument with the foil in a *salle d'armes*.

Leon Bertrand, the last of the illustrious Bertrand family of fencing masters, observed:

It can be said that no one is too old to fence. I could cite numerous cases of fencers whose ages range between sixty-five and seventy and whose ardor remains undimmed, and I question whether any other sport can produce representatives of similar age so active, so virile and possessing the stamia of these warriors.

The game does not develop or produce unsightly bunches of muscle, but makes for suppleness, grace of movement, and agility. Its greatest attraction lies in its combined physical and mental training. Demanding the highest association between brain and muscle, calling for the closest co-ordination between brain, eye, hand, and foot, fencing brings into play almost every body function. A fencer does not toss aside his weapon regretfully at the age of thirty-five or forty. He can look forward to a lifelong enjoyment of this pastime, which is more than can be said of most sporting recreations. Nor does the passing of time see the decline of the swordsman's skill, for he reaches the zenith of his prowess at a stage later than that achieved by any other brand of sportsman.

Because the enthusiast discovers by fencing that he can maintain physical fitness and pursue an art to a ripe age, I find usually that fencing becomes to him a definite and regular incident in his existence. He is enmeshed in the charms of foil, epee, or sabre. Now let him who stands on the brink take the plunge; he will experience a similar fascination, I am sure, and he will never forget his temerity. The genial camaraderie of the fencing-room, the welcome of a happy community, portray in its truest spirit the freemasonry of the sword. One makes lasting friends of perpetual "foes"; the interchange of social amenities creates new associations, new viewpoints are acquired, and very soon the recruit will look upon his visits to the salle as a matter of pleasant habit, his sword-play as a distinct phase of his life.

REFERENCE
Cass, Eleanor Baldwin. *The Book of Fencing*. Boston: Lothrop, Lee, and Shepard, 1930.

LUXBRUDER. A society of swordsmen in Germany.

The Luxbruder, or Fraternity of St. Luke, was an organization of swordsmen that sprang up during the late Middle Ages as Germans sought to structure their fencing into organized and controlled associations. Little, however, is actually known about them. Never as influential as the Marxbruder* or Federfechter,* they seemed to have died out as a group by the fifteenth century.

It is believed that the Luxbruder spawned a species of swordsmen called the *klopffechter*. These stalwart fighters traveled around the country, displaying their fighting talents at fairs.

REFERENCE
Castle, Egerton. *Schools and Masters of Fence.* London: George Bell, 1885.

M

MACHERA. A Greek sword with a long, straight blade.
REFERENCE
Burton, Richard F. *The Book of the Sword*. London: Chatto and Windus, 1884.

MAGIC SWORDS. In ancient lore, magic swords were talismans that both protected their heroic owners from injury and invariably killed or wounded the foe they were directed against. A magic sword might also invoke other powers, such as the power of invisibility, or the ability to travel great distances instantly, to invoke the power of the elements, or to ward off witchcraft.

Roland, Siegfried, Ogier, King Arthur, Perseus, Achilles, Odysseus, Finn, and Charlemagne were all said to own magic swords.
REFERENCE
Leach, Maria, ed. *Funk and Wagnalls Standard Dictionary of Folklore, Mythology, and Legend*. San Francisco: Harper and Row, 1972.

MAGNAN, JEAN-CLAUDE. (c. twentieth century). French fencing champion.

Jean-Claude Magnan's foil team took first at the 1968 Olympics, and third at the 1972 Olympics.

Magnan was world foil champion in 1963 and 1965.
REFERENCES
Palffy-Alpar, Julius. *Sword and Masque*. Philadelphia: F. A. Davis, 1967.
Wallechinsky, David. *The Complete Book of the Olympics*. New York: Penguin Books, 1984.

MAHITO, KUNIMATSU NO. Founder of the earliest named school of Japanese swordplay: *Kashima no tachi* or the Kashima Shrine style of the sword. Kunimatsu no Mahito is sometimes regarded as the founder of *kenjutsu,* or the art of sword fighting, in Japan.
REFERENCE
Sasamori, Junzo, and Gordon Warner. *This Is Kendo.* Vermont: Charles E. Tuttle, 1984.

MAINDROICT. According to the sixteenth-century French fencing master Henry de Sainct Didier,* the *maindroict*—patterned after the Italian *mandritto**—was any cut delivered from the right side.
REFERENCE
Castle, Egerton. *Schools and Masters of Fence.* London: George Bell, 1885.

MAIN GAUCHE. Meaning ''left hand'' in French.
    A weapon of the seventeenth century, the *main gauche* was a left-handed dagger used almost always in conjunction with a sword. It had a straight, double-edged blade; a long, straight crossbar*; a short handle; and a broad, triangular counter guard.*
    While the *main gauche*'s chief purpose was parrying,* it could easily be brought into offensive play when a fencer's sword was stopped by a defensive maneuver.
REFERENCE
Stone, George Cameron. *A Glossary of the Construction, Decoration, and Use of Arms and Armor.* New York: Jack Brussel, 1961.

MAKING AND BREAKING GROUND. Advancing and retreating.
REFERENCE
Morton, E. D. *Martini A–Z of Fencing.* London: Queen Anne Press, 1992.

MAKURA DASHI. Meaning ''pillow sword.''
    The *makura dashi* was a sword hung by the pillow of the master of a Japanese household to be used in case of emergency.
REFERENCE
Stone, George Cameron. *A Glossary of the Construction, Decoration, and Use of Arms and Armor.* New York: Jack Brussel, 1961.

MAL PARE. A parry that touches an attacking blade the same moment the blade touches the target.
REFERENCE
Handelman, Rob. ''Fencing Glossary.'' *American Fencing* (May/June 1978).

MANCHETTE. The cuff of the sword arm. In épée* and sabre* fencing, a valid target* area. In foil, off target.*

REFERENCES

Handelman, Rob. "Fencing Glossary." *American Fencing* (May/June 1978).

U.S. Fencing Association, ed. *Operations Manual.* Colorado Springs, CO: U.S. Fencing Association, 1985.

MANCHETTE CUT. A broadsword attack consisting of cutting at the hand, wrist, and forearm of an opponent with the weapon's inner edge.

REFERENCE

Burton, Richard F. *The Book of the Sword.* London: Chatto and Windus, 1884.

MANCIOLINO, ANTONIO. (c. 1500). Italian fencing master.

Antonio Manciolino was one of Italy's earliest fencing masters of note. Yet, few details are known of his teaching methods. His published book, *Opera Nova* (1531),** deals little with actual fencing methods and instead dwells at length on rules of honor and ways to pick and decide quarrels.

Of his actual teaching style, he draws no distinction between cutting and thrusting; his attacks were almost always delivered on the advance; and only one of his guards appears to have any definite purpose. His greatest advice, it appears, was simply that an attacker should maneuver himself into a position where he could easily strike his opponent.

REFERENCE

Castle, Egerton. *Schools and Masters of Fence.* London: George Bell, 1885.

MANDABOLO. Seventeenth-century Italian fencing master Giuseppe Pallavincini* described this action as an ascending cut with the sword blade's false edge.*

REFERENCE

Castle, Egerton. *Schools and Masters of Fence.* London: George Bell, 1885.

MANDAU. The favorite sword of the Dyaks of Indonesia. The name means "headhunter." It has a short, single-edged blade.

A variation of this weapon has a curved blade, widening near the point.

A *mandau pasir* is a form of the weapon possessing a very wide blade.

Sometimes called a *jimpul.*

REFERENCE

Stone, George Cameron. *A Glossary of the Construction, Decoration, and Use of Arms and Armor.* New York: Jack Brussel, 1961.

MANDOBLE. According to sixteenth-century Spanish fencing master Jeronimo de Caranza,* this action was a cut made from the wrist, executed with a flip of the sword's point.

REFERENCE

Castle, Egerton. *Schools and Masters of Fence.* London: George Bell, 1885.

MANDRITTO. As described by sixteenth-century Italian fencing master Achille Marozzo,* the *mandritto* was any cut delivered from the right—to an adversary's left side—with the right edge of one's blade.

Vincentio Saviolo* later described it simply as a "cross blow."

Also called *mandrittae, mandritti,* and *maindroict.*

REFERENCE

Castle, Egerton. *Schools and Masters of Fence.* London: George Bell, 1885.

MANGIAROTTI, EDOARDO. (1919–   ). Italian fencing champion.

The son of successful fencing master Giuseppe Mangiarotti, Edoardo Mangiarotti began taking fencing lessons when he was eight years old. At the age of seventeen, he was a member of the 1936 Olympic gold medal Italian épée team. In his many years of competition, Mangiarotti won an impressive thirteen Olympic medals.

In Olympic individual foil: 1952 (second place)

In Olympic team foil: 1948 (second place); 1952 (second place); 1956 (first place); and 1960 (second place)

In Olympic individual épée: 1948 (third place); 1952 (first place); and 1956 (third place)

In Olympic team épée: 1936 (first place); 1948 (second place); 1952 (first place); 1956 (first place); and 1960 (first place).

Mangiarotti was also world épée champion in 1951 and 1954.

Edoardo Mangiarotti's older brother Dario was also a fencing champion.

REFERENCES

Palffy-Alpar, Julius. *Sword and Masque.* Philadelphia: F. A. Davis, 1967.

Wallechinsky, David. *The Complete Book of the Olympics.* New York: Penguin Books, 1984.

MANNERS OF THE SWORD. Modern fencing is a game shaped by manners. Conventions and etiquette play a vital part in the continuity of the sport. They give fencing its sense of tradition, reminding the fencer that his roots run deep into a unique and honorable past. On a practical level, manners also give a combatant a point of control from which to begin his encounter.

The manners of the sword, of course, are not a modern concept. They have always played an important part in the life of men dedicated to the blade. In medieval times, knights* knew the value of developing manners in their quest for control over their own actions. The codes of chivalry were the result. The Japanese samurai* came to the same conclusion, creating the concept of Bushido.*

But while samurai manners, inspired by the philosophy of Zen,* were often concerned with the deeper issues of life, the Western approach sometimes was used to convey symbolic meaning. The process of becoming a knight, for instance, had specific manners, which, in fact, were there simply to reinforce a higher level of personal attainment. When taking the oath of knighthood, a new knight would grasp his sword in his right hand, the hand he used to fight with, his hand of power. When being knighted, he would be touched on the shoulder by the king's sword, thereby receiving a portion of the king's nobility and strength. Before a fight, the knight kissed the cross of his sword as a sign of respect for God, his king, and even the weapon itself.

The sword, a bringer of both life and death, was always highly respected. It was not to be drawn without reason or, as the saying went, sheathed without honor. The point of a blade was never to touch the ground. In Japanese traditions, the sword might never even be stepped over, a direct insult to the weapon and its owner.

During the seventeenth century, the convention of saluting one's opponent was introduced by French fencing master Charles Besnard,* an action he referred to as "reverence."

By the eighteenth century, fencing had attained a degree of refinement. Every school of standing had its code of conduct both in and outside the fencing match. According to Egerton Castle* in his *Schools and Masters of Fence* (1885),* "an accomplished fencer was expected to display the utmost regularity, avoid time hits, only riposte when his adversary recovered, so as to avoid wounding his face."

Even the more serious aspect of fencing—the duel—had its prescribed manners and rules. A sword fight, on most occasions, was expected to be fought until the first blood was shed or until the fighters were too tired to continue. In sabre duels, protective bandages were placed at the neck, armpits, wrists, and the stomach to protect vital centers. Also, with the sabre, cuts were allowed, yet thrusting was almost never permitted.

Today, manners play an important role in fencing. According to U.S. Fencing Association rules, "By the mere fact of taking part in a fencing competition, the fencers pledge their honor to observe the regulations and the decisions of the judges."

The saluting of one's opponent and the director of one's bout is a required sign of respect, not only for them but for fencing. In practice bouts, touches are acknowledged as a matter of course; but in tournament play, out of respect for official decisions, such determinations should be left up to the officials.

Other manners are basic common sense to any activity where cooperation is essential to the continued functioning of that activity. Arguing over touches is, of course, frowned upon. Foul language, if repeated, may draw penalties. The same goes for deliberate physical violence.

Continued failure to adhere to the behavior conventions of organized fencing may lead to exclusion from the competition, temporary suspension, or permanent suspension from the U.S. Fencing Association.

REFERENCES

Barber, Richard. *Knights and Chivalry*. New York: Harper and Row, 1974.
Palffy-Alpar, Julius. *Sword and Masque*. Philadelphia: F. A. Davis, 1967.

U.S. Fencing Association, ed. *Operations Manual.* Colorado Springs, CO: U.S. Fencing
    Association, 1985.
Wilson, William Scott. *Ideals of the Samurai.* Burbank, CA: Ohara, 1982.

MANOPLE. A fourteenth- to fifteenth-century Moorish sword.

The *manople* was a sword with a short, slender blade sided by two shorter
blades. The hilt* was of the gauntlet* type, that is, a glove to which a blade
was attached.
REFERENCE
Stone, George Cameron. *A Glossary of the Construction, Decoration, and Use of Arms
    and Armor.* New York: Jack Brussel, 1961.

MARCELLI, FRANCESCO ANTONIO. (c. 1660). Italian fencing master.

A celebrated master of swordplay, Marcelli probably produced the best description of the lunge* in Italian fencing for his time. He is also credited as the
inventor of the *passata sotto* (a pass* made by dropping beneath an opponent's
extended blade). Moreover, he did much to improve the understanding of fencing tempo* (timing).

Marcelli wrote one book, *Regole Della Scherma* (1686).**
REFERENCE
Castle, Egerton. *Schools and Masters of Fence.* London: George Bell, 1885.

MARCHIONNI, ALBERTO. (c. 1800). Italian fencing master.

Founder of the neoclassical Italian school of fencing, which was adapted from
the French school. He wrote *Trattato di scherma sopra un nuovo sistema di
givoco misto di scuolo italiana e francese* (1847).
REFERENCE
Morton, E. D. *Martini A–Z of Fencing.* London: Queen Anne Press, 1992.

MARKER POINT. The fencing world has always been on the lookout for a
reliable way of registering touches—short of using sharp points. One eighteenth-
century method sometimes saw sponges soaked in vermilion and water and
bound over a practice weapon's button to leave a mark of a hit.

During the early twentieth century, the *pointe d'arret* of the épée was sometimes moistened with a red dye, which left a mark on an opponent's jacket.
Because there was no way to remove the resulting stain, each touch had to be
crossed off with a pencil.

Even with the perfecting of the electric scoring machine, as late as the 1950s,
a point marking system was introduced. A Russian invention, it involved a small
head filled with phenolphthalein and ammonia on the end of a blade. When the
head was depressed, a small amount of the liquid was released, creating a stain
that vanished after a few moments. It did not, however, work on metal surfaces,
such as fencing masks.

Marker points are now a thing of the past.
REFERENCE
Morton, E. D. *Martini A–Z of Fencing.* London: Queen Anne Press, 1992.

Francesco Marcelli

MAROZZO, ACHILLE. (c. 1500). Italian fencing master.

Marozzo was known as "a most perfect master" in the art of fencing and is generally looked upon as the first writer of any importance on the subject of swordplay.

While Marozzo's methods have little value by modern standards, they were a considerable improvement over all other schools of combat taught during the early sixteenth century.

With regard to Marozzo's approach to fencing, his various guard positions* end up being not stances meant to aid in any kind of defense but simply attitudes from which to launch attacks. While he talks of parries,* not a single parry is actually ever explained. For defense, he taught basically three things: dodging an opponent's blade, blocking cuts with a buckler* (shield), and counterattacking into attacks.

Marozzo's work was considered very complete and carefully written, yet there is no innovation in his approach to fencing. Indeed, in spite of his popularity as a master of his art, he failed completely to bring any semblance of definite principles into his teachings.

Marozzo produced his celebrated volume on fencing, *Opera Nova,*** in 1536. It saw numerous reprintings after that, the final one appearing in 1568.

REFERENCE

Castle, Egerton. *Schools and Masters of Fence.* London: George Bell, 1885.

MARSH, ANN. (1971–   ). U.S. fencing champion.

A member of both the U.S. Olympic and World Championship fencing teams, Ann Marsh won the U.S. National women's foil championship in 1994. That same year, she also took third place in fencing's World Cup tournament in Marseilles, France.

REFERENCES

Dimond, Jeff, and Annie McDaniel. "Marsh Carries U.S. Medal Hopes To Athens and World Championships." *En Garde* (Summer 1994).

Mar, Colleen Walker. *1993 U.S. Fencing Association Media Guide.* Colorado Springs: ColorTek Printing, 1993.

MARTINGALE. A looped leather strap attached to the grip of a foil or épée just below the guard. By passing his fingers through this arrangement, a fencer sought to strengthen his hold on his weapon, preventing being disarmed by his opponent.

Similarly, another form of the martingale exists as an independent strap. It is employed chiefly by fencers using the Italian foil or épée to secure the grip of their weapon to their wrist, in this case by wrapping them together. Used correctly, it gives support without inhibiting wrist movement.

REFERENCES

Morton, E. D. *Martini A–Z of Fencing.* London: Queen Anne Press, 1992.

Stevenson, John. *Fencing.* London: Briggs, 1935.

Two-handed swordplay espoused by the Marxbruder

MARX, MICHAEL. (1958–   ). U.S. fencing champion.

Michael Marx is a four-time Olympic fencing team member: 1980, 1984, 1988, and 1992. He has also won the U.S. individual foil championship eight times (a record): 1977, 1979, 1982, 1985, 1986, 1987, 1990, and 1993.

At seventeen, Marx was the youngest foil fencer to ever win a national title.

Michael Marx's older brother, Robert, is also a fencing champion.

REFERENCE

Walker, Colleen. *1992 United States Fencing Association Media Guide.* Colorado Springs, CO: ColorTek Printing, 1992.

MARXBRUDER. The Burgerschaft von St. Marcus von Lowenberg, or Fraternity of St. Mark, was a society of swordsmen established initially in Frankfurt, Germany, in the late fourteenth century. The main premise of the group was that if enough able-bodied swordsmen banded together, they might easily monopolize the right to teach fencing in their area—and this they did. Interlopers were immediately confronted by a contingent of Marxbruder—one captain and five masters—and given the opportunity to fight them on an individual basis or as a group. This, of course, was highly successful in keeping competition to a minimum.

Eventually, the influence of the Marxbruder extended throughout Germany. They enjoyed letters of patent given by Emperor Frederick, at Nuremberg, in

1480; Maximilian I, at Cologne, in 1512; Maximilian II, at Augsburg, in 1566; and Rudolf II, at Prague, in 1579.

Athough experts at a number of weapons, the specialty of Marxbruder members was the two-handed sword,* and they held onto this long after the weapon had lost its popularity elsewhere in Europe.

In the late 1500s, Marxbruder strength was challenged for the first time by a rival group, the Freyfechter von der Feder zum Greifenfels, or, simply, the Federfechter.* Advocates of the recently invented rapier,* this new organization vied openly with Marxbruder swordsmen for control of the fencing community—often with drawn blades in the streets.

For years the Marxbruder held on tenaciously to their methods of combat. Yet even with their dogmas and traditions developed over decades, they succumbed to progress in the end. The value of the rapier as an efficient killing tool proved too much for them. By the end of the sixteenth century, while they and the Federfechter continued to maintain separate identities as fraternities, their fighting styles had become indistinguishable.

REFERENCE
Castle, Egerton. *Schools and Masters of Fence.* London: George Bell, 1885.

MARZI, GUSTAVO. (1909–?). Italian fencing champion.

Gustavo Marzi won the Olympic individual foil championship in 1932. That same year, his foil team took second place in the team foil event. In 1936, his Olympic team took first in team foil.

Marzi was world foil champion in 1937.

REFERENCES
Palffy-Alpar, Julius. *Sword and Masque.* Philadelphia: F. A. Davis, 1967.
Wallechinsky, David. *The Complete Book of the Olympics.* New York: Penguin Books, 1984.

MASAMUNE. (1265–1358). Japanese swordsmith.

The greatest of Japan's sword makers, Masamune was highly respected and loved by his countrymen. He produced weapons of the highest quality that were considered priceless by their owners.

It is said that the master cut off the hand of one of his pupils when the student covertly attempted to learn one of his secret blade-making techniques.

In spite of his incredible artistic skill, Masamune rarely signed or decorated his blades.

REFERENCE
Stone, George Cameron. *A Glossary of the Construction, Decoration, and Use of Arms and Armor.* New York: Jack Brussel, 1961.

MASK. Originally, men practiced the art of fencing without any type of protection. Eventually, blunted weapons were employed to minimize injury, but accidents still occurred.

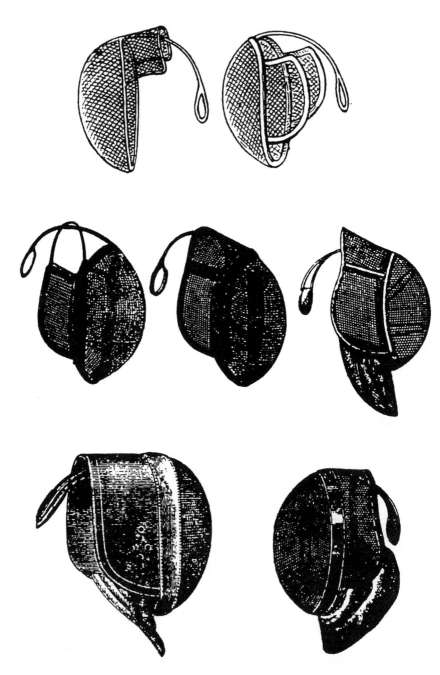

Various incarnations of the fencing mask

The fencing mask, invented by eighteenth-century fencing master La Boessiere* and the celebrated duelist the Chevalier de St. Georges.* These masks were constructed of metal, with wire openings for the eyes, and were tied on with strings.

Still, the mask did not meet with instant acceptance. Fencers continued to rely on their skill to keep from harming an opponent. With form and control becoming focal points of sword handling, a fencer would have been disgraced for life if he wounded an opponent.

Masks were not universally adopted until the end of the eighteenth century. By this time, they had assumed the wire mesh design seen today.

The modern fencing mask is subject to the regulations of the Federation Internationale d'Escrime.* Because of a growing number of serious accidents in the past few years regarding masks, special attention has been paid to the subject. Mask mesh for all fencing masks must be able to withstand a prescribed amount of pressure, the present designation now being twelve kilograms (26.4552 pounds). Also, the mask's bib* must be sewn in.

"Safety" masks with plexiglass faces have been designed but have never gone beyond the experimental stage. Their main drawback has been that they fog up easily when a fencer begins to exert himself.

Specialized masks are made for each weapon of fencing.

REFERENCES

Castle, Egerton. *Schools and Masters of Fence.* London: George Bell, 1885.
Clery, Raoul. "Apropos D'Un Accident." *American Fencing* (September/October 1983).
Palffy-Alpar, Julius. *Sword and Masque.* Philadelphia: F. A. Davis, 1967.

MASTERS OF DEFENSE. A company of English fencing masters incorporated by King Henry VIII in 1540. Divided into a number of levels of attainment—scholar, free scholar, provost, and master—the Masters of Defense had a virtual monopoly on the teaching of fencing in England for decades. The four senior masters of the group were called "the Four Ancient Masters." Their hold on the art of the sword was eventually destroyed by immigrating fencing masters from Italy.

REFERENCES

Castle, Egerton. *Schools and Masters of Fence.* London: George Bell, 1885.
Morton, E. D. *Martini A–Z of Fencing.* London: Queen Anne Press, 1992.

MAUPASSANT, GUY DE. (1850–1893). French short story writer and novelist.

A powerful writer of the human condition, Maupassant practiced his craft for over a decade, until his untimely death at the age of forty-two of syphilis.

It is not surprising that the subject of swordplay should find its way into Maupassant's writing, since he was an enthusiastic fencer and sometime duelist.

In his novel *Bel Ami* (1885), he devotes a number of pages to the description of a fencing tournament, giving the reader a good idea of what an old-time contest must have been like.

There were two professionals, two good second class teachers. They stepped onto the strip, both sparsely built, with military airs, and somewhat stiff motions. Having gone through the salute with machine-like movements they began to attack each other, resembling in their white costumes of duck and leather two soldier-pierrots fighting for fun.

From time to time one could hear the word "Touche!" and the six gentlemen of the jury nodded with the air of connoisseurs. The public saw nothing but two live puppets moving and extending arms; they understood nothing, but they were satisfied.

Maupassant has been called "one of the most moving story tellers of his time."

REFERENCES

Baldick, Robert. *The Duel.* New York: Spring Books, 1970.

Maupassant, Guy de. *Selected Short Stories.* Translated by Roger Colet. London: Penguin Books, 1971.

———. "The Exhibition." Translated by Peter Paret. *American Fencing* (September/October 1981).

MAYER, HELENE. (1910–1953). German-born amateur fencing champion.

Generally acknowledged as the greatest woman fencer who ever lived, if not one of the greatest fencers of all time, Helene Mayer was, at the height of her career, a world sports figure of vast importance.

Born in Offenbach, Germany, in 1910, of a Jewish father and a Christian mother, Helene Mayer showed an early affinity for the sport of fencing, developing a classical style out of the Italian-German school.

At the age of thirteen, she won the women's fencing championship of all Germany. At seventeen, she easily captured a gold medal at the 1928 Olympics in Amsterdam, Holland, winning eighteen bouts and losing only two. A year later, she became the women's fencing champion of the world. She repeated this feat again in 1931.

At the 1932 Olympics in Los Angeles, Mayer was not at her best. She finished fifth. This has been attributed to the stress from growing anti-Jewish sentiments in her homeland. After the games ended, these worries influenced a decision on her part to stay in America to study at Scripps College and later to teach German at Mills College in Oakland. Mayer's fears were not unfounded. In 1933, because of her parentage, she was officially (and publicly) removed from the rolls of her fencing school, the Offenbach Fencing Club.

With the approach of the 1936 Berlin "Nazi" Olympics,* controversy found its way into the sports world. Would Germany allow Jewish athletes to compete on its team? Should the United States boycott the games? For Helene Mayer, the issue grew complicated. As early as 1934, the U.S. Olympic Committee urged her to take part. Jewish groups in the United States attempted to dissuade her from fencing.

Back in Germany, while numerous Jewish athletes were being shunned, the

Fencing great Helene Mayer

Hitler regime suddenly did an about-face on the subject of Helene Mayer. Whether, as some say, it was because of pressure exerted by the U.S. government, or because Germany, in its quest to prove Nazi superiority to the world, was willing to disregard her ancestry in favor of her proven fencing skill is not completely clear. Perhaps it was a bit of both.

In 1935, Helene Mayer officially issued a statement announcing she would be pleased to represent Germany at the 1936 Olympics; furthermore, she said, she wanted to visit her family. Behind this tug-of-sports were rumors of veiled threats against her relatives if she did not comply with Germany's wishes. Was there any truth in this? No one really knows. Helene Mayer remained silent on the subject for the rest of her life.

Whatever the reality of the matter, when the games finally commenced, Helene Mayer was once again competing for Germany. Overshadowed today by the legendary exploits of runner Jesse Owens during the games, the German fencer's performance was among the most closely monitored of any athlete at the competition. Her last bout in the tournament, which was fought to a tie, was called "the most dramatic fencing match of the age."

When the fencing was over, there was a three-way tie for first place. To decide who was to get the gold medal, indicators (touches received versus touches delivered) were counted. Mayer ended up in second place, edged out narrowly by European champion Ilona Schacherer-Elek of Hungary.

Determined to win back her spot as the top fencer in the world, Helene Mayer, at great personal financial sacrifice, journeyed from her home in California to Paris for the 1937 World Fencing Championships. This time, she defeated all her opponents, including the 1936 Olympic champion. Having reestablished herself as the world's best woman fencer, she retired permanently from international competition.

On the U.S. fencing scene, Helene Mayer was virtually an unstoppable force. She entered the U.S. Nationals nine times between 1934 and 1947, winning eight of those competitions. After losing the 1947 women's foil championship in the last bout of the finals to, according to *American Fencer Magazine,* "an inspired Helene Dow," she never again fenced in this top U.S. tournament.

Although she had put the competitive life behind her, Mayer continued to fence at the San Francisco school of her longtime friend Hans Halberstadt. She kept this up until 1951, when she was diagnosed as having breast cancer. At this point, she was forced by her doctor to give up fencing completely.

In 1952, she returned to Germany for treatment for her affliction. There, she married (her first marriage) a Stuttgart engineer, Erwin Falkner von Sonnenburg.

Helene Mayer died on October 15, 1953, in Frankfurt, West Germany.

REFERENCES
De Capriles, Miguel. "Helene Mayer." *American Fencing* (January/February 1984).
Grombach, John V. *The 1972 Olympic Guide.* New York: Paperback Library, 1972.
Mandell, Richard D. *The Nazi Olympics.* New York: Macmillan, 1971.
Silver, Roy J., *Pursuit of Excellence: The Olympic Story.* Connecticut: Grolier Enterprises, 1983.
Wallechinsky, David. *The Complete Book of the Olympics.* New York: Penguin Books, 1984.

McARTHUR, JOHN. (c. 1750). British naval officer and fencing master.

McArthur is perhaps best known for his efforts to reestablish the British navy's use of the sword in combat enounters with the enemy. His efforts, however, were in vain.

McArthur wrote *The Army and Navy Gentleman's Companion* (1780), in which he focused on actual fighting techniques rather than theoretical niceties. He also recommended practicing while blindfolded to develop a feel for an opponent's weapon.

From John McArthur's *The Army and Navy Gentleman's Companion* (1780)

REFERENCES

Castle, Egerton. *Schools and Masters of Fence.* London: George Bell, 1885.

Wise, Arthur. *The Art and History of Personal Combat.* Greenwich, CT: Arma Press, 1971.

McBANE, DONALD. (c. 1720). Scottish fencing master.

Donald McBane was a professional swordsman and no gentleman. He received much of his early experience in actual encounters rather than a fencing school. But, finding himself in so many fights, he quickly decided to take lessons. In time, he became a fencing master.

Some years later, while serving in the British army on the Continent, McBain set about opening a string of establishments that combined fencing schools with brothels. But it was not until he fought twenty-four duels with competitors that he was able to gain a firm foothold in the business community.

Wrote McBain of this experience:

We set up all sorts of gaming Tents, we had not above sixty Campaign Ladies in the Quarters. Sixteen Professors of the Sword resolved to go to the Emperor's Quarters where we got fourteen brave Dutch Lasses as a reinforcement. Next day came twenty-four Swordsmen and demanded the Ladies again. We had a drink, fought Two and Two, eleven Dutch killed and seven of our Men. I fought eight running, we buried our Dead and parted.

After leaving the military, McBane became a champion prizefighter (when prizefights involved swords). He fought thirty-seven times. In his last fight, at the age of sixty-four—sporting a silver plate in his head—he wounded his opponent seven times and broke his arm with his sword.

McBane's main advice to his pupils: "Trust nobody."

His fencing style basically concentrated on the physical: constant movement, beats, and short lunges that made recovery a simple task. "Four or five inches of steel," he noted, "discourage an adversary just as much as a thrust clean through the body."

In 1728, McBane wrote *The Expert Sword-Man's Companion.***

REFERENCES

Castle, Egerton. *Schools and Masters of Fence.* London: George Bell, 1885.

Wise, Arthur. *The Art and History of Personal Combat.* Greenwich, CT: Arma Press, 1971.

MEASURE. In old-time fencing, "measure" referred to distance.* Proper measure meant, essentially (1) never attempting an attack without being within striking distance and (2) keeping out of easy reach of an opponent when on the defensive. It was, as one might expect, considered the most important aspect of swordplay.

Today, distance is simply called distance. Measure has a new meaning: the length of time it takes to complete a fencing movement.

REFERENCES

Castle, Egerton. *Schools and Masters of Fence.* London: George Bell, 1885.

Palffy-Alpar, Julius. *Sword and Masque.* Philadelphia: F. A. Davis, 1967.

MEDIOTAJO. In the seventeenth-century Spanish style of fencing, *mediotajo* was a cut from the elbow.

REFERENCE

Castle, Egerton. *Schools and Masters of Fence.* London: George Bell, 1885.

MEDIO TAJO Y MEDIO REVES. In the Spanish style of swordplay as described by seventeenth-century fencing master Don Luis Pacheco de Narvaez,* these were half-cuts, or reverses, specifically, flipping cuts made, in turn, from the right or the left.

REFERENCE

Castle, Egerton. *Schools and Masters of Fence.* London: George Bell, 1885.

MEI. In Japan, the name of a sword maker inscribed on his work.

REFERENCE

Stone, George Cameron. *A Glossary of the Construction, Decoration, and Use of Arms and Armor.* New York: Jack Brussel, 1961.

MEL PUTTAH BEMOH. A sword of southern India.

The *mel puttah bemoh* was a two-handed sword,* with a long, rapierlike* blade, two guards* (the lower one round, the upper one shaped like a figure eight), and a large pommel* to offset the weight of the blade.

REFERENCE

Stone, George Cameron. *A Glossary of the Construction, Decoration, and Use of Arms and Armor.* New York: Jack Brussel, 1961.

MENSUR. The name for the dueling carried on by German students in the nineteenth century.
REFERENCE
Morton, E. D. *Martini A–Z of Fencing*. London: Queen Anne Press, 1992.

MENTOK. A sword of Java.
The *mentok* had a slightly curved blade, widest near the tip.
REFERENCE
Stone, George Cameron. *A Glossary of the Construction, Decoration, and Use of Arms and Armor*. New York: Jack Brussel, 1961.

MENUKI. Ornaments on the sides of a Japanese sword hilt.*
Also called *menugi.*
REFERENCE
Stone, George Cameron. *A Glossary of the Construction, Decoration, and Use of Arms and Armor*. New York: Jack Brussel, 1961.

MEYER, JOACHIM. (c. 1550). German fencing master.
A member of the famed Marxbruder* fencing society, Meyer was one of Germany's most celebrated teachers of swordplay. But, while ostensibly devoted to the use of the national weapons of his homeland—the two-handed sword* and the *dusack*—he was not above traveling to Italy to learn the workings of the rapier when it began its sweep across Europe. Indeed, Meyer was doubtlessly most responsible for introducing the thrusting weapon to German fencing.
In 1570, Meyer wrote his celebrated volume on fencing, *Grundtliche Beschreibung der freyen Ritterlichen und Adelichen kunst der Fechtens in allerly gebreuchlichen Wehren mit vil schonen und nutzlichten Figuren gezieret und furgestellet.***
REFERENCES
Castle, Egerton. *Schools and Masters of Fence*. London: George Bell, 1885.
Wise, Arthur. *The Art and History of Personal Combat*. Greenwich, CT: Arma Press, 1971.

MEZZA CAVAZIONE. An Italian term for passing from the high line* to the low line* with one's blade.
Originally, the term, as used by sixteenth-century Italian fencing master Salvator Fabris,* was *meggia cavatione.*
REFERENCE
Castle, Egerton. *Schools and Masters of Fence*. London: George Bell, 1885.

MEZZO CERCHIO. An old Italian name for a parry* covering the low-inside line,* with the sword hand held in supination.
Also called a "half-circle."
REFERENCE
Castle, Egerton. *Schools and Masters of Fence*. London: George Bell, 1885.

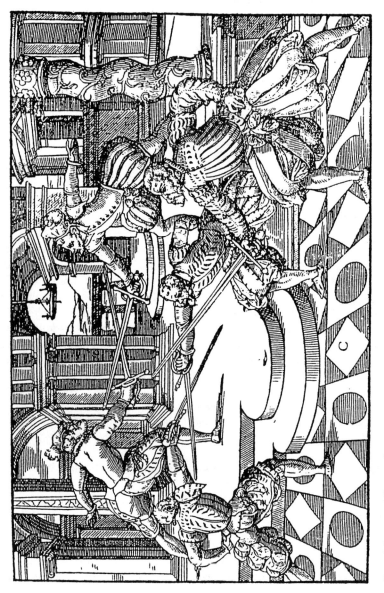

Swordplay according to German master Joachim Meyer

MEZZO DRITTO. According to seventeenth-century Italian fencing master Francesco Alfieri,* a time thrust delivered to the wrist of an opponent.
REFERENCE
Castle, Egerton. *Schools and Masters of Fence.* London: George Bell, 1885.

MEZZO TEMPO. As described by Italian fencing master Marco Doccolini* in 1601: ''When thine enemy thrusts at thee, break [block] thou his thrust, striking him at the same time.''
Basically a ''time hit.''*
REFERENCE
Castle, Egerton. *Schools and Masters of Fence.* London: George Bell, 1885.

MI. In Japanese, a blade.
REFERENCE
Stone, George Cameron. *A Glossary of the Construction, Decoration, and Use of Arms and Armor.* New York: Jack Brussel, 1961.

MICHELANGELO. (1475–1564). Italian artist of the Renaissance.
Aside from creating countless works of art—such as painting the Sistine Chapel, sculpting the *Pieta,* and designing the dome for St. Peter's basilica—Michelangelo found time to engage in the study and practice of fencing.
Also, many of the illustrations in the fencing book by Camillo Agrippa*—*Trattato di scienta d'arme* (1553)**—have been attributed to the famed artist.
REFERENCES
Castle, Egerton. *Schools and Masters of Fence.* London: George Bell, 1885.
Heusinger, Lutz. *Michelangelo.* Florence: Officine Grafiche, 1972.

MIFUNE, TOSHIRO. (1920–   ). Japanese actor.
Toshiro Mifune is one of Japan's greatest† and most versatile actors. Best known for his roles in samurai films, he projects a strength of character that can never be misunderstood. His characterizations are never one-dimensional and often possess an ironic sense of humor.
Mifune's skill with the sword, while admittedly a theatrical invention, is, nevertheless, a joy to behold. Watching him work, it is entirely understandable why he has become Japan's greatest film swordsman.
While Mifune's gruff, loner samurai character in *Yojimbo* (1961) and *Sanjuro* (1962) is quite possibly his most popular creation, his most inspiring performance came in *The Samurai Trilogy* (1954/1955), based on the novel *Musashi* (1935–1939) by Eiji Yoshikawa.
The films—*Samurai, Duel at Ichijoji Temple,* and *Musashi and Kojiro*—also starring Kaoru Yachigusa, Mariko Okada, Kuroemon Onoe, Takashi Shimura, and Koji Tsuruta, tell the story of Japan's greatest swordsman, Miyamoto Musashi,* as he progresses from his earliest times as a brutal, undisciplined boy to his eventual metamorphosis into a mature warrior.

In the opening film, Musashi (Mifune) is directed onto his path of understanding by an old priest who locks him in a cell filled with philosophy books. Here, he learns Bushido, the code of the samurai.

The second film deals with Musashi's famous duel at the Ichijoji Temple, where he single-handedly crosses swords with dozens of armed foes.

Musashi meets his greatest opponent, Kojiro Sasaki, in the final film. In a monumental duel on Ganryu Island, Musashi battles and defeats Kojiro with a wooden sword he has fashioned from a boat oar.

Other Mifune film credits include *Roshomon* (1950), *Pirates* (1951), *Sword for Hire* (1952), *Seven Samurai* (1954), *Rainy Night Duel* (1956), *Throne of Blood* (1957), *Yagyu Secret Scroll* (1957), *The Hidden Fortress* (1958), *Gambling Samurai* (1960), *Daredevil in the Castle* (1961), *The Loyal Forty-Seven Ronin* (1962), *Samurai Pirate* (1964), *Samurai Assassin* (1965), *Rise Against the Sword* (1966), *Samurai Banners* (1969), *Band of Assassins* (1970), *Red Sun* (1971), and *Zatoichi Meets Yojimbo* (1971).

REFERENCES

Katz, Ephram. *The Film Encyclopedia.* New York: Perigee Books, 1979.

Mintz, Marilyn. *The Martial Arts Film.* New York: A. S. Barnes, 1978.

MILITARY SWORDS. Swords designed especially for use in warfare.

Military swords have always been plainer and bulkier than swords whose expressed purpose was civilian-style combat. Certainly, the possibility of encountering less intricate fighting techniques on the battlefield argued against the need for complicated sword designs. Too, because the emphasis on the battlefield was always on function, elaborate designs were a needless extravagance. The heaviness of military blades, of course, kept them from breaking under stress.

Massive, two-handed swords,* by their very nature, were ideal for pitched encounters. A man wielding a sword with a five- or six-foot-long blade could cut a wide swath in enemy lines. Later, however, as the nature of warfare demanded a more mobile soldiery, less ponderous weapons became a must.

The sturdy basket-hilted broadsword* became a favorite military weapon by the seventeenth century. Used extensively during the English civil wars of 1642–1648, they were employed by both Royalist and Roundhead cavalry regiments. Later, the style was preserved among the Scottish Highlanders following Bonnie Prince Charlie in his attempt to regain the English throne for the house of Stuart in 1745. Sometimes called the claymore,* it has become the sword most associated with Scotland.

British infantrymen carried swords until 1786, when—with the exception of a few Scottish regiments—they were withdrawn from use by enlisted men. Officers, however, continued to carry blades (of the smallsword variety) as a sign of their leadership.

Hefty sabres* became standard cavalry issue. Heavy cavalry units carried straight-bladed swords. Light cavalry units possessed broad, slightly curved-bladed weapons with a simple, rounded hand guard. During the early nineteenth century, sabres with a pronounced curve in their blade and a narrower hand guard were the common design.

World War I saw the last swords being carried into combat, when—faced by the murderous efficiency of modern weapons of destruction, like the machine gun—they were abandoned as so much excess weight.

Today, by and large, military swords have been relegated to the level of ceremonial decorations.

REFERENCE
Wilkinson, Frederick. *Swords and Daggers.* New York: Hawthorn Books, 1967.

MISERICORDE. The "dagger of mercy."

The *misericorde* was carried to administer the coup de grace** to a fallen adversary. It had a long narrow blade well suited for thrusting between armor plates.

Simply the visual threat of the *misericorde* was often used to induce an enemy to give up struggling and beg for his life.

REFERENCES
Castle, Egerton. *Schools and Masters of Fence.* London: George Bell, 1885.
Stone, George Cameron. *A Glossary of the Construction, Decoration, and Use of Arms and Armor.* New York: Jack Brussel, 1961.

MISURA LARGA. As explained by sixteenth-century Italian fencing master Salvator Fabris,* *misura larga* (wide measure) referred to being at a fencing distance where an adversary could be hit by taking a single step forward.

REFERENCE
Castle, Egerton. *Schools and Masters of Fence.* London: George Bell, 1885.

MISURA STRETTA. Salvator Fabris,* sixteenth-century Italian fencing master, defined *misura stretta* (close measure) as being at a fencing distance where one would be able to hit an opponent simply by extending the sword arm. This distance was not to be attempted without immediately delivering a thrust or making a feint to ward off a time hit.

REFERENCE
Castle, Egerton. *Schools and Masters of Fence.* London: George Bell, 1885.

MONOKIRI. In Japan, the edge of a sword blade.

REFERENCE
Stone, George Cameron. *A Glossary of the Construction, Decoration, and Use of Arms and Armor.* New York: Jack Brussel, 1961.

MONTANT. A sixteenth-century English term for an upward cut.

REFERENCE
Morton, E. D. *Martini A-Z of Fencing.* London: Queen Anne Press, 1992.

MONTANTE. An Italian term referring to a vertical cut delivered upward.
REFERENCE
Morton, E. D. *Martini A-Z of Fencing.* London: Queen Anne Press, 1992.

MONTANTE SOTTO MANO. An ascending cut with the false edge of a sword blade, according to seventeenth-century Italian fencing master Giuseppi Pallavicini.*
REFERENCE
Castle, Egerton. *Schools and Masters of Fence.* London: George Bell, 1885.

MONTANTO. An early Italian name for a cutting sword.
REFERENCE
Morton, E. D. *Martini A-Z of Fencing.* London: Queen Anne Press, 1992.

MONTE CRISTO FILMS. Alexandre Dumas's* classic novel *The Count of Monte Cristo* (1844) has furnished the movies with much material, some of it more fantastic than even Dumas himself might have imagined.

The original story was not a swashbuckling tale but a romantic melodrama dealing with the theme of revenge. Edmond Dantes, a young man falsely charged with a political crime, is sentenced to life imprisonment in the Chateau D'If. He eventually escapes—twenty years later—and, with the aid of a treasure he finds on the island of Monte Cristo (bequeathed to him by an elderly prison mate, the Abbe Faria), he carries out an intricate plan of revenge against those who wronged him. Some swordplay ensues, although it is not of a dashing nature, as in *The Three Musketeers* (1844),* but rather a plainly grim affair. In the end, Dantes completes his act of vengeance but finds it a joyless, hollow victory.

Of course, when the movies got hold of the book, it was inevitable that the approach to the work should be one of adventure. The story of Edmond Dantes was filmed fourteen times: in 1908, 1910, 1911, 1912 (twice), 1915, 1917, 1922, 1934, 1943, 1954, 1955, 1961, and 1975.

The most successful *The Count of Monte Cristo* film, by far, was the 1934 version, starring Robert Donat, Elissa Landi, Louis Calhern, and Sidney Blackmar. Following a much pruned down story line, Edmond Dantes is even allowed to have a happy Hollywood ending, bravely vanquishing his foes and winning the girl.

Dantes meets one of his adversaries, Mondego, in a sword duel. Staged by fencing master Fred Cavens,* the fight, while fast-paced, is somewhat rigid. At one point, apparently to add some "variety" to the scene, the film print was merely reversed, causing the combatants to suddenly—and inexplicably—become left-handed.

Not content with reworking the original story, Hollywood set about milking the theme for all it was worth. In time, the Count of Monte Cristo's entire assemblage of descendants was called upon to pick up the sword and further the swashbuckling heritage begun by their movie-altered predecessor.

Following the illustrious Count came *The Son of Monte Cristo* (1940), *The Return of Monte Cristo* (1946), *The Wife of Monte Cristo* (1946), *Sword of the Avenger* (1948), *The Treasure of Monte Cristo* (1949), *Sword of Monte Cristo* (1951), *Island of Monte Cristo* (1952), *Mask of the Avenger* (1953), and another *The Treasure of Monte Cristo* (1960).

Swordplay, as to be expected, played an important part in most of these yarns—some of it good, some of it not so good.

REFERENCES

Dumas, Alexandre. *The Count of Monte Cristo.* New York: Thomas Y. Crowell, 1901.

Richards, Jeffrey. *Swordsmen of the Screen.* Boston: Routledge and Kegan Paul, 1977.

MORTUARY SWORD. Many British basket-hilted* military swords of the mid-seventeenth century were decorated with embossed heads that, some believed, represented the executed King Charles I of England. For this reason, these weapons were described as mortuary swords.

REFERENCE

Wilkinson, Frederick. *Swords and Daggers.* New York: Hawthorn Books, 1967.

MOTET. (c. 1730). French fencing master.

The fencing teacher of Henry Angelo* (son of the famed Domenico Angelo*). Motet, situated in Paris, was known all over Europe for the strength of his parry. He was, for his time, a highly popular fencing master.

REFERENCE

Castle, Egerton. *Schools and Masters of Fence.* London: George Bell, 1885.

MOULINET. A French term meaning "small mill," "turnstile," or "winch," that is, something possessing a circular, turning movement.

In fencing, specifically sabre fencing, a *moulinet* is a circular action of the blade that moves, first, toward and, then, away from the body. It is guided specifically by a swing of the forearm and a rotation of the wrist.

The *moulinet* could be employed in the execution of an attack (to add a spectacular flurry to the action) or when defending (creating a response that encompassed both a parry and a counterattack in a single, flowing arc).

An integral part of the Italian style of sabre play common to the early part of the twentieth century, the *moulinet* has since become obsolete. As sabre fencers sought to develop an approach to their weapon encompassing tighter, more economic movement, the *moulinet*—with its wide, sweeping nature that, on reflection, continually exposed the sword arm to stop hits—fell into disfavor.

Today, the *moulinet* has been relegated, by and large, to the realm of spectacular theatrical fencing moves.

Also called a "bastard *molinello*," or a "whirl."

REFERENCE

Palffy-Alpar, Julius. *Sword and Masque.* Philadelphia: F. A. Davis, 1967.

MOVIE FENCING TECHNIQUES. Fencing in the movies can be divided into two categories: theatrical style and historical style.

The theatrical method ends up being a compendium of everything that has ever been known about fencing—moves strung together in a way to produce a dramatic and artistic effect. This includes fencing techniques that might be anachronistic to a film's represented time period (i.e., a full lunge during the Middle Ages). When done well, the end product could be likened to a dance routine.

Said Fred Cavens,* Hollywood's most successful arranger of sword fights during Hollywood's golden age: "The routine should contain the most spectacular attacks and parries it is possible to execute while remaining logical to the situation. In other words, the duel should be a fight and not a fencing exhibition, and should disregard at times classically correct guards and lunges."

Good examples of the theatrical style of movie fencing can be found in *The Prisoner of Zenda* (1937),** *The Adventures of Robin Hood* (1938),** *The Mark of Zorro* (1940),** *The Three Musketeers* (1948),** *The Court Jester* (1956),** and *The Princess Bride* (1987).**

The historical style is a more modern approach to movie fencing. It attempts, as closely as possible, to reproduce swordplay as it might have been in bygone days, stripping away the romance of the sword by showing it for what it was— a device for killing. The overall effect, brutal and ugly as it might be, can produce a highly effective dramatic statement. Such a view of fencing can be found in *Romeo and Juliet* (1968), *The Four Musketeers* (1975),** *Robin and Marian* (1976), and *The Duellists* (1977).**

Yet, as observed by William Hobbs,* one of the leading exponents of the historical movie duel: "One should, however, let the period play a secondary part to what is theatrical. If a fast-moving and exciting fight is required . . . and the correct stance on the period tends to hamper the movement, then it is best to compromise."

There is, of course, room for both types of movie fencing. Ultimately, the deciding factor of which type to use is what sort of atmosphere is to be arrived at—lighthearted swashbuckling or serious, deadly violence.

REFERENCES

Halliwell, Leslie. *Halliwell's Filmgoer's and Video Viewer's Companion.* New York: Charles Scribner's Sons, 1988.

Hobbs, William. *Techniques of the Stage Fight.* London: Studio Vista, 1967.

Richards, Jeffrey. *Swordsmen of the Screen.* Boston: Routledge and Kegan Paul, 1977.

MOVIES, FENCING IN. The sword has always commanded a unique place in the world of the cinema. From the silent days of Douglas Fairbanks, Sr., to the present, swordplay and fencing have become synonymous with romance and adventure, brave deeds and justice.

Early attempts at fencing in movies have been characterized as little more than disorganized "knife sharpenings" by film expert Rudy Behlmer in his article, "Swordplay on the Screen" (*Films in Review,* 1965). But, in 1920, Hollywood finally began to take its staged sword encounters seriously. Douglas Fairbanks, Sr.'s,* *The Mark of Zorro*** is generally regarded as the first film to employ an actual fencing master to stage its fight scenes. Henry Uyttenhove,* a Belgian master who, at the time, was coaching at the Los Angeles Athletic Club, was hired to do the honors. While the action was rather primitive by today's standards, it was still the first time distinct fencing moves could be discerned in a filmed sword duel. Uyttenhove also handled the fencing in *The Three Musketeers* (1921)** and *Robin Hood* (1922).**

As movie techniques in general improved, so did the filmed depiction of fencing. By the mid-1920s, swordplay was as expertly choreographed as dance routines, mostly due to the efforts of one man, fencing master Fred Cavens.* Cavens knew how to handle actors. Above all, he had a sense of drama and timing that translated well before a movie camera. He stressed proper technique enhanced by the spectacular, and this formula rarely failed him. In such classics as *The Black Pirate* (1926),** *The Adventures of Robin Hood* (1938),** *The Sea Hawk* (1940),** *The Mark of Zorro* (1940),** *The Adventures of Don Juan* (1949),** and *Cyrano de Bergerac* (1950),** we find instances of some of the best swordplay Hollywood has ever produced, action that never falters in its flow toward a satisfying resolution or strays from its intent to be anything other than what it is meant to be.

In the 1930s and 1940s, much time was given over to preparing actors—the Errol Flynns and Basil Rathbones and Tyrone Powers—for their roles as film swordsmen. If they did not look good while they fenced, the movie did not look good. Of course, they did not have to be experts. Fred Cavens once noted that he knew Olympic fencing champions who had such poor form that audiences would have laughed at them. Actors needed just enough fencing knowledge coupled with grace and form.

This was clearly demonstrated when dancer Gene Kelly took on the role of D'Artagnan in the 1948 version of *The Three Musketeers.*** While not an experienced fencer, the grace and timing Kelly brought to his part from years of dancing made his athletic performance with a sword, staged by fight arranger Jean Heremans, one of the most memorable ever captured on film.

Fencing master Ralph Faulkner,* known in Hollywood for over fifty years as "swordsman to the stars," put together countless fencing scenes for films. He was a stickler for preparing his actors with proper training. Planning duels often took weeks. Shooting them sometimes took months.

Faulkner, who guided the sword clashes in major productions like *The Prisoner of Zenda* (1937),** *The Thief of Bagdad* (1940), *The Bandit of Sherwood Forest* (1946),** and *The Court Jester* (1956),** believed it was essential to instruct his actors in the basics of fencing, not just give them a strung-together set of meaningless moves to practice. He likened learning to fence to learning a foreign language, and if an actor could readily "speak" fencing, he would be able to establish a sense of realism in his performance that audiences would perceive and appreciate.

While big budgets often ensured quality film swordplay, neat little fencing scenes sometimes turned up in lesser-quality productions if the action was handled by someone in the know. Such instances occur in *Frenchman's Creek* (1944), *Prince of Foxes* (1949), *Mark of the Renegade* (1951), *The Black Castle* (1952), and *The Purple Mask* (1955).

One device that was used extensively in the 1930s and 1940s to enhance fencing scenes was "undercranking." This is the procedure of passing film through a camera at a slower than normal rate of speed so that it records fewer frames of movement per second. When the film is then shown at a normal running speed, the action speeds up. In many cases, as in *The Corsican Brothers* (1941),** this produced a pleasing effect of lightning-fast combat. Occasionally, however, when undercranking was overdone, the subsequent speedup could create a cartoonlike display of movement. Undercranking was an involved process, and only by rehearsing scenes carefully was it likely to be successful.

By and large, films have taken a very theatrical approach when it comes to fencing. While the assembled actions may be correct in terms of basic technique, the final product is often an exaggerated compilation of everything that has ever been learned about fencing. Authenticity of style with regard to history has often been sacrificed in favor of the dramatic. A lunge, which did not appear until the 1500s, might turn up in a medieval sword fight. Or a twentieth-century fencing sabre might be used in a nineteenth-century duel.

In recent years, there has been a growing trend in the staging of movie fencing to produce historically correct fights with regard to both technique and weapons. While this has not always created a pleasing effect, *The Three Musketeers* (1974)** and its sequel, *The Four Musketeers* (1975),** are two films in which history and theatricality were blended successfully. The fencing, arranged by British fencing master William Hobbs, projected a feeling of what dueling might have been like in the 1600s and still preserved the lighthearted swashbuckling flavor of Alexandre Dumas's classic story.

Another film to follow this line was *The Duellists* (1977). Lacking any sense of romance, this film focuses on the ugly side of dueling. Sabre fights, smallsword exchanges, swordplay on horseback, and pistol duels highlight the action. The encounters are strained, bloody affairs, underlining the true savage nature of personal combat.

It is unfortunate that much of the fencing being produced for films today—regardless of its historical or theatrical intent—lacks the flair of yesterday's efforts. The reasons vary. Because of insufficient time spent in preparation, a shortage of money, ignorance, or just plain incompetence, necessary attention is not always given to the details in scenes where broadsword, rapier, or sabre are to be employed. The results of such projects can be sadly unconvincing, as in *Master Gunfighter* (1975), *Swashbuckler* (1976), *The Fifth Musketeer* (1977), *The Last Re-Make of Beau Geste* (1977), *Zorro, the Gay Blade* (1981), *The Pirate Movie* (1982), *Nate and Hayes* (1983), *Yellowbeard* (1983), and *Pirates* (1985).

Still, the ability to interject old-time style into movie swordplay is not beyond some of today's filmmakers. This has been proven by artistically successful vehicles such as the *Star Wars* movies (1977, 1980, and 1983), *The Princess Bride* (1987), *Willow* (1988), *Hook* (1991), and *By the Sword* (1993).

Other films in which swordplay of varying degrees of quality appears include:

To Have and to Hold (1922)

Trifling Women (1922)

Monte Cristo (1922)

The Three Must-Get-Theres (1922)

Rupert of Hentzau (1923)

Ashes of Vengeance (1923)

The Fighting Blade (1923)

Dangerous Maid (1923)

Monsieur Beaucaire (1924)

Dorothy Vernon of Haddon Hall (1924)

The Sea Hawk (1924)

Don Q, Son of Zorro (1925)

Dick Turpin (1925)

Don Juan (1926)

Bardleys the Magnificent (1926)

Senorita (1927)

When a Man Loves (1927)

The Fighting Eagle (1927)

She's a Sheik (1928)

The Iron Mask (1929)

The Private Life of Don Juan (1934)

Treasure Island (1934)

The Count of Monte Cristo (1934)

Cleopatra (1934)

The Crusades (1935)

The Three Musketeers (1935)

Captain Blood (1935)

The Prince and the Pauper (1936)

Anthony Adverse (1936)

Romeo and Juliet (1936)

Fire over England (1936)

The Bold Caballero (1937)

Under the Red Robe (1937)

If I Were King (1938)

Zorro's Fighting Legion (1939)

The Man in the Iron Mask (1939)

The Three Musketeers (1939)

Flash Gordon (1940)

The Son of Monte Cristo (1940)

The Black Swan (1942)

Arabian Nights (1942)

Henry V (1944)

Gipsy Wildcat (1944)

Ali Baba and the Forty Thieves (1944)

The Spanish Main (1945)

Captain Kidd (1945)

The Return of Monte Cristo (1946)

The Gallant Blade (1946)

The Exile (1946)

Monsieur Beaucaire (1946)

Captain from Castile (1947)

The Swordsman (1947)

The Foxes of Harrow (1947)

The Gallant Blade (1947)

Forever Amber (1948)

Sword of the Avenger (1948)

Hamlet (1948)

The Black Arrow (1948)

The Adventures of Casanova (1948)

Joan of Arc (1948)

Port Said (1948)

Macbeth (1948)

The Adventures of Don Juan (1948)

Black Magic (1949)

The Fighting O'Flynn (1949)

Pirates of Capri (1949)

Lorna Doone (1950)

Rogues of Sherwood Forest (1950)

The Fortunes of Captain Blood (1950)

Tripoli (1950)

The Flame and the Arrow (1950)

Barbary Pirate (1950)

Bagdad (1950)

The Desert Hawk (1950)

Mask of the Avenger (1951)

Anne of the Indies (1951)

Flame of Araby (1951)

Quo Vadis (1951)

The Prince Who Was a Thief (1951)

Ivanhoe (1951)

Captain Horatio Hornblower (1951)

The Sign of Zorro (1951)

The Sword of D'Artagnan (1952)

The Prisoner of Zenda (1952)

Jack and the Beanstalk (1952)

Scaramouche (1952)

The Crimson Pirate (1952)

Son of Ali Baba (1952)

The Brigand (1952)

At Sword's Point (1952)

Against All Flags (1952)

The Golden Hawk (1952)

Captain Phantom (1953)

Knights of the Round Table (1953)

The Master of Ballantrae (1953)

Mississippi Gambler (1953)

Veils of Bagdad (1953)

The Iron Mistress (1953)

Crossed Swords (1953)

The Sword and the Rose (1953)

Captain Scarlet (1953)

Casanova's Big Night (1954)

Prince Valiant (1954)

The Black Knight (1954)

Bandits of Corsica (1954)

The Golden Blade (1954)

The Saracen Blade (1954)

Valley of the Kings (1954)

Princess of the Nile (1954)

Prince of Pirates (1954)

Captain Kidd and the Slave Girl (1954)

The Iron Glove (1954)

The Student Prince (1954)

Quentin Durward (1955)

Star of India (1955)

Pirates of Tripoli (1955)

The Black Shield of Falworth (1955)

The Warriors (1955)

Diane (1955)

The Conqueror (1956)

Richard III (1956)

The Swan (1956)

Son of Robin Hood (1958)

The Seventh Voyage of Sinbad (1958)

The Vikings (1958)

The Moonraker (1958)

Dangerous Exile (1958)

Morgan the Pirate (1960)

The Sign of Zorro (1960)

Zorro the Avenger (1960)

Robin Hood and the Pirates (1960)

The Hellfire Club (1960)

Spartacus (1960)

Fury at Smuggler's Bay (1960)

The Thief of Bagdad (1960)

Sword of Sherwood Forest (1961)

Snow White and the Three Stooges (1961)

Swordsman of Siena (1961)

El Cid (1961)

Jack the Giant Killer (1961)

Duel of the Titans (1961)

Duel at the Rio Grande (1962)

Sodom and Gomorrah (1962)

The Shadow of Zorro (1962)

Battles of the Gladiators (1962)

The Pirates of Blood River (1962)

The Magic Sword (1962)

Marco Polo (1962)

Seven Seas to Calais (1962)

Captain Sinbad (1962)

Son of Captain Blood (1962)

Zorro Versus Maciste (1963)

Tom Jones (1963)

The Castilian (1963)

Jason and the Argonauts (1963)

Zorro at the Court of Spain (1963)

Comedy of Terrors (1963)

California (1963)

Zorro and the Three Musketeers (1963)

Arrow of the Avenger (1963)

Sword of Lancelot (1963)

The Scarlet Blade (1964)

Cyrano and D'Artagnan (1964)

The Great Race (1965)

The War Lord (1965)

El Greco (1966)

The King's Pirate (1967)

The Assassination Bureau (1968)

Romeo and Juliet (1968)

Julius Caesar (1969)

Start the Revolution Without Me (1970)

The Love Machine (1971)

Macbeth (1971)

Kidnapped (1972)

Theatre of Blood (1973)

The Golden Voyage of Sinbad (1973)

The Mark of Zorro (1974)

The Count of Monte Cristo (1975)

Monty Python and the Holy Grail (1975)

Royal Flash (1975)

Wind and the Lion (1975)

Sherlock Holmes's Smarter Brother (1975)

Zorro (1975)

Barry Lyndon (1975)

Robin and Marian (1976)

The Seven Per Cent Solution (1976)

Prince and the Pauper (1977)

The Man in the Iron Mask (1977)

Sinbad and the Eye of the Tiger (1977)

The Bastard (1978)

Hawk the Slayer (1980)

Excalibur (1981)

Conan the Barbarian (1982)

My Favorite Year (1982)

Sword and the Sorcerer (1982)

Swords of the Wayland (1983)

My Wicked, Wicked Ways (1983)

Monty Python's Meaning of Life (1983)

Conan the Destroyer (1984)

The Corsican Brothers (1984)

Warrior and the Sorceress (1984)

Sword of the Valiant (1984)

The Highlander (1985)

The Mission (1986)

Jewel of the Nile (1986)

Masters of the Universe (1987)

Outrageous Fortune (1987)

Without A Clue (1988)

Dangerous Liaisons (1988)

Henry V (1989)

Cyrano de Bergerac (1990)

Treasure Island (1990)

Robin Hood, Prince of Thieves (1991)

Highlander II (1991)

Merlin and the Crystal (1991)

Robin Hood (1991)

The Addams Family (1992)

Stay Tuned (1992)

By the Sword (1993)

The Three Musketeers (1993)

Ring of Steel (1993)

REFERENCES
Behlmer, Rudy. "Swordplay on the Screen." *Films in Review* (June/July 1965).
Halliwell, Leslie. *Halliwell's Filmgoer's and Video Viewer's Companion.* New York: Charles Scribner's Sons, 1988.
Maltin, Leonard. *Leonard Maltin's Movie and Video Guide: 1993.* New York: Penguin Books, 1993.
Richards, Jeffrey. *Swordsmen of the Screen.* Boston: Routledge and Kegan Paul, 1977.
Thomas, Tony. *The Great Adventure Films.* Secaucus, NJ: Citadel Press, 1976.

MOZART, WOLFGANG. (1756–1791). Austrian composer.

Mozart has been called the greatest composer of classical music of all time, a musical genius. As a child prodigy, he astounded Europe with his musical skills. As an adult, his output has never been equaled for creativity and power.

As a child of thirteen, Mozart was known to take fencing lessons, doubtlessly encouraged by his father to give his son a physical outlet for his abundant energies and to round out his personality, fencing, by that time, being considered a character-building activity.

REFERENCE
Bishop, Claire Huchet. *Mozart: Music Magician.* IL: Garrard, 1968.

MUETTE. A fencing lesson given without verbal commands.

Also known as a "silent lesson."

REFERENCE
Handelman, Rob. "Fencing Glossary." *American Fencing* (May/June 1978).

MUNE. The back of a Japanese sword blade.

There are three shapes: *maramune* (rounded), *mitsumune* (three-sided), and *iboremune* (shaped like the roof of a small temple).

Also called *mine.*

REFERENCE
Stone, George Cameron. *A Glossary of the Construction, Decoration, and Use of Arms and Armor.* New York: Jack Brussel, 1961.

MUNI-UCHI. Striking the back of a Japanese sword blade.
REFERENCE
Stone, George Cameron. *A Glossary of the Construction, Decoration, and Use of Arms and Armor.* New York: Jack Brussel, 1961.

MURAMASA. (c. 1340). Japanese sword maker.

While an undisputed master craftsman, Muramasa is often left off the lists of celebrated sword makers because of the unsavory reputation of the weapons he produced. It was said that Muramasa blades were bad luck, thirsting continually for blood. Always restless in their scabbards, they supposedly impelled their owners to kill others or to commit suicide.

Only the blade maker Masamune* produced swords of a higher quality.
REFERENCE
Stone, George Cameron. *A Glossary of the Construction, Decoration, and Use of Arms and Armor.* New York: Jack Brussel, 1961.

MUSASHI, MIYAMOTO. (1584–1645). Japanese swordsman.

Known as Kensei, or sword saint, Miyamoto Musashi is by far Japan's most celebrated swordsman. It was Musashi's quest to develop perfect technique with his sword, and he set about the task by engaging in duel after duel. By the age of thirty, he had fought and won more than sixty sword fights.

Musashi's most famous contest took place in 1612, against his arch rival Sasaki Kojiro. Kojiro had developed a deadly fencing technique known as Tsu-bame-gaeshi (swallow counter), patterned after a swallow's tail in flight, and it was long argued which man was the better fighter. It was inevitable that the two should meet, and eventually a contest was arranged to take place on a small island off the coast of Japan. In preparation for the fight, Musashi fashioned a wooden sword* out of an oar as he sat in the boat being rowed across to the island. It was Musashi's belief that a skilled swordsman could fight with any object and win. When the two enemies met on the beach, Kojiro greeted Musashi by throwing his scabbard dramatically into the sea. Musashi, seizing on this psychological moment, taunted Kojiro that he had already lost the fight, for he knew he no longer had need of the sheath. Kojiro, enraged, rushed at Musahi, who brought the oar down on his foe's head, killing him instantly.

After that, Mushashi retired from his life as a duelist and set about formulating his personal philosophy of the sword. In 1645, he wrote *A Book of Five Rings,*** which discussed, in detail, his beliefs about the nature of combat strategy, both individual and on a large scale. He died a few weeks after the volume was completed.

Musashi's life has been dramatized numerous times over the years in book and film.
REFERENCES
Musashi, Miyamoto. *A Book of Five Rings.* Translated by Victor Harris. New York: Overlook Press, 1974.
Sasamori, Junzo, and Gordon Warner. *This Is Kendo.* Vermont: Charles E. Tuttle, 1984.

Legendary Japanese swordsman Miyamoto Musashi

Musketeers at play

MUSKETEER. In a general sense, a musketeer was any soldier armed with a musket.

In its more specialized and, doubtlessly, popular usage, the term refers to a member of the French royal household bodyguard during the seventeenth and eighteenth centuries, as illustrated in Alexandre Dumas's* classic novel *The Three Musketeers* (1844).**

It is safe to say that the best-known musketeer of all time is Dumas's fictional hero D'Artagnan.* The image of a musketeer, then, ends up being that of a dashing swordsman.

REFERENCE

Benet, William Rose. *The Reader's Encyclopedia.* New York: Thomas Y. Crowell, 1964.

MUSO RYU. A technique of swordplay founded in thirteenth-century Japan by Shinenobu Hayashizaki, involving the rapid drawing of the sword from its scabbard. The Muso ryu style quickly became a vital part of samurai* combat.

The formal name for this unique school of fighting is Shimmeimuso-ryu.

The Hoki school, founded by Hisayasu Katayama, was an improvement on the Muso ryu approach.

REFERENCE

Sasamori, Junzo, and Gordon Warner. *This Is Kendo.* Vermont: Charles E. Tuttle, 1984.

MUTU GITAI. Considered the best method of Japanese blade making. A soft bar of steel was doubled, welded, and forged to an original piece of metal. The process was then repeated numerous times. The resulting piece of metal was eventually shaped, cemented, hardened, and tempered. It is said that the final product was composed of 4,194,304 layers.

REFERENCE

Stone, George Cameron. *A Glossary of the Construction, Decoration, and Use of Arms and Armor.* New York: Jack Brussel, 1961.

NADI, ALDO. (1899–1965). Italian fencing champion.

While he lived somewhat in the shadow of his famous brother Nedo, Aldo Nadi was by no means an inferior fencer. Indeed, for a number of years, Aldo was looked upon as the rising champion of the Italian school of fencing. It is said that his footwork made him nearly unbeatable.

Nadi was a firm believer in the technical approach to fencing, that is, perfecting the execution of fencing actions—both offensive and defensive—and the mastery of distance. He also believed in simplicity of action in combat. In his final fencing tournament before retiring from competition, he won first place by employing, for the final touch, nothing more than a simple disengage. Said Nadi, "My reflexes of thirty years made that touch, not I."

Nadi's thoughts on fencing were instilled in him by his fencing teacher/father Beppe, who demanded dedication and discipline in his puplis. The elder Nadi was a strict believer in developing mechanical skills, which, of course, take time and infinite practice to master. Aldo noted that his father never allowed his pupils to begin bouting until they had undergone at least one year of technical training. Competition required two years of lessons.

Aldo Nadi took second place in individual sabre at the 1920 Olympics. His 1920 foil, sabre, and épée teams all took first place.

Following in his father's and brother's footsteps, Aldo became a professional fencing master in 1921. In his new guise as teacher, his methodology was firm and clear:

Curb your adversary's aggressiveness by attacking every time he comes too near during the preparation of his own offensive. The best strategy is to keep holding the initiative, upsetting with threats, early parries and effective mobility any and all attempts of your opponent to gain ground. Your aim is to compel him to attack under the worst possible conditions, not upon his own choice of timing.

In 1935, Maestro Nadi moved to the United States, opening the Aldo Nadi Fencing Academy in New York City. He stayed there until 1943, when he moved to Los Angeles to teach his sport and work in the film industry.

Aldo Nadi worked on a number of movies as the master of swordplay. His credits include *Frenchman's Creek* (1944),** *Captain from Castile* (1947),** and *Mississippi Gambler* (1953).**

Throughout his lengthy career in fencing, Aldo was held in high regard by his peers. Famed French fencing champion Lucien Gaudin* once called him "the thoroughbred of Italian fencing." Giorgio Santelli,* one of the great fencing masters of modern times, said of him, "I have been fencing for four and a half decades and the only person I have seen who approaches perfection in form, technique and execution is Aldo Nadi."

Aside from his normal fencing pursuits, Aldo Nadi once fought a duel, which was sparked, ironically, by the result of a fencing bout. Held in 1924, the contest in question was a highly publicized encounter between French foilist Lucien Gaudin and the reigning Italian professional champion Candido Sassone. The focus of great nationalistic pride, it was an occasion that generated much heated emotion. Reportedly, Gaudin won easily, and Aldo Nadi, Italian but ever the sportsman, praised him for his victory. Conversely, the Italian newspaper editor, Adolfo Cotronei, in a fit of misplaced patriotism, erroneously reported in his writings that Sassone had won the bout nine touches to seven. He also began making rather unflattering remarks about Nadi. Nadi then challenged the journalist to combat. Soon after, the two men met and fought with dueling swords. The exchange, lasting for nearly seven minutes, ended with Aldo's opponent, who'd been wounded several times, giving up. "Oh, Aldo," he announced, "I have had enough! Thank you!" They later drank wine together.

Aldo Nadi wrote two books: *On Fencing* (1943) and his autobiography, *Mask Off*, which has not been published to date.

REFERENCES

Gaugler, William. "Technical Versus Tactical Lessons." *The Sword* (June 1993).
———. "Aldo Nadi's Classic *On Fencing*." *American Fencing* (Spring 1994).
Nadi, Aldo. "The Nadi-Cotronei Duel." *American Fencing* (April/May/June 1992).
Wallechinsky, David. *The Complete Book of the Olympics*. New York: Penguin Books, 1984.

NADI, NEDO. (1894–1940). Legendary Italian fencer.

The son of Italian fencing master Beppe Nadi, Nedo Nadi began studying fencing at an early age. At eighteen, he won his first Olympic gold medal at the 1912 Stockholm games in individual foil, giving Italy its first Olympic victory over the French in that weapon.

During the 1920 Antwerp Olympics, Nadi turned in one of the greatest fenc-

Italian fencing champion Nedo Nadi

ing performances of all time, winning a total of five gold fencing medals: individual foil (first place), team foil (first place), team épée (first place), individual sabre (first place), and team sabre (first place). No other fencer has ever come close to this achievement.

Following his magnificent 1920 performance, Nadi gave up amateur fencing, becoming a distinguished fencing master. Among his students was the famous teacher Leon Bertrand.

An interesting side note on Nadi's early training was how he developed his skill with the épée, which eventually won him an Olympic gold medal. His maestro father's forbidding any of his students to fence with the épée, which he considered an undisciplined weapon, led Nedo and his friend Leo Nunes to sneak out and bout with the épée in secret, improving their technique through mutual critique.

While an avowed and successful professional swordsman, Nedo Nadi did not remain one. In an unprecedented move in 1931, he was returned officially to the ranks of amateurism by the powers-that-be so that he could assume the prestigious post of president of the wholly amateur Italian Fencing Federation, a position he held until his death in 1940.

Nadi's younger brother Aldo was also an accomplished fencer. Said the latter of Nedo's fencing, "The only fault in his defense lay in its lack of variety. He hardly ever broke the line, and seldom made a counter-of-sixte. The very fact that he did not exploit sufficiently the devastating stop-thrust was additional proof that, at times, he was unable to dictate his will to his hand—for it ran away with its counters."

REFERENCES

Capriles, Miguel de. "Ramon Fonst and Nedo Nadi." *American Fencing* (September/October 1976).
Gaugler, William. "Aldo Nadi's Classic *On Fencing.*" American *Fencing* (Spring 1994).
Morton, E. D. *Martini A–Z of Fencing.* London: Queen Anne Press, 1992.
Wallechinsky, David. *The Complete Book of the Olympics.* New York: Penguin Books, 1984.

NAGATACHI. An early-style Japanese long sword.
REFERENCE
Stone, George Cameron. *A Glossary of the Construction, Decoration, and Use of Arms and Armor.* New York: Jack Brussel, 1961.

NAKAGO. The tang of a Japanese sword blade.
  Also called a *komi* or *kuki.*
REFERENCE
Stone, George Cameron. *A Glossary of the Construction, Decoration, and Use of Arms and Armor.* New York: Jack Brussel, 1961.

NAMRAL. A sword of western Tibet.
  Also called *ragee.*
REFERENCE
Stone, George Cameron. *A Glossary of the Construction, Decoration, and Use of Arms and Armor.* New York: Jack Brussel, 1961.

NARVAEZ, DON LUIS PACHECO DE. (c. 1600). Spanish fencing master.
A student of Jeronimo de Carranza,* Don Luis Pacheco Narvaez was the foremost exponent of his master's style, an approach to fencing based on traversing an imaginary circle and on an overblown mystical philosophy.

While both cuts* and thrusts* were employed in the Carranza-Narvaez school of fencing, the lunge was, apparently, unknown to the Spaniards.

While highly artificial in its approach, the Carranza-Narvaez school of swordplay nevertheless held sway in Spain during the whole of the sixteenth and seventeenth centuries. Even though it was never taken very seriously as a fighting discipline anywhere else in Europe, the Spanish enjoyed the reputation of being highly dangerous duelists. It is believed that this was so not so much because of the Carranza-Narvaez technique itself but because its highly methodical approach to combat developed one of the most important elements necessary to a successful fighter: a sense of focused calmness.

Narvaez and his mentor gained a special notoriety as fencing masters when dramatists of the time period began using them as characters in their plays. In Ben Johnson's *Every Man in His Humour* (1598), Captain Bobadil can talk of nothing but the Spanish masters: ''They had their time and we can say they were, so had Carranza, so had Don Lewis . . . Don Lewis of Madrid is the sole master now of the world.''

Don Luis Pacheco de Narvaez wrote a number of volumes on fencing. The first appeared in 1608; the last, in 1672.

REFERENCE

Castle, Egerton. *Schools and Masters of Fence.* London: George Bell, 1885.

NAWAZ KHANI. An Indian sword, much like the popular *firangi.** The blade was back-edged and slightly curved.

REFERENCE

Stone, George Cameron. *A Glossary of the Construction, Decoration, and Use of Arms and Armor.* New York: Jack Brussel, 1961.

NAZI (BERLIN) OLYMPICS. The 1936 Berlin ''Nazi'' Olympics was notable as a world mass event, with Germany's ''master race'' rise to power underscoring the Nazi quest for athletic evidence of its own superiority over other peoples and races.

For the sport of fencing, in particular, the Nazi Olympics was a time of controversy and change.

A major dispute of international proportions arose around a tall, willowy blond German fencer by the name of Helene Mayer,* who also happened to be half-Jewish. With Germany's purging of Jews from its athletic rolls, Mayer became a highly visible target of Nazi hatred. A world champion fencer by the age of seventeen, she had been publicly expelled from her German fencing club in 1933 and was further excluded from representing Germany in any fencing contests.

Yet, after settling in California following the 1932 Olympics in Los Angeles, Mayer seemed far removed from Nazi obsessions. Nevertheless, as the 1936 Olympics drew closer, numerous rumors began revolving around the fencer. First, it was said that the U.S. government was attempting to force Germany to allow her to fence for the good of organized sport but that Germany refused to let a ''Jew'' onto its team. Then, when Germany did an about-face and decided to overlook her ''Jewishness,'' formally ''inviting'' her to fence for her homeland, it was suddenly suggested that she was being blackmailed to do so by a government bent on winning as many medals as possible in an effort to dem-

Controversial fencer Helene Mayer (left) competing in the finals of the 1936 Berlin Olympics

onstrate the superiority of the ''Aryan'' people. Would Helene Mayer fence? Should she fence? The U.S. government encouraged her to do so. Jewish organizations attempted to persuade her to refuse.

In 1935, amid heated debates, accusations, and rumors, Helene Mayer quietly agreed to compete on the German fencing team, stating that she would be happy to represent Germany again and that she looked forward to seeing her family in Germany.

Finally, Helene Mayer went to Berlin and fenced in the Olympics, taking second place in an exciting contest that has been called one of twentieth-century fencing's most dramatic moments. That the winners of the gold and silver medals had to be decided by counting indicators—that is, touches received by a fencer, as opposed to direct wins and losses—shows how close the contest actually was.

What actually led half-Jewish Helene Mayer to compete at the Nazi Olympics? Blackmail? Pressure from the U.S. government? Or simply the desire of an athlete to have the opportunity to express her talents? No one really knows. She never gave a reason.

The Nazi games were also significant as the point in history that electrical weapons and electrical scoring equipment were first introduced for Olympic épée. While it would be a number of years before foils and sabres would be so fitted, fencing had—for better or worse—entered the age of technology.

During the games themselves, an unpleasant incident marred the men's épée competition. A Mexican fencer, Haro Oliva (thought by many to be the Western Hemisphere's greatest competitor since the celebrated Cuban Ramon Fonst), reaching the finals and seemingly headed for a championship, to the obvious consternation of the European community, was suddenly blocked in his quest for a gold medal not by superior fencing but by petty officialdom's fearing a non-European win. Just before the finals were to begin, Oliva's weapons were examined by Italian and German officials, who found that one of his blades was one-fifth of an inch too long. Whether he had been using this particular épée was never proven, but Olivia was ordered by the directors of the competition to fence all his bouts—from the preliminary round on—over again. Needless to say, there was no time to do this before the last bouts got under way, and the Mexican was excluded from further fencing.

For all its posturing, Germany collected only three fencing medals during the Berlin Olympics, and none of them gold: men's team foil (third place), men's team sabre (third place), and women's individual foil (second place).

REFERENCES
Grombach, John V. *The 1972 Olympic Guide.* Paperback Library, 1972.
Mandell, Richard D. *The Nazi Olympics.* New York: Macmillan, 1971.
Wallechinsky, David. *The Complete Book of the Olympics.* New York: Penguin Books, 1984.

NENUKI TSUBA. A Japanese sword guard that is perforated.
REFERENCE
Stone, George Cameron. *A Glossary of the Construction, Decoration, and Use of Arms and Armor.* New York: Jack Brussel, 1961.

NERI TSUBA. Japanese sword guards* made entirely of lacquered animal hide.
REFERENCE
Stone, George Cameron. *A Glossary of the Construction, Decoration, and Use of Arms and Armor.* New York: Jack Brussel, 1961.

NETABA. A Japanese term for the edge of a sword blade.

REFERENCE
Stone, George Cameron. *A Glossary of the Construction, Decoration, and Use of Arms and Armor.* New York: Jack Brussel, 1961.

NEUTRAL. A sword hand position where it can be deemed neither in supination nor pronation. It is a halfway point for the sword hand, with the thumb being placed at twelve o'clock.

REFERENCE
Morton, E. D. *Martini A–Z of Fencing.* London: Queen Anne Press, 1992.

NEW YORK FENCERS CLUB. Founded in 1882, the New York Fencers Club was the first organization devoted exclusively in the United States to the sport of fencing. Its coach, Louis Vauthier, a graduate of Joinville-le-Pont, France's great school for fencing masters, was responsible for America's earliest interest in fencing.

REFERENCES
Grombach, John V. *The 1972 Olympic Guide.* New York: Paperback Library, 1972.
Walker, Colleen. *United States Fencing 1992 Media Guide.* Colorado Springs, CO: ColorTek Printing, 1992.

NIEDERKIRCHNER, ODON. (1904–1987). Hungarian-born American fencing master.

Odon Niederkirchner graduated from the Royal Hungarian Fencing Master's School in Budapest in 1928. He was later appointed fencing master and sports officer in the Hungarian army. After World War II, he emigrated to the United States.

During his years in the United States, Maestro Niederkirchner taught numerous champions, including Ed Richards, Silvio Giolito, George Masin, and Tibor Nyilas. According to the U.S. Fencing Association (USFA), he had one or more students on every U.S. Olympic team from 1952 to 1976.

In 1975, Odon Niederkirchner was awarded the Certificate of Merit by the USFA.

REFERENCES
Kestler, Jeff. "Maestro Odon Niederkirchner." *American Fencing* (July/August 1975).
Tishman, Jeff. "Odon Niederkirchner." *American Fencing* (June/July/August 1987).

NINJA. Japanese warriors trained during that country's feudal days to be spies and assassins. Ninja were experts in all kinds of survival techniques and fighting arts, including the use of the sword. Because of their ability to move undetected among their enemies, ninja were sometimes called "shadow warriors" or "invisible warriors."

In olden times, rather than one single group of ninja, there were numerous clans all across Japan. Probably the most celebrated ninja group was the Iga clan, with its leader Hanzo Hattori, who was an adviser to seventeenth-century shogun Teyasu Tokugawa.

In modern times, ninja have been romanticized in Japanese adventure movies like *Ninjutsu* (1958) and *Daredevil in the Castle* (1961).

Moreover, the way of the ninja, ninjutsu,* has resurfaced as a popular form of martial arts. The leading exponent of the ninja life is Dr. Masaaki Hatsumi,* who, for many years, almost single-handedly spearheaded the movement.

REFERENCES

Hatsumi, Masaaki. *Ninjutsu.* Burbank, CA: Unique, 1981.

Mintz, Marilyn D. *The Martial Arts Film.* New York: A. S. Barnes, 1978.

NINJA KEN. The sword of the ninja.

The *ninja ken* was a single-edged, short-bladed sword. The *tsuba* (hand guard) was a plain, square metal plate. The weapon was shorter than the average samurai sword,* because fighting in close quarters was part of ninja technique.

While it was considered the ninja's primary fighting tool, the *ninja ken* was not relied on to the point that, if disarmed, the ninja was without recourse.

Because many ninja could not afford the work of expert sword makers, they resorted to making their own weapons on forges set up at home. For this reason, the weapons often have a stark, utilitarian look about them.

Also called *shinobigatana.*

REFERENCE

Hatsumi, Masaaki. *Ninjutsu.* Burbank, CA: Unique, 1981.

NINJUTSU. The art of the ninja.

Ninja were expert spies and assassins in feudal Japan; to this end, they developed techniques—both physical and spiritual—that they employed against their designated foes.

The fighting arts of ninjutsu include the use of the sword (*ninja ken**), the staff (*bo-jutsu*), throwing blades (*shuriken-jutsu*), spear fighting (*yari-jutsu*), and unarmed combat (*tai justsu*).

On the noncombative side, ninjutsu included knowledge of disguise and impersonation (*henso-jutsu*), horsemanship (*ba-jutsu*), stealth and entering skills (*shinobi-iri*), strategy (*bo-ryaku*), spying (*cho ho*), escape and concealment (*inton-jutsu*), meteorology (*ten-mon*), and geography (*chi-mon*).

The attainment of spiritual refinement (*seishin teki kyoyo*) was also part of ninjutsu, as it was believed that without an understanding of himself, the ninja would be less effective in understanding and overcoming others.

Ninjutsu, while essentially a phenomenon of Japan's feudal era, has found new life in modern times as a martial arts discipline. The guiding force behind the reborn movement is a Japanese doctor, Masaaki Hatsumi,* who inherited his title of grand master from his teacher, Toshitsugu Takamatsu. The line of ninja masters, of which Hatsumi is the thirty-fourth, is said to have been established during the twelfth century by Daisuke Togakure.

In the West, the foremost instructor of ninjutsu is Stephen K. Hayes, the only

American to be awarded the ninjutsu title of *shidoshi,* or "teacher." Hayes is a writer, lecturer, and movie consultant.

REFERENCES

Hatsumi, Masaaki. *Ninjutsu.* Burbank, CA: Unique, 1981.

Hayes, Stephen K. *Ninjutsu, The Art of the Invisible Warrior.* Chicago: Contemporary Books, 1984.

NITEN-ICHI-RYU. A fencing style devised by famed Japanese swordsman Miyamoto Musashi* involving the use of two swords—one long and one short.

REFERENCE

Sasamori, Junzo, and Gordon Warner. *This Is Kendo.* Vermont: Charles E. Tuttle, 1984.

NIVEN, DAVID. (1909–1983). British film actor.

Suave and debonair, David Niven specialized in playing the light, romantic lead in numerous Hollywood comedies during the 1930s, 1940s, and 1950s. From time to time, he also appeared in costume adventures.

Niven's first swashbuckler role was a supporting one in the 1937 *Prisoner of Zenda,** which starred Ronald Colman.* While not actually in the thick of the adventure, Niven was highly effective in a supporting, slightly comic relief part.

In 1947, he starred in *Bonnie Prince Charlie* as the Bonnie Prince. In his book, *The Moon's a Balloon* (1972), Niven recalled accidentally sticking his sword through the leg of an extra. Luckily, he observed, the man had a wooden leg.

In 1950 came *The Elusive Pimpernel,* a remake of *The Scarlet Pimpernel* tale of a British nobleman saving French aristocrats from execution during the French Revolution.

The King's Thief (1955) brought Niven a rare role reversal when he took the part of the picture's chief villain, who, incidentally, was, of course, an "expert" swordsman. Not exactly a regular to the swashbuckler genre, Niven's fencing was nevertheless adequate to the situation.

At the time of his death in 1983, David Niven had appeared in over ninety films.

REFERENCES

Halliwell, Leslie. *Halliwell's Filmgoer's and Video Viewer's Companion.* New York: Charles Scribner's Sons, 1988.

Niven, David. *The Moon's a Balloon.* New York: G.P. Putnam's Sons, 1972.

NO-DACHI. Meaning "field sword."

In Japanese early feudal days, this very long and heavy sword was used by men who were extremely strong. It was, in fact, 25 percent longer than an ordinary sword.

Because of its size, the *no-dachi* had to be carried on one's back, where it was strapped in place by a narrow belt.

REFERENCE
Stone, George Cameron. *A Glossary of the Construction, Decoration, and Use of Arms and Armor.* New York: Jack Brussel, 1961.

NO MIND. In Japanese swordsmanship, the concept of ''no mind'' refers to a state of consciousness in which the swordsman and his weapon blend into one, where, it is said, conscious thought is left behind. Action comes naturally and freely, creating a perfect flow of energy and movement. Fencing simply becomes an act of ''doing.''

REFERENCE
Suzuki, Daisetz. *Zen and Japanese Culture.* Princeton, NJ: Princeton University Press, 1973.

NONCONVENTIONAL WEAPON. Of the three weapons of modern fencing—the foil,* the épée,* and the sabre*—only the épée is a nonconventional weapon; that is, it lacks any kind of rules establishing the ''right'' of one fencer over another to be the attacker or where an attacking fencer might hit with his blade.

Because épée fencing was patterned along the lines of actual combat—where the object would always be to simply hit an opponent anywhere on the body before he hits you—interjecting any artificial conventions about how the épée itself might be used (other than that the weapon must strike only with the point) would have been to interfere with the game's original intention: to create an ''anything goes'' atmosphere in which a swordsman could prepare himself for dueling.

REFERENCES
Palffy-Alpar, Julius. *Sword and Masque.* Philadelphia: F. A. Davis, 1967.
Vebell, Edward. *Sports Illustrated Book of Fencing.* Philadelphia: J. B. Lippincott, 1962.

NONRESISTING PARRY. A parry that gives way to an opponent's forceful responses—specifically, beats, binds, and heavy parries—rather than fighting against them. While resistance tends to trap energy, nonresisting responses immediately turn the energy of heavy actions into motion, allowing the attacked fencer to channel the force away from him. This frees up the fencer, allowing for an immediate counterattack.

Nonresisting parries are particularly important to a fencer who finds himself with an opponent who uses brute force. Giving way means never having to fight on the other's terms. Thus, he can continually sidestep his adversary's strength.

Sometimes known as ''parrying by yielding,'' ''ceding parry,'' *cedute,* ''non-opposing parry,'' and ''parrying by giving blade.''

REFERENCES
Palffy-Alpar, Julius. *Sword and Masque.* Philadelphia: F. A. Davis, 1967.
Stevenson, John. *Fencing.* London: Briggs, 1935.

NUMERICAL NOMENCLATURE. Referring to the numbering of the various lines* into which the body is divided in fencing: prime* (1), seconde* (2), tierce* (3), quarte* (4), quinte* (5), sixte* (6), septime* (7), and octave* (8).

In the early days of fencing, there was much confusion about the numerical order of the lines, each fencing master assigning his own number to a given location. This differed not only from master to master but from country to country. Such an approach, of course, proved highly inadequate and confusing to the teaching of fencing.

Eventually, standardization of the numerical nomenclature of fencing occurred when the desire to simplify and clarify fencing became greater than the egos involved that were fragmenting it.

Today, the French and Italian schools of fencing have only a few differences in numerical nomenclature. The Italians, for instance, regard the line of French quinte as high septime. The French view Italian quinte to be low quarte.

Customarily, modern fencing masters teach quarte, sixte, septime, and octave as the primary positions of fencing.

REFERENCES
Castle, Egerton. *Schools and Masters of Fence.* London: George Bell, 1885.
Palffy-Alpar, Julius. *Sword and Masque.* Philadelphia: F. A. Davis, 1967.

NUNES, LEO. (1893–1974). Italian-born American fencing champion.

Leo Nunes began fencing in Italy under the tutelage of the great master Beppe Nadi,** father of Nedo Nadi* and Aldo Nadi,* two of Italy's greatest international fencing competitors.

A classical fencer of the highest order, Leo Nunes came to the United States in the 1920s and immediately made a name for himself in U.S. fencing.

In U.S. national championships, he took first place in individual épée in 1917, first in sabre and épée in 1922, first in foil and épée in 1924, first in sabre and épée in 1926, first in épée in 1928, first in sabre in 1929, and first in épée in 1932.

REFERENCE
Every, Dernell. "Leo Nunes 1893–1974." *American Fencing* (July/August 1974).

NYILAS, TIBOR. (1914–1986). Hungarian-born American fencing champion.

Tibor Nyilas began fencing in Hungary at an early age. Coming to the United States in 1939, he was a top performer in American sabre fencing for more than twenty years.

Nyilas was U.S. national sabre champion seven times between 1946 and 1956. He was also a U.S. Olympic team member four times, in 1948, 1952, 1956, and 1960.

At the 1948 London Olympics, his sabre team took third place.

REFERENCE
Blum, Robert. "Tibor Nyilas." *American Fencing* (July/August 1986).

O

OATH IN EARLY ITALIAN SCHOOLS OF FENCING. A student entering an Italian fencing school during the sixteenth century was usually required to swear a sacred oath upon the cross hilt of a sword never to take up arms against his master, a doubtlessly practical demand in the days when everyone carried a weapon.

The student also had to promise never to teach any of his master's secrets without permission. This was to be expected, as each teacher of swordplay, attempting to establish and maintain his own reputation, staunchly protected those moves that he believed set him apart from his contemporaries.
REFERENCE
Castle, Egerton. *Schools and Masters of Fence.* London: George Bell, 1885.

OCTAVE. The line of eight.

Octave covers the low-outside portion of the target area.* The sword hand* is in supination* (palm up).
REFERENCE
Palffy-Alpar, Julius. *Sword and Masque.* Philadelphia: F. A. Davis, 1967.

ODACHI. A fourteenth-century Japanese long sword. The blade was four or five feet in length. Like the *no-dachi,* it was carried over the shoulder attached to a leather strap.
REFERENCE
Stone, George Cameron. *A Glossary of the Construction, Decoration, and Use of Arms and Armor.* New York: Jack Brussel, 1961.

OFFENSE. A group of actions intended to produce a touch against an adversary.
REFERENCE
Handelman, Rob. "Fencing Glossary." *American Fencing* (May/June 1978).

OFFENSES, COMMON FENCING. In foil* and sabre* fencing, a warning may be given if a fencer initiates body contact (*corps a corps**)—either accidentally or on purpose—between himself and his opponent. In épée,* a warning is given if a fencer initiates violent body contact between himself and his opponent. Once warned for either type of body contact, a fencer can be penalized one touch for every subsequent violation during that particular bout.

In fencing with any of the three weapons, a warning may be given if a fencer uses his unarmed hand or arm in either an offensive or defensive manner. Once warned, a fencer can be penalized one touch for every subsequent violation during that particular bout.

A warning may also be given if a fencer leaves the fencing strip (*piste*) to avoid being hit. In leaving the strip, a fencer is penalized one meter in foil and two meters in sabre and épée.

In foil, a warning can be given if a fencer replaces a valid target area* with a nonvalid target* area, such as covering his chest with an arm to avoid a touch. Once warned, a fencer may be penalized a touch for every subsequent violation during that particular bout.
REFERENCES
Lacombe, Claude. *Fencing*. Canada: Les Publications Eclair, 1976.
U.S. Fencing Association, ed. *Operations Manual*. Colorado Springs, CO: U.S. Fencing Association, 1985.

OFF TARGET. In modern fencing, an area of the body not designated as a valid place to strike is considered off target.

In foil* fencing, the mask, arms, and legs are off target. In sabre* fencing, everything below the waist is off target. In épée* fencing, there is no such thing as off target, because the entire body may be attacked.
REFERENCE
Palffy-Alpar, Julius. *Sword and Masque*. Philadelphia: F. A. Davis, 1967.

OGISAKI. A rounded point on a Japanese sword blade.
REFERENCE
Stone, George Cameron. *A Glossary of the Construction, Decoration, and Use of Arms and Armor*. New York: Jack Brussel, 1961.

O'HARA, MAUREEN. (1920–   ). Irish-born film actress.
In the swashbuckler film genre, dominated by male images, Maureen O'Hara managed to create a persona that has positioned her alongside such luminaries as Errol Flynn* and Tyrone Power.* While starring in a wide range of movies over the years, her costume adventure roles are her most colorful—first, as the

fought-over heroine in such productions as *The Black Swan* (1942)** and *The Spanish Main* (1945) and then as a female swashbuckler in *At Sword's Point* (1952) and *Against All Flags* (1952). Her feisty, but feminine, image was well suited to either role.

Maureen O'Hara's film fencing ability was superior to that of many of her male contemporaries.

REFERENCE

Richards, Jeffrey. *Swordsmen of the Screen.* Boston: Routledge and Kegan Paul, 1977.

OLIVIER, LAURENCE. (1907–1989). Distinguished British stage and film actor.

An actor of incredible depth and range, Laurence Olivier could play hero and villain with equal facility. Often described as the greatest actor of the twentieth century, he could step from Shakespeare into a modern drama without losing stride.

It was natural, considering his background in the classics of the theater— from *Hamlet* to *King Lear*—that Olivier should have found his way into at least a few costume productions on the screen. While most of them were Shakespearean in origin, he nevertheless imparted a sense of dash to his portrayals, a necessary ingredient of the swashbuckler genre.

Olivier's fencing abilities were honed by years of stage experience. Yet, he was not without humor regarding his skill. In a foreword to William Hobbs's* book *Techniques of the Stage Fight* (1967),** he recalled: "My training and experience in the art of fence has been largely grounded on the clockwork technique of 'one, two, three; two, one, four'; or 'bish, bash, bosh; bash, bosh, bish; no, no, no, you should not be doing bosh there, it is bash first, then bosh.'"

Moreover, his efforts were not without incident over the years, as the actor noted: "1 broken ankle," "untold slashes including a full thrust razor-sharp sword wound in the breast," "three ruptured Achilles tendons," and "landing from considerable height, scrotum first, upon an acrobat's knee," to name a few of his assorted injuries.

Films in which Laurence Olivier fenced include *Fire over England* (1937), *Henry V* (1944), *Hamlet* (1948), and *Richard III* (1955).

REFERENCES

Halliwell, Leslie. *Halliwell's Filmgoer's and Video Viewer's Companion.* New York: Charles Scribner's Son's, 1988.

Hobbs, William. *Techniques of the Stage Fight.* London: Studio Vista, 1967.

OLYMPIC FENCING. The Olympics have always been looked upon as the highest attainment a fencer could reach. Because they have had such a long history and have been surrounded by so much pomp and celebration, even the world fencing championships hold a slightly less lofty position—if only in the mind and not in actual fencing achievement.

Fencing has been included in the Olympic makeup from the very first game

Women's foil team event—USA versus China—at the 1992 Olympics. Photograph by Roger Mar used courtesy of USFA

in 1896, and while not one of the more important sports in America's eyes, to the European community it has always been every bit as important as track and field and gymnastics.

Olympic fencing, of course, has had its share of giants: Christian d'Oriola,* Ramon Fonst,* Lucien Gaudin,* Pal Kovacs,* Edoardo Mangiarotti,* Helene Mayer,* Nedo Nadi,* and Ilona Schacherer-Elek,* to name a few.

Individual country leaders in Olympic fencing have been France, Italy, and Hungary. Other countries winning Olympic medals include Russia, Cuba, Belgium, Poland, Greece, Mexico, and the United States.

U.S. fencers who have won either individual or team medals in the Olympics include Hugh Alessandroni, Norman Armitage, Albert Axelrod,* Henry Breckinridge, George Calnan,* Dean Cetrulo,* Miguel de Capriles, Dernell Every, James Flynn, Arthur Fox, William Grebe, Francis Honeycutt, Tracy Jaeckel, Joseph Levis,* Arthur Lyon, Tibor Nyilas,* William Scott O'Conner, Harold Rayner, Frank Righeimer, Robert Sears, Curtis Shears, Richard Steere, Charles Tatham, Fitzhugh Townsend, Albertson Van Zo Post, Peter Westbrook,* and George Worth.

International rules to govern Olympic fencing were not adopted until 1919. Also, women were not allowed to fence in the Olympics until 1924, and it was not until 1960 that they were permitted a team event.

REFERENCES

Grombach, John V. *The 1972 Olympic Guide.* New York: Paperback Library, 1972.

Wallechinsky, David. *The Complete Book of the Olympics.* New York: Penguin Books, 1984.

OLYMPIC FENCING RESULTS.

I.   1896, Athens

    INDIVIDUAL FOIL

       1. Eugene-Henri Gravelotte (France)

       2. Henri Callot (France)

       3. Perikles Pierrakos-Mavromichalis (Greece)

    INDIVIDUAL SABRE

       1. Jean Georgiadis (Greece)

       2. Telemachos Karakalos (Greece)

       3. Holger Nielsen (Denmark)

    MASTERS FOIL FENCING (Discontinued)

       1. Leon Pyrgos (Greece)

       2. M. Perronnet (France)

II. 1900, Paris

    INDIVIDUAL FOIL

       1. Emile Coste (France)

       2. Henri Masson (France)

       3. Marcel Jacques Boulenger (France)

    INDIVIDUAL ÉPÉE

       1. Ramon Fonst* (Cuba)

       2. Louis Perree (France)

       3. Leon See (France)

    INDIVIDUAL SABRE

       1. Georges de la Falaise (France)

       2. Leon Thiebaut (France)

       3. Siegfried Flesch (Austria)

    MASTERS FOIL FENCING (Discontinued)

       1. Lucien Merignac (France)

       2. Alphonse Kirchhoffer (France)

       3. Jean-Baptiste Mimiague (France)

    MASTERS ÉPÉE FENCING (Discontinued)

       1. Albert Ayat (France)

       2. Emile Bougnol (France)

      3. Henri Laurent (France)

    AMATEURS AND MASTERS ÉPÉE (Discontinued)

      1. Albert Ayat (France)

      2. Ramon Fonst (Cuba)

      3. Leon See (France)

    MASTERS SABRE FENCING (Discontinued)

      1. Antonio Conte (Italy)

      2. Italo Santelli* (Italy)

      3. Milan Neralic (Austria)

III.   1904, St. Louis

    INDIVIDUAL FOIL

      1. Ramon Fonst (Cuba)

      2. Albertson Van Zo Post** (United States)

      3. Charles Tatham** (United States)

    TEAM FOIL

      1. Cuba

      2. United States

    INDIVIDUAL ÉPÉE

      1. Ramon Fonst (Cuba)

      2. Charles Tatham (United States)

      3. Albertson Van Zo Post (United States)

    INDIVIDUAL SABRE

      1. Manuel Diaz (Cuba)

      2. William Grebe** (United States)

      3. Albertson Van Zo Post (United States)

    SINGLE STICKS (Discontinued)

      1. Albertson Van Zo Post (United States)

      2. William Scott O'Conner** (United States)

      3. William Grebe (United States)

1906, Athens (An unofficial "Olympics")

    INDIVIDUAL FOIL

      1. Georges Dillon-Cavanagh* (France)

      2. Gustav Casmir (Germany)

      3. Pierre d'Hugues (France)

    INDIVIDUAL ÉPÉE

      1. Georges de la Falaise* (France)

      2. Georges Dillon-Cavanagh (France)

3. Alexander van Blijenburgh (Holland)

TEAM ÉPÉE

1. France

2. Great Britain

3. Belgium

INDIVIDUAL SABRE

1. Jean Georgiadis (Greece)

2. Gustav Casmir (Germany)

3. Federico Cesarano (Italy)

TEAM SABRE

1. Germany

2. Greece

3. Holland

THREE-CORNERED SABRE (Discontinued)

1. Gustav Casmir (Germany)

2. George van Rossem (Holland)

3. Peter Toth (Hungary)

MASTERS ÉPÉE FENCING (Discontinued)

1. Cyrille Verbrugge (Belgium)

2. Mario Gubiani (Italy)

3. Ioannis Raissis (Greece)

IV.   1908, London

INDIVIDUAL ÉPÉE

1. Gaston Alibert (France)

2. Alexandre Lippman (France)

3. Eugene Olivier (France)

TEAM ÉPÉE

1. France

2. Great Britain

3. Belgium

INDIVIDUAL SABRE

1. Jeno Fuchs* (Hungary)

2. Bela Zulavszky (Hungary)

3. Vilem Goppold von Lobsdorf (Bohemia)

TEAM SABRE

1. Hungary

2. Italy

3. Bohemia

V. 1912, Stockholm

    INDIVIDUAL FOIL

      1. Nedo Nadi* (Italy)

      2. Pietro Speciale (Italy)

      3. Richard Verderber (Austria)

    INDIVIDUAL ÉPÉE

      1. Paul Anspach* (Belgium)

      2. Ivan Osiier (Denmark)

      3. Philippe La Hardy de Beaulieu (Belgium)

    TEAM ÉPÉE

      1. Belgium

      2. Great Britain

      3. Holland

    INDIVIDUAL SABRE

      1. Jeno Fuchs (Hungary)

      2. Bela Bekessy (Hungary)

      3. Ervin Meszaros (Hungary)

    TEAM SABRE

      1. Hungary

      2. Austria

      3. Holland

VI.   1916, Berlin—Canceled

VII. 1920, Antwerp

    INDIVIDUAL FOIL

      1. Nedo Nadi (Italy)

      2. Philippe Cattiau* (France)

      3. Roger Ducret* (France)

    TEAM FOIL

      1. Italy

      2. France

      3. United States

    INDIVIDUAL ÉPÉE

      1. Armand Massard (France)

      2. Alexandre Lippman (France)

      3. Gustave Buchard (France)

    TEAM ÉPÉE

      1. Italy

      2. Belgium

      3. France

INDIVIDUAL SABRE

   1. Nedo Nadi (Italy)

   2. Aldo Nadi* (Italy)

   3. Adrianus de Jong (Holland)

TEAM SABRE

   1. Italy

   2. France

   3. Holland

VIII.   1924, Paris

INDIVIDUAL FOIL

   1. Roger Ducret (France)

   2. Philippe Cattiau (France)

   3. Maurice van Damme (Belgium)

TEAM FOIL

   1. France

   2. Belgium

   3. Hungary

INDIVIDUAL ÉPÉE

   1. Charles Delporte (Belgium)

   2. Roger Ducret (France)

   3. Nils Hellsten (Sweden)

TEAM ÉPÉE

   1. France

   2. Belgium

   3. Italy

INDIVIDUAL SABRE

   1. Sandor Posta (Hungary)

   2. Roger Ducret (France)

   3. Janos Garay (Hungary)

TEAM SABRE

   1. Italy

   2. Hungary

   3. Holland

WOMEN'S INDIVIDUAL FOIL

   1. Ellen Osiier* (Holland)

   2. Gladys Davis (Great Britain)

   3. Grete Heckscher (Denmark)

IX. 1928, Amsterdam

INDIVIDUAL FOIL

   1. Lucien Gaudin* (France)

   2. Erwin Casmir (Germany)

   3. Giulio Gaudini* (Italy)

TEAM FOIL

   1. Italy

   2. France

   3. Argentina

INDIVIDUAL ÉPÉE

   1. Lucien Gaudin (France)

   2. Georges Buchard (France)

   3. George Calnan* (United States)

TEAM ÉPÉE

   1. Italy

   2. France

   3. Portugal

INDIVIDUAL SABRE

   1. Odon Tersztyanszky (Hungary)

   2. Attila Petschauer (Hungary)

   3. Bino Bini (Italy)

TEAM SABRE

   1. Hungary

   2. Italy

   3. Poland

WOMEN'S INDIVIDUAL FOIL

   1. Helene Mayer* (Germany)

   2. Muriel Freeman (Great Britain)

   3. Olga Oelkers (Germany)

X. 1932, Los Angeles

INDIVIDUAL FOIL

   1. Gustavo Marzi (Italy)

   2. Joseph Levis* (United States)

   3. Giulio Gaudini (Italy)

TEAM FOIL

   1. France

   2. Italy

   3. United States

INDIVIDUAL ÉPÉE

  1. Giancarlo Cornaggia-Medici (Italy)

  2. Georges Buchard (France)

  3. Carlo Agostoni (Italy)

TEAM ÉPÉE

  1. France

  2. Italy

  3. United States

INDIVIDUAL SABRE

  1. Gyorgy Piller (Hungary)

  2. Giulio Gaudini (Italy)

  3. Endre Kabos (Hungary)

TEAM SABRE

  1. Hungary

  2. Italy

  3. Poland

WOMEN'S INDIVIDUAL FOIL

  1. Ellen Preis* (Austria)

  2. J. Heather Guinness (Great Britain)

  3. Erna Bogathy Bogen (Hungary)

XI. 1936, Berlin

INDIVIDUAL FOIL

  1. Giulio Gaudini (Italy)

  2. Edward Gardere (France)

  3. Giorgio Bocchino (Italy)

TEAM FOIL

  1. Italy

  2. France

  3. Germany

INDIVIDUAL ÉPÉE

  1. Franco Riccardi (Italy)

  2. Saverio Ragno (Italy)

  3. Giancarlo Cornaggia-Medici (Italy)

TEAM ÉPÉE

  1. Italy

  2. Sweden

  3. France

INDIVIDUAL SABRE

1. Endre Kabos (Hungary)
2. Gustavo Marzi (Italy)
3. Aladar Gerevich* (Hungary)

TEAM SABRE

1. Hungary
2. Italy
3. Germany

WOMEN'S INDIVIDUAL FOIL

1. Ilona Schacherer-Elek* (Hungary)
2. Helene Mayer (Germany)
3. Ellen Preis (Austria)

XII.   1940, Tokyo—Canceled

XIII. 1944, London—Canceled

XIV.   1948, London

INDIVIDUAL FOIL

1. Jehan Buhan (France)
2. Christian d'Oriola* (France)
3. Lajos Maszlay (Hungary)

TEAM FOIL

1. France
2. Italy
3. Belgium

INDIVIDUAL ÉPÉE

1. Luigi Cantone (Italy)
2. Oswald Zappelli (Switzerland)
3. Edoardo Mangiarotti* (Italy)

TEAM ÉPÉE

1. France
2. Italy
3. Sweden

INDIVIDUAL SABRE

1. Aladar Gerevich* (Hungary)
2. Vincenzo Pinton (Italy)
3. Pal Kovacs* (Hungary)

TEAM SABRE

1. Hungary

2. Italy

3. United States

WOMEN'S INDIVIDUAL FOIL

1. Ilona Elek (Hungary)

2. Karen Lachmann (Denmark)

3. Ellen Muller-Preis (Austria)

XV.   1952, Helsinki

INDIVIDUAL FOIL

1. Christian d'Oriola (France)

2. Edoardo Mangiarotti (Italy)

3. Manlio Di Rosa (Italy)

TEAM FOIL

1. France

2. Italy

3. Hungary

INDIVIDUAL ÉPÉE

1. Edoardo Mangiarotti (Italy)

2. Dario Mangiarotti** (Italy)

3. Oswald Zappelli (Switzerland)

TEAM ÉPÉE

1. Italy

2. Sweden

3. Switzerland

INDIVIDUAL SABRE

1. Pal Kovacs (Hungary)

2. Aladar Gerevich (Hungary)

3. Tibor Berczelly (Hungary)

TEAM SABRE

1. Hungary

2. Italy

3. France

WOMEN'S INDIVIDUAL FOIL

1. Irene Camber (Italy)

2. Ilona Elek (Hungary)

3. Karen Lachmann (Denmark)

XVI. 1956, Melbourne

    INDIVIDUAL FOIL

        1. Christian d'Oriola (France)

        2. Giancarlo Bergamini (Italy)

        3. Antonio Spallino (Italy)

    TEAM FOIL

        1. Italy

        2. France

        3. Hungary

    INDIVIDUAL ÉPÉE

        1. Carlo Pavesi (Italy)

        2. Giuseppe Delfino* (Italy)

        3. Edoardo Mangiarotti* (Italy)

    TEAM ÉPÉE

        1. Italy

        2. Hungary

        3. France

    INDIVIDUAL SABRE

        1. Rudolf Karpati (Hungary)

        2. Jerzy Pawlowski (Poland)

        3. Lev Kuznyetsov (Soviet Union)

    TEAM SABRE

        1. Hungary

        2. Poland

        3. Soviet Union

    WOMEN'S INDIVIDUAL FOIL

        1. Gillian Sheen (Great Britain)

        2. Olga Orban (Romania)

        3. Renee Garilhe (France)

XVII. 1960, Rome

    INDIVIDUAL FOIL

        1. Viktor Zhdanovich (Soviet Union)

        2. Yuri Sissikin (Soviet Union)

        3. Albert Alexrod* (United States)

    TEAM FOIL

        1. Soviet Union

        2. Italy

        3. Germany

INDIVIDUAL ÉPÉE

   1. Giuseppe Delfino* (Italy)

   2. Allan Jay (Great Britain)

   3. Bruno Khabarov (Soviet Union)

TEAM ÉPÉE

   1. Italy

   2. Great Britain

   3. Soviet Union

INDIVIDUAL SABRE

   1. Rudolf Karpati (Hungary)

   2. Zoltan Horvath (Hungary)

   3. Wladimiro Calarese (Italy)

TEAM SABRE

   1. Hungary

   2. Poland

   3. Italy

WOMEN'S INDIVIDUAL FOIL

   1. Heidi Schmid* (Germany)

   2. Valentina Rastvorova (Soviet Union)

   3. Maria Vicol (Romania)

WOMEN'S TEAM FOIL

   1. Soviet Union

   2. Hungary

   3. Italy

XVIII. 1964, Tokyo

INDIVIDUAL FOIL

   1. Egon Franke (Poland)

   2. Jean-Claude Magnan* (France)

   3. Daniel Revenu (France)

TEAM FOIL

   1. Soviet Union

   2. Poland

   3. France

INDIVIDUAL ÉPÉE

   1. Grigory Kriss (Soviet Union)

   2. Henry Hoskyns (Great Britain)

   3. Guram Kostava (Soviet Union)

TEAM ÉPÉE

1. Hungary

2. Italy

3. France

INDIVIDUAL SABRE

1. Tibor Pezsa (Hungary)

2. Claude Arabo (France)

3. Umar Mavlikhanov (Soviet Union)

TEAM SABRE

1. Soviet Union

2. Italy

3. Poland

WOMEN'S INDIVIDUAL FOIL

1. Ildiko Ujlaki-Rejto* (Hungary)

2. Helga Mees (Germany)

3. Antonella Ragno (Italy)

WOMEN'S TEAM FOIL

1. Hungary

2. Soviet Union

3. Germany

XIX.   1968, Mexico City

INDIVIDUAL FOIL

1. Ionel Drimba* (Romania)

2. Jeno Kamuti (Hungary)

3. Daniel Revenu (France)

TEAM FOIL

1. France

2. Soviet Union

3. Poland

INDIVIDUAL ÉPÉE

1. Gyozo Kulcsar (Hungary)

2. Grigory Kriss (Soviet Union)

3. Gianluigi Saccaro (Italy)

TEAM ÉPÉE

1. Hungary

2. Soviet Union

3. Poland

INDIVIDUAL SABRE

1. Jerzy Pawlowski (Poland)

2. Mark Rakita (Soviet Union)

3. Tibor Pezsa (Hungary)

TEAM SABRE

1. Soviet Union

2. Italy

3. Hungary

WOMEN'S INDIVIDUAL FOIL

1. Yelena Novikova (Soviet Union)

2. Maria del Pilar Roldan (Mexico)

3. Ildiko Ujlaki-Rejto* (Hungary)

WOMEN'S TEAM FOIL

1. Soviet Union

2. Hungary

3. Romania

XX.   1972, Munich

INDIVIDUAL FOIL

1. Witold Woyda (Poland)

2. Jeno Kamuti (Hungary)

3. Christian Noel (France)

TEAM FOIL

1. Poland

2. Soviet Union

3. France

INDIVIDUAL ÉPÉE

1. Csaba Fenyvesi (Hungary)

2. Jacques la Degaillerie (France)

3. Gyozo Kulcsar (Hungary)

TEAM ÉPÉE

1. Hungary

2. Switzerland

3. Soviet Union

INDIVIDUAL SABRE

1. Viktor Sidiak (Soviet Union)

2. Peter Maroth (Hungary)

3. Vladimir Nazlymov* (Soviet Union)

TEAM SABRE

1. Italy

2. Soviet Union

3. Hungary

WOMEN'S INDIVIDUAL FOIL

1. Antonella Ragno-Lonzi (Italy)

2. Ildiko Bobis (Hungary)

3. Galina Gorokhova (Soviet Union)

WOMEN'S TEAM FOIL

1. Soviet Union

2. Hungary

3. Romania

XXI.   1976, Montreal

INDIVIDUAL FOIL

1. Fabio Dal Zotto* (Italy)

2. Aleksandr Romankov (Soviet Union)

3. Bernard Talvard (France)

TEAM FOIL

1. Germany

2. Italy

3. France

INDIVIDUAL ÉPÉE

1. Alexander Pusch (Germany)

2. Jurgen Hehn (Germany)

3. Gyozo Kulcsar (Hungary)

TEAM ÉPÉE

1. Sweden

2. Germany

3. Switzerland

INDIVIDUAL SABRE

1. Viktor Krovopuskov (Soviet Union)

2. Vladimir Nazlymov (Soviet Union)

3. Viktor Sidiak (Soviet Union)

TEAM SABRE

1. Soviet Union

2. Italy

3. Romania

WOMEN'S INDIVIDUAL FOIL

1. Ildiko Schwarczenberger (Hungary)

2. Maria Consolata Collino (Italy)

3. Yelena Belova (Soviet Union)

WOMEN'S TEAM FOIL

1. Soviet Union

2. France

3. Hungary

XXII. 1980, Moscow

INDIVIDUAL FOIL

1. Vladimir Smirnov* (Soviet Union)

2. Paskal Jolyot (France)

3. Aleksandr Romankov (Soviet Union)

TEAM FOIL

1. France

2. Soviet Union

3. Poland

INDIVIDUAL ÉPÉE

1. Johan Harmenberg (Sweden)

2. Erno Kolczonay (Hungary)

3. Philippe Riboud (France)

TEAM ÉPÉE

1. France

2. Poland

3. Soviet Union

INDIVIDUAL SABRE

1. Viktor Krovopuskov (Soviet Union)

2. Mikhail Burtsev (Soviet Union)

3. Imre Gedovari (Hungary)

TEAM SABRE

1. Soviet Union

2. Italy

3. Hungary

WOMEN'S INDIVIDUAL FOIL

1. Pascale Trinquet (France)

2. Magda Maros (Hungary)

3. Barbara Wysoczanska (Poland)

WOMEN'S TEAM FOIL

1. France

2. Soviet Union

3. Hungary

XXIII. 1984, Los Angeles

INDIVIDUAL FOIL

1. Mauro Numa* (Italy)

2. Matthaias Behr (Germany)

3. Stefano Cerioni (Italy)

TEAM FOIL

1. Italy

2. Germany

3. France

INDIVIDUAL ÉPÉE

1. Philippe Boisse (France)

2. Bjorne Vaggo (Sweden)

3. Philippe Riboud (France)

TEAM ÉPÉE

1. Germany

2. France

3. Italy

INDIVIDUAL SABRE

1. Jean-Francois Lamour (France)

2. Marco Marin (Italy)

3. Peter Westbrook* (United States)

TEAM SABRE

1. Italy

2. France

3. Romania

WOMEN'S INDIVIDUAL FOIL

1. Luan Jujie* (China)

2. Cornelia Hanisch (Germany)

3. Dorina Vaccaroni (Italy)

XXIV. 1988, Seoul

INDIVIDUAL FOIL

1. Stephano Cerioni (Italy)

2. Udo Wagner (East Germany)

3. Aleksandr Romankov (Soviet Union)

TEAM FOIL

1. Soviet Union
2. Germany
3. Hungary

INDIVIDUAL ÉPÉE

1. Arnd Schmitt (Germany)
2. Philippe Riboud (France)
3. Andrei Chouvalov (Soviet Union)

TEAM ÉPÉE

1. France
2. Germany
3. Soviet Union

INDIVIDUAL SABRE

1. Jean-Francois Lamour (France)
2. Janusz Olech (Poland)
3. Giovani Scalzo (Italy)

TEAM SABRE

1. Hungary
2. Soviet Union
3. Italy

WOMEN'S INDIVIDUAL FOIL

1. Anja Fichtel (Germany)
2. Sabine Bau (Germany)
3. Zita Funkenhauser (Germany)

WOMEN'S TEAM FOIL

1. Germany
2. Italy
3. Hungary

XXV.   1992, Barcelona

MEN'S INDIVIDUAL FOIL

1. Philippe Omnes (France)
2. Serguei Goloubitski (Unified Team/formerly USSR)
3. Elvis Gregory (Cuba)

MEN'S TEAM FOIL

1. Germany
2. Cuba
3. Poland

MEN'S INDIVIDUAL ÉPÉE

    1. Eric Srecki (France)

    2. Pavel Kilobkov (Unified Team/formerly USSR)

    3. Jean-Michel Henry (France)

MEN'S TEAM ÉPÉE

    1. Germany

    2. Hungary

    3. Unified Team/formerly USSR

MEN'S INDIVIDUAL SABRE

    1. Bence Szabo (Hungary)

    2. Marco Marin (Italy)

    3. Jean-Francois Lamour (France)

MEN'S TEAM SABRE

    1. Unified Team/formerly USSR

    2. Hungary

    3. France

WOMEN'S INDIVIDUAL FOIL

    1. Giovanna Trillini (Italy)

    2. Huifeng Wang (China)

    3. Tatiana Sadovskaia (United Team/formerly USSR)

WOMEN'S TEAM FOIL

    1. Italy

    2. Germany

    3. Romania

REFERENCES

Mar, Colleen Walker. *1993 U.S. Fencing Association Media Guide.* Colorado Springs: ColorTek, 1993.

Roch, Rene, ed. *Internationale d'Escrime.* France: Federation Internationale d'Escrime, 1991.

Wallechinsky, David. *The Complete Book of the Olympics.* New York: Penguin Books, 1984.

ONE-TWO. A composed or compound attack.*

The one-two is made up of a feint* (false thrust) of disengage followed by a deception* (evasion) of one lateral parry. The deception of the lateral parry is established by dropping one's blade beneath the movement of the parry.

The one-two is sometimes called a ''double disengage'' or a ''simple-single.''

In a progression of lateral parries deceived after a feint of disengage, the one-two is extended into the following:

Two lateral parries deceived: one-two-three

Three lateral parries deceived: one-two-three-four

Four lateral parries deceived: one-two-three-four-five, and so on.

REFERENCE
Palffy-Alpar, Julius. *Sword and Masque*. Philadelphia: F. A. Davis, 1967.

ON GUARD. In fencing, being in a position of equal offensive and defensive readiness.

During fencing's early days, guard positions had little to do with defensive readiness and were little more than fanciful positions from which a fencer might launch his attack.

The eighteenth-century standardization of a set on-guard position—with the sword hand placed in a pivotal position central to all lines—did much to simplify and clarify fencing.

The standard, modern on-guard position as it relates to foil, the training weapon of fencing, consists of: (1) the right foot and left foot are placed at right angles and then separated by a distance of a foot to a foot and a half; (2) both knees are bent; balance remains equal on both legs; (3) the sword arm is bent slightly; (4) the sword hand is held at chest level, the thumb at a one o'clock position; (5) the point of the weapon is held at the height of one's eyes; (6) the free arm, angled from the left shoulder at a forty-five-degree angle, is bent upward at the elbow; and (7) the free hand hangs limply.

REFERENCES
Castle, Egerton. *Schools and Masters of Fence*. London: George Bell, 1885.
Palffy-Alpar, Julius. *Sword and Masque*. Philadelphia: F. A. Davis, 1967.

OPEN LINE. A section of a fencer's target area that has been enlarged either voluntarily (called an invitation) or without specific intent, by moving one's blade away from that position.

In either case, an attack may well be directed into the less-guarded line.

Also called an "invitation" or simply, *invito.*

REFERENCE
Palffy-Alpar, Julius. *Sword and Masque*. Philadelphia: F. A. Davis, 1967.

OPERA NOVA. (1536). A fencing book written by the Italian fencing master Achille Marozzo.*

This book was considered the first book of note on the art of swordplay. More than any other volume of its time, it explained the systems of sixteenth-century fighting methods. While a theoretically imperfect book by modern standards, it was nevertheless very complete and well written.

Coming on guard in the seventeenth century

Opera Nova was republished in 1550 and 1568.

A more expanded version of the book, published under the title *Arte dell Armi de Achille Marozzo,* came out in 1568.
REFERENCE
Castle, Egerton. *Schools and Masters of Fence.* London: George Bell, 1885.

OPI. A Malayan sword. The hilt* was usually of horn, with a very large pommel* decorated with long strands of hair.

The *opi* was used especially on Wetter Island.
REFERENCE
Stone, George Cameron. *A Glossary of the Construction, Decoration, and Use of Arms and Armor.* New York: Jack Brussel, 1961.

OPPOSITION PARRY. A parry that blocks an attack with direct force, as opposed to lightly knocking it away (beat parry*) or giving way to the action (nonresisting parry*).

Also may be called a "pressure parry," "resisting parry," or "push parry."
REFERENCE
Palffy-Alpar, Julius. *Sword and Masque.* Philadelphia: F. A. Davis, 1967.

ORBAN, ALEX. (1939–   ). Hungarian-born American fencing champion.

Alex Orban began fencing in Hungary at the age of fourteen. In the next few years, he rose to first-class ranking.

He came to the United States in 1957, at the age of eighteen, and immediately began to dominate the sabre fencing scene. Orban won the U.S. national sabre championship five times: in 1965, 1969, 1970, 1971, and 1972. He was also a member of the 1968, 1972, and 1976 U.S. Olympic fencing teams.
REFERENCES
Lyons, Dan. "Alex Orban." *American Fencing* (November/December 1972).
Wallechinsky, David. *The Complete Book of the Olympics.* New York: Penguin Books, 1984.

ORIKAMI. A certificate of a Japanese sword expert containing the name of the maker and description and value of the blade or mounting. It was signed by the expert (*mekike*) and marked with his seal. It was also written on a special kind of soft, thick paper called *kaga-bosho.*
REFERENCE
Stone, George Cameron. *A Glossary of the Construction, Decoration, and Use of Arms and Armor.* New York: Jack Brussel, 1961.

ORTHOPEDIC GRIP. A fencing weapon grip with small prongs or horns around which a fencer wraps his fingers.

An orthopedic grip

Called "orthopedic" because it was originally designed for a hand that had been damaged (i.e., missing fingers) or weakened muscularly, today it has gained popularity as a grip that promotes power.

The original orthopedic handle, the Belgian grip, has been joined in recent years by a number of other orthopedic designs: the Visconti, the Spanish, the Rambeau, the American, the Gardere, and the German.

Often referred to as a "pistol" grip due to its distinctive shape, it may also be called an "anatomical" grip because the shape fits snugly into the hand.

Some traditionally minded fencing masters look down at this type of grip because, by its very design, it creates rigidity in the hand, fostering wide, powerful blade actions rather than light, efficient manipulation and point control.

Yet, the seductive lure of added strength in one's fencing has pretty much won the day, and the orthopedic grip has taken over as the most popular weapon handle among fencers. In his book *Martini A–Z of Fencing,* E. D. Morton calls this family of grips "this monstrous brood."

REFERENCES

Morton, E. D. *Martini A-Z of Fencing.* London: Queen Anne Press, 1992.

Palffy-Alpar, Julius. *Sword and Masque.* Philadelphia: F. A. Davis, 1967.

OSIIER, ELLEN. (1891–?). Danish women's fencing champion.

Ellen Osiier was the first women's Olympic fencing champion. She took first place in women's individual foil at the 1924 Olympics.

REFERENCE

Wallechinsky, David. *The Complete Book of the Olympics.* New York: Penguin Books, 1984.

OTOSHIZASHI. The fashion of wearing the *tachi** (old-style long sword) through the belt instead of hung from it.

REFERENCE

Stone, George Cameron. *A Glossary of the Construction, Decoration, and Use of Arms and Armor.* New York: Jack Brussel, 1961.

OUT OF DISTANCE. A fencer is described as being out of distance when neither he nor his opponent are close enough to each other to make a touch by simply extending the sword arm and lunging.

REFERENCE

Morton, E. D. *Martini A–Z of Fencing.* London: Queen Anne Press, 1992.

OUTSIDE LINE. Those lines on the knuckle side of the sword hand. This includes both high-* and low*-outside lines.

The outside line includes the high-outside lines of tierce* (3) and sixte* (6) and the low-outside lines of seconde* (2) and octave* (8).

Tierce and seconde are achieved with the sword hand in pronation* (palm down); sixte and octave, with the sword hand in supination* (palm up).

Also called *esterna* and *dehors.*

REFERENCE

Palffy-Alpar, Julius. *Sword and Masque.* Philadelphia: F. A. Davis, 1967.

OVERLUNGE. To lunge* with the knee far out past the ankle, instead of being directly over it.

An overlunge ends up throwing the entire weight of a fencer's body forward, making it difficult, occasionally even impossible, to recover from the lunge.

Overlunging also tends to tire out the front leg very quickly because of the unnecessary extra body weight it must contend with.

REFERENCE

Stevenson, John. *Fencing.* London: Briggs, 1935.

𝒫

PALACHE. A seventeenth-century Polish sabre.* The blade could be straight or slightly curved. The crossbar* was short and usually curved toward the blade.
REFERENCE
Stone, George Cameron. *A Glossary of the Construction, Decoration, and Use of Arms and Armor.* New York: Jack Brussel, 1961.

PALFFY-ALPAR, JULIUS. (1908–   ). Hungarian fencing master.
    A fencing master of international repute, Maestro Palffy-Alpar taught fencing at the Hungarian Military Academy from 1935 until 1945. He was also a coach for the 1936 Hungarian Olympic championship team.
    In 1943, he won the three-weapon championship for Army Fencing Masters. Over the years, he has taught fencing in Paris, Canada, and San Francisco.
    Julius Palffy-Alpar wrote a highly readable study of fencing, *Sword and Masque,* in 1967.
REFERENCE
Palffy-Alpar, Julius. *Sword and Masque.* Philadelphia: F. A. Davis, 1967.

PALLAGHY, CHABA. (c. twentieth century). U.S. Fencing Association* (USFA) national director and Federation Internationale d'Escrime* (FIE) vice president.
    Born in Hungary, Chaba Pallaghy fenced in his homeland until he emigrated to the United States in 1957. Continuing to fence and now representing the United States, he won a gold medal as a member of the 1963 Pan-American sabre team.

A year later, his fencing career was cut short when he tore his Achilles tendon while bouting.

Pallaghy then turned his fencing interests toward the official side of fencing, first as a tournament director and later as an executive of the USFA.

In 1993, Pallaghy was elected to the prestigious position of vice president of the FIE, the organization governing fencing around the world.

REFERENCE

Mar, Colleen Walker. *1993 U.S. Fencing Association Media Guide.* Colorado Springs, CO: ColorTek Printing, 1993.

PALLAVICINI, GIUSEPPI MORSICATO. (c. 1650). Italian fencing master.

A student of the great master Matteo Gallici, Pallavicini traveled all over Europe learning the particulars of contemporary fencing and fencing masters. In 1670, he wrote *La Scherma illustrata,*** in which he detailed his findings. From him came many bits of fencing trivia, information that paints an interesting picture of the everyday study of swordplay.

Pallavicini notes that in his time period, fencers used swords fitted with a protective button, "which, when wrapped in leather, was about the size of a musket ball." He also describes cardboard plastrons worn for protection by fencers. He does not mention masks, however.

As to be expected, being Italian himself, Pallavicini lauds the Italian school of fence over all others. Of his specific teaching methods, his ideas differ little from those of other masters of his day.

REFERENCE

Castle, Egerton. *Schools and Masters of Fence.* London: George Bell, 1885.

PARADE DE POINTE VOLANTE. A lateral parry* employing a slight retraction of the arm followed by a riposte* by *coupé.**

REFERENCE

Morton, E. D. *Martini A–Z of Fencing.* London: Queen Anne Press, 1992.

PARADE EN CONTRE DEGAGEANT. A counterparry* employed against a disengage.*

REFERENCE

Morton, E. D. *Martini A–Z of Fencing.* London: Queen Anne Press, 1992.

PARADE EN FINALE. A parry executed at the last possible moment.

Also known as *en finale.*

REFERENCE

Handelman, Rob. "Fencing Glossary." *American Fencing* (July/August 1978).

PARADOXES OF DEFENCE. (1599). A fencing book by George Silver.*

In *Paradoxes of Defence,* English fencing master George Silver champions

Printed at London for I.T. and are to be fold at his Shoppe.

An illustration from George Silver's *Paradoxes of Defence*

the old-style sword combat of his homeland against that of the encroaching, newfangled, foreign rapier play of the Italians.

Silver spends a good deal of time discrediting any Italian masters—both professionally and about their character—who made the "mistake" of setting up shop in England. He speaks at length of the follies of "Signior Rocco" (Bonetti),* Signior Rocco's son Jeronimo,* and Maister Vincentio (Saviolo),* none of whom, according to Silver, came to pleasant ends—all, of course, at the hands of brave ("verie tall") Englishmen.

For instance, of Signior Rocco he announces, "At Queene Hithe, he drew his Rapier upon a waterman, where he was thoroughly beaten with Oares and Stretchers." Of Jeronimo he admits he "was valliant . . . but howsoever with all the fine Italienated skill Jeronimo had, Cheese [his English opponent] with his Sword with two thrusts ran into the body and slue him." As for Vincentio, he describes an encounter with an English fencing master in which the Italian, threatened with a blackjack and ''having nothing but his guilt Rapier, and Dagger about him'' refused to fight, even when insulated.

In his text regarding actual swordplay, he lauds the old-fashioned cutting sword and explains how it is superior to the thrusting rapier. ''I have knowne a gentleman hurt in Rapier fight, in nine or ten places through the body, armes and legges, and yet hath continued his fight, and afterwards slaine the other . . . and is yet living. But the blow being strongly made, taketh sometimes cleane away the hand from the arme, hath manie times been seen. Againe upon the head or face with a sharpe sworde, is most commonly death.'' He further notes, ''Bring me a Fencer, I will bring him out of his fence trickes with good downe right blowes.''

Silver talks at length about fighting methods, but even at this he is never far from a disparaging observation about rapier play. He expounds on ''The False Resolutions And Vaine Opinions of Rapier Men, And Of The Danger of Death Thereby Ensuing.''

In the end, it is apparent that Silver is a jealous man fighting hopelessly against the tide of progress. He was, in fact, the last gasp of a dying breed of fighter. The old methods of combat—methods that depended more on a stout arm than science and reason—were on the way out, and there was really no way of stopping them. Before long, England, too, succumbed to the efficiency of the thrusting weapon over the cutting weapon.

REFERENCES

Burton, Richard F. *The Book of the Sword.* London: Chatto and Windus, 1884.

Castle, Egerton. *Schools and Masters of Fence.* London: George Bell, 1885.

Wise, Arthur. *The Art and History of Personal Combat.* Greenwich, CT: Arma Press, 1971.

PARANG BEDAK. A short sword of Borneo.

The *parang bedak* had a heavy, single-edged blade, convex on the edge, with a back rather straight to within just a few inches of the tip, where it became concave.

REFERENCE

Stone, George Cameron. *A Glossary of the Construction, Decoration, and Use of Arms and Armor.* New York: Jack Brussel, 1961.

PARANG JENGOK. A sword used by thieves among the Kalentan Malays.

Sometimes called a ''peeping knife,'' the *parang jengok* had a sharp peak at the tip, which stood out, almost at a right angle, to the rest of its blade.

The sword was employed by a robber who, just walking past a man, strikes back over his shoulder with the sword, catching his victim totally unaware in the back of the head with the peak. According to Hugh Clifford's *Court and Kampong* (1896): The victim ''can then be robbed with ease and comfort, and whether he recovers from the blow or dies from its effects in his own affair.''

REFERENCE
Stone, George Cameron. *A Glossary of the Construction, Decoration, and Use of Arms and Armor.* New York: Jack Brussel, 1961.

PARANG NABUR. A Malayan sword.

It had a short blade curved toward the tip, with its widest section at the curvature. The hilt* was often made of bone. The hand guard* was usually made of brass or iron.

REFERENCE
Stone, George Cameron. *A Glossary of the Construction, Decoration, and Use of Arms and Armor.* New York: Jack Brussel, 1961.

PARANG PANDIT. A sword used by the seafaring Dyaks of Borneo.

The *parang pandit* had a short, heavy, single-edged blade, with an iron hilt.*

REFERENCE
Stone, George Cameron. *A Glossary of the Construction, Decoration, and Use of Arms and Armor.* New York: Jack Brussel, 1961.

PAREUR. A fencer who relies mainly on his defensive game. Basically, one who parries* a lot.

REFERENCE
Morton, E. D. *Martini A-Z of Fencing.* London: Queen Anne Press, 1992.

PARIEING AND THRUSTING A PLAIN THRUST. A form of conventional exercise* to teach proper parrying,* as set down by seventeenth-century Scottish fencing master Sir William Hope.*

While he was an advocate of such exercises, Hope felt the existing method used in the fencing schools—placing a fencer who was to practice parrying with his back, or left shoulder, close to a wall so that he could not avoid being hit by leaning backward—was a poor teaching method. Instead, he recommended simply placing a fencer into a comfortable on-guard position and making chalk marks on the floor by his feet "so he may not, without being observed, move them out of their place in parieing, and thereby, in place of fairly parieing, cunningly evite [avoid] the thrust."

REFERENCE
Castle, Egerton. *Schools and Masters of Fence.* London: George Bell, 1885.

PARRIES IN RAPIER PLAY. According to seventeenth-century Italian fencing master Ridolfo Capo Ferro:*

Parries are made sometimes with the right edge [of the blade], sometimes, though rarely, with the false [edge]; in a straight line as well as obliquely; now with the point high, now with the point low; now under, now over, according to the attack or thrust. But it is to be borne in mind that all parries ought to be done with a straight arm, and must be accompanied by the right leg, followed by the left. When the "dui tempi"* [separating the riposting action from the parry] are observed, as the parry is made, the left foot must be brought up against the right, and then, as the attack is returned, the right foot must move forward.

REFERENCE

Castle, Egerton. *Schools and Masters of Fence*. London: George Bell, 1885.

PARRY. The act of deflecting or stopping an opponent's attacking blade. The parry, then, is always a defensive act.

In the Middle Ages, armor performed all defensive needs. Parries were unknown. However, when armor was discarded, defensive maneuvers, by necessity, were taken up by the sword.

Early on, the parry and its accompanying counterattack* were accomplished in a single action of blocking an attacker's blade and hitting him at the same moment. Called *stesso tempo,** or single time, this approach was considered necessary because weapons were too heavy to accommodate parries separated from ripostes. While the term "parry" was often mentioned at this time, it was never described in detail.

In time, the lightening of weapons allowed for the parry and counterattacks to be carried out as two distinct actions, called *dui tempi,** or double time. Still, for a number of years, many fencing masters frowned on the latter technique because they felt it slowed down a swordsman's response time, leaving him open to devastating counter-counterthrusts.

During the seventeenth century, Italian fencing master Ridolfo Capo Ferro* taught what he deemed a "universal parry,"* a move useful in a melee or in the dark. It was a sweeping parry, crossing all the lines from tierce to seconde and passing through quarte.

For many years, an alternative method of parrying was to employ various implements in the free hand for blocking an adversary's blade. The original method was to use a small shield called a buckler*; but this proved inadequate with the introduction of the thrusting rapier.* The most popular method of parrying after the buckler was the dagger. But cloaks,* a second sword,* and gloved hands* were also brought into play.

By the beginning of the nineteenth century, the only accepted style of parrying was with the blade itself.

Three types of parries developed over the years: lateral parries* (which moved in a straight line), counterparries* (which moved in a complete circle), and semicircular parries* (which circumscribed only a half circle). At the same time, as to be expected, attacks were devised to evade each type of parry.

Parries might be accomplished by using force (opposition parries*), by lightly beating a blade aside (beat parries*), or by giving way to forceful actions (nonresisting parries*). Moreover, the parry should always be followed by an immediate counterattack called a riposte.*

There are eight lines (positions) to be covered by parries in fencing: prime,* seconde,* tierce,* quarte,* quinte,* sixte,* septime,* and octave.* Because these

Parrying an attack

can be covered by eight lateral parries or eight counterparries, a total of sixteen parries may be employed in defending one's target area.

To make a valid parry in modern fencing, the point of an opponent's blade must merely be deflected from one's target area.

The parry may also be called by the names "parade," *parrade,* the "block," and the *parata.*

REFERENCES

Castle, Egerton. *Schools and Masters of Fence.* London: George Bell, 1885.

Palffy-Alpar, Julius. *Sword and Masque.* Philadelphia: F. A. Davis, 1967.

U.S. Fencing Association, ed. *Operations Manual.* Colorado Springs, CO: U.S. Fencing Association, 1985.

PARRY BY DISTANCE. Stepping back out of the reach of an opponent's attack rather than defending with one's weapon.

Also called "passive defense."

REFERENCE

Morton, E. D. *Martini A–Z of Fencing.* London: Queen Anne Press, 1992.

PARRYING ONESELF. By not paying attention to an opponent's responses, an attacking fencer may, upon making a feint,* continue with his action even when no parry* has been executed. In this situation, the attacker often ends up running into his adversary's still-unmoving blade, creating an involuntary parry.

The experienced fencer, of course, carefully notes his opponent's responses and gauges his own movements accordingly, so that he is not working against himself.

REFERENCE

Morton, E. D. *Martini A–Z of Fencing.* London: Queen Anne Press, 1992.

PARRY OF DESPAIR. Any parry* employed in a state of panic in other words, an out-of-control parry, always heavy and almost never followed by a riposte.

Such a parry is considered highly reactive—without thought—and thus becomes easily evaded.

The parry of quinte (5) often becomes such a last-ditch defensive move.

REFERENCE

Stevenson, John. *Fencing.* London: Briggs, 1935.

PARRY WITH THE POINT. To parry* with the point of one's blade threatening an opponent's target area.

REFERENCE

Morton, E. D. *Martini A–Z of Fencing.* London: Queen Anne Press, 1992.

PARTI PRIS. A fencing decision made in advance of an attack, without taking into account the actions of one's opponent.

REFERENCE
Handelman, Rob. "Fencing Glossary." *American Fencing* (May/June 1978).

PAS D'ANE. A hand guard* formed of loops surrounding the blade of a sword. The *pas d'ane* first appeared during the fourteenth century but did not become common until the sixteenth century.

The *pas d'ane* protected a swordsman's fingers when they were wrapped around the crossbar (quillons) of his rapier.

It has been suggested that the name *pas d'ane* was adopted because of the loops' close resemblance to the hoofprints of an ass.

Also called "the eyes of the hilt."

REFERENCES
Castle, Egerton. *Schools and Masters of Fence.* London: George Bell, 1885.
Stone, George Cameron. *A Glossary of the Construction, Decoration, and Use of Arms and Armor.* New York: Jack Brussel, 1961.

PASS. In the early days of fencing, before the lunge was invented, the only method of getting within striking distance of one's opponent was to step forward by bringing the rear foot to the front. Seventeenth-century Italian fencing master Ridolfo Capo Ferro* noted, "But the true nature of passing is to walk naturally, always taking care that the right shoulder be kept forward, and that when the left foot goes across, its point be turned to the left."

Passing was often carried out by moving around one's opponent in circular fashion.

The Spanish referred to passes in terms of distance covered: the basic pass was a step of about twenty-four inches; the "simple" pass was about thirty inches; and the "double" pass was made up of two passes accomplished with alternate feet.

Passes were also employed with body evasions,* that is, moving one's body in such a manner as to avoid an opponent's weapon.

Passing continued to be an accepted part of fencing well into the eighteenth century, although by then the lunge had become the standard method of delivering an attack.

Also called a *passe, passado, passata,* and a "cross step."

REFERENCE
Castle, Egerton. *Schools and Masters of Fence.* London: George Bell, 1885.

PASSATA SOTTO. A time thrust* made into the low line* by passing beneath an opponent's attacking blade point in the outside high line.*

As an opponent attacks, the fencer carrying out the *passata sotto* drops downward, extending his blade forward, his sword hand in pronation. Here, he rests his body weight on his left hand, which touches the floor next to his right foot. The left leg is stretched backward to achieve extra depth. The head is lowered to shoulder level to avoid being hit in the mask.

The *passata sotto*

The *passata sotto* was among the favorite *botte** of sixteenth-century Italian fencing master Salvator Fabris.*

Also called *sbasso, passa di sotto, ferita di prima,* the "acrobatic lunge," *botte de nuit, cartoccio,* a *vouclousant,* an "under stop thrust," a *passer dessous,* and a "stop hit with three points."

REFERENCES

Castle, Egerton. *Schools and Masters of Fence.* London: George Bell, 1885.

Morton, E. D. *Martini A–Z of Fencing.* London: Queen Anne Press, 1992.

PASSE. Where the point of a blade slides or brushes along a valid target but never hits directly. This is not considered a touch.

REFERENCE

Handelman, Rob. "Fencing Glossary." *American Fencing* (May/June 1978).

PASSIVE CONTROL. Knowingly allowing an opponent to set up an attack with the intention of exploiting it.

REFERENCE

Morton, E. D. *Martini A–Z of Fencing.* London: Queen Anne Press, 1992.

PASSO OBLIQUO. A diagonal step away from the line of attack.

REFERENCE

Morton, E. D. *Martini A–Z of Fencing.* London: Queen Anne Press, 1992.

PASSO RECTO. A step forward to close distance with an opponent.

REFERENCE

Morton, E. D. *Martini A–Z of Fencing.* London: Queen Anne Press, 1992.

PATA. The Indian gauntlet sword.*

The *pata* had a long, straight blade, usually double-edged. The guard, in the form of a metal gauntlet,* may reach up as far as the elbow and is most often strapped to the arm to keep it in place.

Such a sword, while unquestionably protecting the hand and arm, had its drawbacks. It deprived a swordsman of the use of his wrist and so would be an awkward weapon to fence with. It was most likely used on horseback in the same fashion as a lance.

The *pata* was the favorite weapon of the Mahrattas of India.

REFERENCE

Stone, George Cameron. *A Glossary of the Construction, Decoration, and Use of Arms and Armor.* New York: Jack Brussel, 1961.

PATENOSTRIER. (c. 1570). Italian fencing master.

Patenostrier, the great fencing master of Rome, was the first to speak of *filo* (the blade) and *coule d'épée* (an attack made by entering within an adversary's guard by the opposition of the forte* to foible*).

He also advocated reducing the number of guard* positions to two by finding happy mediums between high* and low lines.* Moreover, he was in the forefront of defining attacks not merely by their beginning position but also by reference to the area they were directed to. "This," as noted by Egerton Castle* in his *Schools and Masters of Fence*** (1885), "is indeed the commencement of rational fencing: the number of botte* will increase, their definition and limitation will become more accurate, and, in presence of the multiplicity of attacks, proper parries will be defined."

REFERENCE

Castle, Egerton. *Schools and Masters of Fence.* London: George Bell, 1885.

PATER. (c. 1600). French fencing master.

The most famous fencing master in the time of Louis XIII.* His successful pupil, Jean Baptiste Le Perche,* was the first Frenchman to produce a study of fencing of any note.

REFERENCE

Castle, Egerton. *Schools and Masters of Fence.* London: George Bell, 1885.

PATERNOSTER BLADE. A sword blade with round indentations made in the metal to lighten it. The name "paternoster" came from the depressions' resemblance to the beads on a rosary.

REFERENCE

Burton, Richard F. *The Book of the Sword.* London: Chatto and Windus, 1884.

PATTINADO. An attack movement that is a combination of a step and a lunge. The execution, however, is slightly different from the lunge on the advance.* On the step of the lead (right) foot, the toes of that foot are kept up off the floor until the back (left) leg follows with its part of the step. Then, both feet are simultaneously stamped on the ground. This is followed immediately by a lunge.

Also called a "step-lunge."

REFERENCE

Palffy-Alpar, Julius. *Sword and Masque.* Philadelphia: F. A. Davis, 1967.

PATTISA. A sword used in southern India. It had a straight, broad, double-edged blade, widest near the point. The hilt* possessed a round pommel* and a broad guard.*

Also, the name of a two-handed Indian ax.

REFERENCE

Stone, George Cameron. *A Glossary of the Construction, Decoration, and Use of Arms and Armor.* New York: Jack Brussel, 1961.

PATTON, GEORGE. (1885–1945). U.S. Army general.

Known for his outstanding tactical tank maneuvering against the Germans during World War II, George Patton was also a member of the 1912 U.S. Olympic team, participating in the individual modern pentathlon, which comprises events in fencing, shooting, swimming, riding, and running.

Patton, placing fifth overall, might have won the pentathlon if he had not been such a poor marksman. He placed twenty-first in a field of thirty-two in the shooting competition.

On the other hand, an avid fencer, he placed fourth in the fencing.

REFERENCE

Wallechinsky, David. *The Complete Book of the Olympics.* New York: Penguin Books, 1984.

PAUL, LEON. (c. twentieth century). French fencing master.

Once a fencing master in the French army, Leon "Papa" Paul established in 1931 one of London's most successful and popular modern fencing schools. The achievements of his many students crowd the annals of British and international fencing.

Leon Paul's sons Raymond and Rene and his grandsons Graham and Barry were all champion fencers in their own right.

REFERENCE

Morton, E. D. *Martini A–Z of Fencing.* London: Queen Anne Press, 1992.

PAWLOWSKI, JERZY. (1933–   ). Polish fencing champion.

Jerzy Pawlowski won the Olympic individual sabre championship in 1968.

His team took second place in Olympic team sabre in 1956 and 1960 and third place in 1964.

Pawlowski was world sabre champion in 1957, 1965, and 1966.

REFERENCES

Palffy-Alpar, Julius. *Sword and Masque*. Philadelphia: F. A. Davis, 1967.

Wallechinsky, David. *The Complete Book of the Olympics*. New York: Penguin Books, 1984.

PEDANG DJAWIE BESAR. A sword of Borneo possessing a straight, double-edged blade, widening near the point. The hilt* was straight; the crossbar,* slightly curved.

REFERENCE

Stone, George Cameron. *A Glossary of the Construction, Decoration, and Use of Arms and Armor*. New York: Jack Brussel, 1961.

PEL. A stout, six-foot post planted firmly in the ground on which knights practiced sword cuts.

Also called a *post quintain*.

REFERENCE

Stone, George Cameron. *A Glossary of the Construction, Decoration, and Use of Arms and Armor*. New York: Jack Brussel, 1961.

PENTATHLON, MODERN. An event of the modern Olympics in which fencing is part. Other activities include shooting, swimming, riding, and running.

The imaginary scenario of the pentathlon has a military slant. Basically, a soldier is ordered to deliver a message. He starts out on horseback but has to dismount and fight his way through enemy lines, first with a sword, then a pistol. He escapes. He then must swim across a river. Finally, this accomplished, he ends his task with a run through the woods.

In the early days of the modern pentathlon, its participants were, by and large, actual military people; however, this is no longer always the case.

The fencing weapon used is the épée. As in the early days of épée, bouts are fenced for just a single touch.

Perhaps one of the biggest controversies of the Olympic modern pentathlon occurred in 1976, when a Soviet fencer was found to have been using an electric épée that had been wired with a push-button circuit breaker that allowed him to register touches on the electric scoring machine whether a hit was actually made or not. The Soviet fencer was, of course, disqualified. (He was never seen outside the USSR after that.)

The most famous person ever to participate in the modern pentathlon was doubtlessly George Patton,* who later became a highly decorated and successful World War II general.

REFERENCE

Wallechinsky, David. *The Complete Book of the Olympics*. New York: Penguin Books, 1984.

PEPYS, SAMUEL. (1633–1703). English diarist.

As a politician and a patron of the powerful earl of Sandwich, Pepys was in

THE ATTACK OF THE PEL.

A.D.1300.

The pel

a perfect position to observe the goings-on of his day. As a member of Parliament and the president of the Royal Society, he was able to meet the outstanding individuals of the English social scene, and all that he encountered was set down in his diaries. His writing, while never meant for the public eye, nevertheless paints a vivid picture of an uninhibited age.

It is no wonder, then, that Pepys should have written about sword fighting, which was an everyday part of English life. In 1662, for instance, he described attending a stage prizefight* (with swords): "Walked to the New Theatre. . . . And here I come and saw the first prize fight I ever saw in my life; and it was between one Mathews . . . and one Westwicke, who was soundly cut several times both on the head and legs, that he was all over blood; and other deadly

blows they did give and take . . . til Westwicke was in a sad pickle. They fought at eight weapons, three bouts at each weapons . . . in good earnest.''
REFERENCES
Benet, William Rose. *The Reader's Encyclopedia.* New York: Thomas Y. Crowell, 1965.
Wise, Arthur. *The Art and History of Personal Combat.* Greenwich, CT: Arma Press, 1971.

PERSIAN SWORDS. The sword of the Persians was called an *acinace.* Different varieties existed: some had long, double-edged blades; others were short daggerlike weapons that tapered from an extremely wide bottom to a narrow, sharp point. Handguards for the former were most often downward curving quillons*; for the latter, a thick, ridged, straight crossbar known as a ''crutch'' (because its ample size caused a sword to resemble a crutch). Some *acinaces* came without a handguard. Grips were either straight or slightly concave in shape.
REFERENCE
Burton, Richard F. *The Book of the Sword.* London: Chatto and Windus, 1884.

PERSONAL COMBAT, HISTORY OF. Personal combat can be categorized as a life-and-death struggle between two adversaries marked by intimacy and a sense of responsibility. This is opposed to mass warfare. Personal combat is as old as mankind.

While personal combat over the centuries has taken many forms, the sword fight has been the predominant form of executing this bloody ritual. Killing based on skill and mastery of an art, rather than random violence, was the hallmark of such encounters.

Personal clashes in ancient times are preserved for us in myths and legends. The Old Testament of the Bible speaks of how the champion of one nation would pit himself against the champion of another nation. Homer's *Iliad* is a detailed account of who fought and killed whom in the Trojan Wars.

Later, personal combat took the form of gladiatorial clashes in Roman arenas. Medieval knights,* via tournaments, took up where the Romans left off.

By the 1500s, personal armed conflicts were part of everyday life. Men wore swords everywhere and expected to use them. Schools of fencing, ready and eager to teach the latest methods of destruction on an individual level, flourished.

As weapons became more streamlined, the styles for fighting on a personal level grew more refined and potentially deadlier. During the eighteenth century, sword-handling techniques reached a pinnacle of efficiency.

This was not to last, though. Fashions change. By the end of the eighteenth century, the sword was no longer king of personal combat. The gun, that weapon of indiscriminate, impersonal slaughter, had supplanted the blade as the weapon of choice for dispatching one's enemy. Killing from a distance made killing more easily accomplished. Certainly, less acquired skill was needed to shoot a pistol or rifle than to wield a rapier.

The grim reality of personal combat

From this point on, personal combat, more often than not, became more a technological event than a test of human ability.

REFERENCES

Baldick, Robert. *The Duel.* New York: Spring Books, 1970.

Wise, Arthur. *The Art and History of Personal Combat.* Greenwich, CT: Arma Press, 1971.

PESO. In the old Italian school of swordplay, *peso* meant balance.* *Peso* was considered perfect if the weight of the body was on the left leg when on guard and on the right when attacking.

A proper on-guard* attitude was attained by bending the left knee, while the right leg was kept nearly straight.

REFERENCE

Castle, Egerton. *Schools and Masters of Fence.* London: George Bell, 1885.

PETER PAN. A popular character created by the writer J. M. Barrie in 1904, first for a play and then for a novel.

Peter, the boy hero of the adventure, brings Wendy, Michael, and John Darling to his home in Neverland, a magical place where aging does not occur. Many adventures ensue, especially with the evil Captain Hook and his pirate crew. There is much swordplay. Eventually, Peter meets Hook in a final, climactic duel:

> Without more words they fell to and for a space there was no advantage to either blade. Peter was a superb swordsman, and parried with dazzling rapidity; ever and anon he followed up a feint with a lunge that got past his foe's defence, but his shorter reach stood him ill stead and he could not drive the steel home. Hook, scarcely his inferior in brilliancy, but not quite so nimble in wrist play, forced him back by the weight of his onset, hoping suddenly to end all with a favorite thrust, taught to him long ago by Barbecue at Rio.

In the end, Peter Pan is triumphant, sending his opponent to a well-deserved fate, supposedly in the stomach of a large crocodile.

In staging *Peter Pan,* the role of Peter has traditionally been taken by actresses, notably, Maude Adams, Pauline Chase, and Mary Martin.

Peter Pan was made into a cartoon by Walt Disney in 1953.

A movie reworking of the Peter Pan story, called *Hook* (1991), was produced by Steven Spielberg. The film starred Robin Williams.

Hook, as a Peter Pan story, has proven to be one of the best modern swashbuckler films to date. The story deals with a grown-up Peter Pan—now an uptight, middle-aged, workaholic lawyer, Peter Banning—whose children are kidnapped by a still-alive Captain Hook in an effort to force Peter to return to Neverland for one last battle. The problem: Peter Banning has forgotten that he was ever Peter Pan. So, before he can save his children, he must reclaim his former self. Eventually he does and an epic battle between good and evil ensues. Good, of course, comes out on top.

Robin Williams's buoyant personality made him a perfect Pan. He gives an energetic performance that is both childlike and heroic, somewhat reminiscent of Danny Kaye in the classic film *The Court Jester* (1956). Dustin Hoffman, as James Hook, is the epitome of villainous movie pirate captains.

While the style of swordplay was decided upon by Steven Spielberg, the fencing itself was guided by fencing master Ted Katzoff. The outcome was creative and expertly executed. It was, in fact, on a par with the best of Hollywood's old-time film duels. Katzoff has remarked that he felt the swordplay worked especially well because of the selection of the blade moves he employed in the routines.

Robin Williams, who was personally coached by Katzoff, performed his sword fight routines with a facility and grace one might expect of Errol Flynn* or Douglas Fairbanks, Sr.* Dustin Hoffman, while doubled heavily in the combat, performed his on-camera sword bits admirably.

Maestro Katzoff, of Southern California's Westside Fencing Center, began his fencing career at the age of twelve and earned his teaching diploma through the Fencing Masters Program at San Jose State University.

REFERENCES

Benet, William Rose. *The Reader's Encyclopedia.* New York: Thomas Y. Crowell, 1965.
Cragg, Tom. "Hooked on Hook; Or, Where Did All This Sword Fighting Come From?" *American Fencing* (April/May/June 1992).

PETERS, JEAN. (1926–   ) American film actress.

Acting most often in modern dramas, Jean Peters starred in one swashbuckler film, *Anne of the Indies* (1952), as a lady pirate.

Anne of the Indies, also starring Louis Jordan, was an entertaining fictional account of the life of female pirate Anne Bonnie—in the film her name was altered to Anne Providence—who plundered the West Indies in the early 1700s.

Bringing a definite flair for the melodramatic to her role, Peters proved herself equal to the task of swashing and buckling. Her fencing, coached and directed by Fred Cavens,* was perhaps the best of any woman fencer in films to date.

REFERENCE

Richards, Jeffrey. *Swordsmen of the Screen.* Boston: Routledge and Kegan Paul, 1977.

PETITE COUSSIN. The "little cushion" inside a sword guard. It protects the fingers from occasional heavy impacts that might otherwise cause minor injury or pain. In Italian, *cuscinetto.*

REFERENCE

Stevenson, John. *Fencing.* London: Briggs, 1935.

PHASGANON. The ancient sword known as the *phasganon* possessed a two-edged, leaf-shaped blade. When written about, massive handles are often mentioned.

The name *phasganon,* which appears often in Homer's *Odyssey,* means "slaughter" or "to slay with the sword."
REFERENCE
Burton, Richard F. *The Book of the Sword.* London: Chatto and Windus, 1884.

PHOENICIAN SWORD. The Phoenician sword is described as being of the Egyptian *khopsh* (sickle-shaped) variety.
Sometimes called a *harpé.*
REFERENCE
Burton, Richard F. *The Book of the Sword.* London: Chatto and Windus, 1884.

PHRASE. A series of offensive and defensive (also counteroffensive) moves that take place between two fencers in the course of combat.
Also called *phrase d'armes* or a "fencing phrase."
REFERENCE
Handelman, Rob. "Fencing Glossary." *American Fencing* (May/June 1978).

PICKING. In épée,* making a series of quick stabs at an opponent's arm.
REFERENCE
Morton, E. D. *Martini A–Z of Fencing.* London: Queen Anne Press, 1992.

PIED FERME. Means "standing firm." *Pied ferme* refers to executing fencing actions without moving the feet.
REFERENCE
Handelman, Rob. "Fencing Glossary." *American Fencing* (May/June 1978).

PIED LEVE. Means "lifted foot." *Pied leve* refers to a deception* (evasion) of a parry* executed on the final part of a lunge*—when the right (front) foot has already been lifted off the ground.
REFERENCE
Handelman, Rob. "Fencing Glossary." *American Fencing* (May/June 1978).

PILLOW SWORD. Used during the first quarter of the seventeenth century, the pillow sword was hung by the pillow of the master of the house in case of emergency. It was straight-bladed with a straight cross guard.
The Japanese employed a special sword, also called a pillow sword, for the same purpose.
REFERENCE
Stone, George Cameron. *A Glossary of the Construction, Decoration, and Use of Arms and Armor.* New York: Jack Brussel, 1961.

PIRA. A Malayan sword with a blade like that of a falchion,* that is, a slightly curved blade that is wider at the tip than it is at the guard.*
The *pira* had a long projection from the pommel.*

REFERENCE
Stone, George Cameron. *A Glossary of the Construction, Decoration, and Use of Arms and Armor.* New York: Jack Brussel, 1961.

PIROUETTE. A 180-degree spin, whereby a fencer turned away from his opponent and counterattacked from behind his back or over his shoulder.

The pirouette is no longer a valid action in fencing. Besides, in a contest where a fencer would be hooked up to an electrical scoring machine via his body cord and cable, such a maneuver would doubtlessly result in a tangle preventing further movement.
REFERENCE
Morton, E. D. *Martini A–Z of Fencing.* London: Queen Anne Press, 1992.

PISO ECCAT. A short-bladed (twenty-inch) sword of the Battak people of Malaya. The hilt* is of deer horn.
REFERENCE
Stone, George Cameron. *A Glossary of the Construction, Decoration, and Use of Arms and Armor.* New York: Jack Brussel, 1961.

PISO GADING. A short-bladed (eighteen-inch) sword of the Battak people of Malaya. The hilt* is of fluted ivory.
REFERENCE
Stone, George Cameron. *A Glossary of the Construction, Decoration, and Use of Arms and Armor.* New York: Jack Brussel, 1961.

PISO HALASAN. A short-bladed sword of the Battak people of Malaya. The blade is curved. The hilt* is made from a cylindrical piece of staghorn.
REFERENCE
Stone, George Cameron. *A Glossary of the Construction, Decoration, and Use of Arms and Armor.* New York: Jack Brussel, 1961.

PISO PODANG. A sabre* of the Battak people of Malaya. The blade length is twenty-four inches. It has a cross guard* and a large pommel.*
REFERENCE
Stone, George Cameron. *A Glossary of the Construction, Decoration, and Use of Arms and Armor.* New York: Jack Brussel, 1961.

PISTOL. A firearm used with one hand.

Pistols have been used in combination with swords since the sixteenth century. Indeed, they have been built into the construction of swords; these were called combined weapons.*
REFERENCE
Stone, George Cameron. *A Glossary of the Construction, Decoration, and Use of Arms and Armor.* New York: Jack Brussel, 1961.

PISTOL GRIP. The name commonly applied to any of the modern foil and épée orthopedic or anatomical type grips, whose shape resembles a pistol.

Also called a "revolver grip."

REFERENCE

Morton, E. D. *Martini A–Z of Fencing.* London: Queen Anne Press, 1992.

PISTOL HANDLE. On a sword, a type of grip shaped like the handle of a pistol. It may be found on many Middle and Far Eastern weapons.

REFERENCE

Stone, George Cameron. *A Glossary of the Construction, Decoration, and Use of Arms and Armor.* New York: Jack Brussel, 1961.

PISTOL SHIELD. Pistols fixed into the center of shields were also fairly common during the sixteenth century.

These were also called *gonnes.*

REFERENCE

Stone, George Cameron. *A Glossary of the Construction, Decoration, and Use of Arms and Armor.* New York: Jack Brussel, 1961.

PLAIN THRUST. A seventeenth-century fencing term referring to lunging, in practice, at a fixed target.

REFERENCE

Morton, E. D. *Martini A–Z of Fencing.* London: Queen Anne Press, 1992.

PLANE. In sabre* fencing, the "line of attack."

REFERENCE

Morton, E. D. *Martini A–Z of Fencing.* London: Queen Anne Press, 1992.

PLAQUE. Where the point of the blade hits sideways and flat, slapping against a valid target area. For foil and épée, this is not a touch.

Also called a "place on."

REFERENCE

Handelman, Rob. "Fencing Glossary." *American Fencing* (May/June 1978).

PLASTRON. A breast covering worn in fencing or sword combat.

In battle, the plastron was of iron. For fencing, it could be made of either leather or padded cloth, although seventeenth-century Italian fencing master Giuseppi Pallavicini* talks of fencers using cardboard plastrons in practice.

Today, it is customary for only the fencing master to wear a plastron (again, either of leather or padded cloth). The student's fencing jacket should provide enough protection for bouting.

Also called a "chest protector."

REFERENCES
Castle, Egerton. *Schools and Masters of Fence.* London: George Bell, 1885.
Stone, George Cameron. *A Glossary of the Construction, Decoration, and Use of Arms and Armor.* New York: Jack Brussel, 1961.

PLAY. A term used to describe the combined actions and interactions of a sword fight or fencing, such as swordplay, rapier play, and foil play.
REFERENCE
Stevenson, John. *Fencing.* London: Briggs, 1935.

POIGNEE. The French term for the grip of a sword.
REFERENCE
Stevenson, John. *Fencing.* London: Briggs, 1935.

POINT. The tip of a sword blade.

A sword with a rounded point on its blade is sure to be a cutting weapon. A sword with a sharp point is doubtlessly a thrusting (foining) weapon. Some sharp-pointed swords, however, may also have cutting edges (*fil-et-pointe*).

The point may also be called *la pointe, la punta, die Spitz,* and *der Ort.*
REFERENCE
Burton, Richard F. *The Book of the Sword.* London: Chatto and Windus, 1884.

POINT CONTROL. The ability to place one's blade point successfully onto an opponent's valid target* area.

Before the implementation of fencing masks,* point control was of the utmost importance. A fencer's skill was judged by his ability to repeatedly plant touches on his adversary's chest. To accidentally hit an opponent on the face in a practice bout, for instance, would have disgraced a fencer for life.

Today, with the use of electric weapons, point control has the added necessity of establishing a completely straight trajectory onto an opponent's target area. Without this direct approach, the flat, depressible button* of an electric foil* or épée* blade tip will not push inward, a necessity for a touch to be registered on the scoring machine.*
REFERENCES
Castle, Egerton. *Schools and Masters of Fence.* London: George Bell, 1885.
Stevenson, John. *Fencing.* London: Briggs, 1935.
Volkman, Rudy. *Electrical Fencing Equipment.* Arvee Press, 1975.

POINTE D'ARRET. In the early days of épée* fencing, a three-pronged metal cap—the *pointe d'arret*—was attached to the blade point to ensure that touches to the wrist and arm would be sure to stick.

The *point d'arret* was also sometimes composed of rings or a flat cone.

Also known as a ''tin-tac.''
REFERENCE
Morton, E. D. *Martini A–Z of Fencing.* London: Queen Anne Press, 1992.

Practicing point control during the eighteenth century

POINT IN LINE. When the point of a fencer's blade menaces any portion of an opponent's target area,* it is said to be in line.*
REFERENCE
Stevenson, John. *Fencing.* London: Briggs, 1935.

POINT PRESSURE. The amount of pressure it takes to successfully depress the button* on the tip of an electric foil* or épée.* For a foil, the amount of pressure must equal 500 grams (17-5/8 ounces). For épée, the amount of pressure must equal 750 grams (26.45 ounces).
REFERENCE
U.S. Fencing Association, ed. *Operations Manual.* Colorado Springs, CO: U.S. Fencing Association, 1985.

POINT WEAPON. Any sword designed to be used exclusively or primarily in a thrusting* manner. Also known as "foining"* or "foyning" weapons.* The first modern point weapon was the rapier,* although thrusting swords were also used in ancient times. The smallsword, with its razor-sharp tip, became the very symbol of the point weapon.

Other point weapons included light rapiers, known as transition rapiers* (because they came between the heavier regular rapier and the light smallsword*), and the *colichemarde.**

Point weapons also go under the names of *estoc,** *espada,** *espe,*** *espee,*** *épée,** tuck,*** *tucke,*** stuck,** stock,** *flamberg,*** and *flamberge.**

In modern sport fencing, the foil* and épée* are exclusively point weapons. The sabre,* while mainly a cutting weapon, may be used as a point weapon.
REFERENCES
Burton, Richard F. *The Book of the Sword.* London: Chatto and Windus, 1884.
Castle, Egerton. *Schools and Masters of Fence.* London: George Bell, 1885.
Palffy-Alpar, Julius. *Sword and Masque.* Philadelphia: F. A. Davis, 1969.

POKER. A fencing weapon with a particularly stiff, heavy blade.

Also, a poor fencer, without technique, who merely tries to hit his opponent by employing jabbing thrusts.
REFERENCE
Morton, E. D. *Martini A–Z of Fencing.* London: Queen Anne Press, 1992.

POMMEL. A metal weight on the rear of a sword.

The pommel—meaning "little apple" because of its resemblance to an apple on some swords—acts, first, as a counterbalance on the sword and, second, as a tightening device, screwed onto to the tang of the sword (the narrow portion of the blade that fits through the handle) to keep all parts of the weapon—blade, guard, and grip—fitting snugly together.

Early pommels were often simply flat metal washers. Later, they came as half-circles, wheels, and spheres. It is from the spherical style, though, that the pommel derived its name. Pommels came in both plain and decorated forms.

While usually made of metal, pommels were sometimes made of jasper or other mineral compounds. These special types were usually fitted on swords of the highest quality.

The term to "pommel" or "pummel" someone—which means to beat or hit—comes from the sometime use of the pommel as an offensive part of the sword. When a swordsman found himself too close to an adversary to strike with his blade, the pommel portion of the weapon could be employed to strike a serious blow to the head or face.

Also called the "pummel," *le pommeau, il pomolo, der Knauf, der Knopf, pomo,* and *plumet.*

REFERENCES

Burton, Richard F. *The Book of the Sword.* London: Chatto and Windus, 1884.

Stone, George Cameron. *A Glossary of the Construction, Decoration, and Use of Arms and Armor.* New York: Jack Brussel, 1961.

Wilkinson, Frederick. *Swords and Daggers.* New York: Hawthorn Books, 1967.

POOL. An average fencing tournament* might have forty fencers signed up to compete. Rather than being forced to cross blades with every fencer in a competition—which would take days to accomplish—fencers are organized into small groups called pools. Thus, each fencer must fence only against the contestants he faces within the framework of his own specific pool.

As an example, in a tournament with thirty fencers competing, six pools of five fencers each might be set up for the preliminary (opening) bouts. The three top fencers from each pool might then go on to the semifinal bouts, leaving eighteen fencers in the tournament. Next, the eighteen semifinalists might be organized into three pools of six fencers. Here, the top three fencers from each of these groupings would go on to the final bouting, putting a total of nine fencers into the last stage of the tournament. At this point, the pooling concept is dropped, as each finalist must fence with every other finalist to arrive at a tournament winner.

REFERENCE

U.S. Fencing Association, ed. *Operations Manual.* Colorado Springs, CO: U.S. Fencing Association, 1985.

POSITIONS. The various locations where the sword hand may be placed in covering the four lines of the body. The four supination* (palm up) positions are quarte* (4), sixte* (6), septime* (7), and octave* (8). The four pronation* (palm down) positions are prime* (1), seconde* (2), tierce* (3), and quinte* (5).

In sabre,* there are five basic positions (all in pronation): prime (1), seconde (2), tierce (3), quarte (4), and quinte (5).

REFERENCE

Handelman, Rob. "Fencing Glossary." *American Fencing* (May/June 1978).

A Polish stamp commemorating fencing at the 1956 Olympics

POSTAGE STAMPS, FENCING ON. Fencing has been a popular subject for postage stamps over the years. The first fencing stamp was issued by Hungary in 1925. Since then Poland, the Soviet Union, France, Monaco, the Netherlands, Spain, Cuba, Luxembourg, San Marino, Japan, Austria, Bulgaria, Romania, Belgium, and Niger have all issued stamps featuring fencing.

The United States issued its first fencing stamp in conjunction with the 1984 Olympic games in Los Angeles.

Usually, the countries that do best in international fencing competitions issue the most fencing stamps.

REFERENCES

Harmer, Gordon, ed. *Scott's Standard Postage Stamp Catalogue.* New York: Scott, 1964.

Hoobing, Bob. *Golden Moments.* Washington, DC: U.S. Postal Service, 1984.

POSTURA. As explained by sixteenth-century Italian fencing master Salvator Fabris,* *postura* referred to any given position of the body.

Against any position assumed by an opponent, Fabris advised a similar one, which he termed a *counterpostura.*

REFERENCE

Castle, Egerton. *Schools and Masters of Fence.* London: George Bell, 1885.

POWER, TYRONE. (1913–1958). American film actor.

Tyrone Power proved to be one of those actors who fit neatly into the swashbuckling genre without seeming at all out of place. He could wear a costume

Tyrone Power (right) in *The Mark of Zorro*

easily and handle a sword reasonably well (at least well enough to make the public believe he was good).

Power's best swashbuckling effort came in 1940, with *The Mark of Zorro,*** which also starred Linda Darnell and Basil Rathbone. A remake of an earlier film starring Douglas Fairbanks, Sr., it is truly one of the great adventure films of all time.

The Mark of Zorro tells the tale of Don Diego Vega, who, coming home to old California from years of school in Spain, finds his homeland crushed under the oppression of a wicked dictator. Diego, a champion swordsman and horseman, decides immediately to fight the injustice he sees around him. He then assumes the character of a masked outlaw, Zorro. To keep his enemies off-balance while he harasses the powers-that-be, Diego hides his true self behind the guise of a languid fop. Eventually, he leads a revolt and disposes of the villains. In the end, peace and justice are returned to the land.

The swordplay, guided by fencing master Fred Cavens,* was a technical and artistic triumph. Admittedly, Power was doubled extensively during the action by Cavens's own son Albert; yet, the overall impression of Power's being a magnificent swordsman is never lost.

The Black Swan (1942), which also starred Maureen O'Hara, George Sanders, Anthony Quinn, and Laird Cregar, is another example of Tyrone Power's considerable ability as a swashbuckler. Dennis Belafonte, in his book *The Films of Tyrone Power,* called the film "the model against which nearly all other pirate movies are judged." Tyrone Power plays a recently reformed buccaneer who sets out to rid the Caribbean of the treacherous pirate Captain Billy Leech. There are many sea battles and much swordplay. The final duel, between Power and George Sanders, while not as stylish as the fight between Power and Basil Rathbone in *The Mark of Zorro* (1940), still manages to display some nice touches.

Other adventure films in which Tyrone Power fences include *Captain from Castile* (1947),** *Prince of Foxes* (1949), and *Mississippi Gambler* (1953).**

REFERENCES

Belafonte, Dennis. *The Films of Tyrone Power.* Secaucus, NJ: Citadel Press, 1979.
Parish, James Robert, and Don E. Stanke. *The Swashbucklers.* Carlstadt, NJ: Rainbow Books, 1976.

PREIS, ELLEN. (1912–   ). Austrian women's fencing champion.

Ellen Preis won the women's individual foil event at the 1932 Olympics. She took third at the 1936 and 1948 Olympics.

Preis was women's world individual foil champion in 1947, 1949, and 1950.

REFERENCES

Palffy-Alpar, Julius. *Sword and Masque.* Philadelphia: F. A. Davis, 1967.
Wallechinsky, David. *The Complete Book of the Olympics.* New York: Penguin Books, 1984.

PREPARATIONS. Movements of the blade and body that precede an offensive, defensive, or counteroffensive action. They may be used to mislead or confuse an opponent or to find out how an opponent might react to a specific situation.

Also known as "preludes."

REFERENCES
Handelman, Rob. "Fencing Glossary." *American Fencing* (May/June 1978).
Palffy-Alpar, Julius. *Sword and Masque*. Philadelphia: F. A. Davis, 1967.

PRESA DI FERRO. Engagement (firm contact) with an opponent's blade.

Also known as *prise-de-fer,* "taking the blade," a "press," or simply "pressure."

REFERENCE
Morton, E. D. *Martini A–Z of Fencing*. London: Queen Anne Press, 1992.
Stevenson, John. *Fencing*. London: Briggs, 1935.

PRESENTATION SWORD. A sword given as an award or to commemorate a special event. Often such weapons are mounted on wall plaques.

Today, the Wilkinson Sword Company,* founded in 1772, is the most notable maker of presentation swords.

REFERENCE
Wilkinson Sword Company. *Swords by Wilkinson Sword.* London: Wilkinson Sword, 1973.

PRESSION. Lateral pressure exerted against an opponent's blade.

REFERENCE
Handelman, Rob. "Fencing Glossary." *American Fencing* (May/June 1978).

PREVOST, PIERRE. (c. 1850). French fencing master.

A popular fencing master who taught at the London Fencing Club during the mid-nineteenth century, he also wrote *The Theory and Practice of Fencing* (1860).

Pierre's son, Camille, who taught in Paris, was regarded as one of the great masters of his time. It was he who, in the latter years of the 19th century, set down the precepts that would eventually become the basis for international fencing rules.

REFERENCE
Morton, E. D. *Martini A–Z of Fencing*. London: Queen Anne Press, 1992.

PRICES, SWORD. The highest price ever paid for a sword was $145,000. This was for a gold sword of honor presented to General Marie Joseph Lafayette by the American Continental Congress of 1779. It was sold at Sotheby, Parke, Burnet in New York City on November 20, 1976.

Now, go back over eight hundred years to the year A.D. 1272. In an official document from that time, we find an English nobleman, John of Bretagne, ordering thirty-eight swords from Peter the Furbisher. The price per sword was seven silver pennies.

Meyrick's *A Critical Inquiry into Ancient Armour* (1824), lists a sword and dagger set being valued at six pounds in 1608. In that same record, a silver-hilted rapier cost sixty shillings.

During the seventeenth century, English weapon maker Matthew Boulton produced sword hilts which ranged in price from two pounds to ten pounds.

To put these prices in perspective, we need to know something about English money. From the year 775, the English issued silver pennies as their currency. Two hundred forty pennies were minted from one pound of silver; hence, two hundred forty pennies equalled one pound. After the Norman invasion of England in 1066, the pound was further divided into twenty shillings for bookkeeping purposes. In modern times, until World War I, the pound was valued at $4.76 U.S. dollars.

For many years in this century, modern sport foils, épées, and sabres could be purchased for $10 each. The present prices average out as follows: $35 for standard foils, $60 for electric; $50 for standard épées, $70 for electric; and $50 for standard sabres, $85 for electric.

Antique swords run in price from a few hundred dollars into the thousands, depending on the age and condition of the weapon in question. Reproductions of historical swords, for which there is a big demand among collectors these days, range in price from around $100 to as high as $400.

REFERENCES

American Fencers Supply. *Price List.* San Francisco: American Fencers Supply Company, 1993.

Meyrick, Samuel Rush. *A Critical Inquiry into Ancient Armour.* London: Robert Jennings, 1824.

Museum Replicas Limited. *Battle-Ready Swords, Daggers, Axes, Shields, and Helmets.* Conyers, Georgia: Atlanta Cutlery, 1993.

Russel, Alan. *1987 Guinness Book of World Records.* New York: Bantam Books.

Wilkinson, Frederick. *Swords and Daggers.* New York: Hawthorn Books, 1967.

PRIMARY ATTACK. Any attack where intent to hit an opponent is directed into the initial lunge.

Also known as "first intention."

REFERENCE

Stevenson, John. *Fencing.* London: Briggs, 1935.

PRIME. The line of one.

The earliest mention of the line of prime came from seventeenth-century French fencing master Charles Besnard.* He talked of a thrust in prime by saying, "It is given from above and downwards, the wrist being held higher than the head."

In modern foil* and épée fencing, the line of prime is the position that covers the low-inside portion of the body, with the sword hand in pronation and the blade point lower than the hand.

In modern sabre* fencing, prime covers the left side of the body, with the sword hand thumb pointing downward and the blade point lower than the hand.
REFERENCES
Castle, Egerton. *Schools and Masters of Fence*. London: George Bell, 1885.
Handelman, Rob. "Fencing Glossary." *American Fencing* (May/June 1978).

PRINSE. In swordplay, as explained by sixteenth-century French fencing master Henri de Sainct-Didier,* the seizing of an opponent's sword.
REFERENCE
Castle, Egerton. *Schools and Masters of Fence*. London: George Bell, 1885.

PRINTERS. Early European printers, as suppliers of books, ranked highly in Renaissance society. In some cases, they were, by royal edict, permitted to wear swords at court in recognition of the importance of their craft.
REFERENCE
International Typographical Union, ed. *ITU Lessons in Printing*. Indianapolis: International Typographical Union, 1957.

PRIZEFIGHTING. During the seventeenth and eighteenth centuries, professional swordsmen fought legally on the stage for prizes of money. Their weapons included the backsword, sword and dagger, sword and buckler, the falchion, and the quarterstaff. The weapons were sharp, and there was often much bloodletting. Prizefights were a highly popular form of public entertainment.
Prizefighting with swords was eventually replaced by boxing.
REFERENCE
Castle, Egerton. *Schools and Masters of Fence*. London: George Bell, 1885.

PROFESSIONAL FENCER. One who makes his living from fencing, as either a competitor or teacher.
In England during the late seventeenth and early eighteenth centuries, professional fencers vied for cash prizes on stage in gruesome displays of sword skill that promised "a broken head or a bellyfull" with backsword* and falchion.* These men were often little more than butchers, hacking bits off one another with grim and practiced determination. The redoubtable James Figg* was probably the greatest of this ilk. While lauded during their day, professional sword hacks were a thing of the past by the mid-1700s.
Competitive professional swordsmen—now with foil, sabre, and épée in hand—resurged in the late nineteenth century and continued well into present times. These men were the best that Europe, especially Italy and France, had to offer. Their bouts were highly publicized affairs. The lure, of course, was money. Illustrious fencers the likes of Nedo* and Aldo* Nadi, Alphonse Kirchhoffer, Jean-Baptiste Mimiague, Eugenio Pini,* and Lucien and Emile Merignac took part in professional tournaments.

The first two Olympics, in 1896 and 1900, included fencing events for professionals.

Today, a professional fencer is more likely to be a teacher of fencing rather than a competitor, although pro tournaments are still held occasionally around the world.

Technically speaking, the U.S. Fencing Association* defines a professional fencer as one who gains a profit from fencing instead of engaging in it purely for pleasure, relaxation, or for health.

REFERENCES

Castle, Egerton. *Schools and Master of Fence.* London: George Bell, 1885.

Morton, E. D. *Martini A–Z of Fencing.* London: Queen Anne Press, 1992.

U.S. Fencing Association. *Operations Manual.* Colorado Springs, CO: U.S. Fencing Association, 1991.

PROFESSIONAL FENCING TEACHER. In general terms, a professional fencing teacher is one who makes his living teaching the sport of fencing. According to the U.S. Fencing Association,* a professional fencing teacher is one who derives cash profits from his teaching.

However, there are exemptions: Physical education teachers who teach fencing as part of their curriculum; members of the armed forces who are assigned to give fencing instruction; summer camp counselors who teach fencing as part of their camp duties; and teachers of fencing who have been given permission by the U.S. Fencing Association to receive a fixed and defined financial compensation for their work, according to U.S.F.A. bylaws.

REFERENCES

U.S. Fencing Association. *Operations Manual.* Colorado Springs, CO: U.S. Fencing Association, 1985 and 1991.

PROGRESSION OF LEARNING IN MODERN FENCING. Traditionally, the foil is the first weapon tackled by a fencing student. Because of the way in which the game of foil fencing has been designed—based on the commonsense application of sharp pointed weapons—mastery of the foil gives a fencer control over himself and, hopefully, his opponent in a combat setting. Through the many conventions of the foil, one learns a sense of discipline, timing, strategy, balance, foot work, and an efficient use of a weapon. While the rules of foil fencing are sometimes perceived by unknowledgeable fencers as limiting or confining, in fact they are like a bull's eye on a target that, once regularly hit, confer an expert grasp of situations encountered on a fencing strip. The foil creates a solid foundation upon which all other fencing wisdom may be confidently structured.

The épée should be the second weapon studied by a fencing student because, like the foil, it is a weapon that (1) strikes only with its point, and (2) is guided by the fingers; hence, its manipulation is not confusing for the fencer who has first trained with the foil. Yet unlike the foil, the épée has few rules governing its use. Its application reflects the "anything goes" nature of a real sword fight.

It is a weapon in which inspiration and the ability to take advantage of momentary flaws in another's defensive posture are immensely vital talents. Simply put, the épée is a highly improvizational tool. Nevertheless, it is a paradox that, with only minor dictums placed upon it, the épée demands even more personal control than the foil to be utilized successfully. The free form quality of its employment requires supreme point control and timing to follow the épée's guiding premise: to hit one's opponent without being hit in return. This control of self and weapon should have already been instilled by fencing with the foil and should not be a stumbling block for any fencer following the correct mode of education. Moreover, the continued honing of one's point control through épée practice tends to reflect back on the foil, improving its implementation greatly.

The final weapon to be approached is the sabre. It is primarily a cutting instrument, therefore the arm and wrist, rather than the fingers (as with foil and épée), must guide the bulk of its manipulation. It is the most divergent of the three sport weapons and requires the greatest amount of preparation. If the sabre is picked up too soon in a fencer's career, this "arm" feature of its game may thoroughly disrupt any attempt to develop the finger work needed for able foil and épée play. When fencing sabre, the blade tip is periodically exploited so that the point control one has already derived from foil and épée practice will be of real value. The conventions one has mastered with the foil likewise apply to the sabre.

In developing one's skills in this step-by-step manner, a fencing student will readily find that the foil, épée, and sabre actually end up complimenting each another. Instead of confusing matters, the differing elements of each weapon remain unique personality traits that spice up the overall experience of fencing.

REFERENCES

Palffy-Alpar, Julius. *Sword and Masque.* Philadelphia: F. A. Davis, 1967.
Stevenson, John. *Fencing.* London: Briggs, 1935.
Vebell, Edward. *Sports Illustrated Book of Fencing.* Philadelphia: J.B. Lippincott, 1962.

PROGRESSIVE ATTACK. An attack that combines the feint,* deception,* and lunge* into one smooth action.

REFERENCE

Morton, E. D. *Martini A–Z of Fencing.* London: Queen Anne Press, 1992.

PRONATION. The position of the sword hand when the palm is turned downward.

REFERENCE

Handelman, Rob. "Fencing Glossary." *American Fencing* (May/June 1978).

PSYCHOLOGY, FENCING. Part of the science of fencing deals with the psychological manipulation of one's opponent. To be aware of an opponent's mental workings—whether he reacts without thought or shows controlled responses—and to be able to formulate an effective strategy to use against him are of utmost importance to a successful encounter. Indeed, one cannot fence effectively without a clear picture of that person on the other side of the fencing strip.

Some fencers are easily manipulated and respond to any sort of overt offensive action; others take special handling. Exploratory feints give one an idea of how an adversary is likely to react. The feint becomes a question: "What are you going to do, and how are you going to do it?"

As to the actual manipulation of another fencer, feints may be used to threaten and misdirect. Beats can be employed to break concentration and to irritate.

Body language, popularized by author Julius Fast in the early 1970s, can be used to influence a fencer on a subconscious level. An obvious relaxing of one's muscles for even a moment can lull an opponent into letting down his guard, at which point an attack may be launched. Even a slight lean of one's body can focus an opponent's attention in a given direction, even throw off his balance slightly.

As to one's own psychological outlook, a relaxed mental approach to bouting is the best one. To be able to look at an opponent's attack as simple movement to be dealt with, rather than an aggressive, threatening act, is the key to maintaining balance. This mind-set, of course, can take years of fencing to achieve.

Both overconfidence and a defeatist mentality are equally dangerous. Overconfidence, based on a superior attitude, rarely takes into account the actual fencing situation at hand and leaves one open to all sorts of manipulations and surprises. Likewise, a feeling that one cannot win will surely achieve that outcome.

Anger is another pitfall. In any sport this is true, but in fencing, where a clear mind is essential, it is especially so. It has been said that a fencer reaches his peak in his mid-thirties. This is because an emotional maturity is expected to eventually overtake the impulsive and overly emotional nature of immature youth. Anger blinds an unwary fencer to everything that is going on in front of him and leads to making mistakes. This, of course, only makes him more angry and even more susceptible to error. Nothing good comes out of anger.

Calmness, deliberation, and a thoughtful and realistic examination of each competitive situation end up being the best psychological approach to fencing.

REFERENCES

Fast, Julius. *Body Language.* Philadelphia: M. Evans, 1970.
Palffy-Alpar, Julius. *Sword and Masque.* Philadelphia: F. A. Davis, 1967.
Szabo, Laszlo. *Fencing and the Master.* Budapest: Franklin Printing House, 1977.

PULITI, ORESTE. (c. 1900). Italian fencing champion.

Oreste Puliti won a number of Olympic medals. In 1920, his team took first place in team foil and team sabre. In 1924, his team took first in team sabre. In 1928, his team took first in team foil and second in team sabre.

Puliti was world foil champion in 1927 and 1929.

In 1924, Puliti fought a duel with a Hungarian judge from the Paris Olympics. The dispute was over the Hungarian's having accused Puliti's teammates of having thrown their matches with Puliti so that he might win the gold medal. Incensed by this accusation, Puliti had threatened the judge and was disqualified from the event. Two days later, when the two met, Puliti smacked the Hungarian in the face. Four months after that, the two fought a duel. Following an hour of hacking away at each other with swords, the fight was ended. Puliti and his opponent shook hands and made up.

REFERENCES

Palffy-Alpar, Julius. *Sword and Masque.* Philadelphia: F. A. Davis, 1967.

Wallechinsky, David. *The Complete Book of the Olympics.* New York: Penguin Books, 1984.

PULOUAR. An Indian sword. The hilt* had a very short crossbar* that curved toward the blade, a hemispherical pommel,* and no counterguard. The blade was curved and, on an average, twenty-nine inches long.

REFERENCE

Stone, George Cameron. *A Glossary of the Construction, Decoration, and Use of Arms and Armor.* New York: Jack Brussel, 1961.

PUNTA DRITTA. As explained by sixteenth-century Italian fencing master Angelo Viggiani,* *punta dritta* was a thrust delivered from the right (with the sword hand in pronation).

Punta dritta ascendente was a thrust delivered from the right (with the sword hand in pronation) and upward.

Punta dritta descendente was a thrust delivered from the right (with the sword hand in pronation) and downward.

Punta dritta ferma was a thrust delivered from the right (with the sword hand in pronation) and straight ahead.

REFERENCE

Castle, Egerton. *Schools and Masters of Fence.* London: George Bell, 1885.

PUNTA ROVESCIA. As explained by sixteenth-century Italian fencing master Angelo Viggiani,* *punta rovescia* was a thrust delivered from the left (with the sword hand in supination).

Punta o rovescia ascendente was a thrust delivered from the left (with the sword hand in supination) and upward.

Punta o rovescia descendente was a thrust delivered from the left (with the sword hand in supination) and downward.

Punta o rovescia ferma was a thrust delivered from the left (with the sword hand in supination) and straight ahead.

REFERENCE

Castle, Egerton. *Schools and Masters of Fence.* London: George Bell, 1885.

PUNTA SOPRAMANO. As explained by sixteenth-century Italian fencing master Angelo Viggiani,* the *punta sopramano* was the first clearly described execution of a lunge in fencing literature: "See that the right foot advance one great step, and immediately let thy left arm fall, and let the right shoulder at the same time press the arm forwards, dropping the point slightly downwards from above, and aiming the while at my chest, without in any way turning the hand. Push thy point as far as thou canst."
REFERENCE
Castle, Egerton. *Schools and Masters of Fence.* London: George Bell, 1885.

PUSCH, ALEXANDER. (1955–   ). German fencing champion.
Alexander Pusch won the Olympic individual épée championship in 1976. That same year, his team took second place in the team épée event.
Pusch was world épée champion in 1975.
REFERENCE
Wallechinsky, David. *The Complete Book of the Olympics.* New York: Penguin Books, 1984.

PYLE, HOWARD. (1853–1911). American artist, illustrator, and author.
Howard Pyle was a prodigious artistic talent, producing a huge amount of art, much of which was of an adventurously heroic nature. He did drawings and paintings for both books and magazine stories. He also wrote and illustrated his own books, including tales of the Knights of the Round Table and Robin Hood adventures. His colorful pirate art is without equal for its sense of power and period.
Pyle was the founder of the famous Brandywine School of Art, which produced such successful artists as N. C. Wyeth and Maxfield Parrish.
REFERENCE
Pitz, Henry C. *Howard Pyle.* New York: Bramhall House, 1965.

Q

QUADDARA. A Persian broadsword. The double-edged blade is nearly twenty-nine inches long. It is wide, abruptly narrowing to a sharp point. The hilt* is often made of animal horn. There is no hand guard.*
REFERENCE
Stone, George Cameron. *A Glossary of the Construction, Decoration, and Use of Arms and Armor.* New York: Jack Brussel, 1961.

QUALITY OF FENCING. Between the years 1905 and 1925, points were awarded in fencing matches, in addition to points scored, for the quality of one's bouting, a similarity to Japan's kendo, where form and spirit are held as the most important elements of the game.

Form, once stressed as a prerequisite for control—and embodied in the classical styles of such fencers as Lucien Gaudin* and Aldo Nadi*—is no longer perceived as important as the elements of power and speed; hence, the quality of modern fencing is a highly physical activity, lacking somewhat in the traditional qualities that once made fencing as much an art as a sport.
REFERENCE
Morton, E. D. *Martini A–Z of Fencing.* London: Queen Anne Press, 1992.

QUARTE. The line of four.

In foil* and épée* fencing, quarte is the line covering the high-inside section of the target area, with the sword hand in supination. When parrying, one's weapon's point is higher than the sword hand.

In sabre* fencing, quarte is the position that protects the left side. The point is higher than the sword hand, the cutting edge of the blade turned to the left, the thumb turned up.

Also, *carte* or simply "four."

REFERENCE

Handelman, Rob. "Fencing Glossary." *American Fencing* (May/June 1978; July/August 1978).

QUARTING OFF THE STRAIGHT LINE. The equivalent of the French *volte.** A thrust while stepping to the right with the left foot and twisting the body into an extreme sideways position to avoid an opponent's attack.

From the old Italian term *incartata.*

Also, *quarting.*

REFERENCE

Castle, Egerton. *Schools and Masters of Fence.* London: George Bell, 1885.

QUARTING UPON THE STRAIGHT LINE. Describes the precaution of keeping the body upright and the head well back to avoid a counterthrust in the face.

Also, *ecarting.*

REFERENCE

Castle, Egerton. *Schools and Masters of Fence.* London: George Bell, 1885.

QUILLON. The crossbar on a sword.

The quillons may be either straight or curved. When they bend upward toward the blade tip, they are called *à antennas.* They may be long or short.

The quillons may exist as the only form of guard on a sword. They may be joined by a group of counterguard bars, or they may be set under a cup or shell guard.

While serving mainly as a hand protection and incidentally for wrapping the fingers around to increase one's grip strength, the quillons could also, on occasion, be thrust into the face of an adversary.

Also called the "cross guard," "cross hilt," *les quillons, le vette,* and *die Stichblatter.*

REFERENCES

Burton, Richard F. *The Book of the Sword.* London: Chatto and Windus, 1884.

Castle, Egerton. *Schools and Masters of Fence.* London: George Bell, 1885.

QUINTE. The line of five.

In foil* and épée* fencing, quinte is the high-inside section of the target area, with the sword hand in pronation. When parrying, the point of the weapon is always higher than the sword hand.

In sabre* fencing, quinte is the position that protects the head and shoulders.

The sword hand is to the right, the palm facing forward, the cutting edge of the blade is up, and the blade itself is almost completely horizontal.

Sometimes simply called "five."

REFERENCE

Handelman, Rob. "Fencing Glossary." *American Fencing* (July/August 1978).

QUOTATIONS, SWORD. Many, many quotations exist regarding the sword. They turn up periodically throughout man's long history. The Bible and the plays of Shakespeare include numerous references. Such remarks take into account both the strengths and follies of humanity.

Every man's sword was against his fellows.

—1 Samuel

Many have fallen by the edge of the sword; but not so many as have fallen by the tongue.

—Ecclesiastes

They shall beat their swords into plowshares.

—Isaiah

Every man's sword shall be against his brother.

—Ezekiel

Let all the fighting men draw near and attack. Beat your plowshares into swords and your pruning hooks into spears. Let the weak say I am strong.

—Joel

I came not to send peace, but a Sword.

—Matthew

All they that take the sword shall perish with the sword.

—Matthew

He that hath no Sword, let him sell his garment and buy one.

—Luke

I came forth as his child from his sword.
                    —*The Egyptian Book of the Dead* (1500 B.C.)

If there were no sword, there would be no word of Mohammed.
                    —Old Arab Saying

Nothing is high and awful as the Sword.
                    —*Lod. della Vernaccia* (1200 A.D.)

Let none presume to tell me that the pen is preferable to the sword.
                                —Miguel de Cervantes' *Don Quixote* (1605)

Our swords will play the orators for us.
                                —Christopher Marlowe (1564–1593)

Lay on our royal sword your banished hands.
                                —William Shakespeare's *Richard II* (1595)

Full bravely hast thou flesh'd
Thy maiden sword
                                —William Shakespeare's *Henry IV* (1597–1598)

Why then the world's mine oyster
Which I with sword will open.
                                —William Shakespeare's *Merry Wives of Windsor* (1598)

Keep your bright swords, for dew will rust them.
                                —William Shakespeare's *Othello* (1604)

Why should I play the Roman fool, and die
on mine own sword?
                                —William Shakespeare's *Macbeth* (1606)

When valor pray on reason
it eats the sword it fights with.
                                —William Shakespeare's *Anthony and Cleopatra* (1607)

Upon your sword sit laurel victory,
and smooth access.
                                —William Shakespeare's *Anthony and Cleopatra* (1607)

Slander, whose edge is sharper than the sword.
                                —William Shakespeare's *Cymbeline* (1610)

The pen is worse than the sword.
                                —Robert Burton (1577–1640)

One sword keeps another in its sheath.
                                —George Herbert (1593–1633)

The sword within the scabbard keep
And let mankind agree
                                —John Dryden (1631–1700)

Time will rust the sharpest sword.
—Sir Walter Scott (1771–1832)

The pen is mightier than the sword.
—Edward Bulwear-Lytton (1803–1873)

The voice of every people is the Sword
That guards them, or the Sword that beats them down.
—Alfred, Lord Tennyson (1809–1892)

The history of the sword is the history of humanity.
—Sir Richard F. Burton (1821–1890)

Yet each man kills the thing he loves,
By each let this be heard,
Some do it with a bitter look,
Some with a flattering word.
The coward does it with a kiss,
The brave man with a sword.
—Oscar Wilde (1854–1900)

So will the sword always be, and remain till the end of the world, the final decisive factor.
—German Crown Prince Friedrich Wilhelm Victor August Ernst
(1882–1951)

The sword is the axis of the world.
—Charles de Gaulle's *Le Fil de l'Épée* (1934)

REFERENCES
Bartlett, John. *Familiar Quotations*. Boston: Little, Brown, 1992.
Benet, William Rose. *The Reader's Encyclopedia*. New York: Thomas Y. Crowell, 1965.
Burton, Richard F. *The Book of the Sword*. London: Chatto and Windus, 1884.
Seldes, George. *The Great Quotations*. New York: Pocket Books, 1969.

RACCOGLIMENTO. In Italian, an envelopment.

Also, a *riporto*.
REFERENCE
Morton, E. D. *Martini A-Z of Fencing*. London: Queen Anne Press, 1992.

RACCOURCI. Making an offensive action with an incomplete extension of the sword arm.

Also known as a "bent-arm attack."
REFERENCE
Handelman, Rob. "Fencing Glossary." *American Fencing* (July/August 1978).

RADDOPPIO. A continuous string of lunges* executed by lunging, bringing the rear leg forward to establish a new on-guard position,* then immediately lunging again, bringing the rear leg forward again, and so on.
REFERENCE
Palffy-Alpar, Julius. *Sword and Masque*. Philadelphia: F. A. Davis, 1967.

RAFFINE. The term for a sixteenth- and seventeenth-century French duelist who made it a practice to fight over the most insignificant matters.
REFERENCE
Morton, E. D. *Martini A-Z of Fencing*. London: Queen Anne Press, 1992.

RAGEE. A western Tibetan sword.

Also, *namral.*

REFERENCE
Stone, George Cameron. *A Glossary of the Construction, Decoration, and Use of Arms and Armor.* New York: Jack Brussel, 1961.

RAM DA'O. A Nepalese sword used in animal sacrifices. It had a broad, heavy blade (27 inches long), incurved at the tip, with an eye inlaid on each side. The greater part of the weight of the weapon was set near the tip to facilitate easy cutting. The grip was straight.

REFERENCE
Stone, George Cameron. *A Glossary of the Construction, Decoration, and Use of Arms and Armor.* New York: Jack Brussel, 1961.

RAMROD-BACK SWORD BLADE. An unsuccessful British blade design. The back of the blade was round and thick, and from this "rod" extended a thin, sharp edge. The sudden change in blade thickness made equal tempering of the metal difficult.

Moreover, because of its oddly distributed weight, it proved ineffective in sword fights and was soon abandoned as a blade style.

REFERENCE
Stone, George Cameron. *A Glossary of the Construction, Decoration, and Use of Arms and Armor.* New York: Jack Brussel, 1961.

RAPIER. The thrusting sword of the mid-sixteenth and seventeenth centuries. The word rapier has several possible origins, which include the German *rappen* ("to tear out") and the Spanish *raspar* ("to scrape").

It has been suggested that the rapier came about because of a need of fifteenth-century foot soldiers for a weapon that could be used in combat situations where there was little room for the maneuvering of a cutting sword. A thrusting sword, of course, was the obvious answer.

The rapier first appeared in England around 1560, although it was used much earlier on the Continent by the Italians and Spanish. At first, there was much contention between swordsmen who favored old-style cutting swords and those who preferred the rapier as to which weapon was best. But it soon became apparent to all concerned that the thrust of the rapier was much superior to the cut of the sword in its stopping power.

Early rapiers had both points for thrusting and sharp edges for cutting, but the latter was quickly dropped in favor of play based entirely on thrusting.

In the latter portion of the sixteenth century it became the fashion among swordsmen to employ rapier blades of such length—up to six feet in some cases—that they became both difficult to wield and a public nuisance. In England, an edict was finally passed to limit the rapier's blade length to no more than three feet.

The rapier in its initial form had a heavy blade. Moreover, the guard was usually very complicated, made up of combinations of cups, shells, bars, and

A seventeenth-century Italian rapier

loops. These weapons, being quite heavy, were employed primarily on an offensive basis. Defensive actions were carried out with a cloak, a glove, a dagger,
a second sword, or a small shield called a buckler.

However, as more efficiency was called for, the design of the rapier was
altered. The blade was shortened and lightened, and the hilt design was simplified. When this occurred, fighting tactics improved. Suddenly new attacking

methods were introduced. Also, it became possible to use the blade itself for defensive purposes.

As the seventeenth century drew to a close, further lightening of the rapier blade and simplifying of the hand guard occurred. Eventually, the weapon was transformed to such a degree that a new sword form emerged: the smallsword.

The rapier might also called a "tock," "tuck," "stuck," "stock," *estoc, flamberge,* "Spanish sword," and a *feder.*

REFERENCES

Castle, Egerton. *Schools and Masters of Fence.* London: George Bell, 1885.

Stone, George Cameron. *A Glossary of the Construction, Decoration, and Use of Arms and Armor.* New York: Jack Brussel, 1961.

Thomas, Bruno, Ortwin Gamber, and Hans Schedekmann. *Arms and Arms of the Western World.* New York: McGraw-Hill, 1964.

RAPIER FIGHT, SEVENTEENTH-CENTURY. A seventeenth-century rapier duel, while differing much from sword contests of previous centuries, should in no way be looked on in the light of a modern fencing encounter. Actions were still too broad and the weapons too heavy for this ever to be the case.

A rapier fight might transpire as follows:

Both swordsmen, as was the custom, would come on guard covering their outside line. Armed with his trusty rapier, each would hold the weapon horizontal to the ground. The right or left foot might be placed forward, depending on the individual and the moment. To begin the duel, one man might execute a simple feint of a thrust at his opponent's sword arm, testing his mettle and his reflexes. Here the other could retreat a step or, perhaps, make a parry. If he parried, a counterthrust, delivered with a forward step, would most certainly follow. This would be met with a parry also followed by a counterthrust. If possible, neither swordsman would parry without thrusting at the same instant. This maneuver, known as *stesso tempo,** was the approved method of dealing with an adversary's assault. Thrusts, delivered by either stepping or lunging, were made to targets opened by various disengagements and counter disengagements. Occasionally, to add an element of surprise to the proceedings, one might parry with his free hand, or a body evasion might be instituted to evade a thrust. Footwork, primarily of a circular nature (the conventional method of advancing and retreating during the first part of the seventeenth century) took on a decidedly linear approach more and more. This byplay, with minor variations, would continue until one man was hit.

REFERENCE

Castle, Egerton. *Schools and Masters of Fence.* London: George Bell, 1885.

RASSEMBLEMENT. A position where a fencer has drawn both legs and feet together. It may be done as part of a salute or as a counteroffensive* movement in conjunction with a stop thrust.

REFERENCE
Handelman, Rob. "Fencing Glossary." *American Fencing* (July/August 1978).

RATHBONE, BASIL. (1892–1967). British film actor.

Perhaps most famous for his portrayal of Sherlock Holmes, Basil Rathbone was also one of the great screen villains. As Levasseur in *Captain Blood* (1935),** Guy of Gisbourne in *The Adventures of Robin Hood* (1938),** and Captain Esteban Pasquale in *The Mark of Zorro* (1940),** he proved the perfect wicked balance for the swashbuckling of Errol Flynn* and Tyrone Power.* While his characters were obviously bad people, they were nevertheless eminently strong, giving the heroes they opposed a worthy obstacle to overcome.

It is ironic that Basil Rathbone should have died in most of his screen duels, because he was considered the best fencing actor in Hollywood. An avid fencer from his public school days in England, he later renewed his interest when in Hollywood. After his initial plunge as a film swordsman in *Captain Blood,* he took regular lessons, many of them from fencing master Fred Cavens.* This, of course, proved to be most beneficial to his film personae. His sabre duel with Tyrone Power in *The Mark of Zorro* is the finest example of movie swordplay Hollywood has ever produced.

Basil Rathbone also fenced in *Romeo and Juliet* (1936), *Casanova's Big Night* (1954), and *The Court Jester* (1956).

REFERENCES
Druxman, Michael B. *Basil Rathbone.* New York: A. S. Barnes, 1975.
Thomas, Tony. *Cads and Cavaliers.* New York: A. S. Barnes, 1973.

REBATED SWORD. A sword with a blunted tip used in fencing practice. This forerunner of the modern foil, as noted by fencing historian Egerton Castle* in his *Schools and Master of Fence,* was "certainly a severe enough sort of implement, eliciting vague ideas of pokers and crowbars."

REFERENCE
Castle, Egerton. *Schools and Masters of Fence.* London: George Bell, 1885.

RECOVER FORWARD. Rather than reestablishing the on-guard position* following a lunge* by propelling oneself backward by a push from the front leg, the rear leg is, instead, brought forward.

Recovering forward is done to gain ground on a retreating opponent and perhaps then continue one's attack.

REFERENCE
Stevenson, John. *Fencing.* London: Briggs, 1935.

RECOVERY. The point of returning to the on-guard position* following a lunge.*

The recovery is accomplished by propelling oneself backward by a push from the front leg and a quick lifting and bending of the free arm. At the same

Basil Rathbone (left) with his stunt double on the set of *The Court Jester*

moment, the sword arm is bent, and the point of one's blade is raised to eye level.

Also called a "return to guard."

REFERENCE

Stevenson, John. *Fencing*. London: Briggs, 1967.

REDOUBLEMENT. A continuation of an attack—in the opposite line from the initial attack—after a successful parry has been made. In doing the action, one's weapon point is replaced without withdrawing the sword arm.

The redoublement should only be executed when an opponent does not follow his parry with an immediate counterattack (riposte). This is because, by hesitating, the defender has failed to claim his right to hit. An immediate riposte, however, always takes precedence over a redoublement.

The redoublement, as a continued attack, is especially called for when, along with the lack of a riposte, the line in which the parry has been made is forcefully closed.

Another interpretation of the redoublement describes it specifically as a repeated feint, thrust, or disengage delivered with one or more new lunges against an opponent who retreats as he parries.

Still another definition includes the *coupé* as a possible way to execute the redoublement.

A final explanation of the redoublement simply states that it is a new attack made against an opponent who has parried without riposting or who has avoided the first offensive action by retreating or dodging out of the way of the blade.

Also called *rimessa di filata.*

REFERENCES

Morton, E.D. *Martini A–Z of Fencing*. London: Queen Anne Press, 1992.

Palffy-Alpar, Julius. *Sword and Masque*. Philadelphia: F.A. Davis, 1967.

Stevenson, John. *Fencing*. London: Briggs, 1935.

U.S. Fencing Association. *Operations Manual*. Colorado Springs: United States Fencing Association, 1985.

REEL. In electrical fencing,* the reel is the halfway point between the fencer and the scoring machine.* It is made of a box housing inside of which is a long electrical line that is attached to a fencer's own electrical hookup (weapon and body cord*). The line, connected to a spring, pulls out or retracts into the housing as a fencer advances or retreats.

The reel is connected, via a long cable, to the scoring machine.

REFERENCE

Volkman, Rudy. *Electrical Fencing Equipment*. Arvee Press, 1975.

REFEREE. Modern name replacing the names of "president" or "director," although the job is still the same: guiding the fencing on the piste.*

REFERENCE
Fencing Officials Commission. "FIE and USFA Adopt Bold New Rules." *American Fencing* (Summer 1993).

REFUSING THE BLADE. Avoiding an opponent's attempts to offensively take one's blade.
REFERENCE
Morton, E. D. *Martini A–Z of Fencing.* London: Queen Anne Press, 1992.

REMISE. A continuation of an attack—in the same line as the initial attack—after a successful parry has been made. In doing the action, one's weapon point is replaced without withdrawing the sword arm.

The *remise* should be executed only when an opponent does not follow his parry with an immediate counterattack (riposte).* This is because, by hesitating, the defender has failed to claim his right to hit. An immediate riposte, however, always takes precedence over a *remise.*

The *remise,* as a continued attack, is called for when, along with the lack of a riposte, the line in which the parry has been made stays open.

Also called a *rimessa* and a "replacement."
REFERENCE
Stevenson, John. *Fencing.* London: Briggs, 1935.

RENEWED ATTACK. A continuation of an attack after a successful parry* has been made.

In the normal sequence of fencing actions, the riposte* (counterattack) should always follow immediately on the heels of a parry. This forces the initial attacker back on guard to defend himself before he can attack again. But when the defending fencer either hesitates before launching his riposte or fails to riposte altogether, the initial attacker may, according to the rules of fencing, renew his attack at once. Renewed attacks are valid, then, when they take advantage of the faulty fencing practice of not instantaneously claiming one's right to hit an opponent.

There are three types of renewed attacks: the remise,* the redoublement,* and the reprise.*

An immediate riposte always takes precedence over a renewed attack.
REFERENCES
Palffy-Alpar, Julius. *Sword and Masque.* Philadelphia: F. A. Davis, 1967.
Stevenson, John. *Fencing.* London: Briggs, 1935.

RENVERS. A backhanded cut with one's blade.
REFERENCE
Morton, E. D. *Martini A–Z of Fencing.* London: Queen Anne Press, 1992.

REPARTEE. Repeated jabbing motions made by withdrawing and extending the sword arm. This often occurs when fencers have missed each other several times.
REFERENCE
Palffy-Alpar, Julius. *Sword and Masque.* Philadelphia: F. A. Davis, 1967.

REPRISE. An immediate continuing of an attack following an initial attack that has fallen short of its target. The reprise is preceded by a return to the on-guard position,* often in the form of a forward recovery—that is, following a lunge,* the rear leg is brought forward to establish a new on-guard position to put the attacker closer to his opponent.

Following a recovery, a fencer may also step before he lunges as part of a reprise.

Also called a *reprise d'attaque* and *doppia botta di rimessa.*
REFERENCE
Palffy-Alpar, Julius. *Sword and Masque.* Philadelphia: F. A. Davis, 1967.

RESTING GUARD. An old-time sabre on guard position where the sword hand is held so low that the weapon actually touches the thigh of the fencer.
REFERENCE
Morton, E. D. *Martini A–Z of Fencing.* London: Queen Anne Press, 1992.

RETRACTION. In épée* fencing, the retraction is drawing the right (front) foot backward from the normal on-guard position to keep from being hit by an opponent's attack.
REFERENCE
Palffy-Alpar, Julius. *Sword and Masque.* Philadelphia: F. A. Davis, 1967.

RETREAT. In fencing, to step backward.

The retreat is executed by first stepping back with the rear foot and then the front foot. To maintain a proper balance while retreating, one's weight should be maintained equally on both legs, and both feet should cover an equal distance.

The main objective of the retreat, of course, should be to maintain a safe defensive distance from one's opponent. The retreat, however, should not be used in place of the parry as a fencer's chief defensive maneuver. In fact, in a competitive setting, a continual retreat will eventually be cut short when a fencer reaches the end of the fencing strip.

May also be termed *retrait, rompre,* and "breaking ground."
REFERENCES
Palffy-Alpar, Julius. *Sword and Masque.* Philadelphia: F. A. Davis, 1967.
Stevenson, John. *Fencing.* London: Briggs, 1935.

REVERENCE. The salute with the sword before fencing, as described by seventeenth-century French fencing master Charles Besnard.* This was the beginning of the more gentlemanly aspects now generally associated with fencing.
REFERENCE
Castle, Egerton. *Schools and Masters of Fence.* London: George Bell, 1885.

REVERSE. In the days when swordsmen fought in a circular fashion, to reverse meant to change the direction of one's approach to one's opponent.
REFERENCE
Morton, E. D. *Martini A–Z of Fencing.* London: Queen Anne Press, 1992.

RICASSO. The squared-off and flattened part of a sword blade near the hand guard. It was devised so that a finger might easily be hooked around it and over the cross guard* to improve one's grip.
First appearing during the mid-fourteenth century, the ricasso did not become a regular feature on sword blades until the sixteenth century.
On the rapier, the ricasso is found between the cup guard* and the quillons.*
Also known as the *tige.*
REFERENCES
Castle, Egerton. *Schools and Masters of Fence.* London: George Bell, 1885.
Wilkinson, Frederick. *Swords and Daggers.* New York: Hawthorn Books, 1967.

RICAVATIONE. According to sixteenth-century Italian fencing master Salvator Fabris,* the *ricavatione* was the deception of a counterparry, or *contra cavatione.*
Today, the *ricavatione* action is called a *doublé.*
REFERENCE
Wise, Arthur. *The Art and History of Personal Combat.* Greenwich, CT: Arma Press, 1971.

RIGHT-HANDED/LEFT-HANDED FENCING. Left-handed fencers have traditionally been difficult for right-handed fencers to work with. This is due to the fact that the on-guard position* for the left-hander is the opposite of what the right-hander is normally used to. In effect, it turns everything around with regard to lines* of attack and defense for him. Where the inside line usually is, the right-hander finds an outside line; and where the outside usually is, he finds an inside.
The overriding problem for the right-hander is, of course, the scarcity of left-handed fencers to practice on, while left-handers fence mostly against right-handers and so are used to the difference. It is ironic that the most difficult opponent for a left-handed fencer to deal with is another left-handed fencer.
Old-time fencing masters recommended that the best approach to dealing with left-handed fencers was to learn to fence with either hand.
Eighteenth-century fencing master Domenico Angelo* in his *School of Fenc-*

ing (1763)* added the advice, "When the right-handed and left-handed fencer are together, they ought to be attentive, both of them, to keep on the outside of the sword; this side being the weakest."

During the early twentieth century, fencing master Professor Leonardo F. Terrone of the University of Pennsylvania stressed that students should learn to fence with both hands in order to achieve correct physical development. He reasoned that this could be accomplished only if both sides of the body and both hemispheres of the brain should receive equal cultivation. His work was described in *Right and Left Handed Fencing* (1959).

REFERENCES

Angelo, Domenico. *The School of Fencing.* London: H. Angelo, 1787 edition.

Goldstein, Ralph, ed. *American Fencing* (September/October 1976).

Palffy-Alpar, Julius. *Sword and Masque.* Philadelphia: F. A. Davis, 1967.

RIGHT-OF-WAY. Right-of-way in fencing deals with who has the right to hit whom at any given moment in an exchange between two fencers. The concept, however, applies only to foil* and sabre.* Épée* is fenced without right-of-way.

The idea of right-of-way is a form of common sense worked into the rules. It teaches when it is advisable to try to hit and when it is advisable to be defensive—as if the weapons being used had sharp points or edges. For instance, trying to hit an opponent when knowing full well that one's opponent was going to strike would be foolish. With sharp blades, even going for a double touch (tie) would make little sense. By adhering to the principle of right-of-way, then, a fencer gains offensive and defensive control over his actions.

Also known as "priority."

REFERENCE

U.S. Fencing Association, ed. *Operations Manual.* Colorado Springs, CO: U.S. Fencing Association, 1985.

RIGHT-OF-WAY IN ÉPÉE FENCING. There is no right-of-way in épée* fencing. With the épée, the concept is for a fencer to simply hit before his opponent does, as in a real fight situation.

REFERENCE

U.S. Fencing Association, ed. *Operations Manual.* Colorado Springs, CO: U.S. Fencing Association, 1985.

RIGHT-OF-WAY IN FOIL FENCING. In foil* fencing, the right to hit an opponent is established offensively between two fencers when one fencer extends his sword arm straight and menaces his opponent's target area with the point of his weapon before his opponent does. At this time, he has established right-of-way and may attack.

Defensively, a fencer claims the right-of-way from his attacking opponent by making a successful parry of the attack, that is, making a parry that deflects the attacker's blade point away from his target area. If he ripostes (counterattacks) without pause, then he has established his right to hit.

When one fencer is standing on guard with his arm already straight and his point menacing his opponent's target area, the opponent is required to move that point out of line—so that it is no longer in a threatening position—before he may attack with right-of-way in his favor.

When two fencers attack and hit simultaneously—and no right-of-way has been established—neither fencer is awarded a touch.

Right-of-way is negated offensively when an attacking fencer either bends his formerly straight sword arm or moves his point away from his opponent's target area. Right-of-way is negated defensively when a fencer who has successfully parried hesitates before riposting or fails to riposte at all.

In recent years, the "straight" arm principle for determining right-of-way has been reinterpreted as an arm "straightening during an attack" rather than a "fully straight arm before the attack commences."

Many traditional teachers of foil fencing feel that this new approach, while supposedly simplifying the attacker-defender relationship, actually weakens the overall aspect of offensive right-of-way and proper defensive-counteroffensive timing by blurring the reason for the straight arm in the first place—that is, to give the attacker his greatest reach while attacking, a reach that cannot be taken advantage of by his opponent. Beginning an attack with an arm that is not fully straightened, then, for a moment, puts the attacker in a position that is not, in fact, compatible with the commonsense approach to fencing that the old concept of "straight arm first" was supposed to define and promote.

REFERENCES

Gaugler, William. "Right of Way and Fencing Timing." *American Fencing* (July/August 1986).

U.S. Fencing Association, ed. *Operations Manual.* Colorado Springs, CO: U.S. Fencing Association, 1985.

RIGHT-OF-WAY IN SABRE FENCING. In sabre* fencing, right-of-way may be claimed offensively with either the cut (blade edge) or the thrust (blade point).

According to the Federation Internationale d'Escrime, an attacker with right-of-way is one who:

1. Extends his sword arm before an opponent does.

2. Menaces the opponent's valid target area with the point or cutting edge of his weapon.

3. Menaces the opponent's valid target area continuously.

4. Develops the threat to an opponent within attacking (advance-lunge) distance.

Defensively, sabre right-of-way follows the same form as foil fencing: a successful parry of an attack followed by an immediate riposte.

When two fencers attack simultaneously—where no right-of-way has been established—no touches are awarded.

When one fencer is standing on guard with his arm straight and his point menacing his opponent's target area, the opponent is required to move that point out of line—so that it is no longer in a threatening position—before he may attack with right-of-way behind his action.

Right-of-way is negated offensively on a cut when a fencer makes a momentary pause that allows his opponent to make a successful countercut or thrust against him; on a thrust, when a fencer bends his sword arm or moves his blade point away from his opponent's target area. Right-of-way is negated defensively when a fencer who has successfully parried hesitates before riposting or fails to make a riposte at all.

Because of numerous simultaneous attack situations occurring in modern sabre fencing, a rule was instituted in the early 1980s that was designed to do away with the continual failure on the part of either fencer to establish right-of-way in a bout situation. The rule states that following one simultaneous attack, the very next simultaneous action brings a flip of a coin to determine who then has priority in the attack.

REFERENCES

Huddleson, Mary, ed. "New Sabre Rule." *American Fencing* (November/December 1982).

Orban, Alex, and Jack Keane. "The New View of Sabre Directing." *American Fencing* (September/October 1984).

U.S. Fencing Association, ed. *Operations Manual.* Colorado Springs, CO: U.S. Fencing Association, 1985.

RINGS. During the fourteenth century, it was sometimes the fashion to carry one's sword passed through sturdy metal rings attached to the belt. While the weapon was exposed to the elements, it was held securely and could be drawn more quickly than from a scabbard.

REFERENCE

Stone, George Cameron. *A Glossary of the Construction, Decoration, and Use of Arms and Armor.* New York: Jack Brussel, 1961.

RIPOSTE. The counterattack* after a parry* has been made.

Early ripostes—if they could even be called that—were simply counterattacks that simultaneously performed the action of blocking (parrying) an opponent's cut or thrust. Due to the heavy nature of old-style swords, to even think of separating the counterattack from the parry was unheard of for two reasons. First, the second action would have been too slow to be effective (that either it would have provoked an immediate counter-counterattack, or, as suggested by seventeenth-century Italian fencing master Salvator Fabris,* it would have given one's opponent more than enough time to safely recover from his failed attack).

Second, to maintain a constant offensive nature was considered the best form of defense.

However, when swords were lightened sufficiently to make them responsive to intricate, efficient maneuvering, it became a simple matter to offset the riposte from the parry. Now, the parry could be followed by an immediate counteroffensive movement without any appreciable hesitation between the two actions.

Of course, in modern fencing practice, the riposte should always immediately follow the parry to discourage an opponent from continuing his attack mode. For this reason, the riposte is sometimes called "the echo of the parry."

To perform a riposte, one must first make a successful parry. Once that has been accomplished, the way is open to counterattack. As one's blade recoils off (bounces away from) the opposing weapon, the sword hand should be turned immediately into a completely supinated position (thumb at three o'clock). This takes control of the recoil and keeps one's weapon point in line with the opponent's target area. Turning the sword hand into supination also causes one's blade point to immediately drop to the level of one's sword hand. Finally comes an extension of the sword arm. While the sword arm does not have to be completely straight, it should continue moving forward until one's weapon point either hits or is itself parried.

Normally, the riposte is made without lunging, because one's opponent has already lunged and is therefore already within striking distance.

Also called an "after thrust" or "after cut," a "return" or "return thrust," and a *risposta*.

REFERENCES

Castle, Egerton. *Schools and Masters of Fence.* London: George Bell, 1885.

Palffy-Alpar, Julius. *Sword and Masque.* Philadelphia: F. A. Davis, 1967.

Stevenson, John. *Fencing.* London: Briggs, 1935.

RIPOSTE, DIRECT. A riposte* made in the same line* as the successful parry* that preceded it, for instance, a riposte into an opponent's line of quarte following a parry covering one's own line of quarte.

Also called a "straight riposte."

REFERENCE

Palffy-Alpar, Julius. *Sword and Masque.* Philadelphia: F. A. Davis, 1967.

RIPOSTE BY COULE. A type of direct* riposte.*

Following a successful parry,* a riposte may be made along an opponent's blade without losing blade contact.

Also called a *risposta del filo* or simply a "riposte along the blade."

REFERENCE

Palffy-Alpar, Julius. *Sword and Masque.* Philadelphia: F. A. Davis, 1967.

RIPOSTE BY COUPÉ. A type of indirect* riposte.*

The *coupé* riposte is made into the opposite line* from the successful parry* that preceded it by passing over the top of an opponent's blade. This action is meant to deceive (evade) an opponent's lateral* parry.

REFERENCE

Stevenson, John. *Fencing*. London: Briggs, 1935.

RIPOSTE BY DISENGAGE. A type of indirect* riposte.*

The disengage* riposte is made into the opposite line from the successful parry* that preceded it by passing beneath an opponent's blade. This action is meant to deceive (evade) an opponent's lateral* parry.

REFERENCE

Stevenson, John. *Fencing*. London: Briggs, 1935.

RIPOSTE BY DOUBLÉ. A type of indirect* riposte.*

The *doublé* riposte is executed following a successful parry* by first making a feint of disengage* and then deceiving* (evading) a counterparry.* When it has been completed, the *doublé* riposte will have evaded one lateral parry* and one counterparry.*

REFERENCE

Stevenson, John. *Fencing*. London: Briggs, 1935.

RIPOSTE BY ONE-TWO. A type of indirect* riposte.*

The one-two riposte is executed following a successful parry* by first making a feint* of disengage* and then deceiving* (evading) a lateral parry.* When it has been completed, the one-two riposte will have evaded two lateral parries.

REFERENCE

Stevenson, John. *Fencing*. London: Briggs, 1935.

ROBIN HOOD. The famous medieval English archer-swordsman.

While there is much controversy as to whether Robin Hood actually existed or not, there is no doubt as to the popularity of his legend.

The character of Robin Hood first appeared 600 years ago in a series of poems titled *Robin Hood and the Monk* (1450), although short references to him can be found as early as 1377.

Robin Hood and the Potter (1503) and *A Lyttel Geste of Robin Hood* (1510) firmly established Robin as a folk hero.

Over the centuries, the stories were polished and expanded on, with characters being added as the tale grew.

With minor differences, Robin Hood, as either a Saxon nobleman or commoner, is outlawed for defying the powers-that-be. Most often set during the reign of Richard the Lion-Hearted, his adventures always bring forth such colorful characters as Little John, Friar Tuck, Will Scarlet, Guy of Gisborne, Maid Marian, Allan-A-Dale, and the Sheriff of Nottingham.

The modern concept of Robin Hood includes his stealing from the rich and giving to the poor, punishing evildoers, winning archery tournaments, and de-

Robin Hood and Guy of Gisborne—an eighteenth-century illustration

fending the English throne for his king. Many of these deeds, however, date from as late as the eighteenth century.

By the twentieth century, the Robin Hood saga was pretty much fixed.

Books dealing with Robin Hood include *Ivanhoe* (1819), by Walter Scott; *Robin Hood, Prince of Outlaws* (1872), by Alexandre Dumas; *The Merry Adventures of Robin Hood* (1883), by Howard Pyle; *Robin Hood and His Merry Outlaws* (1904), by J. Walker McSpadden; *Robin Hood and His Men of the Greenwood* (1911), by Henry Gilbert; *The Adventures of Robin Hood* (1965), by E. Charles Vivian; and *Robin and Marian* (1976), by James Goldman.

The actor Errol Flynn doubtlessly furnished the world with the most lasting image of Robin Hood in the 1938 film classic *The Adventures of Robin Hood.*
REFERENCES
Benet, William Rose. *The Reader's Encyclopedia.* New York: Thomas Y. Crowell, 1965.
Holt, J. C. *Robin Hood.* London: Thames and Hudson, 1982.
Richards, Jeffrey. *Swordsmen of the Screen.* Boston: Routledge and Kegan Paul, 1977.

ROBIN HOOD FILMS. The medieval legends of Robin Hood have furnished Hollywood with an abundance of material over the years: Robin Hood the expert archer, Robin Hood the swordsman, Robin Hood the outlaw, Robin Hood the romantic. Some of the films have been excellent; some, pitifully bad. Robin Hood has even spawned celluloid sons and daughters, who have carried on his Greenwood outlaw tradition with varying degrees of swashbuckling aplomb.

Films that follow the Robin Hood tale to one degree or another include:

Robin Hood and His Merry Men (1908)

Robin Hood Outlawed (1912)

Robin Hood (1912)

Robin Hood (1922)

The Adventures of Robin Hood (1938)

Prince of Thieves (1948)

Tales of Robin Hood (1951)

The Story of Robin Hood (1952)

Men of Sherwood Forest (1954)

Sword of Sherwood Forest (1961)

Wolfshead: The Legend of Robin Hood (1973)

Robin and Marian (1976)

Robin Hood, Prince of Thieves (1991)

Robin Hood (1991)

The 1938 *Adventures of Robin Hood,* starring Errol Flynn,* is, by far, the best of these films.

The use of the Robin Hood character, however, has not ended with the medieval stories. The outlaw has found his way into a host of other films:

Ivanhoe (1953): from the novel by Sir Walter Scott

Robin Hood and the Pirates (1961): an Italian film, with Robin Hood joining a band of pirates

Robin and the Seven Hoods (1964): modern update

Robin Hood (1973): a Disney cartoon with anthropomorphic animals

The Zany Adventures of Robin Hood (1984): an unfunny comedy

Robin Hood: Men In Tights (1993): a comedy

Children of Robin Hood emerged in:

The Bandit of Sherwood Forest (1946): a son

The Rogues of Sherwood Forest (1950): a son

The Son of Robin Hood (1958): a daughter

REFERENCES
Druxman, Michael B. *Make It Again, Sam.* New York: A. S. Barnes, 1975.
Maltin, Leonard. *Leonard Maltin's Movie and Video Guide: 1993.* New York: Penguin Books, 1993.
Richards, Jeffrey. *Swordsmen of the Screen.* Boston: Routledge and Kegan Paul, 1977.

ROMAN SWORDPLAY. The Roman writer Vegetius informs posterity that the victories of the Roman legions were won with the sword point rather than the cut. The men of the infantry were trained in the use of sword and shield and honed their skills in sham fights with wooden swords.

Livy, the most famous of Roman historians (59 B.C. to A.D. 17), described a duel between a Roman soldier and a barbarian. The Roman soldier was armed with a shield and a Spanish *spatha.* His opponent, a huge Gaul, was likewise fitted. The latter held forth his shield with his left hand and planted an ineffectual cut of the sword with a loud crash upon the armor of the advancing Roman. The soldier, raising his sword point after forcing aside the lower part of his enemy's shield with his own, closed with him and delivered two quick thrusts at the giant's belly and groin, killing him. This workmanlike quality to Roman sword combat was probably typical of the form.
REFERENCE
Burton, Richard F. *The Book of the Sword.* London: Chatto and Windus, 1884.

ROMAN SWORDS. The Roman sword was, for the most part, much longer, larger, and heavier than the earlier Greek swords. The Romans called their swords *ensis, gladius,* and *spatha.*

The *ensis* was an early form of Roman sword. Double-edged and fashioned of bronze, it came in a number of shapes and sizes. For the most part, however, it was, as compared with later swords, quite short.

The *gladius* was a leaf-shape-bladed sword of iron (nineteen to twenty-six inches long) used for both thrusting and cutting by the Roman legionnaire. It had a small plate hand guard, a narrow grip, and a wide pommel.

The *spatha* was a long, straight, single-edged iron or steel cut-and-thrust sword* (up to twenty-seven inches long) used by the Roman cavalryman.
REFERENCES
Ashdown, Charles. *European Arms and Armor.* New York: Brussel and Brussel, 1967.
Burton, Richard F. *The Book of the Sword.* London: Chatto and Windus, 1884.

ROMARY, JANICE YORK. (1932–   ). U. S. fencing champion.

Janice York Romary fenced in every Olympic from 1948 to 1968. She was also U.S. women's foil champion ten times: 1950, 1951, 1956, 1957, 1960, 1961, 1964, 1965, 1966, and 1968.

Romary was Commissioner of Fencing for the 1984 Olympic Games in Los Angeles.
REFERENCES
Jackson, Donald Dale. "The Athletes Remember." *Official Olympic Souvenir Program.* Los Angeles: U.S. Olympic Committee, 1984.
Walker, Colleen. *1992 U.S. Fencing Association Media Guide.* Colorado Springs: ColorTek Printing, 1992.

RONDACHE. A round shield carried on the arm. It was a common defensive tool in sword fights during the seventeenth century.
REFERENCE
Stone, George Cameron. *A Glossary of the Construction, Decoration, and Use of Arms and Armor.* New York: Jack Brussel, 1961.

RONDELLE A POIGN. A small buckler* (shield) used in swordplay.
REFERENCE
Stone, George Cameron. *A Glossary of the Construction, Decoration, and Use of Arms and Armor.* New York: Jack Brussel, 1961.

RONDELLE, LOUIS. (1864–?). French fencing master.

One of the first fencing masters of France to teach in America.

Rondelle wrote *Foil and Sabre* (1892).
REFERENCE
Cass, Eleanor Baldwin. *The Book of Fencing.* Boston: Lothrop, Lee, and Shephard, 1930.

ROSTAND, EDMOND. (1868–1918). French dramatist.

While Rostand wrote numerous plays, he is best remembered for his classic romantic play *Cyrano de Bergerac,* which tells the story of Savinien Cyrano de Bergerac, seventeenth-century French swordsman, poet, playwright, and soldier.

Cyrano, the greatest swordsman in all of France, is in love with his beautiful cousin Roxanne. His main obstacle: he has an incredibly large, ugly nose. To make matters worse, Roxanne is attracted to the handsome Christian de Neuvillette, a young recruit in Cyrano's regiment. Because he feels he cannot win Roxanne for himself, Cyrano decides to help the tongue-tied Christian secure Roxanne's love.

Perhaps the most rousing moment in the play is Cyrano's "sword duel in rhyme." Composing a ballad as he fights, he ends the poem by running his adversary through.

The play *Cyrano de Bergerac* was a huge success from the very start, so much so that it has never lost momentum as a theatrical production.

The story of Cyrano has been made into a movie six times: in 1909, 1925, 1946, 1950, 1976, and 1990. The 1950 version, starring Jose Ferrer, is perhaps the most notable of all.

A musical adaption of the play was produced in 1973. The star, Christopher Plummer, was praised for his characterization, but the overall production received poor reviews and closed quickly. The fencing, according to a short article in *American Fencing Magazine,* the official magazine of the U.S. Fencing Association, was "excellently staged."

REFERENCES
Goldstein, Ralph, ed. "Cyrano on Broadway." *American Fencing* (January/February 1974).

Rostand, Edmond. *Cyrano de Bergerac.* Edited by Oscar H. Fidell. New York: Washington Square Press, 1968.

ROTTELLA. A type of buckler* (shield) that covered the whole forearm. It was attached to the arm by two straps.

REFERENCE
Castle, Egerton. *Schools and Masters of Fence.* London: George Bell, 1885.

ROUSSEAU, AUGUSTIN. (c. 1780). French fencing master.

The last of a famous fencing master family that, for decades, taught at the highest level of French nobility (Louis XIV, Louis XV, and their relatives).

Augustin Rousseau's fencing career was cut short, literally, when he was guillotined during the French Revolution's reign of terror, simply because he had given lessons to members of the royal family.

It has been reported that, when on the way to the guillotine, fencing master Rousseau was met with the singular jeer from one of the revolutionary judges: "Parry that one, Rousseau!"

REFERENCE
Morton, E. D. *Martini A-Z of Fencing.* London: Queen Anne Press, 1992.

RUDIS. A wooden sword or rod used in practice by Roman gladiators.

REFERENCE
Burton, Richard F. *The Book of the Sword.* London: Chatto and Windus, 1884.

RULES. The conventions* of fencing.

For foil* and sabre,* the rules seek to establish certain commonsense behavior patterns that would be most advantageous if the weapons being used had sharp points or cutting edges. Following the rules, then, helps develop personal control.

For épée,* the rules establish the approach needed for a real sword fight, where the regulated concepts of foil and sabre would not apply.

Fencing rules also set up personal behavior codes (manners)* to which a fencer must—for the sake of order and honor—adhere.

Without rules, most fencing today would probably resemble the violent, undisciplined sword combat of the sixteenth century.

REFERENCES

Castle, Egerton. *Schools and Masters of Fence.* London: George Bell, 1885.

Stevenson, John. *Fencing.* London: Briggs, 1935.

U.S. Fencing Association, ed. *Operations Manual.* Colorado Springs, CO: U.S. Fencing Association, 1985.

RYONOME. Large, scattered spots on a Japanese sword blade.

REFERENCE

Stone, George Cameron. *A Glossary of the Construction, Decoration, and Use of Arms and Armor.* New York: Jack Brussel, 1961.

S

SABATINI, RAFAEL. (1875–1950). Italian-born English novelist.

A best-selling writer of historical adventure stories, Rafael Sabatini was the master of his genre. His stories have been called flowery and absurd but invariably irresistible.

Sabatini books incorporate a strong hero, a heroine to be won, and a villain to be overcome. There is usually an abundance of swordplay.

An example of Sabatini's swordplay from *Master-at-Arms* (1940):

Redas said no more. But even through the meshes of his mask the baleful glare of his eyes could be discerned. . . . He began to pay for the hot pace he had made in his rash confidence that the engagement would be a short one. . . . Morlaix tested him by a sudden riposte, which he was barely in time to parry. . . .

. . . And now Redas, half-winded, weary, and dispirited, found himself giving ground before an attack pressed by an opponent who was still comparatively fresh. It broke upon him in answer to an almost despairing lunge in which the master had extended himself so fully and with such disregard of academic rules that he employed his left hand to support him on the ground. A counterparry swept his blade clear, and a lightning riposte planted the prongs of the arresting point high upon his breast.

A murmur rippled through the assembly as he recovered, with the blood trickling from that superficial wound.

Other Sabatini novels include *Scaramouche* (1921), *Captain Blood* (1922), *The Sea Hawk* (1923), *Captain Blood Returns* (1930), *The Black Swan* (1931), and *The Fortunes of Captain Blood* (1936).

Many of Sabatini's works have been turned into successful films.

REFERENCES
Benet, William Rose. *The Reader's Encyclopedia.* New York: Thomas Y. Crowell, 1965.
Sabatini, Rafael. *Master-at-Arms.* New York: Ballantine Books, 1968.

SABIDORO. The protective coating of clay placed over all but the edge of a Japanese blade when it is being heated and quenched to harden it.

REFERENCE
Stone, George Cameron. *A Glossary of the Construction, Decoration, and Use of Arms and Armor.* New York: Jack Brussel, 1961.

SABRE. A single-edged sword with a slightly curved blade. While it might be used for thrusting, its main purpose is as a cutting weapon.

The sabre was usually a military weapon, especially used on horseback by cavalry. The sabre, then, proved itself most effective in combat where the close proximity of opponents might preclude the use of a sword's point.

The sabre is the direct descendant of the Persian *shamsheer,* a weapon from which the better-known curved-bladed scimitar was based. Brought to Europe in the sixteenth century by invading Turks, the scimitar was eventually adapted into a more sturdy form suited to muscular Western combat. By the eighteenth century, the sabre had become the national sword of Hungary. From this incarnation of the weapon the modern sabre gained its familiar look.

By the mid-eighteenth century, more than 80 percent of all European swords were of the sabre design.

REFERENCES
Palffy-Alpar, Julius. *Sword and Masque.* Philadelphia: F. A. Davis, 1967.
Stone, George Cameron. *A Glossary of the Construction, Decoration, and Use of Arms and Armor.* New York: Jack Brussel, 1961.

SABRE, SPORT. Early sport sabres of the latter half of the nineteenth century were extremely heavy weapons, closely resembling their ponderous military counterparts. Among their proponents they were considered to be a ''real man's weapon.''

It is not surprising that when the modern sport sabre, with its thin, light blade, was first introduced in the early twentieth century, it was looked upon with scorn by many established fencers. Alfred Hutton,* one of England's well-known sabre men, called the interloper ''a silly, little toy.''

Just the same, the streamlined weapon provided a much more energetic, complex game and soon became the sabre of choice in the fencing world.

REFERENCE
Morton, E. D. *Martini A–Z of Fencing.* London: Queen Anne Press, 1992.

SABRE FENCING. Sabre fencing is a game of both cuts and thrusts, although the primary function of the weapon favors the former. It is the only sport weapon that is always held with the hand in pronation (palm down). The weapon itself should be held at about a forty-five-degree angle. The free hand is held on the

The modern sport sabre

hip to keep it out of the way of possible cuts. The on-guard stance is normally assumed in the tierce line, putting one's blade into a position that can move easily into either an offensive or defensive mode.

Generally speaking, the middle of the sabre blade should be reserved for beats, while its forte should be used for parrying.

REFERENCES

Palffy-Alpar, Julius. *Sword and Masque.* Philadelphia: F. A. Davis, 1967.

Vebell, Edward. *Sports Illustrated Book of Fencing.* Philadelphia: J. B. Lippincott, 1962.

SABRE FENCING—HUNGARIANS. From the turn of the century until the 1960s, Hungarian sabre fencers led the world in championship fencing performances. After that, their performance was not quite so strong, but their presence continues to be felt to this day.

On an Olympic fencing level, Hungarians took first place in the individual sabre event in 1908, 1912, 1924, 1928, 1932, 1936, 1948, 1952, 1956, 1960, 1964, 1990, and 1992.

In Olympic team sabre, they won the gold medal in 1908, 1912, 1928, 1932, 1936, 1948, 1952, 1956, 1960, and 1988.

With regard to world championships, Hungarian fencers placed number one in individual sabre in 1925, 1926, 1927, 1929, 1930, 1931, 1933, 1934, 1935, 1937, 1951, 1953, 1954, 1955, 1959, 1962, 1965, 1970, 1977, 1985, and 1990.

They produced world champion sabre teams in 1930, 1931, 1933, 1934, 1935, 1937, 1951, 1953, 1954, 1955, 1957, 1958, 1966, 1973, 1978, 1981, 1982, and 1991.

REFERENCES

Mar, Colleen Walker. *1993 U.S. Fencing Association Media Guide.* Colorado Springs: ColorTek Printing, 1993.

Roch, Rene, ed. *Internationale d'Escrime.* France: Federation Internationale d'Escrime, 1991.

SABRE HALBARD. A German pole arm of the sixteenth century.

This form of halbard possesses a sabre* blade instead of the more common spike.

REFERENCE

Stone, George Cameron. *A Glossary of the Construction, Decoration, and Use of Arms and Armor.* New York: Jack Brussel, 1961.

SABRE HAND GUARD, SPORT. In earlier times the hand guard of the sport sabre might be embellished with etched patterns or decorative holes. These guards eventually were made illegal for use because of the danger they posed: an opponent's weapon tip might get hung up on them, sometimes causing a broken blade. Since then, the guard of the sport sabre is perfectly smooth.

Modern sabre hand guard styles include the "Hungarian," the "Olympic," and the "Schultz." Guards are made from both steel and aluminum.

REFERENCE
Morton, E. D. *Martini A–Z of Fencing*. London: Queen Anne Press, 1992.

SABRE—MODERN SPORT WEAPON. The sport sabre is a weapon used for both cutting and point work.

The total length of a sabre is 41-⅜ inches. Its weight is 17-⅝ ounces. The maximum length of the blade is 34-⁴¹⁄₆₄ inches. The hand guard is of a solid, curved design, that includes a knuckle guard.

The sabre blade is basically of triangular design. Grooves in the blade increase its lightness and flexibility.

REFERENCES
Palffy-Alpar, Julius. *Sword and Masque*. Philadelphia: F. A. Davis, 1967.
U.S. Fencing Association, ed. *Operations Manual*. Colorado Springs, CO: U.S. Fencing Association, 1985.

SABRE PARRIES. There are five parries* used in sabre fencing: prime (one), seconde (two), tierce (three), quarte (four), and quinte (five).

Prime, which places the sabre's point lower than the sword hand, covers the inside line, defending the chest and left shoulder. Seconde, also with a low point, covers the low-outside line, defending the flank. Tierce, with the sabre's point higher than the hand, covers the high-outside line, defending the right side of the mask and sword arm. Quarte, also with the point higher than the sword hand, covers the inside line, defending the chest, abdomen, inner arm, and the left side of the mask. Quinte covers the top of the mask.

The parries in sabre perform three functions: to divert vertical cuts,* lateral or horizontal cuts, and straight thrusts.*

REFERENCE
Vebell, Edward. *Sports Illustrated Book of Fencing*. Philadelphia: J. B. Lippincott, 1962.

SABRE RULES. The sabre, like the foil,* is a conventional weapon.* This means that when fencing with a sabre, rules must be followed regarding its usage. The foremost rule is that of right-of-way,* or the establishment of attacking priority. Essentially, this rule determines who has the right to hit whom at any given time. Once a fencer has confirmed himself as the attacker either by beginning a cutting attack in a straight line before his opponent does so or by placing his point "in line" (i.e., extending his arm straight and menacing his opponent's target area with his point), his opponent, by the rule of right of way, automatically becomes the defender. The attacker then has the right to try to make a touch until his opponent performs a successful parry followed immediately by a riposte (counterattack).

Sabre touches may be scored with the blade's point, cutting edge, or upper portion of the back edge.

The target area in sabre fencing is the body from the waist up, including the head and arms. This particular target area reflects the cavalry origins of the weapon; two combatants sitting on moving horses would naturally direct their attacks at each other's upper torso rather than, say, each other's feet.

A sabre bout, like that of foil and épée,* is fought for five touches, the duration of that bout being six minutes maximum.

REFERENCES

Palffy-Alpar, Julius. *Sword and Masque.* Philadelphia: F. A. Davis, 1967.

U.S. Fencing Association, ed. *Operations Manual.* Colorado Springs, CO: U.S. Fencing Association, 1985.

Vebell, Edward. *Sports Illustrated Book of Fencing.* Philadelphia: J. B. Lippincott, 1962.

SABRE SCHOOLS. In 1868, the Italians founded their first sabre school, run by the fencing master Giuseppe Radaelli, whose book, *Istruzione per la Scherma di Spada e di Sciabola* (1876), set down the basics of the Italian style for the first time. Luigi Barbasetti and Eugenio Pini were two highly successful sabre masters who worked with Radaelli. Barbasetti, following Radaelli's lead, wrote his own book—*Das Säbelfechten*—in 1899, which proved to be the best sabre manual for its time period.

The Hungarian school* of sabre fencing had its official beginnings in 1851, when Joseph Keresztessy,* known as ''the father of Hungarian sabre fencing,'' opened his school to teach a style that involved simple, short cuts and parries that emanated from circular wrist motions.

In 1896, Italo Santelli,* an Italian fencing champion of great renown, was invited by the Hungarian government to come to Hungary to teach sabre. He adapted his style to the Hungarian method to create an approach to sabre fencing that made the Hungarians nearly invincible for decades. Other Hungarian masters who added elements to their country's sabre style were Borsody,* Gerentser, Gerevich,* Schlotzer, and Tusnady.

REFERENCE

Palffy-Alpar, Julius. *Sword and Masque.* Philadelphia: F. A. Davis, 1967.

SABRE STYLES. Sabre fencing developed into two distinct styles: the Italian and the Hungarian.

The Italian school of sabre fencing, incorporating sweeping, dramatic cuts and parries, and traditional footwork was highly popular during the beginning of the twentieth century. However, it was eventually supplanted by the Hungarian approach, which employed short, simple movements directed from the wrist and powerful, athletic footwork.

REFERENCE

Palffy-Alpar, Julius. *Sword and Masque.* Philadelphia: F. A. Davis, 1967.

SAFETY. Safety in fencing can be ensured to a great degree by cultivating a respect for fencing and its traditions. This basically means taking lessons from a knowledgeable instructor, learning and following the conventions of the sport, and always wearing the proper gear in good repair.

REFERENCE
Stevenson, John. *Fencing.* London: Briggs, 1935.

SAGE-O. A flat silk cord that was passed through a fitting on a Japanese sword scabbard. It was used to attach the scabbard to a belt or, when fighting, to tie back one's sleeves.

Also called *tusaki.*
REFERENCE
Stone, George Cameron. *A Glossary of the Construction, Decoration, and Use of Arms and Armor.* New York: Jack Brussel, 1961.

SAGE-OBI. A belt with slings for a *tachi** (the old-style Japanese long sword).
REFERENCE
Stone, George Cameron. *A Glossary of the Construction, Decoration, and Use of Arms and Armor.* New York: Jack Brussel, 1961.

SAIF. A broad-bladed Arab sabre,* with a hooked pommel.* Blade lengths varied between twenty-five and twenty-nine inches.

The *saif* is found in all countries in which Arabs live, although each area has its own variety.

Also called *sayf.*
REFERENCE
Stone, George Cameron. *A Glossary of the Construction, Decoration, and Use of Arms and Armor.* New York: Jack Brussel, 1961.

SAINCT DIDIER, HENRY DE. (c. 1550). French fencing master.

The first French writer of note on the subject of fencing. However, Sainct Didier's teachings are little more than reworkings of the Italian approach to swordplay, especially those theories of Achille Marozzo, Camillo Agrippa, and Giacomo Grassi.

Sainct Didier's one innovation to the teaching of fencing was to adopt the method of referring to two opposing combatants in order to explain their respective actions.

Sainct Didier's book on swordplay, *Traicte Contenant les Secrets du Premier Livre sur L'Espee Seule,*** was published in 1573.
REFERENCES
Castle, Egerton. *Schools and Masters of Fence.* London: George Bell, 1885.
Wise, Arthur. *The Art and History of Personal Combat.* Greenwich, CT: Arma Press, 1971.

SAINT-GEORGES, CHEVALIER DE. (c. 1750). French nobleman and swordsman.

Besides fighting countless duels, the Chevalier de Saint-Georges was the co-originator, along with French fencing master la Boessiere,* of the fencing mask.*

French fencing master Henry de Sainct Didier

Despite the fact that he was a gifted swordsman, Saint-Georges was never known to take advantage of his skill. Once, while visiting at the home of some friends, he was confronted by a young officer of hussars, who, not realizing who he was, boasted of having crossed swords with, and beaten, the famous Saint-Georges many times. Saint-Georges, knowing this to be false, calmly asked the young man to fence with him, which the unfortunate soldier readily agreed to do, thinking he would impress the ladies who were present. Saint-Georges then proceeded to make one hit after another, virtually at will. He ended the exhibition with a dramatic disarm. At this point, Saint-Georges revealed to his shamed opponent who he actually was. The young officer left the house immediately and never returned.

REFERENCES

Castle, Egerton. *Schools and Masters of Fence.* London: George Bell, 1885.
Baldick, Robert. *The Duel.* New York: Spring Books, 1965.

ST. GEORGE'S GUARD. A head parry* of the eighteenth century. As the story goes, it was named after the position in which St. George held his arm while slaying the dragon.

REFERENCE

Castle, Egerton. *Schools and Masters of Fence.* London: George Bell, 1885.

SAINT-MICHEL, CONFRERIE ROYALE ET CHEVALIERE DE. An organization of gentlemen swordsmen begun at Ghent, Belgium, in the first years of the seventeenth century and devoted to the study of fencing. In 1613, the group became rather exclusive, allowing none but the noblest names as members.

While the association's headquarters was damaged during the French Revolution, it continued to function as an institution well into the nineteenth century.

REFERENCE

Castle, Egerton. *Schools and Masters of Fence.* London: George Bell, 1885.

SAKA-TE. In Japanese sword fighting, *saka-te* referred to holding the sword with its point downward.

REFERENCE

Stone, George Cameron. *A Glossary of the Construction, Decoration, and Use of Arms and Armor.* New York: Jack Brussel, 1961.

SALAPA. An Indian sword with a projecting arm from the hilt* that could be used as a hand rest.

REFERENCE

Stone, George Cameron. *A Glossary of the Construction, Decoration, and Use of Arms and Armor.* New York: Jack Brussel, 1961.

SALLE D'ARMES. Formal name, in French, for a school of fencing.

REFERENCE

Curry, Nancy. *The Fencing Book.* New York: Leisure Press, 1984.

SALTO INDIETRO. In Italian, the jump backward, sometimes depicted as executed from a full lunge.

REFERENCE

Morton, E. D. *Martini A–Z of Fencing.* London: Queen Anne Press, 1992.

SALUTE. A courtesy of fencing.

In medieval times, knights, before doing battle, would kneel and kiss the hilt of their down-turned sword, doubtlessly as a prayer to God and, perhaps, in respect to their liege lord or king.

The salute according to Domenico Angelo

The salute resurfaced during the seventeenth century, introduced by the French fencing master Charles Besnard,* as fencing began taking on more gentlemanly qualities than it had previously enjoyed during its earlier roughhouse period, when fencing schools were packed to overflowing with the dregs of society.

As noted by the great master Domenico Angelo* in his book *The School of Fencing* (1763): "The salute is a civility due to the spectators, and reciprocally to the persons who are to fence."

During the seventeenth century, the salute was often performed not only with the sword but by doffing one's hat.

In time, though, given the human quality of complicating what should be basic and to the point, the salute became so intricate, comprising so many moves, that it became a skill simply to perfect it. According to historian Arthur Wise, in his book *The Art and History of Personal Combat* (1971), "It was not apparently sufficient to send a man to the next world with expedition, it must also be done with finesse."

Today, the salute has returned to its simplified form, as a brief respectful acknowledgment, performed with the sword at the outset of one's bout—as Maestro Angelo would have it—of one's opponent and the director and judges presiding over the contest.

One also salutes one's teacher before taking a lesson.

It has been observed that, psychologically, the salute, in its pure state, has an extremely important function in personal combat of allowing a fencer/duelist a pause, a brief moment of calming reflection when he could focus his energies toward the task ahead. Without this important check, he might run off recklessly into an engagement where rash strategic decisions, guided by anger, could conceivably result in defeat or death.

REFERENCES

Angelo, Domenico. *The School of Fencing*. London: H. Angelo, 1787 edition.

Stevenson, John. *Fencing*. London: Briggs, 1935.

Wise, Arthur. *The Art and History of Personal Combat*. Greenwich, CT: Arma Press, 1971.

SAMEZAYA. A Japanese sword scabbard* covered with sharkskin.

REFERENCE

Stone, George Cameron. *A Glossary of the Construction, Decoration, and Use of Arms and Armor*. New York: Jack Brussel, 1961.

SAMURAI. The warrior class of feudal Japan.

The samurai was expert in the use of numerous weapons, especially the sword, which came to represent his inner spirit.

Following a special code of behavior called Bushido,* or the way of the warrior, the samurai was not unlike the European knight* in his quest for physical and spiritual excellence.

Among the most famous samurai in Japanese history are Miyamoto Musashi,* Bokuden Takamiki Tsukahara,** Kagehisa Ittosai, Mitsuyoshi Yagyu,** and Kurando Marume.**

REFERENCES

Nitobe, Inazo. *Bushido: The Warrior's Code*. Burbank, CA: Ohara Books, 1975.

Sasamori, Junzo, and Gordon Warner. *This Is Kendo*. Vermont: Charles E. Tuttle, 1964.

SAMURAI FILMS. The samurai film of Japan is a highly stylized, ritualized movie genre. It embodies the tenets of honor and bravery and often deals with either the concept of spiritual growth of the samurai or revenge. Swordplay, of course, is an ever-present element and usually the vehicle by which all conflict, both spiritual and physical, is settled.

Leading makers of this type of film include Akira Kurosawa,* Hiroshi Inagaki, Masaki Kobayashi, and Kenji Mizoguchi.

The most prominant actor of samurai films is doubtlessly Toshiro Mifune.* Other popular samurai film actors are Tomisaburo Wakayama and Shintaro Katsu.

A samurai duel, as depicted by the artist Kunioshi

Samurai films include:

The Wandering Gambler (1928)

A Swordsman's Picture Book (1929)

Three Jesting Ronin (1930)

Chuji Kunisada (1933)

Matchless Sword (1937)

Miyamoto Musashi (1940)

Snake Princess (1949)

Rashomon (1950)

A Tale of Genji (1951)

Pirates (1951)

Sword for Hire (1952)

Ugetsu (1953)

Gate of Hell (1953)

Seven Samurai (1954)

Samurai (1954)

Duel at Ichijoji Temple (1955)

Musashi and Kojiro (1955)

New Tales of the Taira Clan (1955)

Rainy Night Duel (1956)

Yagyu Secret Scroll (1957)

Ninjutsu (1958)

The Loyal Forty-Seven Ronin (1958)

The Hidden Fortress (1958)

Samurai Saga (1959)

Gambling Samurai (1960)

Daredevil in the Castle (1961)

A Woman Using a Short Sword (1961)

Yojimbo (1961)

Sanjuro (1962)

Samurai Pirate (1963)

Samurai Assassin (1965)

Sword of Doom (1966)

Rise Against the Sword (1966)

The Blind Swordsman's Vengeance (1966)

The Blind Swordsman's Rescue (1967)

Zatuichi (1968)

Samurai Banners (1969)

Devil's Temple (1969)

Band of Assassins (1970)

Red Sun (1971)

Sword of Vengeance (1972)

The Wanderers (1974)

The Yakuza (1975)

Shogun (1980)

Bushido Blade (1980)

The Shadow Warrior (1981)

REFERENCES

Halliwell, Leslie. *Halliwell's Filmgoer's and Video Viewer's Companion.* New York: Charles Scribner's Sons, 1988.

Mintz, Marilyn D. *The Martial Arts Film.* New York: A. S. Barnes, 1978.

SAMURAI SWORD. In popular understanding, the *katana** is the traditional sword of the samurai. The standard samurai sword had a blade between twenty-four and thirty inches long. While the sword of the samurai could be used for thrusting, it was essentially a cutting weapon.

The samurai considered his sword to be his soul and accorded it great respect. Others, too, were expected to treat his weapon with honor, and anything less was considered an insult.

REFERENCES

Brinkley, F. *Samurai: The Invincible Warrior.* Burbank, CA: Ohara, 1975.

Nitobe, Inazo. *Bushido: The Warrior's Code.* Burbank, CA: Ohara, 1979.

SANDERS, GEORGE. (1906–1972). British film actor.

George Sanders made a living of playing scoundrels, cads, and villains for over thirty years. Occasionally, his suave persona took him into the swashbuckler genre. However, as he hated physical activity of any kind, his fencing scenes were usually heavily doubled.

Sanders was set to play the part of Zorro's main adversary in the 1940 classic *The Mark of Zorro,* which starred Tyrone Power. But because of his well-known inactive nature, fencing master Fred Cavens* suggested that the role be given to Basil Rathbone, who, indeed, got the role.

George Sanders's costume adventure films include *Son of Monte Cristo* (1940), *The Black Swan* (1942), *Forever Amber* (1947), *Ivanhoe* (1952), *King Richard and the Crusaders* (1954), and *The King's Thief* (1955).

REFERENCES

Halliwell, Leslie. *Halliwell's Filmgoer's and Video Viewer's Companion.* New York: Charles Scribner's Sons, 1988.

Thomas, Tony. *Cads and Cavaliers.* New York: A. S. Barnes, 1973.

SANTELLI, GIORGIO. (1897–1985). Hungarian-born Italian fencing master.

Son of the famous fencing master Italo Santelli,* Giorgio Santelli began fencing at the age of six. "When I was a youngster," he once explained, "fencing was part of every young man's education. People learned to fence not for sport, but because they might have to go into a duel."

By the time he was twenty-five, Giorgio had won the Austrian foil and sabre championships and the Hungarian sabre championship. He began teaching at the age of twenty-eight.

During the 1924 Olympics, Giorgio's father, who coached the Hungarian fencing team, was involved in a controversy that eventually culminated in a duel for Giorgio. The elder Santelli, present at an argument between an Italian fencer and a fencing judge over an awarded touch, was asked to resolve the matter when the Italian denied his role in the affair. Reluctantly siding with the judge, Italo was later accused by the Italian team of testifying against them because he feared the Italians would defeat his Hungarian team. When he learned of this insult to his honor, Italo, who was over sixty years old, challenged the Italian team captain, Adolfo Cotronei, to a duel. But, before the two could meet in combat, Giorgio, in accordance with the dueling code, demanded to fight in his father's place. Finally, the younger Santelli fought Cotronei with heavy sabres. In an exchange that lasted for two minutes, Giorgio cut his opponent deeply on the head, which brought an end to the conflict.

That same year, 1924, Giorgio came to the United States to coach at the New York Athletic Club, then the center of fencing in America. Later, he created his own school, Salle Santelli. In time, he also coached five U.S. Olympic teams in 1928, 1932, 1936, 1948, and 1952 and produced numerous champions.

Santelli admitted about his teaching style that he was less concerned with the "whys" of fencing than the "hows." He said that he doubtlessly frustrated some of his students; but, he added, "Fortunately there have been enough Santelli champions through the years to bear out the validity of this system."

As for his psychological approach to fencing, Santelli gave advice to students that was often simple and to the point. He explained that in competition a fencer should just fence to his best ability, with the same mental calmness he might generate in friendly bouts at his fencing school. "After all," he once said, "victory should not mean too much. It is when you measure up to what you have got and have the ability to bring that out in yourself which should give you the real inner satisfaction."

He also taught actors appearing on Broadway, notably Jose Ferrer in his successful starring role in *Cyrano de Bergerac* in 1946.

In later years, Santelli noted, "Being my age, I cannot move very fast. But the moment I put a foil in my hand, I start to move. I get a kick seeing myself hopping around."

With his colleague and friend Edward Lucia, Giorgio Santelli wrote one book, *Engravings in Steel,* in 1980.

Giorgio Santelli died in November 1985.

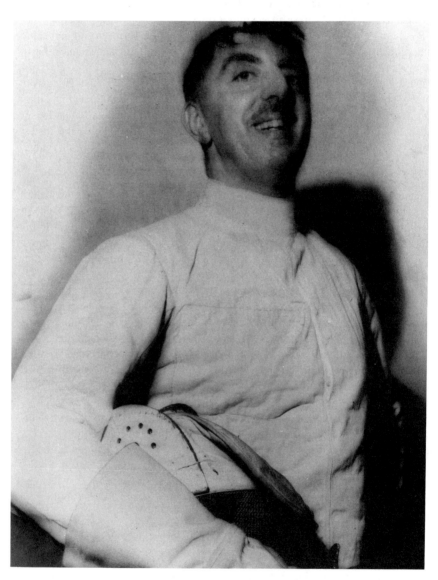

Fencing great Giorgio Santelli

REFERENCES
Black, David. "The Black Musketeer." *Rolling Stone* (1984).
Huddleson, Mary, ed. "Santelli Remembered." *American Fencing* (May/June 1986).
Santelli, Giorgio, and Edward Lucia. "Engravings in Steel." *American Fencing* (May/June 1980).

SANTELLI, ITALO. (1871–1945). Italian fencing master.

Italo Santelli was one of the greatest of modern fencing masters.

Fencing at the Scuola Magistrale di Scherma in Rome, where he developed beyond all his peers and teachers, Santelli brought various fencing styles into a single method, which, by the end of the nineteenth century, made Italians the best swordsmen in Europe.

In 1896, when Italo was twenty-five, he was asked by the Hungarian government to develop fencing in that country. He agreed and established the foundation of the Hungarian style of sabre fencing, turning the Hungarians into the most successful sabre fencers of the twentieth century.

Santelli taught for almost fifty years in Budapest. His service to Hungarian fencing was recognized with the award of knighthood.

Italo Santelli never wrote a book on fencing. His reason: "Fencing is something that you do, not write."

REFERENCES
Evangelista, Nick. "The Italian Side of Fencing." *American Citizen* (October 1986).
Palffy-Alpar, Julius. *Sword and Masque*. Philadelphia: F. A. Davis, 1967.

SAPARA. An ancient Assyrian sword. It had a curved blade and no hand guard.*

REFERENCE
Stone, George Cameron. *A Glossary of the Construction, Decoration, and Use of Arms and Armor*. New York: Jack Brussel, 1961.

SAPOLA. An Indian sabre with a point that is separated into two separate parts. The crossbar* is straight and possesses a knuckle guard.*

Also called a *sapola talwar.*

REFERENCE
Stone, George Cameron. *A Glossary of the Construction, Decoration, and Use of Arms and Armor*. New York: Jack Brussel, 1961.

SASHI-ZOE. In the pair of swords (*daisho*) carried by a samurai*—one long (*katana*)* and one short (*wakizashi*)*—the *sashi-zoe* was a variety of the latter weapon.

REFERENCE
Stone, George Cameron. *A Glossary of the Construction, Decoration, and Use of Arms and Armor*. New York: Jack Brussel, 1961.

SAVIOLO, VINCENTIO. (c. 1590). Italian fencing master.

A fencing master who taught the art of rapier fighting in England at the end of the sixteenth century. While not bringing anything original to fencing theory, Saviolo was nevertheless a highly competent teacher who managed to glean the best ideas from a number of styles of fencing to produce a technique that was both sound and logical.

Disliked among English masters—partially because he represented the changing world of swordplay by teaching the use of a weapon they hated and partially because he enjoyed a popularity among their countrymen—Saviolo was sometimes pushed to fight for his honor. After his death, he was viciously maligned in print by fencing master George Silver* in his attack on rapier play and rapier masters, *Paradoxes of Defence* (1599).**

REFERENCES

Castle, Egerton. *Schools and Masters of Fence.* London: George Bell, 1885.

Wise, Arthur. *The Art and History of Personal Combat.* Greenwich, CT: Arma Press, 1971.

SAYA. A Japanese sword scabbard,* almost always made of Honoki wood (magnolia). Such a scabbard is invariably lacquered. Mountings (artistic metal decorations) are present to varying degrees. The only essential mounting, however, was the *kurikata*—a knob on the side of a scabbard designed to keep it from slipping completely through the belt in which it was carried.

It was not uncommon in ancient Japan to have numerous scabbards for one sword, each one being used for a different occasion.

REFERENCE

Stone, George Cameron. *A Glossary of the Construction, Decoration, and Use of Arms and Armor.* New York: Jack Brussel, 1961.

SAYA-ATA. In old Japan, *saya-ata* referred to striking one's scabbard* against the scabbard of another. It was a form of presenting a challenge to an enemy.

REFERENCE

Stone, George Cameron. *A Glossary of the Construction, Decoration, and Use of Arms and Armor.* New York: Jack Brussel, 1961.

SAYAMAKI. A Japanese sword scabbard* wound with colored cord.

REFERENCE

Stone, George Cameron. *A Glossary of the Construction, Decoration, and Use of Arms and Armor.* New York: Jack Brussel, 1961.

SCABBARD. The carrying cover for a sword. It may be made of metal, leather, or wood.

Also called a "sheath."

REFERENCE

Reid, William. *Weapons Through the Ages.* London: Peerage Books, 1984.

SCANDAGLIO. Preliminary experimenting, through feints* and false attacks,* to discover how a fencing opponent will handle himself defensively.
REFERENCE
Morton, E. D. *Martini A–Z of Fencing*. London: Queen Anne Press, 1992.

SCANNATURA. According to the seventeenth-century Italian fencing master Ridolfo Capo Ferro,* the *scannatura* was basically a parry followed immediately by a counterattack.
REFERENCE
Castle, Egerton. *Schools and Masters of Fence*. London: George Bell, 1885.

SCELTA DI TEMPO. Timing an attack to the slightest perceived opening created by an opponent.
REFERENCE
Morton, E. D. *Martini A–Z of Fencing*. London: Queen Anne Press, 1992.

SCHACHERER-ELEK, ILONA. (1907–). Hungarian women's fencing champion.
Thought by some to be the greatest woman fencer of all time, Ilona Schacherer-Elek won the women's individual foil gold medal at the 1936 Olympics in a dramatic encounter with another great fencer, Helene Mayer.* She also took first in women's individual foil at the 1948 Olympics (she was forty-one years old at the time). She took second at the 1952 Olympics.
Schacherer-Elek was the women's world individual foil champion in 1934, 1935, and 1951.
REFERENCES
Palffy-Alpar, Julius. *Sword and Masque*. Philadelphia: F. A. Davis, 1967.
Wallechinsky, David. *The Complete Book of the Olympics*. New York: Penguin Books, 1984.

SCHERMA. The Italian term for fencing.
REFERENCE
Burton, Richard F. *The Book of the Sword*. London: Chatto and Windus, 1884.

SCHIAVONA. A Venetian broadsword* of the sixteenth century.
The *schiavona* had a broad, straight blade set onto a heavy, elaborate basket hilt. The overall length of the sword was as much as forty-one inches. Blade lengths varied between thirty-five and thirty-eight inches.
The name *schiavona* was derived from the Italian word *schiavoni*, which means "hired soldiers"; that is, the weapon's name was derived from the men who used it.
The Scottish broadsword* of the seventeenth and eighteenth centuries was patterned after the *schiavona*.

REFERENCES
Stone, George Cameron. *A Glossary of the Construction, Decoration, and Use of Arms and Armor.* New York: Jack Brussel, 1961.
Wilkinson, Frederick. *Swords and Daggers.* New York: Hawthorn Books, 1967.

SCHLAEGER. The dueling sword employed by German university students, especially during the last half of the nineteenth century.

The *schlaeger* is a basket-hilted* weapon, with a long, straight, pointless, flat blade that has been sharpened on the edge for seven or eight inches near the tip. The hand guard* is an extremely large basket hilt, designed so as to allow free use of the wrist during play. The grip* is very thin near the blade and thick near the pommel.*

Also called a *schlager, schleger, schlaegar,* and *schlagar.*

REFERENCE
Castle, Egerton. *Schools and Masters of Fence.* London: George Bell, 1885.

SCHLAEGER PLAY. Schlaeger* play was a highly physical affair, depending less on strategy than simple physical endurance. In such a duel, the face and head were the only valid target areas.

To begin with, the opponents would fall on guard within a very close distance, presenting their weapons in a position of high prime (the sword hand held slightly above the head, the schlaeger point below at mouth level), with the sword arm fully extended.

In most cases the eyes would be protected by special goggles, and occasionally, metal caps were used to protect the head.

The play itself, although brutal in its delivery, was without much variety. Basically, it was expressed in flipping cuts delivered from the wrist. Parries were performed by merely raising the sword high above the head to block oncoming cuts.

Cuts* were exchanged quickly and energetically, until a wound was finally administered to one combatant.

REFERENCE
Wise, Arthur. *The Art and History of Personal Combat.* Greenwich, CT: Arma Press, 1971.

SCHMID, HEIDI. (1939–). German women's fencing champion.

Heidi Schmid, a twenty-one-year-old music teacher, won the women's individual foil championship at the 1960 Olympics. In 1964, her team took third in team foil.

REFERENCE
Wallechinsky, David. *The Complete Book of the Olympics.* New York: Penguin Books, 1984.

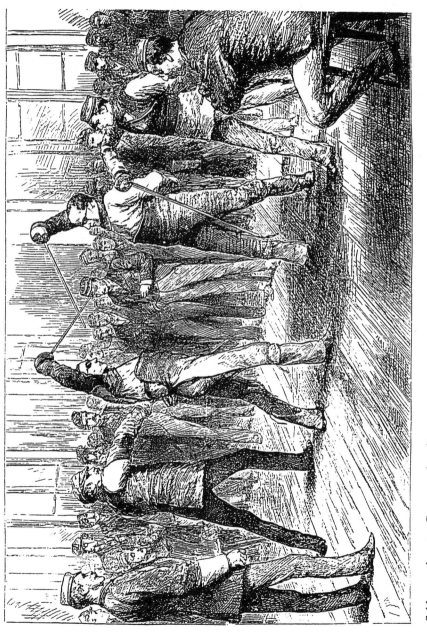

Schlaeger play at a German university

SCHWERDT. The German term for sword. It referred specifically to the heavy two-handed sword that was popular in Germany until the latter part of the sixteenth century.
REFERENCE
Castle, Egerton. *Schools and Masters of Fence.* London: George Bell, 1885.

SCIABOLA DI TERRENO. In Italian, the sabre* used in dueling.
REFERENCE
Morton, E. D. *Martini A–Z of Fencing.* London: Queen Anne Press, 1992.

SCIABOLA IN MANO. An Italian term meaning ''sabre in hand.'' This refers to the condition of holding the sabre correctly so that it may be employed to its fullest extent.
    Also called ''sword in hand.''
REFERENCE
Morton, E. D. *Martini A–Z of Fencing.* London: Queen Anne Press, 1992.

SCORE. Keeping track of the touches delivered and received between two competing fencers.
REFERENCE
U.S. Fencing Association, ed. *Operations Manual.* Colorado Springs, CO: U.S. Fencing
    Association, 1985.

SCORING, ELECTRIC. A specially designed electrical sensing machine is used to register the touches between two opposing fencers. Presently, there are scoring machines for all three fencing weapons—foil, épée, and sabre.
    Touches are acknowledged via flashing lights and buzzers. On-target touches are shown with red and green lights; off-target touches, with white lights (except for épée and sabre scoring machines, which simply block out off-target contact).
REFERENCES
Romeo, Sidney. ''Safety and Electric Sabre—Recommendations and Compliance.''
    American Fencing (June/July/August 1988).
Volkman, Rudy. *Electrical Fencing Equipment.* Arvee Press, 1975.

SCOT'S PLAY. A system of fencing taught by Sir William Hope* during the late seventeenth century. It was fully explained in the fencing master's book, *Scots' Fencing Master* (1687).**
    Said Hope of his approach: ''It runneth all upon binding and securing your adversary's sword before you offer a thrust, which maketh your thrust sure and your adversaries incapable of giving you a contretemps.''
REFERENCE
Castle, Egerton. *Schools and Masters of Fence.* London: George Bell, 1885.

SCOTT, SIR WALTER. (1771–1832). Scottish novelist and poet.
    Drawing heavily on history as the source of his writing inspiration, Sir Walter

Scott produced over thirty novels of romance and adventure. He was, by far, the most popular author of his day.

Scott's best-known work includes *Waverley* (1814), *Rob Roy* (1817), *Ivanhoe* (1819), and *Quentin Durward* (1823).

Swordplay in Scott's work is not uncommon, as pictured in *Ivanhoe:* ''The masterly horsemanship of the Disinherited Knight and the activity of the noble animal which he mounted, enabled him for a few minutes to keep at sword's point his three antagonists . . . and rushing now against the one, now against the other, dealing sweeping blows with his sword, without waiting to receive those which were aimed at him in return.''

Many of Scott's adventures have been made into movies by Hollywood.
REFERENCES
Benet, William Rose. *The Reader's Encyclopedia.* New York: Thomas Y. Crowell, 1965.
Scott, Sir Walter. *Ivanhoe.* New York: Allyn and Bacon, 1926.

SCRAMASAX. An old German single-edged, broad-bladed sword. The *scramasax* varied in blade length from six to thirty inches. One example of the larger form weighed 4.5 pounds.

The blade of the *scramasax* was grooved on both sides.
REFERENCE
Wilkinson, Frederick. *Swords and Daggers.* New York: Hawthorn Books, 1967.

SCUOLA MAGISTRALE DI SCHERMA. A fencing school founded in Rome during the nineteenth century to train fencing masters for the Italian army.
REFERENCE
Palffy-Alpar, Julius. *Sword and Masque.* Philadelphia: F. A. Davis, 1967.

SCUTOR. A *scutor* was a Roman gladiator in armor who carried both a sword and a shield.
REFERENCE
Stone, George Cameron. *A Glossary of the Construction, Decoration, and Use of Arms and Armor.* New York: Jack Brussel, 1961.

SCYMITAR. Sabrelike weapon of the Middle East. The blade always has a pronounced curve in it. The average blade length is around thirty-five inches.

The name scimitar is derived from the Persian *shamshir.*

Also called a *scimeter, scymiter,* and *scimitar.*
REFERENCE
Stone, George Cameron. *A Glossary of the Construction, Decoration, and Use of Arms and Armor.* New York: Jack Brussel, 1961.

SEASHELL SWORDS. Especially in old Polynesia, seashells were attached to wooden sword blades to produce sharp cutting edges.
REFERENCE
Burton, Richard F. *The Book of the Sword.* London: Chatto and Windus, 1884.

SEAX. The curved sword of the Anglo-Saxons.
REFERENCE
Stone, George Cameron. *A Glossary of the Construction, Decoration, and Use of Arms and Armor.* New York: Jack Brussel, 1961.

SECONDARY INTENT. An attack in which a fencer means not to hit with his opening lunge* but with a parry*-riposte* action following the initial attack.

A secondary intent maneuver begins with a primary attack that is false, that is, an offensive ploy made only as a feint to draw an opponent's parry and riposte. When the parry and riposte are forthcoming, the counterattack is itself parried and riposted against. All this takes place while the initial attacker is still in the lunge position. Into this "secondary" action, then, one's "intention" to hit is placed.

The secondary intent is a useful strategy when a fencer is unable to get past an opponent's parry-riposte response. The foreknowledge that he is about to be parried gives him the conscious opportunity to defend himself more quickly after his attack has been stopped. This, in turn, provides an opportunity to lauch a counter-counterattack with greater speed. The secondary intent, in effect, is a timing enhancement maneuver.

Also called "second intention" and *seconda intenzione.*
REFERENCES
Palffy-Alpar, Julius. *Sword and Masque.* Philadelphia: F. A. Davis, 1967.
Stevenson, John. *Fencing.* London: Briggs, 1935.

SECONDE. The line of two.

In modern foil* and épée fencing, the line* of seconde is the position that covers the low-outside line, with the sword hand in pronation and the blade point lower than the hand.

In modern sabre* fencing, seconde is the position covering the right side of the body, taken with the weapon point lower than the sword hand, which is pronated. This places the cutting edge of the weapon to the right.
REFERENCE
Handelman, Rob. "Fencing Glossary." *American Fencing* (July/August 1978).

SECONDE, QUARTE EN. According to seventeenth-century French fencing master Charles Besnard,* quarte en seconde was a thrust* in the line of seconde, with the sword hand in supination (palm up).
REFERENCE
Castle, Egerton. *Schools and Masters of Fence.* London: George Bell, 1885.

SECONDE, TIERCE EN. Tierce en seconde was a thrust* in the line of seconde with the sword hand in pronation (palm down).
REFERENCE
Castle, Egerton. *Schools and Masters of Fence.* London: George Bell, 1885.

SECRET THRUST. Many early fencing masters purported themselves to be the possessor of a secret attack, a devastating maneuver that would penetrate any defense. Fencing historian Egerton Castle,* in his *Schools and Masters of Fence* (1885),** noted that such moves were "to the fencer of those times what the philosopher's stone was to the alchemist."

These moves, when they actually did exist, were, more often than not, simply some favorite trick of the fencing master, but they were still carefully guarded from the common crowd. Still, they might be procured for a sum of money, if it was large enough, and for a pledge from the student that he would never use his new "secret" information against the teacher.

Also known as a *botte secrete* or a *botta segreta.*
REFERENCE
Castle, Egerton. *Schools and Masters of Fence.* London: George Bell, 1885.

SECURING THE SWORD. An old-time term used to describe a disarming* technique involving grabbing an opponent's weapon just below the guard. Such actions, of course, are not allowed in modern fencing.
REFERENCE
Morton, E. D. *Martini A–Z of Fencing.* London: Queen Anne Press, 1992.

SEME. The sword of the Masai of East Africa.

The *seme* had a heavy, double-edged blade, widening near the point. The grip* was without a hand guard.*

The weapon was usually about twenty inches long, although sometimes longer.
REFERENCE
Stone, George Cameron. *A Glossary of the Construction, Decoration, and Use of Arms and Armor.* New York: Jack Brussel, 1961.

SENAC, REGIS. (c. nineteenth century). French fencing master.

America's most widely known nineteenth-century fencing master. Opening the first New York City fencing school in 1874, Senac continued teaching his art for over thirty years.

The master's son Louis continued in his father's famous footsteps.
REFERENCE
Cass, Eleanor Baldwin. *The Book of Fencing.* Boston: Lothrop, Lee, and Shephard, 1930.

SENANGKAS BEDOK. A Malayan sabre* with a heavy, slightly curved blade. It had no hand guard.*
REFERENCE
Stone, George Cameron. *A Glossary of the Construction, Decoration, and Use of Arms and Armor.* New York: Jack Brussel, 1961.

SENESE, ALEXANDER. (c. 1640). Italian fencing master.

Senese wrote a book, *A Treatise on the True Management of the Sword*

(1660).** Despite its title, it added no new knowledge to the art of fencing. It merely adapted old principles to the lighter swords of Senese's time.

His name is sometimes spelled as "Alessandro Senesio."
REFERENCE
Castle, Egerton. *Schools and Masters of Fence.* London: George Bell, 1885.

SENTIMENT DU FER. Meaning the sentiment, or feeling, of the blade. Specifically, this feeling exists when the weapon becomes—through concentration, relaxation, and technique—part of the fencer, so that there is no separation between it and his nervous system. In effect, the fencer and his blade become one.
REFERENCE
Stevenson, John. *Fencing.* London: Briggs, 1935.

SEPARATING SWORD. In ancient traditions of many countries, when a man and woman who were not married, for some reason, had to sleep together, a sword was placed between them as a symbol and guarantee of their chastity.
REFERENCE
Leach, Maria, ed. *Funk and Wagnalls Standard Dictionary of Folklore, Mythology, and Legend.* San Francisco: Harper and Row, 1972.

SEPARAZIONE. The act of removing one's blade from an engagement.*
REFERENCE
Morton, E. D. *Martini A–Z of Fencing.* London: Queen Anne Press, 1992.

SEPPA. Washers placed on either side of a Japanese sword guard (*tsuba**).
REFERENCE
Stone, George Cameron. *A Glossary of the Construction, Decoration, and Use of Arms and Armor.* New York: Jack Brussel, 1961.

SEPTIME. The line of seven.

In modern foil* and épée* fencing, the line* of septime is the position that covers the low-inside portion of the body, with the sword hand in supination.

A parry,* known as high septime, catches an opponent's blade in the low line and lifts it over the defender's head in the extreme high line. This also may be referred to as "lifted septime."
REFERENCES
Handelman, Rob. "Fencing Glossary." *American Fencing* (July/August 1978).
Palffy-Alpar, Julius. *Sword and Masque.* Philadelphia: F. A. Davis, 1967.

SETTO. A sword given by the emperor of Japan to the commander in chief of his army as a symbol of his commission.
REFERENCE
Stone, George Cameron. *A Glossary of the Construction, Decoration, and Use of Arms and Armor.* New York: Jack Brussel, 1961.

SHAKESPEARE, WILLIAM. (1564–1616). English dramatist.

William Shakespeare has been called the greatest of all playwrights. His work is both universal and intimate, possessing the sweep and depth of the human condition. But because his work was staged for the common man, there is often much physical action included in his plays. Sword fights were a daily fact of life in Shakespeare's world, so it is not unusual that they should have been often included in his dramatic creations.

Shakespeare's use of fencing can be found in *Romeo and Juliet* (1596), *Henry V* (1598), and *Macbeth* (1606).

The climactic duel in *Hamlet* (1601) is a classic example of Shakespeare's melodramatic use of sword combat. The two opponents, Hamlet and Laertes, cross rapiers. Hamlet's sword tip has been covered. Laertes's sword tip is exposed and has been dipped in poison. Hamlet touches Laertes. "A hit, a very palpable hit," cries the judge of the match. Then come two more touches by Hamlet. A moment later, Laertes wounds Hamlet. Here, they scuffle, exchanging weapons. Now, Hamlet wounds Laertes. Laertes dies, confessing his treachery. Hamlet, after a bit more bloodletting—this time on his uncle/stepfather—also dies. The ending is not a happy one.

Shakespeare's work continues to be popular even in today's hip, modern world.

REFERENCES

Benet, William Rose. *The Reader's Encyclopedia.* New York: Thomas Y. Crowell, 1965.
Shakespeare, William. *Hamlet.* New York: F. P. Collier, 1901.

SHAMSHIR. A Persian sabre.*

The blade of the weapon was curved and narrow. The hilt* was made up of a simple crossbar* and plain handle.

The *shamshir* was used only as a cutting weapon.

Also called a *shamsheer* and *chimchir.*

REFERENCE

Stone, George Cameron. *A Glossary of the Construction, Decoration, and Use of Arms and Armor.* New York: Jack Brussel, 1961.

SHAMSHIR SHIKARGAR. A Persian hunting sword. Like a normal *shamshir,* except that the blades are decorated with hunting scenes.

REFERENCE

Stone, George Cameron. *A Glossary of the Construction, Decoration, and Use of Arms and Armor.* New York: Jack Brussel, 1961.

SHARPS. A foil* with a quarter-inch of point beyond the button.* As suggested by seventeenth-century Scottish fencing master Sir William Hope,* it was useful to employ sharps when one wished to interject an air of seriousness into one's foil play.

Blunts* was the term for foils with completely dulled tips.

REFERENCE

Castle, Egerton. *Schools and Masters of Fence.* London: George Bell, 1885.

SHASHQA. The sword of the Caucasus region of Russia. The blade (twenty-nine inches long) is usually straight; the hilt, guardless.

Also called a *chacheka.*

REFERENCE

Stone, George Cameron. *A Glossary of the Construction, Decoration, and Use of Arms and Armor.* New York: Jack Brussel, 1961.

SHEARING SWORD. A popular sword of the sixteenth and seventeenth centuries with a light, flexible, double-edged blade.

REFERENCE

Castle, Egerton. *Schools and Masters of Fence.* London: George Bell, 1885.

SHELL GUARD. Originally, a guard that was fashioned in the form of two separate, shallow, rounded shells or plates. These took the place of some of the curved bars on the rapier guard used to protect the hand.

In time, the shells were joined to form a single shell.

When the shell was enlarged and deepened, the guard was called a cup.*

Today, the term shell guard merely refers to the guard of a modern fencing weapon.

REFERENCE

Castle, Egerton. *Schools and Masters of Fence.* London: George Bell, 1885.

SHERIDAN, RICHARD BRINSLEY. (1751–1816). Irish-born English dramatist.

Richard Sheridan was one of the most popular playwrights of his time, producing works such as *The Rivals* (1775) and *The School for Scandal* (1779).

Sheridan, an avid fencer and student of the famous London-based Italian master Domenico Angelo,* fought two smallsword duels during his life. At the age of twenty, he found himself embroiled in an affair of honor with a Captain Matthews, who attempted to force his attentions on a Miss Linley, Sheridan's soon-to-be wife. When Sheridan stepped in to halt the older man's advances, insults were exchanged, and a duel was forthcoming.

The two met one evening in the upper room of a London tavern and fought by candlelight. Sheridan ended the fight almost before it began by beating Matthews's blade aside, grabbing the hilt of his sword, and threatening him with the point of his own weapon. As little as he liked it, Matthews was forced to give up. And that was that.

Unfortunately, word leaked out about Matthews' loss, and to save face, he was forced to challenge Sheridan again. This second duel took place near Bath and proved to be much less academic than the first encounter.

Matthews, cautioned by his previous experience, worked at bearing down on Sheridan, causing him to constantly retreat. When Sheridan sought to repeat his winning move from the first fight, Matthews merely fell back a step, causing his opponent to fall upon his sword point. Sheridan was wounded only slightly.

Here, the fight abruptly lost all relationship to strategic combat. Matthews seized Sheridan; Sheridan seized Matthews. Scuffling about, they dropped their swords, which broke, and fell to the ground, where they wrestled unceremoniously in the dirt. Then, grabbing their respective weapons, they began stabbing viciously at each other. In the end, Matthews climbed on top of Sheridan and nailed him to the earth by thrusting his broken blade through his neck.

Surprisingly, Sheridan was not seriously injured and recovered after a rather lengthy convalescence.

REFERENCES

Benet, William Rose. *The Reader's Encyclopedia.* New York: Thomas Y. Crowell, 1965.

Wise, Arthur. *The Art and History of Personal Combat.* Greenwich, CT: Arma Press, 1971.

SHIELD. A defensive plate carried by knights and soldiers used to ward off sword blows, lances, arrows, and so on. It was often used in conjunction with the sword.

Shields were made of wood, leather, metal, wicker, and cloth, or combinations thereof. They came in a variety of shapes: round, oval, triangular, and rectangular. Moreover, they could have either flat or curved surfaces.

Types of shields include the buckler,* target,* *dhal, kliau, manteau d'armes,* pistol shield or *gonne, rondelle a poign, rotella, scutum,* and *ysgwyd.*

REFERENCE

Stone, George Cameron. *A Glossary of the Construction, Decoration, and Use of Arms and Armor.* New York: Jack Brussel, 1961.

SHIKOME-ZUE. A Japanese sword case.

REFERENCE

Stone, George Cameron. *A Glossary of the Construction, Decoration, and Use of Arms and Armor.* New York: Jack Brussel, 1961.

SHINAI. The bamboo sword of kendo* (Japanese fencing).

The *shinai* was designed by Chuta Nakanishi in the mid-eighteenth century in an effort to create an atmosphere of safety for the learning of swordplay.

The earliest form of the weapon was made from soft reeds that had been split into as many as thirty-two strips and covered with heavy cloth. However, this practice weapon was too light for effective use.

Nakanishi eventually redesigned the *shinai,* fashioning the blade out of four strips of polished bamboo. The strips were fitted together to form a cylinder and fastened together with leather strips. A *tsuba* (hand guard) made of thick hide was fitted on the *shinai*'s handle.

WILL™ LONGUESPEE   EARL OF SALISBURY,

A.D.1224.

From *Meyrick's Ancient Armor*, a knight with his shield

In the beginning, there were no regulations as to how long a *shinai* might be, and some were well over six feet in length. Eventually, a weapon of thirty-nine inches was adopted as the proper length for the *shinai*.

REFERENCE

Sasamori, Junzo, and Gordon Warner. *This Is Kendo*. Vermont: Charles E. Tuttle, 1964.

SHINAI—PARTS.

Tsuru: bamboo blade sections.

Sakigawa: leather covering for tip (*kissaki*) of weapon.

Nakayui: leather cord for binding blade sections together.

Himo: string running the length of the blade, the purpose of which is to aid in keeping all points taut.

Tsuba: hand guard.

Tsuka: leather covering on the handle of weapon.

REFERENCE
Sasamori, Junzo, and Gordon Warner. *This Is Kendo.* Vermont: Charles E. Tuttle, 1964.

SHINAI-UCHI. A Japanese term for fencing.
REFERENCE
Stone, George Cameron. *A Glossary of the Construction, Decoration, and Use of Arms and Armor.* New York: Jack Brussel, 1961.

SHINKEN. In Japan, a metal sword as opposed to a wooden one.
REFERENCE
Stone, George Cameron. *A Glossary of the Construction, Decoration, and Use of Arms and Armor.* New York: Jack Brussel, 1961.

SHINODARI. The symbolized swords of Fudo, Japanese god of wisdom and mercy.
REFERENCE
Stone, George Cameron. *A Glossary of the Construction, Decoration, and Use of Arms and Armor.* New York: Jack Brussel, 1961.

SHIRASAYA. A plain wooden scabbard* in which fine Japanese sword blades were stored when not in use.
REFERENCE
Stone, George Cameron. *A Glossary of the Construction, Decoration, and Use of Arms and Armor.* New York: Jack Brussel, 1961.

SHIRA TACHI. An old-style Japanese long sword with silver mountings (decorations). It was carried by the four highest levels of nobles during the Ashikaga period (from 1336 to 1568).
REFERENCE
Stone, George Cameron. *A Glossary of the Construction, Decoration, and Use of Arms and Armor.* New York: Jack Brussel, 1961.

SHIRAZAYA. A Japanese sword scabbard* covered with tiger-, bear-, or deer-skin. It came to be used only by officers of higher rank.

REFERENCE
Stone, George Cameron. *A Glossary of the Construction, Decoration, and Use of Arms and Armor.* New York: Jack Brussel, 1961.

SHOTEL. An Abyssinian sword. It had a double-edged blade, curved almost in a half-circle. The grip* was a simple, wooden handle.

The *shotel,* an extremely awkward weapon for fencing, was used mainly to strike around, over, or under the edge of an opponent's shield.
REFERENCE
Stone, George Cameron. *A Glossary of the Construction, Decoration, and Use of Arms and Armor.* New York: Jack Brussel, 1961.

SIBAK. A type of Malay sword.
REFERENCE
Stone, George Cameron. *A Glossary of the Construction, Decoration, and Use of Arms and Armor.* New York: Jack Brussel, 1961.

SICA. A short Roman sword, either curved or straight. Because it was easy to conceal on one's personage, it was a favorite of assassins.
REFERENCE
Burton, Richard F. *The Book of the Sword.* London: Chatto and Windus, 1884.

SIDE RING. A ring-shaped guard projecting from the side of a sword hilt.* It first appeared during the sixteenth century.
REFERENCE
Castle, Egerton. *Schools and Masters of Fence.* London: George Bell, 1885.

SILENT LESSON. A lesson given by a fencing master in which no verbal commands are given. The student must, then, rely on his own fencing sense as the teacher serves up various actions.
REFERENCE
Morton, E. D. *Martini A–Z of Fencing.* London: Queen Anne Press, 1992.

SILVER, GEORGE. (c. 1560). English fencing master.

George Silver was one of the last vocal bastions of old-style, cutting sword-play in an age of rapidly changing dueling practices. As the thrusting rapier* swept across Europe as the sword of choice, Silver, seeing his world slipping away, attacked not only the weapon but everyone who taught its implementation or used it.

In his *Paradoxes of Defence* (1599),** Silver vented his hatred and jealousy on the leading rapier masters teaching in his homeland—Rocco Bonetti,* Vincentio Saviolo,* and Jeromimo Bonetti.* He also expounded on "the false resolutions and vaine opinions of Rapier-Men, and of the danger of death thereby ensuing," after which he discussed the proper approach to sword fighting, which was, needless to say, his approach.

In spite of Silver's energetic attempt to stem the use of the rapier, the thrusting weapon won the day. The fencing master's arguments proved to be nothing more than a hollow death knell for weapons and techniques that no longer met the needs of the world.

REFERENCE

Castle, Egerton. *Schools and Masters of Fence.* London: George Bell, 1885.

SIME. The sword of East Africa. The form varied from tribe to tribe. One variety possessed a blade four feet long and an inch and a half wide, which was said to be based on the sword of the Knights Templar.

REFERENCE

Stone, George Cameron. *A Glossary of the Construction, Decoration, and Use of Arms and Armor.* New York: Jack Brussel, 1961.

SIMPLE ATTACK. An attack made up entirely of timing and speed, where the attacker simply hits his opponent before he can respond defensively.

Simple attacks include the straight hit* or cut,* the disengage,* the *coule,** and the *coupe.**

Said famed fencing master Julio Castello* of the simple attack:

The straight thrust and disengage with the foil, and the simple cutting attack with the sabre, if done properly within distance, cannot be parried. The reason is one of simple mathematics. The distance to be traveled by the point or edge of the attacking weapon to the target is a little longer than the line traveled by the parry. But the initiative taken by the attacker is sufficient, in terms of reaction time, to make up for the distance easily.

To produce the proper effect, he added, "In the perfect simple action, the lunge will follow the extension of the arm; notice I did not say that these two parts of the action are simultaneous. The action can be perfected only with extensive practice, so that the lunge will be a prolongation of the extension."

Also called "simple actions" and "single actions."

REFERENCES

Castello, Julio M. "Revolution, or Evolution—or What?" *American Fencing* (March/April/May 1988).

Stevenson, John. *Fencing.* London: Briggs, 1935.

SIMULTANEOUS ACTIONS. A fencing exchange in which both fencers execute their offensive maneuvers at exactly the same moment, resulting in touches that arrive together. Because neither fencer has established himself as the legitimate attacker by being the first to perform a properly executed attack, the hits are annulled. This is true for both foil* and sabre* play.

In épée* fencing, because there are no rules regarding the priority of one attack over another, when a simultaneous action takes place, both fencers score a touch against each other.

Also known as *tempo commune,* a "double hit or touch," and *incontro.*

REFERENCE
U.S. Fencing Association, ed. *Operations Manual.* Colorado Springs, CO: U.S. Fencing
   Association, 1985.

SINCLAIR, CAPTAIN. (c. 1800). British fencing master.

Sinclair, a captain in the British Forty-Second Regiment, wrote a popular book on the art of broadsword fighting and singlestick play at the beginning of the nineteenth century.

A description of Sinclair's book, *Cudgel-Playing Modernized and Improved* (1800), noted, "An attentive perusal of this work will qualify the Reader to handle a sword or stick with Grace, enable him to correct abuse, repel Attack, and secure himself from Unprovoked insult."

REFERENCE
Castle, Egerton. *Schools and Masters of Fence.* London: George Bell, 1885.

SINGLESTICK. A wooden stick fitted with a basket-type hand guard.

Initially, in eighteenth-century England, the singlestick was employed as a practice weapon for the more dangerous backsword. However, during the nineteenth century, singlestick play became a highly popular sport pastime, especially among the lower classes.

In singlestick fencing—sometimes referred to as "backswording" because of its origins—the two combatants, called "gamesters," were placed at a very close distance to one another, hence, no lunge was necessary. Cuts were delivered in a flipping manner from the wrist. No point work at all was involved. The free arm was used to protect the head. Winning was achieved when one singlestick participant drew blood from the head of his opponent.

The singlestick continued to be used in English schools into the first quarter of the twentieth century.

REFERENCE
Morton, E. D. *Martini A–Z of Fencing.* London: Queen Anne Press, 1992.

SIROHI. The favorite sword of the Rajputs of Indian. The blade of the *sirohi,* slightly curved and single-edged, was famous for its temper.

Also called *serye.*

REFERENCE
Stone, George Cameron. *A Glossary of the Construction, Decoration, and Use of Arms
   and Armor.* New York: Jack Brussel, 1961.

SITTING DOWN. Bending the knees in the on-guard* position.

REFERENCE
Morton, E. D. *Martini A–Z of Fencing.* London: Queen Anne Press, 1992.

SIXTE. The line of six.

In modern foil* and épée* fencing, the line of sixte is the position covering the high-outside portion of the body, with the sword hand in supination* and the blade point higher than the hand.

Singlestick play

REFERENCE
Handelman, Rob. "Fencing Glossary." *American Fencing* (July/August 1978).

SLIP. In the terminology of backsword fencing, to slip meant to deceive or evade. Specifically, it meant to withdraw a portion of the body at which an opponent has directed a cut.
REFERENCE
Castle, Egerton. *Schools and Masters of Fence.* London: George Bell, 1885.

SMALLSWORD. Essentially a French weapon, the smallsword was the final incarnation of the dueling sword. It was popular during the eighteenth century.

First appearing at the close of the seventeenth century, the smallsword usually had a triangular blade (average length: thirty inches), which was used exclusively for thrusting. The chief advantage of the weapon was its lightness, which allowed for numerous fencing maneuvers that had hitherto been unthinkable when employing the heavier rapier.*

The hilt* of the smallsword was a simple affair: a plain shell guard,* a straight grip,* and a light knuckle guard.*

The smallsword was the last sword to be worn regularly as part of civilian dress.

REFERENCES

Castle, Egerton. *Schools and Masters of Fence.* London: George Bell, 1885.
Wilkinson, Frederick. *Swords and Daggers.* New York: Hawthorn Books, 1967.

SMALLSWORD FIGHT, EIGHTEENTH-CENTURY. An eighteenth-century smallsword fight might, on the surface, bear a close resemblance to modern fencing. However, because of the obviously disastrous consequences one could easily suffer by committing the slightest error in form or judgment, the resulting by-play in such a contest must have been approached with more care and deliberation than any twentieth-century foil bout.

A smallsword duel might go like this:

When two opposing swordsmen began their assault, they would immediately come on guard covering their high, outside line of tierce. The outside line was the closest to an adversary's sword point; hence, it was the first to be protected. Sword arms would be held nearly straight; sword hands, at chest level; sword tips, at eye level. Advancing and retreating followed a straight line, with no circular approaches to attacking as in previous ages. Since the smallsword was designed exclusively for thrusting, the only effective attack was one launched straight into an enemy's body (angled advances greatly minimized the momentum of one's forward thrust). The play exchanged after falling on guard was uncomplicated—made up of beats, simple thrusts, and disengagements. The lunge, which invariably delivered the attack, looked amazingly like a lunge as it would be performed today. Parries came in both lateral and circular varieties. Ripostes were executed completely and distinctly separate from the parry (known as *dui tempi**). Exchanges between opponents were quick and well-defined. While the free hand might occasionally be used to parry with, this practice was avoided more and more as the eighteenth century progressed in favor of a completely blade-oriented defense. The same attitude was directed toward body evasions. The fight continued, back and forth, until one man was either injured or dead. Quite often, in actions of this type, both men ran a good chance of being at least wounded.

REFERENCES

Angelo, Domenico. *The School of Fencing.* London: H. Angelo, 1887.
Castle, Egerton. *Schools and Masters of Fence.* London: George Bell, 1885.

Smallsword play during the eighteenth century

SMIRNOV, VLADIMIR. (1954–1982). Soviet fencing champion.

A world and Olympic fencing champion, Vladimir Smirnov was killed in a fencing accident at the 1982 World Championships in Rome.

Smirnov's highly publicized death occurred when his opponent's foil, snapping against the Soviet's chest, flipped up and smashed through his fencing mask. The broken blade passed above his left eye and into his brain. He died a few days later.

Immediately after the accident, a brief uproar transpired in the world fencing community when the pistol grip**—a weapon handle promoting forceful, un-yielding pressure and a muscular, resistive, sometimes violent style of fencing—was implicated as one of the prime causes of the tragedy. Some talked of banning all types of pistol grips from the fencing scene. This, however, did not occur, and, before long, the controversy died away.

To fencing's credit, however, since Smirnov's death, both fencing mask and clothing safety standards have been increased. There have also been advancements in blade durability.

REFERENCES

Clery, Raoul. "A Propos d'un Accident." *American Fencing* (September/October 1983).

Huddleson, Mary, ed. "In Memoriam: Vladimir Smirnov 1954–1982." *American Fencing* (September/October 1982).

SOCIETY FOR CREATIVE ANACHRONISM (SCA). An organization created in the late 1960s out of an interest in researching and re-creating the Middle Ages. Events are held, and members attend in period costumes. Events include tourneys, sword combat, armoring, archery, and equestrian. They also produce publications dealing with medieval topics.

Today, the SCA is a worldwide organization.

REFERENCE

Clark, Bernadine, ed. *Writer's Resource Guide.* Cincinnati, OH: Writer's Digest Books, 1983.

SOCIETY OF SWORDSMEN IN SCOTLAND. Founded in 1692 in Scotland, the Society of Swordsmen (sometimes "Sword-men") was organized to encourage the art of fencing. Although it never received the official sanction it sought from the English government, the society flourished for a number of years as a private group.

One of the group's founders, Sir William Hope,* was one of the most distinguished fencing masters of his time.

REFERENCE

Castle, Egerton. *Schools and Masters of Fence.* London: George Bell, 1885.

SORI. The curve of a Japanese sword blade.

REFERENCE

Stone, George Cameron, *A Glossary of the Construction, Decoration, and Use of Arms and Armor.* New York: Jack Brussel, 1961.

SOSUN. A straight Indian sword. The hilt* was fitted with a cup pommel* with a spike on it.

REFERENCE

Stone, George Cameron. *A Glossary of the Construction, Decoration, and Use of Arms and Armor.* New York: Jack Brussel, 1961.

SOSUNPATTAH. A broad-bladed Indian sword with a padded hand guard* and a spike on the pommel.*

REFERENCE

Stone, George Cameron. *A Glossary of the Construction, Decoration, and Use of Arms and Armor.* New York: Jack Brussel, 1961.

SOUBISE. An eighteenth-century black fencing master who worked initially for the famed Angelo school. Although highly popular, he was eventually dis-

missed for his personal excesses. Moving to India, Soubise founded a highly successful fencing school of his own.
REFERENCE
Morton, E. D. *Martini A–Z of Fencing.* London: Queen Anne Press, 1992.

SOVIET FENCERS, NOTED.

Men

Mikhail Burtsev, Vladimir Denissov, Grigory Kriss, Viktor Krovopuskov, Lev Kuznyetsov, Umar Mavlikhanov, Mark Midler, Viktor Modzalensky, Alexandr Mozhaev, Vladimir Nazlymov, Mark Rakita, Aleksandr Romankov, Sabirynan Ruziev, Yakov Rylsky, Guram Saccaro, Viktor Sidiak, Yuri Sissikin, Vladimir Smirnov, Vassily Stankovich, German Sveshnikov, Boris Tyshler, David Tyshler, Viktor Zhdanovich

Women

Galina Gorokhova, Yelene Novikova, Valentina Raskovorova, Valentina Sidorova

REFERENCE
Wallechinsky, David. *The Complete Book of the Olympics.* New York: Penguin Books, 1984.

SPADACINO. An old Italian term for a swordsman.
REFERENCE
Castle, Egerton. *Schools and Masters of Fence.* London: George Bell, 1885.

SPADA SOLA. A term referring to the rapier* being used alone.
REFERENCE
Castle, Egerton. *Schools and Masters of Fence.* London: George Bell, 1885.

SPADONE. A sixteenth-century two-handed sword.
The name *spadone* derives from the Latin term *spatha,* which the Romans applied to the long sword of the Gauls.
REFERENCE
Castle, Egerton. *Schools and Masters of Fence.* London: George Bell, 1885.

SPADROON. A light sword adapted for both cutting* and thrusting.*
It was said that the spadroon was ideal for a swordsman who mastered both the smallsword* and broadsword,* as its particular characteristics made it possible to unite techniques of both weapons.
REFERENCE
Stone, George Cameron. *A Glossary of the Construction, Decoration, and Use of Arms and Armor.* New York: Jack Brussel, 1961.

SPADROON GUARD. The arm was extended horizontally, the hand was in supination,* the point of the sword was low.
The spadroon guard was rarely used, except with very light weapons.

REFERENCE
Castle, Egerton. *Schools and Masters of Fence.* London: George Bell, 1885.

SPADROON PLAY. A form of cut-and-thrust play* with the English back-sword. Spadroon play was based on principles devised by the Italians and Germans.

Spadroon combat was quite simple, but it required a good sense of distance and a great amount of strength in the forearm and fingers. Attacks* were generally delivered with chopping actions. Parries,* of which there were five, were always of a lateral* nature, never circular.*

REFERENCE
Castle, Egerton. *Schools and Masters of Fence.* London: George Bell, 1885.

SPANISH FOIL. The main feature of the Spanish foil, as it developed at the end of the nineteenth century, was two small prongs on either side of the grip—these were the last vestige of the quillons* (crossbars) of an earlier time of rapiers* and smallswords.* These projections were touted as giving the fencer a stronger grip on his weapon.

Also called a "Portuguese foil."

REFERENCE
Morton, E. D. *Martini A–Z of Fencing.* London: Queen Anne Press, 1992.

SPANISH SCHOOL OF FENCING. The Spanish school of fencing, built around an artificial construction of pompous metaphysical philosophy and geometric patterns, was the product, basically, of two sixteenth-century masters, Jeronimo de Carranza and his pupil Don Luis Pacheco de Narvaez. Their teachings, which took the complicated and made it obscure, were later expounded upon in greater detail by the French fencing master Girard Thibault, who attempted, unsuccessfully, to entrench the Spanish method of combat in his homeland.

The Spanish style of swordplay set up patterns for footwork that followed interconnecting lines drawn through a large circle (the "mysterious circle"). These "pathways," if adhered to, were said to both protect their user and practically force an opponent to be impaled on one's sword. While Spanish footwork practice was without equal in the realm of oddness, the use of the sword itself followed traditional theories of cut and thrust.

The Spanish school never caught on outside Spain. Yet, in that country, it reigned supreme for 200 years. The eighteenth-century French master P. J. F. Girard described the Spanish method of combat as it had come down nearly unchanged from Carranza and Narvaez:

They [the Spanish] are fond often to give cut on the head, and immediately after deliver a thrust between the eyes and throat. Their guard is almost straight, their longe [lunge] very small; when they come in distance they bend the right knee and straighten the left,

Rapier play according to Thibault

and carry the body forward; when they retire they bend the left knee and straighten the right; they throw the body back well, in a straight line with that of the antagonist, and parry with the left hand, or slip the right foot behind the left.

Their swords are near five feet long from hilt to point, and cut with both edges; the shell is very large, and behind it is crossed with a small bar, which comes out about two inches on each side; they make use of this to wrench the sword out of the adversary's hand, by binding or crossing his blade with it, especially when they fight against a long sword; but it would be very difficult for them to execute this against a short sword. Their ordinary guard is with their wrist in tierce, and the point in a line with the face. They make appels or attacks with the foot, and also half thrusts to the face, keep their bodies back, and form a circle with the point of their swords to the left, and straightening their arm, they advance their body to give the blow on the head, and recover instantly to their guard, quite straight, with their point in a direct line to their adversary's face.

Fencing master Don Juan Nicolas Perinat was the first Spanish master to break with the old Spanish school by bringing the smallsword to his country in 1758.

By the beginning of the nineteenth century, Spain's mystical, fanciful style of combat, begun in swordplay's infancy, had been entirely abandoned, to be replaced by the modern French and Italian systems of fencing.
REFERENCES
Castle, Egerton. *Schools and Masters of Fence.* London: George Bell, 1885.
Morton, E. D. *Martini A–Z of Fencing.* London: Queen Anne Press, 1992.

SPARIZIONE DI CORPO. Simply put, a body evasion.
REFERENCE
Morton, E. D. *Martini A–Z of Fencing.* London: Queen Anne Press, 1992.

SPIGOLI. An Italian term for the edges of a sword blade.
REFERENCE
Morton, E. D. *Martini A–Z of Fencing.* London: Queen Anne Press, 1992.

SPRATICO. Known as the "beginner's assault." The fencing master alternately attacks and creates openings for the pupil to respond to offensively. None of the teacher's actions are performed with full intent, but with the notion of simply giving the student his first taste of bouting.
REFERENCE
Morton, E. D. *Martini A–Z of Fencing.* London: Queen Anne Press, 1992.

SQUALEMBRATO. A slanting, downward cut with one's blade.
REFERENCE
Morton, E. D. *Martini A–Z of Fencing.* London: Queen Anne Press, 1992.

STAGE FIGHT. A highly popular public entertainment in England in the 1700s, the stage fight would be looked on as nothing short of legalized butchery by today's standards. Basically, men met in open arenas to have at each other with weapons of various kinds.

While full of theatrical bluster on the part of the combatants, the fight itself quite often ended up being a blood-soaked affair, as was proved by a newspaper (*The Spectator*) description of a stage fight between Timothy Buck and James Miller on July 21, 1712:

The Combatants met in the Middle of the Stage. . . . Buck regarding his own defence, Miller chiefly thoughtful of annoying his Opponent. It is not easie to describe the many Escapes and imperceptible Defences between Two Men of quick Eyes and ready limbs: but Miller's Heat laid him open to the Rebuke of the calm Buck, by a large Cut on the Forehead. Much Effusion of Blood covered his Eyes in a moment, and the Huzzas of the Crowd undoubtedly quickened his anguish. . . . As soon as his Wound was wrapped up, he came on again in a little Rage, which still disabled him further . . . a decisive Stroke on the Left Leg of Miller. . . . The Wound was exposed to the view of all who could delight in it, and sowed up on Stage.

In spite of the gore, there seemed to be few fatalites involved in these stage fights. Some swordsmen, like the famous James Figg and John Parks, participated in dozens of such encounters, remaining physically fit to the ends of their lives.

While the backsword* was the acknowledged favorite weapon of the stage fighter, other methods of combat included the sword and dagger,* the sword and buckler,* falchion* play, and the quarterstaff.

Fighting with swords on stage was eventually replaced by the sport of boxing.

REFERENCES

Castle, Egerton. *Schools and Masters of Fence.* London: George Bell, 1885.

Wise, Arthur. *The Art and History of Personal Combat.* Greenwich, CT: Arma Press, 1971.

STAGE FIGHTERS. The stage fighter of the eighteenth century was the equivalent of our modern boxer, except that he fought with weapons rather than his fists.

The most famous stage fighter (and self-proclaimed master of all weapons) during the heyday of stage fighting was James Figg. Figg, described by contemporaries as "the Atlas of the Sword," was reported to "spare no man who took up [a weapon] against him." Figg also became a champion pugilist when boxing came into vogue.

Other well-known stage-fighting swordsmen, as noted in Castle's *Schools and Masters of Fence,*** included John Terrewest, John Stokes, William Gill, and John Delforce. John Parks, who was listed as an expert in the use of the backsword, sword and dagger,* sword and buckler,* single falchon,* case* of falchions, and quarterstaff, fought 350 stage fights.

REFERENCES

Castle, Egerton. *Schools and Masters of Fence.* London: George Bell, 1885.

Wise, Arthur. *The Art and History of Personal Combat.* Greenwich, CT: Arma Press, 1971.

STAR TREK. A popular science fiction television series from 1967 to 1969. Dealing with the interplanetary travels of the starship *Enterprise,* the show constantly thrust its lead characters—Captain Kirk (William Shatner), Spock (Leonard Nimoy), Dr. McCoy (deForest Kelly), Scott (James Doohan), Chekov (Walter Koenig), and Sulu (George Takei)—into situations of conflict and danger.

From meetings with warlike aliens and menacing, intelligent energy forms, to experiencing time travel problems and moral dilemmas, *Star Trek* managed to hit on most of the mainstays of the "space opera" genre, including occasional encounters with swordplay.

Fencing was a featured component in four episodes of the series: "The Squire of Gothos," "Day of the Dove," "Bread and Circuses," and "All Our Yesterdays."

In spite of the high regard many people have for the series, the fencing was, nevertheless, not very good. Little more than blade wacking, such poorly staged action did little to enhance the characters' overall air of competency.

REFERENCE

Gerrold, David. *The World of Star Trek.* New York: Ballantine Books, 1979.

STEAM FOIL. Slang for the standard, nonelectric foil, so called, perhaps, because one had to see that a touch was registered under one's own "steam" rather than through electricity.

REFERENCE

Morton, E. D. *Martini A–Z of Fencing.* London: Queen Anne Press, 1992.

STECCATA. The Italian term for the place of combat.

Also called *champs clos.*

REFERENCE

Castle, Egerton. *Schools and Masters of Fence.* London: George Bell, 1885.

STEINER, MAX. (1888–1971). Austrian-born film composer.

Because of his wide range of musical scope and expert grasp of movie mood, Max Steiner occasionally found himself scoring costume-adventure films, such as *The Three Musketeers* (1935),** *The Adventures of Don Juan* (1949),** and *The Flame and the Arrow* (1950).** His rousing, brassy themes were a perfect accompaniment to the swordplay in these films.

REFERENCE

Katz, Ephraim. *The Film Encyclopedia.* New York: Parigee Books, 1979.

STEP-IN PARRY. To step forward while parrying an opponent's attack.

REFERENCE

Morton, E. D. *Martini A–Z of Fencing.* London: Queen Anne Press, 1992.

STEP OUT. To move to the edge of the fencing strip rather than remaining in the middle.

REFERENCE

Morton, E. D. *Martini A–Z of Fencing.* London: Queen Anne Press, 1992.

STESSO TEMPO. Meaning single time. *Stesso tempo* meant to block an opponent's attack and counterattack in single action rather than to separate the parry and counterattack into two distinctly separate maneuvers. The latter approach was called *dui tempi* or *en deux temps.*

Old-time fencing masters were vehemently against the concept of *dui tempi,** as they believed it created too many openings for an opposing fencer. Only with the development of very light, easily manipulated swords was *dui tempi* thought to be acceptable over *stesso tempo.*

REFERENCE

Castle, Egerton. *Schools and Masters of Fence.* London: George Bell, 1885.

STEVENSON, ROBERT LOUIS. (1850–1894). Scottish novelist, poet, essayist.

Best known for his swashbuckling adventure stories, such as *Treasure Island* (1883), *Kidnapped* (1886), *The Black Arrow* (1888), and *Master of Ballantrae* (1888).

Stevenson stated in one of his many essays that the works of Alexandre Dumas were a major influence on his own writing and that Dumas's character of D'Artagnan was, perhaps, his favorite in all of literature.

Swordplay was sometimes an integral part of Stevenson's stories, as in *Kidnapped:* "But there was Alan, standing as before; only now his sword was running blood to the hilt. . . . The sword in his hands flashed like quicksilver into the huddle of our fleeing enemies."

Hollywood has produced numerous film versions of Stevenson's novels.
REFERENCES
Benet, William Rose. *The Reader's Encyclopedia.* New York: Thomas Y. Crowell, 1965.
Stevenson, Robert Louis. *Essays and Reviews.* Boston: Charles A. Lind, 1906.

STIRRUP HILT. A simple sword hilt* of the eighteenth century made up of a straight crossbar* and knuckle guard.*
REFERENCE
Morton, E. D. *Martini A–Z of Fencing.* London: Queen Anne Press, 1992.

STOCCATA. According to sixteenth-century Italian fencing master Vincentio Saviolo,* the *stoccata* was a thrust* that reached an adversary beneath the sword, hand, or dagger and might be delivered with the hand in pronation.*
REFERENCE
Castle, Egerton. *Schools and Masters of Fence.* London: George Bell, 1885.

STOCCATA LUNGA. Delivering an attack with a lunge,* according to sixteenth-century Italian fencing master Nicoletto Giganti.*
REFERENCE
Castle, Egerton. *Schools and Masters of Fence.* London: George Bell, 1885.

STONE SWORDS. Previous to the implementation of metal, swords were occasionally made of stone, especially flint and sandstone. They were used for both jabbing and striking.

In primitive societies outside Western civilization, stone was also used to enhance the edge of wooden swords. The types of stone most frequently employed were agate, chalcedony, rock crystal, quartz, flint, basalt, lava, jade, and obsidian.
REFERENCE
Burton, Richard F. *The Book of the Sword.* London: Chatto and Windus, 1884.

STOP CUT. A counterattack* in sabre* fencing that stops the attacker from proceeding with his offensive action employing the cutting edge of the weapon.

A stop cut is made at an attacking opponent's sword arm (no lunge included). To be valid,* however, the stop cut must land before the final movement of the attacker's action.

The stop cut is useful against slow or hesitant opponents or those who execute their attacks with exaggerated motions.

Also known as a *coup au tranchant.*

REFERENCE

Palffy-Alpar, Julius. *Sword and Masque.* Philadelphia: F. A. Davis, 1967.

STOP HIT. Any counterattack* made by extending one's blade point or cutting edge into an opponent's attack.

A stop hit may be either a stop thrust, a stop cut, a time thrust, or a time cut.

REFERENCES

Morton, E. D. *Martini A–Z of Fencing.* London: Queen Anne Press, 1992.

Palffy-Alpar, Julius. *Sword and Masque.* Philadelphia: F. A. Davis, 1967.

STOPPING. In Japanese swordsmanship, the concept of stopping referred to focusing on a single aspect of an opponent's attack, instead of letting one's mind flow beyond that action. This was said to freeze the mind, creating a block of one's creative responses.

The proper approach was simply to "perceive" and move forward without calculating thoughts of any sort. This would allow one to move naturally into the encounter, performing whatever needed to be accomplished without hesitation.

It was said that to go beyond "abiding" on the moment created a mental state where it was possible to turn an opponent's own blade against him, making his sword, in effect, yours. The term for this situation was "no sword," because it was as if one's enemy possessed no weapon.

REFERENCE

Suzuki, Daisetz. *Zen and Japanese Culture.* Princeton, NJ: Princeton University Press, 1973.

STOP POINT. A counterattack* in sabre* fencing that stops an incoming offensive action employing the weapon's point.

A stop point is an extension of one's blade—point first rather than a cut—into an opponent's attack (no lunge included). To be valid, however, the stop point must land before the final movement of the attacker's action.

The stop point is useful against slow or hesitant fencers or fencers who advance with wide, careless movements.

REFERENCE

Palffy-Alpar, Julius. *Sword and Masque.* Philadelphia: F. A. Davis, 1967.

STOP SHORT. A sudden halt in one's actions to throw an opponent off guard, to draw an attack to be taken advantage of, or simply to test his reactions.
REFERENCE
Morton, E. D. *Martini A–Z of Fencing.* London: Queen Anne Press, 1992.

STOP THRUST. A counterattack* that stops the attacker from proceeding with his offensive action. As the name implies, the action hits with the point of the blade.

Basically, a stop thrust is an extension of one's blade toward an attacking opponent (no lunge included). To be valid, however, because there is no attempt to divert the oncoming blade, the stop thrust must land before the final movement of the attacker's action.

The stop thrust may incorporate a body evasion of the attacking blade to ensure the avoidance of being hit.

The stop thrust is highly useful against a fencer who insists on attacking with a bent arm or with his point drawn away from his opponent's target area.

Also called a *coup d'arret* and a *colpo d'arresto.*
REFERENCES
Palffy-Alpar, Julius. *Sword and Masque.* Philadelphia: F. A. Davis, 1967.
Stevenson, John. *Fencing.* London: Briggs, 1935.

STRAIGHT ARM. One of the requirements for establishing priority—the right to hit one's opponent—in foil fencing. It is also a requirement for establishing right-of-way when attacking with the point in sabre fencing.

The straightened sword arm ensures an attacking fencer will have his full reach at his disposal when he lunges at his opponent. Moreover, it ensures that the opponent, if he extends his sword arm, will not have the longer reach and, hence, the advantage in the transpiring action.

The straight arm tends to improve both point control and the ability to evade effectively a defender's parries. The straighter the sword arm is during an attack, the more difficult it becomes to employ it in maneuvering one's weapon. This eliminates sweeping, muscular motions that destroy control, guiding blade use, by necessity, into the fingers. Fingerplay always promotes precise, efficient point movement.

Famed Italian fencing master Aldo Nadi,* in his book *On Fencing* (1943), firmly underscored the importance of the straight arm: "The arm must extend before the right foot moves for execution of the lunge—a rule that must remain engraved in your mind forever. Hand before foot, always."
REFERENCES
Gaugler, William. "Right of Way and Fencing Time." *American Fencing* (July/August 1986).
Stevenson, John. *Fencing.* London: Briggs, 1935.
U.S. Fencing Association, ed. *Operations Manual.* Colorado Springs, CO: U.S. Fencing Association, 1985.

STRAIGHT CUT. A form of simple attack* with the sabre,* whereby a cut* is directed to any portion of an opponent's target area* without passing over or under his blade.

Also called a "direct cut."
REFERENCE
Stevenson, John. *Fencing.* London: Briggs, 1935.

STRAIGHT HIT. An attack delivered immediately in the same line* in which the sword arm is extended. There is no feint or blade contact.

The straight hit is considered a simple attack.*

Also called a "direct thrust" and a *coup droit.*
REFERENCE
Stevenson, John. *Fencing.* London: Briggs, 1935.

STRAMAZONCELLO. According to seventeenth-century Italian fencing master Giuseppe Pallavicini,* the *stramazoncello* was a tearing cut with the extreme point of the sword.

In earlier times it was simply called *stramazone, tramazone,* or *estramacon.*
REFERENCE
Castle, Egerton. *Schools and Masters of Fence.* London: George Bell, 1885.

SUKO-HIRO. A celebrated Japanese sword maker during the late seventeenth century.
REFERENCE
Stone, George Cameron. *A Glossary of the Construction, Decoration, and Use of Arms and Armor.* New York: Jack Brussel, 1961.

SULTANI. A heavy, clumsy Indian sword of the eighteenth century. The blade was slightly curved.
REFERENCE
Stone, George Cameron. *A Glossary of the Construction, Decoration, and Use of Arms and Armor.* New York: Jack Brussel, 1961.

SUPINATION. The sword hand palm up.

Partial supination is usually described as having the thumb placed at one o'clock; complete supination, with the thumb at three o'clock.

Having one's sword hand in a supinated position, normally speaking, gives a fencer a lighter touch than does a pronated (palm down) position.
REFERENCE
Stevenson, John. *Fencing.* London: Briggs, 1935.

SUPPLEMENTARY PARRY. In the Italian style of sabre* fencing, the parry* of low tierce.*
REFERENCE
Morton, E. D. *Martini A–Z of Fencing.* London: Queen Anne Press, 1992.

SURAI. A sword of the Mahrattas of India. The blade was straight for two-thirds of its length and curved for the final third.
REFERENCE
Stone, George Cameron. *A Glossary of the Construction, Decoration, and Use of Arms and Armor.* New York: Jack Brussel, 1961.

SURFACE. A term referring to the valid target* area of a fencer's body.
REFERENCE
Handelman, Rob. "Fencing Glossary." *American Fencing* (July/August 1978).

SUTOR, JACOB. (c. 1580). German fencing master.

Notwithstanding his reputation as a fencing master of great repute, especially in the teaching of rapier play, Jacob Sutor held theories that were simply pale imitations of those of his Italian contemporaries.

Sutor wrote a book, *New Kunstliches Fechtbuch,*** detailing his approach to fencing, in 1612.
REFERENCE
Castle, Egerton. *Schools and Masters of Fence.* London: George Bell, 1885.

SWASHBUCKLER. In its original usage, "swashbuckler" was a term of derision, applied to fencers of the late-1500s who, as noted by fencing historian Egerton Castle, "were looked upon with dislike and suspicion by the quieter portion of the community." These men of the sword were most often noisy, swaggering thugs who spent a good portion of their time brawling and bullying.

According to writer and clergyman Thomas Fuller (1608–1661) in his book *The History of the Worthies of England* (1662), swordsmen in the West Smithfield section of London were the original recipients of the title "swashbuckler." It came from the habit of these individuals of "swashing [swaggering] and making a noise on the buckler [a small shield worn on the wrist]."

West Smithfield (also known as "Ruffian Hall") was, it seems, one of the few places in London where fencers were tolerated. Here, men fought openly and regularly. Observed Fuller, "[S]uch men usually met, casually or otherwise, to try mastery with sword and buckler; more were frightened than hurt, hurt than killed."

In modern times, a swashbuckler has come to mean someone who lives with an adventurous flair. Sometimes it is used to describe a flamboyant, dashing actor, such as Douglas Fairbanks, Sr., Errol Flynn, or Ronald Colman.

A variation on swashbuckler was "swingbuckler."
REFERENCES
Benet, William Rose. *The Reader's Encyclopedia.* New York: Thomas Y. Crowell, 1965.
Castle, Egerton. *Schools and Masters of Fence.* London: George Bell, 1885.
Meyrick, Samuel Rush. *A Critical Inquiry into Ancient Armour.* London: Robert Jennings, 1824.

Villainous swashbucklers, from a sixteenth-century German print

SWASHBUCKLER MOVIE. A type of adventure film in which fencing invariably plays a pivotal role. Indeed, the sword fight is the reason for this type of movie to exist. In the end, everything else in the story melts away when hero and villain, locked in some private place, draw their swords and pit themselves against each other for one final contest.

Prime examples of swashbuckler films at their best include *The Black Pirate* (1926),** *The Adventures of Robin Hood* (1938),** *The Mark of Zorro* (1940),** *The Three Musketeers* (1948),** *The Court Jester* (1956),** *The Four Musketeers* (1975),** and *The Princess Bride* (1987).**

REFERENCE

Richards, Jeffrey. *Swordsmen of the Screen.* Boston: Routledge and Kegan Paul, 1977.

SWEEPING PARRY. A parry* taken from the low line to the high line, and vice versa. They normally move from septime* to quarte* or from quarte* to septime.*

The advantage of the sweeping parry is that it can pick up almost any kind of attack.

REFERENCE

Palffy-Alpar, Julius. *Sword and Masque.* Philadelphia: F. A. Davis, 1967.

SWEPT HILT. A type of rapier* hand guard* popular during the seventeenth century. It was formed by a number of intertwining bars that formed a basket that ''swept'' around the hand.

REFERENCE

Stone, George Cameron. *A Glossary of the Construction, Decoration, and Use of Arms and Armor.* New York: Jack Brussel, 1961.

SWORD. ''Sword'' once referred specifically to a long-bladed, sharp-edged offensive weapon, with a simple cross hilt, used specifically for making cuts. Once, then, the thrusting rapier would not have been looked upon, strictly speaking, as a sword—it was a rapier, with its own individual characteristics, just as an ax was an ax. In time, though, ''sword'' simply came to be a generic designation for a wide variety of weapons.

A sword consists of two parts: the blade and the hilt. The blade handles the offensive-defensive chores of the sword. The hilt, which contains the guard and the grip, protects the hand holding the sword.

Some swords are double-edged; some are single-edged. Swords come in both curved-bladed and straight-bladed varieties. The curved-bladed sword is nearly always a weapon used purely for cutting. Straight-bladed ones, depending on the time period in which they were made, might be of either cutting or thrusting types. Occasionally, swords were constructed to incorporate both functions, but while they had a certain versatility in combat, they were never as efficient as weapons designed for a single purpose.

Weapons that fall into the sword family include the arming sword, backsword,

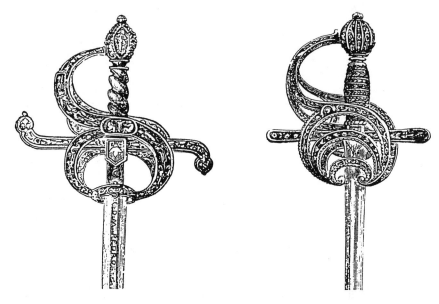

Rapiers with swept hilts

baselard, bastard sword, *boku-to, braquemar,* broadsword, *colichemarde, dha, dusack,* épée, *espadon, falchion,* foil, gauntlet sword, *jin-tache, katana, kledyv, khopsh, lansquenette, nimcha, parang bedak,* pillow sword, rapier, sabre, *schlae-ger,* scymitar, smallsword, spadroon, *spatha, talwar,* and *zweyhander.*

The term sword has its equivalent in a number of languages: the Scandinavian *svard,* the Danish *svaerd,* the Anglo-Saxon *sweord* and *suerd,* the Old German *svert,* and the Old English and Scottish *swerd.*

Additional sword names one might encounter include: *skeyne, sabir, sapara, sayf, sabrenn, sciabla, sabala, sabel, sablja, szablya,* and *yataghan.*

REFERENCES

Burton, Richard F. *The Book of the Sword.* London: Chatto and Windus, 1884.

Castle, Egerton. *Schools and Masters of Fence.* London: George Bell, 1885.

Stone, George Cameron. *A Glossary of the Construction, Decoration, and Use of Arms and Armor.* New York: Jack Brussel, 1961.

SWORD, DEVELOPMENT OF THE. The sword as a weapon evolved from the simple to the complex and then back to the simple again.

It has been suggested that the earliest swords evolved from the flint dagger of the Neolithic period. The first swords were made of copper, and then bronze and, for the most part, had leaf-shaped blades. Sword design was basic: an edged blade for cutting set onto a plain grip.

A major step in sword design took place when the blade was continued in an extension (tang*) that fit into the sword grip. This strengthened the overall weapon and prevented it from being broken apart by a blow.

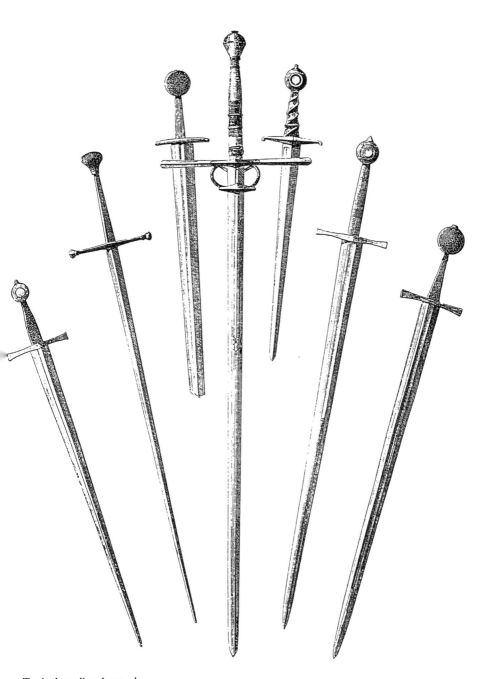

Typical medieval swords

Bronze swords were followed by ones of iron. Here, some hand protection was added to the hilt in the form of a simple, short bar, although it was not until the Middle Ages that this device became fully developed.

The Vikings from Scandinavia introduced sword blades of carbonized steel. These swords were of exceptional strength and temper.

During medieval times, swords had long, straight, double-edged blades and were used exclusively as offensive cutting weapons. The sword hand was protected by a rigid set of crossbars (quillons*) that were either straight or slightly curved toward the blade.

In time, metal rings were added to the hilt to increase hand protection.

When the rapier* was introduced to combat, the hand guard* grew more complicated. A series of rings and intertwined bars created an effect that resembled a cage for the hand. However, this soon proved ineffective in deterring thrusts, so shells or large cups were added to the arrangement.

As the sword shrank down in size, becoming, at last, the smallsword,* the hand guard was cut down to a small plate, short crossbars, and a knuckle guard.

REFERENCE

Wilkinson, Frederick. *Swords and Daggers.* New York: Hawthorn Books, 1967.

SWORD, PARTS OF THE.

Blade

Forte: strong part of the blade.

Foible: weak part of the blade.

Tip: point of the blade.

Edge: cutting surface of the blade.

False edge: cutting surface on the back side of the blade.

Ricasso: flat portion of blade near the hilt.

Tang: portion of blade that fits through the grip.

Hilt

Quillons: cross guard.

Counterguards: curved, intertwined bars.

Rings: circular pieces of metal set about the upper portion of the hilt.

Coquille: shell guard.

Knuckle bow: curved metal bar extending from the quillons to the end of the grip.

Poignee: grip.

Pommel: counterweight on the end of the grip.

REFERENCE

Wilkinson, Frederick. *Swords and Daggers.* New York: Hawthorn Books, 1967.

SWORD BELT. A belt to which a sword scabbard* was attached. It either fastened around the waist or was hung over the shoulder.
REFERENCE
Stone, George Cameron. *A Glossary of the Construction, Decoration, and Use of Arms and Armor.* New York: Jack Brussel, 1961.

SWORD BREAKER. A dangerous-looking dagger reportedly, by its design, able to catch and break a sword blade. Described as a dagger of the *main gauche* variety—a long, tapered, sharp-pointed blade set on a hilt with an extra long crossbar and a wide, triangular knuckle guard—this weapon, in truth, was never employed in the manner in which it was purported to be used, according to fencing historian Egerton Castle,* in his book *Schools and Masters of Fence* (1885).**

Said Castle: "They are decidedly inferior to any ordinary dagger. If they were ever used at all, it was probably in the right hand and alone, not in conjunction with the rapier. No mention of them is ever made in old books of fence, and their date must be ascribed as anterior to the sixteenth century."
REFERENCE
Castle, Egerton. *Schools and Masters of Fence.* London: George Bell, 1885.

SWORD CANE. A hollowed cane into which a sword blade has been inserted. The cane body, in effect, becomes a scabbard. Sword canes became popular when the custom of wearing a sword as part of civilian dress had passed away.

The blade of the sword cane—normally of the triangular épée variety—is attached to the crook part of the cane, or the cane knob, and may easily be drawn from its position if needed.

A well-designed sword cane customarily looks no different from an ordinary cane, concealment being an important function of the weapon.
REFERENCE
Stevenson, John. *Fencing.* London: Briggs, 1935.

SWORD DANCE. A display of skill in the management of the sword performed to the accompaniment of music. Often executed by men's sworn societies, these symbolic displays frequently point to either pagan fertility rites or victories over ancient enemies.

The concept of the sword dance can be traced back to rituals of ancient Greece and Rome, where war dances were performed with swords. Such entertainments were also highly popular in Anglo-Saxon days. As a vital part of all English festivities, they continued well into the fourteenth century.

Various forms of the sword dance are still performed today in various parts of the world: India (*Coorg Dance*), Turkey (*Danse du Sabre*), Russia (*Lezginka*), Spain (*Paloteo* and *Torneo*), Italy (*Bal de Baston*), Lithuania (*Mikita*), Hungary (*Kanasz Tanc*), Finland (*Skin Kompasse*), Scotland (*Gilly Callum*), Austria (*Perchtentanz*), France (*Matachins*), and Mexico (*Moros*).

REFERENCES
Castle, Egerton. *Schools and Masters of Fence*. London: George Bell, 1885.
Leach, Maria, ed. *Funk and Wagnalls Standard Dictionary of Folklore, Mythology, and Legend.* San Francisco: Harper and Row, 1972.

SWORD FIGHT, SIXTEENTH-CENTURY. When two swordsmen would meet in personal combat during the sixteenth century, their encounter did not at all resemble modern fencing.

The combatants would generally fall on guard with their sword points menacing each other's face. Either foot might be held forward depending entirely on the guard position assumed. Attacks were executed by stepping toward one's enemy rather than lunging. For some time, the two would circle around one another, periodically changing their sword guards. One moment the blade might be held high, the next low. All the while, of course, they would be looking for some small opening, some weakness, in their enemy's defensive posture. When that opening was perceived, an attack would be delivered by passing, or advancing one foot in front of the other. Once within reach of his opponent, the attacker would cut at an exposed part of the other's body. In response to this overt offensive maneuver, the defender might either attempt to dodge the advancing blade or deliver his own attack. The latter response would be expected to both block the initial attack and wound simultaneously. If neither action landed, the duel would carry on in this manner until one man was either badly wounded or killed outright.

REFERENCE
Castle, Egerton. *Schools and Masters of Fence*. London: George Bell, 1885.

SWORD KNOT. A loop of leather or cord fastened to the sword hilt. Before drawing the sword, the hand was passed through the loop, which was then given a turn or two to make it secure. A swordsman, so fitted, could not be disarmed.

REFERENCE
Stone, George Cameron. *A Glossary of the Construction, Decoration, and Use of Arms and Armor.* New York: Jack Brussel, 1961.

SWORD MAKERS—JAPANESE. The Japanese sword maker was an artist who approached his task with religious intent. His aim was to create not only a beautiful work but an object that would become, spiritually, an extension of its owner. The best sword makers were revered and honored in their homeland, and their work was much sought after.

The most celebrated sword makers include:

Amakuni of Yamato	A.D. 700
Amasa of Yamoto	700
Shinosuke of Bizen	720
Jiniki of Mutsu	750

Yasutsune of Hoki	800
Sanemori of Hoki	820
Sanetsugu of Chikuzen	850
Hisakuni of Yamashiro	1190
Yukihira of Bungo	1200
Kuniyasu of Yamashiro	1236
Yoshimitsu of Yamashiro	1275
Kunihide of Yamashiro	1288
Masamune of Sagami	1290
Yoshihiro of Echizen	1320
Kuniyoshi of Yamashiro	1325

The work of the sword maker Muramasa, who worked around 1340, is not generally included in lists of celebrated sword makers because his work was considered to be "ignoble, bloodthirsty, and of evil spirit." It was often noted that when a Muramasa blade was drawn, it could not be sheathed until it had spilled blood and that if it did not taste blood often enough, it would bring ill luck to its owner.

REFERENCE

Stone, George Cameron. *A Glossary of the Construction, Decoration, and Use of Arms and Armor.* New York: Jack Brussel, 1961.

SWORD-MAKING CENTERS. Centers of sword making, like those of armor making, sprang up in areas where the natural resources supported such industries.

Sword-making centers included Solingen, Passau, and Cologne in Germany; Poitou and Bordeaux in France; Milan and Brescia in Italy; and Toledo in Spain.

REFERENCE

Wilkinson, Frederick. *Swords and Daggers.* New York: Hawthorn Books, 1967.

SWORD NAMES. The heroes of antiquity often personified their blades by giving them names. These weapons—often said to be of magical origins—became personal extensions of their own superior natures.

Famous swords include:

Frithiof's *Angurvadal* (Stream of Anguish): fourteenth century

Ogier's *Courtain* and *Savaigne:* eighth century

Lancelot's *Ar'ondight:* sixth century

Siegfried's *Balmung* and *Gram* (Grief): pre-eleventh century

El Cid's *Colada:* eleventh century

Edward the Confessor's *Curtana:* eleventh century

Orlando's *Durandan* (the Inflexible): eighth century

King Arthur's *Excalibur* (to Liberate from the stone): sixth century

Charlemagne's *Floberge* (the Flame-Cutter) and *Joyeuse:* eighth century

Sir Bevis's *Morglay* (Big Sword): sixth century

Roland's *Durandel:* eighth century

Oliver's *Glorius:* eighth century

REFERENCES
Benet, William Rose. *The Reader's Encyclopedia.* New York: Thomas Y. Crowell, 1965.
Leach, Maria. *Standard Dictionary of Folklore, Mythology, and Legend.* San Francisco: Harper and Row, 1972.

SWORD OF DISCRIMINATION, THE. The Hindu deity Bodhisattva Manjushri (Beautiful Lord) is pictured with a sword called "the Sword of Discrimination," which, according to mythologist-philosopher Joseph Campbell,** symbolizes discerning the difference between the mortal and the eternal.

Desire and fear fall within the range of the mortal. The eternal has to do with achieving a still calmness within oneself that has been defined as "the firmly burning flame that is not rippled by any wind." It has also been defined as a "state of grace" and "flow."

When an athlete achieves this, his performance becomes, observed Campbell, "masterly." He added: "That's what the samurai does. And the real athlete."

REFERENCE
Osborn, Diane K. *A Joseph Campbell Companion.* New York: HarperCollins, 1991.

SWORD OF MYSTERY. The great sixteenth-century Japanese sword master Yagyu Tajima no kami called the mind "the Sword of Mystery." Ordinary people, he noted, think in one-sided terms. When they see an ending, they fail to see a beginning; when they see a beginning, they fail to see an ending. But the expert swordman's mind sees both at the same time. He sees that an ending is also a beginning and that a beginning is also an ending. This, then, was the mystery.

This more advanced state of mind, according to Yagyu Tajima, led to a fluidity of thought that created an unobstructed approach to swordplay. Movements, he said, are like flashes of light, with no interval between them.

REFERENCE
Suzuki, Daisetz T. *Zen and Japanese Culture.* Princeton, NJ: Princeton University Press, 1973.

SWORD OF NO-ABIDING MIND. An approach to Japanese swordplay created by Hariya Sekiun during the sixteenth century. This method, which sprang from the teachings of Zen,* stated that there was no need in swordplay to depend on technique. When a swordsman was in the proper state of mind—"enthroned in the seat of Heavenly Reason''—he would be free and independent and able to cope with any kind of fencing style.

Basically, the term ''no-abiding'' refers to an emptiness of mind.

REFERENCE

Suzuki, Daistz T. *Zen and Japanese Culture*. Princeton, NJ: Princeton University Press, 1973.

SWORD OF NO SWORD. A nineteenth-century Japanese sword approach devised by Yamaoka Tesshu that sought to unleash inner strength through demanding physical activity. This was achieved by inundating oneself in personal combat, specifically, taking part in numerous daily fencing contests, one right after the other, without letup. The usual method consisted of 100 bouts in the morning and 100 more in the afternoon for as many days as it took to achieve enlightenment. It was a very severe trial, and permission to attempt it was not readily granted by the fencing master.

When approached successfully, the process, producing a sense of impending death, was said to increase both mental clarity and physical prowess to an amazing level. This transformation of spirit over the physical, then, was said to be ''the sword of no sword.''

REFERENCE

Suzuki, Daisetz. *Zen and Japanese Culture*. Princeton, NJ: Princeton University Press, 1973.

SWORD OF TRUTH. The Japanese swordsman's concept that his sword is, above all, the path through which all truths of life and death are perceived.

REFERENCE

Herrigel, Eugen. *Zen in the Art of Archery*. New York: Vintage Books, 1971.

SWORDPLAY. A common term for the use of a sword in personal combat.

REFERENCE

Castle, Egerton. *Schools and Masters of Fence*. London: George Bell, 1885.

SWORDSMAN. One who is skilled in the use of swords.

Despite the image put forth by romantic literature of swordsmen as gallant, dashing heroes, historically speaking, the vast majority of the early followers of fence were a rough lot, thought to be little better than bullies, robbers, and murderers. As was noted by fencing historian Egerton Castle* in his *Schools and Masters of Fence* (1885),** ''Men who professed to excel in the practice of fighting could hardly escape the suspicion of making better use of it, for their own ends.''

It was not until the eighteenth century that swordsmen were able to gain even a semblance of respectability among the populace when fencing schools became centers of culture and manners. It was not until the twentieth century that

Early swordsmen

swordsmen, in the guise of competitive athletes, managed to elicit a lasting public regard for their unique, if not anachronistic, skills.

REFERENCES

Castle, Egerton. *Schools and Masters of Fence.* London: George Bell, 1885.

Palffy-Alpar, Julius. *Sword and Masque.* Philadelphia: F. A. Davis, 1967.

SWORDSMITH. One who makes swords.

Early bladesmiths were not always efficient or capable, producing swords of varying quality. As their experience grew, however, the quality of their weapons improved. Greater ability in metalworking led to lighter weapons, which, as expected, influenced the way in which weapons were used.

Swordsmiths were joined in the production of swords by the hilt makers and blade finishers.

Famous swordsmiths include Melchior Diefstetter, Andrea Ferrara,* John Gill, Thomas Gill, Sabastian Harrantiz, Antonio Piccinino, Sabastian Ruiz, Daniel and Emmanuel Sadeler, Sahagom, and Otto Wetter.

REFERENCE

Wilkinson, Frederick. *Swords and Daggers.* New York: Hawthorn Books, 1967.

SWORD SWALLOWING. A trick of ancient jugglers thought to have originated in Egypt. The sword swallower would throw back his head and blithely lower a sword blade (traditionally straight) down his throat as far as it would go. Certainly the real trick was not to pierce the stomach with the weapon's point or pull one's head forward too soon.

The historian Richard Burton, in his comprehensive *The Book of the Sword* (1884), tells us that sword swallowing was still being practiced during the nineteenth century by certain holy men of the Middle East.

REFERENCE

Burton, Richard F. *The Book of the Sword.* London: Chatto and Windus, 1884.

SYMBOLISM OF THE SWORD. On a basic, psychological level, the sword with its long, straight blade is a masculine symbol, obviously phallic in nature. Consequently, it further becomes a symbol of male power. Among Germanic tribes in the early centuries A.D., the sword was a symbol of high rank and command, just as it is in modern military institutions.

Because of its very nature as a tool of combat, more than any other weapon the sword has been characterized as a symbol of war. The ancient Scythians, Chadeans, and Babylonians, emphasizing this connection, worshipped the image of a sword as a representation of their war gods. Yet, from war comes not only conflict but resolution; so the sword may equally lay claim to symbolizing peace.

This dualistic nature of the sword goes on to identify it—with its equal ability to heal or slay, liberate or subjugate, create or destroy—as a symbol of both freedom and bondage.

A more esoteric view of the sword symbolizes it as a wound, or the ability to wound. Further arcane thought explains it as the embodiment of physical extermination (death) and psychic decision (spiritual evolution). When a sword appears in association with fire, it stands for purification. Composed of two joined elements, blade and guard, it might even be a symbol of conjunction. It also serves as a simple symbol of bravery.

Medieval Europe employed the sword to typify high social attainment, often displaying it on seals of state and coats-of-arms. A figurative, as well as actual, prerogative of the noble and knightly, the weapon was uniformly forbidden by law to the peasant. In feudal Japan, the sword was chiefly a symbol of the warrior class, the samurai.* As in the West, it could not be possessed by a member of the lower classes.

Tarot cards,* an ancient method of predicting the future, often use the sword and its association with war as a symbol of ill boding. Sword cards, of which there are fourteen in the tarot deck, represent death, pain, failure, sickness, destruction, exile, loss, and hatred. Occasionally the cards denote more upbeat aspects of life, such as triumph, hope, confidence, and harmony.

In recent times, famed psychoanalyst Carl Jung (1875–1961) looked upon the sword as a symbol of the "self."

Some sword symbolism holds that the oriental sword, with its curved blade, is lunar in aspect, and hence feminine.

REFERENCES

Burton, Richard F. *The Book of the Sword.* London: Chatto and Windus, 1884.

Cerlot, J. E. *A Dictionary of Symbolism.* New York: Philosophical Library, 1983.

Velikovsky, Immanuel. *Worlds in Collision.* New York: MacMillan, 1950.

Waite, Arthur Edward. *The Pictorial Key to the Tarot.* New York: University Books, 1959.

T

TAC. A beat parry, that is, a parry that lightly knocks an opponent's attacking blade out of line.
REFERENCE
Handelman, Rob. ''Fencing Glossary.'' *American Fencing* (July/August 1978).

TAC AU TAC. An exchange of beat parry-direct riposte actions between two fencers.

Also known as a ''Bertrand riposte'' (named after nineteenth-century fencing master Francois-Joseph Bertrand, who popularized the action).
REFERENCE
Stevenson, John. *Fencing.* London: Briggs, 1935.

TACHI. The earliest form of single-edged sword in Japan. The length of the *tachi* blade was officially fixed in 1730 at between 17.5 and 26.5 inches.

In many ways the *tachi* is quite similar to its successor, the *katana.* The main physical difference between the two is in the way they were decorated. Another distinction was in the way they were worn. The *tachi* was hung, blade edge downward, from a belt. The *katana* was thrust through a sash and carried blade edge upward.

While it is sometimes stated that the *tachi* blade is more curved than that of the *katana,* * this, upon examination, proves to be false.
REFERENCE
Stone, George Cameron. *A Glossary of the Construction, Decoration, and Use of Arms and Armor.* New York: Jack Brussel, 1961.

TACHI BUKURO. A case or box for a *tachi.**
REFERENCE
Stone, George Cameron. *A Glossary of the Construction, Decoration, and Use of Arms and Armor.* New York: Jack Brussel, 1961.

TACHI HANAGU. A *tachi** with mounts (decorations) of gold or gilded copper.
REFERENCE
Stone, George Cameron. *A Glossary of the Construction, Decoration, and Use of Arms and Armor.* New York: Jack Brussel, 1961.

TACHIUCHI. In medieval Japan, a fencing match employing real swords.
REFERENCE
Sasamori, Junzo, and Gordon Warner. *This Is Kendo.* Vermont: Charles E. Tuttle, 1984.

TAGA DHARA SHANI. A type of Indian sabre.*
REFERENCE
Stone, George Cameron. *A Glossary of the Construction, Decoration, and Use of Arms and Armor.* New York: Jack Brussel, 1961.

TAGA TALWAR. An Indian sabre* with a *hukim khani* hilt* (short quillons,* drooping projections over the blade, a short grip,* and a disk pommel*).
REFERENCE
Stone, George Cameron. *A Glossary of the Construction, Decoration, and Use of Arms and Armor.* New York: Jack Brussel, 1961.

TAIKEN. In Japanese, carrying a sword slipped through the belt.
REFERENCE
Stone, George Cameron. *A Glossary of the Construction, Decoration, and Use of Arms and Armor.* New York: Jack Brussel, 1961.

TAKAHI. In Japanese, a sword hilt.*
REFERENCE
Stone, George Cameron. *A Glossary of the Construction, Decoration, and Use of Arms and Armor.* New York: Jack Brussel, 1961.

TAKONA-GATANA. A type of Japanese bamboo sword used in fencing practice.
REFERENCE
Stone, George Cameron. *A Glossary of the Construction, Decoration, and Use of Arms and Armor.* New York: Jack Brussel, 1961.

TAKOUBA. The sword of the nomadic Tuareg people of the central Sahara Desert.

The *takouba* has a straight, single-edged blade and no hand guard.* There is, however, a crosspiece below the pommel,* which has no defensive purpose.
REFERENCE
Stone, George Cameron. *A Glossary of the Construction, Decoration, and Use of Arms and Armor.* New York: Jack Brussel, 1961.

TALIBON. A sword used by the Christian natives of the Philippines.

The heavy blade of the *talibon* is straight on the back and curved on the edge, with a longish point. The grip,* which has no crossbar* over it, has a marked curve in it.
REFERENCE
Stone, George Cameron. *A Glossary of the Construction, Decoration, and Use of Arms and Armor.* New York: Jack Brussel, 1961.

TALWAR. The generic name for the Indian sabre.* It includes nearly all the curved swords used in India.

Great care was taken among the fighting men of India to keep their *talwars* in perfect condition. Whenever a sword was taken off, it was wrapped in oiled muslin. Moreover, only leather scabbards* were used, rather than steel, to keep the blades from becoming dull.

Talwar blades vary in size, curvature, and quality. Hilts* possess short, heavy crossbars* and disk pommels.* Some have knuckle guards*; some do not.
REFERENCE
Stone, George Cameron. *A Glossary of the Construction, Decoration, and Use of Arms and Armor.* New York: Jack Brussel, 1961.

TAMPEI. A type of Japanese short sword.
REFERENCE
Stone, George Cameron. *A Glossary of the Construction, Decoration, and Use of Arms and Armor.* New York: Jack Brussel, 1961.

TANG. The portion of a sword blade that fits inside the grip.

Also called the "tongue," *la soie, la spina,* and *il codolo.*
REFERENCE
Burton, Richard F. *The Book of the Sword.* London: Chatto and Windus, 1884.

TARGET. A large, round shield with loops on the back. The arm passed through one loop; the hand held the other. The target dates back to the twelfth century.

The target, which was most often made of wood and covered with leather, also possessed a central spike, which often measured as long as ten inches.

This type of shield found its greatest popularity among the Scots as late as the nineteenth century.

REFERENCE

Stone, George Cameron. *A Glossary of the Construction, Decoration, and Use of Arms and Armor.* New York: Jack Brussel, 1961.

TARGET AREA. The portion of a fencer's body relegated to valid touches* by the conventions* of fencing.

In foil* fencing, the target area consists of the trunk of the body. In sabre* fencing, it is from the waist upward, including the head and arms. In épée* fencing, the entire body is considered the target area.

REFERENCE

Stevenson, John. *Fencing.* London: Briggs, 1935.

TAROT CARDS. Picture cards used to divine the future.

The first historical references to tarot cards appear in the late fourteenth century, although it has never been clear as to where they actually originated.

The tarot deck, which is made up of seventy-eight cards, is separated into two categories: the major arcana and the minor arcana.

The major group possesses twenty-two individual cards: the Magician, the High Priestess, the Empress, the Emperor, the High Priest, the Lovers, the Chariot, Fortitude, the Hermit, the Wheel of Fortune, Justice, the Hanged Man, Death, Temperance, the Devil, the Tower, the Star, the Moon, the Sun, the Last Judgment, the Fool, and the World.

The minor group is divided into four categories: Swords, Cups, Batons, and Coins. Of these, the Sword is linked with Air, the Cup with Water, the Baton with Fire, and Coins with the Earth.

The suit of Swords is generally an unlucky sign, because the sword, as a weapon, suggests war, bloodshed, and death. It is associated with intellect and instability.

The suit of Cups is the luckiest of the four suits. Its connection is with things feminine. It mainly covers love, marriage, emotion, and pleasure.

The suit of Batons (also Wands, Rods, and Staffs) is related to things masculine. It often deals with creative energy regarding business, enterprise, and moving forward in life.

The suit of Coins, as one might expect, deals with money, as well as property, earning a living, status, and security.

Each suit is further portioned into thirteen cards: King, Queen, Page, Ten, Nine, Eight, Seven, Six, Five, Four, Three, Two, and Ace.

Every card in the tarot deck has its own specific meaning and, when read in a group of cards, according to those proficient in reading them, is supposed to give a detailed projection of future happenings.

REFERENCES

Cavendish, Richard. *The Tarot.* New York: Harper and Row, 1975.

Waite, Arthur Edward. *The Pictorial Key to the Tarot.* New York: University Books, 1959.

The Nine of Swords

TAU-KIEN. Chinese weapons with hilts* like swords and heavy metal bars in place of blades. Some weigh as much as ten pounds.
REFERENCE
Stone, George Cameron. *A Glossary of the Construction, Decoration, and Use of Arms and Armor.* New York: Jack Brussel, 1961.

TEBUTJE. A type of sword used by the Gilbert Islanders. It was a light club fitted, on either side, with rows of shark teeth.
REFERENCE
Stone, George Cameron. *A Glossary of the Construction, Decoration, and Use of Arms and Armor.* New York: Jack Brussel, 1961.

TEGHA. A sabre* used by the Mahrattas and Rajputs of India. It had a broad, curved blade and a hilt* resembling that of a *talwar.**
REFERENCE
Stone, George Cameron. *A Glossary of the Construction, Decoration, and Use of Arms and Armor.* New York: Jack Brussel, 1961.

TELEVISION, FENCING ON. It has been said that television reduces everything to its lowest common denominator, and this has been especially true with theatrical fencing. Today, when an actor on a television series is called on to fence, the finished product is apt to be disappointing from both a technical and dramatic standpoint. Such displays, for the most part, are usually forgettable encounters. There have been numerous examples graphically illustrating this unfortunate situation over the years.

The lack of preparation that goes into most television fencing scenes is the main reason for the proliferation of such mediocrity. This is somewhat understandable when a show must be created from scratch in a single week. It could be offset somewhat if an actor already had some fencing training, but most modern thespians are minus this expertise. Add to this a lack of technical understanding on the part of those directing the swordplay, and the resultant blade hacking and waving and unfencer-like postures become inevitable.

Series like the 1960s "Star Trek,"* the 1970s "Happy Days," and the 1980s "Fantasy Island," "Hart to Hart" and "Magnum P.I."** turned out fencing scenes that ranged in quality from poor to extremely poor.

There have, however, been exceptions to this rule. During the 1950s, various anthology series occasionally produced shows that included fencing in the story line. Because the fencing was handled by people who took it seriously, the action was often surprisingly well mounted. In 1957, Louis Jordan** starred in "The Man Who Beat Lupo" on the Ford Theatre. The story dealt with a nobleman who becomes a professional fencing master to win prize money to support his aged mother. In 1959, James Mason** had the title role in "A Sword for Marius" on the Alcoa Goodyear Theatre. This tale centered on a philosophy teacher who is also a fencing master and how he handles his personal philosophy of nonviolence with an aggressive student. In both cases, the fencing, guided by fencing master Ralph Faulkner,* was both clean and well paced.

The fencing on the Walt Disney series "Zorro"** (1958–1959) was another notable exception to the often inferior swordplay created for television. The show's star, Guy Williams,** trained by veteran film fencing master Fred Cavens,* regularly turned in performances with the sword that displayed above average ability.

Another show that produced fencing of a highly competent nature was the short-lived 1980s series "The Master," starring Lee Van Cleef, which dealt with the adventures of a modern American ninja master wandering across the United States. The sword fights were ably staged by Van Cleef's costar, Sho Kosuji.

In a few cases of swashbuckler movies made for television, there has fortunately been a greater concern for creating competent fencing scenes than that shown on weekly series. While not necessarily excellent efforts, they at least manage to rise above the completely forgettable. Bigger budgets, longer shooting schedules, and more fencing training for the actors involved in the action are the main reasons for increased fencing quality. Examples include *The Man in the Iron Mask* (1977), starring Richard Chamberlain*; *The Scarlet Pimpernel* (1982), starring Anthony Andrews; *Ivanhoe* (1982), again starring Anthony Andrews; and *The Corsican Brothers* (1985), starring Trevor Eve.

REFERENCES
Halliwell, Leslie. *Halliwell's Filmgoer's and Video Viewer's Companion.* New York: Charles Scribner's Sons, 1988.
Richards, Jeffrey. *Swordsmen of the Screen.* Boston: Routledge and Kegan Paul, 1977.

TEMPIST. An old term describing a fencer of much subtlety.
REFERENCE
Morton, E. D. *Martini A-Z of Fencing.* London: Queen Anne Press, 1992.

TEMPO. A combination of speed and movement employed to achieve a particular result in fencing. The speed aspect of timing has less to do with actual quickness than the way the speed is used. The movement aspect may include both blade and body motion.

The purpose of timing, as explained by fencing historian Egerton Castle* in his *Schools and Masters of Fence* (1885),** was to "reduce motions of weapon and body to the strictly necessary, both in number and extent, so as to employ the least possible time in attack and parry; secondly, to balance these actions carefully with the adversary's in order to seize at once the least opportunity and to reduce the number of hits to a minimum."

Also called "timing" or, simply, "time."
REFERENCES
Castle, Egerton. *Schools and Masters of Fence.* London: George Bell, 1885.
Stevenson, John. *Fencing.* London: Briggs, 1935.

TEMPO INDIVISIBLE. According to seventeenth-century Italian fencing master Alexander Senese,* tempo indivisible was defined as timing expressed in a parry*-riposte* action in which the riposte resulted from a parry without any pause.
REFERENCE
Castle, Egerton. *Schools and Masters of Fence.* London: George Bell, 1885.

TEMPS PERDU. A riposte* or counterriposte* that is not executed immediately after a parry.* The term means "lost time."
REFERENCE
Handelman, Rob. "Fencing Glossary." *American Fencing* (July/August 1978).

TENNIS. Sixteenth-century French fencing master Henry de Sainct-Didier* included in his fencing book, *Traicte Contenant les Secrets du Premier Livre sur l'Espee Seule* (1573),** a parallel between fencing and tennis, in which he applied various fencing expressions to methods of receiving the ball in tennis.
REFERENCE
Castle, Egerton. *Schools and Masters of Fence.* London: George Bell, 1885.

TETE. A sabre* term referring to the top of the mask, which, for that weapon, is part of the target area.
REFERENCE
Handelman, Rob. "Fencing Glossary." *American Fencing* (July/August 1978).

THEATRICAL FENCING. Combat with swords, for theatrical purposes, in which the moves have been carefully planned out and rehearsed well in advance of the actual encounter. In most cases, such swordplay has been both enlarged and exaggerated: first, for dramatic effect and, second, so that the audience can easily follow the action. Sometimes, theatrical duels follow a historical bent; more often than not, however, they are simply a distillation of everything that has ever been learned in fencing so as to create the most dramatic and satisfying fight possible.

Theatrical fencing may be for either stage or film.
REFERENCE
Hobbs, William. *Techniques of the Stage Fight.* London: Studio Vista, 1967.

THEATRICAL STAGE FENCING. Rehearsed sword fights on the theatrical stage.

Fencing has appeared on stage since the days of William Shakespeare. It was often looked upon as an integral part of the story, perhaps because the sword used to be a part of everyday life. Actors, of course, were expected to have fencing skills because of this.

In the early days of stage fencing, duels were simple affairs of little more than whacking blades together. In time, though, routines that worked well were repeated enough times until they became a familiar part of theatrical combat. They had names like the "Round Eights," the "Glasgow Tens," and the "Long Elevens."

Theatrics were always highly important to these combats. Flint was sometimes attached to sword blades to produce sparks. Weapons were even wired with electricity to produce even "grander" effects.

Plays featuring sword fights were highly popular during the 1800s, so much so that more than one play was hastily written as a vehicle for a grand sword fight.

Modern stage fencing, rather than relying on melodramatic histrionics, usually follows a more polished theatrical approach: either a dancelike choreographed style of swordplay, with an emphasis on elegant form and grace, or a historically oriented fight, with the brutal reality of combat being its underlying orientation.

REFERENCES

Hobbs, William. *Techniques of the Stage Eight.* London: Studio Vista, 1967.

Palffy-Alpar, Julius. *Sword and Masque.* Philadelphia: F. A. Davis, 1967.

Richards, Jeffrey. *Swordsmen of the Screen.* Boston: Routledge and Kegan Paul, 1977.

THEATRICAL SWORD. A fencing weapon designed specifically for theatrical fencing. Broadswords and sabres are dull-edged. Rapiers and smallswords are dull-pointed. In the case of the latter two weapons, while the hilts are true to a specific time period, the blades are often of the modern sport variety (specifically, épée).

REFERENCE

Richards, Jeffrey. *Swordsmen of the Screen.* Boston: Routledge and Kegan Paul, 1977.

THIBAULT, GIRARD. (c. 1600). French fencing master.

Girard Thibault, although French by origin, taught the highly artificial, esoteric method of fencing developed by the Spanish during the sixteenth century.

His *The Academy of the Sword*** (1628), which took fifteen years to produce, was a huge, magnificently illustrated tome detailing the virtues of geometrically inspired fencing (the Mysterious Circle*) and the odd metaphysical philosophies originated by Jeronimo de Carranza* and Don Luis Pacheco de Narvaez.* For all its serious expounding, however, the book had no effect at all on the development of fencing in France, or, for that matter, any other country. It remains, as noted by fencing historian Egerton Castle* in his *Schools and Masters of Fence* (1885),** nothing more than "a bibliographic curiosity."

Thibault's name is also found spelled "Thibaust" and "Thibauld."

REFERENCE

Castle, Egerton. *Schools and Masters of Fence.* London: George Bell, 1885.

THREE MUSKETEERS FILMS. The quintessential swashbuckler story, Alexandre Dumas's* classic romantic, historical adventure of D'Artagnan and his

French fencing master Girard Thibault

An illustration by artist Maurice Leloir for an 1895 edition of *The Three Musketeers*

musketeer comrades—Athos, Aramis, and Porthos—has been one of Hollywood's favorite literary targets over the years.

The Three Musketeers has found its way onto the movie screen over a dozen times: 1908, 1911, 1913, 1914, 1916, 1921, 1935, 1939, 1948, 1952, 1953, 1961, 1974, and 1975. It was also parodied in a 1922 comedy, *The Three Must-Get-Theres.*

The numerous versions of the tale invariably follow the familiar Dumas story line: D'Artagnan,* fresh from his country home in Gascony, arrives in Paris, meets the famous three musketeers, duels, engages in court intrigues, and eventually becomes a full-fledged musketeer.

The first film version of note was Douglas Fairbanks, Sr.,* 1921 energetic salute to swashbuckling. The film also starred Marguerite de La Motte, Leon Barry, George Siegmann, and Eugene Pallette. This *Musketeers* was a combination of Dumas's story line and Douglas Fairbanks's personality. The fencing, staged by Henry Uyttenhove, was flavored with numerous acrobatic enhancements and exhilarating sword stunts.

The first sound version of *The Three Musketeers* appeared in 1935 and starred Walter Abel, Paul Lukas, Ian Keith, Onslow Stevens, Ralph Forbes, and Margot Grahame. The film, although somewhat slow-moving at times, nevertheless caught the sense of comradeship and honor so prevalent in Dumas's story. Walter Able came nowhere near Douglas Fairbanks's vital, hyperactive performance as D'Artagnan. Instead, he gave a rather low-key performance as a simple, but brave, country boy out to make good. The fencing, staged by Fred Cavens,* was simple and clean.

In 1939, Hollywood produced a musical comedy version of *The Three Musketeers,* starring Don Ameche, Binnie Barnes, Lionel Atwill, and the Ritz Brothers. Don Ameche was a singing D'Artagnan. The Ritz Brothers impersonated the famous musketeers. Ameche handled his part well. Although the overall film lacked vitality, the fencing was, in fact, exciting.

The Gene Kelly* version of *The Three Musketeers,* made in 1948, is, perhaps, the most dashing, glittering sound version to date. The film also starred June Allyson, Van Hefflin, Gig Young, Robert Coote, Vincent Price, and Lana Turner. Kelly was an inspired choice for D'Artagnan. The dancer's expert sense of timing and acrobatic skills helped create a larger-than-life heroic image of D'Artagnan that, for both vitality and humor, rivals Douglas Fairbanks's cinematic creation. Fencing master Jean Heremans* was also in top form. His "duel behind the Luxembourg," an intricate blend of fine swordplay and comedy stunts, ranks as one of Hollywood's all-time classic film sword fights.

Richard Lester's 1974 *The Three Musketeers,* starring Michael York, Oliver Reed, Frank Finlay, Richard Chamberlain, Raquel Welch, Christopher Lee, and Faye Dunaway, was a stunning deviation from the usual "fairy tale" rendering of the story. Going for a uniquely historical approach to the subject matter, it had much less of the purely romantic than simple nitty-gritty realism. There were grime and lust and blood aplenty. The swordplay, created by fight arranger William Hobbs,* was a smorgasbord of period styles of combat. While vastly different in feeling from standard theatrical fencing, it nevertheless was the proper approach for the type of film Richard Lester was making.

This latter version of *The Three Musketeers* was followed the next year with a sequel, *The Four Musketeers.* While the overall effort was more dour and slow-moving than its predecessor, the fencing continued in an inventively brutal vein.

D'Artagnan, Athos, Aramis, and Porthos continued their swashbuckling ways in various renditions of *The Man in the Iron Mask: The Man in the Iron Mask* (1928), *The Iron Mask* (1929), *The Man in the Iron Mask* (1939), *Prisoner of the Iron Mask* (1962), *The Man in the Iron Mask* (1977), and *The Fifth Musketeer* (1977).

Other musketeer-related films include *The Sword of D'Artagnan* (1950), *Lady in the Iron Mask* (1952), *Zorro and the Three Musketeers* (1963), and *Cyrano and D'Artagnan* (1964). Progeny of the musketeers turned up in *At Sword's Point* (1952).

As expected, fencing is a staple of all these films.

REFERENCES

Druxman, Michael B. *Make It Again, Sam.* New York: A. S. Barnes, 1975.

Richards, Jeffrey. *Swordsmen of the Screen.* Boston: Routledge and Kegan Paul, 1977.

THREE MUSKETEERS, THE. (1844). Novel by Alexandre Dumas.

The Three Musketeers is one of the world's greatest and most popular novels. Based on an eighteenth-century volume, *Memoires of M. d'Artagnan, Captain-Lieutenant in the First Company of King's Musketeers* (1700), written by Gatien de Courtilz, the book has become the archetypical historical romance.

D'Artagnan, a young Gascon swordsman, comes to Paris to seek his fortune. His hope is to join Louis XIII's musketeer regiment. Almost at once, he becomes friends with the three best swordsmen in France: Athos, Porthos, and Aramis—the three musketeers.

After numerous adventures, D'Artgnan achieves his goal and is admitted to the ranks of the king's musketeers.

As expected, there is much swordplay along the way. For example:

[D'Artagnan] fought like a furious tiger, turning ten times round his adversary, and changing his ground and guard twenty times. Jussac was, as they expressed it in those days, a fine blade, and had much practice; nevertheless, it required all his skill to defend himself against an adversary, who, active and energetic, departed every instant from received rules, attacking him on all sides at once, and yet parrying like a man who had the greatest respect for his own skin.

This contest at length exhausted Jussac's patience. Furious at being held in check by him whom he had considered a boy, he grew hot, and began to make mistakes. D'Artagnan, who, though wanting in practice, had a good theory, redoubled his agility. Jussac, anxious to put an end to this, springing forward, aimed a terrible thrust at his adversary, but the latter parried it, and, while Jussac was recovering himself, glided like a serpent beneath his blade, and passed his sword through his body. Jussac fell like a dead mass.

The Three Musketeers, because of its vast and lasting appeal, has been dramatized on stage and in film numerous times.

REFERENCES

Benet, William Rose. *The Reader's Encyclopedia.* New York: Thomas Y. Crowell, 1965.

Dumas, Alexandre. *The Three Musketeers.* New York: D. Appleton, 1925.

Maurois, Andre. *Alexandre Dumas.* New York: Alfred A. Knopf, 1955.

THREE STOOGES, THE. America's slapstick kings—Larry, Moe, and Curly, sometimes Shemp; and later Curly Joe—almost by necessity, due to the vast quantity of story lines generated by the team over the years (the Stooges made well over 200 films), hit on swashbuckling as a vehicle for their comedy nonsense.

The Three Stooges picked up the sword in *Restless Knights* (1935), *Scotched in Scotland* (1954), *Knutzy Knights* (1954), and *Snow White and the Three Stooges* (1961). The fencing was always incredibly silly, as well it should have been.

REFERENCE
Howard, Moe. *Moe Howard and the Three Stooges.* Secaucus, NJ: Citadel Press, 1977.

THRUST. An offensive extension of one's sword toward an opponent.

REFERENCE
Stevenson, John. *Fencing.* London: Briggs, 1935.

TIERCE. The line of three.

In foil* and épée* fencing, tierce is the high-outside line with the sword hand held in pronation.* The weapon point is always higher than the sword hand. Before the end of the nineteenth century, the on-guard position in tierce was the only one used.

In sabre* fencing, tierce is the position covering the right side of the body. It is taken with the point higher than the sword hand and the blade cutting edge turned toward the right. The sword hand is in pronation.

Also known as *terza*.

REFERENCE
Handelman, Rob. "Fencing Glossary." *American Fencing* (July/August 1978).

TIGISHI. In Japan, a man who sharpens sword blades.

Also called a *togiya*.

REFERENCE
Stone, George Cameron. *A Glossary of the Construction, Decoration, and Use of Arms and Armor.* New York: Jack Brussel, 1961.

TIME CUT. In sabre* fencing, a counterattack* in the form of a cut to the arm of an attacking opponent, followed by a step backward, a parry* of the attacker's cut, and a riposte.*

REFERENCE
Morton, E. D. *Martini A–Z of Fencing.* London: Queen Anne Press, 1992.

TIME HIT. Either a time thrust* or a time cut.* These counterattacking actions block or intercept an opponent's attacking blade and strike a touch at the same moment.

Basically, a parry and riposte in a single action.

REFERENCE
Morton, E. D. *Martini A–Z of Fencing*. London: Queen Anne Press, 1992.

TIME THRUST. A type of time hit* involving a thrusting, point-oriented action.

A time thrust is an extension of one's blade into an opponent's attack that both blocks the course of the offensive action (which protects the fencer who executes the time thrust) and strikes the attacker.

There are four forms of the time thrust: the *appuntata,* the *inquartata,* the *imbroccata,* and the *passata sotto.*

The time thrust may also be called a *coup de temps,* a "time touch," an "attack by interception," a "covered stop hit," and an "attack in opposition."
REFERENCES
Morton, E. D. *Martini A–Z of Fencing*. London: Queen Anne Press, 1992.
Palffy-Alpar, Julius. *Sword and Masque*. Philadelphia: F. A. Davis, 1967.

TIRER AU MUR. In French, "lunge to the wall."

As described by eighteenth-century French fencing master Guillaume Danet,* this was a fencing exercise where one fencer executed a series of disengagements against another. The latter would then, for the sake of experience, either parry or let an action hit. Furthermore, attacks could be practiced in any line. Often executed slowly and with much deliberation, these maneuvers could be studied and weighed for their effectiveness. Care was always given to form.

Such academic training might also be engaged in employing a target on a wall rather than a partner.

Tirer au mur was, in fact, an early form of conventional exercises.*

Interestingly, the Japanese developed similar learning approaches to their fencing.
REFERENCES
Castle, Egerton. *Schools and Masters of Fence*. London: George Bell, 1885.
Stone, George Cameron. *A Glossary of the Construction, Decoration, and Use of Arms and Armor*. New York: Jack Brussel, 1961.

TJOEDRE. A type of Malay sword.
REFERENCE
Stone, George Cameron. *A Glossary of the Construction, Decoration, and Use of Arms and Armor*. New York: Jack Brussel, 1961.

TO HAVE A HAND. The act of parrying* well.
REFERENCE
Morton, E. D. *Martini A–Z of Fencing*. London: Queen Anne Press, 1992.

TOKONOMA. A place of honor in a Japanese room, often an alcove, where racks of swords were frequently placed.

REFERENCE
Stone, George Cameron. *A Glossary of the Construction, Decoration, and Use of Arms and Armor.* New York: Jack Brussel, 1961.

TOUCH. To make contact with an adversary's target area* with the point or cutting edge of one's weapon.

Valid touches* make contact with an opponent's prescribed target area. Invalid touches* are outside the limits of the prescribed target area.

Also called *touche, toucher, tocada, toccata,* and *tocco.*
REFERENCE
Handelman, Rob. "Fencing Glossary." *American Fencing* (July/August 1978).

TOUR DE BRETTEUR. A blade with an overly pronounced bend in it.
REFERENCE
Morton, E. D. *Martini A–Z of Fencing.* London: Queen Anne Press, 1992.

TOURNAMENT. The official title given to all competitions held at the same place, at the same time, and for the same reason.
REFERENCE
U.S. Fencing Association, ed. *Operations Manual.* Colorado Springs, CO: U.S. Fencing Association, 1985.

TOURNAMENTS, MAJOR FENCING. While fencing tournaments can always be found on a local level across the country, there are also numerous high-level competitions to which a fencer may aspire. Some are held in other countries besides the United States.

Major fencing tournaments include The National Championships, the Olympic Games,* the Pan-American Games, the World Championships, the Martini-Rossi Tournament, Junior Olympic Championships, the U.S. Olympic Festival, the World University Games, Junior World Championships, and the World Cup.

Such tournaments include all three weapons of fencing—the foil, the sabre, and the épée—and are participated in by both men and women.
REFERENCES
MacConaugha, Candi, ed. *American Fencing* (Summer 1993).
Mar, Colleen Walker. *1993 U.S. Fencing Association Media Guide.* Colorado Springs, CO: ColorTek Printing, 1993.

TRANCHANT. The designated "cutting edge" of the sport sabre.*

Also called the *taille.*
REFERENCE
Handelman, Rob. "Fencing Glossary." *American Fencing* (July/August 1978).

TRANSITION RAPIER. Toward the end of the seventeenth century, the rapier* blade had been cut down in length and weight, and its hand guard had been simplified in design to such a degree that it led naturally to the next step in dueling swords—the smallsword.*

The simplest form of the transition rapier guard consisted of a shallow cup guard,* quillons,* a knuckle guard,* and a *pas d'ane.**
REFERENCE
Castle, Egerton. *Schools and Masters of Fence.* London: George Bell, 1885.

TRIALAMELLUM. A triangular smallsword* blade that was deeply grooved on all three sides. It was highly popular because it was both light and stiff.

Also called a "Biscayan" blade.
REFERENCE
Stone, George Cameron. *A Glossary of the Construction, Decoration, and Use of Arms and Armor.* New York: Jack Brussel, 1961.

TROJAN SWORD. Richard Burton tells us in his *The Book of the Sword* (1884) that the only "sword" found in the excavations of Troy during the nineteenth century was a copper fragment measuring five and two-thirds inches long and two inches wide.

The Greek poet Homer makes mention in his classical account of the Trojan War, *The Iliad,* of the Trojan hero Hector, with his sharp sword, both "huge and strong," hanging below his loins.
REFERENCE
Burton, Richard F. *The Book of the Sword.* London: Chatto and Windus, 1884.

TROMPEMENT. A deception* (evasion) of an opponent's parry.*

Also called *tromper.*
REFERENCE
Palffy-Alpar, Julius. *Sword and Masque.* Philadelphia: F. A. Davis, 1967.

TROVARE DI SPADA. To make contact with an opponent's blade.
REFERENCE
Morton, E. D. *Martini A–Z of Fencing.* London: Queen Anne Press, 1992.

TSUBA. The hand guard* on a Japanese sword, typically a plate of metal.

The earliest *tsuba,* which date from around the eighth century, were plain and utilitarian. Later examples were highly decorated and treated as works of art in their own right.

Tsuba come in a variety of shapes and sizes.
REFERENCE
Stone, George Cameron. *A Glossary of the Construction, Decoration, and Use of Arms and Armor.* New York: Jack Brussel, 1961.

TSUBA MAKERS. While the Japanese viewed their sword as the best of killing tools, they also regarded it as an object worthy of aesthetic appreciation; and, as such, no portion of the weapon could be overlooked in an attempt to create

Japanese sword guards

ornamental perfection. The handguard, or *tsuba*,* received no less attention to artistic expression than did the sword blade. To this end, numerous schools of *tsuba* design were founded.

Famous *tsuba* makers include:

Yujo Goto (fifteenth century): Founded Japan's most illustrious family of *tsuba* and sword mounting designers. The Goto clan flourished until the end of the nineteenth century.

Shozui Hamando (1659–1769): Depicted battle scenes on the *tsuba* he designed. Founded a school that produced many noted artists.

Hirataharunari (seventeenth century): Made *tsuba* noted for their enamel coatings.

Kizayemon Jakuchi (eighteenth century): Founded a school of *tsuba* makers who decorated their work with Chinese landscapes.

Katsumi (1829–1879): The official *tsuba* maker of Japan's last shogun.

REFERENCE
Stone, George Cameron. *A Glossary of the Construction, Decoration, and Use of Arms and Armor.* New York: Jack Brussel, 1961.

TSUBA-SHI. In Japan, a maker of *tsuba*.*
REFERENCE
Stone, George Cameron. *A Glossary of the Construction, Decoration, and Use of Arms and Armor.* New York: Jack Brussel, 1961.

TSUCHI. A small hammer used for disassembling Japanese swords.
REFERENCE
Stone, George Cameron. *A Glossary of the Construction, Decoration, and Use of Arms and Armor.* New York: Jack Brussel, 1961.

TSUJIGIRI. In Japan, a random killing in the street to test a new sword blade.
REFERENCE
Stone, George Cameron. *A Glossary of the Construction, Decoration, and Use of Arms and Armor.* New York: Jack Brussel, 1961.

TSUKA. The hilt* of a Japanese sword.
REFERENCE
Stone, George Cameron. *A Glossary of the Construction, Decoration, and Use of Arms and Armor.* New York: Jack Brussel, 1961.

TSUKA GASHIRA. The pommel* of a *tachi*.*
Also called a *kabuto gane*.
REFERENCE
Stone, George Cameron. *A Glossary of the Construction, Decoration, and Use of Arms and Armor.* New York: Jack Brussel, 1961.

TSUKA-ITO. The silk cord wound around the hilt* of a Japanese sword.
REFERENCE
Stone, George Cameron. *A Glossary of the Construction, Decoration, and Use of Arms and Armor.* New York: Jack Brussel, 1961.

TSUKURI. The ornaments of a Japanese sword.
REFERENCE
Stone, George Cameron. *A Glossary of the Construction, Decoration, and Use of Arms and Armor.* New York: Jack Brussel, 1961.

TSUKURI-SORI. A strongly curved Japanese sword blade.
REFERENCE
Stone, George Cameron. *A Glossary of the Construction, Decoration, and Use of Arms and Armor.* New York: Jack Brussel, 1961.

TSUKURI-SUGU. A slightly curved Japanese sword blade.
REFERENCE
Stone, George Cameron. *A Glossary of the Construction, Decoration, and Use of Arms and Armor.* New York: Jack Brussel, 1961.

TSURUMAKI GATAME NO SHI TO. An old-style method of wearing one's sword in Japan. The weapon was slipped horizontally through a small basket called a *tsurumaki*. If a knife was also carried, it was slipped vertically through the *tsurumaki*.
REFERENCE
Stone, George Cameron. *A Glossary of the Construction, Decoration, and Use of Arms and Armor.* New York: Jack Brussel, 1961.

TUBAL-CAIN. A Biblical character from the Book of Genesis.
Tubal-Cain, the son of Lamech and Zillah, was the first metalsmith. He has since been identified in legend as the inventor of the sword.
REFERENCE
Burton, Richard F. *The Book of the Sword.* London: Chatto and Windus, 1884.

TWO-HANDED SWORD. A sword designed to be used specifically with two hands. While this type of weapon was a favorite for a number of centuries, by 1499 it had lost much of its appeal as a military sword and was replaced in battle by the pike and halbard.

In the Western world, the two-handed sword, such as the claymore, was usually a double-edged weapon used for cutting. Blades were flat and up to seventy-eight inches long. They were, more often than not, because of their bulkiness, used on foot.

Other swords of this type include the *spadone*, the *espadon*, the *zweyhander*, and the *flamberge*.

Fighting with two-handed swords

The *estoc* was an exception to the "cutting" rule, being a triangular-bladed, two-handed sword used exclusively for thrusting.

In Japanese fighting traditions, most swords were used with two hands, although not generally because of their size and weight, as was the case with Western swords. The grip of the Japanese sword was designed specifically to foster two-handed fighting—as suggested by Daisetz T. Suzuki in his book *Zen and Japanese Culture* (1973)—to promote a purely offensive form of swordplay that would lead a samurai to meet his opponent with the concept of *ai-uchi,* that is, with no thought of surviving the fight. This mentality was supposed to free him from the fear of death so that he might strike his opponent with the full force of his being. In any event, most fighting techniques in Japan revolved around the use of both hands on the sword.

The Japanese did, however, have one large sword—the *no-dachi,* or field sword—which, because of its size, could be used only with two hands.

REFERENCES

Castle, Egerton. *Schools and Masters of Fence.* London: George Bell, 1885.

Stone, George Cameron. *A Glossary of the Construction, Decoration, and Use of Arms and Armor.* New York: Jack Brussel, 1961.

Suzuki, Daisetz T. *Zen and the Japanese Culture.* Princeton, NJ: Princeton University Press, 1975.

TYRFING. A magical sword* of Scandinavian epic poetry that fought by itself. It could not be beaten, but it was said to bring death to anyone who held it.

REFERENCE

Leach, Maria, ed. *Funk and Wagnalls Standard Dictionary of Folklore, Mythology, and Legend.* San Francisco: Harper and Row, 1972.

𝒰

UDENUKI CORD. The Japanese sword knot.

The *udenuki* cord was passed through two openings in the *tsuba** (guard) of the *katana** and then wound around the wrist, thereby preventing being disarmed.

REFERENCE

Stone, George Cameron. *A Glossary of the Construction, Decoration, and Use of Arms and Armor.* New York: Jack Brussel, 1961.

UJLAKI-REJTO, ILDIKO. (1937–   ). Hungarian women's fencing champion.

Ildiko Ujlaki-Rejto won the women's individual foil championship at the 1964 Olympics. That same year, her team took first in team foil. In 1968, she took third in individual foil; her team took second place. In 1972, her team took second in team foil. In 1974, her team took third in team foil.

Ujlaki-Rejto was born deaf. She began fencing at the age of fourteen, her coaches communicating instructions in writing.

REFERENCE

Wallechinsky, David. *The Complete Book of the Olympics.* New York: Penguin Books, 1984.

UNCOVER. To open up a particular line* with the idea of directing an attack into that line.

Also called an "invitation."

REFERENCE

Stevenson, John. *Fencing.* London: Briggs, 1935.

UNDERARM PROTECTOR. A padded sleeve worn under a fencing jacket, on the sword arm, to protect the armpit from thrusts. It is a required piece of equipment when a fencer takes part in official fencing contests.
REFERENCE
U.S. Fencing Association, ed. *Operations Manual.* Colorado Springs, CO: U.S. Fencing Association, 1985.

UNDERCOUNTER. According to seventeenth-century fencing master Sir William Hope,* the undercounter was a type of bind.

"After you have overlapped your adversary's sword, in this you must go quite under his sword, turning your hand into tierce, and bring up his sword, giving him the thrust."
REFERENCE
Castle, Egerton. *Schools and Masters of Fence.* London: George Bell, 1885.

UNDERLUNGE. In a normal lunge,* the knee of the front (leading) leg should end up directly over the front ankle. This helps to create a well-proportioned action that establishes the lunge's full potential in its extension toward an opponent.

When, in a lunge, the knee ends up behind the ankle, the lunge is held back; that is, the action does not establish the lunge's full potential of its reach. This is an underlunge.

The underlunge may be generated by a subconscious fear of committing to an attack, which causes one to physically hold back. Or, by simply overestimating one's lunging capabilities, the front foot ends up being thrust too far forward for a proper lunge to be executed.
REFERENCES
Palffy-Alpar, Julius. *Sword and Masque.* Philadelphia: F. A. Davis, 1967.
Stevenson, John. *Fencing.* London: Briggs, 1935.

UNIFORM, FENCING. A standard uniform for a fencer includes a white fencing jacket,* white knickers* (pants), white socks, athletic shoes, a glove* for the sword hand, and a fencing mask.*

For a fencing master, the uniform is basically the same as for the fencer, although the teacher's clothing may be of colored material (especially black or blue) to indicate his importance among his students.
REFERENCE
Vebell, Edward. *Sports Illustrated Book of Fencing.* Philadelphia: J.B. Lippincott, 1962.

UNIVERSAL PARRY. A parry that was said to be able to stop an attack into any line.

Seventeenth-century Italian fencing master Ridolfo Capo Ferro taught his version of the universal parry as a sweeping action that moved from tierce, passing through quarte, and into seconde. Eighteenth-century French fencing master Guillaume Danet taught a wide counterparry as a universal parry. Other versions existed.

REFERENCE

Castle, Egerton. *Schools and Masters of Fence*. London: George Bell, 1885.

URA. The side of the tang* of a Japanese sword blade that is outward when the sword is slung edge downward. *Tachi* tangs were signed by their makers on this side. *Katana* tangs were signed on the opposite side.

REFERENCE

Stone, George Cameron. *A Glossary of the Construction, Decoration, and Use of Arms and Armor*. New York: Jack Brussel, 1961.

URTO. A type of Chinese sword.

REFERENCE

Stone, George Cameron. *A Glossary of the Construction, Decoration, and Use of Arms and Armor*. New York: Jack Brussel, 1961.

U.S. FENCERS, PROMINENT MEN.

FOIL

Hugh Allesandroni, Albert Axelrod,* Ed Ballinger, Carl Borack, Nick Bravin, Henry Breckinridge, Daniel Bukantz, George Calnan,* Dean Cetrulo, Ed Donofrio, Warren Dow, Dernell Every, Silvio Giolito, Gene Glazer, Harold Goldsmith, Dean Hinton, Francis Honeycutt, John Hurd, Byron Kreiger, Martin Lang, Joseph Levis,* Peter Lewison, Zaddick Longenbach, Nat Lubell, Arthur Lyon, Brooke Makler, Michael Marx,* Joseph Paletta, William Pecora, Rene Peroy, John Potter, Austin Prokop, Harold Rayner, Frank Righeimer, Robert Sears, Sewall Shurtz, Richard Steere, Jack Tichacek, Alan Weber, and Ed Wright.

ÉPÉE

Ed Barnett, Andrew Boyd, Scott Bozek, Henry Breckinridge, George Breed, George Calnan,* Jose de Capriles, Miguel de Capriles, Ray Dutcher, Joe Elliott, Tim Glass, Gustave Heiss,* Tracy Jaeckel, Arthur Lyon, Brooke Makler, Robert Marx, George Masin, Allen Milner, Jon Normile, Chris O'Laughlin, Paul Pesthy, Miles Phillips, Harold Rayner, Frank Righeimer, William Russel, Robert Sears, Curtis Shears, Lee Shelley, Leon Shore, Sewell Shurtz, Joe Socolof, Robert Stull, and Donald Waldhaus.

SABRE

Donald Anthony, Paul Apostol, Norman Armitage, Thomas Balla, Robert Blum, Roscoe Bowman, Peter Bruder, Robert Cottingham, David Cox, F. J. Cunningham, Michael D'Asaro,* Miguel de Capriles, Bela de Nagy, John Dimond, Ralph Faulkner,* James Flynn, C. Bradford Fraley, John Friedberg, Paul Friedberg, E. G. Fullinwidder, Eugene Hamori, John Huffman, Stephen Kaplan, Anthony Keane, Attila Keresztes, Allan Kwartler, Michael Lofton, Thomas Losonczy, Arthur Lyon, Alfonso Morales, Steve Mormando, Nicholas Muray, Tibor Nyilas,* Alex Orban, Tom Orley, J. Brooks Parker, Chris

Reohr, Sam Stewart, David Stollman, Alex Treves, Harold van Buskirk, C. J. Walker, Peter Westbrook,* and George Worth.

REFERENCES

Menke, Frank. *The Encyclopedia of Sports.* New York: A. S. Barnes, 1955.

Walker, Colleen. *1992 U.S. Fencing Association Media Guide.* Colorado Springs: ColorTek Printing, 1992.

Wallenchinsky, David. *The Complete Book of the Olympics.* New York: Penguin Books, 1984.

U.S. FENCERS, PROMINENT WOMEN. Tanya Adamovich, Jana Angelakis, Shiela Armstrong, A. Baylis, Catlin Bilodeaux, Vincent Bradford, X. Brown, Elaine Cheris, Natalia Clovis, Polly Craus, Gay D'Asaro, J. De Tuscan, W. H. Dewar, Helene Dow, Niki Tomlinson Franke, Kathryn Furu, Adeline Gehrig, Jennifer Gilbert, Jane Hall, Rachel Haugh, T. Hopper, Harriet King, Teresa Lewis, Marion Lloyd, Dorothy Locke, Rachel McDaniel, Ann Marsh, Margaret Martin, Leslie Marx, Helene Mayer, Margo Miller, Maxine Mitchell, Sharon Monplaisir, Ann O'Donnell, Mary Jane O'Neill, Susan Paxton, Jessie Pyle, P. Roldan, Janice York Romery, F. Schoonmaker, Laurel Skillman, Elisabeth Spilman, S. Stern, M. Stimson, D. Stone, Molly Sullivan, P. Sweeney, E. Takeuchi, Barbara Turpin, E. Van Buskirk, A. Voorhees, Florence Walton, D. Waples, Wendy Washburn, Ruth White, and Jennifer Yu.

REFERENCE

Mar, Colleen Walker. *1993 U.S. Fencing Association Media Guide.* Colorado Springs: ColorTek Printing, 1993.

U.S. FENCING ASSOCIATION. In 1981, the Amateur Fencers League of America* (AFLA), founded in 1891, changed its name to the U.S. Fencing Association (USFA) in an effort to modernize its image. The basic functions of the organization, however, remained the same: to hold tournaments, to promote fencing, to organize and disseminate fencing information, and to develop champion-level U.S. fencers.

REFERENCES

Johnson, Emily. "From the President." *American Fencing* (March/April 1981).

Richards, Carla-Mae. "U.S.F.A.: A New Name, A New Direction." *American Fencing* (September/October 1981).

Walker, Colleen. *1992 United States Fencing Association Media Guide.* Colorado Springs: ColorTek Printing, 1992.

U.S. NATIONAL FENCING CHAMPIONS, MEN'S ÉPÉE.

1892—B. F. O'Conner	1896—A.V.Z. Post
1893—G. M. Hammond	1897—C. G. Bothner
1894—R. O. Haubold	1898—No competition
1895—C. G. Bothner	1899—M. Diaz

1900—W. D. Lyon

1901—C. T. Tatham

1902—C. T. Tatham

1903—C. T. Tatham

1904—C. G. Bothner

1905—W. S. O'Conner

1906—W. Grebe

1907—W. D. Lyon

1908—Paul Benzenberg

1909—A. de la Poer

1910—A. de la Poer

1911—George Breed

1912—A.V.Z. Post

1913—A. E. Sauer

1914—F. W. Allen

1915—J. A. MacLaughlin

1916—W. H. Russell

1917—Leo G. Nunes

1918—No competition

1919—W. H. Russell

1920—R. W. Dutcher

1921—C. R. McPherson

1922—Leo G. Nunes

1923—George Calnan

1924—Leo G. Nunes

1925—W. H. Russell

1926—Leo G. Nunes

1927—H. Van Buskirk

1928—Leo G. Nunes

1929—F. S. Righeimer

1930—M. Pasche

1931—Miguel de Capriles

1932—Leo G. Nunes

1933—Gustave Heiss

1934—Gustave Heiss

1935—Thomas Sands

1936—Gustave Heiss

1937—Thomas Sands

1938—Jose de Capriles

1939—L. Tingley

1940—F. Seibert

1941—Gustave Heiss

1942—Henrique Santos

1943—R. Driscoll

1944—Miguel de Capriles

1945—Max Gilman

1946—A. Wolff

1947—James Strauch

1948—Norman Lewis

1949—Norman Lewis

1950—Norman Lewis

1951—Jose de Capriles

1952—A. Menendez

1953—Donald Thompson

1954—Sewell Shurtz

1955—A. Cohen

1956—A. Cohen

1957—R. Berry

1958—R. Berry

1959—H. Kolorat

1960—D. Micahnik

1961—R. Beck

1962—Gil Eisner

1963—L. Anastasi

1964—Paul Pesthy

1965—Joseph Elliott

1966—Joseph Elliott

1967—Paul Pesthy

1968—Paul Pesthy

1969—S. Netburn

1970—Joseph Elliott

1971—Jamie Melcher

1972—Jamie Melcher

1973—Scott Bozek

1974—D. Cantillon

1975—Scott Bozek

1976—George Masin
1977—Leonard Dervbinsky
1978—Brooke Makler
1979—Tim Glass
1980—Leonard Dervbinsky
1981—Lee Shelley
1982—Lee Shelley
1983—Paul Pesthy
1984—Paul Soter
1985—Robert Marx

1986—Lee Shelley
1987—Tim Glass
1988—Jon Normile
1989—Robert Stull
1990—Robert Stull
1991—John Normile
1992—Robert Stull
1993—Ben Atkins
1994—Sean McClain

REFERENCES

Mar, Colleen Walker. *The 1993 U.S. Fencing Association Media Guide.* Colorado
Springs: ColorTek Printing, 1993.

U.S. NATIONAL FENCING CHAMPIONS, MEN'S FOIL.

1892—W. O'Conner
1893—William T. Heintz
1894—C. G. Bothner
1895—A.V.Z. Post
1896—G. Kavanaugh
1897—C. G. Bothner
1898—No competition
1899—G. Kavanaugh
1900—F. Townsend
1901—C. T. Tatham
1902—J. P. Parker
1903—F. Townsend
1904—C. G. Bothner
1905—C. G. Bothner
1906—S. D. Breckinridge
1907—C. Waldbott
1908—W. L. Bowman
1909—O. A. Dickinson
1910—G. K. Bainbridge
1911—George Breed

1912—Sherman Hall
1913—P. J. Meylan
1914—S. D. Breckinridge
1915—O. A. Dickinson
1916—A. E. Sauer
1917—Sherman Hall
1918—No competition
1919—Sherman Hall
1920—Sherman Hall
1921—F. W. Honeycutt
1922—H. M. Raynor
1923—R. Peroy
1924—Leo Nunes
1925—George Calnan
1926—George Calnan
1927—George Calnan
1928—George Calnan
1929—Joseph Levis
1930—George Calnan
1931—George Calnan

1932—Joseph Levis

1933—Joseph Levis

1934—Hugh Alessandroni

1935—Joseph Levis

1936—Hugh Alessandroni

1937—Joseph Levis

1938—Dernell Every

1939—Norman Lewis

1940—Dernell Every

1941—Dean Cetrulo

1942—W. A. Dow

1943—W. A. Dow

1944—A. Snyder

1945—Dernell Every

1946—Jose de Capriles

1947—Dean Cetrulo

1948—Nathaniel Lubell

1949—Daniel Bukantz

1950—Silvio Giolito

1951—Silvio Giolito

1952—Daniel Bukantz

1953—Daniel Bukantz

1954—Joseph Levis

1955—A. Axelrod

1956—S. Shurtz

1957—D. Bukantz

1958—A. Axelrod

1959—J. Paletta

1960—A. Axelrod

1961—L. Anastasi

1962—Ed Richards

1963—Ed Richards

1964—H. Cohen

1965—R. Russell

1966—M. Geuter

1967—H. Okawa

1968—H. Okawa

1969—Carl Borack

1970—A. Alexrod

1971—Uriah Jones

1972—J. Freeman

1973—Ed Ballinger

1974—H. Hambarzumian

1975—Ed Ballinger

1976—Ed Donofrio

1977—Michael Marx

1978—Martin Lang

1979—Michael Marx

1980—Greg Massialas

1981—Mark Smith

1982—Michael Marx

1983—Mark Smith

1984—Mike McCahey

1985—Michael Marx

1986—Michael Marx

1987—Michael Marx

1988—Greg Massialas

1989—Peter Lewison

1990—Michael Marx

1991—Nick Bravin

1992—Nick Bravin

1993—Michael Marx

1994—Nick Bravin

REFERENCES

Mar, Colleen Walker. *The 1993 U.S. Fencing Association Media Guide.* Colorado Springs: ColorTek Printing, 1993.

Menke, Frank. *The Encyclopedia of Sports.* New York: A. S. Barnes, 1955.

U.S. NATIONAL FENCING CHAMPIONS, MEN'S SABRE.

1892—R. O. Haubold

1893—G. M. Hammond

1896—C. G. Bothner

1897—C. G. Bothner

1898—No competition

1899—G. Kavanaugh

1900—J. L. Ervin

1901—A.V.Z. Post

1902—A.V.Z. Post

1903—A.V.Z. Post

1904—A. G. Anderson

1905—K. B. Johnson

1906—A. G. Anderson

1907—A. G. Anderson

1908—G. W. Postgate

1909—A. E. Sauer

1910—J. T. Shaw

1911—A. G. Anderson

1912—C. A. Bill

1913—A. G. Anderson

1914—W. V. Bluenburgh

1915—Sherman Hall

1916—Sherman Hall

1917—Arthur Lyon

1918—No competition

1919—Arthur Lyon

1920—Sherman Hall

1921—C. R. McPherson

1922—Leo Nunes

1923—L. M. Schoonmaker

1924—J. E. Gignoux

1925—Joseph Vincc

1926—Leo Nunes

1927—Nicholas Muray

1928—Nicholas Muray

1929—Leo Nunes

1894—G. M. Hammond

1895—C. G. Bothner

1930—N. C. Armitage

1931—J. R. Huffman

1932—J. R. Huffman

1933—J. R. Huffman

1934—N. C. Armitage

1935—N. C. Armitage

1936—N. C. Armitage

1937—J. R. Huffman

1938—J. R. Huffman

1939—N. C. Armitage

1940—N. C. Armitage

1941—N. C. Armitage

1942—N. C. Armitage

1943—N. C. Armitage

1944—Tibor Nyilas

1945—N. C. Armitage

1946—Tibor Nyilas

1947—James Flynn

1948—Dean Cetrulo

1949—Umberto Martino

1950—Tibor Nyilas

1951—Tibor Nyilas

1952—Tibor Nyilas

1953—Tibor Nyilas

1954—George Worth

1955—R. R. Dyer

1956—Tibor Nyilas

1957—D. Magay

1958—D. Magay

1959—T. Orley

1960—E. Hamori

1961—M. Davis

1962—Mike D'Asaro

1963—E. Hamori

1964—A. Keresztes

1965—Alex Orban

1966—A. Morales

1967—A. Morales

1968—A. J. Keane

1969—Alex Orban

1970—Alex Orban

1971—Alex Orban

1972—Alex Orban

1973—Paul Apostol

1974—Peter Westbrook

1975—Peter Westbrook

1976—Tom Losonczy

1977—Tom Losonczy

1978—Stan Lekach

1979—Peter Westbrook

1980—Peter Westbrook

1981—Peter Westbrook

1982—Peter Westbrook

1983—Peter Westbrook

1984—Peter Westbrook

1985—Peter Westbrook

1986—Peter Westbrook

1987—Steve Mormando

1988—Peter Westbrook

1989—Peter Westbrook

1990—R. Cottingham

1991—Michael Lofton

1992—Michael Lofton

1993—David Mandell

1994—John Friedberg

REFERENCES

Mar, Colleen Walker. *The 1993 U.S. Fencing Association Media Guide.* Colorado Springs: ColorTek Printing, 1993.

Menke, Frank. *The Encyclopedia of Sports.* New York: A. S. Barnes, 1955.

U.S. NATIONAL FENCING CHAMPIONS, WOMEN'S ÉPÉE.

1981—Sue Badders

1982—Vincent Bradford

1983—Vincent Bradford

1984—Vincent Bradford

1985—Cathy McClellan

1986—Vincent Bradford

1987—Donna Stone

1988—Xandy Brown

1989—Cathy McClellan

1990—Donna Stone

1991—Margo Miller

1992—Barbara Turpin

1993—Leslie Marx

1994—Donna Stone

REFERENCE

Mar, Colleen Walker. *The 1993 U.S. Fencing Association Media Guide.* Colorado Springs: ColorTek Printing, 1993.

U.S. NATIONAL FENCING CHAMPIONS, WOMEN'S FOIL.

1912—A. Baylis

1913—Mrs. W. H. Dewar

1914—M. Stimson

1915—Jessie Pyle

Adeline Gehrig

1916—Mrs. C. H. Voorhees

1917—Florence Walton

1918—No competition

1919—No competition

1920—Adeline Gehrig

1921—Adeline Gehrig

1922—Adeline Gehrig

1923—Adeline Gehrig

1924—Mrs. C. H. Hopper

1925—F. Schoonmaker

1926—F. Schoonmaker

1927—S. Stern

1928—Marion Lloyd

1929—F. Schoonmaker

1930—Mrs. E. Van Buskirk

1931—Marion Lloyd

1932—Dorothy Locke

1933—Dorothy Locke

1934—Helene Mayer

1935—Helene Mayer

1936—Mrs. J. de Tuscan

1937—Helene Mayer

1938—Helene Mayer
1939—Helene Mayer
1940—H. Mroczkowska
1941—Helene Mayer
1942—Helene Mayer
1943—H. Mroczkowska
1944—Madaline Dalton
1945—Maria Cerra
1946—Helene Mayer
1947—H. Dow
1948—H. Dow
1949—Polly Craus
1950—Janice-Lee York
1951—Janice-Lee York
1952—Maxine Mitchell
1953—Paula Sweeney
1954—Maxine Mitchell
1955—Maxine Mitchell
1956—Jan York Romary
1957—Jan York Romary
1958—Maxine Mitchell
1959—P. Roldan
1960—Jan York Romary
1961—Jan York Romary
1962—E. Takeuchi
1963—Harriet King
1964—Jan York Romary
1965—Jan York Romary
1966—Jan York Romary

1967—Harriet King
1968—Jan York Romary
1969—Ruth White
1970—Harriet King
1971—Harriet King
1972—Ruth White
1973—Tanya Adamovich
1974—G. Jacobson
1975—N. Tomlinson
1976—A. O'Donnell
1977—Shiela Armstrong
1978—Gay D'Asaro
1979—Jana Angelakis
1980—N. Tomlinson Franke
1981—Jana Angelakis
1982—Jana Angelakis
1983—D. Waples
1984—Vincent Bradford
1985—Molly Sullivan
1986—Caitlin Bilodeaux
1987—Caitlin Bilodeaux
1988—Sharon Monplaisir
1989—Caitlin Bilodeaux
1990—J. Yu
1991—M. J. O'Neill
1992—Caitlin Bilodeaux
1993—Felicia Zimmerman
1994—Ann Marsh

REFERENCE

Mar, Colleen Walker. *The 1993 U.S. Fencing Association Media Guide.* Colorado Springs: ColorTek Printing, 1993.

U.S. OLYMPIC FENCING. From the earliest days of the Olympic Games,* the United States has not fared as well in fencing competitions as it has in other competitive areas, such as track and field and gymnastics. Nevertheless, the United States has won more than a few medals.

Still, the only time the United States has managed to really shine on a large scale in Olympic fencing was during the 1904 St. Louis games, when, because of the "out-of-the-way" location of the affair, combined with the poor manner in which it was perceived to be run, most European countries kept their fencers at home. Here, the Americans, without much competition, racked up ten fencing medals: second (Albert Van Zo Post) and third place (Charles Tatham) in men's individual foil; second place in men's team foil; second (Charles Tatham) and third place (Albert Van Zo Post) in men's individual épée; second (William Grebe) and third place (Albert Van Zo Post) in men's individual sabre; and first (Albert Van Zo Post), second (William Scott O'Conner), and third place (William Grebe) in men's singlesticks.

After this, the United States was not able to garner another fencing medal until the 1920 Antwerp games, when it managed to grab a third place in men's team foil.

The next fencing medal came in 1928 at the Amsterdam Games—a third place in men's individual épée (George Calnan*).

In 1932, at the Los Angeles games, the United States captured three medals: second place in men's individual foil (Joseph Levis*); a third place in men's team foil; and another third place in men's team épée.

At the 1948 London games, the United States won a third-place medal in men's team sabre.

The United States did not pick up another fencing medal until the 1960 Rome games. It was another third place, this time in men's individual foil (Albert Axelrod*).

The last U.S. Olympic fencing medal, to date, was acquired at the 1984 Los Angeles games—a third place in men's individual sabre (Peter Westbrook*).

REFERENCE

Walker, Colleen. *1992 U.S. Fencing Association Media Guide.* Colorado Springs: ColorTek Printing, 1992.

Wallechinsky, David. *The Complete Book of the Olympics.* New York: Penguin Books, 1984.

UYTTENHOVE, HENRY. (c. twentieth century). Belgian fencing master.

Henry Uyttenhove, a graduate of Belgium's Military Institute of Physical Education and Fencing, became the first professional master of swordplay to be employed by the film industry in the production of a movie. Douglas Fairbanks, Sr.,* hired him to guide the combat in his classic *The Mark of Zorro*** (1920).

Uyttenhove was also the fencing adviser on *The Three Musketeers* (1921),** *The Prisoner of Zenda* (1922), *To Have and to Hold* (1922), *Robin Hood* (1922),** *Trifling Women* (1922), *Monte Cristo* (1922), *Rupert of Hentzau* (1923), and *Scaramouche* (1923).

The Belgian's film fencing style was characterized by a clean, workmanlike—though not particularly creative—quality. He was succeeded by Fred Cavens* as Hollywood's premier stager of sword fights.

Henry Uyttenhove

Henry Uyttenhove was also the longtime fencing master for the Los Angeles Athletic Club. He wrote one book, *Foil Fencing* (1936).

REFERENCE

Behlmer, Rudy. "Swordplay on the Screen." *Films in Review* (June/July 1965).

$\mathcal{V}$

VAGINA. A Roman sword sheath.
REFERENCE
Burton, Richard F. *The Book of the Sword.* London: Chatto and Windus, 1884.

VALDIN, M. (c. 1700). French fencing master.
His addition to fencing was the innovation of limbering-up exercises before fencing.
REFERENCE
Morton, E. D. *Martini A–Z of Fencing.* London: Queen Anne Press, 1992.

VALID TOUCH. Any touch* that is delivered with the proper portion of a weapon on the target area designated for that weapon.
A valid touch in foil* fencing is made with the foil's point on the trunk of an opponent's body. A valid touch in épée* fencing is made with the épée's point anywhere on an opponent's body. A valid touch in sabre* fencing is made with either the sabre's point or cutting edge on an opponent's body from the waist up.
REFERENCE
U.S. Fencing Association, ed. *Operations Manual.* Colorado Springs, CO: U.S. Fencing Association, 1985.

VENTRE. In sabre* fencing, the lower left part of the chest.
REFERENCE
Handelman, Rob. "Fencing Glossary." *American Fencing* (July/August 1978).

VERDADERA DESTREZA. The old Spanish art of swordsmanship with all its esoteric philosophy and mysterious geometric movement.
REFERENCE
Castle, Egerton. *Schools and Masters of Fence.* London: George Bell, 1885.

VERDUN. A type of dueling sword used toward the end of the sixteenth century. It was named after the town in France where it was made.

Minus cutting edges, the slender, diamond-shaped blade was designed exclusively for thrusting. Because of the way it was constructed, the Verdun could be lengthened dramatically without destroying the weapon's rigidity or increasing its weight. These swords were so long that they could not be worn. Their owners had them carried by servants who walked behind them.
REFERENCE
Castle, Egerton. *Schools and Masters of Fence.* London: George Bell, 1885.

VEST, ELECTRIC. The metallic vest worn over a standard fencing jacket. Covering every portion of the valid target area, it is used to indicate on-target touches. Basically, when the vest, which is inlaid with copper threads, is touched with an electric fencing weapon, an electrical circuit is completed that sets off an on-target signal on the electric scoring machine.

Electric vests are used for both foil and sabre fencing and are mandatory for all official (U.S. Fencing Association) fencing tournaments.

Also called "metallic plastrons" and "overjackets."
REFERENCE
U.S. Fencing Association, ed. *Operations Manual.* Colorado Springs, CO: U.S. Fencing Association, 1985.

VIGGIANI, ANGELO. (c. 1560). Italian fencing master.

Viggiani was the first fencing master to profess the use of the lunge (*punta sopramano*). He was also an early advocate of the thrust, which he considered superior to the cut. He did not, however, apply his innovative theories to all the attacks he taught, so most of his teachings were mere reflections of his contemporaries.

Viggiani's book on fencing, *Lo Schermo d'Angelo Viggiani* (1575),** was actually published a number of years after the fencing master's death. A later edition of his book was issued in 1588, with Viggiani's name spelled "Vizani."
REFERENCE
Castle, Egerton. *Schools and Masters of Fence.* London: George Bell, 1885.

VIGGIANI GUARDS. Sixteenth-century Italian fencing master Angelo Viggiani* called a guard position "perfect" when it allowed for the delivery of a thrust.* He termed a guard "strait" when a sword point was held in line with one's opponent. In an "open" guard, a sword point was held away from one's

A guard position according to Angelo Viggiani

opponent. In an ''offensive'' guard, the sword was held on the right side. In a ''defensive'' guard, the sword was held on the left side.
REFERENCE
Castle, Egerton. *Schools and Masters of Fence.* London: George Bell, 1885.

VIKING SWORD. While perhaps more at home with a battle axe, the Viking warrior was nevertheless proficient in the use of the sword. The Viking sword, furthermore, was a formidable piece of weaponry. It had a medium-length blade, tapered to a point, making it lighter at the tip and easier to wield. It could be used for either cutting or thrusting.

Early Viking sword blades were made of bronze; later they were made of iron. It was, in fact, the Vikings who introduced sword blades of carbonized iron. Blades were sometimes embellished with runes, or magic writing, and were given savage names like *Gramr* ("Fierce") and *Fotbitr* ("Leg-biter") by their owners.

By the sixth century A.D., the Viking sword, with its double-edged, straight blade, plain crossbar handguard, simple grip, and large pommel, had assumed a classic form that it would keep for a thousand years.

REFERENCES

Burton, Richard F. *The Book of the Sword.* London: Chatto and Windus, 1884.

La Fay, Howard. *The Vikings.* Washington, D.C.: National Geographic Society, 1972.

Norman, A.V.B., and Don Pottinger. *English Weapons and Warfare, 449–1660.* Englewood Cliffs, N.J.: Prentice-Hall, 1979.

VISION, FENCING. The point upon which a fencer rests his attention. Some have suggested this should be an opponent's sword hand; others, his blade tip; a few, his feet. A more reasonable course is to develop a keen general (holistic) awareness—an awareness that takes into account an opponent's overall demeanor.

Focusing on any single aspect of an opponent's personage may lead to overlooking other vital pieces of information regarding his fencing that might feasibly be used against him.

REFERENCES

Morton, E. D. *Martini A–Z of Fencing.* London: Queen Anne Press, 1992.

Stevenson, John. *Fencing.* London: Briggs, 1935.

VOLTE. A sideways step to the right with the back (left) foot, which turns the torso away from an oncoming blade. Basically, the *volte* is a displacement of the target to avoid being hit. The turn is usually accompanied by a thrust (counterattack).

The *volte* was a common form of defense during the eighteenth century, although the lightness and maneuverability of swords toward the end of that century rendered the move somewhat dangerous. The famous eighteenth-century French fencing master Guillaume Danet disapproved strongly of the action.

The *demivolte,* or half turn, was an abbreviated form of the *volte.*

REFERENCE

Castle, Egerton. *Schools and Masters of Fence.* London: George Bell, 1885.

VOLTE-COUP. A feint* in a given line* followed by a thrust* in the most directly opposite line.

REFERENCE

Castle, Egerton. *Schools and Masters of Fence.* London: George Bell, 1885.

VOLTEX. A complete turn to avoid being hit.

REFERENCE

Handelman, Rob. "Fencing Glossary." *American Fencing* (July/August 1978).

The *volte*

W

WAKIZASHI. A Japanese short sword. The blade was about eighteen inches long. It was sometimes called the "guardian of honor," because it was the sword used for ceremonial suicide.
REFERENCE
Stone, George Cameron. *A Glossary of the Construction, Decoration, and Use of Arms and Armor.* New York: Jack Brussel, 1961.

WALKING SWORD. Any type of sword deemed suitable for personal use during the days when wearing a sword was part of a gentleman's daily apparel.
REFERENCE
Morton, E. D. *Martini A–Z of Fencing.* London: Queen Anne Press, 1992.

WARD. An eighteenth-century fencing term similar to "line" in modern fencing.
Also called a parry (a ward), and the act of parrying (to ward).
REFERENCES
Castle, Egerton. *Schools and Masters of Fence.* London: George Bell, 1885.
Morton, E. D. *Martini A–Z of Fencing.* London: Queen Anne Press, 1992.

WASTER. A wooden sword used for practice by the common people in sixteenth-century England. It was sometimes used with the buckler (shield).
Also called a "wafter."
REFERENCE
Castle, Egerton. *Schools and Masters of Fence.* London: George Bell, 1885.

WEDDING CEREMONY AND THE SWORD. During medieval times the sword was considered such a compelling masculine symbol in general, and a personal symbol of self in particular, that the weapon of a man to be wed was sometimes used at his marriage ceremony to represent him in his absence.
REFERENCE
Burton, Richard F. *The Book of the Sword.* London: Chatto and Windus, 1884.

WELLES, ORSON. (1915–1985). American actor, director, producer.

While most famous for his film *Citizen Kane* (1940), the story of the rise and fall of a newspaper publisher, Orson Welles also managed to find his way into the occasional swashbuckler film, although never as the hero.

Studying fencing as a young man, the flamboyant actor was bound to pick up the sword at some time during his film career. His most dramatic—or melodramatic—effort was *Black Magic* (1949), which was based on Alexandre Dumas's nineteenth-century novel *Joseph Balsamo.* Welles starred as Cagliostro, an evil gypsy mesmerist whose hatred of aristocrats drives him to use his hypnotic powers against the French nobility in the late 1700s. After nearly toppling the throne of France, Cagliostro is unmasked as a traitor. Escaping, the villain is then trapped on the rooftops of Paris, where he fights a sword duel with a young army officer—"You cannot defeat my eyes!" "I'm looking at your sword point!"—who kills him.

Welles also starred in a film version of Shakespeare's *Macbeth* (1948) and *Othello* (1951).

During the 1940s, Welles had hopes of doing a film version of *Cyrano de Bergerac,* but the project never materialized. It was finally put to rest when Jose Ferrer did Cyrano in a 1950 film.
REFERENCES
Evangelista, Anita. *Dictionary of Hypnotism.* Westport, CT: Greenwood Press, 1991.
Halliwell, Leslie. *Halliwell's Filmgoer's and Video Viewer's Companion.* New York: Charles Scribner's Sons, 1988.
Leaming, Barbara. *Orson Welles.* New York: Penguin Books, 1985.

WESTBROOK, PETER. (1952–). U.S. fencing champion.

Peter Westbrook has long been one of America's premier fencers. He was a member of the U.S. Olympic sabre team in 1976, 1980, 1984, 1988, and 1992. At the 1984 Olympics in Los Angeles, he won a bronze medal in men's individual sabre, becoming the first U.S. fencer to win an Olympic fencing medal in twenty-four years.

He has won the U.S. National Individual Sabre Championship twelve times (a record): 1974, 1975, 1979, 1980, 1981, 1982, 1983, 1984, 1985, 1986, 1988, and 1989.

At the 1989 World Championships, Westbrook finished eighth in men's individual sabre.

U.S. fencing champion and Olympic medal winner Peter
Westbrook. Photograph courtesy of USFA

REFERENCE
Walker, Colleen. *1992 U.S. Fencing Association Media Guide.* Colorado Springs:
  ColorTek Printing, 1992.

WEST SMITHFIELD. Called "Ruffian Hall" by those who knew it well, West
Smithfield was an area of London during the sixteenth century noted as a hang-
out for dangerous swordsmen. It was mostly frequented by sword and buckler*
men.
REFERENCE
Castle, Egerton. *Schools and Masters of Fence.* London: George Bell, 1885.

WHEELCHAIR FENCING. Developed for athletes confined to wheelchairs.
Fencers approach each other at angles, rather than straight on. To watch it is,
in a way, rather remindful of swordsmen on horseback.

REFERENCE
Axelrod, Albert, ed. *American Fencing* (September/October/November 1988).

WHEEL POMMEL. A large, disk-shaped pommel found on some medieval swords.

REFERENCE
Morton, E. D. *Martini A–Z of Fencing.* London: Queen Anne Press, 1992.

WHYFFLER. A two-handed swordsman who cleared the way for a procession.

REFERENCE
Stone, George Cameron. *A Glossary of the Construction, Decoration, and Use of Arms
    and Armor.* New York: Jack Brussel, 1961.

WILDE, CORNEL. (1915–1990). American film actor.

A college fencing champion, Cornel Wilde starred in a number of swashbuckler films during the 1940s, 1950s, and 1960s. These films include *A Thousand and One Nights* (1945); *The Bandit of Sherwood Forest* (1946), *Forever Amber* (1947), *At Sword's Point* (1952), *The Scarlet Coat* (1955), *Star of India* (1956), *Omar Khyyam* (1957), *Constantine and the Cross* (1962), *The Sword of Lancelot* (1963), *The Fifth Musketeer* (1977), and *The Norseman* (1977).

It was almost a trademark in Wilde's film fencing for him to fight with either hand, showing off his ambidexterity. Sometimes, in the course of the action, he would be wounded in his normal fencing arm and have to change; sometimes he would simply switch hands for no particular reason. This was particularly apparent in *The Bandit of Sherwood Forest, At Sword's Point, The Sword of Lancelot,* and *The Fifth Musketeer.*

The Bandit of Sherwood Forest is, perhaps, Wilde's best swashbuckler vehicle. A "son-of-Robin Hood" movie, it is both well mounted and exciting. The story: a cruel tyrant attempts to usurp the English throne, and Robin Hood, Jr., stops him in his tracks.

The swordplay, staged by "fencing master to the stars" Ralph Faulkner,* was highly effective, although Faulkner's doubling for the film's villain (Henry Daniell*) during most of the action scenes was rather obvious.

Cornel Wilde was a good-enough fencer to make the U.S. Olympic fencing squad in 1936. But, for some unknown reason, he was always rather contemptuous of his swashbuckler film roles.

REFERENCES
Parish, James Robert, and Don E. Stanke. *The Swashbucklers.* Carlstadt, NJ: Rainbow
    Books, 1976.
Richards, Jeffrey. *Swordsmen of the Screen.* Boston: Routledge and Kegan Paul, 1977.

WILKINSON COMPANY. One of the world's foremost makers of ceremonial swords.*

The Wilkinson Sword Company has been making swords for over 150 years.

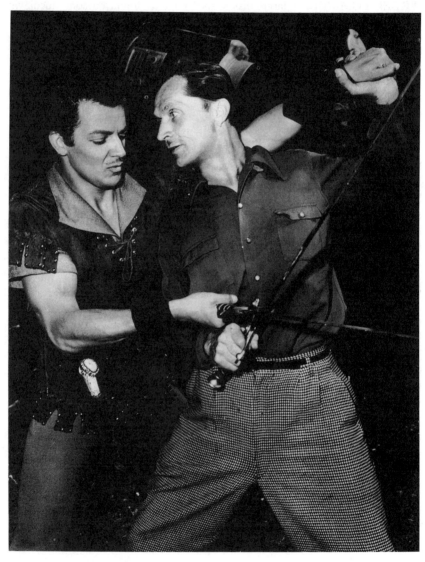

Cornel Wilde (left) being coached for a scene in *The Bandit of Sherwood Forest*. Photograph courtesy of Ralph Faulkner

It traces its history back to 1772, when Henry Nock, a noted maker of swords and guns, had a shop in London. Apprenticed to Nock was James Wilkinson, who was later to became his partner. Wilkinson eventually inherited the business in 1805.

From the start, the Wilkinson Company had a reputation for producing quality products, a reputation that continues to this day. Of the two dozen sword cutlers active in England during the eighteenth and nineteenth centuries, only the Wilkinson business still exists.

Wilkinson makes swords for the military services in England, swords for special ceremonies, and swords for presentation and commemoration. In an average year, they produce over 8,000 swords.

REFERENCE

Wilkinson Sword Company. *Swords by Wilkinson.* Surrey, England: Biddles, 1973.

WITHOUT FENCING MASKS, FENCING. While the invention of the fencing mask officially dates back to the early eighteenth century, it was not employed with any great regularity until the mid-nineteenth century. Fencing, even with rebated weapons could, of course, be a risky endeavor, yet the use of masks was deemed both unmanly and an excuse for sloppy technique. An invitation to put on fencing masks before bouting was an insult of the highest order.

It was recognized that fencing during its earliest times could leave a swordsman covered in bruises, minus an eye or teeth, or even dead; therefore, as swordplay evolved into a more sportlike activity, it took on an extremely academic flavor. Movement became polished and studied exercises in control. A fencer's fear of wounding an opponent severely, as was noted by author Egerton Castle* in his history of fencing, *Schools and Masters of Fence* (1885), "could only act detrimentally on his velocity of movement, however it might tend to keep up his form." Any fencer who even accidentally hit an adversary in the face was scorned and ostracized for his lack of skill.

In practice, an attack would always be undertaken from proper distance. Parries were firm, but not heavy. Ripostes would only be put into play when an attacker had fully recovered from his lunge. No stop thrusts were allowed, and any touch was expected to be placed on target deliberately, the ubiquitous "palpable touch."

The nineteenth-century explorer and writer Richard Burton,* himself a respected fencer, is reported to have undertaken a match with a celebrated French fencing champion in which he chose (obviously showing off) to compete maskless. In Fawn Brodie's biography of Burton, *The Devil Drives* (1967), the author described the encounter:

With a grandiloquent gesture Burton disdained the mask, and kept the crowd gasping as he fought one bout after another—seven in all—each time disarming his masked opponent's sword and receiving himself but a single prod on the neck. The Frenchman, unnerved by the bravado as much by skill, finally refused to continue, saying his wrist was nearly dislocated.

This colorful account can be read in two separate ways. On one hand, one might say simply that Richard Burton was indeed an incredibly talented swordsman. In light of the situation, however, it could also be suggested that the Frenchman, mindful of any misstep on his part against his maskless adversary, was sufficiently thrown off in his own fencing game to be easily beaten.

Today, any fencer who decides to bout without a mask should be avoided at all costs. Needless to say, the rules of the U.S. Fencing Association* strictly forbid this thoughtless practice.

REFERENCES

Brodie, Fawn M. *The Devil Drives.* New York: W. W. Norton, 1967.

Castle, Egerton. *Schools and Masters of Fence.* London: George Bell, 1885.

Morton, E.D. *Martini A–Z of Fencing.* London: Queen Anne Press, 1992.

U.S. Fencing Association. *Operations Manual.* Colorado Springs: U.S. Fencing Association, 1985.

WOMEN AND THE SWORD. Through the centuries, countless sword fights have been fought over women. Literature, from *Three Musketeers* (1844)** to *Captain Blood* (1922)** to *The Princess Bride* (1973),** abounds with tales of swordsmen fighting for the love of a woman. The female, then, is often placed in the passive role when we think of women and the sword.

This, however, is not a complete picture of the subject.

Historically, women have, at times, picked up the sword on their own behalf. Perhaps the most famous, or infamous, female swordsperson was the seventeenth-century French actress Julie de Maupin. Having learned to fence from one of her many lovers, who happened to be a fencing master, she is said to have killed in duels a number of men whom she felt had insulted her.

While the sport of fencing was traditionally considered a man's sport for many years, by the end of the nineteenth century, women were crossing swords with each other as an exercise of good breeding—but never, of course, with men.

It was not until the 1924 Olympics, however, that women were allowed to compete on an international basis. During this event, a thirty-three-year-old Danish fencer, Ellen Osiier,* won the women's individual foil event by winning all sixteen of her bouts.

The 1929 World Championship tournament was the first of its kind to include women. The great German fencer Helene Mayer* won the foil event. She subsequently won it two more times, in 1931 and 1937.

Other woman fencers to shine in the fencing world were Ilona Schacherer-Elek* of Hungary and Ellen Preis of Austria.

While the first World Champion team event was held for women in 1932, women were not given a team event in the Olympics until 1960. On this occasion, the team foil competition was won by the USSR.

The United States has produced a number of fine women fencers over the years, including Caitlin Bilodeaux, Vincent Bradford, Polly Craus,** Adeline Gehrig, Harriet King, Margo Miller, Maxine Mitchell, Sharon Monplaisir, Molly Sullivan, Jan York Romary,* and Ruth White.

A nineteenth-century fencing school for women

In the past, the foil was traditionally the only weapon women were allowed to use on an official basis. However, since the 1980s, women have been competing regularly in sabre and épée, although, of the two weapons, the épée is the only one thus far to be recognized in major tournaments.

Also, while men's bouts have always consisted of five touches, for many years, women's bouts were made up of just four touches. Today, women, too, fence for five touches.

REFERENCES

Baldick, Robert. *The Duel.* New York: Spring Books, 1970.

Walker, Colleen. *U.S. Fencing Association Media Guide.* Colorado Springs: ColorTek Printing, 1992.

Wallechinsky, David. *The Complete Book of the Olympics.* New York: Penguin Books, 1984.

WOMEN FENCERS IN FILM, ASIAN. In films from both Japan and China, women have long held a position of martial proficiency, much more so than in films from Western countries.

Women swordspersons in Japanese films tend to be, on the whole, extremely cold and calculating and usually more dangerous than most of the men they encounter. Often, although not always, they are ninja, the assassins of old Japan. Japanese films featuring women with swords include *A Woman Using a Short Sword* (1961), *Sword of Vengeance* (1972), *Snowblood* (1974), and *The Wanderers* (1974).

In Chinese films, while women fighters tend to be portrayed in a mostly sympathetic light, they are rarely second to men in their combat skills. Chinese films in which women martial artists employ swords include *The Rivals* (1968), *Lady Hermit* (1969), *Lady of the Law* (1969), *The Invincible Eight* (1970), *The Young Avenger* (1970), and *The Fate of Lee Khan* (1973).

REFERENCES

Glaessner, Verina. *Kung Fu, Cinema of Vengeance.* London: Lorrimer, 1974.

Mintz, Marilyn D. *The Martial Arts Film.* New York: A. S. Barnes, 1978.

WOMEN FENCERS IN FILM, WESTERN. While the trend in Hollywood swashbuckler films has been that of "hero, sword in hand, saves helpless female," there have been exceptions to this rule.

At times, the actress/heroine has been given the opportunity either to equal or to surpass the fencing capabilities of her leading man.

In the silent era of film, Marion Davies carried a sword in *When Knighthood Was in Flower* (1923). Norma Talmadge fenced in a scene for *Ashes of Vengeance* (1923). Other movies that incorporated fencers include *Senorita* (1927) and *She's a Sheik* (1928).

In more modern times, Binnie Barnes cut an impressive swath with her swordplay as a lady pirate in *The Spanish Main* (1945), as did Maureen O'Hara in *Against All Flags* (1951) and Jean Peters in *Anne of the Indies* (1952).

Stick sword combat in ancient Egypt

Lenore Aubert, as the wife in *The Wife of Monte Cristo* (1946), actually took the lead from her wounded husband and took care of most of the swordplay throughout the film.

Other modern films with women fencers include *Port Said* (1948), with Gloria Henry; *At Sword's Point* (1951), with Maureen O'Hara (1951); *Mask of the Avenger* (1951), with Jody Lawrence; and *Princess of the Nile* (1954), with Debra Paget.

More recently, Genevive Bujold fenced with a feminist flair in *Swashbuckler* (1976). This was soon followed by militant sword wielders Sandahl Bergman in *Conan the Barbarian* (1982) and Brigitte Nielson in *Red Sonja* (1985), both proving once again that women could take an active role in filmed fencing encounters.

REFERENCES

Behlmer, Rudy. "Swordplay on the Screen." *Films in Review* (June/July 1965).
Halliwell, Leslie. *Halliwell's Filmgoer's and Video Viewer's Companion.* New York: Charles Scribner's Sons, 1988.
Richards, Jeffrey. *Swordsmen of the Screen.* Boston: Routledge and Kegan Paul, 1977.

WOODEN SWORD. Wooden swords existed before metal swords and have continued, in one form or another, in conjunction with them in both civilized and primitive areas around the world.

Wooden stick swords were used as a form of sport combat in ancient Egypt. Romans employed short wooden swords as practice weapons for their gladiators. Primitive, premetal Ireland produced wooden swords for combat.

Japan has the *bokken,* a wooden sword fashioned of red oak, white oak, or loquat. Used for centuries in the teaching of swordplay, this wooden implement, while essentially a practice and tournament weapon, could easily be turned to more deadly pursuits. Today, the *bokken* is a used as an aid to perfect one's fencing form.

Wooden swords—paddle-shaped, sabre-shaped, club-shaped, and leaf-shaped—have also been part of the weaponry of Africa, South America, Mexico, Australia, and the Pacific islands. Such woods as rosewood, *chonta*-wood, eucalyptus, oak, and palm wood were frequently used. Unfortunately, the wooden blade, no matter how hard, made a poor cutting weapon. So, more than occasionally, these weapons were fitted with sharp stones, bone, teeth, or horn to increase their destructive power.

During the eighteenth and nineteenth centuries, the singlestick (or cudgel), a basket-hilted stick sword often made of ash, was employed as a practice and sport weapon in England. Singlesticks at last found their way into popular use in modern fencing competition during the 1904 Olympics, and they existed well into the 1920s in British public schools.

REFERENCES

Burton, Richard F. *The Book of the Sword.* London: Chatto and Windus, 1884.

Castle, Egerton. *Schools and Masters of Fence.* London: George Bell, 1885.

Wallechinsky, David. *The Complete Book of the Olympics.* New York: Penguin Books, 1984.

WOOTZ. Natural Indian steel that was much prized for sword blades in Persia and Afghanistan.

Also, *wutz.*

REFERENCE

Burton, Richard F. *The Book of the Sword.* London: Chatto and Windus, 1884.

WORLD FENCING CHAMPIONS, MEN'S INDIVIDUAL ÉPÉE.

1906—de la Falaise (France)	1933—Bouchard (France)
1921—Gaudin (France)	1934—Dunay (Hungary)
1922—Heide (Norway)	1935—Drakenberg (Sweden)
1923—Brouver (Holland)	1937—Schmetz (France)
1926—Tainturier (France)	1938 Pecheux (France)
1927—Bouchard (France)	1947—Artigas (France)
1929—Cattiau (France)	1949—Mangiarotti (Italy)
1930—Cattiau (France)	1950—Luchow (Denmark)
1931—Bouchard (France)	1951—Mangiarotti (Italy)

1953—Sakovics (Hungary)

1954—Mangiarotti (Italy)

1955—Angelsio (Italy)

1957—Mouyal (France)

1958—Hoskyns (England)

1959—Khabarov (USSR)

1961—Guittet (France)

1962—Kausz (Hungary)

1963—Losert (Austria)

1965—Nemere (Hungary)

1966—Nyikancsikov (USSR)

1967—Nyikancsikov (USSR)

1969—Andrzejewski (Poland)

1970—Nyikancsikov (USSR)

1971—Kriss (USSR)

1973—Edling (Sweden)

1974—Edling (Sweden)

1975—Pusch (W. Germany)

1977—Harmenberg (Sweden)

1978—Pusch (W. Germany)

1979—Riboud (France)

1981—Szekely (Hungary)

1982—Pap (Hungary)

1983—Borrmann (W. Germany)

1985—Boisse (France)

1986—Riboud (France)

1987—Fischer (W. Germany)

1989—Pereira (Spain)

1990—Gerull (W. Germany)

1991—Chouvalov (USSR)

Any year not included in the preceding list was not a year in which a world championship men's individual épée tournament was held.

REFERENCES

Palffy-Alpar, Julius. *Sword and Masque*. Philadelphia: F. A. Davis, 1967.

Roch, Rene, ed. *Internationale d'Escrime*. France: Federation Interationale d'Escrime, 1991.

WORLD FENCING CHAMPIONS, MEN'S INDIVIDUAL FOIL.

1906—Dillon-Cavanagh (France)

1922—Heide (Norway)

1926—Chiavacci (Italy)

1927—Puliti (Italy)

1929—Puliti (Italy)

1930—Gaudini (Italy)

1931—Lemoine (France)

1933—Guaragna (Italy)

1934—Gaudini (Italy)

1935—Gardere (France)

1937—Marzi (Italy)

1938—Guaragna (Italy)

1947—D'Oriola (France)

1949—D'Oriola (France)

1950—Nostini (Italy)

1951—Di Rosa (Italy)

1953—D'Oriola (France)

1954—D'Oriola (France)

1955—Gyuricza (Hungary)

1957—Fulop (Hungary)

1958—Bergamini (Italy)

1959—Jay (England)

1961—Parulski (Poland)

1962—Sveshnikov (USSR)

1963—Magnan (France)

1965—Magnan (France)

1966—Sveshnikov (USSR)

1967—Putyatyin (USSR)

1969—Wessel (W. Germany)

1970—Wessel (W. Germany)

1971—Sztankovics (USSR)

1973—Noel (France)

1974—Romankov (USSR)

1975—Noel (France)

1977—Romankov (USSR)

1978—Flament (France)

1979—Romankov (USSR)

1981—Smirnov (USSR)

1982—Romankov (USSR)

1983—Romankov (USSR)

1985—Numa (Italy)

1986—Borella (Italy)

1987—Gey (W. Germany)

1989—Koch (W. Germany)

1990—Omnes (France)

1991—Weissenborn (Germany)

Any year not included in the preceding list was not a year in which a world championship men's individual foil tournament was held.

REFERENCES

Palffy-Alpar, Julius. *Sword and Masque.* Philadelphia: F. A. Davis, 1967.

Roch, Rene, ed. *Internationale d'Escrime.* France: Federation Internationale d'Escrime, 1991.

WORLD FENCING CHAMPIONS, MEN'S INDIVIDUAL SABRE.

1906—Georgiadis (Greece)

1922—de Jong (Holland)

1923—de Jong (Holland)

1925—Garay (Hungary)

1926—Gombos (Hungary)

1927—Gombos (Hungary)

1929—Glykais (Hungary)

1930—Piller (Hungary)

1931—Piller (Hungary)

1933—Kabos (Hungary)

1934—Kabos (Hungary)

1935—Gerevich (Hungary)

1937—Kovacs (Hungary)

1938—Montano (Italy)

1947—Montano (Italy)

1949—Dare (Italy)

1950—Levavasseur (France)

1951—Gerevich (Hungary)

1953—Kovacs (Hungary)

1954—Karpati (Hungary)

1955—Gerevich (Hungary)

1957—Pawlowski (Poland)

1958—Rilszkij (USSR)

1959—Karpati (Hungary)

1961—Rilszkij (USSR)

1962—Horvath (Hungary)

1963—Rylsky (USSR)

1965—Pawlowski (Poland)

1966—Pawlowski (Poland)

1967—Rakita (USSR)

1969—Szigyak (USSR)

1970—Pezsa (Hungary)

1971—Maffei (Italy)

1973—Montano (Italy)

1974—Montano (Italy)

1975—Nazlymov (USSR)

1977—Gerevich (Hungary)

1978—Krovopuskov (USSR)

1979—Nazlymov (USSR)

1981—Wodke (Poland)

1982—Krovopuskov (USSR)	1987—Lamour (France)
1983—Etriopolski (Bulgaria)	1989—Kirienko (USSR)
1985—Nebald (Hungary)	1990—Nebald (Hungary)
1986—Mindirgazov (USSR)	1991—Kirienko (USSR)

Any year not included in the preceding list was not a year in which a world championship men's individual sabre tournament was held.

REFERENCES

Palffy-Alpar, Julius. *Sword and Masque.* Philadelphia: F. A. Davis, 1967.

Roch, Rene, ed. *International d'Escrime.* France: Federation Internationale d'Escrime, 1991.

WORLD FENCING CHAMPIONS, MEN'S TEAM ÉPÉE.

1906—France	1965—France
1930—Belgium	1966—France
1931—Italy	1967—USSR
1933—Italy	1969—USSR
1934—France	1970—Hungary
1935—France	1971—Hungary
1937—Italy	1973—W. Germany
1938—France	1974—Sweden
1947—France	1975—Sweden
1949—Italy	1977—Sweden
1950—Italy	1978—Hungary
1951—France	1979—USSR
1953—Italy	1981—USSR
1954—Italy	1982—France
1955—Italy	1983—France
1957—Italy	1985—W. Germany
1958—Italy	1986—W. Germany
1959—Hungary	1987—USSR
1961—USSR	1989—Italy
1962—France	1990—Italy
1963—Poland	1991—USSR

Any year not included in the preceding list was not a year in which a world championship men's team épée tournament was held.

REFERENCE
Roch, Rene, ed. *Internationale d'Escrime*. France: Federation Internationale d'Escrime, 1991.

WORLD FENCING CHAMPIONS, MEN'S TEAM FOIL.

1929—Italy	1965—USSR
1930—Italy	1966—USSR
1931—Italy	1967—Romania
1933—Italy	1969—USSR
1934—Italy	1970—USSR
1935—Italy	1971—France
1937—Italy	1973—USSR
1938—Italy	1974—USSR
1947—France	1975—France
1949—Italy	1977—W. Germany
1950—Italy	1978—Poland
1951—France	1979—USSR
1953—France	1981—USSR
1954—Italy	1982—USSR
1955—Italy	1983—W. Germany
1957—Hungary	1985—Italy
1958—France	1986—Italy
1959—USSR	1987—W. Germany
1961—USSR	1989—USSR
1962—USSR	1990—Italy
1963—USSR	1991—Cuba

Any year not included in the preceding list was not a year in which a world championship men's team foil tournament was held.

REFERENCE
Roch, Rene, ed. *Internationale d'Escrime*. France: Federation Internationale d'Escrime, 1991.

WORLD FENCING CHAMPIONS, MEN'S TEAM SABRE.

1906—Germany	1934—Hungary
1930—Hungary	1935—Hungary
1931—Hungary	1937—Hungary
1933—Hungary	1938—Italy

1947—Italy	1970—USSR
1949—Italy	1971—USSR
1950—Italy	1973—Hungary
1951—Hungary	1974—USSR
1953—Hungary	1975—USSR
1954—Hungary	1977—USSR
1955—Hungary	1978—USSR
1957—Hungary	1979—USSR
1958—Hungary	1981—Hungary
1959—Poland	1982—Hungary
1961—Poland	1983—USSR
1962—Poland	1985—USSR
1963—Poland	1986—USSR
1965—USSR	1987—USSR
1966—Hungary	1989—USSR
1967—USSR	1990—USSR
1969—USSR	1991—Hungary

Any year not included in the preceding list was not a year in which a world championship men's team sabre tournament was held.

REFERENCE

Roch, Rene, ed. *Internationale d'Escrime.* France: Federation Internationale d'Escrime, 1991.

WORLD FENCING CHAMPIONS, WOMEN'S INDIVIDUAL ÉPÉE.

1989—Straub (Switzerland)	1991—Horvath (Hungary)
1990—Chappe (Cuba)	

Women's individual épée was not included in a world championship fencing tournament until 1989.

REFERENCE

Walker, Colleen. *1992 U.S. Fencing Association Media Guide.* Colorado Springs: ColorTek Printing, 1992.

WORLD FENCING CHAMPIONS, WOMEN'S INDIVIDUAL FOIL.

1929—Mayer (Germany)	1931—Mayer (Germany)
1930—Addams (Belgium)	1933—Nelligan (Great Britain)

1934—Elek (Hungary)

1935—Elek (Hungary)

1937—Mayer (Germany)

1938—Sediva (Czechoslovakia)

1947—Preis (Austria)

1949—Preis (Austria)

1950—Preis (Austria)

1951—Elek (Hungary)

1953—Camber (Italy)

1954—Lachmann (Denmark)

1955—Domolki (Hungary)

1957—Zabelina (USSR)

1958—Kiszeljova (USSR)

1959—Jefimova (USSR)

1961—Schmid (Germany)

1962—Szabo-Orban (Romania)

1963—Rejto (Hungary)

1965—Gorokhova (USSR)

1966—Szamuszenko (USSR)

1967—Zabelina (USSR)

1969—Novikova (USSR)

1970—Gorokhova (USSR)

1971—Demaille (France)

1973—Nikonova (USSR)

1974—Bobis (Hungary)

1977—Sidorova (USSR)

1978—Sidorova (USSR)

1979—Hanisch (W. Germany)

1981—Hanisch (W. Germany)

1982—Giljazova (USSR)

1983—Vaccaroni (Italy)

1985—Hanisch (W. Germany)

1986—Fichtel (W. Germany)

1987—Tufan (Romania)

1989—Velitchko (USSR)

1990—Fichtel (W. Germany)

1991—Trillini (Italy)

Any year not included in the preceding list was not a year in which a world championship women's individual foil tournament was held.

REFERENCES

Palffy-Alpar, Julius. *Sword and Masque.* Philadelphia: F. A. Davis, 1967.

Roch, Rene, ed. *Internationale d'Escrime.* France: Federation Internationale d'Escrime, 1991.

WORLD FENCING CHAMPIONS, WOMEN'S SABRE. At present, neither women's individual sabre nor team sabre events are included in world championship fencing tournaments.

REFERENCE

Mar, Colleen Walker. *1993 U.S. Fencing Association Media Guide.* Colorado Springs: ColorTek Printing, 1992.

WORLD FENCING CHAMPIONS, WOMEN'S TEAM ÉPÉE.

1989—Hungary

1990—Germany

1991—Hungary

Women's team épée was not included in a world championship fencing tournament until 1989.

REFERENCE

Walker, Colleen. *1992 U.S. Fencing Association Media Guide.* Colorado Springs: ColorTek Printing, 1992.

WORLD FENCING CHAMPIONS, WOMEN'S TEAM FOIL.

1932—Denmark	1965—USSR
1933—Hungary	1966—USSR
1934—Hungary	1967—Hungary
1935—Hungary	1969—Romania
1936—Germany	1970—USSR
1937—Hungary	1971—USSR
1947—Denmark	1973—Hungary
1948—Denmark	1974—USSR
1950—France	1975—USSR
1951—France	1977—USSR
1952—Hungary	1978—USSR
1953—Hungary	1979—USSR
1954—Hungary	1981—USSR
1955—Hungary	1982—Italy
1956—USSR	1983—Italy
1957—Italy	1985—W. Germany
1958—USSR	1986—USSR
1959—Hungary	1987—Hungary
1961—USSR	1989—W. Germany
1962—Hungary	1990—Italy
1963—USSR	1991—Italy

Any year not included in the preceding list was not a year in which a world championship women's team foil tournament was held.

REFERENCE

Roch, Rene, ed. *Internationale Escrime.* France: Federation Internationale d'Escrime, 1991.

WORSHIP OF THE SWORD. Sword worship is an ancient practice dating back to man's earliest historical times. The Babylonians, Chaldeans, and Sythians all worshipped the gods Nergal, Ares, and Mars, who were essentially the same deity.

The Chaldeans worshipped Nergal, whom they called both "the Great Warrior" and "Sword-God." Nergal, it was believed, was the instigator of massive heavenly upheaval, including brimstone, flame, storm, and the reeling of the sky.

According to the fifth century B.C. writer Herodotus, the Sythians worshipped the god Ares in the form of an iron sword with a curved, scymitar-like blade. They frequently made human sacrifices to the sword, pouring fresh blood over it. Solinus, a historian living in the third century A.D., said of the Sythians in his *Polyhistor,* ''The god of these people is Mars; instead of images they worship the sword.''

The god Mars was greatly feared among the Babylonian people, who believed him to bring war and pestilence. Even the later Romans looked upon him as an unpleasant, martial figure. Mars was always depicted with a menacing sword in his hand.

REFERENCE

Velikovsky, Immanuel. *Worlds in Collision.* New York: MacMillan, 1950.

WYETH, N. C. (1882–1945). American illustrator.

A student of the successful illustrator Howard Pyle, N. C. Wyeth produced a wide range of art, much of it of a highly heroic nature. While his work included Indians and cowboys, scenes of American history, and country life, his most striking work includes swashbuckling scenes of adventure and swordplay. He illustrated volumes of classic literature, including *Treasure Island* (1911), *Kidnapped* (1913), *Robin Hood* (1917), *Westward Ho!* (1920), *The White Company* (1922), *Legends of Charlemagne* (1924), *David Balfore* (1924), and *The Boy's King Arthur* (1945). He also illustrated numerous magazine stories.

Wyeth invokes a grandeur that few other artists have managed to achieve. His art possesses a vitality that draws the viewer quickly into the picture. His characters move with a life and power that create movement.

N. C. Wyeth was the father of famed painter Andrew Wyeth.

REFERENCE

Allen, Douglas, and Douglas Allen, Jr. *N. C. Wyeth.* New York: Bonanza Books, 1972.

XIPHOS. One of Homer's names for the sword.

The blade of the *xiphos* was double-edged and widest at a point about a third of its length from the tip.

REFERENCE

Stone, George Cameron. *A Glossary of the Construction, Decoration, and Use of Arms and Armor.* New York: Jack Brussel, 1961.

XIPHOS, SPANISH. A long, two-edged sword of the second century.

The Spanish *xiphos,* or *gladius* Hispanus, was so called because it was made in Spain—especially Toledo (Toletum)—where materials existed to create steel of superior temper.

The weapons that came out of this area played a significant part in Rome's later conquests.

REFERENCE

Burton, Richard F. *The Book of the Sword.* London: Chatto and Windus, 1884.

XIPHOS-GLADIUS. A short Roman sword of the second century. It was much like the sword of the Greeks, only shorter.

REFERENCE

Burton, Richard F. *The Book of the Sword.* London: Chatto and Windus, 1884.

Y

YAGEN DOSHI. A short, heavy, Japanese sword used especially for smashing armor.
REFERENCE
Stone, George Cameron. *A Glossary of the Construction, Decoration, and Use of Arms and Armor.* New York: Jack Brussel, 1961.

YAGYU FAMILY, THE. A family of great Japanese sword masters.

Founded by Muneyoshi Yagyu (1527–1606), the Yagyu school of swordsmanship swiftly became the most famous in all Japan. Muneyoshi was eventually appointed fencing master to the last Ashikaga shogun.

Muneyoshi's son, Munenori (1571–1646), was every bit as successful as the elder Yagyu. As the fencing master to Shogun Ieysu Tokugawa, he was transformed into one of Japan's most colorful folk heros.

Other notable Yagyu family members include Mitsutoshi Yagyu and Mitsuyoshi Yagyu (1607–1650). The latter, commonly known as *Jubei,* developed the Yagyu style of sword combat into its highest, most effective form.
REFERENCE
Sasamori, Junzo, and Gordon Warner. *This Is Kendo.* Vermont: Charles E. Tuttle, 1984.

YAKBANDI. A sword belt of India.
REFERENCE
Stone, George Cameron. *A Glossary of the Construction, Decoration, and Use of Arms and Armor.* New York: Jack Brussel, 1961.

YAKUZA. Japanese gangsters.

Coming into their own right after the samurai system fell apart in Japan in the late nineteenth century, the *yakuza* lived by their own strict code of behavior. However, rather than professing allegiance to country or a lord, the loyalty of the *yakuza* was aimed toward his gang, or group.

The *yakuza* carried swords and were proficient in their use.

Today, the *yakuza* is depicted in numerous Japanese films of a highly violent nature. These include *The Gambling Samurai* (1960), *The Notorious Dragon* (1972), and *The Wanderers* (1974).

REFERENCE

Mintz, Marilyn D. *The Martial Arts Film.* New York: A. S. Barnes, 1978.

YASURIME. File marks left on the tang* of a Japanese sword blade. Their purpose was to keep the tang from slipping inside the grip.

REFERENCE

Stone, George Cameron. *A Glossary of the Construction, Decoration, and Use of Arms and Armor.* New York: Jack Brussel, 1961.

YATAGAN. A Turkish sabre* with an incurved blade. It had no hand guard.* It was designed with a forward weight especially useful for making cuts from the wrist.

The *yatagan* was normally worn thrust through the belt, and when going into combat, its owner would throw away the sword's scabbard. The reasoning was that if he won, he would have plenty of time to locate it, and if he lost, he would not really care.

Yatagan-type swords were also found in India.

REFERENCE

Stone, George Cameron. *A Glossary of the Construction, Decoration, and Use of Arms and Armor.* New York: Jack Brussel, 1961.

YORKE, ROWLAND. (c. 1550). A noted English villain.

A "desperado," according to historical accounts, who betrayed the town of Devanter, Holland, to the Spanish in 1587, Rowland Yorke is credited—sometimes discredited—with introducing the thrusting sword—the rapier*—to England.

REFERENCE

Castle, Egerton. *Schools and Masters of Fence.* London: George Bell, 1885.

YOSHIMITSU. (c. 1400). Japanese sword maker.

One of Japan's most celebrated sword makers.

REFERENCE

Stone, George Cameron. *A Glossary of the Construction, Decoration, and Use of Arms and Armor.* New York: Jack Brussel, 1961.

Z

ZAFAR TAKIEH. Meaning "the cushion of victory."

A short sword with a crutch-shaped pommel.* It was carried by Indian princes while they gave audiences.

In some cases, the crutch made up the entire hilt.

Also called *zafar takieh salapa.*

REFERENCE

Stone, George Cameron. *A Glossary of the Construction, Decoration, and Use of Arms and Armor.* New York: Jack Brussel, 1961.

ZAMAN. (c. 1600). Arab swordsmith.

A celebrated sword maker of Ispahan and pupil of the legendary craftsman Assad Ullah.

REFERENCE

Stone, George Cameron. *A Glossary of the Construction, Decoration, and Use of Arms and Armor.* New York: Jack Brussel, 1961.

ZEN AND THE SWORD. The Buddhist philosophy of Zen is the profound realization of experience. Its goal is to be one with all things, the universe, and thereby achieve enlightenment, called satori.

Zen, which favors intuition over intellect, became the way of spiritual growth for the samurai in ancient Japan, and many approaches were used to achieve this goal. The "Sword of No-abode," the "Sword of Mystery," the "Sword of No Sword," and the "Sword of Life and Death" were terms used to describe such paths toward true Zen understanding.

Swordsmanship became the perfect tool for the practice of Zen because its use involved the experience of life and death in its most intimate and personal form. To be faced with death, to be aware that any mistake, even the slightest slip, could bring immediate destruction, brought a swordsman into a situation where he needed Zen not in any theoretical sense but in the most practical manner possible. Zen dealt with the transcending of reason, thereby placing the thoughts of mortality beyond importance. At this point a swordsman was said to act naturally, and all his maneuvers, rather than guided by technique or strategy, would flow from his being in perfect accordance with the situation. Basically, by placing himself outside the realm of worldly concerns, he would triumph in his lethal encounter.

REFERENCES

Herrigal, Eugen. *Zen in the Art of Archery.* New York: Vintage Press, 1971.
Suzuki, Daisetz T. *Zen and Japanese Culture.* Princeton, NJ: Princeton University Press, 1973.

ZHDANOVICH, VIKTOR. (1938–). Soviet fencing champion.

Viktor Zhdanovich was the first Soviet fencer to win an Olympic gold fencing medal. He won the individual foil championship in 1960.

REFERENCE

Wallechinsky, David. *The Complete Book of the Olympics.* New York: Penguin Books, 1984.

ZIMMERMAN, FELICIA. (1975–). U.S. fencing champion.

Felicia Zimmerman was a member of the U.S. Olympic fencing team, as an alternate, in 1992. In 1993, she won the U.S. National women's individual foil championship. In 1994, she became the first U.S. woman fencer in the history of organized fencing to make the individual finals in a World Championship tournament, taking seventh place.

REFERENCES

Dimond, Jeff, and Annie McDaniel. "Late Breaking News." *En Garde* (Summer 1994).
Mar, Colleen Walker. *1993 U.S. Fencing Association Media Guide.* Colorado Springs, CO: ColorTek Printing, 1993.

ZORRO. A heroic, swashbuckling character created by writer Johnston Mc-Culley in 1919 for his serial pulp magazine story "The Curse of Capistrano."

Zorro (the Fox), the dashing alter ego of nobleman Diego Vega, was a kind of old Californian Robin Hood, championing peasants oppressed by a corrupt government. The character became the archetypical avenging masked swordsman.

Over the years, McCulley produced seventy-seven Zorro stories.

Since his creation, Zorro has been dramatized numerous times, mostly in the movies. Douglas Fairbanks, Sr.'s* successful *The Mark of Zorro*** (1920) is such an example.

Actor Guy Williams as Zorro

Perhaps Zorro's most popular incarnation came in the 1950s with Walt Disney's "Zorro"** television series, starring Guy Williams.

Over the years, Zorro has also turned up in cartoons, in comic books, on trading cards, in board games, on puzzles, on T-shirts, and on lunch boxes.
REFERENCE
Yenne, Bill. *The Legend of Zorro*. New York: Mallard Press, 1991.

ZORRO FILMS. Zorro, the masked swordsman of old California, has been a favorite film subject—along with Robin Hood, the three musketeers, and the count of Monte Cristo—since Hollywood's silent days.

The original film story of Zorro, based on a 1919 story, "The Curse of Capistrano," by Johnston McCulley,** followed lines that have since become familiar: Don Diego Vega, returning from years of schooling in Spain, finds his Californian homeland crushed under a cruel dictator. A champion horseman and swordsman, he decides at once to fight against the oppression as Zorro, hiding behind the guise of a languid fop to keep himself free from suspicion.

Beginning in 1920, with Douglas Fairbanks, Sr.'s popular film, *The Mark of Zorro,** the character of Zorro the avenger was firmly set in the public's mind. As a swashbuckler production, it was rather primitive when compared with later films of the genre. Yet, it remains a classic, mostly because of Douglas Fairbanks himself. In usual Fairbanks style, the story line is merely an excuse for an endless string of "Doug" stunts—leaping and climbing and fencing—executed with a wild, childlike grace and enthusiasm that have rarely been equaled on screen.

Fairbanks reprised his Zorro role in 1925 in *Don Q, Son of Zorro,* in which he played both old Zorro and his son Don Cesar.

The first sound version of the Zorro saga, *The Bold Caballero,* featuring Robert Livingston, was produced in 1937. A very low-budget epic, it was a disappointing blend of histrionics and a poor script.

Following this, numerous serials featuring Zorro descendants were produced from the late 1930s to the late 1940s. Starting with *Zorro Rides Again* (1937), the story line moved on to *Zorro's Fighting Legion* (1939) and from there to *Zorro's Black Whip* (1944), *The Son of Zorro* (1947), and, finally, *The Ghost of Zorro* (1949).

The next version of *The Mark of Zorro* (1940),** starring Tyrone Power* and Basil Rathbone,* is one of the truly great swashbuckler films of all time. Power made an excellent Don Diego/Zorro character, and Rathbone was in top form as the villain. The final duel of the film, staged by Fred Cavens,* was flawlessly executed, the movement both tightly knit and technically sound.

The year 1958 saw the beginning of a highly popular Walt Disney–produced Zorro television series, starring Guy Williams. Episodes of the show were eventually collected into two films, *The Sign of Zorro* (1960) and *Zorro the Avenger* (1960). The fencing, which was plentiful, was highly adequate.

Numerous Zorro films came out of Europe, beginning in 1952 with *The Sign of Zorro,* starring Walter Chiari. Next came an awkward reworking of the Zorro theme in *Duel at the Rio Grande* (1962), which starred Sean Flynn, Errol Flynn's son. This was followed by *The Shadow of Zorro* (1962), with Frank Latimore; *Zorro Versus Machiste* (1963), with Pierre Brice; *Zorro at the Court of Spain* (1963), with George Ardisson; and the improbable *Zorro and the Three Musketeers* (1963), with Gordon Scott.

Alain Delon starred in an ambitious French-produced *Zorro* (1975), which set the action in South America instead of Los Angeles. While the swordplay was fierce, it lacked a creative touch.

In 1974, Hollywood cranked out a remake of the 1940 *Mark of Zorro* starring Frank Langella. Pale and lifeless when compared with the earlier production, the film had neither originality nor energy going for it. The fencing was merely adequate.

A 1981 Zorro comedy called *Zorro, the Gay Blade,* starring George Hamilton, was well received by the public, mostly because of Hamilton's campy performance. But the film's overall impact on the swashbuckler genre was minimal. The fencing, which should have reflected at least some of the humorous aspect of the film, was flat and mechanical.

A new Zorro television series surfaced in 1982. An ill-fated flop called "Zorro and Son," the show was canceled after a brief airing.

Then, in 1989, New World Productions came out with still another Zorro television show, this time titled "The New Zorro." Starring Duncan Regehr, as a sort of swashbuckling "Father Knows Best," this latest offering was more "social relevance" than adventure. The fencing in the introductory episode, handled by Peter Diamond,* was reasonably well done. Later swordplay, unfortunately, often descended into a hodgepodge of meaningless blade waving and dubbed-in sword-wacking sounds.

REFERENCES
Richards, Jeffrey. *Swordsmen of the Screen.* Boston: Routledge and Kegan Paul, 1977.
Yenne, Bill. *The Legend of Zorro.* New York: Mallard Press, 1991.

ZU'L-FIKAR. Meaning "lord of cleaving."

Zu'l-Fikar was the sword given by the archangel Gabriel to the Prophet Mohammed, founder of Islam, and by him to his son-in-law Ali ben Ali Talib.

REFERENCE
Stone, George Cameron. *A Glossary of the Construction, Decoration, and Use of Arms and Armor.* New York: Jack Brussel, 1961.

ZWEYHANDER. The German two-handed sword** popular during the sixteenth century.

REFERENCE
Castle, Egerton. *Schools and Masters of Fence.* London: George Bell, 1885.

APPENDIXES

A. Types of Swords

Ama Goi Ken

Aor

Arming Sword

Asidevata

Asil

Aswar

Ayda Katti

Babanga

Backsword

Badelaire

Badik

Bakkur

Bandol

Baselard

Bastard Sword

Beheading Sword

Beladah

Bhawani

Bilbo

Blunt

Bokken

Boku-To

Bolo

Brand

Brandestoc

Braquermar

Broadsword

Campilan

Celtic Sword

Chalcos

Chasse-Coquin

Chereb

Chikuto

Chisa Katana

Choku-To

Chundrik

Chura

Cinctorium

Cinqueda

Cladibas

Claymore

Cluden

Colichemarde

Congo Sword

Court Sword

Coustil a Croc

Craquemarte

Crusader Sword

Cudgel

Curtana

Cutlass

Cutting Sword

Dacian Sword

Dagger Sword

Daisho

Dalwel

Damascus Sword

Dankali Sword

Danpira

Dao

Das	Goliah	Kongavel
Dha	Guddara	Kora
Dhoup	Gupti	Kubikuri
Dirk	Gupti Aga	Kuge-No-Tachi
Djoemloeng	Hakase	Kusari Tachi
Dodhara	Halab	Lading Belonajoeng Lamah
Dohong	Hammasti	Lall-I-Wall
Dress Sword	Hanger	Landsknecht
Dueling Sword	Hausa Sword	Long Sword
Dukn	Hebrew Sword	Machera
Duku	Herebra	Magic Sword
Dusack	Heyazashi	Makura Dashi
Efu No Tachi	Hiebcoment	Mandau
Electric Épée	Hoken	Manople
Electric Foil	Italian Foil	Mel Puttah Bemoh
Electric Sabre	Ito Maki Tachi	Mentok
Elephant Sword	Jin-Tachi	Mortuary Sword
Épée	Jinto	Nagatachi
Épée de Combat	Jumgheerdha	Namral
Épée de Passot	Kairagai	Nawaz Khani
Épée de Salle	Kamashimo Zashi	Ninja Ken
Espada	Kantschar	No-Dachi
Espadin	Kapee Dha	Odachi
Espadon	Kaskara	Opi
Estoc	Kastane	Palache
Falchon	Katana	Parang Bedak
Firangi	Ken	Parang Jenok
Fist Sword	Kenuki Gata Tachi	Parang Nabur
Flamberge	Khadja	Parang Pandit
Flyssa	Khanda	Pata
Foil	Khandoo	Pattisa
French Foil	Khopsh	Pedang Djawie Besar
Gagne-Pain	Khyber Knife	Phasganon
Gallic Sword	Kilij	Pira
Gauntlet Sword	Kindachi	Piso Eccat
Gladius	Kledyu	Piso Gading
Goddara	Klewang	Piso Halasan

Piso Podang

Poker

Presentation Sword

Pulouar

Quaddara

Ragee

Ram Da'o

Ramrod Backsword

Rapier

Rebated Sword

Rudis

Sabre

Saif

Salapa

Sapara

Sapola

Schavona

Schlaeger

Schwerdt

Sciabola di Terreno

Scramasax

Scymitar

Seax

Seme

Senangkas Bedok

Separating Sword

Setto

Sharp

Shashqa

Shearing Sword

Shinai

Shinken

Shira Tachi

Shotel

Sibak

Sica

Sickle Sword

Sime

Singlestick

Sirohi

Smallsword

Sosun

Sosunpattah

Spadone

Spadroon

Spanish Foil

Stone Sword

Sultani

Surai

Sword Cane

Tachi

Tachi Hanagu

Taga Dhara Shani

Taga Talwar

Takona-Gatana

Takouba

Talibon

Talwar

Tampei

Tau-Kien

Tebutje

Tegha

Tjoedre

Tyrfing

Urto

Verdun

Wakizashi

Waster

Wooden Sword

Xiphos

Xiphos-Gladius

Xiphos-Spanish

Yagen Doshi

Yatagan

Zafar Takieh

Zu'l-Fikar

Zweyhander

B. Fencing Masters

FOURTEENTH CENTURY THROUGH EIGHTEENTH CENTURY

Agrippa, Camillo (Italy)

Alfieri, Francesco (Italy)

Angelo, Domenico (England)

Angelo, Harry (England)

Besnard, Charles (France)

Capo Ferro, Ridolfo (Italy)

Carranza, Jeronimo de (Spain)

Cavalcabo, Heronimo (Germany)

Danet, Guillaume (France)

Fabris, Salvator (Italy)

Giganti, Nicoletto (Italy)

Grassi, Giacomo di (Italy)

Hope, William (England)

Kahn, Anton (Germany)

Kreussler, Wilhelm (Germany)

Labat (France)

La Boessiere (France)

La Tousche, Philibert de (France)

Le Perche, Jean (France)

Liancour, Andre de (France)

McBane, Donald (England)

Manciolino, Antonio di (Italy)

Marozzo, Achille (Italy)

Meyer, Joachim (Germany)

Narvaez, Don Luis Pacheco de (Spain)

Pallavicini, Giuseppe (Italy)

Rada, Lorenz de (Spain)

Sainct-Didier, Henry de (France)

Saviolo, Vincentio (England)

Schmidt, Johann (Germany)

Silver, George (England)

Sutor, Jacob (Germany)

Swetnam, Joseph (England)

Thibault, Girard (France)

Underwood, James (England)

Valeria, Diego de (Spain)

Villardita, Giuseppe (Italy)

NINETEENTH CENTURY

Angelo, Henry Charles (England)

Angelo, William Henry (England)

Barbasetti, Luigi (Italy)

Bertrand, Baptiste (England)

Bertrand, Felix (England)

Bertrand, Francois-Joseph (France)

Bonnafous, Justin (United States)

Corbesier, A. J. (France)

Gouspy, Emile (United States)

Hutton, Alfred (England)

Jacoby, H. H. (United States)

Jean-Louis (France)

Keresztessy, Joseph (Hungary)

La Boessiere (France)

Lafaugere, Louis (France)

Merignac, Emile (France)

Nadi, Beppe (Italy)

Prevost, Pierre (France)

Radaelli, Giuseppi (Italy)

Roland, George (England)

Rondelle, Louis (United States)

Santelli, Italo (Hungary)

Senac, Regis (United States)

Vauthier, Louis (United States)

TWENTIETH CENTURY

Alaux, Michael (United States)

Aurial, Yves (United States)

Balogh, Bela (Hungary)

Beaumont, Charles de (England)

Beke, Zoltan (Hungary)

Bertrand, Leon (England)

Castello, Julio (United States)

Crosnier, Roger (England)

Csiszar, Lajos (United States)

D'Asaro, Michael (United States)

Di Rosa, Livio (Italy)

Elthes, Csaba (United States)

Faulkner, Ralph (United States)

Ganchev, George (United States)

Geller, Alfred (Hungary)

Gerevich, Aladar (Hungary)

Halberstadt, Hans (United States)

Imregi, B. (Hungary)

Kogler, Aladar (United States)

Lucia, Edward (United States)

Lukovich, Istvan (Hungary)

Nadi, Aldo (Italy)

Nadi, Nedo (Italy)

Nazlimov, Vladimir (Soviet Union)

Palffy-Alpar, Julius (United States)

Paul, Rene (England)

Pinchart, Rene (France)

Santelli, Giorgio (United States)

Simmonds, A. T. (England)

Szabo, Laszlo (Hungary)

Tusnady (Hungary)

Vass, Imre (Hungary)

C. Noted Swashbuckler Films

Adventures of Don Juan, The (1949)

Adventures of Robin Hood, The (1938)

Bandit of Sherwood Forest, The (1946)

Black Pirate, The (1926)

Black Swan, The (1942)

Captain Blood (1935)

Corsican Brothers, The (1941)

Court Jester, The (1956)

Cyrano de Bergerac (1950)

Don Juan (1926)

Exile, The (1946)

Iron Mask, The (1929)

Man in the Iron Mask (1939)

Mark of Zorro, The (1920)

Mark of Zorro, The (1940)

Prisoner of Zenda, The (1937)

Scaramouche (1952)

Sea Hawk, The (1940)

Three Musketeers, The (1921)

Three Musketeers, The (1948)

Three Musketeers, The (1974)

D. Actors Who Fenced in Movies

Barrymore, John

Chamberlain, Richard

Colman, Ronald

Derek, John

Fairbanks, Douglas, Jr.

Fairbanks, Douglas, Sr.

Ferrer, Jose

Flynn, Errol

Granger, Stewart

Heston, Charlton

Kaye, Danny

Kelly, Gene

Lee, Christopher

Mason, James

O'Hara, Maureen

Peters, Jean

Power, Tyrone

Rathbone, Basil

Reed, Oliver

Wilde, Cornel

Williams, Guy

Williams, Robin

York, Michael

E.   Film Fencing Masters

Anderson, Bob
Cavens, Fred
Crean, Patrick
Diamond, Peter
Faulkner, Ralph
Heremans, Jean
Hobbs, William
Uyttenhove, Henry

F. Historical Fencing Organizations

BELGIUM

Confrerie Royale et Chevaliere de Saint-Michel, 17th century

BRITISH ISLES

Corporation of Maisters of Defence, 16th century
Society of Sword-Men in Scotland, 16th century

FRANCE

Academie d'Armes du Languedoc (Academy of Toulouse), 16th century
Compagnie des Maitres en fait d'Armes des Academies du Roi en las Ville et Faubourg de Paris, 16th century
Academie d'Armes du Strasbourg, 17th century
Ecole d'Joinville le Pont, 19th century

GERMANY

Fraternity of St. Luke (*Lux Bruder*), 15th century
Fraternity of St. Mark (*Burgerschaft von St. Marcus von Lowenberg*, or Marxbruder), 15th century
Company of St. Matthew, 16th century
Federfechter (*Freyfechter von der Feder zum Greifenfels*), 16th century

ITALY

Accademia Nazionale di Scherma di Napoli, 19th century
Scuola Magistrale di Scherma, 19th century

SPAIN

La Real Academia de Cavalleros Guardias Marinas, 18th century

G. Modern Fencing Organizations

AMATEUR

International

British Empire Fencing Association
Federation Internationale d'Escrime
International Fencing Committee (defunct)

Canada

Canadian Fencing Association

France

Federation Francaise d'Escrime

Germany

Deutcher Fechter Bund

Great Britain

Amateur Fencing Association
Combined Services Fencing Association
Ladies Amateur Fencing Union

Ireland

Irish Amateur Fencing Federation
Northern Ireland Amateur Fencing Union

Italy

Federazione Italiana di Scherma

Scotland

Scottish Amateur Fencing Union

Spain

Real Federacion d'Escrima

United States

Intercollegiate Fencing Association
National Intercollegiate Women's Fencing Association
U.S. Fencing Association (formerly Amateur Fencers League of America)

Wales

Welch Amateur Fencing Union

PROFESSIONAL

International

Academie d'Armes Internationale

Algeria

Academie d'Armes d'Algerie

Australia

Australian Academy of Arms

Austria

Akademie der Fechtkunst Osterreichs

Belgium

Academie Rayale d'Armes de Belguque

Canada

Canadian Academy of Arms

France

Academie d'Armes de France

Germany

Akademie der Fechtkunst Deutschkands
Weltmesisterschaften der Fechtmeister

Great Britain

British Academy of Fencing
Ladies Professional Fencing Association

Greece

Academie d'Armes de Grece

Hungary

Hongrie

Ireland

Irish Academy of Arms

Italy

Associatione Italiana di Scherma

Malaysia

National Fencing Academy of Malaysia

Netherlands

Nederlandse Akademie van Schermleraren

Portugal

Academie d'Armes de Portugal

Spain

Academie d'Armes d'Espagne

Sweden

Academie d'Armes de Suede

Switzerland

Academie d'Armes de Suisse

United States

Society of American Fight Directors
United States Fencing Coaches Association

Index

Page numbers in **bold type** refer to main entries in the encyclopedia.

About the Author

NICK EVANGELISTA is a Fencing Master who was trained in Europe and the United States and who teaches both sport and theatrical fencing. In addition, he is a freelance writer and has been a fencing technical consultant to the film industry.